HUBERT WOLF

The NUNS of SANT'AMBROGIO

Hubert Wolf, born in 1959, is professor of medieval and modern church history at the University of Münster, Germany. He was honored with the Leibniz Prize of the German Research Foundation (DFG), the Communicator Award, and the Gutenberg Award, and he was fellow at the Historisches Kolleg in Munich.

A NOTE ABOUT THE TRANSLATOR

Ruth Martin has a PhD in twentieth-century German literature and philosophy from the University of London, where she also lectured. She is now a full-time translator and has translated several nonfiction books from German.

The NUNS *of*
SANT'AMBROGIO

The NUNS of SANT'AMBROGIO

✳

THE TRUE STORY
OF A CONVENT IN SCANDAL

HUBERT WOLF

Translated by Ruth Martin

VINTAGE BOOKS
A Division of Penguin Random House LLC
New York

This work has been supported by a one-year research residency at the Historisches
Kolleg in Munich. The Historisches Kolleg is financed by the Free State of Bavaria.
The research stipend was provided by the Fritz Thyssen Foundation.

The translation of this work was funded by Geisteswissenschaften International—
Translation Funding for Humanities and Social Sciences from Germany, a joint
initiative of the Fritz Thyssen Foundation, the German Federal Foreign Office,
the collecting society VG WORT, and the Börsenverein des Deutschen
Buchhandels (German Publishers & Booksellers Association).

The Library of Congress has cataloged the Knopf edition as follows:
Wolf, Hubert.
[Nonnen von Sant'Ambrogio. English]
The nuns of Sant'Ambrogio : the true story of a convent in scandal / Hubert Wolf ;
translated by Ruth Martin.—First United States Edition.
pages cm
Includes bibliographical references and index.
1. Sant'Ambrogio della Massima (Monastery : Rome, Italy).   2. Nuns—Italy—
Rome—History.   3. Convents—Italy—Rome—History.   4. Scandals—Italy—
Rome—History.   5. Catholic Church—Italy—Rome—History.
6. Monasteries—Italy—Rome—History.   I. Title.
BX4220.I8W6513 2014   271′.973045632—dc23   2014001625

Vintage Books Trade Paperback ISBN: 978-0-8041-6980-6
eBook ISBN: 978-0-385-35192-8

Author photograph © Norbert Enker
Book design by Maggie Hinders

www.vintagebooks.com

Contents

Dramatis Personae

PRINCESS KATHARINA VON HOHENZOLLERN-SIGMARINGEN
A German aristocrat. Spends fifteen months as the novice Luisa Maria in the convent of Sant'Ambrogio, where her knowledge of convent secrets puts her life in danger.

GUSTAV ADOLF ZU HOHENLOHE-SCHILLINGSFÜRST
The titular archbishop of Edessa and a confidant of Pope Pius IX. Also Katharina's cousin and her savior.

MARIA AGNESE FIRRAO
Founder of the convent, whose inhabitants honor her as a saint. Convicted by the Holy Office of false holiness.

MARIA LUISA
The convent's beautiful young novice mistress and madre vicaria. Has visions and is regarded as a saint.

MARIA VERONICA
Abbess of Sant'Ambrogio, thanks to Maria Luisa.

LUIGI FRANCESCHETTI
The lawyer responsible for the convent's legal affairs.

AGNESE ELETTA
The niece of Agnese Firrao, a nun who shares Maria Luisa's bed.

MARIA GIACINTA
Franceschetti's sister, a nun who also shares Maria Luisa's bed.

AGNESE CELESTE
A novice and a doctor's daughter, who knows about medicines and poisons.

MARIA FRANCESCA
A novice with heavenly handwriting.

xii · *Dramatis Personae*

MARIA GIUSEPPA
A nurse with the keys to the convent dispensary.

MARIA IGNAZIA
A novice and Maria Luisa's accomplice.

MARIA FELICE
A novice and another of Maria Luisa's accomplices.

PETER KREUZBURG
"The Americano." Possessed by the devil (and by Maria Luisa).

GIUSEPPE LEZIROLI
A Jesuit priest, the spiritual director and principal father confessor
of Sant'Ambrogio; believes in both its saints.

GIUSEPPE PETERS
A Jesuit priest and the second father confessor of Sant'Ambrogio;
admirer of Maria Luisa. Is more than he seems.

KARL AUGUST, COUNT REISACH
Cardinal and sometime spiritual guide to Katharina; has a weakness
for women with stigmata.

MAURUS WOLTER
A Benedictine priest and Katharina's new spiritual guide; persuades
her to submit a complaint to the Inquisition.

COSTANTINO PATRIZI
Cardinal protector of the convent; cardinal vicar of the Roman
Curia; keeper of secrets.

VINCENZO LEONE SALLUA
A Dominican; investigating judge of the Roman Inquisition.

PIUS IX
Pope from 1846 to 1878; believes the Virgin Mary does intervene
in the world.

MARY
The mother of Jesus Christ; supernatural manifestation and
correspondent.

The NUNS *of*
SANT'AMBROGIO

Prologue

"Save, Save Me!"

"Shortly after eight o'clock on Monday, July 25, the Archbishop of Edessa—sent by the Lord—finally came to me. There was no time for waiting; this was the one and only time to get saved. To him, I had to reveal everything and had to implore him to help me escape the convent as swiftly as possible. It all went well: my prayers were fulfilled, and I was understood."[1] These dramatic words were set down by Princess Katharina von Hohenzollern-Sigmaringen in a complaint she submitted to the pope in summer 1859. They were written barely five weeks after her escape from the convent of Sant'Ambrogio in Rome—or rather, after her cousin, Archbishop Gustav Adolf zu Hohenlohe-Schillingsfürst, managed to secure her release—and they describe the sensational conclusion to her adventure inside the walls of a Roman Catholic convent. It was an adventure for which she had narrowly avoided paying with her life.

She had been humiliated, isolated from her fellow nuns, cut off from the outside world, and—since she was party to the convent secrets and therefore regarded as a danger—somebody had tried to silence her. They had even made several attempts to poison her. At half past three in the afternoon on July 26, 1859, after almost exactly fifteen months, she finally left Sant'Ambrogio della Massima. Her life as Sister Luisa Maria of Saint Joseph, a nun in the Regulated Third Order of Holy Saint Francis in Rome, had begun so promisingly. And now here she was, being saved in the nick of time, rescued from imminent danger of death.

In her written complaint, the princess gave her failure as a nun and her thrilling escape from the convent a typically pious interpretation, casting it as salvation by Christ the Lord. This somehow made the experience bearable for her. But the final dramatic episode, and the preceding months she had spent under the constant fear of death, would come to define her whole life. After July 26, 1859, nothing would ever be the same again. Her plight had been genuinely existential: her life really was threatened in Sant'Ambrogio. Even years later, she was still traumatized by the attempts to poison her. This is all brought vividly to life in her *Erlebnisse* (Experiences), a book written by her close collaborator Christiane Gmeiner in 1870, more than a decade after the terrible events in Rome.[2] According to this autobiographical source, Katharina had managed to smuggle a letter out of the convent during the night of July 24, 1859. This was handed to Archbishop Hohenlohe in the Vatican.

> The princess waited in a state of great anxiety until she was called into the parlor at half past seven in the morning. Fearful and almost breathless, the princess hurried downstairs to the archbishop, to whom she called out in great agitation: "save, save me!" At first, he did not understand her, and was almost afraid his cousin had run mad, but by and by she managed to convince him that she was mistress of her senses, and that her fear was not unfounded. Now he understood her pleas to leave the convent, and he promised to do everything in his power to arrange this as soon as possible— though the first appointment he was able to make was not until the following day.

The words are Christiane Gmeiner's, recounting in the third person what the princess had told her in her own words.[3]

Katharina von Hohenzollern-Sigmaringen's account sounds like a story from the depths of the Middle Ages, and confirms many of the common clichés and prejudices about life in Catholic convents and monasteries. But this story takes place in the modern world of the mid-nineteenth century. And the setting isn't a secluded mountain convent at the world's edge, but the center of the capital city of Christianity, little more than half a mile from the Vatican—home to the representative of Jesus Christ on earth.

What really happened in Sant'Ambrogio? Were these poisonings simply the fantasy of a highly strung aristocrat, or were they genuine attempts on Katharina's life? She was a princess of the house of Hohenzollern and a close relative of Wilhelm I, the man who would later become king of Prussia and the German emperor. So how did Katharina come to take her vows in such a strict religious order in the first place—and why in Rome?

CHAPTER ONE

"Such Turpitudes"

Katharina von Hohenzollern Complains to the Inquisition

ROME AS A HEAVENLY JERUSALEM

Johann Wolfgang von Goethe and Johann Joachim Winckelmann both longed for Italy, intoxicated by the idea of Rome, the stronghold of classical antiquity. But it wasn't this idea that drove Katharina there.[1] Nor was she following in the footsteps of the great German royal houses, from the Karolingers to the Staufer Carolingians, who had come to the city on the Tiber to take the emperor's crown. Katharina's destination was an order of pious women, so her motivation for coming to the pope's city must have been largely religious.

But, starting in the mid-eighteenth century, Rome had undergone a dramatic decline as a religious center.[2] Situated in the middle of Italy, the Papal States covered at least a quarter of the Apennine Peninsula, and, as their secular prince, the pope was increasingly drawn into political and military conflicts to protect his rule. This left him less and less able to take care of his duties as spiritual head of the Catholic Church. Toward the end of the century, religious respect for papal authority sank to an all-time low. In 1773, the European powers even managed to force Clement XIV to dissolve the Jesuit order, his most important political supporters within the Church. Napoleon Bonaparte annexed the pope's lands, and forced Pius VII into French exile. Following the pope's return, the 1815 Congress of Vienna restored the Papal States as an independent entity. But although Cardinal Secretary of State Ercole Consalvi promised the Congress that in return, reforms would be implemented in the areas of governance, legislation, education, and the economy, these never materialized.[3] The Papal States remained the most backward political entity in the whole of Europe.

However, following the Wars of Liberation, the Restoration had become a dominant movement in Europe, and the pope was able to regain the people's respect for him as a moral and religious authority. He had suddenly become the only monarch in Europe to have defied the beast Napoleon, earning a spell in exile for his convictions. All the other rulers had made deals with the French emperor. To the Romantic mind, papal authority was a guarantee of eternal values, in particular of the divine right of kings. It was a protective force against the chaos and uncertainty of the French Revolution, with its liberal understanding of constitutional law and human rights. Leo XII was particularly adept at utilizing this desire for security. The Eternal City would once again become the most sacred place on earth.

German Catholics were increasingly turning toward Rome in the wake of secularization and the destruction of the old Imperial Church with its prince-bishoprics. Most had become the subjects of Protestant princes, and were seeking salvation through a closer connection with the pope. After the July Revolution of 1830, there was a phase of growing Ultramontanism within the Catholic Church. Catholics were starting to look *ultra montes*, beyond the mountains, to Rome. Roman piety, Roman liturgy, and Roman theology were increasingly regarded as the only true realizations of Catholicism, legitimated by the pope in his role as *Vicarius Christi*.

With this movement in full swing, the Catholic press began to style Rome as the bride of Christ, the holy city, a heavenly Jerusalem on earth. This religious elevation of the papacy didn't stem from the popes and the Roman Curia itself: it was brought to the pope from outside. The pontiff became the surface onto which people could project their need for religious security in an age of upheaval, doubt, and revolution. During this period, people began to rediscover the idea of making a pilgrimage to Rome. Having a personal encounter with the pope, praying over the graves of the apostles Peter and Paul—and the religious self-assurance this brought with it—became markers of a genuine Catholic faith.

The members of the Roman Curia utilized this new orientation toward Rome in very different ways. The College of Cardinals split into *Zelanti* and *Politicanti*. The first group, the zealots, wanted to use the new enthusiasm for Rome to suppress any kind of reform in the Church and the Papal States, increasingly absolutizing the pope as the infallible sacred monarch. The other members, the pragmatists, were rather more skeptical, seeing that this represented a threat to their program of reconciliation between the Church and the world. There were mighty clashes between "hawks" and "doves"—particularly when it came to electing a new pope. Hard-liners and moderates scored alternate victories in the conclaves.

Katharina von Hohenzollern and her mother also headed for Rome, as part of a procession of pilgrims largely drawn from the higher echelons of society. They entered Rome for the first time in 1834, during the pontificate of Gregory XVI, who was a *Zelant*. The pope and his circle harbored a general mistrust of the modern world, with all its progressive political ideas, scientific discoveries, and economic developments.[4] During his reign, he built the holy city into a kind of spiritual fortress against the diabolical powers of liberalism, since the repercussions of the French July Revolution hadn't spared the theocratic Papal States. Gregory XVI was deeply traumatized by the revolution, and consequently persecuted all innovators within the Catholic Church. For this pope, anything that looked remotely like freedom, reform, or modern education had a whiff of brimstone about it. He believed the Catholic Church should be concentrated on Rome, and furnished as a "house full of glory." The Church would stand up to modernity and would eventually emerge victorious against it, through the *Triumph of the Holy See*—as the title of a book written by the pope would have it.[5]

Following on from this Restoration pontiff, Giovanni Maria Mastai-Ferretti was elected pope on June 16, 1846. He was a moderate *Politicant*, and consequently took the name of his predecessor's predecessor, becoming Pius IX.[6] The new pope, a man of great personal charm, began his pontificate by pushing through a series of reforms. He decreed an amnesty for political prisoners, set up a civilian government, and promised his subjects a constitution that would give them a say in the political life of the Papal States. This liberal stance met with broad approval from the Roman population. But sparks from the 1848 March Revolution in the German states landed in the pope's city: people became radicalized, and Pius IX was ultimately forced to flee to Gaeta, in the Kingdom of Naples. It was only after French troops had put down the uprising that the pope was able to return to the Vatican, in 1850.

The trauma of the 1848 Revolution shaped his pontificate from then on. All reforms were rescinded; policy in the Papal States, and the Church's magisterium, became distinctly reactionary. Like his predecessor, Gregory XVI, the pope felt persecuted and threatened from all sides. He developed an almost apocalyptic fear of the Papal States' occupation by Italian nationalist troops. Only foreign troops could secure Pius IX's temporal power in the Papal States against the *Risorgimento*, the national unification movement that saw Rome as the natural capital of a new Italian nation-state.

This siege mentality extended to the religious sphere.[7] At the start of Pius IX's pontificate, he had listened to liberal cardinals and prelates as well as hard-liners and intransigents, but now the balance shifted toward the latter. In the first half of the nineteenth century, Rome had been a city of religious pluralism. The various factions and theological movements that existed in Germany and France, for example, were reflected in the offices and congregations of the Roman Curia. Some members of the Curia sought reconciliation between Church and world, modern philosophy and Catholic faith; others were Romantics and new scholastics, who saw the only conceivable basis for Catholicism in the philosophy of Saint Thomas Aquinas. The Jesuit order and the Collegio Romano, whose faculty it dominated, increasingly became a stronghold for hyper-orthodoxy and Rome's new scholastics, while the Benedictine abbey of Saint Paul Outside the Walls prescribed a more open, pluralistic model of piety and theology, incorporating newer philosophical approaches.

From 1848, the pope increasingly came down on the side of the conservatives, ordering the Inquisition and the Congregation of the Index to pursue any divergent theological opinions. Numerous modern theologians found themselves on the *Index of Forbidden Books*. During the time of Pius IX, the *Index* went from being a means of controlling the book market to a means of disciplining independent thinkers within the Church.

Different theological and political orientations within the Church corresponded to quite different religious practices and mentalities. The reactionary, Romantic faction sought to restore Baroque Catholicism's exalted forms of devotion. They rediscovered mysticism, which had been discredited during the Enlightenment, and looked for miracles at every turn. The liberal elements of the Curia preferred a more sober piety: a faith that could endure the demands of the modern age of reason. Here, too, Pius IX's preferences were very clear: the pope firmly believed that heavenly powers could intervene in the here and now. As a child, he had fallen into a raging river, and he attributed his rescue directly to a helping hand from the Mother of God.[8]

This was the environment that Katharina von Hohenzollern entered when she finally decided to move to Rome in 1857. At this point, the city of Rome was small and manageable. When Gregorovius, the city's chronicler, arrived at the Tiber for the first time in 1852, he noted in his diary: "Rome is so entirely silent that one can live in heavenly tranquility and think and work."[9] Gregorovius's impression is unsurprising, given that the city had just 180,000 inhabitants.[10] Of these, around 7,500 were priests and nuns. There was no compulsory education, though the elementary schools ensured that roughly a third of the population could read and write. Of the five and a half square miles of the city that lay within its fourteen miles of ancient walls, a good third was built up. The remaining land was given over to farming—the Forum Romanum was used to pasture cattle. There were 14,700 buildings, housing 39,000 families who belonged to fifty-four different parishes. Gas lamps weren't installed on the streets until 1854, and there was no railway. The nineteenth century's industrialization and subsequent economic boom had touched neither the Eternal City nor the sixteen thousand square miles and 3.2 million inhabitants of the Papal States.

The disparity in income was immense. A high prelate in the Curia earned just under 2,000 scudi per year, while a middle-class family of six needed around 650 scudi, and a farming family of the same size survived on 250 scudi. An agricultural laborer earned 72 scudi a year, and a shepherd boy received 32 scudi.

A ROAD-TO-DAMASCUS EXPERIENCE AND ITS CONSEQUENCES

Katharina's first encounter with Rome, in the year 1834, represented a crucial turning point in her life.[11] She had been born in Stuttgart on January 19, 1817, to Prince Karl Albrecht III zu Hohenlohe-Waldenburg-Schillingsfürst, and his second wife, Leopoldine zu Fürstenberg. Her parents had her baptized into the Catholic faith.[12] They separated a few years after her birth, her father withdrawing to live on his Hohenlohe estates, and the princess spent most of her childhood in Donaueschingen, with her mother and her Fürstenberg relatives. Her strictly orthodox biographers speak with deep regret about a very liberal upbringing in Baden, lamenting that she had no "real religious guidance" throughout her childhood and youth.[13]

When the seventeen-year-old Katharina traveled to Rome with her mother in 1834, she had a road-to-Damascus experience. In the pope's city, Katharina embraced the Catholic faith in its strictest form, and the liberal young girl became a pious Catholic noblewoman. The transformation was due in no small part to Karl August, Count von Reisach.[14] Reisach, born on July 6, 1800, was a member of the Swabian-Franconian nobility, like Katharina von Hohenlohe-Waldenburg-Schillingsfürst. He had had a difficult start in life. His father, who was constantly on the brink of financial catastrophe, had been accused of misappropriation of funds, and had relieved himself of his responsibilities by committing suicide in 1820. This must have been a formative experience in the life of the young count. Reisach studied law, but his hopes of a professorship in Landshut were dashed, and his marriage plans also came to nothing. Reisach, searching for orientation, and a foothold in the world, then fell under the influence of two men. The first was Clemens Maria Hofbauer,[15] a Redemptorist Catholic priest who had converted from Protestantism. The second was Adam Müller,[16] a professor of constitutional law in Göttingen, who advocated a Romantic, corporative model of society, with the pope at its head. Reisach decided to head for Rome, to take refuge from the uncertainties of his life. He wanted to become a priest, and went to study theology in the only place where, in his view, he would receive orthodox tuition. In October 1824, he became the first German to enter the Collegio Romano since German secularization. The college had recently been reopened by Leo XII, and later became the Pontifical Gregorian University. Reisach moved into the Collegium Germanicum, the Roman seminary for German candidates for the priesthood.[17] Under the influence of the Jesuits, Reisach developed into a zealot. Ordained in 1828, he was also awarded a doctorate in

This portrait was painted in 1848, when Katharina was thirty-one.
She married Prince Karl von Hohenzollern-Sigmaringen the same year.

theology, and became rector of the Propaganda Fide College, part
of the Congregation for the Propagation of the Faith. He formed a
particularly close and faithful relationship with its prefect, Cardinal
Mauro Cappellari. The two men were united by a strictly restorative
orientation, and a rejection of all reforms, which Reisach viewed as
a "tightly woven conspiracy of liberal theologians and philosophers,
with the aim of abolishing the Catholic Church."[18] After Cappellari
took the papal throne as Gregory XVI, Reisach became his closest
ally in the struggle against Church reformers, particularly those in
the southwest of Germany, Katharina's home.

Katharina must have been fascinated by this young priest. Reisach
immediately became her father confessor and spiritual guide, thereby
gaining a decisive influence over her future. The princess not only
promised to open her soul to him in the sacrament of confession, but
from thenceforth to turn to him for advice and guidance in all things.
An intense correspondence developed between confessor and penitent. In her youthful exuberance, Katharina was eager to follow Reisach into the battle for the Church, and expressed her desire to enter a

Dominican convent in Rome. But Reisach seems to have opposed this idea. He probably saw it as the whim of a seventeen-year-old, rather than a mature religious decision. She should do her duty as a wife and mother first—as befitted her status as a young noblewoman.[19]

And Katharina von Hohenlohe duly put on a wedding dress instead of a nun's habit. Her niece, Marie von Thurn und Taxis-Hohenlohe,[20] later wrote that Katharina had "fallen passionately in love with a Count Ingelheim, whom my grandparents would not countenance as a husband: the young man, who was otherwise very agreeable, was thought to be a consumptive. But Aunt Katharina got her way, and married him in spite of all resistance."[21] The wedding took place in 1838. Count Erwin von Ingelheim[22] really did die young, in 1845, and the marriage remained childless. Three years later, Katharina entered the state of holy matrimony once more, though this time it seems to have been a marriage of convenience. In 1848 she married Prince Karl von Hohenzollern-Sigmaringen,[23] who was thirty-four years her senior. His first marriage had been to Antoinette Murat, a niece of Napoleon Bonaparte's brother-in-law. Prince Karl brought several stepchildren to the marriage, almost all of them older than his second wife. But this marriage didn't last long, either. The prince contracted typhus on a journey through northern Italy, and died in Bologna on March 11, 1853. After only five years of marriage, Katharina, who was now thirty-six, had been widowed for a second time. From her husband's family, she received an estate in Bistritz, Bohemia, as her dower residence, and a pension of 12,000 Rhenish guilders, which later rose to 15,000. There was also a lump-sum payment of 100,000 guilders. She used this to set up a fund from which she intended to finance the founding of a convent later in life.[24]

But first, she fulfilled her heart's desire, the ambition she had first expressed in Rome in 1834. Katharina became a nun. On December 18, 1853, she entered the community of the *Dames du Sacré-Cœur* in Kintzheim, Alsace. In many ways, the nuns of the Sacred Heart were like the English Ladies. Their congregation was also dedicated to the education of girls, inspired by a Jesuit concept of pedagogy, and people thought of them as a kind of female equivalent of the Jesuits.[25] On March 11 of the following year, Katharina was clothed as a novice. However, it soon became clear that the princess was neither physically nor mentally equal to the strains of serving in the school. She felt overtaxed and, with her dream of cloistered life shattered, she reacted by falling ill. Medical treatments and rest cures brought her no relief. Was this reaction a typical pattern of behavior for the princess, when faced with failure? Might this not suggest she could have made up a story about poisoning a few years later in a Roman convent? This would mean she wouldn't have to confess that, once again, she had failed as a nun and become seriously ill.

In any case, her spiritual guide, Reisach, consulted with her doctors and suggested that she withdraw immediately from the convent in Alsace. In the nineteenth century, during Germany's "convent Spring," many women joined religious orders and congregations in order to become teachers or nurses—jobs from which they would otherwise have been barred. But this clearly wasn't the right path for Katharina. Reisach, who had become bishop of Eichstätt in 1836, and archbishop of Munich and Freising in 1846, thought her "not inclined to or trained for the educational profession." In his view, this teaching order was simply unsuitable for a "sickly widow, doubly bowed by her life's tribulations."[26] The sources don't clarify exactly what the princess's health problems were. In his 1912 biography of Katharina, Karl Theodor Zingeler speaks of a "dropsy"—an abnormal collection of fluid in the body—from which the corpulent princess suffered all her life.[27]

Following Reisach's advice, Katharina left the Sacred Heart convent in November 1855, and spent the winter in Kupferzell and Baden-Baden. She then returned to Bistritz, her widow's seat. In summer, her disease led her to seek out the convent of Lichtenthal, near Baden-Baden. Her health stabilized somewhat over the following year, and she recalled Reisach's words to her, written from Rome following her departure from Kintzheim. Pius IX had made him a cardinal of the Roman Curia on December 17, 1855. "In a few years, come to Rome, when your health has improved."[28] In summer 1857, the princess moved to the Eternal City. She took up residence in the Palazzo alle Quattro Fontane, right next to the Quirinal Palace, the pope's city residence outside the Vatican.[29]

In contrast to her first visit to Rome in 1834, there were now plenty of German speakers in the Curia for Katharina to approach. Many candidates for the priesthood left Germany for Rome's Collegium Germanicum to study theology, and the Vatican offices employed an increasing number of Germans. Most important, a close relative of Katharina's, Gustav Adolf zu Hohenlohe-Schillingsfürst, had been a member of Pius IX's entourage since 1846.[30] Born on February 26, 1823, he was the product of an interdenominational marriage. His father, Prince Franz Joseph, was a Catholic, while his mother, Constanze, Princess zu Hohenlohe-Langenburg, was Protestant. According to the Prussian Civil Code of 1794, the daughters inherited their mother's faith, while the four sons—among them the future imperial chancellor Chlodwig zu Hohenlohe-Schillingsfürst[31]—followed their father's religion. In spite of his liberal upbringing, Gustav Adolf fell under the influence of the Breslau Prince-Bishop Melchior von Diepenbrock[32] and chose to enter the priesthood. He first studied Catholic theology in Breslau and Munich, and was possibly influenced by an encounter with the Munich church historian Ignaz von Döllinger.[33] Gustav then decided to begin his ecclesiastical career in the Roman Curia, as befitted his status—a choice that met with vehement resistance from his Protestant mother. She was afraid her son would be spoiled by the Jesuits who dominated the Curia. But Gustav's brother Chlodwig was able to reassure their mother: a spell in Rome wouldn't automatically make him a Jesuit. And in fact, Gustav managed to resist the charms of the Society of Jesus. The openminded, irenic education he had received in Breslau and Munich won through.

Hohenlohe quickly ascended through the Roman Curia. In 1847, he entered the Accademia dei Nobili, the training institute for the Curia's leaders and prospective papal diplomats. In 1848, he accompanied Pius IX as he fled to Gaeta. There, he was ordained as a priest and succeeded in building a friendship with Pius IX. The pope, who "loved him personally and had him as his favorite companion" set great store by Hohenlohe's opinion.[34] He took on the function of a Secret Chamberlain participating, and being a member of the pope's household gave him direct access to Pius IX. When Katharina came to Rome in 1857, she was able to witness her cousin being consecrated as a bishop in the Sistine Chapel. Hohenlohe rose to become the titular archbishop of Edessa. As the pope's almoner, he administered the pontiff's alms fund, and coordinated his charitable work.

Even so, Katharina remained true to her long-standing spiritual guide and confessor, Cardinal Reisach, and didn't consider Hohenlohe for this role. By staying with Reisach, she was allying herself to a particular theological and political orientation—though without really being aware of the nuances of the different philosophies for which Reisach and Hohenlohe stood.

We can't be certain which of the two arranged Katharina's first meeting with the pope. In any case, Katharina was intrigued to find him charming and likable. He invited Katharina to see him on numerous occasions, and granted her several private audiences. Pius IX was clearly gratified even by the fact that she was closely related to the Protestant king of Prussia, and he hoped to influence Berlin's religious policy through her.

In one private audience, the pope is said to have made a joke about her extremely stately appearance, which was due to her tremendous girth.[35] The Italians referred to her in mocking tones as a *matrone*. Her niece, Marie von Thurn und Taxis, also spoke of her aunt's "shocking corpulence." She described Katharina as a "peculiar, engaging and awe-inspiring character," who was "tall and very fat." Her rosy face was "broad and bloated," though it retained "traces of great beauty" and lent her a "serene and regal" air. "Her wide light blue eyes looked directly at you; they spoke of a quick, lively mind, absolute correctness, and a masterful, passionate will. [She had] thick, blond eyebrows, a straight, pretty nose, a small mouth which could smile so gently, showing small, white, regular teeth, and dimples in her cheeks. . . . She had a strong Swabian accent, with a quaint, sing-song tone. Out of this imposing body came a very high, soft, almost childlike voice." To Marie, her aunt seemed a "confident woman with a burning faith, never afraid to draw her sword to defend her rights."[36]

A ROMAN CLOISTERED IDYLL

Katharina and her spiritual guide, Cardinal Reisach, began the search for a suitable convent as soon as she arrived in Rome. The pope himself seems to have made the first suggestion, directing Katharina toward the Visitandines.[37] Central to their devotional practice was the worship of the Sacred Heart of Jesus—a cult that had declined during the Enlightenment, but underwent a revival in the nineteenth century. Pius IX encouraged the worship of the Sacred Heart, turning it into a beacon of his crusade against modernity. The Sacred Heart cult became a symbol of Catholics' retreat inward, toward a self-ghettoization into the countersociety of the Catholic milieu. It became a "symbol of identification for Catholics' contemporary sufferings." The Catholics had lost the battle against the modernization processes of the modern era.[38] While modern science declared the brain to be the most important organ in the human body, Catholics clung to the idea of the heart "as the central organ of physical life, and the bearer of moral life."[39]

But urgent repairs to the Visitandines' recently purchased convent buildings made it impossible for the princess to join their order. This meant that Reisach was able to redirect Katharina's interest to a convent that he may well have had in mind for her from the beginning: Sant'Ambrogio della Massima. This was an enclosed convent of the "strictest order," which led Marie von Thurn und Taxis to describe its inhabitants as *sepolte vive*—buried alive.[40] Reisach's suggestion is surprising, given that he had considered the much less strict setup of the convent in Alsace too taxing for the sickly, unhappy princess. One would rather have expected he would suggest that Katharina seek spiritual refuge in an independent religious community for noblewomen.

But the cardinal gave Katharina the impression that he believed the piety and strict discipline that ruled Sant'Ambrogio would suit her very well. And Katharina duly undertook a *retraite* at the Franciscan convent over Easter 1858. Her first impression was overwhelmingly positive. It was "a place of cloistered peace and holy order," and she was convinced she had reached "the goal of her fierce longing for convent life." To make absolutely sure that this was somewhere she could achieve the long-sought-after "undisturbed union with her soul's bridegroom," Jesus Christ, the princess asked permission to extend her stay in Sant'Ambrogio by becoming a postulant. This meant she wouldn't yet formally enter the convent, or have to wear the convent habit.[41] A number of people warned her against this, particularly those allied to her cousin, Archbishop Hohenlohe, who doubted that the sickly princess would "survive in a strict convent." But Katharina remained there, wearing her own clothes, for several more months.[42]

During this time, Reisach also introduced her to a new confessor, as his many duties left him with no time to continue looking after Katharina. He remained her spiritual guide, but handed over day-to-day matters and regular confession to a close Jesuit acquaintance of his: the forty-seven-year-old Padre Giuseppe Peters. Peters had, in any case, some years ago begun taking confession from other nuns in Sant'Ambrogio to relieve the pressure on the convent's spiritual director his fellow Jesuit Giuseppe Leziroli, who was sixty-three and in poor health. This way, the princess could continue to receive spiritual guidance from the Jesuit order.

Later, Katharina had the highest praise for her trial period in Sant'Ambrogio. According to her *Erlebnisse*, "Life in the convent . . . left nothing to be desired, and seemed exemplary." Rules were followed to the letter; there was a good balance between work and prayer, with prayers starting at four o'clock in the morning; the *clausura* was strictly maintained. The princess was also pleased with Sant'Ambrogio's architectonics: "Hardly a sound from the city at whose center it lay penetrated this quiet, private world." She was particularly taken with the Franciscans' poverty and simplicity. The majority of their income came from gardening and "artistic embroidery for church decoration." The nuns were completely sealed off from the world; even the priests who came to give Communion or take confession were not permitted to enter the enclosure. As is usual in a strictly enclosed order, they remained separated from the nuns by iron bars.[43]

The princess was also more than satisfied with "the people who managed and led this quiet, well-ordered, unworldly community." In particular, she thought the abbess, Sister Maria Veronica, was "a fine example of obedience to the sacred rules, and a woman of gentle, quiet character," who inspired in her a sense of great trust from the very beginning. It was easy "to obey her like a child," and Katharina felt "very drawn to her." But she was still more fascinated by the novice mistress, who was also the abbess's deputy: Madre Vicaria Maria Luisa of Saint Francis Xavier. "This young nun (she was still only twenty-seven years old) possessed a striking physical beauty and grace, and such a lovely, winning nature that all hearts soon felt drawn to her." The princess, too, willingly gave in to the "magic of her loveliness"; she was truly "enchanted by [this] likable nun."[44]

As a member of the German aristocracy, however, Katharina felt a clear division between her own mentality and education, and those of the Italian nuns, who mostly came from simpler stock than herself.[45] To her mind, they were women "without knowledge of the world or its people," with no "refined education, or even some knowledge that would have been imparted by the most rudimentary schooling." As the princess recalled, they had never even seen a toothbrush before.[46] At the time, there was a widespread belief that the devil and evil spirits tried to force their way in through a person's orifices, in order to take possession of him. The nuns were baffled by Katharina's toothbrush. They worried that it might be the work of the devil, and debated whether Katharina should be allowed to carry on using it. After consulting the abbess and the father confessors, the princess was permitted to keep the toothbrush, which was deemed spiritually harmless. The cotton that Katharina used for her needlecraft was also completely unknown to her Roman sisters.[47] They earnestly believed, as they told Katharina on several occasions, that "such stuff grew on the heads of Germans."[48] But the princess interpreted this cultural ignorance as *sancta simplicitas*. And holy innocence was a very becoming trait in humble nuns, particularly the daughters of the *Poverello*, Saint Francis of Assisi.

After a trial period of just over six months, Katharina came to a firm decision. She believed she had found the end point of "her fierce longing for convent life."[49] On September 29, 1858, having contributed a dowry to the convent, she was officially clothed as a novice.[50] Cardinal Costantino Patrizi performed the liturgical ceremony, and Cardinal Reisach "gave an address on withdrawing from the world."[51] This marked the princess's admission to the convent of Regulated Franciscans of the Third Order.[52] Katharina was now ruled by the abbess and the novice mistress, who was her immediate superior, and had to follow their instructions with absolute obedience.

When the princess entered the convent, it was home to around three dozen nuns.[53] Most of them came from Rome itself, or the surrounding area of Latium. A few were from other parts of the Papal States. Katharina was the only foreigner in Sant'Ambrogio. The princess was also an exception in terms of her social background. The German noblewoman was now living with women who came mostly from the middle classes, and whose families were able to raise the substantial dowry necessary for their daughters' admission. All the sisters could read and write; one was a lawyer's sister, another the daughter of a surgeon; at least one of them could speak French. The forty-one-year-old Katharina found that they were divided into three age groups. A handful were in their early sixties, having lived in the convent since it was founded. Then there were a dozen or so sisters of around forty years old. But life in Sant'Ambrogio was shaped by its numerous younger sisters. About twenty of them were aged just twenty, or even younger; their presence was mostly down to a successful recruitment drive by the novice mistress, Maria Luisa.

SALVATION FROM A CLOISTERED HELL

But the idyll of Sant'Ambrogio proved deceptive. The little piece of paradise inside the convent walls must quickly have become hell on earth for Katharina. There is no other explanation for her desperate call for help, her cry of "save, save me!" to her cousin, Archbishop Hohenlohe, on July 25, 1859. Even getting him to Sant'Ambrogio had involved taking a huge risk: she had smuggled a letter to the Vatican out of the enclosure without the knowledge of the convent's superiors, which was against the rules. Less than a year after entering the convent, there seemed to be nothing left of her "childlike obedience" to the abbess.

What happened inside the walls of Sant'Ambrogio, in the ten months from September 1858 to July 1859? The archbishop couldn't make head nor tail of what his cousin said when he met her in the convent on July 25. He thought she had become confused and was talking nonsense—at least, Katharina's *Erlebnisse* describes his reaction in these terms.[54] At first, he could see no danger to the princess's life. Hohenlohe seemed convinced that Katharina had overtaxed herself again, just as she had at the convent in Kintzheim, and was seeking some way of extricating herself from the situation. It was no coincidence that he had written to her at the start of July 1859, urging her "to show perseverance in her chosen profession."[55] To his mind, it was simply out of the question for her to leave another convent. He had, of course, been against her entering Sant'Ambrogio in the first place. He knew what a delicate state her health was in, but she had listened to her spiritual guide, Reisach, instead of him.

In spite of all his persuasion, Hohenlohe was unable to reassure his cousin, and when she carried on talking about poisoning and how she feared for her life, he reluctantly decided to help her. He went to the pope and begged permission for the princess to leave the convent the following day, on grounds of ill health. Pius IX granted his wish immediately.[56] This speedy solution was only made possible by the direct access to Pius IX that Hohenlohe was granted as a Secret Chamberlain. Anyone else would have had to set in motion a lengthy process in order to fulfill the requirements of canon law for being released from a convent.[57]

On July 26, 1859, Archbishop Hohenlohe collected Katharina von Hohenzollern-Sigmaringen from the convent and had her taken to his estate at Tivoli. In these rural surroundings, she would be at peace, and then they could see what was to be done. Katharina believed she had managed to convince her cousin "that her fears were not unfounded," and that there had been real attempts on her life.[58] However, it isn't certain whether Hohenlohe grasped the true extent of the scandal that had played out in Sant'Ambrogio. It may merely have been pity that prompted him to let Katharina draw a line under her second attempt at convent life.

The Villa d'Este, Hohenlohe's summer residence in Tivoli, lay some eighteen miles northeast of Rome. Its gardens, with their fountains and sprawling parklands, were an ideal place for Katharina to recover from the tribulations of her life in the convent. Here, she could finally bring the Sant'Ambrogio chapter of her life to a close. But she needed to get back on her feet in more than the physical sense. She also had to work through what had happened to her inside the walls of the Roman convent from a spiritual point of view. Although Cardinal Reisach visited Hohenlohe in Tivoli at the end of July, Katharina didn't open up to her long-term spiritual guide.[59] Instead, she started talking to a Benedictine padre from Saint Paul Outside the Walls, a Catholic abbey in Rome. He was taking a rest cure in Tivoli, to escape the heat of the Roman summer. Rudolf Wolter had been born in Bonn in 1825, obtained his doctorate in philosophy from the university there in 1849, and was ordained in 1850.[60] In 1856, he followed his brother Ernst[61] into the abbey of Saint Paul Outside the Walls, taking the religious name Maurus. The abbot at the time, Simplicio Pappalettere, was very receptive to modern ideas.[62] His aim was to create a synthesis of Benedictine spirituality and contemporary philosophy within Saint Paul Outside the Walls, a counterbalance to the Jesuit-dominated Gregorian University. He was guided in this by the thought of the Viennese priest and philosopher Anton Günther.[63]

Maurus Wolter clearly made a big impression on the princess. His spirituality, and his exuberant enthusiasm for the cause of Saint Benedict, the "flame that consumed him," was as great a source of fascination for Katharina as the young Reisach had been in 1834.[64] Wolter became her new spiritual guide and confessor almost overnight. When his rest cure in Tivoli came to an end, the princess wrote to his superiors "with the urgent plea to grant an extension to Don Mauro Wolter's holiday with us." It had been a great comfort to her to have found a countryman, whom providence had "delivered for my spiritual guidance." She implored them "not to rob me of such a father confessor."[65] And a month later, she thanked the "sons of Saint Benedict" for "graciously listening to the humble pleas of a poor Franciscan child." They had, she said, "shown a deep understanding of her painful orphaned state, kindly [allowing her] to find her homeland in the hearts of German priests."[66]

During these pastoral conversations, which sometimes took place in the sacramental context of confession, the idea took shape in Katharina's mind that—as she reported in her *Erlebnisse*—she "should not be content with her own rescue from Sant'Ambrogio." It was her duty to bring "the abuses there to the attention of the Holy See."[67] A few weeks after Archbishop Hohenlohe had rescued her, Katharina von Hohenzollern-Sigmaringen contacted the Holy Tribunal of the *Sanctum Officium*, and made serious allegations against the nuns of Sant'Ambrogio.

DENUNCIATION AS A MORAL DUTY

The first files in the case of Sant'Ambrogio date from August 23, 1859.[68] On this day, Katharina von Hohenzollern appeared in person before the investigating judge of the Roman Inquisition (known as the *Sanctum Officium,* or Holy Office), First *Socius* Vincenzo Leone Sallua. Sallua, a highly experienced inquisitor, accepted the denunciation and questioned the "denunciator" about her allegations.[69] The interview took place in Archbishop Hohenlohe's apartment in Rome.

The princess first placed her hand on the Gospels, and swore to tell the truth. Then she said: "It is out of a moral duty, imposed by my current father confessor, that I turn to this holy tribunal." She explained that the German mother tongue she shared with her new spiritual guide, Padre Wolter, had allowed them to discuss at length all the "doubts and anguishes" that had plagued her during her stay in Sant'Ambrogio. With his help, she had finally managed to impose a degree of order on the confusing events of that period. As Katharina told the inquisitor, four issues had taken shape in her mind during these discussions, and she wanted to bring them to the attention of the highest tribunal. First, there was the forbidden cult of the nun who had founded the Franciscan community of Sant'Ambrogio, Maria Agnese Firrao. She had been found guilty of "false holiness" by the Holy Office at the start of the nineteenth century. Despite this, the nuns doggedly persisted in venerating her as a saint, both while Firrao was still alive, and to an even greater extent after her death. The second issue was the highly suspect relationship that the young novice mistress and madre vicaria, Maria Luisa of Saint Francis Xavier, had conducted with "Pietro N., called the Americano," under the pretext of attempting to free him from demonic possession. The third was this same Maria Luisa's claim to sainthood. She gave the appearance of having an "extraordinary soul." She was said to be capable of "supernatural things," and to possess "heavenly gifts." Katharina's fourth point encompassed all the things that had "befallen" her in the convent, up to and including the attempts on her life.

Following "careful consideration" and "thorough reflection," her confessor had declared it her absolute moral duty "to denounce everything to this *Supremo Tribunale*." She therefore sat down and wrote about her experiences in German, "*in modo narrativo*," before translating this into Italian. The princess added that she wanted to submit her denunciation in written form, since she would find it "far too oppressive and complex to do this verbally."

The incendiary power of this *Denunzia* was not fully revealed in Katharina's verbal complaint. Clandestine relationships between attractive men and beautiful young nuns—women whose parents or guardians had often forced them to enter a convent against their will—were, after all, a classic and frequently aired rumor. The Nun of Monza from Alessandro Manzoni's *The Betrothed,* and Denis Diderot's novel *The Nun* are probably the best known literary examples of these stories.[70] And Katharina was a "stately" matron, making allegations against an attractive young novice mistress with "angelic looks": Sallua couldn't entirely rule out envy as a possible motive.

But the allegation of "pretense of holiness" against Maria Luisa must have made the inquisitor prick up his ears. Combating women who claimed to be living saints, or were honored as such by their devotees, was one of the Holy Office's "sacred duties." And Katharina was making a double accusation: first against the dead founder, and secondly against the young madre vicaria. The Inquisition had to act on this. Katharina's use of the words *affettata santità*, for the religious offense of feigned holiness suggested she had received professional advice. This must have come from either Hohenlohe or Wolter. If the princess hadn't been able to name a specific offense against the Faith—if she had continued to focus on the poisoning attempts—then her complaint wouldn't have fallen within the Inquisition's remit. Her cousin and her new spiritual guide had considered this carefully. They also seem to have coached Katharina on the reason for making her complaint, which she cited several times: she was simply fulfilling the moral obligation that had been laid out for her in confession.

THE SECRET OF SANT'AMBROGIO

Sallua was confronted with the monstrous scale of Katharina's accusations against the convent only on careful reading of her written denunciation. It must have taken his breath away.

Sant'Ambrogio had a secret. At first, Katharina had no idea what this might be. But three months after she entered the convent on March 27, 1858, she knew that something that "frequently occupied the community" had been kept from her.[71] Through her conversations with the madre vicaria, she became aware of the existence of "some kind of secret." "She led me to understand that the father confessor had decided it was not yet time to reveal it to me." She soon sensed this was somehow connected with "influences of a supernatural kind," but comforted herself with the thought that "such naïve souls" as her new Roman sisters could more easily obtain their spiritual edification from those miraculous tales than from abstract theological tracts.[72]

Of course, had she been able to interpret Reisach's cryptic remarks, she might have been forewarned about this, as Katharina remarked self-critically in her *Erlebnisse*. Before she entered the convent, the cardinal had explained to her that in a southern country such as Italy one was frequently confronted with unusual or supernatural occurrences. "Strange and remarkable things might take place around her." The Italians' lively characters would make things seem very different from what she was used to, coming from cool, rationalist Germany. But in a place like Rome, where a "living faith grasps and maintains everything with a freshness and strength that we Germans can hardly conceive of . . . there also exist struggles and temptations quite alien to our experience." Reisach had warned Katharina not to let herself "be unsettled or disturbed by such things."[73]

The cardinal's words reveal his own enthusiasm for Latin European sentimental forms of Catholic devotion, and his rejection of an Enlightened, rational religious practice that was common in Germany. He was particularly fascinated by transcendental religious phenomena: in every single hour he was prepared for manifestations of the Sacred, especially in Rome. There was no doubt in his mind that "poor souls," the spirits of the dead, could take up contact with this world from the other side at any time.[74] So the princess saw nothing unusual in the fact that the refectory readings in Sant'Ambrogio often mentioned "ecstasies, miracles and apparitions." Admittedly, she criticized these readings for overstimulating the imagination of her fellow nuns, and would have preferred solid "religious instruction." This might have imparted the necessary basic Christian knowledge that the nuns of Sant'Ambrogio were wholly lacking—as the princess soon noticed.[75] But, following Reisach's advice, she put their enthusiasm for supernatural religious phenomena and miracles down to their southern mentality and their lack of educational achievement. At first, she didn't see anything dangerously heretical. And her new father confessor, Padre Peters, managed to allay the princess's "first serious concerns."[76]

However, the nuns were still hiding something from her: they would stop talking abruptly when Katharina approached them; they would slip into a Roman dialect that the princess didn't understand; they dropped obscure hints. It was only after she was admitted as a novice on September 29 that Padre Peters and Cardinal Reisach were finally prepared to come clean and lift the veil of secrecy. They had kept from her the fact that the founder of the Franciscan community of Sant'Ambrogio, Mother Agnese Firrao, had been condemned as a false saint by the Roman Inquisition, and sent into exile. They evidently feared that this revelation would have kept the princess from entering the convent.

This secret was the first point of Katharina's denunciation. She complained that despite her conviction, Agnese Firrao was still being honored as a real saint in Sant'Ambrogio. The nuns, and in particular Padre Peters, had played down the implications of the Holy Office's verdict on their mother founder. Once Katharina had become a novice, they referred to Firrao in her presence as *La Beata Madre* and venerated her as a saint, even though the Church stipulated that this kind of cult was only for people it had officially beatified. "They showed me her scourges, and other instruments of mortification, and told me of the three pounds of raw flesh that fell from the Mother after a single flagellation. They always praised her extraordinary virtue," the princess noted in her report. "In this convent they don't even blush when they proclaim the holiness of Sister Maria Agnese; she surpasses almost all other saints." In Sant'Ambrogio, the Inquisition was criticized for having passed a clearly wrong judgment when it found Agnese Firrao guilty of false holiness. According to Katharina, the nuns regarded numerous items owned by their "saint" as contact relics: clothes, embroidery, and in particular three portraits done in oils. The confessors were working on a "saint's life" of Firrao, which would be read aloud to the community once it was finished. The founder's prayers, mottoes, letters, and messages had been painstakingly collected. On high feast days, "poems were recited, glorifying the blessed Maria Agnese, depicting her surrounded by angels, and nuns who had passed on." On these occasions, "words of praise for the current madre vicaria were put into the mouth of the 'Beata Madre,' calling her 'her joy, her treasure, the brightest of her stars.'"

A POSSESSED SEDUCER OF NUNS

The second of the princess's allegations came under the mysterious heading "Report on the Possessed Man."[77] Maria Luisa, the novice mistress, had told stories about an attractive man whom she called

Pietro, or just "The Americano." This man, who had apparently been educated at a Jesuit school in Fribourg, Switzerland, had been close to the convent's second confessor, Padre Peters, since his early youth. The mysterious American was actually a native German speaker, as Katharina discovered, and was probably from Tyrol. He was said to be in his mid-thirties, and a doctor by profession. He had come to Rome to rid himself of five demons, which Peters could "clearly distinguish," as he had given them names. Maria Luisa was convinced that, once the Americano had been healed (through tough penance and fasting), he could do a great deal of good for the Jesuits, and would "convert thousands of people." "On July 11, 1858, the madre vicaria told me he had prayed for 11 hours at the grave of St Ignatius, where the saint had appeared and praised the madre vicaria, expressing his joy that Pietro was under her guidance."

This last phrase caught the princess's attention. It seemed to be Maria Luisa, and not one of the confessors, who was undertaking the exorcism to free him from his demons: an unheard-of idea for Katharina. According to canon law, exorcisms were only to be performed by very experienced clerics. Under no circumstances should they be carried out by women, whom the Church had regarded as particularly susceptible to the temptation of evil ever since the fall of Eve. And in fact, on several occasions the novice mistress told her how much she had suffered because of this possessed man. In her written complaint, Katharina reported several meetings between Maria Luisa and the American. "One day, when she came back from a meeting with him, she limped into my cell, her eye closed up, her tongue swollen, her head covered in bruises. She announced that she had fought him and had eventually emerged victorious, forcing him to make five signs of the cross on the ground with his tongue."

The whole thing seemed highly suspicious to Katharina. As she tried to explain to the inquisitor, whenever she saw the novice mistress, she did her best to avoid this delicate subject. However, Maria Luisa wanted to impress her new novice with this exorcism, and on several occasions she showed Katharina letters from Pietro, composed in bad Italian. A letter in German at the end of October was addressed both to Maria Luisa, and to Luisa Maria (Princess Katharina von Hohenzollern). It made a play on the similarity of the two nuns' names, and used lewd terms to suggest that Luisa Maria could become a "mother without a husband" like Maria Luisa. Maria Luisa didn't speak German, so she gave this letter to the princess to translate. Katharina was "highly indignant" at its many erotic innuendos and "extremely obscene expressions." Pietro more or less explicitly asked both nuns to engage in sexual acts with him. The letter concluded by saying that the madre vicaria would be tormented by one of the American's demons—"the demon of impurity"—for seven months; she would "suffer so much that she would have to seek his help as a doctor, though she wouldn't have to lose her virginity."

Katharina was shocked, and her trust in the novice mistress was shaken. She told her confessor, Padre Peters, that she was "astonished to see a young nun's chaste eyes under threat of reading such turpitudes." Peters, as Katharina recalled in her *Denunzia*, admitted to her that Maria Luisa had also shown him a letter of the Americano. "But he claimed that he either didn't read Pietro's letters, or destroyed them immediately." The princess ended her remarks on the "Possessed Man" with the cryptic assertion that following the "sad events" that had taken place as a result of her informing the confessor about this, Peters and Maria Luisa had stopped mentioning Pietro in her presence. These words contained at least an indirect accusation that the Jesuit had reported to the novice mistress everything Katharina had told him in their pastoral conversations.

A FALSE SAINT

The princess's third allegation related directly to Sister Maria Luisa, whom she accused of nothing less than "false" and "feigned holiness."[78] But first, she presented a very interesting character sketch of this young nun.

Maria Luisa is 27 years old and has been in the convent since she was 13. She has a very pleasant physiognomy and an almost irresistible charm—which, however, is rather more like that of a worldly person than of a virgin dedicated to God. In addition to this quality, she is constantly busy and thinking about everyone and everything. She has a superior elegance and ease in conversation, and displays the utmost delicacy in her dealings with others, along with a sharp wit and cunning—though without any sententious affectation—and a tense, composed manner. You can hear the madre vicaria chatting away in the convent almost all the day; she is quite incapable of staying quiet or keeping a secret. The consequence of this is garrulity, volatility, a tendency to lie easily, alongside extreme cunning, an intriguing mind, jealousy and effrontery. But all this seems to vanish beneath a mysterious allure, a sweet lovability and a kind of affected ingenuousness and liveliness. Among all the offices she holds—though she is far too young for them—are the important positions of cellarer, vicaress and novice mistress. She pays hardly any heed to the convent rules. She seldom shows her face in the choir, the refectory or at the daily devotions. In addition to this she has access to all the keys, and to all the convent's rooms during prayers and mealtimes, in which she almost never participates. Her duties make it very easy for her to spend long periods in the parlatory, conducting long, confidential conversations with outside persons, and gaining her impressive knowledge of all that is going on in politics and in the city. She is able to satisfy her boundless passion for control and command over everything. This ambitious pride drives her to use everyone as an instrument for her projects to diminish the authority of the mother abbess, even to remove it, by speaking ill of her and countermanding her instructions with orders of her own.

The princess added an observation that sounds very much like the "crushes, 'breakdowns' and exuberance" typical of a girls' boarding school in the nineteenth century—ways in which young girls expressed their enthusiasm for a teacher or more experienced pupil, while also channeling their "erotic desires."[79] Maria Crocifissa, a twenty-year-old novice, followed the novice mistress everywhere, "as if drunk with love. She is always caressing her, kissing her hand, laughing and doing a thousand crazy things without the madre vicaria stopping her. The tender, jealous affection most of the novices display towards their mistress is also reprehensible: they frequently gather round her bed until late into the night. I cannot and must not make an ultimate judgment on her methods of educating the novices. But what I do know is that the novices are largely left to their own devices."

After this, Katharina von Hohenzollern raised her real allegation: the madre vicaria's pretense of holiness. Maria Luisa enjoyed "the reputation of an extraordinary penitential spirit. In the convent she is known for hardly ever taking sustenance." The confessor had told Katharina that "there was no natural explanation for how little she ate." Katharina was not convinced: "Outside the refectory, I have seen otherwise." She must have observed Maria Luisa eating between the official mealtimes. "She also gives the appearance of spending her nights in prayers, meditations, and in terrible privations and sufferings, emerging from these mysterious nightly struggles with her tongue swollen and of different colors. And here I must sadly confess that in 16 months I never saw her pray during the day before the Blessed Sacrament, or in any other place."

The way Maria Luisa spoke about senior figures in the Catholic Church struck Katharina as high-handed, and out of keeping with the humble bearing of a nun. Still, Maria Luisa had "the reputation, particularly with the father confessor, of possessing unusual and wonderful graces, which showed themselves in a heavenly wisdom, a superhuman knowledge of secret things, both inside and outside the convent ... [and] through miracles, namely the ability to heal the sick. The madre vicaria also often prophesies, with an indifferent expression on her face, that at a certain hour her guardian angel would leave something for her in the rota at the convent gates[80]—sometimes sweets, or other things. And the items she mentioned really did appear at the appointed hour, to the great wonderment of the novices, who would eat them with great reverence and devotion."

After a refectory reading on the life of a saint who exuded a pleasant, sweet fragrance for three weeks, the madre vicaria smelled so strongly of rose essence "that it induced a headache, because the whole convent was filled with it." The princess didn't share the opinion of many in the convent that Maria Luisa was able to draw the pain and suffering of other nuns to herself with an almost magnetic force, and could even heal the sick using a ring of "mysterious power." She didn't know how the vicaress had come by this ring, but one of the nuns who had supposedly been healed by it later said: "It is certainly a strange thing that our madre vicaria received a ring of such extraordinary size, when the ring Saint Catherine received from the Savior was so small and hardly visible." Katharina went on: "After I had complained about all this to the father confessor, she stopped wearing the ring when I was there. This ring is about an inch and a half in size, and they say it is made of diamonds and rubies! And here I cannot conceal the suspicion that this mysterious ring came from the possessed Pietro."

It was impossible for anyone in Sant'Ambrogio to express doubts about Maria Luisa's holiness. The abbess and the convent's spiritual director, Padre Leziroli, always had explanations at the ready. "The fragrance of sainthood which surrounds the madre causes people to associate her authority with a particular hatred of the devil—as if any skepticism about her perfection were inspired by Satan." For many years, the confessors had been rebutting any doubt about Maria Luisa's virtues, calling it "diabolical machination." The novices in particular felt they were "placed under a good deal of pressure" by the madre vicaria. But Leziroli and the abbess had explained to them that if they thought they had seen Maria Luisa doing anything unjust, this was in reality "a manifestation of the devil, who took on the appearance of the madre vicaria."

Katharina's father confessor, Padre Peters, also rejected her doubts about the madre vicaria's "truthfulness" and her "character." He believed Maria Luisa completely incapable of "deception." This prompted a confrontation between the novice and the novice mistress, during which Maria Luisa denied ever having spoken to Katharina about the possessed Americano, let alone having shown her a letter from him, "and certainly not the above-mentioned German letter." Both confessors declared "that what had happened was impossible to explain, unless by a most frequent apparition of the demon in the guise of the madre vicaria." Katharina could "give no credence" to this explanation. In her view, all the facts fitted "very well with the character and the behavior of the madre vicaria." She had become well acquainted with these over fifteen long months, during which: "I can say with the greatest certainty that I did not see her perform *a single virtuous deed.*"

To Katharina's mind, the only plausible explanation was the obvious one: Maria Luisa was pretending a holiness she didn't deserve. She was a false saint, and thus a heretic. But how had she managed to convince the other nuns and the confessors of her holiness? Katharina's denunciation also provided an answer for this. She took the confessors' diabolical explanation, and turned it around: Maria Luisa was no victim of Satan; she was in league with him. "Considering all of this together, I feel obliged to express my most painful concern that the above-mentioned madre vicaria, Maria Luisa, was only able to achieve her reputation for extraordinary holiness in the convent of Sant'Ambrogio with the help of the devil. In the future, she could call up endless misery not only for this convent, but for more distant regions too." Katharina also put the attempt on her own "poor life" down to this.

POISONING

The princess began to feel increasingly isolated in the convent. The nuns viewed her as an unbeliever, for her lack of faith in the "convent saint." And this, as she soon learned, was a dangerous thing to be. In a letter she submitted to Sallua, Katharina gave a detailed description of how the madre vicaria's "whole hatred" increasingly fell on her; how Maria Luisa's "impassioned tone" and her "screeching voice" "froze the marrow in [her] bones."

Katharina reported that on December 8, 1858, she finally confronted the novice mistress. "When I was alone with her, I threw myself at her feet and begged her to honor the Lord and retract." But Maria Luisa refused. She demanded absolute faith and obedience from Katharina. She told the princess she had to accept her supernatural gifts as genuine, and above all believe that the devil repeatedly took on her form. It had been Satan, and not her, who had shown the princess the Americano's obscene letter. Now it was Katharina's turn to refuse. The abyss seemed unbridgeable the madre vicaria told her: "Your behavior shows that you are not guided by the spirit of God. You will always be one among us who doubts."[81]

Katharina's predicament now became a matter of life and death: immediately after the abortive conversation on December 8, she fell gravely ill, and it seemed likely she would die. Was this a coincidence? Was there something more behind it? Or had the princess simply become overexcited?

Katharina herself blamed her sudden illness on several attempts to poison her. And she believed the person behind these attempts was none other than the madre vicaria. She laid out this belief at some length in her fourth and final allegation, in which she accused Maria Luisa and her accomplices of attempting to murder her on several occasions.[82]

The princess told the inquisitor that her argument with Maria Luisa had badly unsettled her stomach. On December 9, she was therefore grateful when somebody brought her a cup of black tea after lunch, supposedly on the abbess's instructions. She drank it down and was immediately gripped by severe "stomach pains, dizziness and vomiting." She was too weak to stand, and had to take to her bed. In the evening, two novices brought her a cup of chamomile tea, which she hoped would alleviate her symptoms. But she was put off by its acrid taste and revolting aroma. She had one of the novices taste it, and she, too, found it entirely unpalatable. Then the madre vicaria suddenly appeared and chastised the novice, saying this sort of behavior wasn't permissible when caring for the sick. On December 10, Katharina said, she was given castor oil, and she recovered a little.

On the morning of December 11, the madre vicaria herself brought the princess a cup of beef tea, which tasted "*amarissimo e pizzicante,*" extremely bitter and acrid. With a huge effort, she overcame her misgivings and finished the cup "as a test of her obedience." She immediately suffered severe stomach pains, a headache, and nausea, and felt intoxicated. One of the two convent doctors prescribed almond milk with gum arabic. She was given this emulsion, which she had taken many times before, in the afternoon. Katharina was horrified to discover that this had "the same acrid taste and unpleasant smell" as the beef tea. She drank only a little of it, and at once felt extremely unwell. The pot of almond milk remained in her cell. When the doctor returned, a novice who was devoted to Maria Luisa came and hid the pot. That evening, the novice mistress brought her a plate of rice soup, but this also had "the same bitter taste." Again, the princess refused to eat, at which the madre vicaria was very indignant.

On December 12, the novices brought her beef tea again. Katharina managed to put some of it into a glass vial without being seen, and asked her confessor, Padre Peters, to have it analyzed. He promised he would. But Peters was unable to share the princess's suspicion that the madre vicaria was trying to poison her. On the contrary, he was quite vexed over her accusations, and did his best to reassure her. And initially—as Katharina reported—he was successful in this. But that night she was struck by a sudden recollection: she had once asked the novice mistress for an ammonia solution to treat insect bites, and Maria Luisa had said: "Know that this is a powerful poison: you could kill a lot of people with this little bottle." The princess had laughed and replied that nobody could bear to swallow the stuff because of its repulsive smell. But now Maria Luisa's seemingly incidental remark gained a new meaning in Katharina's mind.

December 13 passed peacefully. The princess ate and drank almost nothing. In the evening, the confessor came and told her that alum had been found in the beef tea. But, he continued, this had clearly been used accidentally by somebody in the convent kitchen who had mistaken it for salt. Alum wasn't a deadly poison, so she could be reassured. Katharina was unconvinced by his argument: black tea, chamomile tea, beef tea, rice soup—all of them with alum instead of salt? This was too much to be a coincidence or an accident.

The following day, the princess claimed, she was told to take an electuary of cassia and tamarinds. The madre vicaria, and Katharina's fellow novice Maria Ignazia, had both asked her if she was familiar with the taste.

They warned me that this remedy would taste bad, and so once again I had an awful suspicion. I asked for Holy Communion before this, which I was granted. On that Monday night, my night light went out; when I lit it again, I noticed that the ampule of ammonia solution was not in its place. I searched for it all night, but could not find it in my chamber. My knees trembled, and my heart raced. At four o'clock on Tuesday morning the mother abbess visited me, and I assured her that I was better. She told me I could not take Holy Communion as I was ill in bed; other people who were ill did not have it brought to their beds, either. I tried to stay as calm as I could, and to strengthen my faith in God, when Maria Felice brought me the medicine. I invoked the holiest names as I ate, taking six spoonfuls of it. The taste was revolting, but I could not tell what it was. I cannot say what state I was in afterwards. I suffered very much and, an hour later, the rumor went round the convent that I had had a stroke and was close to death. The effects of the illness, after I had taken this medicine, were as follows: protracted sickness with nausea, heavy dizziness in the head, a terrible fever, a racing pulse, a severe rumbling in my stomach and heavy, black stools. The two doctors who cared for me were Doctor Riccardi and Doctor Marchi. I cannot describe exactly the course of the illness after this day, as my memory is not entirely clear, and I cannot now tell the days of December 14 and 15 apart.

Katharina received the last rites: absolution, provisions for the journey, and extreme unction. She was also asked if she wanted to profess her vows ahead of time, as she was on her deathbed, which she gratefully did. "I asked for my crucifix, a book and a burning candle. I stayed quiet and composed for some time. But in my soul, there was a growing suspicion and a fear of death. The agonies were getting worse. They let my blood four times; and although I consented willingly, I was devoured by the fear that they were extracting too much of my blood, hastening my end or at least robbing me of my senses." When Katharina sat up in bed during the night, her veins opened up again, and she was afraid they hadn't bandaged her properly on purpose, to hasten her death. "Frightened, I called for the father confessor, who was in the adjoining room. He came in and saw to it that my bandages were renewed. When I tried to touch my bandaged arm, the confessor held me back, which offended me more than a little. He seemed to believe that I was intending to open the wound deliberately. I was afraid the poison I had been fed was something I had kept in my room. The thought that after my death, people might say I had killed myself with my own poison weighed heavily on me; this idea almost drove me to insanity. I sought for a way to free myself, but in vain."

Katharina survived this terrible night, but there was no end to her agony. When Hohenlohe visited her on December 15, she contemplated asking him to take her away from this danger. "But the thought occurred to me that my words could be dismissed as the product of a high fever. If my suspicion came to light, I would be lost. Fear made me remain silent. . . . I no longer had any faith in myself, and feared sinning before my death." And so the princess allowed her only opportunity to tell somebody outside the enclosure about the poisoning to pass her by.

During the night of December 15, Katharina was left alone with her fears. Her confessor had been sent home. She interpreted this awful night as an attack on her faith by the devil:

> That was the point when the Fiend battled my faith as well. That such things could come to pass in Rome, in one of the best convents, under the eyes of the Church. . . . The *clausura* only serves to draw a veil over such crimes. Where is God, in whom I have placed all my trust, where is my Savior, whom alone I have longed only to serve? Towards morning, at the height of my misery, I found the rosary that Gustav had sent me, lying on my bed. I put it around my neck, in the hope that the merciful Mother would come to my aid. Even if I could not pray, I at least wanted to touch some rosary bead and say an Ave Maria. I tried it, and was saved. I calmed down a little, sensing hope.

When the madre vicaria entered Katharina's cell on the morning of December 16, Katharina asked to speak with her privately. The princess grasped Maria Luisa by both hands and revealed what she knew: that for the past five days, her food and drink had been contaminated with various ingredients. She gave the madre vicaria an urgent warning. Poisoning could be detected after death, through an autopsy, and in her case the Holy Father would undoubtedly order such a procedure to be carried out. "What shame it would bring on the convent, particularly for the father confessors and their order!" She had already proved her love for Sant'Ambrogio by staying silent, even though a single word would have been enough to reveal her situation to the doctors or the archbishop. Katharina asked Maria Luisa to allay her concerns. She wanted permission to seek out her cousin and speak openly with him about her suspicions. The novice mistress would be able to take part in this conversation. Katharina also announced that from then on she would eat and drink nothing that seemed suspicious. "The madre vicaria was completely transformed, kneeling before my bed and begging me to calm myself. Everything would be arranged to allow me to regain my strength, the archbishop would visit me, and I would not have to take any more medicine. The result of this explanation filled me with confidence. On this day I began to hope that the wickedness might finally be at an end."

Katharina placed particular trust in Maria Giuseppa, the sister responsible for the convent dispensary and caring for the sick. When she brought Katharina her medicine, unseen by the others, she gave her a sign that there was nothing mixed into it. "And so I trusted her and drank it. A short while later, Maria Ignazia appeared in a great hurry, completely beside herself. She said I should not take the medicine. I wondered at this." Over the following days, Katharina made an admirably quick physical recovery. But her mental state remained frail. "I still always felt more or less afraid that I might die. I battled against my inner suspicion, and the memory of the things I had suffered. I had somebody fetch all the medicines I had brought with me into the convent—and there was the little bottle of ammonia."

By the time Christmas arrived, things had calmed down somewhat. Katharina continued to be very cautious, and made an effort to be particularly humble with her superiors. She had decided not to speak to anyone on the outside about her terrible suspicions. There was, in any case, no way of doing this from within the convent's strictly enforced enclosure. Until the end of February 1859, neither her cousin Hohenlohe nor her spiritual guide Reisach visited her. But Katharina's strategy didn't work. In the convent, she was still regarded with a high degree of skepticism, and the two confessors, in particular, were still concerned that she might give something away.

Spring 1859 brought fresh fears and uncertainties. Padre Peters and the madre vicaria told Katharina terrible things about the skirmishes taking place on Italian soil, most importantly the tensions between France and Austria over Lombardy and Venetia.[83] Peters and Maria Luisa both saw the "sect of the Freemasons" at work in the attempt to unify Italy, and predicted that their troops would overthrow Rome. There would be terrible atrocities, and priests and members of holy orders would be persecuted. Katharina was convinced they were trying to persuade her to go back to her homeland, as she wrote in her report to the Inquisition.[84] This would have been an elegant way to get rid of somebody who was threatening to reveal the convent's secrets. In far-off Germany, there would be no chance of the princess talking to people with an influence in Rome about what had taken place in Sant'Ambrogio. It would have been impossible for her to make a direct denunciation to the tribunal in Rome, or for them to question her as a witness. And Katharina didn't dismiss this solution out of hand: "I gave thorough consideration to this option, as I hoped I might thereby escape my difficult situation in the convent."

By early summer 1859, Katharina had become extremely agitated: the political situation in Italy was coming to a head. On July 17, Stephanie von Hohenzollern-Sigmaringen,[85] Katharina's step-granddaughter and the queen of Portugal, died of diphtheria, and Katharina fell into an indisposition and into depressive states. The madre vicaria now adopted a new strategy, constantly telling the convent's inhabitants that they had to approach Katharina with great caution and shouldn't interact normally with her. The princess began to fear that the madre vicaria might "have her declared mad on the basis of such fears and agitations." Being locked away in a psychiatric institution would certainly have silenced her once and for all.

However, the madre vicaria's plan didn't come to fruition, and Katharina "had started to entertain the hope of being released in peace," when in summer 1859 there was another dramatic change in the novice mistress's attitude toward the princess. "Her antipathy became apparent again." Once again, Katharina suspected that somebody was trying to murder her. Once, when she had to wait longer than usual for her breakfast, she went into the anteroom to her cell and found Sister Maria Felice there with a cup of chocolate in her hand. The princess believed she was trying to mix something into the chocolate. Despite this, "I drank the chocolate that was brought to me later without any ill effects." Still, her fears remained. "My suspicion continued to grow, so that as soon as I was not being observed, I regularly tipped away my breakfast and my evening soup."

The madre vicaria did her utmost to prevent Katharina making contact with the outside world. In June and July 1859, the princess tried in vain to reach the convent's cardinal protector, Costantino Patrizi, or her cousin Archbishop Hohenlohe. When they both visited Sant'Ambrogio on July 24, they were told that Katharina was ill in bed and could not receive visitors, as entry into the enclosure was not permitted. The madre vicaria also denied the princess any conversation with her confessor. Nor was she allowed to write to her spiritual guide, Cardinal Reisach. "There was no doubt in my mind that I was being kept apart from everyone. I thus feared another attempt on my life. For two days I had been feeling ill. I had pains in my stomach and lower body, and diarrhea, though this was not as severe as during my first illness. . . . The following night was terrible for me. The next morning they wanted to give me cassia; I sent it back and asked for lemonade with cream of tartar." Several times, she was served soup instead of her usual breakfast, and secretly poured it away. Once, Katharina drank a little of the soup in the presence of the novice mistress. Although she couldn't taste anything unusual in it, she suffered severe stomach pains afterward.

Then, on July 25, her salvation arrived in the shape of the archbishop of Edessa. Hohenlohe was her "guardian angel," come to rescue his cousin. "It all went well—my prayers were fulfilled—and I was understood"—as Katharina explained to the inquisitor. "I took off the sacred convent robes with tears in my eyes, and left the convent of Sant'Ambrogio at half past three in the afternoon, on July 26, 1859."

Katharina's written complaint was very nuanced. After studying the text thoroughly, Sallua had only a few questions, which he put to the princess in writing. She answered these by letter, and wasn't required to return to Rome. She was also able to provide information on where certain of the mother founder's papers were hidden.[86]

THE SAVIOR'S PERSPECTIVE

The first person outside the walls of Sant'Ambrogio to whom Katharina spoke about her experiences in the convent was her savior, Archbishop Gustav Adolf zu Hohenlohe-Schillingsfürst. On the road to Tivoli, and during the weeks they spent together at the Villa d'Este, his summer residence, he was able to form a more detailed picture of his cousin's state, and assess the events she related to him.[87]

At his Inquisition hearing, Hohenlohe immediately reminded the inquisitor of the central role Cardinal Reisach had played in Katharina's entry into Sant'Ambrogio. He seemed to have guided her well: at first, everything went splendidly. Katharina was "content and cheerful." Sant'Ambrogio appeared to be the perfect place for his cousin to lead her cloistered life, and her relationships with the other nuns were almost ideal. Then there came a surprising change, toward the end of 1858. "In December a certain Garzia, a servant in the convent, came to me late at night with the news that the princess was in a very

Gustav Adolf zu Hohenlohe-Schillingsfürst rescued his cousin Katharina
from the convent of Sant'Ambrogio.

poor state of health. He did not tell me the exact circumstances; he
only spoke very little." Hohenlohe was unable to leave the Vatican, as
he had duties in the pope's household that he couldn't put off, and he
spent "a very oppressive night."

When Hohenlohe arrived at the convent early next morning, the
abbess and the novice mistress seemed very concerned about the princess's condition. "But they told me flatly that I could not go to her, as
she was out of her mind with pain." The archbishop wasn't put off so
easily, however, and he insisted they tell him more about his cousin's
illness. Finally he received the information that she had suffered a
"syncope." This meant a circulatory collapse, which could have any
number of causes, from impaired circulation in the brain to a cardiac
irregularity, or a metabolic disorder. They told Hohenlohe he should
come back in an hour or two with a blessing from the pope. He went
to Pius IX, obtained his blessing, and, on his return, met Leziroli
in the sacristy, from whom he demanded the right to be allowed to

see his cousin. "He answered abruptly that I would be doing Luisa Maria a great favor if I did not visit her. This was her express wish. She wanted to be alone at this terrible time, and did not wish to be disturbed."

At this moment, as Hohenlohe recalled, it became clear to him that those in charge of Sant'Ambrogio were doing everything in their power to keep him from seeing his sick cousin. He was angered and deeply offended by this, and resorted to invoking his authority as a bishop and close friend of the pope. He accused Leziroli of acting in his "typical girlish way" even in this serious matter. "I needed to see Katharina urgently, and was adamant that I would achieve this." He therefore ordered them to open the door to her cell. After a "remarkably long time" he was finally led into his cousin's chamber. "I found her there with her face aglow, and with a glassy stare; I was shocked at how dazed she was." It was impossible to have a private conversation, as the novice mistress and two other nuns remained in Katharina's cell the whole time. He could sense there was something Katharina wanted to tell him, but couldn't while her guardians were in the room. When he asked about the cause of her illness, she merely pointed to the madre vicaria and said, "Do tell him what I am suffering from!"

The archbishop didn't press her further, instead inquiring whether she needed anything from him or her relatives. Katharina was very "offended" by his apparent reluctance to get to the bottom of the matter, ending the conversation by telling him it would be best for him to follow the rules and refrain from visiting her again. Sant'Ambrogio was a strictly enclosed convent, and its statutes barred visitors from the clausura. The madre vicaria reminded him of this fact forcefully on his way out. "The whole thing left me with a feeling of great sadness, and I went away deeply pained."

This begs the question of why Hohenlohe and his cousin didn't just speak to each other in their native German. The other nuns present in Katharina's cell spoke no German, so the two could have exchanged the relevant information without revealing themselves to the others. In her written complaint, Katharina explained that she had consciously spoken Italian throughout her illness so that Maria Luisa would understand her every word, in an attempt to avoid angering her.[88]

Immediately after his visit, Hohenlohe sought out Katharina's confessor, Padre Peters, in the Jesuit college near the Il Gesù church.[89] He was hoping that Peters could shed more light on his cousin's illness. But in this he was disappointed. The Jesuit merely told him he was certain "she would die the following night, as the sickness in her heart left her with only a few hours to live." These words enraged the archbishop. What made the Jesuit so sure he could predict Katharina's death with such precision?

Several members of the convent, and the doctors treating her, repeatedly advised against Hohenlohe paying Katharina another visit, and he didn't go to see her again for six months. Even Cardinal Patrizi told him the princess wished to be left in peace, and didn't want to see him. What made Cardinal Patrizi side with the abbess, the novice mistress, the confessors, and Katharina's doctors to keep Hohenlohe away and prevent him speaking to her in private? Did they have something to hide, or were they simply trying to protect her?

Hohenlohe heeded the high-ranking cardinal's advice. He only returned to Sant'Ambrogio to see his cousin in the summer of 1859 — but he was denied entry. "The following day she sent me a letter, in which she begged me on Christ's mercy[90] to come to her and have her called to the parlatory. I set off for the convent at once." Several nuns came out to meet him and begged him to dissuade the princess from leaving the convent, because they loved her so much. Finally, Hohenlohe managed to speak to the princess in private. She first thanked him for his letter, in which he had reminded her of her religious calling and encouraged her to remain in her cloistered state. But then she said: "At this moment, it is not a question of my calling; it is simply a matter of saving my life and my soul, as I am afraid I will die here without the presence of the father confessor." Frightened, she told him of that night in December, when she had almost died without Padre Peters looking in on her once, though he had spent all night in the convent.

Finally, Katharina voiced her suspicion "that this illness was brought on by illicit and poisonous substances mixed into her medicines, and her food and drink." Katharina was convinced it was only Hohenlohe's visit in December that had saved her life and prevented further attacks on her person. "She was afraid that something like this would happen again, and begged me for the love of God to take her away from there." She had already written to the cardinal vicar and the Holy Father, begging them to let her leave the convent "on health grounds." She hadn't mentioned to either of them the real reason for her desire to get out of Sant'Ambrogio as quickly as possible: the fact that somebody was trying to murder her.

Hohenlohe also spoke to Katharina's spiritual guide, Cardinal Reisach. The interview with the cardinal must have left him with a very conflicted impression. Hohenlohe thought his cousin's fear of poisoning would be news to Reisach, but the cardinal had been in the picture for months, apparently informed by Peters. Reisach simply hadn't thought it necessary to inform Katharina's closest relative in Rome. Hohenlohe also told the Inquisition that Cardinal Reisach had leapt to defend the convent, especially its beautiful young madre vicaria and the father confessor Peters, against all the accusations. He called Katharina fanciful and thought she had imagined the whole poisoning affair. The noble lady just had "too much imagination." She should subordinate herself once more to the guidance of her confessor "with blind obedience," as befitted a nun.

After much insistence from Hohenlohe, Reisach finally had to concede that poison had been found in Katharina's soup. The cardinal put this down to an "oversight in the kitchen," an accidental "contamination" of the ladle. He dismissed the story about a letter "filled with obscenities and immoral things" that the novice mistress had supposedly given Katharina to read, saying that this was beyond belief. But at least neither of the two clerics was willing to attribute the incident to the influence of the devil.

Hohenlohe remained suspicious. When exactly had Reisach been informed of what was happening in Sant'Ambrogio? Why didn't he step in, as was his duty as Katharina's spiritual guide? Was the Jesuit sympathizer protecting the Jesuit confessor, Padre Peters, even if it meant the possible death of Princess von Hohenzollern?

In Tivoli, Katharina told her cousin she had made a will during her illness, leaving the greater part of her wealth to the convent. The bequest was made on the provision that a new convent would be founded as a daughter institution to Sant'Ambrogio, with the novice mistress, Maria Luisa, as its first abbess. A solid gold heart should go to the Jesuit church Il Gesù. Katharina explained that the madre vicaria had been "very concerned" that the will might fall into Hohenlohe's hands during his visit in December, thinking that he would immediately persuade the princess to alter it. Once she was in Tivoli, Hohenlohe did just that: on his advice, Katharina revoked the will, though she didn't claim back her dowry from the convent.[91]

Their conversations in Tivoli convinced Hohenlohe that his cousin wasn't talking nonsense. By and large, Katharina's denunciation tallied with his perspective on what had taken place in Sant'Ambrogio. He, too, saw the madre vicaria as the main culprit in this affair. The archbishop was certain that Maria Luisa had hated the princess from the moment the latter uncovered her affair with the Americano. But he laid more blame than his cousin did at the feet of the Jesuit confessor Padre Peters. In Hohenlohe's view, Peters's prediction of Katharina's imminent demise made him at least a passive accomplice to the poisoning. And there was more: Hohenlohe also believed that Cardinals Patrizi and Reisach, high-ranking friends of the pope, were caught up in the matter—though how, or to what extent, was not yet clear to him.

CHAPTER TWO

"The 'Delicatezza' of the Matter as Such"

Extrajudicial Preliminary Investigations

INFORMAL QUESTIONING

Once Katharina had presented her report to the Inquisition, the next move was up to Vincenzo Leone Sallua and his officials. They had to decide how to deal with the princess's *Denunzia*. Sallua was born in 1815, took holy orders with the Dominicans in Santa Sabina in Rome, and was ordained as a priest in 1838.[1] The Dominicans had played a major role in the Inquisition and the detection of heretics since the Middle Ages, and people referred to the *Dominicanes* mockingly as *canes Domini*, "God's dogs." The Inquisition of the Middle Ages was very different from the Holy Roman and Universal Inquisition, founded in 1542. The latter had local Inquisitions in many of Italy's episcopal cities, though its headquarters was in Rome. Somebody who had earned his spurs in one of these local organizations was often invited to Rome as a reward. So it was with Sallua, who had begun his career as vicar to the local inquisitor in Lugo. In 1850 he became an investigating judge of the Roman Inquisition and, in 1870, commissary of the Holy Office. He was aided by the second investigating judge, Enrico Ferrari, who was entrusted with keeping the files in the Sant'Ambrogio case. Ferrari was a fellow Dominican. He was born in 1816, and had been in office since the start of 1851.[2]

Giacinto Maria Giuseppe De Ferrari, born in 1804, had been commissary and chief justice of the Inquisition since 1851. He took holy orders in 1821—he was another Dominican—and was ordained as a priest in 1827. In 1839, he became the librarian of the famous Biblioteca Casanatense, the Roman Inquisition's library. He had worked for the Congregation of the Index since 1843, and there was no more dedicated evaluator in the field of Catholic book censorship in the nineteenth century. He appraised over 150 works during his career.[3] While the remaining offices of the Inquisition were occupied by members of various other orders and secular priests, the office of commissary and his two deputies, the investigating judges, were firmly in the hands of the Dominicans.[4]

The assessor, who was the real head of the Inquisition's Tribunal, was the secular priest Raffaele Monaco La Valletta. La Valletta, who was born in 1827, was a canon of Saint Peter's, and became pro-assessor in January 1859, before being promoted to assessor in December 1860.[5]

On September 17, 1859, Sallua informed Pope Pius IX privately of Katharina von Hohenzollern's denunciation.[6] The Dominican viewed the denunciation as a very grave business, "not only due to the *delicatezza* of the matter as such," but because of the wide repercussions that news of the case would have if it spread through Rome. He therefore tried to keep the whole thing as secret as possible.[7]

The Inquisition's files state that the padre *socius* believed he "should lay this denunciation most humbly at the feet of His Holiness," which at first glance seems to suggest that Sallua took this step on his own authority as investigating judge. But it is highly unlikely that a second-ranking inquisitor would have gone straight to the pope without consulting his superiors. Before taking the matter to the pontiff, he would at least have gained the agreement of his immediate superior, Commissary De Ferrari. Tradition suggests that he probably also discussed it at the Inquisition's *Congregazione Particolare*. This meeting was always held on a Saturday, and its main aim was to distribute the pending cases among individual members. As a rule, the assessor, the commissary, the investigating judges, the "fiscal" (who played a similar role to a modern state prosecutor), and a representative from the chancellery all took part in this. This meeting also decided "to whom each matter should be communicated: the consultors, the cardinals, or even the pope."[8] In this case, the *Congregazione Particolare* may have made the decision to inform the pope immediately. This task fell to Sallua, since at this point he was the only one familiar with the case. He was received by the pope in a private audience, and handed him a written summary of the allegations.

Pius IX studied the princess's denunciation and the Dominican's report thoroughly, but remained skeptical about the truth of Katharina's claims. For one thing, she had made allegations against people whom he held in such high regard that he couldn't believe they would be mixed up in this sort of affair: Cardinal August, Count Reisach, Katharina's spiritual guide, and Cardinal Costantino Patrizi, the cardinal protector of Sant'Ambrogio. Or was it possible that the two Jesuit confessors, the abbess, or even the beautiful madre vicaria could have enjoyed a similar prestige with the pope? The "nature of the offences" also placed doubts in the pope's mind. He could scarcely imagine that all these crimes had been committed in a place of pious women, and in such a short space of time.[9]

For Pius IX, this wasn't necessarily a case of heresy, for which the Roman Inquisition would have been responsible. Heresy meant denying a Catholic article of faith, or refusing to let go of a notion that went against Catholic dogma. If a Catholic consciously and stubbornly questioned the dogma, this was a "formal heresy." When this denial happened unconsciously, and the culprit showed a willingness to change, it was classed as a "material heresy."[10]

The pope thought that if there *was* anything in the princess's accusations, then the case was a matter of discipline and smaller criminal offenses. These weren't crimes against the Faith. The pope was also keen to prevent the affair becoming public at all costs, and instructed the Dominican to keep the whole thing under wraps. An Inquisition trial would bring more attention from within the Curia, and create a hotbed of rumor—something the pope was eager to avoid. And so he transferred the case from this larger stage to a smaller one, telling Sallua to hand the matter over to the cardinal vicar.[11]

The cardinal vicar represented the pope in his function as bishop of Rome. He looked after the administration of the diocese of Rome, and had full jurisdiction over all disciplinary aspects of religious life in the Eternal City. The Church officials and courts under his auspices included the Tribunal of the Vicariate. He was provided with administrative support by one vicegerent, who was a titular bishop, and had another for juridical matters. The *Vicarius Urbis* was one of the few officials of the Roman Curia who didn't lose his position when a pope died; a *sede vacante* led to most other offices being lost.[12]

In 1859, the office of cardinal vicar happened to be held by Costantino Patrizi, the cardinal protector of Sant'Ambrogio.[13] Patrizi was born in 1798 in Siena, and belonged to one of Rome's richest families. He studied canon and secular law in Rome, and was ordained in 1819. He quickly rose through the ranks of the Curia, and by 1828 he was titular bishop of Philippi. He was made a cardinal in 1836, and became a member of the Inquisition in 1839. He was cardinal vicar of Rome from 1841 until his death in 1876. A close friend and confidant of Pius IX, he was described as pious and reactionary. His opponents in the Curia held him to be a man of "dull wits," though more than a few commentators saw him as the most influential of the cardinals, and the supporting pillar of Pius IX's "authoritarian system of government." Patrizi had very close links with the Society of Jesus, not least through his brother Saverio, who had gone into the order.[14]

As cardinal protector of Sant'Ambrogio, Patrizi had to supervise the convent. Elections to offices within the convent were only valid when carried out in his presence, and with his blessing.[15] If anyone in the Catholic hierarchy was party to the convent's dark secrets, it would have been Patrizi—particularly with regard to the cult surrounding its founder, Maria Agnese Firrao. If the investigation ordered by the pope had uncovered anything, it would have incriminated the cardinal protector. We should therefore have a degree of skepticism about his objectivity in the case of Sant'Ambrogio. In any event, Pius IX placed the Dominican Sallua at Patrizi's side to keep an eye on him. This was a very smart move by the pope. He had found a compromise that involved the Holy Office, even if the case was officially under the cardinal vicar's jurisdiction. Cardinal Patrizi ordered an initial, cautious, extrajudicial investigation.[16]

Sallua's first task was to question a nun who had been expelled from Sant'Ambrogio a few years previously on disciplinary grounds, and had since been compelled to live in the convent of San Pasquale.[17] He was told to exercise "extreme discretion." It was hoped that she could provide information on any irregularities within the convent.

Sallua also had to collect other information, in secret, "especially on the ominous 'Americano' possessed by the devil." Finally, the Roman authorities tasked the local inquisitor of Gubbio[18] with questioning some of the sisters at the convent of San Marziale in the town.[19] The Holy Office had sentenced Maria Agnese Firrao, Sant'Ambrogio's mother founder, to live in monastic imprisonment there until her death.

This suggests that to start with the investigation was entirely focused on the veneration of Firrao as a saint, and whether she had secretly continued to lead the Catholic community of Sant'Ambrogio from her cell in Gubbio. That was evidently where the authorities in Rome saw the real crime: a woman who had been condemned as a false saint and expelled from Rome by the highest Church tribunal had allowed people to call her *Beata*, and the cult she had inspired among her devotees in Sant'Ambrogio had extended to the driving out of devils and demons.

THE OUTCAST'S TESTIMONY

The nun who had been expelled from Sant'Ambrogio, and whom Sallua was to interrogate, was Sister Agnese Eletta of the Holy Family. The cardinal vicar, acting in his role as cardinal protector of Sant'Ambrogio, had sent her to San Pasquale in August 1857 for disobedience. Here she was to become more spiritual, and practice the virtue of humility. But there had never been a proper investigation of the "difficulties" she had caused in the Franciscan convent; if there had, Patrizi could simply have dug out the old files.[20] This in itself casts the cardinal vicar of Rome in a less than favorable light. Had he neglected his duties as the most senior supervisor of religious life in Sant'Ambrogio? Had he blindly trusted the superiors there, in particular the Jesuit confessors?

In order to gain an initial impression of Agnese Eletta, Sallua first questioned the prioress of the Augustine Sisters of San Pasquale, Sister Maria Luisa of Jesus.[21] They had had a difficult time with Agnese Eletta since she arrived in San Pasquale, the prioress told him. The nuns had required a great deal of patience to deal with her constant "insubordination" and her egotism. She wasn't accustomed to convent practices. Days of abstinence and fasting were clearly unknown to her; in Sant'Ambrogio, as Agnese Eletta said herself, she had often enjoyed fancy foods, "always with butter." She had also dressed a little like a woman of the world. Agnese Eletta's superior—or rather, her convent jailer—painted a picture of a nun who had failed at cloistered life. So how had Agnese Eletta survived for so many years in a strictly enclosed convent?

The following day—October 18, 1859—the Dominican was able to question Agnese Eletta herself.[22] She was forty years old, and her given name was Agnese Corradini. Once Sallua had made her take the oath, the first question he put to her was the usual one: did she know why she had been summoned to this hearing? She answered, "no, sir." He then asked her about the important facts of her life to date, and took down her personal details. She said she was the niece of the founder, Agnese Firrao, and had lived in a convent since she was four, when she had moved into the house in Borgo Sant'Agata run by the reformed nuns of the Third Order of Holy Saint Francis. This was in 1823, and she had moved with them to Sant'Ambrogio in 1828, professing her vows there at the age of twenty.

First and foremost, Sallua was interested in the reasons for her expulsion from Sant'Ambrogio. Agnese Eletta gave an extremely evasive answer, saying she had actually always felt very at home in Sant'Ambrogio. It was only just before she went away that her relationship with the abbess had cooled. The abbess had said to her: "You went into my room, picked up several letters from our mother founder Sister Maria Agnese that were on my desk, took them to your room and tore them up. That is the reason I am angry with you." Agnese Eletta's assurances that she had done nothing of the sort were met with disbelief. She told the inquisitor that she suspected these letters had been placed in her drawer by another nun, the young novice mistress Maria Luisa.

However, this didn't stop Agnese Eletta finishing her hearing by singing the praises of the young madre vicaria. "She has the look of a soul privileged by the Lord." God "gave her the gift of sometimes being able to speak with Him." After they had prayed together on the night before Maundy Thursday, "she started to talk as though the Lord wanted to speak to me and give me a warning." Visions and visitations from heavenly beings had been a daily occurrence for her. According to Agnese Eletta, Maria Luisa was "lovable, warm-hearted and graceful," and showed the novices "great affection and attention."

"Night-time was when she was most often blessed by God; I say this because I slept in her cell for a while, and heard her . . . speaking to the Lord." But Agnese Eletta also stated that she had never truly believed in these supernatural phenomena. It "may have been [Maria Luisa's] imagination" at work here. Eventually, Maria Luisa had become inexplicably cold toward her, and Eletta didn't really know why she had been forced to leave.

Sallua was dissatisfied with the result of this hearing. His principal aim had been to extract information about the cult of Firrao. But Agnese Eletta, the mother founder's niece, had said almost nothing about this. And what she had told him about Maria Luisa remained strangely inconclusive. Agnese Eletta's statement seems to have given her a sleepless night as well: the next day, she went to her prioress and requested another interview with the Dominican.[23]

This took place on October 21.[24] Agnese Eletta admitted that "due to my confusion during the first hearing" there were some things she had forgotten or omitted to say. But her confessor had appealed to her conscience, and convinced her to speak the whole truth.

First I must say that, when Maria Luisa let me sleep in her cell, she did this behind the abbess's back and without her permission. When the abbess realized, she scolded Maria Luisa and tried to stop me sleeping in her room. Maria Luisa called me to her and said that, before I started to sleep there, for three nights she had heard a great commotion of demons in my room. She had risen and gone into my cell to release me. The demon had been furious, telling her that the moment I began to sleep alone in the cell again, he would strangle me. Then she said that I should tell our father confessor and the mother abbess what she had told me. She wanted me to say that I myself had heard the commotion during those nights. I replied that I had heard no such commotion and so could tell neither the father confessor nor the abbess about it. But she insisted: *"On the contrary, you can and must tell them you heard it, because I heard it."* And so I was duty-bound to assure the confessor and the abbess that I really had heard it. As a result, Padre Leziroli ordered the abbess to let me sleep in Maria Luisa's room. I was so afraid of the demons that I sometimes shared her bed. From July to December 1854, and from December to June 1855, I always slept in her cell.

Two young nuns sharing a bed: this fact must have caught Sallua's attention. The sisters always had to address each other by the formal Italian *Lei*; they weren't permitted the familiar *tu*. Personal friendships were forbidden. Two nuns should never have been allowed to share a cell without supervision by an older sister—to say nothing of a bed.[25]

In the course of the interview, the witness kept drawing the inquisitor's attention to the beautiful young novice mistress and her numerous "ecstasies and visions." From the start, her aunt Maria Agnese Firrao, the "mother founder," had been skeptical about Maria Luisa and her affected behavior. While confined in Gubbio, she had warned the abbess and Padre Leziroli several times "that they should watch out, because Maria Luisa's ecstasies and visions were imaginative games, and they should not give into her because she was deluded." And this advice came from a woman who had spent her whole life claiming to have conducted almost daily conversations with heavenly beings, and who assumed that everyone recognized her own visions as the real thing.

Agnese Eletta said that this meant Maria Luisa had to wait until Firrao's death to finally prove the authenticity of her heavenly gift. "After the death of the mother founder in Gubbio, on October 4, 1854, Maria Luisa told me openly that the founder had appeared to her in a vision and begged for her forgiveness. She was sorry for what she had written about her, which was that she believed Maria Luisa's visions and ecstasies were illusions and deceptions. During the time I slept in Sister Maria Luisa's cell, she had ... visions almost every night, and spoke with the Lord or with the founder."

A vision of the convent's founder, Agnese Firrao, seen only by the visionary herself, was supposed to prove that this vision, and the visionary, were both genuine. This kind of circular argumentation should have elicited a skeptical reaction from any theologian who was halfway educated in philosophical logic—as Padre Leziroli would have been after studying with the Jesuits. But Maria Luisa's strategy was unexpectedly successful.

Padre Leziroli believed "in something supernatural and in a vision," as Agnese Eletta reported. She herself, on the other hand, was convinced that Maria Luisa had consciously invoked these heavenly powers in order to get her own way. Whenever an important convent office became available, the beautiful young nun would have a vision proclaiming her God's appointed candidate. This was how she became gatekeeper, novice mistress, and even vicaress.

Padre Leziroli used his priestly authority to see that the heavenly instructions were carried out in each case. Only he could absolve somebody of their sins in the confessional, or deny absolution. This gave him a powerful instrument of control, which he used deliberately: Katharina reported as much in her denunciation. On this point, her testimony tallies with that of the first witness.

Agnese Eletta, at least, saw through Maria Luisa's strategy. And when the latter tried to force her—Agnese Eletta, the niece of the visionary Agnese Firrao, whom people probably assumed to be particularly receptive to supernatural phenomena—to back her by saying she had shared one of her visions, Agnese Eletta refused to play along.

Other nuns also remained skeptical, doubting that Maria Luisa's visitations were genuine. Unsurprisingly, she was greatly angered by their doubt. She challenged these recalcitrant sisters again and again, doing everything she could to convince them she had been blessed by heaven. But as soon as she sensed she had gone too far, she claimed that the devil had "taken her shape" and appeared to the nuns. She herself had done nothing.

To illustrate this, Agnese Eletta recounted something that had happened to two of the older sisters, Maria Caterina and Maria Francesca.

It occurred in the following way: Maria Luisa told me she wanted to speak with the above-mentioned sisters regarding the rearrangement of the choir for Christmas. I advised her against it, because it was not right for her, as a young nun, to do this. But she tried to speak to them anyway, and the nuns complained to the abbess. As soon as I heard this, I informed her; she was surprised, and said it could be made right. A short while later, she told me it had been the devil, and not her, who had spoken to the two nuns. I told her that was impossible, as she had told me of her intentions shortly beforehand, and in any case I had proof, because I had passed by and heard her talking to them. She replied that the voice both I and the other nuns had heard was not her own, but that of the devil, imitating her.

Agnese Eletta was convinced that Maria Luisa had gotten her expelled from the convent "through one of her revelations or something else." Was Maria Luisa trying to get rid of an unbeliever, who wasn't convinced of her supernatural gifts? Or was the mother founder's niece ejected because Maria Luisa saw her as competition for power and influence? Both of these were probably the case.

At the very end of the interview, Agnese Eletta suddenly returned to the delicate topic that had caught Sallua's attention earlier on. She told him that after she left Sant'Ambrogio, Maria Luisa chose the young novice Maria Giacinta to sleep in her cell. She then brought her testimony to an abrupt end: "It seems to me that I have nothing further to say."

TWO NUNS IN A BED

This final statement was nothing less than a blatant lie under oath, and a week and a half later, Agnese Eletta's superior in San Pasquale had to request another interview with Sallua on her behalf. Spiritual exercises and long conversations with her confessor, Padre Andrea Scalzo, had finally convinced her to tell the whole truth.[26]

The third hearing of the outcast from Sant'Ambrogio took place on November 3, 1859. Agnese Eletta submitted a paper written in her own hand. She said that even in the confessional, she had blushed deeply as she told her confessor about the awful things she now wanted to reveal to the Inquisition. She had been terribly ashamed, and "filled with extreme disgust." Padre Scalzo had therefore suggested that "I set down in writing the things that made my cheeks red with shame when I spoke them aloud."[27] The sister read out this text, which Sallua entered into the files. She then had to sign for it.[28]

> In August of the year 1854, Maria Luisa said to me one day: "You must know that you will have a sickness showing itself in your private parts, for which you will have to visit the professors and let them treat you." When I heard this I was horrified, and asked her to pray for me so that I would not fall victim to this shame. She answered that the Lord had told her she should treat me herself, so that I would be released from this punishment. She had to exam-

ine and treat me four times. I said that I currently had no complaint, so at the present time no treatment was necessary, but she added that the malady had already begun, although I myself had noticed nothing yet. I believed this, and with the utmost revulsion and reluctance I allowed her to look at and touch me, thinking that if it was such a trial to show myself to a woman, it would be worse still to show myself to a man. If not for this consideration, I would never have allowed her to do it. Maria Luisa warned me not to speak of this to Padre Leziroli.

A few days later she had one of her usual ecstasies, and I realized she was speaking to the late abbess, Maria Maddalena. At the same moment, she handed me a letter from Maria Maddalena, which she said I was to read at once. I then had to do what the letter told me. But the handwriting was Maria Luisa's. The letter was addressed to me, and was full of praise for her, presenting her as a saint and a favored soul. In order to recognize the great purity of this her daughter (to use the words of the letter), I was to look closely at certain parts of her body.

When I read this, I was horrified, and doubted the letter, thinking it a diabolical deceit. As Christian religious virtue tells us, I was disgusted by the thought of looking at such things. But because of the great respect I had for Maria Luisa, and because it seemed impossible to me for her to want to do me harm, I overcame this thought. I believed that although the deed itself was sinful and I should not commit it, I must follow the order that had been given to me by a heavenly apparition. Eventually I did it—she appeared to be asleep all the while. Afterwards, Maria Luisa told me I should burn the letter and say nothing to Padre Leziroli.

A few weeks later, Maria Luisa told me that Maria Maddalena would come to visit her that night. So I remained very watchful, and I heard her speaking with this dead nun and telling her about the following vision: "This person appeared to me (without saying so, she made it clear that this was the Lord), and out of His side He gave me a liquid that dripped onto my face, then flowed over my whole body, collecting in the lower part of my body, as in a little hollow, where it then remained. Agnese Eletta shall share in this liquid, by joining with me and touching me, so she may be purified and share in this same blessing." And she went on, saying other things like this.

Another night, after one of her ecstasies, she told me that the Lord had appeared to her and had given her a special blessing, so that when she touched me, that part of my body would be healed. And so she wanted me to sleep in the same bed as her, although that repulsed me. And she wanted me to join myself to her person in a very corrupt way (the rest I do not have to explain), saying that the Lord willed it, and that, since it was His will, I was not committing any sin by this act, and that it was necessary so that I might enjoy all the above-mentioned advantages.

But I was not to speak a word of this to Padre Leziroli, or to anyone else. I reluctantly agreed and, believing it really was a heavenly command, I tried to convince myself that although these were forbidden things, the Lord might have commanded them for reasons I did not know. This happened again in different ways, towards the end of September of the same year.

A few months later I discovered I had been deceived, in the following way: the same extraordinary father confessor came who visited every year, and Maria Luisa went into confession before me. As she left the confessional, she said to me: "Confess that you have been in my bed at night, because the father confessor has said that it is a sin." After she said this, I was taken aback, realizing she had deceived me, and realizing the evil she had allowed me to commit for so long. Still, out of false consideration for her honor, I did not tell the confessor in what way she had deceived me, instead letting him believe I was the guiltier one.

Afterwards I asked Maria Luisa how this change of heart had come about, and she told me, in a web of lies, she had not said a word about it to the confessor; it was he who had told her everything.

I then said, greatly surprised: "So you were deceiving me when you allowed me to believe that the Lord commanded you to do this, and had worked a miracle in order to reveal it."

Maria Luisa answered me: "No, it must have been the devil, working to dishonor me. The padre must have taken confession from somebody he believed to be a saint, and this person, having been told about it by a devilish apparition, must then have told the father confessor."

And she reassured me that there was not the least evil in these things, and warned me again not to say anything to Padre Leziroli, and she went on talking until I believed her, although I had many a suspicion regarding this and the other apparitions. As my doubts continued to grow, she became aware of them, and probably feared that I might talk to Padre Leziroli about it after all. Finally she said to me one day that what she had told me about the extraordinary father confessor had been a lie, and that in truth she had been worried, and so had confessed. But she did not have to say anything about me, as I had already confessed.

And so I remained convinced that she had acted purely out of a devilish madness. And I still nursed the suspicion that it was not a desire to repent that had made her confess, but the fear that the regular confessor might hear of it, and that he would then cease to hold her in such high regard. She may have feared that over time, I might start to worry, and so she pretended she was allaying my conscience, thinking that once I had said it, I would never say it again. Perhaps she wanted to reassure herself as well, although I do not know how much use this confession was to her.

So the close friendship that had bound us for more than a year came to an end. It had begun in January 1854, with an aim that seemed holy. Maria Luisa made out that she was there to lift me out of the numbness of my life and set me on the path to perfection, and for my part I took her for a saint, as was the general opinion. I believed that her guidance could help me improve myself. And in the beginning, this really seemed to be the case. But later she proved to be very harmful, because of the temptations and pangs of conscience to which I fell prey. Finally I was hounded out of the convent.

Outwardly Maria Luisa always acted as a friend, and when I accused her of these things she showed humility, but I believe this was all a pretense.

UNCHASTITY AND SODOMY

Reading Agnese Eletta's written testimony, Sallua realized the women had broken their vow of chastity. Like all Catholic nuns, Eletta had professed vows of poverty, chastity, and obedience. Every line of her text speaks of repressed physicality and sexuality. The Church's long tradition of somatophobia was constantly reinforced by Sant'Ambrogio's confessors. Contemporary handbooks "For the Use of Priests and Father Confessors"[29] stressed the need, when addressing the sixth commandment in the confessional, to focus on chastity, abstinence, and honesty. "It is not permitted to allow one's eye to rest unnecessarily on things that one cannot observe without injuring one's modesty and putting oneself in danger of committing some sin of impurity. The dishonest gaze is a mortal sin or a venial sin, according to whether it is more or less dangerous and excites the passions more or less. . . . The same applies to touching, which is even more dangerous than a look, and for this reason can easily be a mortal sin."[30] According to the precepts of Catholic moral theology, a Catholic woman—in particular a nun, who was duty-bound to embody the ideal of "virginal chastity"—should be embarrassed to have her genitals or breasts examined by a doctor.[31]

A Catholic woman became a "victim of shame" when she had to undress for a doctor to look at or touch her, as Agnese Eletta, who was entirely committed to the Catholic ethos of shame, described so tellingly.[32] Maria Luisa made clever use of this taboo to satisfy her own sexual urges. But after a year, she had obviously grown weary of her bedfellow and dropped Agnese Eletta like a hot potato, leaving the nun alone with her guilt and her "sin."

And as if the fact that a virgin dedicated to God had broken the vow of chastity wasn't bad enough, Agnese Eletta's testimony confronted the inquisitor with a much thornier issue: a sexual relationship between women. What resources did he have on hand to help him grasp and judge this phenomenon? A glance through the Roman Inquisition's files would have been no help at all. While cases involving sexual acts between men arose relatively frequently, with these acts often being described as *il pessimo*—the worst possible mortal sin— there was hardly any information on sexual relationships between women.[33] But this was nothing out of the ordinary: in the nineteenth century, relationships between women were very seldom connected with "forbidden sexuality." People were often "entirely convinced that these women satisfied no independent erotic desires beyond reproductive sexuality."[34]

The only thing left for Sallua—who was both a Dominican priest and a confessor—was to consult the relevant handbooks on moral theology. If there was any information on lesbian sexuality, it was sure to be contained in the texts on the sixth commandment.[35] In the Decalogue, this commandment merely stated: "Thou shalt not commit adultery," but over the course of Church history, all possible sexual sins were subsumed under this. Sexuality outside marriage was completely forbidden, and the act of married love had exclusively to serve the conception of children.[36] The lust of a man for a woman, and a woman for a man, was "unchaste" according to the moral theology of the time—though since it served the aim of procreation, it was counted as a venial sin, which could always be forgiven in confession. Homosexual desire between men, on the other hand, was seen as a mortal sin *contra naturam*, and was often termed "sodomy."[37] Until well into the twentieth century, gay men faced criminal prosecution almost everywhere in Europe; occasionally women were prosecuted, too.[38]

The question of whether "unnatural fornication" could even exist between women had been the subject of debate for a long time, both inside and outside the Church—not least because in Europe sexuality was "male-dominated and phallocentric, identified with penetration." The question resulting from this assumption was: "Could women penetrate other [women] without using an implement, and thereby commit the sin of sodomy?"[39] Or did their anatomy make them incapable of this sin?

In his *Summa theologiae*, which became the most important reference work of scholastic-influenced Catholic moral theology in the nineteenth century, Thomas Aquinas laid out four possible forms of unnatural lust. Alongside masturbation, sodomy, and sexual intercourse in an unnatural position, there was also "sleeping with the wrong sex, man with man and woman with woman."[40] The moral theologians were unclear for a long time, however, on how this "concupitus" of two women could be "technically" possible. From a phallocentric point of view, it could only happen if one woman "inserts some wooden or glass object into the belly of another."[41] The moral theologians believed this was the only way the mortal sin of sodomy could be committed by women.[42] Over time, however, as medical knowledge of the female sexual organs improved, they became increasingly convinced that there was "a true sodomy between women," because "mutual rubbing" caused a fluid to accumulate in the vagina without the use of sex aids, and this was interpreted as female ejaculation.[43]

A DOMINICAN WANTS THE DETAILS

In light of this discovery, Sister Agnese Eletta's written testimony wasn't sufficient for Sallua. He had to know more about the sexual practices between the nuns, and on November 3, 1859, he insisted on a further face-to-face interview with the witness under oath. Agnese Eletta gave a detailed explanation in response to the inquisitor's inquiries.[44]

What I said about the letter that Sister Maria Luisa gave me, so that I would read it and follow the heavenly commands, happened when I slept in her cell and was still in the dormatorium, before I went into the novitiate. It happened at night, and so she ordered me to light the lamp and do what the letter said. As she lay there in bed seeming to be out of her senses, I was to undress her and gaze at *all the parts of her body*. She wanted me to look at my own body at the same time, to find out whether we were the same in every way. Before I did all this I was so upset, fearing this was one of the devil's tricks, that I said a few Ave Marias and scattered holy water over her bed. Straight afterwards, she asked me to lie down to sleep in her bed, and from then on we slept together, although I also sometimes slept in my own bed.

Regarding the unions that took place between us which, she said, the Lord had commanded so that I might be healed, she also taught me how I should perform this union with her. This happened in various ways. She told me that the gifts and blessings that she had received from the Lord would be transferred to me when I touched *her private parts* with my hands, and she then repeated the same actions on my body. She also touched first herself, and then me. This had an effect on her sexual parts that I could not observe in my own, and from her behavior and what she said, I gathered that she got great enjoyment from it. She told me I could do these things with a clear conscience, in order to receive the blessings from the

Lord that she had pronounced to me. She said there was no evil in it, as we were pursuing this aim that the Lord had revealed to her.

I will admit that it took a great deal of effort to obey her and subordinate myself to these acts. I will admit that after she and I had confessed to the extraordinary father confessor, we continued to sleep in the same room and sometimes in the same bed, and this gave me some reassurance, as I said in my letter. At the start of our relationship and friendship it appeared that she was training me towards greater obedience and a perfection of the spirit.

Regarding the treatment of *my private parts*, of which I spoke in my letter, Maria Luisa told me she had already spoken to the father confessor about it. She said I should just tell him that she was treating me for a little problem, and this is what I did. At this time she told me that when the Lord appeared to her, He taught her a great many things regarding honesty that she had not known, and He had done this so that if necessary, she could give the novices advice, dispel their doubts, and instruct them in their difficulties. When she finally said all this to Padre Leziroli, he answered that the Lord had told her these things for the healing of souls.

Maria Luisa started having long conversations in the evenings with the novice Sister Maria Giacinta, and I made a few remarks about this. She replied that this novice felt certain difficulties and temptations regarding her purity, and she had to communicate her needs to Maria Luisa, so that she could give her advice. This Maria Giacinta is the same person whom Maria Luisa called to sleep in her cell after I had left it. I knew she used to call one or another of the novices to her at night for them to sleep with her, as she admitted to me herself. However, I do not believe that she shared the same intimacies with them as she had with me, and which I described in my letter.

When she made me leave the novices' wing, I scolded her for what she had done with me, and told her she should be wary of doing these things with other novices, because they would not keep it all a secret as I had done. But I said she should have no doubts about me, as I would never talk about it. In general she was always humble and said I could talk about it if I wished. However, I knew that she would then say the devil had taken her form and done these things, as she had on many other occasions. She told me that the Lord had determined the way everything would be revealed.

I never spoke to Padre Leziroli about this, because he would not have believed me. He was too firmly convinced of Maria Luisa's holiness. However, I told it all to Padre Nicola Benedetti,[45] a Jesuit from Tivoli. At first he wanted permission to speak to Padre Leziroli about it himself, but when he had thought longer about it and taken into consideration that Padre Leziroli was firmly convinced of Maria Luisa's holiness, he said to me: "We will let the Lord do it, He will ensure that all this is revealed." And then he urged me to pray for Maria Luisa. However, I will admit that it took me a great effort to find inner peace, though I eventually did, with God's mercy. . . .

During the final days I spent in Sant'Ambrogio, I avoided listening to Padre Leziroli's sermons, and this caused surprise and scandal in the community. The reason for it was as follows: just before new appointments were made to the community's offices, this padre had given a sermon, and it was all about a favored soul. The mother founder, Sister Maria Agnese Firrao, had revealed to this person who should be appointed to each office, and in particular how the new novice mistress was to conduct herself. She should have the freedom to lead the novices as she wished. . . . Maria Luisa, who was not yet the novice mistress, was not present at the sermon. But the revelation came from her: she had already said this to me and Padre Leziroli, as I have already stated. I remember that on this occasion Leziroli's sermon did not please the older nuns. Later on, I began to hear phrases in Padre Leziroli's sermons that I thought came from Maria Luisa's visions. I was no longer on familiar terms with her, and since I knew that her visions were illusions, this angered me, and I did not want to go and hear any more of his sermons.

I believe this was one of the reasons they forced me to leave the convent, and the cardinal vicar also hinted at this in his reply to one of my letters.

In her hearing on November 3, 1859, Agnese Eletta was talking about events that had taken place five years previously. Following her aunt's death on October 4, 1854, there had been good reason to give her, the mother founder's niece, one of the convent offices. Significantly, her aunt's death came not long after her "friendship" with Maria Luisa had begun in January 1854. From July 1854 to July 1855, their relationship developed into a full-blown affair. On December 15, 1854, in the middle of this period, Maria Luisa was chosen as novice mistress.[46] Along the road to power, Maria Luisa made clever use of visitations from the late mother founder, and befriended the dead woman's closest relative, Agnese Eletta, whom she convinced to vouch for the authenticity of her visions. But in the summer of 1855, after Maria Luisa had ended the affair, Agnese Eletta evidently began to oppose her—partly, perhaps, from feelings of unrequited love. In retaliation, Maria Luisa utilized the confessor in an attempt to discipline her. When this seemed to have failed, and the carousel of Sant'Ambrogio's convent offices was about to revolve once more, she mounted a concentrated campaign, enlisting Padre Leziroli, the abbess, and the convent's cardinal protector, Patrizi, to get rid of Agnese Eletta and thus ensure she kept her mouth shut. Tellingly, Eletta was placed in the conservatory of San Pasquale in Trastevere, which also fell under Costantino Patrizi's jurisdiction as cardinal vicar.[47]

Looking at the respective ages of the two nuns—Agnese Eletta was thirty-five in 1854, and Maria Luisa only twenty-two—it seems very unlikely that Maria Luisa would have been the instigator of this affair. But viewing the liaison as part of a strategy to gain power within Sant'Ambrogio, Agnese Eletta's version of events could make perfect sense.

MANY CONVINCING PROOFS

Even after questioning the outcast Agnese Eletta three times, Sallua had still learned nothing new about the real secret of Sant'Ambrogio: the nuns venerating her aunt as a saint. On the other hand, she had more than substantiated the accusations Katharina von Hohenzollern had made against the madre vicaria, Maria Luisa. The former sister of Sant'Ambrogio laid a lot of the blame for Maria Luisa's behavior on the spiritual director and principal confessor, Giuseppe Leziroli. He not only believed all her supernatural experiences to be real, but forced the nuns to believe in Maria Luisa's holiness, even in the confessional. He was also aware that Agnese Eletta and Maria Luisa were sharing a bed. To Sallua's mind, the homosexual acts that

Maria Luisa had initiated under false pretenses clearly amounted to sodomy. In the language of the highest Church authority, these acts were *rebus pessimi*, the very worst things. Here, he was employing the same terminology that the Inquisition usually used to describe intercourse between men.[48] And Sallua had now also learned that Maria Luisa brought another nun into her bed besides Agnese Eletta.

Before conducting the hearings with Agnese Eletta, the Dominican had received important new information about the "possessed Americano." He was certainly no invention of Katharina's. Padre Maurus Wolter, the princess's new confessor, had written Sallua a letter on September 17, 1859.[49] It was the first and only time he contacted the Dominican. A Prussian priest named Wegener,[50] who lived in the German seminary of the Campo Santo Teutonico[51] next to Saint Peter's, had told Wolter that "Pietro Americano" was actually Peter Kreuzburg. Kreuzburg was a doctor by profession, and Tyrolean by birth. He had been a U.S. citizen for seventeen years, and lived in Cincinnati. To that extent, the term "Americano" was correct. In 1857 he had left his wife and children in America, and traveled to the capital of Christianity to seek help for his spiritual tribulations. Wolter also told Sallua that this Kreuzburg had a long-standing special relationship with the Jesuits, and had a "close friendship" with a "certain Padre Kleutgen."

The priest of San Nicola in Cacere,[52] to whose parish the American belonged, even gave the Dominican Kreuzburg's exact address on October 11, 1859.[53] Pietro Maria Kreusberg—as the Italians spelled his name—was the son of Giuseppe Kreusberg, and lived at number 65, Via di Monte Tarpeo.[54] The priest invited the Americano to visit, and reported that when he saw Kreuzburg, the latter's clothing was in quite a shabby state, and he was living with very disreputable people. All in all, the forty-four-year-old Kreuzburg had made a "pitiful" impression. If we believe the priest's analysis, a kind of religious mania seemed to have driven Kreuzburg to leave his family and job, in the hope of finding true salvation in Rome.[55]

Sallua informed Cardinal Vicar Patrizi of how the investigation stood, in a secret meeting at the start of November 1859. Of course, he couldn't tell the high-ranking cardinal about the involvement in the affair of people whom Pius IX held in high esteem. This would also have meant talking to Patrizi about his role as cardinal protector of Sant'Ambrogio. Instead, he focused on the number and nature of the offenses, and managed to demonstrate that Katharina's *Denunzia* was "an extremely weighty denunciation, backed by many convincing proofs."[56]

Patrizi must have been shocked to his core, as he recognized the full incendiary power of the Sant'Ambrogio affair. There was now a danger that the focus of interest could shift to him: in his role as cardinal protector, the ultimate responsibility for what happened in the convent lay with him. As Sallua put it, Patrizi did not want "to bear the responsibility any longer," and asked the Holy Father to hand the case over to the Holy Office's tribunal, where it could be dealt with *more solito*,[57] in the usual way. Patrizi was probably placing his hopes in the Holy Office's obligation to maintain absolute secrecy about its cases: breaking this silence resulted in the harshest punishment from the Church.[58]

We can guess just how disconcerted Patrizi felt from the fact that, out of the blue, he handed Sallua a raft of documents and letters from Sant'Ambrogio dating from 1848 to 1854.[59] These proved conclusively that the abbess and the confessor had given the cardinal protector regular updates on what was happening in Sant'Ambrogio, with particular reference to the veneration of Maria Agnese Firrao as a saint, and Maria Luisa's supernatural experiences. Patrizi had done nothing about either of these, simply allowing matters to take their course—though he hadn't given any encouragement, either. His behavior could perhaps be explained by the huge support that his mother, the Marquise Kunigunde Patrizi, had given Sant'Ambrogio's founder. During the Inquisition trial against Maria Agnese Firrao, Patrizi's mother had proved herself a true follower of this supposed servant of God, and was one of the few people to take the stand in her favor.[60]

To Sallua's mind, the letters Patrizi gave him provided "a clear argument and firm evidence" for the validity of Katharina's denunciation. Anyone with an ounce of sense should have seen that Maria Luisa's visions and visitations, as reported by Padre Leziroli, had the "character of fictions," and that they were "*supposte rivelazioni*," pretended revelations.[61] Sallua's words contained a tacit criticism of Patrizi himself, who must surely have seen through the whole conjuring trick. This was the only time the Dominican articulated—in a cautious and very

As the cardinal vicar of the Roman Church and protector
of Sant'Ambrogio, it was Costantino Patrizi's duty to keep a watchful eye
on what went on in the convent.

indirect way—his incomprehension over Patrizi's extremely problematic attitude as protector of the convent. As an experienced investigating judge, Sallua used these texts to set in motion a full Inquisition
trial.

AN INQUISITION TRIAL, AFTER ALL

Patrizi's withdrawal put an end to the low-key solution the pope had
initially sought for the case of Sant'Ambrogio. Pius IX must have
realized that an Inquisition trial was now unavoidable. However,

after Sallua had told him about the current state of affairs on November 11, 1859, the pope simply said that *pro nunc*, "for now," he would call a secret meeting in which the cardinals, but not the Inquisition consultors, would be informed of the affair and the "clever and energetic steps" the pope had already taken.[62]

Sallua prepared a detailed report for the cardinals' secret meeting, which took place on November 16, 1859. It left no room for doubt that the case of Sant'Ambrogio fell under the jurisdiction of the Holy Office, as the crimes involved were primarily religious.[63] He saw three valid charges arising from his investigations so far.

First, there was the nuns' continued veneration of Maria Agnese Firrao, whom the Inquisition had convicted of being a false saint. There was also evidence that she had continued to lead the community by means of letters from exile, which was also forbidden. And Leziroli had written a saint's life of Firrao, which he used regularly in his sermons.

Second was Sister Maria Luisa's pretense of holiness—an offense that Sallua regarded as clearly proven. The Dominican was also in no doubt that she had used her visions to gain offices in the convent, shown a marked lack of fellow feeling for the other nuns, and had unstintingly supported the false cult through Leziroli.

Third, Sallua told the cardinals of Maria Luisa's "improper practices," and made a connection between these and the first false saint, Agnese Firrao. She, too, had been accused of grave sexual transgressions—and continued heresy went hand in hand with continued sodomy. It was no coincidence that Sallua's report mentioned the "false dogma *in re venerea*" (in matters of sex) and the "disgraceful acts *sub specie boni*" (under the pretense of doing good). This was his way of bringing the third allegation under the Inquisition's remit as well. It was a matter of false "practical" dogma, and the Holy Office was responsible for Catholic dogma and its protection.

Sallua's arguments convinced the cardinals to a man, and they decided to open an Inquisition trial against the nuns of Sant'Ambrogio and their confessors, the Jesuits Giuseppe Leziroli and Giuseppe Peters. The convent was to be permanently dissolved, and the nuns divided among various other suitable institutions.[64] As the pope wasn't present for this decision, the assessor, Monaco La Valletta, sought an audience to obtain his agreement.[65]

But Pius IX substantially moderated the cardinals' decision. *Ad mentem*,[66] in the spirit of the pope's original decision, there was to be no more talk of the immediate suppression of the convent and a trial against the Jesuit confessors. First, there would be an Apostolic Visitation to Sant'Ambrogio which—and this will come as no surprise—fell under the jurisdiction of Cardinal Vicar Patrizi and his vicegerent, Antonio Ligi-Bussi.[67] The latter was tasked with conducting a thorough inspection of the convent, and for this purpose was allowed to enter the *clausura*. In particular, he was instructed to search for writings from the pen of the late mother founder. The pope told the cardinal vicar to contact Petrus Beckx, the Jesuit general, and "very carefully" broach the subject of dismissing Padres Leziroli and Peters. He should then assign other, non-Jesuit spiritual guides to the nuns of Sant'Ambrogio.[68]

The vicegerent began his search of the convent the following day and, although he found nothing, he did learn that the lawyer Luigi Franceschetti, the convent's legal representative, knew where Firrao's writings were hidden. At their meeting on December 6, the cardinals of the Inquisition decided to invite the lawyer in for questioning. The pope himself gave the order to seize Maria Luisa at once, and have her placed in another convent without any public fuss.[69]

On December 8, Sallua had a private audience with the pope, prostrating himself at the feet of His Holiness, as he reported, in a gesture of humility typical for an inquisitor. He gave a detailed report of the results from the preliminary investigations, setting out a total of eight charges.[70]

First: the nuns had continued to honor the condemned Agnese Firrao as a saint.

Second: the twenty-seven-year-old Maria Luisa had also pretended to be a saint.

Third: the novices had committed improper acts with the novice mistress, exchanging intimacies and kisses. The night before professing their vows, lesbian initiation rites had taken place. The women had also indulged in physical lovemaking, up to and including intercourse (*usque ad consumationem*). All this had happened under the pretense of heavenly "sanctification."

Fourth: there had been attempts to poison and murder Princess Hohenzollern.

Fifth: the nuns had hidden cult objects belonging to "saint" Firrao in the convent.

Sixth: Maria Luisa forced the novices to give confession to her.

Seventh: the novices had disregarded important rules and had, for example, eaten meat on fast days and not taken part regularly in the Liturgy of the Hours. Then there was also the forbidden relationship between Maria Luisa and the Americano.

Eighth: the two confessors, Leziroli and Peters, had tolerated, if not actively supported, these offenses.

Only now did Pius IX really seem convinced that the charges were justified, and he finally authorized the Dominican to open an Inquisition trial.[71] The trial was to cover not only the crimes against the Faith, but all the other felonies relating to the attempted murder, which actually fell within the jurisdiction of other criminal courts in Rome.

In doing this, the pope himself was drawing an overt connection between the two levels of the Sant'Ambrogio affair: the "natural" level of the felonies, and the "supernatural" level of supersensible phenomena. These two planes and their mutual dependence were to become a leitmotif that ran through the whole trial. The judges were confronted with the same conundrum over and over: did incorrect actions lead to incorrect belief? Or was incorrect belief responsible for incorrect actions?

The trial began in December 1859, and ended in February 1862, with the pronouncement of the final judgment. A mighty task lay before the tribunal. Around sixty witnesses had to be questioned—thirty-seven of them the nuns of Sant'Ambrogio[72]—and numerous documents seized, including the saint's life of Maria Agnese from the pen of Padre Leziroli.[73] The witness examinations alone took more than a year.

THE INQUISITION TRIBUNAL: PROCESSES AND PROTAGONISTS

The elements of the modern criminal trial that we take for granted—the public proceedings, the direct confrontation of defendants and witnesses, heated exchanges between defense counsels, prosecutors, and judges, cross-examinations, and the detailed reporting of cases in the media—didn't apply to a trial before the Inquisition, even as late as the nineteenth century. But this didn't mean an Inquisition trial was ruled by pure capriciousness, as various legends and clichés would have us believe.[74] From a historical point of view, there was no such thing as *the* Inquisition. There are three types of Inquisition to be distinguished in the history of the Church.[75] First, there was the Medieval Inquisition, which was largely used to prosecute the Cathars. Second, the Spanish Inquisition, which went down in history for its rigid proceedings against suspected crypto-Muslims and crypto-Jews in Reconquista Spain, and which mainly served to preserve the unity of Spain's newly established kingdom. Third, there was the Holy Roman and Universal Inquisition, founded in 1542 to combat the "Protestant heresy."[76] But the Roman Inquisition was soon given a much more extensive remit, to include control of all Catholics' religious and social behavior.[77] It became an increasingly bureaucratic authority, producing endless reams of paper, like any other modern administrative or juridical apparatus.

But "Inquisition" can also mean a new kind of legal process that, when the pope introduced it in the thirteenth century, was one of the greatest leaps forward in legal history. Among its innovations was the office of state prosecutor. Investigations were now initiated by this office, and not—as had previously been the case—purely on the grounds of an accusation.[78] But the Inquisition's positive impact is largely unknown. When this *inquisitio* was later linked with the use of torture, the progressive "Inquisition trial" gained the negative image it still has today. However, by the second half of the nineteenth century, defendants weren't being shown instruments of torture or subjected to horrific interrogations using them. The trial was purely a written process—which at that time was also a customary feature of trials in certain areas of the secular justice system.

It is impossible to reconstruct the case of Sant'Ambrogio without detailed knowledge of an inquisitorial trial's processes and protagonists. The Inquisition's tribunal had no official rules of procedure.[79] Even the internal document from the nineteenth century, "norms for a procedure in cases for the Holy Office," which is now held in the Archive of the Congregation for the Doctrine of the Faith (as the Holy Office was renamed in 1966), gives hardly any specific instructions for the organization of a trial, the course it should take, and the parties involved.[80] We can therefore assume that the Roman Inquisition had evolved a procedure for criminal trials based largely on customary law and precedent. With nothing set out in writing, the inquisitors would have had a great deal of freedom in how they conducted a trial.[81]

For criminal trials, the Roman Inquisition was divided into two sections. The deciding authority, the court to which the ultimate judgment fell, was identical with the congregation of cardinals assigned to the Holy Office. And then there was the investigating authority, which preceded and was subordinate to the cardinals.

The real head or prefect of the Inquisition was no lesser person than the pope, the most senior legislator and judge of the Universal Church. Unlike the other congregations (the groups of cardinals who oversaw various administrative areas of the Catholic Church), the *Sanctum Officium* had no cardinal prefect; its leader was merely called the cardinal secretary.[82] A dozen or more other cardinals formed the actual court. They met every Wednesday (the so-called *Feria quarta*) without the pope, and on Thursdays (*Feria quinta*) with the pope at their head.[83] Their decisions and judgments are recorded in the *Decreta* files, which, because of the sheer number of issues covered, mostly contain only summary records of the outcome in each case.[84] Preparations for these decisions were made by the consultors, who always met on a Monday (*Feria secunda*). Their meetings included up to three dozen experts, theologians, jurists, and canon lawyers.[85] They wrote reports and votums (petitions) on each batch of issues passed on to them by the cardinals, and often formulated suggested decisions for the congregation's meetings, which the assessor, who led these, set out before Their Eminences.[86] If a decision was made during a Wednesday meeting when the pope was absent, the assessor would seek a private audience with the *Pontifex maximus* to obtain his agreement. The pope often modified or clarified exactly what the assessor had to record in each case, according to his own ideas on the matter.[87] In general—and this is the crucial difference from a modern, secular criminal trial—the entire process was conducted through written rather than verbal proceedings, with the public fundamentally excluded.

The witnesses and the accused never encountered one another

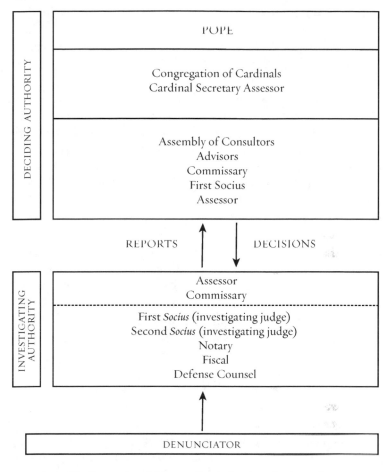

The Roman Inquisition consisted of an investigating and
a deciding authority, with the pope as its ultimate head.

in a courtroom. There was theoretical provision for an unmediated
confrontation, but it was never put into practice. Hearings were conducted with one individual at a time, transcribed by a notary, and
authenticated with a signature from the person who had been questioned. These hearings were also not unusual in secular courts during
the nineteenth century.[88] Nor were the defendants or the witnesses

ever confronted with the tribunal itself—they never had sight of the judges. But the accused had only to look at the annually produced handbook of the Papal States to find out which cardinals were current members of the Inquisition, and were therefore sitting in judgment on them.

Their Eminences arrived at their verdict exclusively on the basis of source evidence, presented to them by the investigative section of the Inquisition. The "Inquisition's perpetually working instructive court"[89] was headed by an "official judge,"[90] the Holy Office's commissary,[91] and two investigating judges, the first and second *socius*.[92] They conducted the trial, received the denunciations, questioned the witnesses, interrogated the defendants, and summarized the results of these hearings and other information for the cardinals in documents known as *Relazioni*. The interrogation transcripts were witnessed by a notary or actuary.[93] The fiscal was another important figure: as the Church's lawyer, he played the same role a state prosecutor would in a secular court.[94] He was responsible for seeing that the trial was properly conducted. In principle, the accused had a defense counsel at their disposal, though in practice he didn't usually play a significant part in the proceedings. All the same, he was entitled to read the investigating judges' summaries once the hearings were over, and then submit a written defense.[95]

The assessor was the main link between the lower, investigating section of the tribunal and its upper, deciding section. He had the right to take part in all hearings—in particular the interrogation of the defendants—and he was always present at the official meetings of the congregation of cardinals. The assessor was the "advisor to the commissary"; he also reported the cardinals' decisions to the pope, and obtained his seal of approval. Last but not least, he signed off on the *Ristretti*, the files containing summaries of the defendants' testimonies, upon which the congregation of cardinals based its verdict. The assessor, the commissary, and his senior deputy, the first *socius* (but not the second *socius*), were also official members of the consultors' conference, thus providing a second link between the investigating and deciding authorities.

Two obvious changes to the composition of the Holy Office's congregation of cardinals were made after the official opening of the Sant'Ambrogio trial in December 1859. On May 21, 1860, Pius IX made Cardinal Reisach a member of the Inquisition.[96] And on October 5 of the same year, the pope named Patrizi, of all people, as the Holy Office's cardinal secretary.[97] This is the only time in the 470-year history of the Holy Office that a cardinal vicar, responsible for the Tribunal of the Vicariate Court of the City of Rome, has also been made cardinal secretary of the Holy Office. In an internal paper from the early nineteenth century, the cardinals of the Inquisition explicitly advised against a coupling of these two offices: "The election of the cardinal vicar as the secretary of the Holy Office could lead to collisions between the ordinary powers of the Vicariate and the extraordinary powers of the Holy Office." For this reason, in the history of the Church there was "not a single example of a cardinal vicar, who is qua office a member of the Inquisition, simultaneously being appointed secretary of the Holy Office."[98]

Why did Pius IX disregard this unwritten rule? The answer is not far to seek: the pope wanted to be certain that the investigation of the Sant'Ambrogio affair remained in the hands of his trusted servant, the supporting pillar of his pontificate. As Patrizi had been unable to deal with the case within the Vicariate, which had been the pope's initial intention, he would now deal with it as head of the Inquisition. This way, the pope could offer more protection to people close to him who were embroiled in this affair. At the same time, he was appointing one of the suspects as supreme judge, thus placing him beyond the tribunal's reach. Similar motives may have played a role in the promotion of Cardinal Reisach to cardinal member of the Inquisition. But wasn't the pope drawing suspicion on himself with these decisions, which he must have made in the knowledge that both men were caught up in what had happened in Sant'Ambrogio? Was he somehow personally involved?

THE SOURCES FROM THE ARCHIVE OF THE CONGREGATION FOR THE DOCTRINE OF THE FAITH

The *Archivo Segreto Vaticano*, the secret archive in the Vatican palace, is reached via the Porta Sant'Anna on the right of Saint Peter's Square. It has been open to researchers since 1881. The material relating to all trials by the Roman Inquisition, meanwhile, remained inaccessible for significantly longer. The files are located in the most secret of all Church archives, the *Archivio della Congregazione per la Dottrina della Fede* (ACDF), the Archive of the Congregation for the Doctrine of the Faith. This archive contains the collections of the Inquisition and the Congregation of the Index. It is situated not in the Vatican's secret archive, but in the Palazzo del Sant'Uffizio, the current home of the Congregation for the Doctrine of the Faith. This building is situated to the left of the colonnades of Saint Peter's Square, right in front of the Campo Santo Teutonico. Pope John Paul II finally opened the archive in 1998, in the run-up to the Holy Year of Jubilee. It contains the document collection of the Congregation of the Index, which was exclusively concerned with book censorship, and the Roman Inquisition's much more extensive collection. In addition to monitoring the book market, and having basic responsibility for deciding all religious questions, it also acted as the highest religious tribunal. The main collection is therefore divided in numerous and diverse subcollections, concerned with general religious questions, disputes on sacramental theology, matrimonial law, dispensations, the relationship between Jews and Catholics, and unresolved issues of every kind.[99]

A little was known about the Sant'Ambrogio case before the archive was opened. It was at least clear that this must have been a matter of feigned holiness. And so one might have expected the files from this case to be housed in one of the relevant archive series on the pretense of holiness.[100] But the search for them there was fruitless. The case of Sant'Ambrogio was finally discovered in the Stanza Storica, the archive's "historical hall," which was principally a collection of material ranging from the sixteenth to the twentieth century.[101] The reams of paper that make up the case files, plus the documents and books confiscated from the convent, take up over six feet of shelf space. In terms of content, there are no recognizable connections between the Sant'Ambrogio files and the bundles on either side of them. There seems to be little logic to shelving the files here, and it may have been a mistake. Or were these incendiary papers deliberately hidden?

Due to the structure of the tribunal, with its two levels linked by individuals and institutions, in every Inquisition trial there are three types of court files. First, the investigation files from the lower section, documenting the work of the commissary and his two deputies. They are handwritten throughout, and comprise the receipt and record of the denunciation, along with transcripts from the witness examinations and the interrogations of defendants. There are also brief notes and remarks from the examining judge, detailing the current position of the trial. These were either made for the judge's own benefit, or in preparation for presenting the case to the upper level of the cardinals, or even the pope. Sometimes there are also letters to the cardinal secretary.

The second type of file comprises important documents from the tribunal's deciding level: transcripts of the assembly of consultors and their suggested decisions, as well as the handwritten *Decreta* from the assembly of cardinals. Where necessary, written reports or judgments from individual consultors on certain specialist topics were brought into the meetings.

The files connecting the investigating and deciding levels are the summaries of witness examinations (*Relazioni*) and the interrogations of defendants (*Ristretti*). These were first drafted by hand, and then multiple copies were printed secretly and internally for the cardinals and consultors. In the *sommario*, it was common for a selection of key passages from the examinations to be presented verbatim. These reports made by the investigative level formed the basis for the judgments made by the cardinals, and ultimately the pope, in all Inquisition trials. Sometimes the verdict was announced publicly; sometimes it was given in secret. One way of announcing the verdict in public was to publish the text of the judgment on large posters, called *bandi*. The *bandi* were pasted to the doors of the main Roman Catholic churches, and put up in the Campo de' Fiori. The other option was to forgo a publication of the judgment, informing only the people involved in the trial. This approach was very frequently chosen, usually to protect the people involved.[102]

In this knowledge, let us take a closer look at the available material on the case of Sant'Ambrogio. First, the files produced by the investigating section of the highest tribunal, which, as usual, start with the *Denunzia*. The denunciator first had to give a valid reason for turning to the Inquisition. The material also had to fall within the Holy Office tribunal's remit, which meant it must largely pertain to the protection of the true Catholic Faith, and the defense against heresy. Egotistical motives like hatred or resentment, and the intention to revenge oneself upon or harm an opponent, weren't recognized. The only acceptable reasons for making a complaint were those of a "superior nature," like the "unburdening of conscience," a "zeal for the Holy Faith," the fear of being excommunicated, and, above all, being instructed to complain by one's confessor.[103]

The acceptance of the denunciation followed a fixed pattern:[104] first, the denunciator gave his personal details and took an oath on the Gospels. Then his verbal complaint was heard in Italian, the first sentence of which had to contain one of the legitimate reasons mentioned above.[105] There were other standard questions, followed by questions from the investigating judge pertaining to the specific case, each of which was asked in Latin and answered by the witness in Italian. Finally, the notary read out the transcript of the denunciation *ad alta voce*, and this was then signed by the denunciator.[106] Later examinations followed a similar format.

The next set of documents in the investigative section of a trial is the transcripts of examinations and interrogations, all of them individual hearings. In the Sant'Ambrogio case, the pope expressly instructed that the interrogations should all be transcribed by the second investigating judge, the Dominican Enrico Ferrari. He had already taken down the denunciation. His job was to act as notary, and vouch for the authenticity of the statements. Each transcript starts with the date. There follows an introduction, with a record of the examinee's personal details, and the oath. Like the investigating judge's questions, both of these were spoken and transcribed in Latin. And as in the *Denunzia*, the answers from the witnesses and defendants were spoken and transcribed in Italian.

The opening question to the witnesses—as in all the hearings, formulated in the third person singular—was always: *"An sciat, vel imaginetur causam suae vocationis, et praesentis examines?"* ("Does he know, or can he imagine, the reason he has been called to this examination?")[107] The witnesses replied in Italian. Agnese Eletta simply answered, *"No, Signore."*[108] Archbishop Hohenlohe's answer was much more positive: "I imagine that it could be to do with Princess Katharina von Hohenzollern, and all that she experienced in Sant'Ambrogio in Rome, when she was there as a novice."[109] The examination of each witness often lasted several days. As far as possible, their testimonies were taken down verbatim, and thus remained in the first person singular.

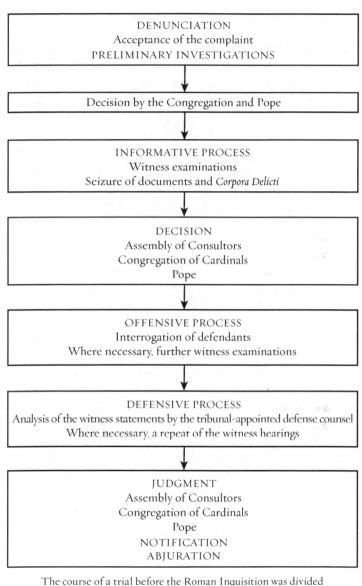

DENUNCIATION
Acceptance of the complaint
PRELIMINARY INVESTIGATIONS

Decision by the Congregation and Pope

INFORMATIVE PROCESS
Witness examinations
Seizure of documents and *Corpora Delicti*

DECISION
Assembly of Consultors
Congregation of Cardinals
Pope

OFFENSIVE PROCESS
Interrogation of defendants
Where necessary, further witness examinations

DEFENSIVE PROCESS
Analysis of the witness statements by the tribunal-appointed defense counsel
Where necessary, a repeat of the witness hearings

JUDGMENT
Assembly of Consultors
Congregation of Cardinals
Pope
NOTIFICATION
ABJURATION

The course of a trial before the Roman Inquisition was divided
into several clearly defined steps.

However, the presence of the transcriber in these documents shouldn't be overlooked. Ferrari was an experienced inquisitor, whose practiced ear may well have heard things implied that a witness didn't actually say. His "anti-heretical" stance may occasionally have made him—and for the most part, this was probably an unconscious action—overhasty in filing away some statements into particular "inquisitorial drawers." This should be borne in mind where the transcripts from the nuns' examinations contain theological terminology that one might not expect to hear from relatively uneducated women.

The defendants' interrogation transcripts are constructed in a very similar way to those of the witness examinations. The investigating judge, Sallua, always took part in the interrogations. His colleague Ferrari transcribed the nuns' hearings, and a substitute notary took over for the interrogation of the confessors. Raffaele Monaco La Valletta, who became the assessor in January 1859, was also present for the latter. Sallua confronted the suspects with compromising statements from the witnesses. Unlike the witness hearings, which were purely a series of questions and answers, here there were heated discussions between the judges and the defendants.

Once the tribunal's lower section had completed the first phase of investigation, the "informative process,"[110] Sallua prepared a *Relazione informativa*, a detailed summary report, for the deciding section. This was first drafted by hand, and then printed secretly and internally in the Vatican and presented to the congregation of cardinals and the consultors. They had to decide whether the informative process had yielded sufficient evidence to move on to an offensive process, and bring formal charges, or whether the trial should be halted.

The Sant'Ambrogio *Relazione informativa* dates from January 1861. It was extremely detailed, and its *sommario* contained a long appendix of word-for-word extracts from the witness examinations. It documented the result of the investigation from the investigating judge's point of view. Sallua's handwritten notes on this are the closest we can get to his personal views on the Sant'Ambrogio case. He prepared these *brevi cenni* for his own use, or as the basis for a report to the pope or the cardinals.

Following on from the informative process, the offensive process was also summarized in printed reports. These *Ristretti*—one for each defendant—were compiled by the investigating judge with the help of a scribe.[111] They were then checked over by the fiscal and, where applicable, the defense counsel, before being passed on to the consultors and cardinals via the assessor.

A third phase of the trial, the defensive process, gave the defense counsel the opportunity to reevaluate the witness statements. This stage was omitted in the Sant'Ambrogio case, as neither the defendants nor their counsel requested it.[112] This meant that the *Ristretti informativi* from the offensive process formed the basis for the verdict by the congregation of cardinals. As usual, a suggested judgment came from the conference of consultors, and the cardinals then came to a decision, which was presented to the pope. Finally, the verdict was announced in a *decreto di condanna*, which as a rule took the form of a notification detailing the names of the people who had been convicted, the offenses, and the reasoning behind the judgment and sentencing in each case. This text was communicated to the guilty parties, either publicly or privately. They were expected to subordinate themselves to the verdict unquestioningly and, if they had been convicted of heresy, to renounce their errors in a ceremonial abjuration. The sentence could be anything up to lifelong monastic imprisonment and, for capital offenses, dismissal from the priesthood. This would mean the accused having to stand trial before a secular court, which could impose the death penalty. When the Inquisition opened the Sant'Ambrogio trial, Maria Luisa, and possibly also her confessors, would have been afraid not only for their reputations, but for their lives and their souls' salvation.

CHAPTER THREE

"I Am the Little Lion of My Reformed Sisters"

The Informative Process and the Devotees of the Mother Founder

THE CONVENT OF SANT'AMBROGIO DELLA MASSIMA

"From the Piazza Mattei, you follow the street that leads to the *Pescheria*; here you see the gate of the new convent, and the outer courtyard with the new church on its far side. . . . On the left is the gate to the enclosure. Passing through it, you enter a little courtyard to the right, from where you access the Rota." This is the start of a description of Sant'Ambrogio della Massima, contained in an Apostolic Visitation report from the year 1710.[1]

The convent, which today serves as the office of the procurator general for the Benedictine Congregation of Subiaco,[2] lies in the *rione XI* (11th district) of Sant'Angelo, in the old city of Rome. It is situated next to the former Jewish ghetto, the Marcellus theater, and the Palazzo Mattei, no more than two dozen paces from the famous "Turtle Fountain," the *Fontana delle Tartarughe*.[3] There is an old legend that says Saint Ambrose's family's home stood here in the fourth century, having been erected on the ruins of a temple to Hercules.[4] Sant'Ambrogio was named after this famous bishop of Milan.[5] The addition "della Massima" appeared for the first time in 1190, though researchers have never agreed on exactly what it refers to. Suggestions range from the convent's proximity to the Cloaca maxima, or the Porticus maximus, to a daughter of Emperor Maximian named Maxima.[6]

In the early Middle Ages, the little convent was renamed, and called after the Virgin Mary or the protomartyr Stephanus, the patrons of the two small adjoining chapels. It seems to have been more or less constantly inhabited by pious women, though it isn't entirely clear which rule they followed. At first this may have been a local Roman community of canonesses. But in the middle of the tenth century, the nuns took on the Rule of Saint Benedict, which they followed until the start of the nineteenth century.[7] After 1606, the church and convent were redeveloped, and from then on they went by their original name of Saint Ambrose. The religious renewal that came with this was largely due to the Torres family of Spanish diplomats, in particular Cardinal Ludovico de Torres and his sister Olympia. She was installed in Sant'Ambrogio as abbess, as the inscription over the entrance still shows today. The building works begun at that time were only concluded at the end of the eighteenth century, so by the nineteenth century no more major restructuring was necessary.[8]

In 1810, the Benedictine tradition that had shaped Sant'Ambrogio for almost a millennium came to an abrupt end. Napoleon had occupied the Papal States in 1809, and on May 7, 1810, he issued a decree dissolving all religious orders in Rome.[9] The Benedictine sisters of Sant'Ambrogio were given a fortnight to leave their convent. Following the fall of Napoleon and the restitution of the Papal States in 1814, Pius VII allowed them to return, but they decided to join another community of Benedictine sisters in the Campo Marzio. The pope then gave the convent over to a congregation of women known as the Virgins of the Conservatory of Saint Euphemia, who left again after only a few years.[10]

FRANCISCANS OF THE THIRD ORDER

This left the way clear for a community of nuns of the Regulated Third Order of Holy Saint Francis, governed by the Rule that Maria Agnese Firrao had re-formed with the help of her confessor. The three orders of Franciscans are fundamentally different:[11] the First Order comprises Franciscan monks; they are further split into moderate "conventuals" and more strict "observants." Later, the Capuchins were also added to this order. The Second Order refers to the

Franciscan nuns called the "Poor Clares," named after Saint Clara. They live cut off from the world, in strict enclosure. The Third Order was originally for "secular people" who tried to practice the Franciscan ideals of poverty and following Christ outside convents, "in the world," in their own families and professions.[12]

But the Third Order's Rule increasingly served as the foundation for communities of cloistered Franciscan nuns. A rash of female Third Order congregations came into being following the Council of Trent at the end of the sixteenth century, with even greater numbers being founded in the nineteenth century. Their members lived together in open convents, which allowed them to pursue charitable work, such as caring for the sick or educating girls, outside the convent walls.

However, there are now contemplative as well as active Tertiaries, often called Regulated or Reformed Franciscans of the Third Order. They are distinguished by absolute enclosure, strict fasting, and communal Divine Office. Their way of life is similar to that of the Second Order, although legally they aren't Poor Clares.[13] Sant'Ambrogio's community was one of Regulated Franciscan Tertiaries.[14] The nuns weren't allowed to leave the enclosure, which contained their cells, the cloister, the refectory, the chapter house, and the nuns' choir. People often referred to them as "walled in" or "buried alive." In Sant'Ambrogio there was no *dormitorium,* or communal sleeping area. Each nun had her own cell. The novices' rooms were in their own wing, the novitiate. Nobody from outside was allowed to enter the enclosure—even the confessor and other people acting in pastoral roles. Very few exceptions were made to this strict prohibition. If a nun was in immediate danger of death, the abbess could grant permission for a doctor to come and treat her, and for a priest to administer the last rites. If urgent repairs to the buildings were necessary, craftsmen were also permitted to enter the enclosure.

The sisters mostly communicated with the outside world through a metal grille. The parlatory in Sant'Ambrogio was divided into a room accessible from outside, and an inner parlor that could be reached from the enclosure, joined by a barred opening in the dividing wall. The confessors also took confession from the nuns through this grille.

The church of Sant'Ambrogio had a dual function: it was used both for the nuns' services, and as a "church of the people" where townsfolk could come to hear Mass. The sisters followed the service from the nuns' choir, which couldn't be seen from the nave. They also took Communion through a barred window.

The daily routine in Sant'Ambrogio was, as in all contemplative convents, structured around the Liturgy of the Hours, when the nuns came together in the choir to praise God.[15] Psalms were recited in Latin. There were seven Offices in total, and in Sant'Ambrogio they began at four in the morning with Matins. Lauds followed at six, or at sunrise. Over the course of the day, work was interrupted three times by the "Little Hours"—Terce, at the third hour (around 9 a.m.), Sext at the sixth hour (around midday), and None at the ninth hour, the time of Jesus's death on the cross (around 3 p.m.). The day ended with Vespers, the evening prayer at 6 p.m., and Compline before bed.

Holy Mass was read every morning after Lauds, which the nuns attended on an empty stomach. After this came breakfast, with lunch after Sext and supper after Vespers. Meals were taken communally in the *refectorium*, the convent's dining room. After lunch there was an hour of leisure time, when the nuns could walk in the gardens or the cloister. Wednesdays and Fridays (the day of Jesus's death) were fasting days. As a rule there was no talking during meals. Instead, there were refectory readings, often taken from the lives of saints. Between Offices, which always lasted from half an hour to forty-five minutes, the sisters did a variety of work. In Sant'Ambrogio, this was principally gardening or sewing vestments and other textiles for liturgical use, the sale of which helped to finance the convent. The chapter house was where the nuns gathered to read the individual chapters of the Rule and the constitutions, for communal discussion of any questions that had been raised, and for the election of sisters to the convent offices.

The community was led by the abbess. She steered the convent in all matters, though she left most of the economic and organizational issues to the vicaress, who in Sant'Ambrogio also took on the role of cellarer. She had the key to the cellar and all the other rooms of the convent. Both women were addressed as "Reverend Mother." The nuns therefore referred to them as the mother abbess, and the madre vicaria (mother vicaress). The novice mistress was responsible for training the novices. There was an infirmary mistress, responsible for the convent dispensary, a nurse, and a quartermistress responsible for the convent's food. There were also the offices of gatekeeper and sacristan.

The religious director and primary confessor of Sant'Ambrogio played a central role in the spiritual leadership of the nuns, among many other things. This office was always occupied by a member of the Society of Jesus, who was supported in his duties by a second confessor, another Jesuit. The cardinal protector supervised the convent, and his office was always held in conjunction with that of cardinal vicar of the diocese of Rome. The cardinal protector had a duty to ensure a strict adherence to the rules and to correct any misbehavior, but also to protect the convent from outside hostility. As the nuns were unable to leave the convent, they employed a lawyer to help them handle legal matters. He represented Sant'Ambrogio's interests, in consultation with the vicaress.

Anyone wishing to become a member of the Sant'Ambrogio community first spent some time in the convent as a postulant. If her mind was still set on entering, and if the convent's superiors (the abbess, vicaress, confessor, and novice mistress) were convinced of her suitability, she would then be clothed as a novice. She had to complete a novitiate lasting at least a year, during which time the novice mistress would provide guidance that allowed her to become absolutely certain about whether she was called to convent life. The novice would have to grapple with the convent's spirit and its customs. Every sister received a new name: her entry into the order meant the start of a new life, with a new identity. After this period of thorough testing came the profession of vows, a ceremony where the novice pledged herself to poverty, chastity, and obedience until death. Nuns were expected to remain in the convent for the rest of their lives, and leaving the order was only possible with a great deal of fuss and an act of mercy by the pope.

Another condition for entering the convent was a dowry of 500 scudi.[16] These dowries formed the basis of the convent's funds. Even in the nineteenth century, some young women's hopes of entering a convent were still dashed by the inability to raise a dowry, especially if they came from the lower classes. Considering that a farmhand in Rome at that time earned just 70 scudi a year, 500 was a considerable sum. Many nuns relied on the support of aristocratic patrons or

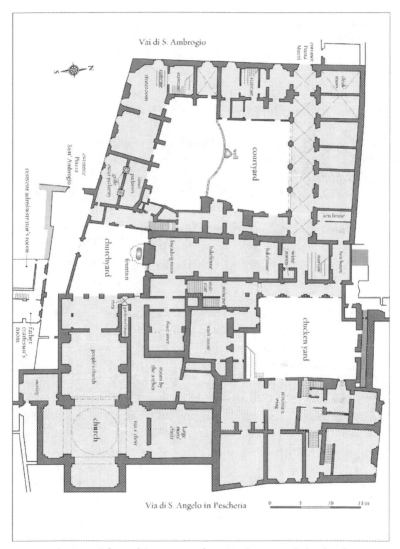

The ground floor of the convent of Sant'Ambrogio, with the church,
inner and outer parlatory, and the rota. The nuns slept on the first floor.

respected middle-class families. As paradoxical as it may sound: in order for a nun to follow in the footsteps of the *Povorello* Saint Francis of Assisi and live in poverty, the convent that housed his followers required a secure financial base.

AGNESE FIRRAO IS VENERATED AS A SAINT

The community of Sant'Ambrogio owed its existence to the reform of Maria Agnese Firrao, who was known to the nuns by the honorific "mother founder."

Lucia Firrao was born on October 6, 1774, in Rome.[17] Her father, Giuseppe Firrao, came from a family that had originally been Jewish—his father had been baptized at the age of three. Her mother was Teresa Vitelli. The Firraos were a respected middle-class family in Rome, and knew people in the Church establishment. Giuseppe Firrao's brother Natale became a priest, and was a close friend of Carlo Odescalchi, who was later made a cardinal. In 1838, Cardinal Odescalchi fulfilled a long-cherished desire that had been frustrated by successive popes, and joined the Jesuit order.[18] Lucia's parents had already found a suitable match for their daughter, who was to marry when she reached sixteen. But Lucia fought their decision, finally getting her own way and entering the convent of Santa Apollonia in Rome as a novice in the early 1790s. This was a Regulated Third Order convent, with a strict enclosure and a ceremonial profession of vows.[19] But a year later, Lucia transferred to Santa Chiara, which was also inhabited by sisters of the Third Order of Holy Saint Francis.[20] There she was given her habit on January 24, 1796, and took the name Maria Agnese.[21]

Incredible stories about the twenty-year-old nun began to appear not long after she had entered the order. On April 30, 1796, the Roman newspaper *Diario ordinario* reported that Maria Agnese had fallen ill and was on her deathbed, the doctors having declared there was nothing more they could do, when she had a vision of Saint Francis and Saint Clara. She begged them to let her die and "rejoice in her bridegroom [Jesus Christ] in paradise," but they denied her request, saying that the Lord still had important work for her in this world.[22]

Against all expectations, the young nun made a full recovery. News of her miraculous healing quickly spread through Rome: it was said that the order's saints, Francis and Clara, had saved their faithful servant from certain death.

Catholics began to make pilgrimages to the convent of Santa Chiara, to see the new "saint." This prompted a trial in 1796 before the Tribunal of the Vicariate, to determine whether the miraculous healing was genuine.[23] All this was done "to the greater glory of God," said the *Diario ordinario*, and quoted from the printed court files to prove to the world "how great God's protection of His faithful creations is, as we experience the miraculous effect of His divine assistance."[24] The young nun was portrayed here as an exemplary recipient of God's mercy, and the Vicariate recognized the miracle as genuine.

Now that the Church and the public had legitimated her miraculous healing, Sister Maria Agnese's spiritual guide, Domenico Salvadori,[25] decided to reveal several supernatural phenomena that she had experienced in the period following her recovery. He spoke of the five bleeding stigmata that Sister Maria Agnese had received on her hands, feet, and breast, and painted a picture of her as a radical ascetic and ideal follower of Christ. Her life, he said, was shaped by the most severe mortification of the flesh: "She trapped her tongue under a heavy stone for five to six minutes" so that no blasphemy might issue from her mouth. Still, demons plagued her day and night, trying to tempt her away from the path she walked with Christ. Maria Agnese often wore an "iron mask containing 54 pointed nails." Playing to a Catholic audience that was seemingly obsessed with miracles, Maria Agnese's confessor claimed she had been sent countless ecstasies and visions. She had even been granted the blessing of a heavenly marriage with Jesus Christ. Supernatural messages had told her that God was threatening "to take the Catholic Faith away from Rome" if the city didn't reform. In subsequent visions, God was severely critical of "the disorder that reigns throughout the clergy, in particular the higher echelons, and above all the pope himself."[26]

The confessor's interpretations of these visions drew implicit parallels between Maria Agnese, at the turn of the nineteenth century, and Saint Catherine of Siena in the second half of the fourteenth century. Maria Agnese lived through Napoleon's first occupation of the Papal States and the city of Rome in 1798, when he threatened the very existence of the papacy. Catherine of Siena, who was born in 1347, had experienced something very similar when the popes were wholly dependent on France. In 1309, at the start of the Church's "Babylonian Captivity," the papal residence had to be moved from Rome to Avignon, into the sphere of influence of the French kings. Like Catherine of Siena, who was very involved in Church affairs and finally succeeded in persuading Gregory XI to return to Rome in 1377, Agnese Firrao was now speaking out against what was, in her view, Pius VI and his successor, Pius VII's, excessive compliance with the French. In 1801, Pius VII had to sign a humiliating concordat with France, and in 1804 he even had to anoint Napoleon as emperor. Both Catherine and Maria Agnese belonged to strict penitential orders; both had received stigmata; both achieved the highest level of mystical union with God through a "heavenly marriage" with Christ. Though they were women, these direct encounters with God legitimated their involvement in the politics of churchmen. Catherine of Siena paid the price for her mystical experiences and her political activity when people accused her of being a heretic and a false saint. It took a long time for the Church authorities to recognize her as a true mystic. Wasn't there a danger that the same fate might await Maria Agnese?

To start with, things seemed to be going well for her. Influential circles of the Roman Curia came out in support of the young visionary. The cardinal protector of Santa Chiara, the influential cardinal Giuseppe Albani,[27] encouraged her and her new confessor, Giuseppe Loreto Marconi,[28] to carry out a reform of the convent. Marconi also secured the support of a network of ex-Jesuits, many of whom became secular priests after their order was suppressed in 1773. Padre Giuseppe Pignatelli,[29] who was later beatified, seemed especially convinced that Firrao's visions were genuine, and helped with the creation of new constitutions for the convent. But very soon, problems began to arise with the implementation of the reform in Santa Chiara. The changes boiled down to a tightening of discipline and enclosure, and there was open resistance to this from nuns who had been there for many years. And so Pius VII allowed Maria Agnese, her biological sister, and two other nuns to leave the convent and found a new institution. In 1804 he gave them a house in the Via Graziosa, near Santa Maria Maggiore.[30] Pope Pius VII considered the proposed Rule for the reformed Franciscan Nuns of the Third Order, and approved it

Maria Agnese Firrao, in an attitude typical of a saint,
with a cross at her breast.

on January 26, 1806. Papal authorization for the ceremonial followed
on April 10,[31] and Maria Agnese became the first abbess.

Even after Firrao had founded her own order, Marconi continued
to inform the public of her numerous visions and miracles. She was
said to have multiplied items of food, in emulation of Jesus' loaves and
fishes miracle,[32] which caused a huge sensation in Rome. But sooner
or later, somebody must have denounced her to the Holy Office.
Saint Catherine of Siena wasn't the only woman whose fate Firrao
now shared; the Roman Inquisition scrutinized almost all women
who founded an order or carried out reforms in the area of organized
female asceticism. Angela Merici,[33] the founder of the Ursulines,
and Mary Ward,[34] the founder of the English Ladies, suffered the
same scrutiny. It wasn't unusual for these devout and driven women
to be accused of dishonest intentions and heretical tendencies, and
for the Church to declare them orthodox only after a long struggle
involving humiliation, allegations, condemnation, and incarceration.
The Church's mistrust of Firrao was in line with the Roman Inquisition's view of nuns and women in general: the daughters of Eve had
to subordinate themselves to the male clerical hierarchy. It had been
the decision to act on her own initiative—as every reader of the Bible
knew—that led to catastrophe for the priordial mother of the female
sex in paradise, laying the way clear for the devil.

AGNESE FIRRAO IS ACCUSED OF FALSE HOLINESS

There is no record of precisely when and why Sister Maria Agnese Firrao was arraigned before the Holy Tribunal. Her devotees tried to play down the whole affair. They simply reported an accusation of 1809, leading to a trial that was stopped before it could really begin, when the French forced the Holy Office's commissary, Angelo Merenda, into exile.[35] Her opponents, on the other hand, attempted to recast Firrao's entire biography as the life of a heretic.[36]

This was also the approach taken by the investigating judge, Vincenzo Leone Sallua, at the end of 1859 and the start of 1860. But before he could start questioning the witnesses in the current Sant'Ambrogio case about the veneration of Firrao, he had to get an overview of the old case.

This undertaking proved difficult, as the Papal States had been occupied by French troops on several occasions between 1798 and 1814. Conditions were so chaotic during the notorious *epoca napoleonica* that the Inquisition had to keep suspending its work.[37] In the history of the old case that Sallua prepared for the Congregation of Cardinals, he evolved a completely different chronology from that suggested by her devotees.[38] He claimed that in January 1806, the Holy Office had begun a *new* trial against Firrao. If this was so, then the proceedings over the miraculous healing of 1796 would have to be seen as her first Inquisition trial, which wasn't true.

In any case, Sallua reported that the Holy Office had reached a verdict against Agnese Firrao in 1806. He claimed that her former spiritual guide, Marconi, who had publicized her miracles, was stripped of his office, and Agnese Firrao was demoted from her role as abbess. Her active and passive voting rights in the convent were also removed. The decree specifically prohibited any further personal or epistolary contact between the confessor and the nun, on pain of excommunication. Sallua remarked ruefully that due to the political confusions of the time, the judgment could not be implemented.

But this interpretation of events is less than convincing. At the time when the Inquisition, with the pope at its head, was supposed to have been passing judgment on Padre Marconi and Agnese Firrao, Pius VII was actually approving the Rule and the ceremonial that

Marconi and Firrao had presented to him. One gets the impression that, whether consciously or unconsciously, the investigating judge was rewriting inquisitorial history in the Holy Office's favor. In his version, its wisdom naturally recognized the false saint's deceit from the very beginning.

Sallua then claimed that February 4, 1808, marked the conclusion of a further Inquisition proceeding—but this is also impossible to substantiate.[39] At this time, the inquisitor stated, "crucial evidence" was found of Firrao's "feigned holiness" and her "lewd behavior" with the priest Pietro Marchetti.[40] In addition to this, there were the "perverse principles of Quietism" that she and her sisters followed. She also caused "dangerous writings" to be produced, publicizing her own holiness. Firrao's spiritual guides and confessors wrote ever more detailed hagiographic texts. The most monumental of these was the seven-volume saint's life from the pen of Padre Marconi, in which the confessor essentially proposed a living woman as a candidate for beatification.[41]

This made the charges brought by the highest religious authority more serious in two respects. First, sexual misconduct was added to the theological misdemeanors—naturally, initiated by the woman, not the priest in question, which was typical of the views of the period. Then the whole thing was classed as heresy, and specifically as Quietism.[42] The Inquisition was looking for a heretical pigeonhole into which they could sort Firrao's behavior, because the phenomena somehow seemed to fit there. There is, however, some doubt about whether Quietists even existed at the start of the nineteenth century, and whether Agnese Firrao had ever heard of their theological system.

As a theological movement and a devotional practice, Quietism was founded on a theory of grace, based on the assumption that man could only find God by negating the self, avoiding all independent activity, and remaining in a state of "absolute inaction" and "total passivity."[43] A person had to be indifferent to everything earthly, and was unable to do anything toward his own salvation. Instead, everything was left up to God. For the Inquisition, Quietism was a sort of crypto-Protestantism.

But once again, Sallua said, there could be no trial, and therefore no judgment: in February 1808, Napoleon reoccupied Rome, taking

Pius VII captive, and sending him into French exile in the summer of the following year. The Napoleonic-era chaos also meant that the nuns were expelled from their home in the Via Graziosa and had to flee. It was only after the pope's return to Rome in May 1814 that they were able to move into a new house in Borgo Sant'Agata, in the district of Monti.[44] And at this point, like other Congregations of the Curia, the Inquisition also resumed its work. The Firrao case was at the top of its list.

From this point on, Sallua's historical rehash of the old Firrao case was able to draw on his authority's files. Abbess Maria Agnese Firrao was immediately arrested and held in a series of convents in Rome. Besides the supernatural phenomena and "boasting of her holiness," the main accusation leveled against her was of sexual misconduct, specifically "lasciviousness and carnality with demons." Finally, they said, this had left her pregnant. Two fetuses were removed from her, causing great pain, by surgeons at the Hospital of the Holy Ghost.[45] In his biography of her, Marconi claimed that her chastity had not been broken by this, because she had been the victim of evil powers. For Sallua, on the other hand, the pregnancies were the result of a long affair with the priest Pietro Marchetti, lasting from the start of 1810 until October 1812. The two had met regularly in the convent's parlor. "She pretended ecstasies, fell on him in an improper way, and gave him wine to drink to enhance his libido."[46]

THE INQUISITION'S 1816 VERDICT

The Holy Office came down entirely on the side of Firrao's opponents and, on February 15, 1816, pasted a poster-sized *bando* on the doors of St. Peter's, the church of Santa Maria Sopra Minerva next to the Pantheon, in the Campo de' Fiori, and in "the other usual places" in Rome. This was how the Inquisition's commissary at that time, the Dominican Angelo Maria Merenda, chose to publicize Firrao's formal conviction for "feigned holiness."[47]

Sister Maria Agnese Firrao of Rome, 42 years old, former nun in the convent of Santa Chiara in Rome, then founder of that institution known as the Reformed Convent of the Third Order of Holy St Francis of Assisi has, through long and cunning efforts, given the appearance of being a saint. She boasted of possessing the wounds of Christ and receiving visions, revelations, ecstasies, visitations and other gifts and special blessings from God. But following the investigation conducted by this Holy Office into the aforementioned matter—after Firrao had been locked up in the conservatory of Santa Maria del Rifugio[48]—it has emerged that the wounds, revelations, visions, ecstasies, visitations and the other above-mentioned things taken to be miraculous and special blessings from God, were nothing but deceptions, boasts, falsifications and simulation of a false reality.

For these misdemeanors, the Inquisition sentenced Firrao to "lifelong imprisonment in a convent of the strictest observance, to be determined by the cardinal vicar. From henceforth she must wear the penitential habit without the black veil, and is strictly obliged to stay away from the grille, the gates and the convent's parlor. She is also forbidden from corresponding with anyone without the express permission of the mother superior." The principal aim of this punishment was to prevent any kind of communication between the former abbess and the nuns of her reformed Third Order. If there was the least breach of the Inquisition's terms, Firrao would automatically be sentenced to a year in a convent jail, and three months of taking only bread and water on Fridays. She also had to pray a Rosary in atonement for her sins every Saturday for the rest of her life.[49] The notification added that once His Holiness and Their Eminences the cardinal inquisitors had decided the matter, "Nobody must dare to claim in the future or continue to believe that the above-named Sister Maria Agnese Firrao is a saint."

This judgment, made in the assembly of the Holy Office cardinals and Pope Pius VII on February 8, largely followed the recommendation of the consultors. They had considered Firrao's case on January 22, and classed her supernatural experiences and supposedly divine gifts as "Molinosism," thus pigeonholing what she had done as a heresy that had been condemned in 1687.[50]

Molinosism was named for Miguel de Molinos, who died in the Inquisition's jail in 1696.[51] The Spanish priest had quickly made a

On February 15, 1816, the Holy Office published Maria Agnese Firrao's formal conviction for "pretense of holiness" on a *bando*.

name for himself as a spiritual leader and confessor in various convents in Rome. This rapid success led envious rivals to accuse him of Quietism—and it didn't end there. Molinos's opponents ramped up the charge, arguing that if he and his followers considered their own moral actions meaningless in terms of their souls' salvation, then they must believe that one could indulge in the worst kind of fleshly debauchery without being called to account on the Day of Judgment.

In the language of the Inquisition, Molinosism meant not just false mysticism but, at least indirectly, serious sexual misconduct.[52] It is very likely that the cardinals and Pius VII consciously avoided using this term in their public judgment: to do so would have been to unleash speculations about erotic adventures behind the convent walls. This was a trope that had been common currency ever since the anti-monastic rhetoric of the Reformation, and it was revived during the Enlightenment.[53]

In the meeting on February 8, 1816, the cardinals also decided to dissolve the convent with immediate effect.[54] Agnese Firrao herself was incarcerated in the convent of the Concezione.[55] However, according to Sallua, her confessor helped the "mother" to remain "in secret and cunning contact" with her "daughters." She induced them to "continue to adhere to the maxims and principles that had been condemned." Her letters gave secret instructions, and prophesied that she would soon be reunited with her daughters. She was therefore summoned once more before the Holy Office's tribunal. The witness statements and documents with which they confronted her were so overwhelming that Firrao confessed to everything they had accused her of, including her long sexual relationship with Monsignore Marchetti. When he was interrogated by the Inquisition, Marchetti himself was forced to admit "that he *in eodem lecto simul turpiter agebat*[56] both with Firrao and Sister Maria Maddalena." In plain English, this meant the priest had had sexual intercourse with two nuns at the same time, in the same bed.

Sallua described how the Inquisition increased its pressure on Firrao. She now "repented of all her wicked deeds, in her own handwriting." The tribunal officially informed Firrao's "daughters" of the judgment and her abjuration, hoping to "disillusion" them. But this didn't stop them venerating her as a saint. Contact between the mother and her daughters continued in secret, and the Inquisition finally decided to transfer Maria Agnese to San Marziale in Gubbio, away from Rome, to break off the forbidden contact once and for all—though this strategy also failed.

The Inquisition generally concluded affairs of this type with a secret internal abjuration. Why did it depart from its usual practice in Firrao's case? Why did it decide to make a public announcement of the judgment? This was principally because since the confirmation of the 1796 miracle, Maria Agnese Firrao's fame had spread right across Europe. In Rome, even members of the College of Cardinals and ladies of the Roman nobility had held her in high esteem.[57] The wounds and ecstasies had turned her into a saint. A public condemnation would draw a line under any further regard for her.

The *Damnatio* of 1816 led to substantial coverage of the case in the international press.[58] Over the course of March that year, people all over Europe were informed of the false saint and the wounds she had inflicted on herself. The Inquisition's verdict even seems to have had consequences in far-off Dülmen, the home of the stigmatized visionary Anna Katharina Emmerick.[59] She had been born in 1774, and had borne bleeding marks from the crown of thorns on her head since 1798. In 1812 she also developed five wounds on her hands, feet, and side, which at first bled regularly, then only on Fridays, and eventually only during Holy Week. But on Good Friday of the year 1816, Anna Katharina Emmerick's stigmata didn't bleed.[60] A connection has been posited between the Roman Inquisition's judgment against Firrao, and Emmerick's fear that her stigmata might be examined.[61] The *Journal de la Province de Limbourg* commented that the Holy Office's judgment against Firrao proved "that this tribunal has allowed itself to be illuminated by the century's Enlightenment." Despite the "deference showed to her by several cardinals and ladies of the Roman aristocracy, the tribunal held her to be a fraud, deserving of the harshest punishment." A surgeon and a pharmacist had also been arrested on suspicion of "causing the stigmata on the body of the alleged saint" and providing her with the "suffocating drug" that could be smelled in the alleged visionary's room, "whenever she claimed to have been tempted by the devil."[62]

THE MIRACULOUS CONVERSION OF LEO XII

Roma locuta—causa finita: Rome has spoken, and that is an end to the matter. The Roman Inquisition must have been convinced this would also hold true for the case of Maria Agnese Firrao. But it was not to be. Her devotees suffered a sore defeat in 1816, but they still weren't prepared to accept the verdict. Members of Rome's noble families (including the Marchesa Costaguti[63] and Signora Faustina Ricci),[64] prelates of the Curia, and even cardinals (Alessandro Mattei's name repeatedly crops up in this context)[65] were apparently still convinced of Firrao's holiness.[66] The king of Sardinia, Charles Emmanuel IV,[67] and his wife, the French princess Marie Clotilde,[68] played a particular role here: the king was a Jesuit sympathizer, and Marie Clotilde was an enthusiastic disciple of Maria Agnese.[69] The royal couple had shared a confessor with the stigmatized nun: the ex-Jesuit Padre Marconi, who died in 1811.[70] There had been a long, difficult period between the point at which the pope had succumbed to pressure from other European powers and suppressed the Jesuit order, and its reinstatement in 1814. During this time, the feeling of solidarity between *i Nostri* in the tight, militaristically organized unit of the Society of Jesus had become even stronger than the order's constitutions had envisaged. The fellow feeling within the Society was greater even than the duty of obedience to the highest religious authority.

At first, the efforts of Firrao's supporters were fruitless; this changed only when Cardinal Lorenzo Litta[71] became cardinal vicar of Rome on September 23, 1818. Litta was convinced of Firrao's innocence, and on April 3, 1819, he managed to persuade Pius VII to revoke his dissolution of the convent in Borgo Sant'Agata. With the exception of their former abbess, the nuns were allowed to return.[72] They elected Maria Maddalena as their new abbess, and Maria Crocifissa as their novice mistress.[73] Litta died on May 1, 1820, and Cardinal Annibale della Genga succeeded him as cardinal vicar on May 6.[74] He had been born in 1760, and came from a noble family with land in the Marches and Umbria. Della Genga was a member of the *Zelanti*, and a firm opponent of the moderate cardinal secretary of state, Ercole Consalvi. He was marked out by a rigorous puritanism and piety, and regularly took part in processions barefoot. The fate of the Regulated Franciscans of Sant'Agata now depended on him.[75] And their prospects didn't look good: della Genga came to the convent in 1822 with the firm intention of "expelling" the nuns.[76] The Franciscans and their confessor saw him as the "worst enemy of the Reform, because of the hatred he bore for Maria Agnese."[77] He was determined to enforce the Holy Office's decision of 1816.

When Cardinal Vicar della Genga arrived at the convent, Abbess Maria Maddalena took him into the chapel, where they both remained for a long time, sunk in prayer before the picture of the

Virgin Mary, the *María Santíssima Consolatrice*. This image showed the Virgin Mary with the baby Jesus, holding the globe in one hand, with his other resting in benediction on the head of the young John the Baptist.[78] The painting was believed to possess miraculous powers, and the Mother of God was said to have spoken to the nuns through it. Following this, they had scraped a few fragments from its edges and ground them into a healing powder.[79] It was reported that, as a child, Cardinal Nicola Clarelli Paracciani had been cured of an illness by this powder.[80]

This painting made a deep impression on della Genga; one might say it worked the miracle of his *mutazione* from firm opponent to firm supporter of the Regulated Franciscan nuns.[81] It was "*un miraculo della Madonna*, who spoke to him from her image." Over the period that followed, Maria Maddalena seems to have become the cardinal's closest confidant. Backed by revelations from the miraculous painting, she apparently prophesied that he would be elected pope the following year. After the death of Pope Pius VII, the conclave really did elect della Genga as the new pope, on September 28, 1823. He took the name Leo XII.

Leo XII came to the convent *in modo privato* several times, to honor the painting and discuss important issues of his pontificate with the abbess. During one of these visits, he is said to have exclaimed: "*Sono il Leoncino delle mie Riformate*"—I am the little lion of my Reformed sisters.[82] Nicholas Patrick Wiseman, the rector of the English College who later became cardinal of Westminster, mentioned Leo XII's visits to the nuns in his memoirs, describing them as a "most unexpected proof of paternal care."[83] On August 19, 1826, the pope crowned the miraculous image of the Virgin with his own hand.[84]

However, the Sant'Agata convent was too small, and entirely unsuitable for enclosure, so in October 1828 the pope presented the community with the convent of Sant'Ambrogio della Massima. This was to become the permanent home of the Regulated Franciscan nuns of the Third Order of Holy Saint Francis, reformed by Agnese Firrao. Leo XII also reinstated the Jesuit network that Giuseppe Marconi had created to protect Firrao's reform at the turn of the century. At the end of 1828, the pope requested that pastoral care and the hearing of confession in Sant'Ambrogio be divided between two Jesuit padres—functions that would remain in Jesuit hands until the convent was dissolved.[85]

This painting hung in the church of Sant'Ambrogio. Many Catholics, including Pope Leo XII, believed it was miraculous.

In 1828, Leo XII also ordered an Apostolic Visitation.[86] The visitator noted that there were nineteen women in the convent at this time. The Rule approved by Pius VII in 1806 was followed in a very strict and exemplary manner, and the visitator had no doubt that the papal approbation of 1806 had been genuine. But the Inquisition's tribunal had disputed this fact in 1816, and was still disputing it in 1861.[87]

The Visitation formed the basis for a very well-meaning brief issued by Leo XII on January 30, 1829. This text solemnly confirmed the reformed Rule of 1806, and the gift of the new convent. "We have given consideration to transferring these sisters to another, larger and more suitable place. And finally we have selected for them the convent called Sant'Ambrogio, in the Flaminio district." The pope also freed the sisters from "any kind of censure, all judgments, the punishment of excommunication and interdict, and every other conviction by the Church, for whatever reason and in whatever matter these may have been effected."[88]

Leo XII died a few days later, on February 10, 1829. After his death Padre Pietro Cinotti,[89] who was the Jesuits' *Vizepreposito,* the second most important man in the Society, gave the nuns his personal condolences. The well-known Jesuit dogmatist Giovanni Perrone[90] led their exercises.[91] Over the period that followed, Leo XII's nephew, Cardinal Gabriele della Genga,[92] kept a protective watch over the nuns. He also had a close relationship with the abbess, Maria Maddalena, whom he held in "high regard."[93] It was no coincidence that when he was enthroned as a bishop on September 15, 1833, the ceremony was held in the church of Sant'Ambrogio, underneath the miraculous painting of the Virgin Mary.[94]

Without saying so explicitly, Leo XII's brief had declared the Roman Inquisition's 1816 verdict invalid. In any case, the pope had overturned the judgment's legal effects, and the question of Agnese Firrao's holiness was open once more.

TRUE AND FALSE HOLINESS

The main goal of the Holy Roman and Universal Inquisition was to fight heresy and maintain the purity of the *sana doctrina*, healthy Catholic doctrine.[95] The "sacred duty" of this authority, which had good reason to be called the Holy Office, was to sniff out heretics of every stripe and to silence anyone who deviated from the official line. When the Christian denominations became more sharply divided following the 1563 Council of Trent, the newly founded Inquisition concentrated on Protestant communities and their protagonists. Over the course of the eighteenth century, and increasingly after the French Revolution, its focus gradually shifted to matters within the inner-Catholic realm. The Holy Office became the disciplinary organ for Church-internal movements away from Rome and the pope, no matter how orthodox their positions were in other respects. The *Index of Forbidden Books* also showed this tendency: more and more Catholic theologians whose thought differed from the prevailing views in Rome were denounced to the Congregation of the Index or the Inquisition by their opponents, and ended up on the "blacklists." Over the nineteenth century, new scholasticism—which had been just one of many theological schools of thought—gradually became the Roman (and therefore true Catholic) theology. All other theological viewpoints were *a priori* suspicious.[96]

The Inquisition turned its "left eye" toward the pursuit of intellectual dissenters in the area of doctrine. Its "right eye," however, had a great deal more to see.[97] Its gaze fell on all phenomena that might very broadly be described as mysticism and the belief in miracles: private revelations, epiphanies, visions, and auditions of divine powers—in particular angels and saints, but most of all apparitions of the Blessed Virgin Mary. There were more than a few Catholics who heard "voices from beyond the grave" or received messages from those "poor souls" who had passed on. Supernatural abilities and miracles were often attributed to these people: they healed the sick through the laying-on of hands, multiplied bread, or averted storms. A few particularly "blessed" among the faithful even bore the stigmata, the wounds being a sign of their special devotion to Christ.

This was a form of religious behavior that largely evaded the rational foundation and controls of the Church. These "mystics"—often women—claimed to have a direct line to God and the saints, and could therefore pose a threat to the Church hierarchy. Anyone who could communicate directly with heaven had only a limited need for the Church as an institution and a mediator of God's blessing and sacrament. If these "blessed" people then claimed to be living saints, or were honored as such by simple Catholics, the Inquisition was forced to impose harsh measures to protect the hierarchy. Where would the Catholic Church be if its flock was able to choose its own saints without the pope's blessing? What would happen if unworldly mystics, who protested long and loud about how the Catholic Church was becoming nothing more than a clerical and judicial institution, were raised to the altars by these "subversive" means?

The Congregation of Rites was founded in 1588, as the sole authority responsible for carrying out the canonization process. At this point the expression "pretense of holiness" appeared for the first time in the catalogue of responsibilities and rubrics of the Holy Office.[98] The pope was laying claim to a new monopoly: it was now only possible to become a saint by decree from the *Summus Pontifex*, rather than through popular devotion.

Following a long period of trial and error, a process for canonization began to develop in 1634, and was given its eventual form by Pope Benedict XIV in 1741. This remained in place until the publication of the *Codex Iuris Canonici* in 1917.[99] At the same time, a new Roman

Catholic model of sainthood was taking shape. The traditional markers of sainthood such as ecstasies, prophecies, and other supernatural apparitions, food for the sensation-hungry masses, retreated into the background. Rome became especially skeptical of stigmata.[100] "Heroic virtue in a moral or social field" was now the crucial criterion.[101]

Since the end of the sixteenth century, the history of canonization shows each pope raising people to the altars according to his own Church-political leanings. If a pope flew the flag for the fight against Protestantism, he would canonize martyrs who had been killed by Protestants. If he was aiming to intensify the Church's missionary work, new saints would be successful evangelists. If a pope wanted to cultivate a close bond with the Society of Jesus, he would canonize a large number of Jesuits.[102] From 1519 to 1758, a total of fifty-two new saints were canonized, forty-one men and eleven women. Only two of them were members of the laity; most belonged to religious orders, or were bishops or archbishops. However, there was only one pope among them: Pius V, canonized in 1712.[103] In 1625, the Holy Office expressly forbade Catholics from honoring any deceased person rumored to have been holy without prior authorization from the apostolic throne.[104]

Unsurprisingly, this monopoly met with both private and public opposition. Many of the faithful didn't agree with their saints being moral rather than magical. They didn't want saints to show special virtue and moral strength in everyday life, but to do something extraordinary: saints were supposed to float through the air, work miracles, heal the sick, and receive secret messages and revelations from the afterlife. A saint was a prophet who could see into the future, go for months without nourishment, or live exclusively off the strength he derived from the Host at Holy Communion. The wounds of Jesus Christ that he bore on his body were an unmistakable sign that he had been chosen by God; they forced him to reenact Christ's Passion over and over again. Mystics who bore the stigmata sometimes caused outbreaks of hysterical devotion, especially in the nineteenth and early twentieth centuries, which saw the emergence of Anna Katharina Emmerick, Therese Neumann von Konnersreuth, and Padre Pio.[105] It is the fascination held by supernatural phenomena with no rational explanation that drives people to create a cult around a (living) saint, and explains the *persistenza del modello mistico.*"[106]

Many men at the top of the Church hierarchy, especially Pius IX, were also susceptible to the fascination of transcendent phenomena. This meant the Church hierarchy didn't always combat the new forms of popular piety as thoroughly as it might. Instead, churchmen put all their energy into channeling and controlling these movements according to their political interests and theological ideas. Even so, the kind of contemplation that was supposed to lead to a mystical vision of God, in the mold of Meister Eckhart or Teresa of Avila, was often viewed as a protest against the utilitarianism of the Counter-Reformation's "heroic" saints. In the eyes of the faithful, a mystic's direct connection with God gave him an advantage over the Church hierarchy, whose power came via the objectivity of the authority that ordained them, and not the charisma of a divine encounter.

The Inquisition's "invention" of the concept of feigned holiness in the sixteenth and seventeenth centuries must be viewed in the context of the changes within the Catholic Church during this period. In the wake of the Counter-Reformation and confessionalization, the Church became more uniform and centralized, with a set hierarchy.[107] The diverse *Catholica* of the Middle Ages had to be subsumed into a unified Roman Catholic Church, in order to distinguish Catholicism from the other Christian denominations. Clear Catholic principles and precepts had to be drawn up, and these were to be guaranteed and overseen exclusively by Rome and the papacy in an attempt to discipline Catholics into denominationally correct behavior.[108]

Feigned or simulated holiness was initially seen as just a moral misdemeanor, a strategy used by the "saint" to gain social, financial, and religious capital. This was dealt with on the level of Church discipline. Over time, however, the Roman inquisitors turned it into a crime against the Faith, which the highest religious authority could punish with the thunderbolt of excommunication. It was frequently ranked alongside the heresies of Molinosism and Quietism. "Until the start of the 17th century, false holiness is *fraud* and deceit, subtle human artifice, then a *sickness*, and finally and above all a *heresy*."[109]

For his history of the Inquisition in Italy, Andrea Del Col found verifiable records of 114 Inquisition trials for feigned holiness between 1580 and 1876. There were at least thirty-two other cases formally handled under the rubric of "*falso misticismo*," where the offense also amounted to feigned holiness. For this period, then, there were twice as many saints condemned as "false" as there were "true" saints raised to the altars.[110]

False or fraudulent holiness, as the Roman source material also calls it, was an especially incendiary matter when the suspect was a woman. The Roman inquisitors regarded women as being particularly susceptible to the devil whispering in their ear. And it was almost a matter of course for the guardians of the Faith to see the demons of sexual seduction at work in cases where women pretended to be saints. But mysticism and extraordinary occurrences were pretty much the only way for women to make their voices heard in the male-dominated Church. Significantly, the overwhelming majority of people who displayed stigmata were women. Of the 321 documented cases up to the end of the nineteenth century, 281 were women and only forty men. Of the fifty to sixty cases of full stigmatization, only two were men: Saint Francis of Assisi and Padre Pio.[111]

The relationship of these "holy" women to their spiritual guides and confessors was an important factor.[112] Agnese Firrao and Domenico Salvadori were certainly no exception in this respect. Confessors provided an interface between the holy mystics and the general public. A confessor might dismiss and suppress his charge's ecstasies, prophecies, miracles, and stigmata as deception and superstition. Or he could become an advocate for her status as an authentic saint. But this didn't necessarily mean he held the position of power in the relationship: the confessor might also have fallen under the influence of the "seer" and become fascinated by her himself. Unsurprisingly, such a close spiritual relationship between a man and a woman sometimes led to physical intimacy and sexual contact. And here, too, the roles were by no means predetermined: the "saint" might have seduced the cleric, or it could be the other way around.

But why are there hardly any known cases of feigned holiness from the nineteenth century?[113] Three possible explanations suggest themselves: the phenomenon may simply have ceased to exist in this period. Or there *were* cases, but these haven't yet attracted the attention of researchers. Or—and the find in the Congregation for the Doctrine of the Faith's archive certainly speaks for this—cases of feigned holiness continued to arise in the nineteenth century, but were frequently handled as something other than *affettata santità*. The offense may, for example, have been *Sollicitatio*, seduction in the confessional.[114] After all, the Inquisition frequently connected the offense of feigned holiness with Molinosism and its attendant sexual misdemeanors. However, the user guide for collections held in the Archive of the Congregation for the Doctrine of the Faith reveals that files dealing with offenses committed in the celebration of the sacraments (the so-called *graviora delicta*) are still classified, and inaccessible to researchers.[115] This makes the case of Firrao a truly valuable find.

PROOF OF THE CONTINUING CULT OF FIRRAO

Tellingly, the continued veneration of Maria Agnese Firrao also formed the kernel of the first strand of the informative process that Pope Pius IX ordered in December 1859. The second part of this investigation focused on the pretense of holiness of Sister Maria Luisa, and the third on the reprehensible moral practices and crimes committed in Sant'Ambrogio. Over the course of the hearings, Sallua gradually formed a more detailed picture of the case, and was able to subdivide each of the three main charges into several *Titoli*. He then presented the result of this process to the cardinals.

In preparation for the hearings, Sallua had composed a historical overview of the old Firrao case for himself and the congregation of cardinals. However, there was one crucial question he failed to ask: did the verdict against Firrao from 1816 still hold even after Leo XII's 1829 brief, which released Sant'Ambrogio from all Church censures and judgments?

If Leo XII's brief had quashed Firrao's conviction for false holiness, then the sisters were doing no wrong in venerating their mother founder. But Sallua's consideration of the case took no account of this brief, thus editing out a fundamental part of the 1816 judgment's history. In Sallua's eyes, the veneration of Firrao was clearly a crime. He just had to prove that it was happening, and the nuns would have committed a punishable offense.

In her denunciation, Katharina von Hohenzollern had referred to a continued cult of the mother founder in spite of her conviction for feigned holiness. Sallua's initial interrogation of Luigi Franceschetti, the convent's legal representative, provided strong evidence to substantiate this.[116] The lawyer said that the young vicaress, Maria Luisa, had told him several times of the founder's extraordinary holiness.

She believed the trial before the Inquisition in the early nineteenth century had been "slanderous." To her mind, it was no coincidence that some of her denouncers had since "suffered an agonizing death": this was a punishment from God. According to Franceschetti, Maria Luisa thought of Agnese Firrao as a true saint. The novice mistress pointed to Firrao's stigmata as hard evidence of her holiness: on Good Friday, sister Maria Agnese had always "suffered the agonies and pains of Jesus' passion"; furthermore, the lawyer said, Maria Luisa had told him that even years after her death and interment in Gubbio, the founder's body remained undecayed.

Here, Maria Luisa was pointing to a typical marker of true holiness. While the apostle Paul said that man's earthly body was "corruptible," Psalm 16 claimed that God would not "suffer thine Holy One to see corruption." At first, this idea was applied exclusively to Jesus, but it was soon extended to the saints. Texts from the Middle Ages often speak of bodies being exhumed intact even decades or centuries after burial. The undecayed body soon became a trope and a sign of sainthood, especially for martyrs and people who were sexually abstinent.[117]

The novice mistress evidently succeeded in convincing Franceschetti that her own visions and revelations were genuine. The lawyer testified: "I believed in them completely."

When the nuns were questioned, they corroborated Franceschetti's testimony. And, as the inquisitor discovered, they were unanimously convinced that the Inquisition had judged the mother founder unfairly. They all spoke of miracles, visitations, and healing the sick; they all believed the founder would guide their souls to heaven when they died. Their testimonies tallied right down to their choice of words—as the Dominican noted in his summary of the hearings of the three dozen nuns, for the cardinals of the Inquisition.[118]

The fifty-five-year-old abbess, Maria Veronica, displayed an initial unwillingness to speak plainly about the whole thing.[119] It was only when the inquisitor confronted her with the other nuns' statements that she gave up "her discretion." Even so, he didn't manage to convince her that the retraction the Inquisition had eventually forced from the mother founder was legal. Maria Veronica continued to refer to the *Beata Madre*, and to speak of Firrao's extraordinary self-discipline in penance and fasting. She termed the founder's practice of flagellating herself until she drew blood exemplary. She herself had cured several illnesses through the laying-on of the mother founder's veil. The abbess admitted that, by way of numerous visions and visitations, the founder had also imparted specific instructions to her for the leadership of the convent. Finally, she also admitted to venerating the founder as a saint. She said that a portrait of Agnese Firrao stood on the novitiate altar between two candles, and that the nuns had venerated it over a period of several days, coming to kneel and pray before it.[120]

The abbess went on to say that in prayers of supplication and litanies,[121] the nuns of Sant'Ambrogio called on the mother founder instead of Saint Clara (the companion of Saint Francis), saying: "Holy Agnese di Gesù, pray for us!" The inquisitor suggested that the nuns had performed "cult acts, which one would usually perform only to a canonized saint," and the abbess replied: "This allegation is correct. We believed she had been glorified by God in heaven, and hoped that one day we would also see her glorified by the Church. These feelings and convictions were shared by the father confessors. For this reason we—and I, in front of the nuns—referred to her as *beata e santa madre*."[122]

The mother founder's first companions and old friends, who had entered the convent under Abbess Agnese Firrao, proved particularly recalcitrant under questioning. They were Sisters Maria Caterina of Saint Agnes, Maria Gertrude of Saint Ignatius, and Maria Colomba of Jesus of Nazareth, who were now all around seventy years old.[123] All three claimed they had witnessed several miraculous healings following the holy founder's intercession, both during her lifetime and after her death.[124] The three old nuns were using these medical miracles to allude to a central element of the official Catholic canonization process: nobody could be raised to the altars without evidence that they had performed at least one miracle, interceding to heal a sick person whose recovery had no medical or scientific explanation. Martyrs were the only exception to this, as they had borne witness to Christ with their blood.[125]

Even forty years after the fact, the founder's three companions believed the Holy Office and Pope Pius VII had made a fatal error in convicting her for feigned holiness. During her interrogation on January 31, 1860, Maria Caterina also stated:[126] "After the founder was convicted by the *Sanctum Officium* and the judgment was read out to us, which said so many serious and terrible things, we, who were witnesses to the Mother's innocence and the falseness of all parts of the judgment, thought the Holy Father had said in his judgment:

'that he condemned her for all the things he had heard from the Holy Office.' And so we said: 'he did not condemn her as the pope and successor to St Peter, but only as the result of things he had heard from the *Sanctum Officium*, which were completely false.' And so we remain convinced of the Mother's holiness and innocence." Maria Caterina believed the pope had erred in his judgment of Maria Agnese because he had spoken as a man, and had been taken in by human errors made by the Roman Inquisition. As evidence of this, she mentioned that the head of the Scottish College in Rome, Paul MacPherson,[127] had told her that "Padre Merenda said on his deathbed: 'The Holy Office committed a grave error in condemning Maria Agnese; if we could undo it, we would.'"

It took a certain amount of chutzpah to tell the investigating judge of the Holy Office that one of his predecessors had admitted to an error of judgment. Padre Merenda was in fact Angelo Merenda, commissary of the Inquisition from 1801 to 1820. It was his signature on the *bando* that proclaimed the judgment against Agnese Firrao.

The three older nuns backed their claim that the Holy Office had made an error in the Firrao case, by saying that senior people in the church hadn't accepted the validity of the notification, either: "More than a few cardinals, who had always venerated Maria Agnese, continued to venerate her after she was convicted." Among them were Placido Zurla, Alessandro Mattei, and Giacomo Filippo Fransoni.[128] Sister Maria Colomba went so far as to say: "Even if you were to cut me into little pieces, I would still say she is a saint."[129]

To Sallua's mind, the remarkable agreement between all the witnesses he had questioned proved the first *Titolo* without a doubt. With one accord, and in spite of formal prohibition, the nuns of Sant'Ambrogio had venerated their condemned mother founder as a saint during her lifetime, and all the more so after her death. And, as the Dominican noted, they were entirely unrepentant, refusing to abandon this false cult even during the trial.

THE SECRET ABBESS

In Sallua's mind, the second *Titolo* arose unavoidably from the first.[130] The judgment of 1816 not only forbade the continuation of the cult; it also threatened to punish any contact between the convent's founder and its nuns. And if the false cult had continued, it was to be suspected that the "mother" and her "daughters" had remained in uninterrupted contact.

Sallua had plenty of forthright witnesses and handwritten evidence for this charge. The principal witnesses were the abbess, the prioress, and the father confessors of San Marziale, as well as some women from Gubbio who had taken dictation from Agnese Firrao in the last years of her life, after she went blind. On November 29, 1859, Sallua asked the local inquisitor of Gubbio to question these witnesses, and after the New Year he informed the head office in Rome of the results.[131]

The abbess of Gubbio, Sister Matilde Bonci, had no doubt that Firrao had been in constant written communication with the nuns of Sant'Ambrogio. "On some occasions all of them, or almost all, wrote to her." They had "a great admiration for her, both as founder of the convent, and due to her reputation for holiness." The prioress of San Marziale, Teresa Serafina Salvi, and other sisters there, corroborated the abbess's statement. Filomena Monacelli, who had taken dictation from Agnese Firrao, stated: "I recall that some of the sisters of Sant'Ambrogio believed Sister Agnese to be a saint; for her part, she thought some of the sisters of Sant'Ambrogio were saints, too"— namely Maria Metilde and Maria Maddalena. Filomena Monacelli read out letters to Firrao from the nuns and a "certain Jesuit Padre Leziroli from Rome." These not only expressed a deep admiration, but also contained statements of accounts, and news that her previous instructions had been carried out. The mother founder had dictated these instructions to her in letters to Rome. Firrao had also exercised a direct influence on the elections to convent offices. From exile in Gubbio, she used the authority of heavenly visions to decide whom the nuns of Sant'Ambrogio should choose as abbess, novice mistress, or vicaress. The same went for the acceptance or rejection of novices. The confessor at San Marziale, Canon Bruno Brunelli,[132] even told the local inquisitor in Gubbio that the nuns of Sant'Ambrogio were "totally dependent" on Firrao, as "daughters depend on their mother."[133]

The San Marziale witnesses were, however, unable to provide evidence of Agnese Firrao's saintly life and death, even though she had lived with them for around forty years. "We never noticed any deeds of special and exceptional virtue," the sisters agreed. Firrao died without being anointed, or receiving absolution and the *Viaticum* of Holy Communion, although she had been ill for more than a year and therefore had ample time to request the last rites.

This was a serious omission. The understanding at that time was that the last rites were the only guarantee that a "good" Catholic would have a good death and safe passage to heaven. Until the mid-twentieth century, death notices commonly contained the words: "died fortified with the last sacraments of the Church."[134]

In fact, Firrao's death frightened her nurses. Filomena Monacelli said that when she died, there was "a great commotion, like the loosening of iron chains." A report on the death of a devout Catholic—a saint, even—would make very different reading. Rattling chains sounded more like a sign of the devil, who might have been at work in Firrao's death.[135] At least, this was how the nurses in San Marziale interpreted it. In spite of this, the nuns of Sant'Ambrogio petitioned to have Firrao brought back to Rome for reburial. She had been laid to rest by the outer wall of the church in San Marziale, away from the nuns' graveyard. The nuns of Sant'Ambrogio wanted her body returned to them, so they could create a saint's tomb as a place of veneration.[136] Their abbess, Maria Veronica, had written to the abbess of Gubbio on June 15, 1859: "We still think of our treasure being with you; you will understand that I speak of our dear and much beloved Mother."

Sallua scrutinized the interrogation transcripts from Gubbio, and concluded that in spite of the lifelong prohibition, there had been continuous contact between the mother founder and the nuns of Sant'Ambrogio from 1816 until Firrao's death in 1854. Even after her banishment, Firrao in effect continued to lead the convent. She was its real, secret abbess.

RELICS

In Catholicism, haptic objects play a natural part in the cult of a saint. Ideally these include the saint's grave, or at least his or her bones.[137] There may also be images and various objects once owned by the saint, as well as clothing—for nuns, this is usually their habit—and the utensils of day-to-day devotional practice, such as rosaries and prayer books. These are known as contact relics.[138] Texts written by the saint are also important relics, in his or her own handwriting where possible. In addition to letters, these may also be prayers, litanies, or instructions for leading a spiritual life. The lives of the saints form their own literary genre, along with other hagiographic texts from the pens of third parties.[139]

The Inquisition suspected that these and other cult objects existed in Sant'Ambrogio. In her denunciation, Katharina von Hohenzollern expressly referred to Firrao's writings and letters, as well as "supposedly miraculous objects" and portraits of the mother founder. When Sallua questioned her about these, she was even able to tell him where writings and objects belonging to the former abbess were hidden: in the archive; in the library whose entrance was behind the organ loft; in a chest in a passageway next to the abbess's room. Two attic rooms above the workshop and the infirmary also served as secret hiding places. According to Katharina, you had to hoist a plank up to the attic in order to climb in.

When they were first questioned, the abbess and most of the nuns denied possessing any such objects.[140] In her first interrogation on January 13, 1860, Abbess Maria Veronica was very reluctant to admit that somewhere in the convent there was a description of Agnese Firrao's life, written by Abbot Marconi.[141] Then she claimed she had already handed this over to the Holy Office. In reality—as Sallua discovered on closer analysis of her statements—she had burned it, along with other texts, shortly before the Apostolic Visitation. The abbess admitted there were also some letters from the mother founder's confessors, but she didn't know where these were currently to be found. The Dominican showed her evidence "that all these papers and the other writings had been retained by her." Finally, she was forced to admit "that some of the sisters still had writings and letters from the founder, and that these writings were regularly used for spiritual readings and instruction, as refectory readings, prayers, subjects for meditation, novenas and other devotional practices." Furthermore, the founder's cilice and scourge, two habits, and various other items of clothing had been preserved, and were said to radiate a "special blessing." The nuns had also hidden two oil paintings and a picture on paper. Under extreme pressure from the inquisitors, the abbess finally confessed to having burned numerous papers to stop them being seized by the Holy Office. She had destroyed the entire correspondence between the founder in Gubbio and Sant'Ambrogio's abbesses and nuns, as well as original instructive texts on the leadership of the convent, Firrao's letters to her confessors—including the Jesuit Pignatelli—and the documents that Leziroli had used to compile his saint's life of Firrao.

Further interrogations revealed that the abbess was employing a salami-slicing strategy with the information she gave the Inquisition. Several times, she even told Sallua outright lies. In his summary for the cardinals of the Inquisition, he noted laconically: "With regret, I am forced to declare here that through her behavior the Mother Abbess has consciously perjured herself."

The older sisters, in particular Maria Gertrude and Serafina, had a similar attitude. They had hidden various texts and objects to which they accorded the status of contact relics. For them, these were real "objects of veneration" that had belonged to the "Holy Mother." Under massive pressure from the investigating court, Serafina finally cracked and gave away their hiding places. After this, the Inquisition was at least able to seize the documents that had not yet been burned:[142] first the convent's death book, which started with the mother founder, and celebrated her "heroic virtues, miracles, fame, visions, and above all her saintly death." This was hidden in the straw sack of a seriously ill nun in the infirmary. Then came the annals of the institute, from its founding to the year 1858. These were tucked behind a tapestry in a sitting room on the ground floor. There was also a little chest full of letters from Firrao and her confessors, a small picture of Padre Pignatelli, numerous "of the Mother Abbess's little dresses, and a cloth that had been dipped into the wound in her ribs." Cups, cutlery, glasses, crucifixes, and rosaries had all been kept as contact relics. The abbess had "collected these objects with reverence and in the hope that they might serve as cult objects and relics if the Church one day raised the mother founder to the altars."

Many of Sant'Ambrogio's nuns said the same thing in their Inquisition hearings, right down to their choice of words. The sixty-two-year-old Sister Maria Maddalena was particularly angry, as her confessor had forced her to show the abbess the places where the mother founder's objects were hidden. She made a bitter accusation against her mother superior: "If she had not talked so much to the investigating fathers, I would not have had to give up so many things." In other words, Maddalena told the inquisitors to their faces that it would have been better to refuse to speak to them. This shows just how devoted this nun was to the cult of the founder and the holiness of her relics—and how little respect she had for the highest religious tribunal. And what harm could come to her, with a saint to intercede for her in heaven?

The seventy-year-old Maria Gertrude took the same line. As the inquisitors were searching the convent once more for Firrao's writings, she said loudly to a fellow nun: "Poor fathers: they really think we'll tell them where we've hidden those things! They'll never find them!"

The nuns' hearings painted a clear picture: a real cult of Saint Agnese Firrao existed in Sant'Ambrogio, involving all kinds of relics, objects of veneration, and things that were said to have miraculous properties. For Sallua, this proved the third *Titolo*.

INSPIRED TEXTS

The fourth *Titolo* dealt with a very specific category of letters, as Sallua reported to the cardinals.[143] "The following facts reveal how great was the nuns' veneration of the mother founder, and how convinced they and the abbess were of her glorification in heaven. This story arose again and again throughout the interrogations. During one hearing, the mother abbess seemed full of reverence and wonder. Looking very shy and secretive, she showed a few rather elegant little letters, which she had apparently found in mysterious places and under wholly unusual circumstances. She said: 'These letters were written by the mother founder in heaven.'"

As proof that these letters were genuine, the abbess said the paper they were written on was not kept in Sant'Ambrogio, and the convent's strict enclosure meant that they couldn't have come from outside. The handwriting clearly belonged to the Blessed Mother, and her letters referred to current events that she couldn't have known about when she was still alive. The abbess was firmly convinced that the mother founder continued to lead the convent from heaven.

The Inquisition's evaluators quickly discovered that Agnese Firrao had claimed her texts were inspired, and the nuns had believed her.[144] The nuns cited the miraculous power of her letters as proof of their divine quality. Every year on Christmas Eve, a strange ceremony took place: "The ceremonial said that the abbess must give a long speech, in which she would be inspired by the Blessed Mother. On this occasion, the statue of the Christ child would move and come alive."

While in common parlance "inspiration" means a creative idea or sudden realization, the theological term comes from the idea that the Holy Scriptures were ultimately written by God.[145] However, in theological history the relationship between God as primary author and the human scribe as instrumental author has been interpreted in a variety of ways. This could either be a verbal inspiration, through which the Holy Ghost not only determined the content, but dictated every single word and punctuation mark to the biblical writers. Or it could be a "real" inspiration, in which God guaranteed the infallibility of the content, though without directly inspiring the words.

In any case, saying that somebody convicted of "false" holiness had written texts inspired by God was quite a claim. This would make these writings sacred texts, and if God was their ultimate author, they should be met with strict obedience and unconditional belief.

But this wasn't simply a case of the founder's daughters believing their mother's texts were inspired: in her letters, the founder herself claimed that God had guided her pen. Agnese Firrao and her confessor had apparently authored Sant'Ambrogio's ceremonial themselves, and this, too, claimed that "even the words and turns of phrase" had been "inspired by God."[146] But the Inquisition's theologians quickly proved that most of the ceremonies and rubrics had simply been copied from the ceremonials of other convents. This was also the case for Maria Agnese's spiritual guidance, which she had compiled from the works of various ascetic authors. As the Dominican concluded, there was no trace of divine inspiration here; this was simple deception. It was aggravated by the fact that Firrao had threatened "harsh punishments, torments and spiritual pain" if the nuns should fail to follow her instructions to the letter.

A "MOTHER CONFESSOR"

Sin and forgiveness play a central role in the Catholic Church in general, and in monastic orders in particular. The sacramental granting of absolution is reserved for priests in the confessional—though this must be differentiated from the "chapter of faults" that takes place in many religious orders.[147] This is when the members of the order gather in the chapter house, and tell the community about their transgressions against the convent rules. The most senior person there—as a rule the abbot or abbess—assigns each sinner particular acts of penance to carry out.

In the Sant'Ambrogio ceremonial, the Inquisitors found a form of confession that took place not in front of the community, but before the abbess alone.[148] "The nuns [were] ordered to confess their sins and lack of virtue to the mother superior, as if they had Christ Himself before them." To the Inquisition, this had all the hallmarks of a "sacramental confession." And Firrao, acting as the mouthpiece of God, did in fact seem to have arrogated to herself the sacramental power to forgive sins—as individual nuns confirmed during their interrogations.

This meant that the mother founder was taking on a role that Catholic doctrine said was reserved solely for officers of the Church. Only clerics—priests and bishops—can act *in persona Christi*. They are the only people to whom a Catholic must accord the obedience due to Christ.[149] Feigned holiness thus had consequences that posed an immediate threat to the structure of the Church hierarchy. Where would it be if nonordained people, and in particular women, were able to dispense divine mercy?

The highest religious tribunal was obliged to intervene here: this was an attack on the Church's sacramental order. To protect the hierarchy, the Inquisition believed it had to act against this woman, whose sacramental powers of absolution did not and could not stem from ordination.

In his report to the cardinals, the Dominican also pointed out the pastoral ramifications of this state of affairs. He spoke of the "serious spiritual difficulties" and the "spiritual disadvantage" that the younger nuns, in particular, had experienced as a result of this dangerous confessional practice. There was a crucial difference between the *Forum externum* (outward discipline), for which the convent leaders were responsible, and the *Forum internum* (inner faith and spirituality), for which the father confessors had sole responsibility. Canon law stipulated that these two areas had to remain separate, and this hadn't been the case in Sant'Ambrogio. The sisters found themselves forced to confess their innermost secrets, without being protected by the seal of the confessional.

"Lay confession" was a part of Catholic history, even if the practice was ever more forcefully suppressed. In the convents of the Middle Ages, it wasn't uncommon for abbesses to take confession from their fellow nuns. Severe criticism of this practice from popes like Innocent III suggests that abbesses were actually granting absolution. In Sant'Ambrogio, Firrao had probably latched onto this tradition even though it had been suppressed by the Church hierarchy. In any case, the strict division between confession and chapter faults should be seen more as wishful thinking by Church leaders than as a historical reality.[150]

THE CONFESSORS PROCLAIM THE FALSE CULT

The conspicuous failure of confessors in this case weighed particularly heavy for the Inquisition.[151] The fact that educated Jesuits were venerating this false saint presented them with a scandal of the first order. How could both confessors have been taken in by such a deception? How could they have failed so badly in their clerical oversight of these devout women?

In their hearings, the nuns proved to be united on this point: "The confessors Leziroli and Peters claimed that the founder, Sister Agnese Firrao, was a saint. They communicated this to the nuns of Sant'Ambrogio through conversations, insinuations, and in various other ways. Padre Leziroli did this for 30 years, and Padre Peters for ten." Sallua made the confessors' responsibility for the continuing cult of Firrao into his fifth *Titolo*.

The matter turned out to be even worse than the Dominican had first feared. He quickly concluded that the confessors were the real initiators of the Firrao cult. "Over many repeated hearings, the nuns stated that everything they had learned, said, taught, read and practiced with regard to the life, miracles, extraordinary holiness, veneration, teachings and spirit of the so-called Blessed Mother, had come from the suggestions of the confessors, in particular Padre Leziroli." And this was in spite of the fact that Leziroli and Peters "knew of Firrao's conviction and her abjuration," as well as the fact that she had been banished and prohibited from contacting the nuns. This meant the confessors had knowingly defied a judgment from the highest religious tribunal—a particularly serious offense in the eyes of the Inquisition.

Under questioning, the abbess emphasized how united she and the confessors had been in their veneration of the mother founder. Padre Leziroli always carried with him a cap that had belonged to Firrao, with which he blessed the sick both inside and outside the convent, healing them via the intercession of "saint" Maria Agnese. Sister Maria Giuseppa spoke of several apparitions of the *Beata Madre*: "When the nuns were renewing their vows and taking Holy Communion, the mother founder appeared to Padre Leziroli as he was laying his hand on their heads." Sister Maria Serafina told how Padre Leziroli had healed a man who had been mortally ill, but was cured through the intercession of Agnese Firrao. Sister Maria Ignazia said: "Padre Leziroli told us nuns that when a padre of the Society of Jesus had been ill, he had taken a little piece of paper with the mother founder's signature upon it, and torn it into tiny pieces. He gave it to the padre to drink. Then he said that this man was healed by her signature." The lawyer Franceschetti confirmed that it was the confessors who were really responsible. He also described Padre Peters's attempts to keep letters from the founder, and the memoir written by Padre Leziroli, out of the Inquisition's hands.

A glance at Leziroli's work, *Sulle memorie della vita di Suor Maria Agnese di Gesù,* convinced Sallua of the pivotal role the confessors had played in the Firrao cult. Leziroli wrote repeatedly of the mother founder's miracles and blessings. "Thus one reads that she flew to heaven, innocent as a newly-baptised child, and later appeared in order to reveal how she had been glorified."[152]

For the Roman Inquisition's investigating judge, this sealed the question of the confessors' guilt in the forbidden cult of Firrao. Padre

Leziroli seemed to be the main culprit, while, judging by the witness statements, Padre Peters appeared to be more of an accomplice.

The Inquisition spent more than a year interrogating the nuns, the other witnesses, and the lawyer Franceschetti. By January 1861, Sallua believed the first charge was clearly proven: Maria Agnese Firrao had been venerated as a saint. There were relics; her texts were treated as if they had been inspired by God; she had been the convent's secret abbess, leading it from exile in Gubbio; she had acted as "mother confessor." The facts of the matter were clear: this was without doubt the offense of venerating a forbidden saint. Sallua was, of course, assuming that the Inquisition's judgment of 1816 was still valid. This claim should first have required proof: Leo XII's brief of 1829, and the chronology of the Regulated Third Order sisters' reform by Maria Agnese Firrao, cast the story in a rather different light. It could be argued that the cult of Firrao was no longer forbidden. Why did Sallua once again bypass this crucial question? Was it simply to protect the Roman Inquisition from having to admit it had made an error of judgment?

CHAPTER FOUR

"Wash Me Well, for the Padre Is Coming"

The Madre Vicaria's Pretense of Holiness

VISIONS ON THE ROAD TO POWER

Madre Vicaria Maria Luisa's pretense of holiness was the second of the three main charges considered in the informative process.[1] Over roughly three dozen hearings with the nuns of Sant'Ambrogio, Sallua was repeatedly confronted with this issue, in more or less unconnected statements. And very soon, a focal point emerged: Maria Luisa was said to have had ecstasies, visions, and other supernatural experiences that bordered on mystical translation.[2]

The testimonies, particularly those of the older sisters, all agreed that Maria Luisa's career as a visionary had begun very early. She was taken into the convent as a postulant at the age of thirteen, and received her novice robes in 1847. People spoke of her even then as "a soul particularly favored by God." During her first year in the convent, Maria Luisa told Maria Veronica, the nun who was then novice mistress (and who later became abbess), that she had had a vision of "the Lord Jesus pierced through with many lances."

The world of ideas in which this young nun was operating was clearly still influenced by the Sacred Heart of Jesus cult, promulgated by Pius IX. In the nineteenth century this symbol, printed on thousands of holy cards and used enthusiastically in religious instruction, was a standard element of Rome-oriented Catholic faith.[3]

But Maria Luisa must soon have started having other, very different, visions. The late abbess, Maria Maddalena, under whose aegis she had entered the convent, seemingly appeared to her frequently. But in her letters from Gubbio, Agnese Firrao cast doubt on the authenticity of these visions. She warned the convent's superiors about Maria Luisa, urging Padre Leziroli to keep a particularly close eye on her, "because this woman seems to be deceived and betrayed by the devil." After Agnese Firrao's death in October 1854, Maria Luisa told the whole convent that the mother founder had appeared to her in a vision, and had "begged her forgiveness for questioning her virtue and favor while she was still alive."

A few weeks later, in December 1854, the current abbess (Agnese Celeste della Croce) also died. Just a few hours after her death, Maria Luisa went to the novice mistress, Maria Veronica, to report something the dead woman had just told her in a vision: Agnese Celeste della Croce had been too mild and gentle. "For this she would have to spend several years in purgatory, and only the intercession and mercy of the mother founder Maria Agnese could free her. The dead woman said: 'Above all, the new abbess must ensure strict adherence to the rules.' Her command was that Maria Veronica should become the new abbess. The novice mistress should become the vicaress, and Maria Luisa should be made novice mistress." This vision was relayed to Padre Leziroli, who—as the nuns' testimonies confirm—spoke at length about it to the voters, instructing them that it was "their duty" to do what the vision had commanded. And so Maria Luisa was elected novice mistress, on the basis of a divine command that she alone had received. Maria Veronica became abbess, for which she ultimately had Maria Luisa to thank.

Sister Maria Gesualda was one of the few witnesses who took a skeptical view of these "divine" appointments, and cast doubt on Maria Luisa's visions. During her witness examination on May 7, 1860, she said:

When I was a novice, Maria Luisa read me part of a letter from the mother founder, in which she reprimanded her for her headaches and visions—things she took for tomfoolery. And in fact, as long as Agnese Celeste della Croce was alive, Maria Luisa was kept in check. But after the deaths of Agnese Firrao and Agnese Celeste

della Croce, Maria Luisa began to speak openly about her supernatural experiences. They included a vision of the mother founder,
pleading for forgiveness because she had not believed her. Even as a
novice, Maria Luisa showed a desire for power. She said: "let me be
mistress for a single hour, and I will make everything right again."

Three years later, in 1857, the vicaress died. Maria Luisa brought a
note to the abbess, Maria Veronica, telling her the Madonna had
"dictated this to her and commanded" she give it to the confessor. He
should then "proclaim the will of the Virgin to the electoral committee." The note read: "It is the will of the Blessed Virgin Mary that
Maria Luisa should be elected as vicaress, and at the same time remain
novice mistress." Once again, Leziroli completed his task without
hesitation, and without calling into question the authenticity of these
commands. This time, however, there were difficulties. Some of the
nuns resisted; they thought Maria Luisa far too young to take over
both convent offices simultaneously, and they doubted the truth of
the revelation. But the confessor forced them all "to suppress their
judgment and remain silent," as Sallua put it. He added that a few of
the sisters were now well aware of Maria Luisa's "artfulness."

A valid election could take place only in the presence of the cardinal vicar, the protector of Sant'Ambrogio.[4] Maria Luisa therefore had
another vision of the Virgin Mary, who gave her a message for the cardinal. The Virgin said that if he didn't come to Sant'Ambrogio on the
day of the election, he would be "poisoned with chocolate" at home by
a servant who had been possessed by the devil. Satan apparently had
a deep hatred of Patrizi, because he had campaigned "so hard for the
dogma of the Immaculate Conception." Leziroli also acted as post-
man on this occasion, and Patrizi did in fact come to Sant'Ambrogio
on October 17, 1857, for the election. As was only to be expected, the
vote fell just as the Virgin had wished.[5] Maria Luisa had used her
visions to put her career plan in Sant'Ambrogio into action. At just
twenty-four years of age, she was already novice mistress and vicaress. The next step was to aim for the office of abbess. But for this she
would have to wait for the present incumbent to die or step down, or
found her own convent.

This accumulation of roles was highly unusual in the history of
religious orders: the offices of vicaress (the convent administrator),

and novice mistress (the new sisters' spiritual leader), weren't really compatible. The fact that Patrizi gave consent to this double election shows how convinced he was of Maria Luisa's qualities.

Maria Luisa also used her supernatural gifts to allocate tasks in Sant'Ambrogio, to influence the convent's philosophy, and, above all, to recruit new blood. A series of younger sisters made corroborating statements to the effect that Maria Luisa had used her hotline to heaven to "entice young women into the convent," and to decide which of the novices were allowed to profess their vows. A few of the witnesses claimed that the very first time they met, the novice mistress revealed she had seen them in spirit long before they entered the convent, and could thus communicate God's will to them. Several of them were admitted to the novitiate, or were even clothed, without having fulfilled the necessary requirements.

Maria Crocifissa provided a telling example of this method of recruitment. On April 25, 1860, the twenty-two-year-old nun gave the following statement:[6]

> I entered this convent thinking that I would leave it again immediately, as one of my sisters was quite ill. But after a few days I changed my mind, which happened by a miracle, as I learned afterwards. When I entered the novitiate, Agnese Eletta, a friend of Maria Luisa's, told me ... that when Maria Luisa had been in the choir at a novena for the Mother Comforter, Jesus Christ had appeared to her. He told her that if I left the convent even for a short time, I would never return. It was His express wish that I remain a nun in this place, and He would therefore show my family special favor if they declared themselves to be in agreement. In confession, Padre Leziroli spoke to me of this same favor, and Maria Luisa's vision—and he added that he himself had delivered a letter to my home, in which this vision and the favor were mentioned. He said this letter had not been signed, and he had named neither the convent nor the person who had given him the letter. He urged me never to speak of it, and never to say who had written the letter. There is no doubt that this was true, because my mother and my uncle told me of it when they came to the convent.

Maria Luisa also claimed that Christ himself had worn her cloak during a vision. Padre Leziroli preserved this cloak as a contact relic, to be brought out whenever important decisions had to be made. Some of the novices claimed that, after the reading of the Rule, Maria Luisa "breathed upon" their faces, "to instill in them the spirit of the institute." In a vision, she herself had been "thrice breathed upon" by the mother founder. Agnese Firrao "thus instilled her spirit in her." Maria Luisa was drawing on the Bible, where Christ breathes on his disciples, saying "receive ye the Holy Spirit."[7] This claim was a signal that the founder had passed her authority on to Maria Luisa, in the same way that Christ gave it to his apostles. But once again, Maria Luisa went beyond the biblical paradigm: a single breath, like Jesus, wasn't sufficient—it had to be three.

And the novice mistress went still further, acting out her God-given authority in quasi-sacramental rituals. One Easter Saturday, when she had spoken to the novices about the Passion of Christ, she took "a large glass, which she called a chalice." After drinking from this glass herself, she passed it to the novices, declaring: "This is the chalice of Christ. . . . My daughters, you must never forget that you have drunk from this chalice, as the apostles did with the Lord. Take courage." The chalice of the Passion tasted (as one young nun put it) extremely bitter. One of the novices suspected a bitter liqueur, another "pistachio ice-cream from the infirmary." Maria Luisa was giving a word-perfect imitation of Jesus at the Last Supper with his disciples, as described in the Gospel of Luke.[8] Maria Luisa cast herself as the Lady of the Supper. The glass of liqueur or pistachio ice cream did, however, lend the whole tableau a note of absurdity.

A series of nuns reported that God had bestowed other heavenly "gifts" on Maria Luisa. Among these were her mystical translations into heaven, hell, and purgatory. Maria Luisa frequently told her fellow nuns that she had been taken up to heaven, where once she had even celebrated the Feast of the Assumption.[9] She had experienced the mystery of the Trinity at close hand, and had other deep mystical experiences there. The Mother of God had also taken her into hell many times, where Maria Luisa had "trampled the devil with her feet" and commanded him not to attempt any more campaigns of deceit. Here, Maria Luisa was using a familiar liturgical trope, which celebrated the Virgin Mary as a warrior who "trampled the head of the hellish serpent."[10]

However, Maria Luisa's actions in hell attracted the devil's "particular hatred." He often came at night to do battle with her. "The morning after, her face and mouth looked terribly bruised; her scapular[11] was torn into long shreds."

Furthermore, Maria Luisa claimed that in purgatory, where she was a frequent visitor, she had released many of her order's sisters, reducing their time in the purifying flames and allowing them to go straight to heaven. There she had also received from God "the privilege ... of being present at the judgment of each sister who died," and thus being able to plead their case. In classical Catholicism, the intercession for the dead at the throne of heaven is one of a saint's most important tasks.[12] By implication: a person who you believe capable of divine intercession should be honored as a saint.

According to the numerous witness statements given by the nuns of Sant'Ambrogio, discussions with heavenly beings were part of Maria Luisa's everyday life. During her mystical fits, she often broke into "prophetic expressions," when she could be heard talking to Christ. And she was always speaking "with the Virgin, and with the angel, and often with the dead mother founder and Maria Maddalena."

Saints are frequently given the gift of prophecy.[13] Maria Luisa made good on this expectation, too, as her fellow nuns told the inquisitor. Of particular interest to the investigating judge was a prophecy concerning Pius IX: Maria Luisa warned that the pope was in danger of falling into "eternal damnation." But she had "secured his salvation through prayer." With all these phenomena, Maria Luisa was building on the tradition of the female mystics of the Middle Ages.

MYSTICISM

In everyday language, the word "mystical" carries a whole raft of undertones. The things we call mystical are typically opaque and shrouded in mystery, magical and occult, hidden and extrasensory, inexplicable and intangible, or even demonic and spiritualist.[14] Mysticism doesn't quite seem to fit into a modern, rational world. But over the last few decades, a new kind of spirituality or esotericism has led to a widespread resurrection of mystical practices—initially outside Christianity, with shamans, Sufis, neo-Hindu gurus, yoga cults, and Zen meditation. And within Christianity, there has also been a revival of forms of devotion influenced by mysticism, as demonstrated by the sightings of the Virgin Mary at Medjugorje in Bosnia and Herzegovina that began in 1981, or the veneration of Padre Pio in Italy.

In the history of the Catholic Church, mystical experiences have been regarded with a high degree of skepticism for both theological and political reasons. According to Catholic belief, Jesus' message of divine revelation was passed from His apostles to their successors, the bishops, forming an unbroken line of witnesses through the ages. The vital task of imparting Jesus Christ's divine revelation thus falls to the Church as an institution. Faith comes from listening to the proclamations of ordained, male witnesses, and Christ only comes in a mediated form, via the office of the Church.[15]

But alongside this there has always been a second, extraordinary and immediate route to Christ, often called mysticism. The mystic movement centered on the unmediated experience of the absolute, the ascension of the soul to God, and its union with Christ.[16] The initiative for this *unio mystica* clearly came from God. The mystic could prepare himself by means of meditation, asceticism, or fasting, but ultimately he would be "graciously seized by the divine reality."[17] This unmediated experience of the divine was very often bestowed upon women, who were then able to use their extraordinary route to Christ to compensate for their exclusion from religious office.[18]

The Church was rather distrustful of these "private" revelations.[19] Many mystics drew political conclusions from their direct experience of God, and went to the hierarchy with calls for reform. As a result, mystics were often met with hostility. Many were prosecuted, locked up, or even executed for heresy. It was only after a long struggle that great mystics like Catherine of Siena, Hildegard of Bingen, and Teresa of Avila gained official Church recognition. From the Inquisition's point of view, real mystical occurrences were rare, and false mysticism was the norm.

The unmediated "vision of God's being" might be a purely spiritual experience for a mystic, but it could also take on physical and even erotic characteristics. The female mystics of the Middle Ages were particularly given to describing their experiences in the erotically charged language of the Old Testament's Song of Songs. The *unio mystica* could be interpreted as a divine wedding to Christ in heaven.[20] As a sign of this bond, some female mystics even received a heavenly ring, to symbolize their marriage to their divine bridegroom.[21]

The "mystical wedding" of Saint Catherine of Siena may be the best known of these bridal experiences.[22] In his *Legenda maíor*, the Dominican Raymond of Capua[23] spoke of this event in detail. Catherine had been praying for a union with her "divine Spouse" Christ "with more fervor than ever." The Lord replied: "I intend ... to celebrate the wedding which is to unite me to thy soul. I am going, according to my promise, to espouse thee in Faith." At this, the Virgin Mary took Catherine by her right hand and gave it to her Son. Jesus "offered her a golden ring, set with four precious stones, at the center of which blazed a magnificent diamond. He placed it Himself on Catherine's finger, saying to her: 'I thy Creator and Redeemer, espouse thee in Faith.' ... The vision disappeared, and the ring remained on the finger of Catherine. *She* saw it, but it was invisible to others!"[24] Raymond of Capua laid particular emphasis on this point. The ring came from heaven, and, as it was only the mystic herself who had been elevated to this sphere, only she was able to see it. It was and remained part of that supernatural reality, even after Catherine returned to earth. Her confessor, who had not been granted a role in this mystical union, was therefore unable to prove the ring's objective existence. It existed only in the mystical world.[25]

As an extraordinary route to Christ, mysticism played a substantial role in Church history until the era of the Reformation. In the seventeenth century, however, it reached a crisis point. At the same time, the Roman Inquisition began to keep a very close eye on mystics—particularly female mystics. The increasing emphasis on the absolute "passivity" of a person undergoing a mystical experience, during which God alone was the active party (which was, apparently, a false understanding of grace), made many members of the Inquisition suspect crypto-Protestantism. The Enlightenment's rationalist outlook then gave rise to a general suspicion of mystical experiences, which were seen as the spawn of irrationalism.

But countermovements also started to spring up. The century of materialism and science saw a rediscovery of the supernatural. The rise of spiritualism, with its séances, mediums, and table-tipping, can be interpreted as an esoteric counterweight to the nineteenth century's rationalist drive toward science and modernity.[26] Enlightenment thought and Romantic art, rationalism and mysticism, secularization and resacralization in private devotional practices were all closely interrelated.[27] Even educated Catholics longed for a "re-enchantment of the world." Some of Romanticism's leading exponents were Catholics, or at least Catholic sympathizers. Clemens Brentano, for example, wrote a literary interpretation of the visions of the stigmatized nun Katharina von Emmerick.[28]

In this context, Christianity made its peace with mysticism once again. Protestantism experienced a renaissance of pietistic movements "inward." The Allgau revival movement is particularly worthy of mention in this respect.[29] Justinus Kerner's 1829 bestseller, *Die Seherin von Prevorst* (The Seer of Prevorst), brought worldwide attention to the case of Friederike Hauffe, a young protestant woman who heard voices from the next world and saw supernatural lights. Divine powers also gave her the ability to make prophecies.[30]

Within Catholicism, the publicist Joseph Görres developed a new concept of the mystical.[31] He was particularly interested in beatific visions that had visible, tangible consequences in this world. During a vision, he said, a person became a medium, a "gateway to the other side—both the good and the evil."[32] Evidence of this mystical union appeared in the form of "wounds," the "lovely fragrance of holiness," or a "halo of ecstasy."[33]

Stigmata were interpreted as proof of God's continuing action in history, and as a miracle of His potent presence. For Catholics, this was an opportunity to challenge modern science, by "producing quasi-scientific evidence of the working of the Holy Spirit, and the factual existence of miracles, in the shape of tangible extraordinary phenomena."[34] Viewed in this way, miracles and apparitions of the Virgin Mary weren't irrational and unexplained at all: they were a deliberate response to the age's materialism and faith in science.

The "physical side-effects" of mystical experiences became increasingly important in this regard.[35] Mystical phenomena were increasingly seen as "explicit, experimentally verifiable confirmation" of the Catholic belief in God.[36] But the devil and the evil side of the supernatural realm were also able to use female mystics as a gateway to the mortal world. This called for caution and constant vigilance, to tell the good from the evil spirits.

This *Glauben an das Wunderbare* (Belief in Miracles—the telling title of a work published in Münster in 1846) became widespread in Catholic circles by the middle of the century. The author, J. W. Karl, spoke enthusiastically of numerous apparitions of the Virgin, ecstasies, and women with stigmata. The time for automatically doubting all revelations and supernatural phenomena was finally over. There was a direct line running from the miracles of Christ and the apostles to the "supernatural apparitions of our century."[37] "Mysticism seems to be opening up again, and things that have long been considered fables and stories are . . . once again being justified as facts."[38] A real miracle came when a supernatural experience wasn't confined to the mystic herself. The "supernatural effects" of a mystical union with Christ then became visible in nature, on the human body of the mystic.[39] According to J. W. Karl, the belief in miracles wasn't just the private opinion of a few theologians, but a "religious truth" that a "Catholic [must] not doubt."[40]

This belief that the supernatural had a tangible effect in nature was a crucial feature of Catholic mysticism in the nineteenth century: the next world materialized here on earth. Stigmata; apparitions of divine beings on earth; the divine fragrance rising from the body of a bride united with Christ in heavenly marriage—all these were a natural part of this belief. For Catherine of Siena, the heavenly ring given as a symbol of this marriage had been immaterial, only visible to her. Now it had to be material, a sign of God's proximity that everyone could see and touch.

The supernatural phenomena of Sant'Ambrogio should be viewed against this background. The "belief in miracles" made visions, ecstasies, and other mystical phenomena an everyday occurrence. In the nuns' refectory readings, holy mystics from Catherine of Siena to Teresa of Avila and Gertrud of Helfta were continually held up to them as role models. So how did Maria Luisa and her miraculous gifts fit into this canon? Was she a true or a false mystic? Or could this even be the work of the devil?

THE EARTHLY ORIGINS OF HEAVENLY RINGS
AND THE SCENT OF ROSES

These were the very questions Sallua put to the nuns and other witnesses.[41] In his letters to Patrizi, which the cardinal vicar had handed over to Sallua at the start of the trial, Padre Leziroli had started talking about Maria Luisa's "marriage to Jesus Christ" in heaven as early as the 1840s. Apparently the Virgin Mary, Saint Francis, and the two late nuns Maria Maddalena and Teresa Maddalena had also been present at this ceremony.[42] Maria Luisa had received a divine ring, which the nuns and the abbess had seen "over the course of several years and on various occasions," as they stated to Sallua when he questioned them. Over time, this ring changed shape and size, each time growing more ornamental and beautiful. Sometimes it was "so large and sparkling that it covered her ring finger almost entirely." At first, it had been a gold ring with a little cross, then one with a larger cross "like a tree trunk." Filled with "embarrassment and blushing in shame," Maria Luisa had revealed the mystery of the heavenly ring's variability. She confided to the abbess that the Lord had "decorated" her with not just one but several rings, and the "most beautiful and brightest" of these had come from the Virgin Mary.

At first, it was only the abbess who knew about the divine wedding and the rings. But of course the entire community had to be informed of the miracle, in a suitably mystical way. The abbess recalled that one day, Maria Luisa had had a headache, which was "regarded by the nuns and the father confessors as something extraordinary and supernatural." The abbess had come upon her lying lifelessly on the bed in her cell. Maria Luisa was wearing two rings, "one more valuable than the other." The abbess sent for Leziroli and inducted the confessor into the "mystery." At once, he fetched a few of the "more pious and careful" nuns into Maria Luisa's cell, and announced to them that the "most valuable and brightest ring, decorated with a lily and rose intertwined, made of rubies and diamonds" was the ring of the Virgin herself, who had given it to her "favored daughter" Maria Luisa. The nuns should therefore "kneel and say some *Ave Marias* in the Virgin's presence." Then they had to kiss the ring with great reverence, which would "free some souls from the fires of purgatory." As a bonus, the nuns were given further evidence of the beautiful young nun's holiness: when the blanket was gently raised from the unconscious woman's chest, "a divine fragrance rose up from her heart and flooded the cell."

After this, the mistress of the rings enlisted the two Jesuit confessors to help her make use of her heavenly regalia. When she had been elected vicaress, Padres Leziroli and Peters were admitted to the enclosure, against the convent's rules. In a festively illuminated chapter house, Padre Peters led a great pageant of veneration, demanding that all the sisters kiss the "miracle ring" with reverence. The two confessors then also kissed the ring on Maria Luisa's hand. During her hearing, Sister Maria Giuseppa made sure the inquisitor was aware of this breach of regulations—men were only allowed to enter the *clausura* in an emergency. "I would like to draw attention to the fact that nobody was ill when the father confessors . . . entered to conduct the celebration; at least, they did not visit any sick nuns." The forty-seven-year-old Maria Giuseppa was the convent nurse, and she was sure about this.

Once Maria Luisa had revealed her *Mysterium*, the confessors instructed her to wear the ring all the time, so that everyone might see it. Padre Leziroli proudly noted in the convent annals that the Virgin Mary's ring was set with sixty-five precious stones.[43] Many of the nuns mentioned that the madre vicaria had worked a number of "miracles" with her rings. In particular, they said she had healed the sick.

Several nuns remembered a refectory reading during a meal they had taken in silence. The text came from the life of a virgin saint, whose "virginal body" had "exuded a divine fragrance." A few days later, Maria Luisa's body had also begun to give off a "strong fragrance," which the witnesses described as being "like a rose extract or a rose essence," according to Sallua's summary. The abbess told the nuns that this lovely scent was obviously divine, and was a sign of Maria Luisa's "purity and holiness." The confessors confirmed this was the case.

The nuns also pinpointed a second source of this fragrance. In the nuns' choir of the church, there were two tiles that gave off this "magnificent scent." The nuns and confessors believed this was because "the Virgin Mary had laid her feet upon them and left the delicate fragrance behind."

But there were also critical voices. The convent doctor, Piazzoli, repeatedly asked the abbess: "What sparkling, valuable ring is that, which the madre vicaria wears on her finger?" The abbess replied that Maria Luisa wore it to bless the novices, and the doctor told her it was "a contradiction of Franciscan poverty." On other occasions, he warned the abbess: "Keep an eye on this madre vicaria, she is prideful." But the voices of doubt remained in the minority. In addition to the convent's two confessors, other Jesuits who came to help with confession also regarded Maria Luisa as a saint, as many of the novices testified.

Maria Luisa completely outstripped the mystics of the Middle Ages. Her ring was visible and tangible to all, as the new mysticism of the nineteenth century dictated it should be. The fact that she owned several heavenly rings at once is unique, as are the miraculous healings she accomplished with the aid of these rings. And Maria Luisa didn't smell like any common or garden-variety saint; she gave off the scent of roses and lilies. Over the course of the century, the rose became the flower of the Virgin, and in Saint Augustine's writings the virgins in the Lord's garden smelled like lilies.[44] Maria Luisa was erring on the side of caution here, too: such a quantity of holy fragrance would ensure nobody continued to doubt her holiness. And in this, she was successful.

Sallua's task was now to unmask Maria Luisa's holiness as a deception. He quickly figured out that the convent's lawyer, Luigi Franceschetti, would be an important source of information on this subject, and Franceschetti was called to give evidence no fewer than five times.[45]

At his first hearing, he stated that his work had brought him into regular contact with the abbess and the vicaress. On one of these occasions, in the fall of 1859, he had learned that the convent was in a state of great upheaval as an Apostolic Visitation had been announced. The mother abbess told him that the Lord was merely testing the convent with this "tribulation." She was convinced that all would be well, and the visitators wouldn't discover anything bad there. There were two reasons for the Visitation: the veneration of the mother founder as a saint, and Maria Luisa's mystical experiences, in particular the heavenly rings. Franceschetti was deeply shaken—and he had every reason to be.

The lawyer was reluctant to come clean about the provenance of the rings. But finally he said that around two years previously, the madre vicaria had asked him to place an order on her behalf with a goldsmith in Rome for a ring with a gold cross on it. She had not, however, informed him of its purpose. A while later, she discreetly commissioned another, more valuable ring, warning him that neither the other nuns nor the confessors were to be told anything about it. Later she ordered a third, far more valuable ring, which was significantly larger and set with precious stones of various colors.

After a time, Maria Luisa told the lawyer that she liked the rings so much she now wanted a bracelet, and another ring. On the ring, she wanted a rose and a lily entwined, with red and white precious stones for the flowers and green for the leaves. The lawyer told Sallua that the vicaress had been delighted with the ring; however, she had pretended it wasn't for her, but for a stranger who wanted to collect it from the convent. Franceschetti finally revealed the names of the goldsmiths—Tofanelli and Colarietti in Rome—as well as the price of the rings. Maria Luisa had also paid him for his role as middleman, with a few gold circlets and some precious stones from broken jewelry. Franceschetti described the appearance of the rings in detail, and Sallua learned that Maria Luisa had asked for a ring that could be opened from underneath. The reason for this, the inquisitor suspected, was so that she could have the ring suddenly vanish from her finger. Maria Luisa had sworn the lawyer to secrecy and told him that if he absolutely had to, he must tell the visitators he had commissioned the ring for a stranger.

Franceschetti also admitted that on several occasions Maria Luisa had asked him to buy rose oil for her. He had obtained a total of seventy or eighty drops at a price of a paolo per drop,[46] from the Sant'Ignazio apothecary. She had told him she needed it to treat a mouth infection of his sister's—she was living in the convent under the name Maria Giacinta.

Of course, Maria Luisa had to find a way to pay for the rings and the rose scent. Luckily for her, one of the vicaress's duties was to look after the convent's funds. This meant she had access to the dowries that the sisters had to pay when they entered the order. The files of the investigating court reveal that she used a lady named Anna Cavazzi, the mother of one of the novices, to sell "a few trifles." When she was questioned, Cavazzi stated that the novice mistress had ordered her, in the strictest confidence, to have a ring and a bracelet repaired. When she brought the jewelry back, Maria Luisa said this had been an errand for Katharina von Hohenzollern. Supposedly acting on the princess's behalf, Maria Luisa had then ordered another four gold rings decorated with crosses. Cavazzi sold several individual pieces of jewelry for the vicaress in order to pay the bills. She also stated that on three occasions she had bought rose oil at Maria Luisa's request, at 10 baiocchi per drop.[47] This, too, was supposedly for the princess.

Further witness hearings finally brought to light the fact that, a

few days before her arrest, Maria Luisa had handed over the rings and
the seal of the Madonna to her confidant, Sister Maria Ignazia, with
strict instructions to hide them in a safe place if there was any danger.
When the novice mistress was arrested, the twenty-year-old Maria
Ignazia took fright, opened the sealed envelope, and found the large
ring, two smaller ones, and the seal of the Immaculate Virgin. She
then threw "these objects and the paper envelope into the opening of
the secret place"—meaning the latrine.

Sallua was now able to begin a targeted search.

After receiving the above-mentioned information, the necessary
judicial measures were taken to come into possession of these
items. The master bricklayer, who had served the Holy Office several times before, was informed under sacred oath of the work he
was to undertake (together with three other men, also under oath)
in the latrines of the convent of Sant'Ambrogio. He proceeded
with discretion and care. The mother abbess was advised to admit
the workmen to the convent and take them to all the places they
wanted to look, as there were some operations they had to carry
out with the utmost secrecy. Under the sacred oath they were not
allowed to reveal who they were and by whom they had been sent,
so she had to ensure that the nuns stayed away from the scene of
the investigations. As the men were not familiar with the locality,
they encountered some difficulties while carrying out their task.
The mother abbess claimed that the latrines emptied out into the
sewer; she did not want to risk the potentially serious damage that
could be caused by making a hole in the convent wall. . . . However,
the Inquisition was determined to see the matter through, and
allayed the abbess's fears about the convent walls, saying that they
would suffer no damage. It was simply necessary to go ahead with
the work. On the second day of the operation the above-named
items were found in the sluice of the latrine, and handed in by the
master bricklayer. The openings in the wall were bricked up, and
the work completed with all due care and secrecy.

This proved the earthly origins of the rings and the rose scent, and
Sallua's *Relazione informativa* for the cardinals shows just how pleased
he was with his demystification of Maria Luisa.[48]

LETTERS FROM THE MOTHER OF GOD

During the hearings of the female witnesses, Sallua was confronted with another mystical phenomenon that went far beyond anything he had seen before. Almost all the nuns of Sant'Ambrogio testified that the Virgin Mary had written letters from heaven, which had appeared in the convent and played a central role in the community's life.[49] In his investigation of the cult of Firrao, Sallua had already come across the "elegant letters" that the mother founder had supposedly written from heaven after her death. Now the Madonna herself was putting pen to paper.

The first question Sallua had to ask himself was how the Virgin's letters got from heaven to the convent of Sant'Ambrogio. The witness statements told him that the heavenly letters usually materialized in a wooden casket, to which Padre Peters held the only key. Every time he opened it, there would be a new letter inside. Anyone who wanted to reply to the Virgin would ask Padre Peters to put their answer in the casket and lock it again. The next day, the letter would have vanished, having been transported to heaven. This little box was probably kept on the altar underneath the miraculous painting of the Virgin Mary, which would mean a direct connection between the letters and the Virgin's presence in the painting.

The second point of interest for the Dominican was the letters' contents. The abbess and the other nuns stated that the heavenly letters frequently mentioned Maria Luisa's glorification by the Virgin. There was "great praise for the subject of this inquiry [Maria Luisa], who was called a *great treasure*, and whose humility and chastity were said to be incomparable," as Sallua summarized. "There would be trouble in store for anyone who contradicted or disparaged her." But the Virgin went even further, giving specific instructions that would enable Maria Luisa to fulfill her aspirations to power, both inside the convent and beyond its walls. The Blessed Virgin threatened draconian punishments in this world and the next to anyone who disobeyed.

Sallua's eye now fell on Padre Peters, the man with the only key to the casket. But why was the Jesuit willingly acting as postillion?

Padre Peters's appointment as second confessor of Sant'Ambrogio had come at the behest of a heavenly letter from the mother founder.

Maria Luisa had passed this on to the abbess, who in turn gave it to the Jesuit general, who carried out the heavenly order immediately. The letter had discredited Padre Benedetti, who at that time was the second confessor. It accused him of having conducted an intimate relationship with the late Sister Maria Agostina. The Jesuit general withdrew Nicola Benedetti, and replaced him with Padre Giuseppe Peters. Sallua mentioned remarks by some of the nuns to the effect that Maria Luisa "preferred Padre Peters and had an extraordinary affection for him." It seems she first met the Jesuit when he came to Sant'Ambrogio as a stand-in to celebrate Mass and take confession.

The Jesuit general had almost total power within the Society of Jesus.[50] The members of the order had to follow his commands with a military obedience. While the classical orders had a lifelong connection to a particular monastery, a uniform habit, and communal Divine Office, Ignatius of Loyola consciously avoided these features of monastic life when he created the original Society of Jesus He wanted to build a new type of order. The Jesuits professed a special fourth vow, which gave them a high degree of flexibility: in addition to poverty, chastity, and obedience, they swore loyalty to the pope. This made them into his mobile response troop, and it was also the reason that a Jesuit could be transferred from one area of responsibility to another at the stroke of a pen. At this point, the general of the Jesuits was Petrus Johann Beckx,[51] who was born in Brabant in 1795. He had been ordained as a secular priest in 1819, and in October of the same year he entered the Jesuit novitiate. He became the provincial of the order's Austrian province in 1852, and was elected general in 1853.

The pope instructed that, due to Beckx's high standing, his hearing before the Inquisition in March 1860 should be conducted not by Sallua, but by the assessor, Monaco La Valletta. The Jesuit general conceded that he had relieved Padre Benedetti of his office in Sant'Ambrogio at the "request of the nuns." He characterized Padre Leziroli as a "simple man," generally believed to be a "good priest who followed the rules." Beckx claimed the same "about Padre Peters, although he did not [enjoy] the same reputation for piety as Padre Leziroli."[52]

Naturally, Sallua was interested in exactly how the correspondence between the Mother of God and Padre Peters had taken place. Apparently, apart from Peters and Maria Luisa, this was something only the

The Blessed Virgin Mary's letter to the Jesuit general Petrus Beckx.

abbess knew.[53] Sallua did everything in his power to get hold of the heavenly missives as evidence, but without success. Maria Luisa and Peters had ensured the letters wouldn't fall into the hands of the Holy Office by burning them all. The Dominican was therefore forced to reconstruct the content of individual letters—there must have been several dozen of these—from the witness statements.

But the inquisitor did have one piece of luck: under questioning from Monaco La Valletta, the Jesuit general revealed that he, too, had received a letter from heaven. At first, of course, he had no clear memory of it. Then he claimed to have burned the letter. When the assessor pressed him further, Beckx promised to have another look for it among his papers. And as luck would have it, after a thorough search the general found the letter and handed it over to the Inquisition.[54] It bore no date, and was written in French. In translation, it read:[55]

Paternité,

With all the ardor of my heart I ask you in the name of God not to hesitate for a moment to separate the unfortunate Passaglia from his Companion Schiader. Remember that in your conscience you are responsible for the Society. Woe, woe to you if you do not free the College at once from the unfortunate Passaglia, and from those who do not behave well, and transfer them to other Houses and appoint another person in place of Passaglia, and you will do the same for the others. You must do this, if you do not want to weep for unhappiness. Take care not to let any other reason or any authority prevent you, for the Society is on your conscience, and for this you will have to answer to God. Be mindful of God's will in this! It is done out of the love I bear for my dear Society, Your Paternité and all your sons. I beseech you once again, send the unfortunate Passaglia and his Companion and all others who have earned such correction away from Rome, or they will bring the wrath of God down upon the Society. So consider that you are the Superior, and God has given you the authority to command at once what I have said. If you want to know who it is that has given you this warning and has written to you, it is

Marie

Why "Marie" didn't choose to write in Latin, the language of the Church, or Aramaic, the dialect of her homeland, is open to debate. French was the diplomatic language of the nineteenth century, and was also used in the Curia,[56] which might have been the reasoning behind the choice of "divine" language. Alternatively, the letter may have been modeled on the widely read missive from the "*mère de Dieu*," written in French in the eighteenth century. Or the Virgin Mary may have chosen French because it was the mother tongue of Petrus Johann Beckx.

In any case, the letter contained an extraordinary number of errors, proving that its author had only a limited command of French, and had probably learned it as a spoken rather than a written language. In spite of this, the letter's commands were in fact carried out in 1857. The "unfortunate" Passaglia was duly separated from his companion, Schiader (actually Schrader). On August 3, 1857, the Jesuit general gave orders for Clemens Schrader to be transferred from the Gregorian University to the Catholic theology faculty of the University of Vienna. Petrus Beckx used his authority to override protests from both Passaglia and Schrader.[57] As a result, Passaglia resigned from all his offices in the Jesuit order, and gave up his professorship at the Gregorian University.

Carlo Passaglia[58] was born in 1812, and was one of Rome's most high-profile Jesuit theologians. He entered the Society of Jesus in 1827 and, once he had been ordained in 1840, served as the prefect of studies at the Collegium Germanicum. In 1844, he was given one of the two chairs for dogmatics at the Gregorian University. There, he became friends with one of his students, Clemens Schrader, who later became his colleague.[59] Schrader was born in 1820 in Itzum, near Hildesheim, and studied at the Germanicum from 1840 to 1848, when he entered the Society of Jesus. That same year, the Roman Revolution forced the Jesuits into exile, and the two men went to Ugbrooke in Devon, England, where they carried on teaching. Passaglia stood for a historical form of Thomism, and therefore found himself increasingly opposed to the new scholastics, who were growing ever stronger in the Gregorian University, and who worked less historically. He also attracted a great deal of skepticism from other members of his order for his pragmatic view of the Italian unification movement, and his attempt to build bridges between the papacy and the nascent Italian state. His works on this topic ended up on the *Index of Forbidden Books*.[60] Passaglia was held in the highest regard by Pius IX, as he had been a strong supporter of papal infallibility, and had done sterling work on the 1854 dogma of the Immaculate Conception. But the term "unfortunate" in the Virgin Mary's letter probably held the unspoken accusation of a homosexual relationship with Clemens Schrader.[61]

Did the letter from the Virgin lead to the separation of Passaglia and Schrader, or was it a kind of *vaticinium ex eventu*, something that claimed to be a prediction of the future, but actually "foretold" an event that had already happened? If it was the latter, it would have to have been written after August 3, 1857, the date that Beckx had Schrader transferred. But if it was written prior to August 3, it might really have influenced the general's decision.

This question must have electrified Sallua: if the Jesuit general—the "black pope"—had really transferred Schrader on the letter's instructions, it would mean he had acknowledged the letter as genuine.

Word of Beckx's letter from the Virgin Mary had clearly spread among the Jesuits, and had also unsettled Padre Leziroli. He instructed Maria Luisa to give him more detailed written information about it. She reluctantly complied, via a letter written on August 5,

1857.[62] Writing "purely out of obedience," she told Leziroli that the Madonna had recently appeared to her in the convent, and told her "the whole story of the Collegio Romano and these two padres." The Virgin said: "Listen: Oh! My daughter. The authorities are in error . . . I have already told you once, you should pray for my dearly beloved Society. I also sent the general a letter regarding the matter of the Collegio, as I told you." The Virgin added that she was sure her "good son Pietro" would make sure "the Collegio was freed from such a monster." The Blessed Virgin passed a judgment of annihilation on Passaglia, and Maria Luisa couldn't entreat her to moderate it. The Madonna simply said, "Well well, poor Carlo, poor Carlo: his great pride drove him into the abyss."

If Maria Luisa answered Leziroli on August 5, this means Beckx's letter from the Virgin was written before this date, and could well have played a role in the Jesuit general's actions against Passaglia. It may seem unlikely today that a heavenly missive could influence the head of an order's decisions about its members. But were letters from the Virgin Mary such an unusual phenomenon in this period? Or did the Blessed Virgin intervene to alter the course of history on an almost daily basis?

THE MARIAN CENTURY

The nineteenth century was the age of the feminization of religion.[63] In civil society, men and women inhabited separate spheres: men took care of politics, while women looked after the household and religion; men's involvement with the Church was via Catholic clubs and movements, while women were frequently overrepresented at Mass and religious festivals. The century's monastic revival was largely based on the establishment of new women's congregations. These performed good works, caring for the poor and the sick, or working in schools and on behalf of girls' education. But it wasn't just that more women were engaging in devotional practices; the practices themselves became increasingly sentimental and emotional, characterized by devotion and humility, but also by hysteria. These were all seen as feminine qualities. This fact was used as a weapon by the anticlerical movements—particularly the opponents of the Jesuits. They frequently questioned the masculinity of devout men, calling women the "Jesuitical sex," while the Jesuits' male adherents were "weak and womanish."[64]

In this context, the Blessed Virgin Mary gained more and more currency as the addressee of prayers. She was invoked in Rosaries, May devotions, and Marian litanies. It wasn't just members of the lower classes who became enthusiastic devotees of the Virgin, but people from society's upper echelons and clerics, all the way up to the pope.

This devotional practice was related to a particular development in theology. Over the course of Church history, the Catholic image of God had been purged of all the feminine characteristics that had existed in the Holy Scriptures. Now they were making a comeback, in the form of the Mother of God. The period from the mid-1800s to the mid-1900s is therefore known as the Marian century, the end point of which is formed by the 1950 dogma of the Assumption of Mary.

Pius IX's dogmatization of the Immaculate Conception, meanwhile, stands as a beacon at its start.[65] This was the question of whether Mary, due to her special position as mother of the Savior and Redeemer Jesus Christ, had been preserved from the stain of original sin, with which every other person is tarnished from the moment of conception.

For a long time, this issue was the subject of a controversial debate within the Church. In the thirteenth century, the Dominicans spoke out against the Immaculata Conceptio of Mary, as there was neither written evidence for it nor any clear proof to be won from Church tradition. But by the nineteenth century there was really no need for dogmatization: the question was no longer being debated. Most people believed in the Immaculata Conceptio and, until this point, the Church had only resorted to dogmatization in order to defend a fundamental religious truth from attack. This was how the great dogmas had come into being, which formed the core of the Catholic creed. The Immaculate Conception, on the other hand, was something new—a "devotional" dogma.

Pius IX was adamant about instituting this dogma. It had been sparked by his expulsion from Rome, following the Revolution of

1848–1849. And in exile in Gaeta, the pope set the doctrinal wheels in motion—seemingly in the genuine hope that the Mother of God would intervene in world history and help him win back his Papal States.

On December 8, 1854, Pius IX dogmatized the *Immaculata Conceptio*, by the sole power of his authority, and in the presence of numerous bishops. In so doing, he anticipated the infallibility that the pope was only to be accorded by the Vatican Council in 1870. "Accordingly, by the inspiration of the Holy Spirit, for the honor of the Holy and undivided Trinity, for the glory and adornment of the Virgin Mother of God, for the exaltation of the Catholic Faith, and for the furtherance of the Catholic religion . . . 'We declare, pronounce, and define that the doctrine which holds that the most Blessed Virgin Mary, in the first instance of her conception, by a singular grace and privilege granted by Almighty God, in view of the merits of Jesus Christ, the Savior of the human race, was preserved free from all stain of original sin, is a doctrine revealed by God and therefore to be believed firmly and constantly by all the faithful.' "[66]

A contemporary editorial in the Jesuit journal *Civiltà Cattolica* viewed the new Marian dogma in political as well as theological terms. Through the dogma, the "principle of authority in society is created anew," and "the judgment of damnation is spoken against the so-called sovereignty of the people."[67] The Immaculate Virgin was styled as a combatant against modernity. "Just as the Immaculata, free from every stain, archetype and paragon of the Church, is victorious over temptation and Satan, so the Church and Catholics shall repel seductive Reason and tempting Liberation, and be victorious over the Revolution."[68]

The new dogma was announced amid a flurry of apparitions of the Virgin.[69] Between 1803 and 1917, there were no fewer than 119 documented sightings. Significantly, 115 took place in Europe. In Italy, apparitions of the Virgin reached an absolute high point in the 1850s. This was seen as a direct consequence of the new dogma, but it also hints at the increasing threat to the Papal States posed by Italian unification. Generally speaking, visions of the Virgin always increase in Catholic countries in times of political or economic crisis. Interestingly, of the 115 European apparitions, only eight were recognized by the Church. Of these, Mary's appearances at La Salette in 1846 and Lourdes in 1858 achieved worldwide fame.

A shift in religious expression during the nineteenth century created an atmosphere in which visions of the Virgin seemed more plausible than they had previously been, and were treated more sympathetically by the Church. "Pius IX's papacy provided evidence that the Church was able to channel powerful outpourings of popular piety effectively; that it could take up and institutionalize the fears and longings released by the apparitions of the Virgin." The pope expertly co-opted these apparitions into his struggle against the modernizers, developing a "remarkable skill in the use of modern methods of communication to further the Cult of the Virgin."[70] The people to whom the Virgin appeared were for the most part women or children from simple stock, whose visions often led to an improvement in their social standing. The fate of an apparition and the person who had seen it, however, still hung on the Church authorities, and was particularly dependent on how the responsible priest dealt with the phenomenon. Seers were often abruptly removed from the limelight and deposited in a convent, when (as at La Salette) their message from the Mother of God turned out to be highly critical of the Church and the clergy.

The corporeality of these appearances was the subject of much controversy and discussion in the theology of the time. While theologians with modern leanings assumed that these visions played out in the heads of the visionaries, many new scholastically oriented theologians were convinced the seers really were able to perceive the Mother of God with their sense organs, and that the heavenly Lady showed herself in tangible form. This idea was part of the more general concept of how the natural and supernatural worlds were related that new scholastic theologians developed during the nineteenth century.

From real corporeal appearances of the Blessed Virgin to the materialization of letters from heaven was—at least in theory—not a huge imaginative leap. And if the supernatural was really manifesting itself in the natural world, then why shouldn't other heavenly beings besides Mary use the written word to convey instructions from the other side?

But all this looked rather different in practice. While a host of apparitions of the Virgin were reported in the nineteenth century, letters from the Virgin were relatively rare. Two categories of Marian letters should be distinguished here: the so-called apocryphal writings that Mary was supposed to have set down during her lifetime in Palestine; and the "heavenly letters," which were apparently written by the Blessed Virgin after her assumption into heaven, and then fell to earth or materialized here. One famous example of the first category is Mary's letter to the people of Messina. This was written in Greek, dated June 27 of AD 42, and supposedly sent from Jerusalem.[71] Its authenticity has been debated by numerous popes.

Heavenly letters from the Virgin have appeared on a number of occasions since the sixth century, often in the context of mystical experiences.[72] These have only ever been a single letter in each case, though this has meant each has attracted a great deal of attention. A letter from Mary written in French was widely circulated in eighteenth-century France. Mary described herself as the *"mère de Dieu, dame des Anges, bénigne et pure, espérance et réconfort de toute bonne créature."*[73]

Apparitions of the Virgin required a human medium, a visionary—somebody to see Mary and hear her pronounce her heavenly message before conveying it to the world. A letter from heaven, by contrast, was itself the medium in which a message from the other side was conveyed in black and white. Visions and auditions were subjective, momentary experiences, but with a piece of heavenly writing there was tangible, lasting proof of the command "from above."

The appearance of written sources as proof of the authenticity of an event has something historicist about it: *Quod non est in actis, non est in mundo.* If something isn't there in black and white in the source material, it doesn't exist. And while the authenticity of apparitions was difficult to prove, with a letter from heaven you had a tangible *Corpus Delicti* in front of you, whose origins could be investigated.

FORGING LETTERS FROM THE VIRGIN

Sallua had come into possession of just one letter. He couldn't rule out the possibility that Beckx really had followed its "divine" instructions, so he had to focus all his efforts on learning more about the letters from the Virgin. Having spent two months denying she knew anything about them, the abbess finally gave him a clue as to how the letters had been produced.[74] Sister Maria Francesca had told her that "she had written these letters on the instructions of Sister Maria Luisa. She received the drafts from her, and the order never to speak of the matter to anybody." When the inquisitor rebuked the abbess for her long silence on this central point, she replied: "I believed I would be committing an error if I were to speak of it, since I had written to ask Padre Peters about this at the start of the hearing. He answered in writing that I should reveal everything. But then he sent Franceschetti to tell me in person that *I was under no obligation to say everything I knew, be it as abbess, or through the seal of the confessional, or anything that might cause harm to another person.*"

Now that the abbess had implicated Sister Maria Francesca, Sallua finally had the leverage he needed to unravel the mystery of the letters. Maria Francesca was "subjected to numerous interrogations over four months," as the Dominican reported to the cardinals. She always "answered with unusual candor" and was able to remember the content of the various heavenly missives very precisely, "down to individual phrases."

This nun was interrogated in February 1860.[75] Maria Francesca a Passione stated that she was twenty-three years old, had been in the convent for three years, and had taken her vows the previous year. The first question she was asked was "whether she knew the reason she had been summoned and why she was being examined, or if she could guess the reason." She answered: "I believe I have been called here to tell you things about the madre vicaria and novice mistress, Maria Luisa." At this, the investigating judge asked her to tell him what she knew, one thing at a time. And Maria Francesca testified:

I had been a postulant in the convent for about a month when Mistress Maria Luisa asked me to write a letter in French to the padre general of the Jesuits, saying bad things about Padre Passaglia, that he was a bad monk who had tainted the Society of Jesus. The general was advised to keep a close watch on this padre, and received the order to excommunicate him from the *Compagnia.* I ended the letter with the following words: "if you want to know who has written to you thus, it is"—then she asked me, without having me write anything else, how you write "Mary" in French. And I told her. Then Maria Luisa took the letter and told me that I should sign it, "Marie." Finally, Maria Luisa forbade me from speaking about this matter to anybody, or saying I knew anything about the origins of this letter.

This cleared up the origin of the Virgin Mary's letter to the Jesuit general, and Sallua was finally able to narrow down the time period in which it had been written. Maria Francesca composed the letter to Beckx in spring 1857—considerably before August 3, the day that Passaglia and Schrader were separated.

But this wasn't the only letter that Maria Francesca had written at the novice mistress's behest in the name of the Virgin and other heavenly powers, so Sallua continued his investigations. First of all, the late mother founder had been made to serve as the author of heavenly letters. Maria Francesca continued.

"A few months later, Maria Luisa told me to copy out many things written by the Mother. But as I was writing out fair copies from these drafts, I soon realized that the Mother was really Maria Luisa." Eventually, the beautiful novice mistress became dissatisfied with the mother founder and the Virgin Mary as correspondents. She decided to go even further up the divine hierarchy:

> Over several months, Maria Luisa would shut me in my cell and order me to write out papers that she had written in her own hand, in which Jesus spoke to her and called her his beloved bride. Then Jesus Christ started addressing her confessor, Padre Peters, and spoke in the third person about a soul whose services, virtues and gifts he described from the day of her birth to the present day. I gave the drafts back to her. I wrote out the letters in this manner on hand-made paper that Maria Luisa bound with a little leather band, on which the name of Jesus was embossed.

Now it wasn't just the Virgin, but Jesus himself who was writing letters. Letters from Jesus do crop up in religious history, but are far rarer than those from the Virgin Mary. There are really only two known cases where He was supposed to have sent a letter from heaven. One was addressed to Clement of Alexandria, who lived in the second half of the second century AD. The other appeared in the sixth century, and spoke in favor of the Sunday observance. There is some debate about whether this text was originally written in Latin or Greek. Later it was even divided into two or three letters.[76]

The young nun also described the way in which these divine letters materialized on earth. There was a little casket "into which Maria Luisa laid the letters I had written"; these were then discovered there and taken to be letters from the Virgin, fallen from heaven. They were addressed to the abbess, Padre Leziroli, and, more frequently, Padre Peters.

One letter that Maria Francesca wrote to Padre Peters "in the role of the Mother of God," said: "Poor son! Do you not smell the scent of my first-born daughter? It does one good to smell it." Maria Francesca added, by way of explanation: "This was at the time when Maria Luisa smelled very strongly of roses." And the Virgin went on: "I am the *rosa mystica*,[77] and my daughter is also a rose, giving off this fragrance that comes from her heart." In the guise of the Virgin Mary, Maria Luisa was giving Peters a Marian interpretation of the rose scent, and drawing a parallel between herself and Christ. Christ is the firstborn son of God; Maria Luisa is the firstborn daughter of the Mother of God. It was a monstrous claim.[78]

In her second hearing, Maria Francesca carried on talking about her work forging heavenly letters.[79] Her testimony was clearly so fascinating and illuminating that the inquisitor didn't want to interrupt her by asking any additional questions. When uprisings began in Bologna and other parts of the Papal States, panic had broken out in Rome,[80] and the Mother of God wrote to Pope Pius IX. "In two letters to the pope, she recommended that he flee to Austria." From the style of the drafts Maria Luisa had given her, Maria Francesca believed they had been prepared by Padre Peters. At the very least, Maria Luisa had used information the Jesuit had given her to write them. The letters to the pope addressed an issue that was widely discussed in Rome at that time: the question of how Pius IX should behave in this delicate political situation.

The witness went on: "At Maria Luisa's request, I wrote Padre Peters a kind of reprimand, in the name of Jesus Christ." Jesus told Peters he should have more faith in the contents of the heavenly letters, especially what they said about the "extraordinary soul"—meaning Maria Luisa. The letters claimed

that on the occasion of her baptism she was taken up to heaven, where God the Father pressed her to his bosom and gave her the name Maria; God the Son called her glorious Agatha,[81] the Holy

Ghost called her holy Gertrude;[82] Father, Son and Holy Ghost gave her over to the Blessed Madonna as her first-born daughter; the Virgin pressed her to her bosom and quieted her 33 times. They said Jesus would often appear to wake her from her sleep, and would fix her hair and eat with her. . . . When she professed her vows, Jesus Christ appeared to her with the Blessed Virgin, and he married her as the daughter of Saint Catherine of Siena. The strength of the love was so great that it broke three of her ribs.

In another letter from the Madonna, Francesca had to say "that the Lord placed Maria Luisa's soul in the hands of Father Confessor Peters; indeed, as he slept, his soul would be transported to paradise and united with the soul of Maria Luisa." Other letters from the Virgin were written in response to the Jesuit padre's replies. From these, Maria Francesca gleaned "that Padre Peters was asking the Virgin to tell him why he had thus far been unable to feel any good effects from such a union. On the contrary, he had felt his emotions become rebellious, and other evil effects. Maria Luisa answered in the name of the Madonna, demanding that he submit to her. This was simply the way it was, and nothing bad was in it. Then I illustrated this union with the symbol of an eagle carrying a dove, and with two lit candles, the better one lending the weaker one its warmth."

Further letters revealed exactly what was meant by this union of the confessor and the novice mistress.

These letters said that Padre Peters was an extraordinary servant of this soul (this was the Madonna speaking). He kissed her in the mouth, and through this act God disclosed himself to her in extraordinary ways. They said Padre Peters, or the Lord, kissed her on the heart, and that there was a special connection between hand and heart. The Madonna also ordered him to give Maria Luisa the extraordinary blessing, which I did not understand—but I learned that this meant the permission or the command that the Madonna gave to Peters, as eternal father and protector of this soul, so that she might visit her accompanied by Jesus Christ.

This *bacio in bocca*, the kiss in the mouth, was nothing less than a divine injunction to perform a French kiss. Catholic moral doctrine strictly forbade this kind of kissing, viewing it as the expression of unbounded lust and animal instincts. Not even a husband and wife were permitted such an intimacy. And here the Mother of God was inviting Peters, an educated theologian, to dispense special heavenly gifts and blessings via a French kiss. This was completely unheard of, and must have aroused his suspicion.

And other letters contained similar commands—as always, written in the name of a guardian angel, Jesus Christ, or the Madonna. "The love of Padre Peters for God has grown so great that, if he presses this soul (*Maria Luisa*) to his heart, he will receive an extraordinary communion." And Francesca went on: "I wrote this several times. Nothing was explained in more detail in the letters; they just said 'you understand,' and other such things."

Maria Luisa was clearly inviting Padre Peters to initiate sexual contact with her. But the Jesuit apparently didn't understand—or perhaps refused to understand—these ambiguous invitations. The heavenly letters expressed Maria Luisa's disappointment over this in no uncertain terms, as Maria Francesca related.

"A few months previously, Peters had spent the night in the convent, to care for Maria Agostina, who then died. At that time I wrote Peters a letter in the name of the guardian angel, which said: 'You have not become acquainted with your first-born daughter: the Lord did not arrange your stay in the convent so that you might care for Maria Agostina, but so that He might disclose Himself to you in an extraordinary way through his first-born daughter.'" In plain English: this death gave you the unique chance to spend the night in the convent, but instead of coming to my cell, you wasted your time on the Office for the Dead. Over the period that followed, Maria Luisa staged several illnesses, which were announced to the confessor in letters from the Virgin. This finally put him where Maria Luisa wanted him: alone with her in her cell, over the course of many nights, where he could provide her with (spiritual) succor. The abbess and the first confessor, Leziroli, gave their express permission for this.

Maria Francesca continued to pour out the contents of these letters in her third hearing. She had written them using the Virgin's handwriting and signature, and they were addressed to Peters.[83] Physical intimacy, and the blessings to be gained through this erotic experience, was a running theme. Again and again, the letters pressured the confessor into performing this "extraordinary communion." But there was also another development: the Virgin now announced that the devil would take Maria Luisa's shape and do bad things to damage her favorite daughter. At the same time, she presented this as a divinely willed test of Maria Luisa's "pure soul." Was this a reference to the poisoning of Katharina von Hohenzollern?

Finally, the letters from the Virgin didn't just legitimate the intimacies between Maria Luisa and her confessor; they also attempted to justify the nuns' lesbian practices. Maria Francesca stated:

> During the time when the princess was ill, Maria Giacinta was also lying ill in the novitiate. And, as mentioned above, I wrote a letter to Padre Peters in the name of the most holy Virgin Mary, saying that the devil had taken on the shape of my best-beloved daughter Maria Luisa, and had been to Maria Giacinta's bed to commit immodest acts. In order to discredit my best-beloved daughter, he had led Maria Giacinta into temptation, and made her say that she had fallen and given in to these immodest acts. I wrote that the Lord permitted Maria Giacinta to do these things, to quash her pride.

The witness continued:

> Now I will tell of what I saw with my own eyes. As I stood in Maria Giacinta's cell, when she was lying ill in bed, I saw Maria Luisa come in. Based on what I saw, I took her to be the devil. She leaned over Maria Giacinta's bed and stroked her face and breast, and they embraced and kissed each other. Maria Giacinta meanwhile raised her waist a little, and I realized that she was exposing herself—then I went out and prayed, and banished the temptation. Sometimes I would see the above-mentioned person come into Maria Giacinta's cell and throw herself at once onto the bed, in a very licentious manner. Then things would proceed as described above, and I would go away. It seemed to me that this went on for the whole of advent, when Maria Giacinta was ill. Sometimes another novice was also present, but I don't remember it all that well now. Since I thought the mistress so reticent and delicate in these matters, I was convinced that the devil was committing these obscenities in her form. The novice Agnese Celeste also said to me:

"Remember those things that Maria Luisa did in bed with Maria Giacinta? Padre Peters told me it was the devil, who took on her shape."

But Maria Giacinta very soon began to feel pangs of conscience, and increasingly doubted the truth of the Virgin Mary's commands, as Maria Francesca stated during her final hearing.[84] Initially, Giacinta had been thoroughly jealous of Katharina von Hohenzollern. When Katharina first entered the convent, the novice mistress had paid a great deal of attention to her—apparently neglecting Giacinta, who had previously been her favorite. In an attempt to soothe her, Maria Luisa told Maria Francesca to write a letter from the Virgin to Peters, saying: "This little daughter of mine was chosen as the companion of my first-born daughter, after Sister Agnese Fletta went away. But reveal nothing of the great things of the mistress to this little daughter." When this piece of flattery didn't do the trick, the Virgin Mary sent a letter to Peters during Advent 1858, instructing him to: "remove the proud Maria Giacinta from her Mother." This was done straightaway, as Maria Francesca recalled.

Sallua managed to coax a statement on the whereabouts of the letters out of Franceschetti: Maria Luisa had handed them over to him when the Apostolic Visitation arrived. He was unsure what to do with them. The abbess and Leziroli declared themselves in favor of burning the letters (a task that Padre Peters would perform), and the lawyer finally left the packet of letters with him.[85]

Sallua was very satisfied with this result. He had not only exposed Maria Luisa as a false mystic, but unmasked her as a forger of "heavenly" letters from the Virgin. But the extremely problematic contents of these letters also suggested that this case of feigned holiness wasn't confined to the areas of faith and religious experience. It also seemed to have affected the realm of practical and sexual behavior.

PASTORAL CARE IN BED

The Madonna's letters ordered Padre Peters to take special care of the beautiful young novice mistress, Mary's "first-born daughter." He was to inhale the scent of the Virgin's favorite daughter, press her heart to his, and receive further divine blessings through union with her. Following Maria Francesca's interrogation, it was clear to Sallua that the heavenly letters reflected Maria Luisa's erotic fantasies and sexual desires. But did this heavenly temptation really succeed?

Sallua was able to drum up several nuns who had observed a close relationship between the confessor and the young novice mistress.[86] Agnese Celeste, Giuseppa Maria, Maria Gesualda, Maria Fortunata, and the abbess all provided juicy details. Sister Agnese Celeste said:[87]

> When Maria Luisa had a headache, Padre Peters would care for her for most of the day, until late at night. Once he spent the whole night in her cell. I recall that on this night somebody closed the door curtain several times, which I kept opening again during the night. I heard noises in the mistress's cell. . . . I was able to see Padre Peters going into the *clausura* and shutting himself in a room near the parlatory with the mistress. In the door to this room there is a glass window to let in light. This happened almost every day; it was very rare that it did not happen. . . . I noticed that they stayed in there a long time, sometimes for half a day. . . . I remember that Maria Ignazia told me that once, when Peters went to the mistress for her headache, she was restless, tossing about in bed, and she was uncovered. When Maria Ignazia tried to cover her up, the padre said to her: *"Leave her, she is still covered by her bodice."*

Sister Agnese Celeste, who was only nineteen, did her best to banish the evil suspicion that there was a sexual relationship going on between Maria Luisa and Padre Peters. Her fellow nun, Giuseppa Maria, was less scrupulous in her hearing on March 31, 1860.[88]

> These headaches usually started in the mornings when it was time to rise, which was at 4 o'clock, and the first thing we had to do was send for Padre Peters, who was called at once. Apart from the midday meal, he would spend the whole day there. When I went to wake her one morning at the usual hour, I found Peters there, and learned that he had spent the whole night with her. She had been speaking to the mother founder, and Peters alone was to hear this speech, so none of the sisters came into that room, and the two of them remained alone for the most part. . . . Peters

stayed overnight in the convent for around two months, and slept in another cell. . . . However, Maria Luisa visited him frequently in this cell.

I, having noticed the frequency of these visits, was able to observe the following: one evening, after the mistress had reassured me that no danger lay in store on this night (the abbess was also present), she said that Peters could be sent to sleep in his usual cell. She convinced the abbess to go to bed, and said that she would go to the novitiate. I, who spent the night in the cell of a nun who was ill, noticed that Maria Luisa was the last to withdraw, but after she had gone in the direction of the novitiate, I saw her turn back and go on tiptoes to Peters' cell. When she saw me, she came into the sick nun's cell and gave me a thorough scolding. She ordered me not to leave the sickroom again. I had to obey, particularly because at the time I was still only a novice, but I suspected she would come back to Peters, so I carried on watching without her seeing me. And indeed I could see very clearly how, after walking past the Padre's cell, she came back on tiptoes and went in. Meanwhile, the sick woman settled down, and I was plagued by thoughts of the mistress and Peters, who were together in this room.

After a few hours or when the night was already half over, the sick nun woke up, and I used the opportunity to divert her attention, by pretending to be afraid that the sick nun might be choking again. Then I banged on the wall with my fist, and Padre Peters came, and when he saw that the sick woman did not need anything, he asked me why I had called him. I answered that I had not been calling him: I wanted the mistress to come and see if anything was needed, so that she could then call the Reverend Father.

He looked unsettled, and answered: "But don't you know yourself if something is needed? And where is the mistress, then?"

And I answered: "The mistress is in your cell, Father."

At which he said: "But she's not in my room."

And I said: "She is—I saw her go in."

Meanwhile, I left the room to fetch something, but he quickly called me back to the sick nun's cell and said that I was not allowed to enter his cell, and that if I needed something I should knock for him to come, but I should not leave the sickbed.

During the night I went barefoot to the door of Peters' cell and leaned against it very carefully, and I could hear them talking in muffled voices, but I could not make out the words.

Maria Luisa often spent time in Peters' cell, either alone or with him; sometimes the abbess knew, and then they would leave the door open, but otherwise they shut it, so that nobody, not even I, would know that they had shut themselves in there. After the mistress had been with the padre on these nights, and particularly on the above-mentioned night, when she came to the sick woman, I noticed as she came closer to me that her hands, shoulders and head smelled very strongly of tobacco. She herself did not consume it, but Peters did, in large quantities. When I kissed the mistress's hand, I said to her: "my mother mistress, you reek of tobacco, did the padre touch you with his tobacco-covered hands?" She did not answer, but smiled. I asked her this question several times. Maria Giacinta asked her the same thing, when she noticed the smell just as I did. Due to the affection that the mistress showed to me and to Maria Giacinta, I also kissed her shoulders, and her head, and everywhere she stank of tobacco.

Giuseppa Maria tried to voice her suspicions to Padre Leziroli in confession. But he firmly rebuffed her concerns, telling her this was the devil at work again, taking the shape of the novice mistress. Over Christmas 1858, Giuseppa Maria then spoke directly to Padre Peters during confession about the smell of tobacco on Maria Luisa:

He admitted that Maria Luisa had been with him on this night and also on other occasions. And he explained to me why she smelled of tobacco. When she spoke of spiritual things, he said, she would start to sway on her chair so much that she would have fallen to the floor if he had not used his arms to hold her upright. And that was why I had smelled the stench of tobacco when I approached her, as this had happened several times. He said: "You don't understand these things, but I, who have studied, know how holy Maria Luisa is from her high talk of paradise."

The relationship between the confessor and the madre vicaria had obviously gone so far that Peters was neglecting his duty to provide spiritual support to the dying. And this, after all, was the official reason he was allowed to spend the night in the enclosure. But the novices guessed what was really going on behind the closed door of their mistress's cell. She no longer had any time for her novices, and only had eyes for the Jesuit padre. During her hearing on May 7, 1860, Maria Fortunata stated:[89]

> A few times we novices complained to each other that we never got to see the mistress, because she was always talking to Padre Peters. They kept shutting themselves away in the parlatory, but I don't know what they were doing in there—though I did see the mistress come out afterwards *quite red,* and sometimes she couldn't even open her eyes. Once, when I said to her: "My mistress, how red you are!" she answered: "Never say such things to me again, or I will give you a hard penance!"

Maria Luisa would beautify herself in preparation for the meetings with her confessor. In the transcript of Sister Maria Fortunata's hearing of May 14, 1860, the novice says:[90] "As a moral obligation I have to say that, when Maria Luisa was lying in bed, she sometimes said to me: 'Wash me well, for the padre is coming.'" She was always in a state of great excitement before meeting the Jesuit. Finally, on May 23, 1860, the abbess was asked whether the confessor's illicit sojourn in the enclosure was connected to the novice mistress's "supernatural pain." She had to admit that she had placed blind faith in Maria Luisa and Padre Peters. After all, these meetings had been foretold in letters from the Mother of God.[91]

A ritual had developed for the confessor's intimate encounters with the novice mistress. The Virgin would write a letter, announcing some fresh mystical struggle or supernatural suffering for her favorite daughter, and saying it was therefore absolutely necessary for her confessor to watch over her day and night. The letter setting out the date and place of this meeting would materialize in the locked casket. Having read it, the Jesuit would then write back to the Madonna, saying he was always ready to provide spiritual support. Then Maria Luisa would get one of her "truly unearthly" headaches, which always heralded the ecstasies and battles with demons that were to follow. The confessor was sent for immediately, and was allowed to enter the enclosure.

Taken together, the nuns' witness statements suggested a new, double offense to Sallua: on the one hand, the intimacies between Peters and Maria Luisa looked like a case of *Sollicitatio*. This charge applied to Peters: if he had seduced his penitent into committing a terrible sin against the sixth commandment before, during, or after confession, or under the guise of pastoral care, he was guilty of a criminal abuse of authority. On the other hand, the beautiful young nun had seduced the confessor and carried out sexual acts with him. She gave the whole thing the "false appearance of the enactment of divine love" by pretending to act "on God's commands."

During these hearings, the Dominican had also stumbled across a scandalous rumor. This was that Peters had given a "life confession" before the Virgin Mary, *vulgo* Maria Luisa, telling her of an affair with a woman named Alessandra. The *Fama* claimed that she had instructed the beautiful novice mistress to bestow upon him "special blessings" following this revelation. He would have divine experiences with Maria Luisa, which would be completely different from the "sinful indecencies" that he had committed with this Alessandra. Would Sallua be able to pin this rumor down, or would it dissolve into air? Only the interrogation of Maria Luisa and Padre Peters could provide an answer to this.

LESBIAN INTIMACIES IN A CONVENT CELL

There was one more allegation to be addressed here: the homosexual acts that Maria Luisa had performed with various partners.[92] Agnese Eletta's statement during the pretrial investigations had already given Sallua significant grounds for suspicion. And numerous witnesses had corroborated her story: when Maria Luisa had grown tired of her bedfellow, she used a vision to get this woman, who knew her most intimate secrets, shut away in San Pasquale.

The real reason Maria Luisa ditched Agnese Eletta, who was thirty-nine at the time, was her new favorite among the novices: Maria Giacinta. At thirty-three, she was six years younger than Agnese Eletta. And like the older nun, Maria Giacinta found herself unable to give a verbal testimony before the Inquisition, due to "the total disgust" she felt at what she had done. Instead, at her hearing with Sallua on March 24, 1860, she submitted a detailed text, which was read out word for word during the hearing, and which she then signed.[93]

The Mother Mistress showed me singular affection from the beginning. She embraced me after I received my habit, she kissed me passionately and called me "my daughter, my heart, my soul, my love," and she told me that Jesus Christ and the Blessed Virgin had a fondness for me, and had instructed her to prefer me in her love. She said the Virgin told her she had great responsibility for my spirit and my body.

When Sister Agnese Eletta had gone—I don't remember exactly when—the Mother Mistress moved me into her cell. After retiring in the evening, we would engage in spiritual conversation; one evening, as I was kneeling by her bed and she was already lying in bed, she asked me to lay my face on her breast, and she showed me how hard her heart was beating, and then she asked me to suck her nipples; this happened every evening, and she always expressed her affection for me. Finally she told me that, although it did not seem so, she was actually fleshless; I might therefore touch her on various parts of her body, and I remember that I also touched her on the shameful parts.

The following night she did not go to bed first, but told me to do as she said and lie down, and on this particular evening she left the lamp burning, as she wanted to look at my whole body, every part of it. She took a medal and made the sign of the cross on my sexual organs. This happened two or three times.

Over those three, four or five months (though I don't remember exactly how much time passed before I professed my vows), she also kissed and embraced me very frequently during the day.

The unchaste acts were committed through touching with our hands, bodies, and two or three times also using my tongue. She was the most keen on touching our bodies together, which she called "giving," and she asked me to lie in a certain position, with my legs raised, while she "entwined" herself with me, as she called it. She then made movements and a sound such as I cannot express in words, and she instructed me to position myself so that I could receive her bodily fluids into me. Or sometimes she wanted me positioned above her, so that we were body to body and mouth to mouth. She said that this bodily fluid had been given to her by God, to heal the sicknesses of these body parts; sometimes, after the act was completed, she wanted me to make the sign of the cross on my body with a damp finger, and when I used my tongue, she also wanted me to suck, because in this way I would be healed. For a few days these acts took place every evening, and lasted for one to two hours in my bed. After this they happened less frequently.

When I suffered from an ailment of the sexual organs that meant I had to apply a poultice, she wanted to do this herself.

One evening, or on the evening immediately before I professed my vows, she came to my bed for the usual acts, and told me that this would be the last time, that it was all over and I was now healed: the final thing she wanted to do was to shave the hair from these parts of my body.

Still, she kept wanting to touch me even after I had taken my vows, and she also wanted me to touch her with my hands, although there were only a few occasions when she demanded all the other acts of love and intimacy. After I had professed my vows, I remarked that although I was now recovered, I still did not feel well, so she resumed her treatment. In answer, she said many things that I now don't remember, except that some part of the sickness still remained.

In the inquisitor's eyes, the exchange of vaginal fluid, the intense passion, and the reference to a "completed act" all amounted to female sodomy. Maria Giacinta also spoke of her pangs of conscience. She found herself faced with an almost impossible dilemma: she was very well aware of the depravity of these sexual acts, but the heavenly voices kept demanding she do things that were forbidden. She wrote:

I did not even want to submit to the very first caresses, because I held them to be a sin, and all the while I repeated to Maria Luisa that these were sinful deeds, and I wanted to confess them. I did not want to carry on living this way. But she did all she could to convince me that I must not say anything to the padre: she said it was not a sin if I did not feel anything and remained like a block of wood. The Lord had given my body over to her, especially that part of it, to cure it of all sensual feeling. She frequently forced me to relent out of obedience to her, and when I then replied that obedience could not force me to sin, she said that something God had commanded could be no sin.

Several times I fended her off, saying: "You are not the Mother Mistress, but a demon who has taken on the shape of the Mother Mistress."

"No," she said, "it is really me."

To make certain of this, I said to her: "Then kiss the crucifix." And she kissed it.

She wore a cross that was said to have miraculous powers, so she probably thought that if she came to me wearing this crucifix I would be happier that it was not the demon, but herself in person.

The crucifix test was evidence enough for Maria Giacinta that she really was in bed with the beautiful madre vicaria herself. The cross was the surest defense against the devil and his demons, and was used in exorcisms.[94] The second nurse, Giuseppa Maria, gave her a rather brutal piece of advice: during the sexual act, she should bite Maria Luisa's face. The following morning everyone would be able to see that it was the novice mistress, and not the devil in her shape, who had done those dreadful things in bed with her. But Maria Giacinta didn't follow this advice.[95]

She did, however, have an urgent need to speak to a priest and unburden her conscience. The path she should have taken to the father confessors was barred to her, as Maria Luisa had forbidden her from speaking to them. But she did eventually have a conversation with Peters, who then seems to have broken the seal of the confessional. "Several times it happened that after I had confessed, the Mother Mistress came to me and repeated something that I had said in confession. Once she even said: 'The father confessor . . .' but then she started over, adding, 'No, another person told me that you confessed so and so.' I have every reason to believe that the Mother Mistress came eavesdropping while we were confessing, as I used to find the little window to the parlatory open (where Padre Peters heard confession), though I was always certain I had shut it as I went in."

But as a novice, she was still dependent on her mistress, and the confessors were no help to her, either. In fact, they took Maria Luisa's stories about the devil at face value. Maria Giacinta's frustration mounted when she was transferred to the infirmary, and was no longer sleeping in the novitiate, under the novice mistress's direct guardianship. When Maria Luisa tried to visit her sickbed, she screamed: "Go away, you evil witch, you idiot, you ass!" At least, on February 22, 1860, Maria Francesca stated under oath that she had heard her use these expressions.[96]

And Maria Giacinta wasn't the only nun with whom Maria Luisa exchanged intimacies. Almost all the novices testified that the novice mistress had kissed, embraced, and caressed them. "At the start of my novitiate, the mistress came to me several times and embraced and kissed me," said Agnese Celeste."[97] Maria Giacinta clearly set an example, as Maria Fortunata related. When Giacinta "impetuously" ran to the madre vicaria, kissed her, and laid her head on her breast, Fortunata and the rest of the novices did likewise.[98]

Several novices also spoke of a kind of lesbian initiation rite in Sant'Ambrogio, which had come into being under the aegis of the novice mistress Maria Luisa. The night before they were clothed as nuns, each novice had to share a bed with the novice mistress. They lay face-to-face and breast-to-breast, often in a fierce embrace. If several novices were professing their vows at the same time, they all slept together in Maria Luisa's cell. "It became a permanent bordello."[99] The novices, dressed only in their nightshirts, would dance around the cell holding hands. After a night spent in this manner, rather than—as the Rule dictated—in prayer, the novices would be led into church by their mistress for their ceremonial profession of vows.

The inquisitor had little to add to the witnesses' statements in his summary report for the cardinals. The lesbian acts committed "under the guise of special virtue" turned out to be yet another consequence of Maria Luisa's feigned holiness.

THE SANT'AMBROGIO SYSTEM

Maria Luisa had developed a "Sant'Ambrogio system," which rested entirely on her authority as saint and mystic, and assured her a unique position of power both inside and outside the convent. When he was interrogated on September 12, 1860, the convent's lawyer, Luigi Franceschetti, said something that made the inquisitor prick up his ears. He stated that the nuns of Sant'Ambrogio had "a completely different system and completely different principles from any other religious community."[100] In his report, the investigating judge laid out six of this system's fundamental distinguishing features.[101]

First, leadership of the convent—both in the areas of outward discipline (which fell under the abbess's jurisdiction) and inner spirituality (for which the confessor had sole responsibility)—lay in the hands of the madre vicaria. Maria Veronica, after all, had only been appointed abbess by the grace of Maria Luisa. When they entered the convent, the novices had to give a "general confession" to the novice mistress, and at other times they were to confess "first to her, and only then to the father confessor." Maria Luisa informed Leziroli of the points on which the novices were "well or ill disposed." And, as the inquisitor summarized from the many witness transcripts, she had also managed to "persuade the abbess to betray to her the nuns' confessions or self-incriminations." Maria Luisa was following a tradition started by the mother founder—though she went significantly beyond anything Maria Agnese Firrao had done. Firrao had never achieved this level of connection between the nuns admitting their sins to her, and confession in the confessional.

Second, the novice mistress accrued responsibilities to herself that went far beyond what was permitted in canon law. She took it upon herself to give the young nuns dispensations from attending the Divine Office. Some of the novices, who really should have been practicing the psalms every day, were released from this for days, weeks, or even months at a time. Maria Luisa also instructed them to disregard the obligation to fast before receiving Holy Communion. The sick received the Eucharistic gift—"frivolously," as Sallua put it— several times a week. The precondition for taking Holy Communion was that absolution had to be given in the confessional immediately beforehand. Sant'Ambrogio's Rule stipulated that the sick could only be given Communion every eight days—though it also said the nuns should have the opportunity to receive Communion every morning. This was already more than the general Rule of the Third Order said: according to this, the sisters were only obliged to take Communion at least three times a year, at Easter, Christmas, and Pentecost.[102]

Third, the religious fasts were not taken very seriously in Sant'Ambrogio. According to the Rule, meager meals were to be served twice a day in winter, and three times a day in summer. During the two fasting periods before Christmas and Easter, as well as on Mondays, Wednesdays, Fridays, and Saturdays, the nuns weren't allowed to consume meat or dairy products.[103] According to statements from many of the novices, Maria Luisa ate meat in their presence on Fridays, and all the other fast days. She claimed to have been released from all obligations, including going to Mass, even on feast days. It seemed that the novice mistress hadn't taken part in any of the prescribed Offices of the Liturgy of the Hours for the past five years.

Fourth, the Sant'Ambrogio system was not solely dependent on the supernatural gifts, blessings, visions, and ecstasies of "saint" Maria Luisa: there were also real objects, which made her holiness tangible in the truest sense of the word. The inquisitor accorded these relics a charge of their own.[104] From one of her trips to heaven, Maria Luisa had brought back a "strand of the Virgin Mary's hair," which was kept in a silver reliquary. Another time, she received a relic from Saint Joseph during a rapture, and then Christ gave her a "substantial piece of the holy cross," which she displayed on Good Friday. The handover of these gifts in heaven was confirmed in letters from the Virgin to Padre Peters, who then saw that the relics were venerated. Sallua managed to obtain from the abbess the reliquary containing the Virgin's hair. Padre Leziroli had written an inscription on a card displayed above Maria Luisa's cloak, which Christ was supposed to have worn during one of their encounters in heaven. The notice read: "No nun should ever put on the cloak, since the Savior of the world condescended to wear it one night, when He was cold." One of the novice mistress's veils was also hailed as miraculous; the nun's habit she had worn at her wedding to Christ in heaven was carefully preserved; the novices guarded the hair cut from her head like a treasure—this was holiness you could actually touch. Here, too, Maria Luisa was following the example of her great role model, Maria Agnese Firrao, but at the same time far surpassing her.

Fifth, the investigating judge placed particular weight on the fact that the two confessors were extremely active in "inculcating, approving and endorsing" these bad "precepts and practices." They had attributed them "to the supposed will of God," supported by the "absolute conviction that they had an extraordinary mystic in the convent," and the "great holiness" of Agnese Firrao and Sister Maria Luisa.[105]

Sixth, the Sant'Ambrogio system was bound up with an absolute and sacramentally sanctioned veil of secrecy. At Maria Luisa's behest, the confessors impressed upon the nuns the need to remain silent about the system to the visitators, and even the inquisitors. Maria Luisa's holiness had to be defended by any means necessary, up to and including perjury. According to Giuseppa Maria, Maria Luisa herself swore the community to absolute secrecy: "It is better to protect the secret, even if you are questioned about these things; I will be the first to set an example, even if I am made to take an oath. The princess is the denouncer, and I would like to ask those in charge to let her come and justify these accusations to us. I close this chapter with the request that you do as I do."[106]

This was a straight request to give false testimony under oath. But Maria Luisa was also able to rely on the authority of the Jesuit fathers, Leziroli and Peters. "The extraordinary events around Maria Luisa were kept as secret as possible on the instructions of the father confessors," the abbess stated on May 19, 1860.[107] And the confessors went even further: not only did they issue a general warning to the sisters not to say anything about the veneration of Maria Luisa; during confession they even instructed individual nuns to perjure themselves as an obligatory penance. Maria Ignazia said in her hearing that Padre Peters had placed her under the "seal of the confessional" with regard to the madre vicaria's "gifts." She was therefore under the impression that she "could swear to and deny everything with complete conviction," even when she wasn't telling the truth. She went so far as to tell the investigating judge that she had the support of her confessor, and would "rather be turned into mincemeat than talk."[108]

In his *Relazione* for the Inquisition's cardinals, written in January 1861, Sallua summed up the results of the witness examinations. "This charge," he said, meaning the feigned holiness of the beautiful young novice mistress and madre vicaria, Maria Luisa, "represents, in its significance and importance, the central point of this extremely serious *Causa*." His reasoning behind this was that "all other charges feed into this or stem from it. It stands at the center of all the accused's actions, and those of all the other people involved in this trial."[109] And as far as the Dominican was concerned, all aspects of this charge had been proved during the informative process.

CHAPTER FIVE

"An Act of Divine Splendor"

Murder on the Orders of the Virgin

THE AMERICANO AND HIS OBSCENE LETTER

Once the investigating judge had dealt with the first two charges in the informative process—these being the veneration of Agnese Firrao as a saint, and the feigned holiness of Maria Luisa—he moved on to the attempts to poison Katharina von Hohenzollern. Sallua was now entering a minefield, even if the pope had intimated his grave doubts over the plausibility of the whole story. Moreover, the Dominican had no expertise in the investigation of capital offenses: other papal courts usually dealt with murder and manslaughter.

The highest religious tribunal's inexperience in handling this type of crime is reflected in how the files on this charge were put together. While the investigative court's argumentation on the religious offenses is notable for its clarity and rigor, Sallua's summaries on the poisonings appear disordered and incomplete. He also slipped up by forgetting the most important testimony on Katharina's poisoning, and had to add this in later.[1] In his *Relazione* to the cardinals of January 1861, he remarked self-critically that he had entered uncharted territory when he investigated the attempted murder. "The trial system of our holy court is quite different from that of the criminal court, which normally handles crimes of such severity and gravity."[2]

Both Katharina and Archbishop Hohenlohe had made serious accusations against the madre vicaria, blaming her for the repeated poisonings. But this was nowhere near sufficient to prove Maria Luisa's guilt. The Dominican needed reliable witness statements and evidence. He had to shed light on the background to the poisoning, in order to discover the motive for the attacks.[3]

Sallua started with Katharina's claim that her relationship with the madre vicaria, which had been very good, was badly damaged when she showed Katharina the obscene German letter from the Americano. He had to find out more about this ominous letter and its author.

Various witnesses told Sallua that Peter Kreuzburg had been introduced to Sant'Ambrogio by Padre Peters, who had apparently known him since he was a child. The Jesuit, they said, had tried to free Kreuzburg from his "five demons" through an exorcism.

In contrast to the present day, exorcisms were a daily occurrence in the nineteenth century—a fact connected to contemporary notions of the devil and demons.[4] The devil wasn't viewed as a second eternal principle alongside God. Satan and his followers, the demons, were seen as angels created by God who had chosen to pursue evil, and had therefore fallen from heaven. People imagined demons and the devil as having airy bodies, meaning they could force their way into humans through any orifice and possess them, in particular during sexual intercourse. Exorcism was the ritual expulsion or banishing of evil spirits (including the devil himself) from people who had been possessed.[5] The *Rituale Romanum* of 1614 reserved the right to perform exorcisms for very experienced priests, who were only permitted to do this after close consultation with their bishops. Amateurs—particularly women—could not drive out devils.

The liturgy of exorcism followed the three steps of word, sign, and seal. First, the name of God was invoked. There followed the direct address to the devil or the demons, using the threat of God, and finally the order to leave. The possessed person would often emit ecstatic cries, and experience cramps, nosebleeds, and exhaustion. The whole thing was rounded off with a laying on of hands, making the sign of the cross, and anointing or breathing on the possessed person. The demons usually put up a fight, and priests had to be prepared for a long struggle with the forces of evil, repeating the exorcism many times in order to free a possessed person completely. Even when the demons had gone, that person was still susceptible to evil.

Kreuzburg met Maria Luisa when he came to Mass in the convent church, which was also open to the public. Peters introduced her as a saint with special divine gifts. After the Jesuit padre had failed to exorcise Kreuzburg, he entrusted Maria Luisa with Kreuzburg's spiritual guidance, and with driving out his demons, which was clearly in contravention of canon law. She met the Americano frequently under this pretext, inside the convent and sometimes even outside its walls, and often returned from these encounters looking very much the worse for wear.

The lawyer Franceschetti, who had also met Kreuzburg through Peters, was able to provide Sallua with further information. "Padre Peters revealed to me in strictest confidence that Doctor Kreuzburg was possessed, and that he had argued about him with one of the Jesuit houses in Switzerland."[6] The argument concerned an unsuccessful exorcism, during which one of the fathers "heard a great rumbling throughout the house; afterwards, they found a very heavy door lying on the floor, even though it had been secured with large iron pegs." Peters told Franceschetti that in his role as confessor he had told Kreuzburg to make reparations for vilifying saints during the failed exorcism. He then saw the American raise himself "into the air" to "clean" the pictures of saints in the church, and thereby "assure them of his obeisance." The American had been "transported across immense spaces" by the devil, "sometimes across the seas, sometimes through the air." There was talk of levitation, a phenomenon also reported of some mystics.[7] But in this case, Peters described the levitation as the work of the devil.

However, Kreuzburg had also received help from the Blessed Virgin, which made Peters believe that he was basically a good soul. Franceschetti mentioned some truly bizarre aspects of Kreuzburg's life. The Americano had tried to convince him, among other things, that he was tormented by the devil in the shape of cats and mice. The lawyer also described his crazy political speeches.[8]

Kreuzburg's demons had also tried to lead Maria Luisa, the saint, into temptation—though they had never really managed to conquer her, as Franceschetti said proudly. Once, he had been present in the parlor when the vicaress performed an exorcism on Kreuzburg. But Kreuzburg had only mocked and laughed at her, as if he were the devil laughing at being ordered about by a woman.

Several nuns and the abbess confirmed there had been an improper relationship between Maria Luisa and Peter Kreuzburg. According to them, the madre vicaria conducted a long correspondence with the so-called Americano, and met with him in secret for hours at a time. Maria Luisa told her astounded sisters implausible stories, such as that he had a nun for a wife. The nuns' testimonies also reveal that, with Padre Peters's consent, she had made the American turn over all his books to her, in particular the medical volumes. Maria Giacinta actually found one of these on the little table in Maria Luisa's cell, and "was greatly confused and curious to see a lot of bad pictures, of the naked sexual organs of men and women."

But Sallua wasn't entirely satisfied with the results of his investigation. He had been able to draw no further conclusions about the content of the obscene letter, let alone get hold of the letter itself. His only evidence was what Katharina had said in her *Denunzia*. And he was unable to question the letter writer: Kreuzburg had escaped the Inquisition's clutches by fleeing back to the United States. But at least the Dominican had been able to establish the fact of a suspicious relationship between Maria Luisa and Kreuzburg.

Kreuzburg's biography is still a puzzle to present-day historians.[9] Peter Maria Kreuzburg came from the Pustertal in Austria, and may have been born there in around 1815. It seems he received his education at the Jesuit boarding school in Brig, the Spiritus Sanctus College, where he must have met Padre Peters. There is no information to be found on his medical studies. Nor did Peter Maria Kreuzburg ever work as a doctor; he probably just passed himself off as one in Rome. What is certain is that he traveled to the United States in about 1840, and applied for American citizenship in Cincinnati in November 1844. In February 1846 he married Gertrud Nurre, who had also emigrated to the United States in 1839. And in 1850, Kreuzburg and his brother-in-law, Joseph Nurre, opened a bookstore in Cincinnati. The marriage produced six children: a daughter, Cesaria, in 1846; Maria in 1849; Joseph in 1854; Mary in 1857; Gertrude in 1861; and finally Angela in 1863. Maria, Joseph, and Mary probably died in childhood. In March 1857, Peter Maria Kreuzburg was issued with the passport he had applied for in order to travel to Europe. According to his application, Kreuzburg was five feet six, with gray eyes, a high forehead, brown hair, and an oval face with a "well-proportioned" nose. He used the passport to go to Rome.

Kreuzburg seems to have returned to the United States at the end of 1859, when the Sant'Ambrogio trial made the streets of Rome a little too hot for him. He and his wife subsequently became farmers in Millcreek Township, in Hamilton County, which today is part of Cincinnati. His brief venture into agriculture was clearly unsuccessful: in 1861 he was back in Cincinnati, working as a publisher and bookseller. In 1862, Kreuzburg and his family left the United States, and probably lived until 1874 in Einsiedeln in Switzerland. He then spent five years in Canada, before finally taking up residence in Jurançon near Pau in France, in 1879. Here, he once again assumed the title *Docteur en médecine*. A year after his arrival, however, he suffered a stroke—at least, his daughter Cesaria said he had become lame. Peter Maria Kreuzburg died on March 14, 1889, in Pau. His wife, Gertrud, died in 1909. Their daughters Cesaria and Angela taught at a school in Pau, which today lies on the "Avenue Kreuzburg."

THE CORD AROUND KATHARINA'S NECK

When Sallua questioned them, several of the sisters confirmed that the princess and the novice mistress had begun to grow apart after Katharina had read the Americano's obscene letter.[10] They told the inquisitor that Maria Luisa had been increasingly exasperated with Luisa Maria (the princess's name as a novice), and continually spoke ill of her. The rumor went around the convent that she had "made [Katharina] read a letter from a German that was unworthy of a nun." Maria Luisa dismissed this as wicked slander on the princess's part and, like the two confessors, claimed it was the result of a "devilish deception." As the rumor continued to spread within the convent walls, Leziroli and Peters spoke to the novice mistress about this alleged letter, but she "vigorously denied everything." However, since "the father confessors established that this letter really existed, and as the other facts of the matter were also impossible to refute, they both judged that it was all an evil ploy by the devil, who had appeared to the novice princess in the shape of Maria Luisa."

But Katharina, to whom most of her fellow nuns attributed genuine "obedience" and "great deference," refused to give in, or to acquiesce to the confessors' interpretation of events. She was "certain of the facts, [and] tried to move the mistress to confess all."

In her denunciation, Katharina gave a detailed account of this attempt, which took place on the morning of the Feast of the Immaculate Conception,[11] December 8—a Wednesday. She approached the novice mistress in the choir of the convent church, probably after Lauds, when the nuns had gathered there for morning prayers. A confrontation took place between the two women. Katharina's account was corroborated by a series of nuns who had witnessed the scene at close hand. Maria Giuseppa, Giuseppa Maria, and Agnese Celeste proved to be particularly good witnesses. On April 2, 1860, Giuseppa Maria told Sallua:[12]

One morning, on the day of the *Immaculata* in 1858, I went down into the lower choir after Communion to call the mistress, who had remained there. There, to my surprise, I saw Luisa Maria, the princess, getting up from where she had been kneeling in front of the mistress, and taking a cord from around her neck.

The mistress left the lower choir with me when I called her, with a distracted expression on her face. As we were walking, she said in a firm voice: "Whoever would have thought that such evil lurked beneath a mantle of goodwill?"

A short while later I asked Maria Giacinta, who was ill, about what had happened. She told me Princess Luisa Maria had had the temerity to lay her cord around her neck in the lower choir, and tell the mistress she had made a full and honest confession about everything to the padre. She told the mistress she had been deceived, and was imagining things. The princess was praying for Maria Luisa, she said, because of all this and for other, similar reasons. She was worried for her soul. But the mistress replied that she had thought the princess was a novice, and the manner in which she had addressed her was presumptuous and rash. The following day, this same Maria Giacinta said that the mistress told her she had seen the Lord during Communion. He was outraged at what

Luisa Maria had said to the mistress, and decreed that the princess would be punished with death.

Two weeks prior to Giuseppa Maria's hearing, on March 17, 1860, Sallua had questioned Sister Maria Giacinta himself. Her statement tallied almost word for word with Giuseppa Maria's.[13] She said that the Lord had appeared to Maria Luisa and revealed to her that "as punishment for her pride, the princess *would die, and He had already arranged this*." Maria Luisa even told Agnese Celeste, with regard to the scene in the choir, that "the princess behaved among the novices as Judas among the apostles."

This way, the novice mistress was likening Katharina's behavior in the choir to Judas Iscariot's betrayal of Jesus. She saw the princess as a female Judas, who was betraying the community of Sant'Ambrogio by refusing to believe in Maria Luisa's holiness. Katharina wanted to turn her over to the Church authorities, just as Judas had turned Jesus over to the high priests. In the world of Catholic ideas, the cord around Katharina's neck was associated with the suicide of Judas Iscariot, who hanged himself when he realized the consequences of his betrayal.

But within religious orders, a cord around the neck had a very different historical significance. Here, it wasn't a sign of betrayal, but a gesture of great humility.[14] When a monk or a nun put the cord or belt that held their habit together around their neck, it meant they were humbling themselves utterly, and putting themselves entirely at the mercy of their superior. This kind of ritual abasement was the only way for a novice to remonstrate with a superior like the novice mistress, to whom she owed strict obedience. The gesture of humility forced the superior to listen to her charge. And placing a cincture around one's neck was a particularly expressive gesture of humility for the Franciscan orders. It was said that Saint Francis of Paola always received holy communion kneeling with his cincture around his neck, and advised his fellow monks to do likewise.[15]

Katharina was consciously following this tradition. But why did Maria Luisa have such an extreme reaction to her remonstrations? The witnesses' statements may not reveal the exact words the two women exchanged, but they were clearly talking about the letter from the Americano. The princess was disgusted by the letter's indecent content, not least because the Americano was also making improper advances toward her, saying she could become a "mother without a husband" like Maria Luisa. She had made a point of this in her *Denunzia*. But why hadn't the madre vicaria simply dismissed the obscene phrases as the sick sexual fantasies of a man possessed by demons, with no bearing on reality? After all, she couldn't be held responsible for the crazy thoughts of a sick mind. Why hadn't she immediately deplored the letter and its contents? The fact that she denied ever having shown Katharina the letter—and later, when the princess insisted she had, started blaming the devil—raises the suspicion that it wasn't just a possessed man's fantasy. There was something behind this crazy talk of "becoming a mother without a husband": probably nothing less than a sexual relationship between the Americano and the madre vicaria.

This was the subject on which Katharina had implored Maria Luisa to speak the truth. She asked her to repent of all her deceptions and lies, including the story about the devil. If she refused, Katharina would have to take up the matter herself, in order to save Maria Luisa's soul. She would reveal the madre vicaria's affair with the Americano. But Maria Luisa wasn't prepared to repent. The attempt to persuade her failed, and the relationship between the two women was permanently destroyed.

HEAVENLY LETTERS FORETELL KATHARINA'S MURDER

Katharina's impending death had hung in the air since the scene in the choir. Christ had already told Maria Luisa of it in a vision, and now all that was missing was written confirmation from above. Once again, the novice mistress set Maria Francesca to work writing letters in the name of the Virgin Mary. Maria Francesca told the investigating judge about the origin of these in her hearing on February 21, 1860.[16]

> What I am about to say is what I told Peters in the name of the Madonna in writing, in several letters: namely, that the devil was able to take on the shape of her favorite daughter, and to slander

her in this way. In this form, he appeared hundreds of times to Sister Luisa Maria (the princess, who in the letters is called Katharina), and harassed her, so she would leave the convent. The letters called her Katharina because she always *acted* like that, *prideful, stubborn and accepting nobody's opinion but her own*. Katharina was supposed to proclaim the glory of the daughter of God. The devil prevented this by appearing to her, but the glory of God only increased by this. *God ordained that Katharina would die suddenly of a stroke, and would be damned.*

In the letters the Blessed Virgin also wrote that Peters should make Katharina's fate known, and also that of his favored daughter, who foresaw Katharina's fate; he might ask Maria Luisa to pray for the princess, as this was now the only thing that could save her.

Another letter said that the Virgin's first-born daughter had prayed for Katharina; she had spent several hours in hell and her prayers had ensured that although Katharina would suffer a stroke, through justice and mercy she would not then die.

But in truth, Katharina (the princess) suffered such a serious attack that we thought she would die.

I wrote several similar letters to Peters in the name of the Madonna: "The devil has taken on the shape of my favorite daughter and convinced the princess that she should be afraid of being poisoned." He appeared in the same form to the novice Agnese Celeste (her father is a doctor) and asked her what the strongest poison was, which would kill a person. She answered him. Then the devil appeared in the same form to Maria Ignazia and the late sister Maria Felice, both of whom were novices at that time. He told them it was the will of God and of Padre Peters that poison should be mixed with the princess's medicine, for she was a soul in God's grace and would be saved through death. The devil, still in the same form, showed Maria Ignazia and Maria Felice, who were looking after the princess, where they should get the poison, namely from the box in Mother Mistress Maria Luisa's room, where she kept her writing things, and from a tin in the pharmacy. I clearly remember writing that the devil in the shape of Maria Luisa went to Katharina's chamber with the two novices and there, with his own hands, put the poison into the container where the princess's medicine was being prepared. The devil also alerted the other nuns, Maria Giuseppa, Maria Giacinta and Giuseppa Maria ... to what the above-mentioned novices Maria Ignazia and Maria Felice were doing, when they gave the princess the poisoned medicine. The three nuns noticed other deceptions by the devil, when they found other cups and little tins contaminated with poison.

All these things happened while the princess was very ill.

The letter from the Madonna ended by saying that Peters' favored daughter knew what the devil was doing, taking on her shape and going to the princess, but she herself remained hidden in order to pray for the princess and her daughters. . . . Finally, I would like to add that, when the princess was well again, Padre Leziroli preached to us *that the devil could take on the appearance of people; he could touch and deceive, and therefore we should believe the servants of God.*

The following day, Maria Francesca resumed her testimony:[17]

To go back to the matter of the poison and the princess, I would like to add by way of making things clearer, that during those days when the princess was ill, and people were talking about her being poisoned, I also wrote a letter to Peters, in the name of the Madonna, saying: "The devil has taken my box to the pharmacy and showed us there a tin of poison. But I would like the box to remain in my daughter's room."

In another letter, the Madonna told Peters he should say to the princess that all the things she had heard from the mistress had been the devil's illusions. Padre Peters should repeat this to his cardinal (His Eminence Cardinal Reisach).

Another letter revealed that Peters was waiting for a sign from the Madonna . . . to convince the princess, as she refused to believe. But the Madonna answered: *"No, I will give no sign! He who does not believe in the servants of God will not believe in miracles either."* Finally, she told Peters that the devil himself would give such a sign. This sign was the inscription of the name of Jesus on a brick in Maria Luisa's chamber. A little later, an inscription of Mary's name appeared on another brick. Padre Peters wrote a prayer to banish the devil, for him and his fellow confessor Padre Leziroli to repeat every three months. I copied out the aforementioned prayer from Padre Peters' handwriting.

Analyzing these supposedly divine letters from the Virgin brings to light the following course of events: Maria Luisa initially tried to protect herself from all future accusations by having the Madonna announce that the devil was appearing to people in her form. Then she built up a stark contrast between the "holy" Maria Luisa and the "unbeliever" Luisa Maria. The latter was condemned to die for her pride; the former was to be glorified by God. Finally, we glimpse how Maria Luisa set about the poisoning operation. Having inquired about strong poisons with Agnese Celeste, the doctor's daughter, she recruited the two novices Maria Ignazia and Maria Felice as her accomplices, again saying this was a divine decree.

The fateful letter was written on December 8, the day of the scene in the choir. Sallua obtained the date from the abbess, who testified that the day before the princess fell ill (meaning December 8) Maria Luisa had come to her looking very worried. She told the abbess:[18] "God wants to punish the princess, and will send her an illness which will take her life." She repeated this several times. "And in fact," the abbess said, "the princess did begin to feel unwell the next day, after dinner, with vomiting and pain in her guts, and by the next morning she was in the grip of that serious illness."

The heavenly announcement of the poisoning was accompanied by prayers. Maria Luisa demanded that the novices pray a novena to the Precious Blood, asking the Lord to strike down a member of the convent with an illness. And the nuns knew very well that this meant none other than the princess.[19] Repeated over nine days, this is a particularly intense form of supplicatory prayer, through which the faithful implore God to fulfill their wish. The fact that the nuns spent nine days wishing the princess dead represented a serious perversion of the Church liturgy, as the inquisitor noted.

THE DRAMATURGY OF A POISONING

Reconstructing the exact sequence of events for the poisonings presented Sallua with some not insignificant problems. Having spent more than a year questioning witnesses, the Dominican found very little agreement on this between the sisters' testimonies. Many of the nuns and novices had only heard rumors and, two years after the fact, were simply padding these out. The information they provided contributed relatively little to the investigation of how the crime had been committed. The inquisitor soon realized there were only a few nuns and novices from whom he could expect a reliable testimony.

At least Maria Francesca's statements had told Sallua which nuns these were. First, there were Maria Luisa's direct accomplices, the novices Maria Ignazia and Maria Felice—although Maria Felice had died in suspicious circumstances shortly after the dramatic events of December 1858. Then there was the doctor's daughter, Agnese Celeste, the nurse, Maria Giuseppa—who was the only one to take a skeptical view of the heavenly letters—and finally Maria Giacinta, who had been ill and confined to bed in December 1858, like Agnese Celeste and Katharina. There was also Giacinta's brother, the lawyer Luigi Franceschetti, who met with the madre vicaria regularly, and whom she could send on errands outside the convent without attracting too much attention.

Extensive questioning of these witnesses provided the inquisitor with the crucial information he had been looking for on the poisoning plot. Their testimonies allowed him to trace how the whole campaign had been staged and, most importantly, to pinpoint a variety of poisons that had been used, in quantities that would have felled an elephant.[20] However, he still failed to present the congregation of cardinals with a convincing chronology for the attacks.

In part, this was because it was the first time the Dominican had been confronted with a criminal case. An experienced investigator would have reckoned with the inconsistency of the witness statements from the start, particularly with regard to timings, and would have attempted a critical comparison of these with the sequence of events presented in Katharina's *Denunzia*. Doing this exposes some of their contradictions as failures of memory, and reveals a relatively clear chronology for the murder plot.[21]

After the incident in the choir, Maria Luisa didn't hesitate for a second before setting in motion her plan to murder Katharina. One of her first steps was to isolate the princess from the other sisters. She thus forbade Katharina from taking part in the deathbed prayers for the mortally ill Maria Saveria, for which the sisters gathered in her cell on December 8. As Maria Giuseppa reported, immediately after

Maria Saveria's death, the madre vicaria fell into a long swoon. When she awoke, she claimed to have been transported to heaven, where she spoke to Christ about Maria Saveria's judgment. In what Jesus had said about Maria Saveria, she "also recognized his judgment of Luisa Maria." The princess would "soon die and be damned," because Maria Luisa's "tears and prayers [had] achieved nothing with God."[22]

That evening, Maria Luisa turned her attention to producing a deadly brew for the princess. Agnese Celeste and some of the other novices observed the mistress breaking up shards of glass. The nuns thought the glass dangerous, and warned Maria Luisa to be careful of her eyes. Depending on their size, splinters of glass can injure the inside of the mouth, the stomach, and even the intestines, causing internal bleeding. The finer the glass is ground, the less obvious the bleeding. At around six o'clock in the evening, during Vespers, Maria Luisa put her plan into action. The nuns had to be in the choir of the church for Divine Office, and she thought nobody would observe her. When Maria Giacinta, who was lying ill in her cell, asked Maria Luisa why she had crept past on tiptoes, she replied sanctimoniously that she hadn't wanted to wake her, as she was ill. "Then I started to suspect that somebody really did want to kill the princess. And more so when I noticed the novices Maria Ignazia, Maria Felice, Agnese Celeste and Mistress Maria Luisa busying themselves over the princess's bed. They had declared themselves the only people responsible for the princess's care."[23]

Maria Ignazia was to give the princess the gruel containing the ground glass on this Wednesday evening. She remembered the novice mistress summoning her:[24]

Maria Luisa began speaking to me as follows: "My daughter, what I am about to tell you must remain absolutely secret; do not tell anybody. I will not say anything to Maria Felice, as she could make things difficult for me. You know that those who are obedient never do anything bad; now we are showing obedience to the padre (I think she meant Peters). So you must take a little piece of *spongia* and put little bits of glass into it, and mix this with the gruel you are taking to Luisa Maria (the princess) this evening."

I was still very confused by her instructions, and answered as best I could: *"My mother mistress, if the Lord has commanded you in this mat-*

*ter, it would be best for you to do it alone, for you know how the command should
be carried out. You can well imagine that Luisa Maria might notice, and the matter would not stay secret."*

The mistress said nothing to this. Shortly afterwards, she asked
me: "Do you know which medicine is also a poison?"

I replied: *"Opium is a poison!!"*

This was how the matter was left on that day, and when Padre
Peters came out of the princess's cell, the mistress accompanied him
to the door. Feeling anxious, I went into the little choir, to confide
in the Lord and the Blessed Virgin, so that they might enlighten
me as to whether I must obey the mistress or not—and whether the
person who had spoken to me was actually the mistress.

After Maria Ignazia's hesitant reaction, Maria Luisa decided to take
matters into her own hands. Agnese Celeste observed her outside
the door to Katharina's cell, "reaching under her collar and drawing
something out" that she mixed into the gruel that was to be given to
the princess.[25] Katharina ate the gruel, which apparently caused her
to feel unwell. On that Thursday morning, December 9, she asked
for a cup of black tea, which was brought to her straightaway. But this
made her feel no better: on the contrary, the tea caused severe stomach pains, nausea, and vomiting.

The sickness may have been caused by tartar emetic in the tea.
Sant'Ambrogio's nurse and apothecary, Sister Maria Giuseppa, told
the inquisitor that the novice mistress had asked her for tartar emetic.
She showed her a little bottle of this, and impressed upon her that
"one small drop is enough to cause severe nausea."[26]

Tartar emetic contains antimony, which belongs to the same chemi-
cal family as arsenic. Potassium antimonyl tartrate tastes unpleasantly
sweet, with a disgusting aftertaste, and causes terrible, unappeasable
nausea. In the nineteenth century, small doses were taken as a decon-
gestant for coughs. The maximum daily dose is 0.5 gram; higher doses
lead to inflammation of the stomach and intestines, severe vomiting
and diarrhea, and the breakdown of the intestinal walls.

Katharina must have been in a desperate state on that Thursday,
and Maria Luisa was unable to conceal her delight. Maria Giacinta,
who was still ill, said the novice mistress had come to her in very high
spirits, saying:[27] "Did you know? The princess is already having pains."

Maria Giacinta went on: "Later I saw Maria Ignazia, and when I inquired about the princess's health, she snapped: 'Yes, she is doing badly. She is lying in bed, mistrustful, with her eyes open, like a hangman. She wants neither medicine nor chamomile tea, and she will hardly even taste her food, sending it back because she thinks she is being poisoned.'

"I was completely astonished, and said: 'What, is this the *Macchia della Faiola* then?'"

The *Macchia della Faiola* had become a byword for a den of *Briganti*, the bands of robbers who were much talked about in nineteenth-century Italy.[28] Maria Giacinta's exclamation shows just how implausible she found the poisoning story.

But Maria Luisa wanted to make absolutely certain the princess would die, and the effects of the ground glass and tartar emetic weren't enough for her. And so, later that day, she enlisted Agnese Celeste as another collaborator. The novice gave the inquisitor a detailed account of their conversation.[29]

In the evening the mistress came to my room, closed the door and told me she had to ask me something. But for heaven's sake, she said, I must say nothing of this, particularly to Maria Giacinta and Padre Peters. I promised, and she said: "As you are the daughter of a surgeon, can you tell me what is needed to kill a person with poison? But so that the cause cannot be found out. The body should not be bloated, for example."

Before I answered, I asked her: "Mistress, have you already tried this using the glass you broke up yesterday evening?"

She replied: "Oh, the glass was not enough."

I: "Does the glass sink to the bottom?"

She: "Yes, the glass sinks."

I: "What if you ground it more finely and stirred it well into the gruel?"

She: "We tried that, but still it sinks."

But although I suspected that the aim of this conversation was to poison the princess, the mistress said to me: "Think nothing of it: a superior may have many reasons for asking such questions."

After this I answered her, saying that a large quantity of opium can cause death, or so I had heard when my sister was ill. When the mistress inquired further, I added that opium was black. She asked about the exact lethal amount, and I said: "Usually you administer a small amount as a medicine, but if you raise that amount just a little, it can be fatal."

I reminded her that Maria Giacinta had once been given two opium pills, and afterwards she had a severe inflammation. Finally she asked me whether I knew of anything else that was lethal.

I answered: "Turpentine, and it is a clear liquid."

To which she said: "You cannot just mix that in, it would be noticed."

It now became clear to me that she wanted to poison the princess.

I also suggested quicklime. . . . I don't recall whether I also mentioned belladonna and quicksilver. She left my room, telling me I should try and think of other possibilities, and to keep the conversation secret.

Turpentine and quicklime corrode the digestive tract and ultimately cause death, but to start with, Maria Luisa had to press ahead using the things she had to hand. On the evening of December 9, Giuseppa Maria was tasked with preparing chamomile tea for the princess, into which Maria Luisa put something from "another smaller cup," as the nurse testified. Katharina tried the tea, but didn't want to drink it. It looked blackish and tasted "disgusting."[30] She asked a novice to try the tea and she, too, found it undrinkable. The novice mistress, appearing unexpectedly in Katharina's cell, gave the novice a terrible scolding, as Maria Ignazia confirmed in her statement: "I would like to add that the chamomile tea the princess was given that day must have had something mixed into it: Giuseppa Maria knows about such things and honestly attests to this, and the mistress shouted at us for tasting it. . . . I actually ran to the princess's chamber to get rid of the cup. The mistress told Sister Maria Nazarena to tell me to do this."[31] The poison couldn't be allowed to fall into other hands. They had to get rid of the *Corpus Delicti*.

From then on both nurses, Maria Giuseppa and Giuseppa Maria, were certain that the madre vicaria was trying to poison the princess. The novice mistress had also asked them about the effects of opium and tartar emetic, and she had demanded the key to the dispensary, which gave her direct, unsupervised access to the poison cupboard. To prevent the worst from happening, the two nuns waited until everyone was gathered in the refectory for supper, and shut themselves in the convent's pharmacy. They "emptied all the containers and tins in which poisonous substances were kept," substituting harmless powders of the same color.[32] They replaced the tartar emetic with cream of tartar, which is the same color, and swapped the opium for licorice. After Vespers, they then obediently handed the dispensary key to the vicaress.

On Friday, December 10, during early Mass, the two of them noticed a light in the dispensary. Soon afterward, Maria Luisa and Maria Ignazia came out, the latter holding a lantern. They clearly hadn't found what they had been looking for. The easiest way to obtain poison inside the convent had thus failed.

That day, as Sister Giuseppa Maria stated, another opportunity unexpectedly presented itself, when the doctors prescribed Katharina a "laxative containing castor oil." Before the princess was given this medicine, the mistress poured a few drops of varnish into the little bottle of castor oil. She took the varnish from the tins of paint and vitriolic acid left in Sant'Ambrogio's refectory by the painters who were working there. Giuseppa Maria saw Maria Luisa, her hands smeared with oil paint, on her way to the infirmary to clean herself up. Katharina took the poisoned castor oil, and once again suffered severe nausea and vomiting.

Afterward, Maria Luisa gave the medicine bottle to Giuseppa Maria, but "because of the color and the smell," she noticed immediately that the medicine Katharina had been given was contaminated with varnish. To make absolutely sure, she asked her fellow nurse Maria Giuseppa to check what was in the bottle. She confirmed it was contaminated straightaway "and, horrified, immediately ran to the abbess with the bottle." The abbess cried out: "This is a betrayal! This is not castor oil. Bring me a spoon, I want to try it." The oil that was left at the bottom of the bottle tasted nothing like castor oil. The abbess therefore ordered Giuseppa Maria to take the little bottle to an apothecary outside the convent for a precise analysis of its contents. She set out immediately, but Maria Luisa stopped her at the gate and took the bottle from her, simply saying, "Somebody gave that poor woman rancid oil."

A nun who was looking after the princess's "bodily needs due to the castor oil she had taken" told the investigating judge that Katharina, "tormented by terrible pains in her intestines," had passed "pieces of white stuff that looked like fat" in her excrement. These may have been pieces of her stomach lining—a result of the tartar emetic. Once her diarrhea had subsided, however, Katharina seemed to recover a little over the course of that Friday.

Meanwhile, Maria Luisa was conducting a fevered search for new poisons to finish the princess off. And she quickly had a bright idea. She told Maria Ignazia:[33] "Sister Agnese Celeste told me that atropa belladonna—that is, belladonna extract—is the most effective poison of all. I myself will order everything from the apothecary this morning, but I will do it via the lawyer Franceschetti and not the estate manager. So as not to arouse his suspicion, I will also have him buy magnesia, tartar and some other things along with the belladonna extract and the opium." And a few hours later, Franceschetti duly handed over the medicines Maria Luisa had requested at the convent gate. As he confirmed in his hearing, he procured nine or ten different substances, including magnesium oxide, tartar, and opium.[34] He had admittedly wondered about one of the items on Maria Luisa's list: atropa belladonna. He doubted the apothecary would even sell him this dangerous poison, but the latter provided it without any objection. Sallua managed to identify the apothecary—Barelli, on the Salita del Tritone—and included the receipt in the files. He also got ahold of the medicines Franceschetti had bought. The convent apothecary said that nobody in Sant'Ambrogio had asked for any medicines at that time: they already had everything they needed for the nuns who were ill. Clearly, the procurement of the poisons was exclusively Maria Luisa's doing.

On the evening of December 10, the novice mistress had another conversation with the doctor's daughter, asking her whether she had thought of any more poisons.[35]

Agnese Celeste replied:

> "If you leave things in copper, they become poisonous."
> She: "Does that have negative effects?"
> "It causes bloating," I told her.
> She: "That's no good to me. Tell me how opium can be administered."

"In pill form," I answered.

She: "No, she will never take it like that."

So I recommended that she mix the opium with cassia, which is the same color. She asked me again about the dosage, and I replied that, when in doubt, it was better to give too much than too little. She warned me again to keep the conversation to myself, and left me. Fearing that the mistress really wanted to poison the princess, I felt bad, but I calmed myself with the thought of how the beautiful Judith murdered Holofernes,[36] which was an act of divine splendor.

Now Maria Luisa just had to wait for a suitable opportunity. For the next few days, she remained extremely cautious, and spoke to no one else about the poisoning, not even her confidantes: the witness statements provide no information about December 11, 12, and 13. On these dates, Maria Luisa brought the princess meat broth and rice soup, both with the same bitter aroma.

Katharina was mistrustful and, as she said in her *Denunzia*, on December 12 she filled a little bottle with some of the meat broth and gave it to Padre Peters, pleading with him to have an apothecary analyze it for poison. Peters claimed the apothecary to whom he had given this task had found no poison—only alum, which in nineteenth-century medicine was used as a caustic agent against hemorrhages, or as a corrosive for the removal of warts. The taste is initially sweet, then bitter, making the mouth contract. Used internally, alum corrodes the lining of the stomach and intestines, and in high doses can be fatal. But how alum, a water-soluble double salt of potassium and aluminum, could have caused the bitter smell of the meat broth remained Padre Peters's secret. Whether he really had the little bottle analyzed is open to question.

A little later, Doctor Luigi Giovanni Marchi visited Katharina's sickbed, and ordered the nuns to give her cassia with tamarind, to detoxify her and stimulate her metabolism. This finally provided Maria Luisa with an opportunity to kill the princess. Agnese Celeste had advised her to mix opium with cassia, as it was the same color and the cassia would mask the smell. Now the doctor was prescribing this very medicine. To Maria Luisa, it must have seemed like an act of divine providence. The madre vicaria told her accomplice, Maria

Ignazia, that Maria Giuseppa had been spreading rumors that she was trying to poison the princess. This meant her hands had been tied for days. And now the doctor had prescribed a medicine that was ideally suited to disguising poisons, and entrusted this to her personally.

On Monday, December 13, Maria Luisa turned the opium into liquid so that it could be mixed with the cassia.[37] Several witnesses observed her going into her cell and dissolving opium in oil, using a tin plate over a pan of charcoal. She poured the liquid into a cup. Maria Ignazia told the inquisitor she had come into Maria Luisa's cell in the evening.[38] "I could smell a strong and very repulsive stench. . . . The mistress noticed the expression on my face. When I told her there was an unbearable stench, she answered: 'But no, no stench, it must be the medicine.' Then she added: 'Tomorrow morning, get up and dress quickly, then dilute the medicine with hot water and take it to the princess.'" Maria Ignazia also noted "that there was now a larger dose of the cassia and tamarind medicine in the glass, and it was a different color."

Then she described in detail her own role in Katharina's poisoning on Tuesday, December 14.

The following morning I got up at the first wake-up call and quickly went to the mistress's cell. I lit the lamp. She said I should call Sister Maria Felice at once and tell her to fetch hot water from the kitchen; I had to stay with her. While Maria Felice went to fetch the hot water from the kitchen to dilute the medicine, the mistress gave me the following speech: "Do you know? I fear that the princess will not take the medicine that was prepared yesterday evening, because there is too much of it and it is too thick. We should therefore prepare this other one, which was actually meant for Sister Agnese Celeste. But I beg you, do not get confused; it should not be given to Agnese Celeste. Take care not to make a mistake."

I replied: "Don't worry. I will not get confused and will not give it to her."

Then she said: "Good, fetch our casket."

I fetched it, and she took the key she had with her. While I held the lamp and she lay in bed, she opened the casket and took out a tin of medicinal clay, which was sealed with red wax and carried the apothecary's stamp, though I cannot describe this. The mistress took a little packet from the tin, cut the wax paper open with scissors and emptied the contents into the glass containing the medicine for Sister Agnese Celeste. The little packet had the inscription "atropa belladonna." The mistress also told me herself that it was belladonna extract.

The mistress instructed me to leave the medicine glass on her little table; she shut the casket and said to me: "Now find a suitable place to throw this tin away, then clean the scissors. You won't have time to take the medicine to the princess, so when Maria Felice comes to me I will get her to take it."

I went into the parlor with the lamp to carry out this task, and when I went in, there was the same stench that I had smelled in the mistress's cell the previous evening. I looked behind the door and saw a plate on the floor. It was dirtied with oil, and some black, melted stuff that I could not identify. I thought other nuns might notice this, so I threw the tin away and carefully washed the plate and the scissors.

When I went back to the mistress's cell, I told her about the plate and the smell, and she replied: "Oh! Yes, I put that there yesterday and forgot to tell you to clean it."

I asked her what the oil and the black stuff were, and she said: "The black stuff was opium; it was so hard that it could not be ground up. It was still in little pieces, so I dissolved it in oil, on the plate that I left in the parlor yesterday evening."

When the final bell rang from the choir stalls, I asked her to go to Matins, but she said: "Off you go. If the princess needs anything, I will have someone call you."

Maria Felice went into Katharina's chamber and proffered her two glasses on a tray. One contained a relatively thick mixture of cassia and the opium Maria Luisa had melted. The second glass of cassia, originally intended for Agnese Celeste, contained the belladonna. The brew was of a thinner consistency, and even a small dose of the deadly nightshade extract would have been fatal. Against expectations, the princess chose the thicker cassia with the opium, rather than the belladonna. "After the sick woman had taken six spoonfuls from Maria Felice's hands, she could drink no more, and fell back on the pillow, as if she had suffered a stroke, quite dazed and panting hard."[39]

At this moment, Maria Luisa entered the princess's chamber, and immediately called Maria Ignazia back from the choir. Maria Ignazia recalled the incident very precisely:

I left the choir stalls straightaway, terribly afraid of what might have happened. When I came to the door of the room by the arches, I recognized the mistress coming towards me, although it was dark. In a low voice, she said: "Run quickly to the princess, for she is dying."

I went and ran to the princess's cell, where I found Maria Felice, supporting the princess's head; she was very scared and said to me: "Dear sister, come quick, look at what has happened."

I saw the princess, much disheartened and dazed, and I called her by her name: "Luisa Maria."

She replied with a gasp, "Maria Ignazia, I am dying."

In a state of great anxiety I left the cell to find somebody. I encountered the mistress, who at once asked me. "how is Sister Luisa Maria?"

"The princess," I answered, "is doing badly; come, for God's sake, we have to call the padre and the doctor."

The mistress said: "Why such a rush? Wait and tell me, where did you leave the other medicine?"

I quickly went to the princess's cell and saw she had taken the medicine that the mistress had mixed with opium the previous evening in her cell. The princess said to me: "See, I have not taken all the medicine!"

And I said to her: "Just leave the medicine there and do not think about it."

I . . . saw the other medicine, which had been prepared the previous morning (as mentioned above) in the mistress's cell; I went back to the mistress and told her that both glasses were in the princess's room and that she had taken just over half of the medicine that had been mixed with opium.

The mistress said to me: "Do not worry about the princess any more; run and take the two medicines and find somewhere suitable to pour them away, then rinse out the glasses."

However, when I told her that even if I rinsed the glass, it would not get rid of the revolting stench, she added: "Go and throw away the glasses and the medicine, wherever you think best, but hurry. If the princess should ask you why you are taking the glasses away, tell her that you want to take the medicine to Sister Agnese Celeste."

I quickly went to the princess and told her that the mistress had instructed me to take the medicine to Agnese Celeste. I ran to a suitable place and emptied the glasses, then I went to the kitchen, to rinse the glasses with hot water. But the stench still remained in one of them; I broke the glass and threw it away.

In the midst of all this, Maria Ignazia had the presence of mind to think about the questions that might be asked later.

I went to the mistress and told her everything, and then said: "What will the nurses say when they find out the novice has not taken the medicine, and one of the glasses is missing?"

She replied: "Tell them you tripped on the stairs of the dormitory, you spilled the medicine and the glass was broken."

This I told to everyone who asked me. I then went back to the princess and found her in a much worse state. I left the room together with the mistress, who was also there, and repeated that we needed to call the doctor.

Again, she said: "Why such a rush? You should wait, but it's your decision. The doctor will come and let her bleed, and then it will all be over."

From her words, I thought she didn't want anyone to call the doctor, because he would task her with something and then it might all go wrong.

I went back to the princess, who was doing so badly that she asked me to fetch her first one bottle, then another that she had in her room, so she could smell them and recover herself. I could see her condition was still worsening, and I wanted to help her in some way, so I set off to see the abbess. I met the mistress on the way, and repeated that the princess was getting worse and worse.

She said to me: "Off you go to the abbess then, and tell her that the princess is not well."

I found the abbess in the choir, and told her about the princess's condition and that I believed she had suffered a stroke.

The abbess replied: "Oh! Lord, here I am."

As we were going to the princess, we saw the mistress; she told us she had already sent for the doctor. The abbess was very alarmed to see the princess in that condition; the two doctors and two father confessors were sent for in a great hurry, and they came.

Then Maria Ignazia described to the court the doctors' diagnosis, and the action the confessors had taken.

First of all, Doctor Marchi came and said, "it is a syncopation of the heart: quick, a good leech treatment"; this was carried out.

When Doctor Riccardi came, he said: "This is a syncopation of the head, which has attacked the fibers of the brain." He called for a second leech treatment straightaway, which was carried out.

When the doctors had gone, the confessors came and quickly brought the princess the last Communion. As her condition was still worsening and her fever was getting higher, she was given extreme unction after the midday meal. She took her vows in the presence of the father confessor, the abbess, the mistress and a few other nuns.

It was common practice to allow mortally ill novices to take their vows on their deathbeds. But somehow, Katharina didn't die. Maria Luisa had no idea how two ounces of opium could have failed to kill her. On the evening of December 14, the novice mistress seemed very ill at ease. "It seems impossible that she should survive this," she told Maria Ignazia. "She could still die tonight, don't you think?"

The hearings of the two convent doctors basically corroborated Katharina's statement, and those of the many witnesses—at least, with regard to the symptoms of her illness.[40] However, the thought that poisoning could have been the cause of Katharina's surprising malady didn't occur to them. Doctor Gregorio Bernardo Riccardi "never had any kind of suspicion that the princess's illness could be down to a misuse of medicines or an intake of food dangerous to her health."[41] Maria Luisa's strategy had worked: the poisons she had used were undetectable. But her real aim still eluded her.

Hoping to hasten the princess's demise, Maria Luisa turned to her confidante Maria Ignazia: "Could you do something for me? When the princess is fast asleep, take this little bottle of chloroform and hold it under her nose, so she falls into an even deeper sleep." Katharina used chloroform[42] regularly for certain "unctions," as she told her doctors. Was this an indirect confession that she was one of many nineteenth-century noblewomen who "sniffed" chloroform to put themselves in an intoxicated state? Whatever the truth of this, the vapor that the chloroform gave off was so strong that Katharina had to ask other nuns to leave the cell when she used it. Eventually, the doctors banned her from using chloroform altogether, saying the Italians "simply could not get used to it." It seems Maria Ignazia didn't want to risk this distinctive smell in Katharina's cell, and she took the little bottle into another room.

Katharina was still alive on the morning of Wednesday, December 15, and Maria Luisa asked Franceschetti to procure another two ounces of opium, which he did immediately. Maria Ignazia stated:

> I saw it in her hand, when she took the tin out of the bag.
>
> "Here," she said to me, "I ordered this; we will mix it with the medicines that the princess has to take."
>
> But the doctors prescribed no more medicines. Katharina's condition had deteriorated greatly, and she was no longer in a fit state to take them. So she could not be given any more opium, and the treatment had to be continued with leeches. I never found out what became of the opium.

Meanwhile, the madre vicaria retreated to the convent dispensary to forage for more poisons. Maria Ignazia said:

> The following morning, Padre Peters went to celebrate Mass. The mistress sent me to the abbess for the key to the dispensary, which she gave me, and I took it to the mistress. The mistress told Sister Maria Felice to stay with the princess and said to me: "Come with me."
>
> And then: "Go to our room, fetch the little tin and bring it to me in the dispensary."
>
> When I had given her the tin, she said: "Stay here by the dispensary door, and watch to see if anyone comes; if Maria Giuseppa comes, let me know at once."
>
> She stayed in there for quite a long time. She left the casket

there, came out and closed the door. Then she said to me: "Well, what a chaotic dispensary we have in Sant'Ambrogio!"

We parted ways. In the evening she took me back to the dispensary, to fetch the tin, which she told me to take back to her cell.

Maria Luisa must have found what she was looking for in the poison cupboard. On Thursday, December 16, she gave Maria Ignazia a paper packet containing a wood-colored powder, saying: "Pour that into the princess's lemonade, for it will make anyone go out of their mind, and causes vomiting." Maria Ignazia took the powder "with a heavy heart." Her statement continues:

Finally I decided to put just a tiny bit into the princess's lemonade, so that she would drink it. I did it, but then it was impossible for me to take the lemonade away before the princess asked me for it, so I had to give it to her. She drank only a sip, without noticing anything and without feeling any ill effects. Then I promptly took the lemon water away. I met the mistress and told her I had done everything she had instructed, and the princess had not had any complaint.

She replied: "I see. I imagine you only put a tiny amount in, and of course that would have no effect."

I gave her the rest of the powder and went away.

After this, Maria Luisa made another attempt at poisoning Katharina's lemonade, this time using opium again. Maria Ignazia was once more entrusted to carry out the task:

As I was also in the room, she said to me: "Put three drops of the opium water into this."

I pointed out to her that this water was dark in color, while the lemonade was white, so this would color it.

But she argued: "You must do it out of obedience."

She left the glass there. She was hardly out of the door when she met Maria Giuseppa and cried loudly: "What is this? What is the meaning of this, what are you trying to claim? Such things do not happen in the house of God."

Maria Giuseppa replied: "But if you have not put anything in the lemonade, then what is Maria Ignazia doing in this room?"

"I was standing at the door," I said. "I am just standing here, not doing anything."

Then the mistress took the glass of lemonade, went to the abbess and said: "What is going on? Maria Giuseppa believes that something has been put into the lemonade. Here, there is nothing in it."

The mistress and the abbess drank the lemonade in the presence of Maria Giuseppa, to show her there was nothing in it. And in fact there was nothing, because I had not yet added the three drops that the mistress told me to put in it.

After this, Maria Ignazia refused to carry out any more orders from Maria Luisa to poison the princess, and told her she wanted to go back to the novitiate. The novice mistress finally agreed. She had now lost her most important accomplice.

But Maria Luisa refused to give up, and revisited Agnese Celeste's idea of using turpentine. She asked Franceschetti to purchase a turpentine pill for the dispensary. However, as he handed it over, the lawyer warned her that "whatever it touches, it will burn at once," and the novice mistress took fright and threw the pill away.[43]

Over the New Year of 1858–1859, the attempts to poison Katharina tailed off, and finally ceased altogether. Whether this was really down to Katharina clearing the air with Maria Luisa on the morning of December 16, as she reported in her *Denunzia*, is open to question.

Katharina slowly recovered from the effects of the various poisons, although over the months that followed she refused almost all the food and drink she was offered. In particular, she no longer drank chocolate at breakfast. She ate only bread and drank water, in the belief that nobody could poison them. But she still suffered from terrible indigestion, and on several occasions during the spring the abbess ordered a "sealed whey-based laxative" from the pharmacist. Sometimes, however, the bottle would arrive with a broken seal. When this happened, the abbess decided not to give the medicine to Katharina—evidently erring on the side of caution. She wanted the princess to feel she was no longer under threat in the order's community. The abbess's aim was to keep her in the convent at all costs: leaving would give Katharina the opportunity to talk about Sant'Ambrogio's secrets and what had happened there to the outside world. The grass must be allowed to grow over the whole affair first.

But in early summer 1859, the madre vicaria resorted to poisoning again. Just before Easter, she had shown her hatred of Katharina to be undiminished, this time expressing it in a liturgical context. While she washed the novices' feet on Maundy Thursday, as Jesus did for his disciples before the Last Supper,[44] the novice mistress told them there was a Judas in their midst, who was not present in the church at that moment. The only nun missing from the liturgy of the Last Supper was Sister Luisa Maria, alias Katharina von Hohenzollern-Sigmaringen. Maria Luisa was reiterating the accusation she had made on December 8, 1858, when Katharina had knelt before her with the cord around her neck.

After Hohenlohe had removed the princess from Sant'Ambrogio, the abbess received a letter from the Virgin, interpreting this event as a divine intervention: "Recognize the great mercy I have shown to you by freeing you from this soul: in the eyes of God, what you took to be gold was in fact vile excrement." The Virgin Mary even assigned the abbess a penance for being so accommodating to the princess during the final six months of her stay in the convent. Padre Peters also received a letter from the Madonna, containing the same divine judgment and penance, which the confessor insisted on observing.

Katharina von Hohenzollern's exit from Sant'Ambrogio must have been a terrible defeat for Maria Luisa. Ever since she had read the Americano's letter to Katharina, she had made every effort to silence or kill her. Now the princess was outside and able to speak freely. And more importantly, Maria Luisa had mixed the poisoned drinks for Katharina and given them to her via her helpers. There were simply too many witnesses: it would be easy to convict her. Her best hope might have been to address the matter head-on with Katharina, beg her forgiveness and try to dissuade her from bringing criminal charges. But Maria Luisa adopted quite a different strategy. She turned once more to the supernatural, though this time to hell rather than heaven.

"IT WAS MOST CERTAINLY THE DEVIL"

Sallua exposed Maria Luisa's devilish exculpation strategy with the aid of an exemplary witness, in the shape of Maria Ignazia. She had already admitted to being Maria Luisa's "accomplice," giving several self-incriminating testimonies. In his *Relazione* for the cardinals, the Dominican remarked that Maria Ignazia's honesty had led "truth to triumph" in the tortuous story of the poisoning.[45]

In her hearing on March 2, 1860, Maria Ignazia painted a compelling picture of the strategy Maria Luisa and the father confessors were using to justify themselves.[46]

One evening, when the princess was well again, I went into the novitiate wing to receive the blessing from Mistress Maria Luisa.

She said to me: "Daughter, be a good girl and do not cause me any trouble like these other novices."

I assured her that I would not say anything to anybody.

She: "Daughter, what do you mean? Do you still have such things in your head? I don't know what you're talking about."

And then I began to cry and reminded her of what she had made me do for her with regard to the princess.

The mistress seemed astonished and said to me, falteringly, "But what? I never said or ordered these things, nor do I know anything about them. Remember the reading that was given in the refectory today, from the life of Sister Veronica Giuliani?[47] These things can happen again."

The reading from the life of Sister Veronica had been about how the devil had taken her shape and thus done many evil things.

Finally, she said to me: "Go to bed, and tomorrow come to me when it is time for morning prayers. I will soon drive this nonsense out of you."

I went to her room punctually the following morning. I repeated to her everything she had said and what she had instructed me regarding poisoning the princess, and recounted all the details, including the places, the exact words, and the people involved.

Then she: "But daughter, I know nothing of all these things."

She said she had suffered greatly from worrying about the princess, and had only been to see her occasionally, to provide comfort with her words.

To me she said: "Take courage, Maria Ignazia."

I said, "Yes, that is true, but it is also true that you said and instructed me to do all the other things."

She: "Daughter, that certainly was not me."

I: "Then who was it? I have done a great deal of harm, and will have to tell the padre everything, will I not?"

She: "No, daughter, you have done no harm. You were obedient. Trust in obedience: remain silent, and never say a word. If you are questioned, always deny. This is the best way to defy the devil."

I replied: "So it was the devil in your shape, Reverend Mother?"

She: *"Alas!* I wish it were not so. The devil has taken on my form on too many other occasions, as he also did in this case. You threw away the cup and did other things that you have described to me. This you can openly deny, as I know that the devil also took on your shape."

I asked her: "Where were you on those days?"

She answered, "I had foreseen everything that would come to pass. And so I withdrew myself and prayed in the little rooms in the lower choir, and left them only when it was absolutely necessary."

She repeated: "Stay calm and do not say a word."

I told her that her words and conscience had reassured me, and I would never say anything.

As Maria Ignazia pointed out, Maria Luisa had resorted to her usual defense: it wasn't me, it was the devil. This claim wasn't entirely implausible to her fellow nuns. They had, after all, learned from their refectory readings that the devil had also tried to shame Saint Veronica Giuliani by taking on her shape. The Capuchin nun from the convent of Città di Castello near Perugia died in 1727, and was finally raised to the altars in 1839, following much debate within the Church. The passage in the life of Saint Veronica to which Maria Luisa was referring furnished her with the perfect precedent:

The devil, despairing of being able to subdue her, conceived the idea of blackening her reputation, and of making her appear a sacrilegious hypocrite, by the following stratagem. He frequently assumed her form, and contrived to be caught in the act of eating greedily and surreptitiously, at improper hours, sometimes in the kitchen, sometimes in the refectory, and sometimes in the dispensary. The nuns were extremely scandalized at this, especially when they once or twice saw Veronica go to Holy Communion after they had witnessed one of these unlawful repasts. But it pleased God to undertake the defense of His servant, by causing the infernal plot to be discovered. One morning, about the time of Holy Communion, some of them found the supposed Veronica engaged in eating, and accordingly ran to the choir to inform the abbess, but there they found their holy sister rapt in prayer. . . . It may be easily conceived how the malice of her infernal enemy increased when he found himself so utterly scorned by Veronica, and when he beheld her at the same time so closely united to her divine Spouse. There was no art to which he did not resort for the purpose of making her unfaithful. He would present to her the most dreadful images of guilt, and in company with other fiends under the forms of wicked young men, he would enact scenes, the very thought of which is abhorrent to nature.[48]

Like Veronica Giuliani's fellow nuns, Maria Ignazia had also been taken in by the devil, and on his orders had tried several times to kill Katharina. She was now left alone with her questions and her guilt: the madre vicaria knew no pity, and had condemned her to absolute silence. But there came a point where it was no longer possible to avoid a conversation between Maria Ignazia and Padre Peters, who had become unsettled by the poisonings. The novice mistress gave her precise instructions for this:

When the princess was returning to health, the mistress called me to her and said to me: "you will be called by Padre Peters. Think about the promise you made me not to say a word about the medicine and the poison for the princess. Say only that I came into her cell now and then to give her courage, and that you and Maria Felice saw me one night at the princess's bed, but you felt a certain dread. Say that the princess behaved strangely, and I reassured her that I had been in bed that night and had not been to her room, and that Maria Giacinta threw me out of the cell in contempt."

I went to Padre Peters and he questioned me about the medicine and the poisoned remedies that were given to the princess. I answered that there was no truth in this and, just as I had promised the mistress, disagreed with everything he said. I denied every point, though he asked me the most detailed questions.

Peters told me he was questioning me in order to find out what lay behind this business. He did not think the mistress capable of such a thing, and he mentioned that she had foreseen it all a long time ago. Furthermore, the princess was supposed to die as a punishment from God, but the devil had interfered to make it look like murder.

He told me about the alum they had found in the bottle of soup. When I asked him how the devil had brought this about, he replied that the devil was truly able do such things, and had mixed it into the soup so that something would be found in it.

Before I went to Peters, the mistress gave me the same explanation, word for word: she said the Lord wanted to punish Luisa Maria and that the devil had interfered to place the blame on the mistress's shoulders.

I spoke to Padre Leziroli about these matters, and he said: "In truth everything that has happened to the princess was the work of the devil; we have carried out the necessary tests and we are sure that it was the devil's art, and that the mistress Maria Luisa neither thought nor said such things, and did not carry out these deeds."

I replied: "So was I speaking to the devil?"

And he: *"Certainly. It was most certainly the devil who caused you these troubles."*

During spiritual exercises, this same Padre Leziroli preached in front of the entire community that the worries that some—in fact almost all—the nuns had experienced with regard to the princess, whom all the sisters knew, had been a deception by the devil. He could assume the shape of other people, and had poisoned the soup and the medicine. He did all this to disrupt the peace of the community. But we should remain calm, as none of us had done any of the things we saw. The princess was present at this sermon.

I know that in the end Leziroli also tried to convince the princess of this deception by the devil. He said she should not judge the mistress so harshly and should not hate her—for if she did, she could not remain in the house of God. Leziroli concluded the above sermon by saying he had firm evidence of the mistress's innocence.

Maria Ignazia's testimony was corroborated by several other nuns and the abbess.[49] Even after Katharina had left, the nuns were repeatedly told that all the poisoning attempts had been the work of the devil.

Maria Francesca had to write another letter for Maria Luisa, this time using the name and handwriting of Maria Felice, who had just died. This letter said that the princess had been a "strange woman" who "carried on with the devil" and falsely believed somebody was trying to poison her. The dead nun complained about having to nurse this peculiar woman during her illness. Maria Stanislaa confirmed that the novice mistress had tasked Maria Francesca with writing out this letter.

In the fall of 1859, when the Apostolic Visitation that the pope had requested was already under way, the confessors instructed the nuns to treat the statement "The devil assumed the shape of Maria Luisa to poison Katharina" like an article of the creed. Any dissenting nuns were pressured and persecuted. Maria Giuseppa was treated particularly harshly for her stubborn refusal to comply with this. When she insisted in the confessional that Maria Luisa was responsible for the poison attacks against Katharina, Leziroli forced her to make a formal retraction. She had to swear to Maria Luisa's "holiness and extraordinary gifts" before Leziroli, with her hand on the gospels, and reject her suspicions as a "great sin." "He said I had to speak his phrase about Maria Luisa's holiness, if I wanted to save my soul," Maria Giuseppa recalled.

Maria Luisa also followed this pastoral strategy, in her own way. Notes suddenly started appearing and being passed around the convent, supposedly originating from the Americano. According to Maria Ignazia, these explained "how the demons took on the shape of the mistress and other sisters, to poison the princess."[50] The Americano addressed the notes defending "the mistress's innocence" to Padre Peters. "She read one out to me, to convince me of her innocence in the poisoning affair. Before the mistress was taken away, she told me I should defend her innocence, just as she would defend mine when I was taken away. Now I know why she said this. She was afraid because of what she had done."

MORE MURDERS

By "what Maria Luisa had done," Maria Ignazia didn't just mean her attempted murder of Katharina von Hohenzollern. The madre vicaria had also made several attempts to kill other nuns.[51]

First, there was the case of Maria Giacinta, which must have played out in the first half of 1859. Luigi Franceschetti's sister had observed Maria Luisa grinding glass and mixing it into the princess's food. She was also well informed about other "deceits" involved in Katharina's poisoning. She spoke to the abbess, Padre Peters, and other nuns about these, and finally confronted Maria Luisa herself with her knowledge: "Yes, I saw it, I saw it."

Maria Luisa started to feel threatened by what Maria Giacinta knew, and decided she had to get rid of her. At once, she gave Maria Francesca instructions to write several letters to Padre Peters in the name of her guardian angel and the Virgin. The Virgin spoke about her former "favorite little daughter" Maria Giacinta, who had been "destined for something great, alongside her mistress." But now she was just another "haughty" and "proud" nun, whom the confessor and abbess had to "humble." Finally, the Virgin announced, "Maria Giacinta will die of her illness; her life will be shortened by many years because she has fallen from the elevated step of glory beside her mistress."

As a result, the confessor placed Maria Giacinta under pressure. She was utterly bewildered and feared for her life, thinking she was about to be poisoned. Giuseppe Maria confirmed this suspicion. Maria Giacinta was then struck down by a severe inflammation of the intestines and ulceration of the throat, from an overdose of opium or something similar. The illness exhausted her, and she was on her deathbed. Franceschetti corroborated the testimonies of Maria Francesca and Giuseppa Maria: two pills of opium, given to his sister by Maria Luisa, had brought her close to death. She would have died, had the convent doctor not given her an antidote at the last minute. The medical man had said this quantity of opium was enough to kill a horse.

This, along with other evidence and witness interviews, gave the Inquisition enough information to prove that in the days after Maria Giacinta was poisoned with opium, the madre vicaria tried to give her an even larger dose of another poison to finish her off. This was probably *vinum colchici seminis*, made from the flowers of the autumn crocus. It was usually used in small doses to treat gout, but in larger quantities it was a deadly poison. Maria Luisa had also announced this murder in a letter from the Madonna to Padre Peters, which foretold the death of a nun as a punishment from God. It even pinpointed the exact timing and the circumstances of the death. However, Maria

Giacinta realized what was afoot and stubbornly refused to take the liquid.

When nothing came of this divine prophecy, Maria Luisa put aside the first letter from the Virgin and wrote another, in which Mary now proclaimed that her firstborn daughter Maria Luisa's prayers, penance, and services had worked, and Maria Giacinta didn't have to die after all.

The same good fortune was not granted to the novice Maria Agostina, whose tragic story played out in October 1858. The young nun was starting to get a reputation for having visions and ecstasies. The mother founder, in particular, had appeared to her several times. A number of the other nuns had started to follow the new visionary and believe her prophecies. Maria Luisa was consumed with envy, and devoted all her efforts to unmasking Maria Agostina's ecstasies as "duplicitous pretenses." First, in her capacity as novice mistress, she made Maria Agostina "unburden her conscience to her as to a father confessor," giving her a biographical confession. The novice mistress then told the other sisters about all the weaknesses and miseries in this young woman's life. She spoke widely and at length about the "shameless relationship" Maria Agostina had conducted in Ferrara with her confessor, the Jesuit Vincenzo Stocchi.[52] Maria Luisa forced the young novice to retract her visions in public—not just in the novitiate, but also in the choir, in front of the whole community of Sant'Ambrogio. But this ritual humiliation still wasn't enough for her. Claiming she was making a zealous attempt to set this lost soul back on the right path, she placed Agostina under massive psychological pressure. She was evidently trying to drive her to madness, and ultimately to death.

In her hearing, Maria Giuseppa recalled that "last summer, the late Sister Maria Agostina ... fell ill. She was young, robust and in good health. But it seemed that her illness had an unnatural cause, and I later began to suspect that something had been mixed into her food. This sister had a constant fever, and she pined away. ... The sick are usually given Holy Communion every eight days, but I remember that she was not given it for quite some time. Around last October, she was taken ill with a severe fever, and they said it brought on a stroke. She was 21 or 22 years old. The stroke left her dazed, and she stuttered. Ulcers built up in her mouth and throat. She wasted away to a skeleton in just a few days, and finally died."[53]

Several witnesses confirmed in their statements that the novice mistress had a crazed notion that Maria Agostina was out to get her. They expressed their unanimous conviction that Maria Luisa had poisoned her. The vicaress hated Agostina so much that she had forbidden Maria Ignazia, the mortally ill woman's biological sister, from visiting her in the infirmary. Maria Ignazia's testimony shows how obedient she was to Maria Luisa: this was the reason the latter had recruited her as an accomplice.[54]

> I never visited my sister, as I knew this would not have pleased the mistress. But in the end, the father confessor and the mistress went to my sister. She made her confession and took Holy Communion. Then I visited her too, but she was close to death, and I do not think that she recognized me.
>
> The reason the mistress brought Padre Peters in to take my sister's confession, was to free her from the demons. The mistress told me that Peters laid a stole on her head and she resisted strongly. Padre Peters drove out her seven demons, and the mistress told me she saw them. After this, my sister lived another eight days, but she was no longer sensible.

Giuseppa Maria was convinced that Maria Luisa had made the sick woman "take a powder orally. This led to inflammation of the chest, made everything appear yellow, caused ulcers in her throat and left her completely dazed."[55] The second nurse was absolutely certain of her facts: she had taken the same powder as a medicine, and had observed the exact same symptoms in herself as in Maria Agostina, with whom she had spoken several times as she was nursing her. In her hearing, she stated:[56]

> So I harbored the suspicion that the mistress had poisoned her food: a few days previously, something similar had happened to me. The doctor prescribed an infusion for my stomachache, of corallium and wormseed. This was prepared in the sick room, where the mistress was always around. The first time I took it, I felt nauseous, got a headache, and my vision misted over in a yellow color. But I said nothing."

The symptoms Giuseppa Maria describes here, in particular the colored vision, confusion, and affected speech, suggest she was poisoned by the santonin contained in the wormseed. Giuseppa Maria went on:

> The following day, I took another dose of the medicine. I felt exactly as I had done the day before; everything looked yellow. I was supposed to take the medicine eight times, but decided not to take it any more.
>
> A day later, I was still feeling bad, and when the doctor came, the mistress was occupied with something else. So I was able to describe my condition to him in person, and Doctor Marchi was astonished. He said this medicine was very mild, and could even be given to animals. It should not have any of these side-effects, and I should stop taking it. It also made me vomit, and I spewed up stuff that burned and caused ulcers in my mouth and throat.

But it didn't end with the murder of Maria Agostina. Maria Felice's death in the fall of 1859 can also be chalked up to Maria Luisa's account. She had been one of the vicaress's two main accomplices in the poisoning of the princess.[57] Once again, Maria Luisa prophesied the death through the usual letters from the Virgin to Padre Peters. She was clearly frightened the young nun would crack under pressure from the Inquisition, and reveal the whole poisoning plot. Once Maria Felice had been laid low by a mysterious illness, the novice mistress even forced her to pray for her own death. She was ordered to simulate pains she didn't have, so the doctors would keep letting her blood and gradually making her weaker. Maria Felice died from the results of this treatment, at barely twenty-two years old.

Maria Felice went far beyond the obedience that canon law dictates a novice must show to her mistress. Hers was a case of religiously motivated dependency, bordering on enslavement. She prayed for her own death and simulated symptoms she didn't have, in order to receive a treatment that would fatally weaken her. These are clear indications of a pathological religious mania. The basic tenet of the Roman Inquisition, as voiced by Sallua several times in the Sant'Ambrogio case files, obviously applied to the facts of Maria Felice's death: false religiousness leads to false morality. And in the worst-case scenario, feigned holiness leads to murder or manslaughter.

According to the testimonies of various nuns, Maria Luisa was also to blame for the death of Sister Maria Costanza in January 1858. Costanza had opposed the election of the young nun as novice mistress in 1854, and had also spoken out against Agnese Eletta's expulsion from Sant'Ambrogio. Maria Costanza suffered from a severe inflammation of the lungs. As her condition deteriorated, the nurse asked Maria Luisa to call a doctor immediately. But Maria Luisa refused several times. When Doctor Marchi finally arrived, the following day, it was too late. The doctor said: "If we had been called in time, we could have saved her. Now there is nothing more we can do." Maria Costanza died of pneumonia on January 23, 1858.

Maria Luisa was now responsible for the deaths of at least three nuns.

PENNIES FROM HEAVEN

Murder and manslaughter weren't the novice mistress's only crimes. There were also counts of embezzlement and other financial misdemeanors to add to the charges—and here, too, divine forces were supposedly at work. Sums of money were always turning up in Sant'Ambrogio in a miraculous manner.[58] In her hearing, Sister Maria Colomba reported Maria Luisa giving her money to take to Padre Peters, who was waiting in the parlor. It was for the payment of doctors' fees for Maria Giacinta. When Colomba went back to say she had completed her task, the novice mistress claimed she knew nothing about the money or the errand. Eventually Maria Luisa said it had probably been the mother founder herself, who had assumed Maria Luisa's form and given Maria Colomba the money. The abbess added that this had been a freshly minted gold coin worth 12 scudi. She preserved this coin as a gift from heaven, and settled the doctors' bill with used, earthly currency.

The mother founder took care of the convent's finances from heaven on several occasions. Once, the abbess received a letter from Maria Agnese Firrao sent "from paradise," the wax seal of which carried the "fingerprint of the Immaculate Virgin." The founder announced that Padre Peters would find money in the little casket that usually contained letters from heaven. The money had been sent from heaven by the late Maria Felice, to repay Sant'Ambrogio for the cost of her illness. And, in the presence of the novice mistress, the Jesuit did indeed open the box to find a roll of coins totalling 100 gold scudi, 50 scudini,[59] and 25 25-paoli pieces. There was also a note, on which was written: *"Alms sent by Maria Felice, in fulfillment of her promise to the Holy Daughter Maria Luisa."*

Twice during the renovation of the convent church, envelopes containing 50 scudi were discovered in the rota (the rotating hatch between the enclosure and the outer area). Following a long investigation by Sallua, the lawyer Franceschetti finally admitted obtaining rolls of 100 new gold scudi in exchange for used money, at Maria Luisa's behest.

Maria Luisa was fairly generous with the convent's money elsewhere, too—money for which she was responsible as the abbess's vicaress. The "heavenly rings," the rose oil, the handmade paper for the heavenly letters, and the valuable casket all had to be paid for. Padre Peters also received large sums on several occasions for penitents of his who found themselves in financial difficulties. Heavenly powers sent the Jesuit 570 scudi for one Vittoria Marchesi; another time it was as much as 700 gold scudi.

Maria Luisa was probably just misappropriating money from the nuns' dowries, which were laid down when they entered the convent, and formed the basis of the institution's wealth.

While Maria Luisa was in charge, the convent's accounts had fallen into chaos, as the lawyer Franceschetti (who was actually supposed to keep an eye on what she was doing), admitted in his hearing on September 12, 1860.[60]

Now I will say something on the administration of the convent of Sant'Ambrogio. As already mentioned, this is completely unlawful. Firstly, there is no general account for income and expenditure. They have a separate arrangement for certain deposits, which are not entered into the main book. Even for the listed deposits there are no receipts. This is particularly clear for the dowry sums— which is to say that these receipts are not specific, or rather, the amounts are not entered as deposits into the reserve assets. Some dowries are not listed at all.

In an attempt to exonerate himself, the lawyer came to the conclusion:

> As well as all these irregularities in the accounts, I have now realized that, unlike all other convents, the superiors here arrogated to themselves the privilege of free and independent administration. Only very recently have I been able . . . to recognize all this.

Sallua could have contented himself with proof of the murders and financial irregularities but, in conclusion to his *Relazione* for the cardinals of the Holy Office, he added a final *Titolo* on a matter that lay particularly close to his heart: the role of the two confessors.

THE CONFESSORS AS CONFIDANTS AND ACCOMPLICES

Casting a critical eye over the witness statements, the Dominican came to the conclusion that "sometimes one, sometimes the other, but often both father confessors were aware of all the criminal acts addressed in this trial."[61] They had been revealed as either "supporters" and confidants or, in some cases, "accomplices." The starting point for the countless crimes committed in Sant'Ambrogio was the false cult propagated with such enthusiasm by Leziroli and Peters. For Sallua, the fact that the two confessors were the "principal supporters of the holiness and the supposed gifts" of Maria Luisa could "clearly be seen from every hearing—one might almost say, from every page of the thirteen volumes of records in this trial."

Leziroli had even gone so far as to tell the abbess that he could "never call into question Maria Luisa's holiness, even if an angel were to tell him the opposite." And Peters said on several occasions that he had "the proof of Maria Luisa's extraordinary gifts and holiness in [his] possession." Collective coercion, for which the confessors were ultimately responsible, was part of the Sant'Ambrogio system. It was the huge pressure applied by Leziroli that got Maria Luisa elected as novice mistress and vicaress. And Padre Peters, in particular, encouraged the cult of contact relics. Such was his blind admiration for the beautiful young nun that, several times, he kissed her feet in public.

Both confessors were aware of the "intimacies and kisses" that Maria Luisa exchanged with various other sisters. They were also extremely careless with information the nuns gave them in confession, telling Maria Luisa afterward about "the penitents' confessions and states of mind." Many of the sisters were "always deeply troubled by this": the mistress frequently "spoke to them about what they had just told the priest in confession." Maria Fortunata made a point of this in her hearing: "The mistress would often mention to me a confession I had just made to Padre Peters. I said to her: 'Either you are eavesdropping on us, Reverend Mother, or Padre Peters has told you.'" Sallua argued that this proved the seal of the confessional had been habitually broken.

Both confessors were also mixed up in the poisoning affair. Maria Luisa had told them "verbally and in writing about the supposed divine revelations and commands regarding the princess's impending sickness and death." "The nuns also informed them of facts connected to the poisoning," as Sallua noted. As evidence for this, he cited the fact that the confessors asked "the doctors treating the princess whether a dose of opium, or some kind of mistake with the medicines, could have led to her illness." The Dominican referred once more to the testimony of the lawyer, Franceschetti, who said that Padre Peters knew the princess was being poisoned and told him "of this matter" from the beginning. Peters had also warned the lawyer about the upcoming hearings before the Inquisition, self-confidently claiming that "I will not be called before the Holy Office, since I am a confessor. But if I am questioned about the poisoning business, I will leave out many facts, citing reasons of conscience and the seal of the confessional."[62]

Leziroli, meanwhile, had forced the abbess to beg Maria Luisa's forgiveness for suspecting her of poisoning the princess. He also forced the two nurses who had observed the mixing of the poisons to give up their positions. In their hearings, the nuns also blamed the confessors for helping to conceive and implement Maria Luisa's defense strategy. They, too, had started claiming the devil had assumed her form to carry out the poisoning attacks. The confessors were also the first to proclaim that Maria Luisa had received "monies from heaven in a miraculous manner." And they openly incited the nuns to perjure themselves during the vicegerent's Visitation and the hearings before the Inquisition.

"As a result of the facts presented thus far," Sallua summarized, "it appears obvious that the above-named father confessors acted as confidants and accomplices in the majority of charges to be brought in the present trial."

THE RESULTS OF THE INFORMATIVE PROCESS

At the end of January 1861, after more than a year of intensive witness examinations, Sallua was finally in a position to summarize the results of the informative process. His *Relazione informativa* presented some clear suggestions on how to proceed in the case of Sant'Ambrogio.[63] But these decisions didn't fall to the lower, investigative section of the Inquisition: they would be made by the upper section of the Holy Office's tribunal, the congregation of cardinals, and, ultimately, the pope. They based their judgments on the extremely detailed *Relazione,* which included an appendix of extracts from the transcripts of the most important witness examinations.

The document in which the Dominican presented the case sticks very closely to the witness statements. His summaries follow the text of each testimony, even reproducing individual phrases. The material is arranged according to the three main charges (the cult of Firrao; the false holiness of Maria Luisa; poisonings and other crimes), and is further divided into a total of fourteen individual charges. On all points, Sallua emphasizes that the facts he is presenting are corroborated down to the smallest detail by the witness statements. The investigating judge's own opinion can only be read between the lines: the cardinals were to make their own judgment on the basis of the materials he had prepared.

It is only on the very last page of his *Relazione* that Sallua makes specific judgment suggestions to the congregation of cardinals—and not without once more emphasizing that "base" motives had played no part in the princess's complaint to the authorities. There had been no mutual enmity between the plaintiff and the defendant, Maria Luisa. Nor had there been any scores to settle between the nuns, Katharina von Hohenzollern, Maria Luisa, and the two confessors. The only motive for planning Katharina's murder was to keep the Sant'Ambrogio system a secret. In this case, there was no suggestion that the Inquisition was being abused in order to exact revenge. At the end of his report, the investigating judge suggested a series of measures to Their Eminences.

First: charges should be brought against the confessors Leziroli and Peters. They had promoted the false cult of Firrao and Maria Luisa; acted as confidants and accomplices in the poisonings and in other "false precepts"; they had carried out "blasphemous practices *sub specie boni et privilegii*" and "continually broken the *clausura*." In the case of Padre Peters, there was also a charge of sexual relations *"ad malum finem"* with his penitent Maria Luisa, and of *Sollicitatio*. Interestingly, there was no specific mention of breaking the seal of the confessional, although several witnesses had raised this more or less directly.

Second: charges should be brought against Abbess Maria Veronica for continual perjury and as an accomplice or at least a confidant in all the above-mentioned offenses.

Third: charges should be brought against Agnese Firrao's old companions, Sisters Maria Gertrude, Maria Caterina, and Maria Colomba, all now around seventy. They had "promoted her condemned holiness, immoral precepts and practices" as well as Maria Luisa's feigned holiness.

Fourth: the other nuns who had spoken for the holiness of Firrao and Maria Luisa should be considered "accomplices," although "some of them have revealed themselves to be more fanatical and obstinate than others." However, Sallua conceded that a number of the younger nuns and novices were "more led astray than spoiled, and actually had no ill intentions." The verger Maria Maddalena; the novice mistress's bedfellow Maria Giacinta; Maria Luisa's accomplice Maria Ignazia; the secretary and scribe of the heavenly letters Maria Francesca; the "poison expert" Agnese Celeste; the second nurse Giuseppa Maria; and Sister Maria Gesualda had all come to realize the scale of the "evil and the deceptions" over the course of their hearings, "and felt honest regret." They had won Sallua's respect with their brutal honesty and openness before the tribunal, and had obviously mollified him. And because of this, they had felt the wrath of the other, more stubborn nuns of Sant'Ambrogio. "They confided in us, saying they found themselves in constant danger." No charges should therefore be brought against them. But if the situation was not thoroughly redressed, Sallua argued, then Sant'Ambrogio would continue to operate just as it had done for the past fifty years.

On February 27, 1861, the congregation of cardinals met without the pope, and discussed the results of the informative process in detail, on the basis of the printed *Relazione*. The cardinals largely followed Sallua's suggestions. More specifically, they decided to bring charges against Abbess Maria Veronica, and to move her from Sant'Ambrogio to the convent of Santa Maria del Rifugio. The two confessors would also be charged, though at first neither of them should be suspended from their priestly offices. The Jesuit general should ensure that Peters and Leziroli couldn't communicate with each other, either in writing or verbally through middlemen. Beckx was also instructed to hand over every piece of writing that could possibly have a bearing on the Sant'Ambrogio case. The defendants were to be interrogated by the assessor, Raffaele Monaco La Valletta, together with the investigating judge, Sallua, and the fiscal, Antonio Bambozzi, supported by a substitute from the Holy Office's Chancellery.[64] Bambozzi's involvement came as a surprise: he had been fiscal from May 1841 until July 1851, before moving to the Secretariat of State and being replaced as fiscal by Giuseppe Primavera. The pope redeployed Bambozzi as fiscal specifically for the Sant'Ambrogio case.[65]

The pope's initial reservations about the validity of Katharina's *Denunzia* were set aside by Sallua's compelling body of evidence. The pope approved the decisions made by the congregation of cardinals the same day, adding that both confessors should have their right to take confession suspended with immediate effect. In a private audience with the assessor, Pius IX made him responsible for sending all the postulants and simple novices, who had not yet professed their vows, away from Sant'Ambrogio immediately. The pope formally gave the assessor, fiscal, and investigating judge the necessary authority to interrogate the defendants and conduct the rest of the trial.[66]

Sallua at once set out his suggestions for how the interrogations should be organized. The cardinals gave their unanimous agreement to them a week later, on March 6, 1861.[67] The course was set for the second phase of the Inquisition trial in the case of Sant'Ambrogio della Massima. The deciding authority, the tribunal's upper section, tasked the investigating authority with carrying out an offensive process, which would concentrate on the interrogation of the four principal defendants.

CHAPTER SIX

"It Is a Heavenly Liquor"

The Offensive Process and the Interrogation of the Madre Vicaria

"I ALWAYS WANTED TO BECOME A NUN"

Unlike the other three main defendants—the two confessors and the abbess—Sant'Ambrogio's vicaress and novice mistress, Sister Maria Luisa of Saint Francis Xavier, had been a suspect ever since the preliminary investigation. She was therefore removed from the convent on December 7, 1859, on the pope's orders, and transferred to the convent of Purificazione, near Santa Maria Maggiore.[1]

After Maria Luisa had spent more than three months there without hearing any news of the case, she became restless, and asked for a hearing before the Inquisition of her own accord. "Even after repeated examination of her conscience," she said, she had been able to find no reason for her "transfer." After consulting her confessor, she asked to make a "voluntary" appearance before the Holy Tribunal. And on March 20 and 26, 1860, Sallua gave her the chance to put forward her side of the story.[2]

The daughter of Domenico Ridolfi and Teresa Cioli, Maria Ridolfi had been born in 1832, in the parish of San Quirico in Rome.[3] The parish is in the Rione Monti, which, in the mid-nineteenth century, had a good twenty thousand inhabitants. Monti was one of Rome's poorest districts, and was home to a lot of the city's day-laborers, winegrowers, and market gardeners. Maria's father was a *ciambellaro*, selling pastries, which put him firmly in Rome's underclass.[4] As a child, Maria attended the Franciscan school, where she was taught the basics of reading, writing, and mathematics. She spent only a few years in school, however, as her mother died young, leaving Maria to take over the management of her father's household. Her two sisters, one older and one younger than herself, remained single, and in 1860 were still living in their father's house.

Maria soon tired of housework. "When I was about six years old, I took the *vow of chastity*, following an inspiration, and on the advice of a good old lady who has since died. Before I took this vow, on several occasions the above-mentioned old lady had taken me to see her father confessor in a church near Monte Cavallo, which can be reached via two staircases." This was the church of San Silvestro di Monte Cavallo, which today is called San Silvestro al Quirinale. The confessor there, whose name Maria Luisa couldn't remember, had advised her to take this step. "I took the eternal *vow of chastity* in that church on the Feast of the Madonna,[5] under the guidance of the above-mentioned old lady, Francesca Palazzi." Maria took her first Communion at the age of nine or ten, in San Quirico's parish church. After this, she developed a desire to do more than just live as a virgin dedicated to God "in the world." She wanted to enter a convent and become a nun. However, her confessor advised her to think very carefully about this decision.

When she was eleven or twelve, Maria made the acquaintance of Maddalena Salvati, the wife of Giacomo Salvati, who lived on the Campo Corleo. Giacomo worked closely with Vincenzo Pallotti (who was later canonized), and had founded a house for vulnerable young girls. The Pia Casa di Carità was housed in the building in Borgo Sant'Agata where Agnese Firrao's reformed Franciscans of the Third Order had originally been accommodated.[6] From her conversations with the Salvatis, it soon became apparent to Maria that the Ridolfis could never afford to place her in a convent. In order to be accepted into a nunnery in Rome at that time, an applicant had to provide evidence that she could contribute a dowry of at least 300–500 scudi. This sum was equivalent to the entire annual budget of a middle-class family in Rome. And as the Ridolfis had to get by on 70–100 Scudi a year, it would have been completely impossible for them to raise this amount. Maria's only hope was to find an upper-class or aristocratic patron to finance her dowry. Her last resort was the archconfraternity of Santissimo Rosario, which offered the annual prize of a dowry for a Roman girl from the lower classes.[7] Maria Ridolfi seems to have been successful in this. Having secured the money, all that remained was to find a suitable convent for her in Rome.

Maria then revealed her intentions to her family, who strongly opposed her decision to enter a convent. But with the help of her confessor, Monsignore Pastacaldi,[8] and Maddalena Salvati, whose apartment became Maria's second home, she finally obtained her father's permission. Maddalena Salvati introduced Maria to several convents, but they all rejected her for being too young. Finally, Mrs. Salvati took Maria Luisa to the convent of Sant'Ambrogio, where she was at least permitted to remain for a day. After pleading with the abbess, she was granted a second day there. This time, she spent most of the day locked in a room. It was only toward evening, when she wanted to leave, that the abbess told her she would have to prove herself. "Then she said that I should wait another year; but after a little while, she wrote to say I could spend that year in the convent. This was how I entered the convent, on April 21, at the age of 13." The year was 1845, and on June 22, 1846, Maria was duly clothed as a novice. After a year in the novitiate, she professed her vows, and took the religious name Maria Luisa.

The unrest in the city during the period of the Roman Republic (1848–1849) meant that the nuns had to leave Sant'Ambrogio and take refuge in the convent of Santi Quattro Coronati,[9] where they remained for almost a year.

After that, we went back to Sant'Ambrogio. While I was there, I held almost every office. In December 1854, I was elected novice mistress; three years later I was elected vicaress of the convent, and held the role of novice mistress together with this other office; I held these two offices until the day I was taken away from Sant'Ambrogio.

On the night of December 7, 1859 (following an announcement from the Monsignore Vicegerent to the Mother Abbess), at around half past twelve or one o'clock in the morning I had to go to the gatekeeper's parlor in Sant'Ambrogio, where I found Your Paternity. You told me to get into the coach; inside were a woman and a man I did not know. I was taken straight to the convent of Purificazione, and entrusted by Your Paternity to the care of the Mother Abbess there.

THE STORY OF AN INNOCENT LAMB

Maria Luisa made use of the four months between early December 1859 and the end of March 1860, while she was being held in the convent of Purificazione, to figure out her defense strategy. On March 20, she submitted an eighty-eight-page report to Sallua, set down in her own hand at the suggestion of her confessor.[10]

The mantra that ran through Maria Luisa's text was that, even after the most thorough examination of her conscience, she could find "no reason" for her removal from Sant'Ambrogio. However, she was evidently well aware of why she had been locked up, and of the fact that the Princess von Hohenzollern had made accusations against her. She therefore painted a picture of Katharina as a high-strung German noblewoman who had been ill at ease and required special care throughout her time in the convent.

First, Maria Luisa broached the subject of the scene in the choir, which the princess herself and various other witnesses had already described. Maria Luisa said that on December 8, 1858, Katharina had knelt before her with the belt of her habit around her neck. (This was confirmation that the "cord" really was the belt that held together the habit of the Franciscan order.) Maria Luisa knew that several of her fellow nuns had witnessed this incident, so she brought it up of her own accord. However, her account of what she and the princess had argued about was completely different from the testimonies of Katharina and the other nuns. Maria Luisa's story made no mention of the Americano's obscene letter as the catalyst for this scene. She claimed Katharina tried to "convert" her in a way that was totally incomprehensible to her. She really hadn't understood what the princess wanted from her. A few days later, Katharina had suffered a stroke or a syncopation of the brain—only, she claimed she was being poisoned. But this had simply been a product of her own fevered imagination.

Maria Luisa said she herself had never visited the princess's bedside during her illness, so there was no way she could have mixed anything into her food or drink. And if anyone claimed to have seen her there, they were either mistaken or they had seen the devil in her form.

Maria Luisa's strategy boiled down to portraying the princess as confused, if not mentally ill, and therefore unfit to testify. She gave a detailed account of all kinds of "mad" things the princess had done during that period. Katharina had apparently conducted a painstaking search "for a way to give her life to save the Holy Father." At this point, there were battles raging in Lombardy, and the possibility that Italian troops might take Rome and imprison Pius IX was much discussed.[11] Maria Luisa also described "certain letters that the princess wrote and sent to the Holy Father, in the name of two peasants. These contained warnings and accusations against the pope." She herself had received numerous "secret assignments" from Katharina—in particular, requests for various pieces of jewelry. For example, the princess asked her to have an "expensive bracelet" made. The task caused Maria Luisa some "difficulties and problems" due to the strict enclosure in Sant'Ambrogio. This was her attempt to explain how a poor daughter of Saint Francis of Assisi had come to be in contact with Roman goldsmiths—a connection arranged by the lawyer, Franceschetti. She had been trying to procure a bracelet for the princess, and not heavenly rings for herself.

Maria Luisa also complained at some length about a second nun: Agnese Eletta, her onetime bedfellow. It was her statement about lesbian practices in the convent that had really set the Inquisition trial in motion. The former vicaress characterized Agnese Eletta—who was, after all, the niece of the revered mother founder—as corruption personified, or possibly even a witch. Her description made use of nineteenth-century Church teaching on witches.[12] Coming to the convent at the age of just four, Agnese Eletta had "improper and blasphemous dealings with the devil since she was first able to reason." Several times she had spoken in detail of her contact with Satan, which lasted over thirty years. Coming to her "in the shape of a very dashing young man," the devil had whispered the "most obscene and repulsive words and intimacies" in her ear, and had "sated all her lusts." Her pact and her coupling with the devil had even been signed "with the blood of her monthly period."[13] With this compact, Agnese Eletta had signed her soul over to the devil for eternity. To please him, she had defiled "holy pictures and the crucifix," and even abused "the sacred Hosts." According to Catholic doctrine, Christ is literally present in the Host after it has been consecrated.[14] "She polluted them by putting them into her private parts, and other things."

Maria Luisa described Agnese Eletta "as a nun without a vocation," whose presence had been a singular "affliction" for the whole community. She herself had tried several times to release her from the devil. At first, she had some success: Agnese Eletta had made "a general confession of her whole life" to her, which was the source of all the information she was now giving to the court. After this, Agnese Eletta had been "virtuous and tractable," and had become one of her "trusted bosom friends." At this point, Maria Luisa wanted to have Agnese Eletta "with her at night as well."

This was the only reference to a possible sexual relationship between the two women. In March 1860, Maria Luisa wasn't prepared to say anything more; she had no way of knowing what Agnese Eletta had already said. In any case—according to Maria Luisa's statement—the conversion was only temporary. Agnese Eletta soon went back to her usual "deceits and villainies with the devil," and had even made "attempts to kill" the novice mistress. It was for this reason alone that she had been removed from Sant'Ambrogio.

Maria Luisa also provided a detailed exposé of Maria Agostina, another nun whose fate she had been responsible for. The novice mistress attributed Agostina's inexplicable sickness and premature death at the age of twenty-one to her pride, and the hubris of the claims she made about having visions and auditions of the mother founder. As the novice mistress, she had been responsible for Maria Agostina, and had to force her to confess these false pretenses and desist from her "tricks." But even after Agostina made her retraction in front of the community, things did not improve. This young nun, the bloom of life itself, had been carried off by Satan and destroyed. Padre Peters performed an exorcism on her, and clearly established that she was possessed by the devil. Hearing this, Agostina just murmured something barely intelligible, which Maria Luisa interpreted as: "Damned Agnese Eletta . . . I am finished." In the end it was either the devil, or Agnese Eletta, possessed by the devil, who had killed Maria Agostina—in any case, it certainly hadn't been Maria Luisa. That was the message Sallua was intended to take away from this.

The investigating judge's commentary was unambiguous. Sallua characterized Maria Luisa's eighty-eight-page text as "a sham of the cleverest and most sophisticated kind," in which the former novice mistress emphasized her own "modesty, patience, chastity, and also her extraordinary gifts from the Lord, and boast[ed] of herself as a brave soldier in the fight against the devil." He believed the entire report from cover to cover was "counterfeit, slanderous, and twist[ed] the truth." It was a systematic attempt to blame others for offenses that Maria Luisa had committed herself.

Sallua also regarded Maria Luisa's personality as pathological, from a religious point of view. The four months she had spent in the convent of Purificazione had, he realized, had almost no effect on her. At the end of her report, she even claimed she had experienced supernatural phenomena during this period of monastic imprisonment. The habit of styling herself as a saint was evidently too much ingrained for her to simply lay it aside like her convent robes. She said she had been "favored by the Lord in these dark days." He had appeared to her in her cell, "in the middle of a consecrated Host, in all His splendor," to comfort her. But the devil, too, had come several times to torment and beat her. He had "ripped her habit to shreds, spilled the ink on the paper she was writing on, and said to her: take that, you ugly witch! Here is the man who was driven out of Sant'Ambrogio . . . you are damned. Oh, welcome—you are the fallen ambrosial giant, the dirty ermine. Victory! Take that, this is for you . . . go, go and preach . . . die a miserable death, take that, go to your damned brothers and tell them, and prepare yourself: it is my will that you should face a trial, which goes from earth to heaven."

The meaning of these cryptic phrases is not immediately obvious. Saint Ambrose, for whom the convent was named, stands for erudition and the courage to stand up for the Church. The ermine, which is white in winter, is a symbol of purity and innocence on the one hand, and of royal majesty on the other. The devil is delighted with Maria Luisa's tainted innocence; she is the fallen giant of Sant'Ambrogio. Her undeserved situation and the Inquisition's unjust accusations against her are ultimately the work of the devil—this is Maria Luisa's message to her judges.

By the end of April 1860, Sallua was convinced that the former vicaress and novice mistress was the main culprit for the whole affair. His submission to the Holy Office's congregation of cardinals was immediately successful: on May 2, 1860, the cardinals acted on his suggestion without further ado, and decreed that Maria Luisa should stand trial. With the utmost secrecy, she was transferred from the convent of Purificazione to the jail of Buon Pastore.[15]

Maria Luisa's interrogation began on June 11, 1860, and lasted until November 12, 1861. The Inquisition also examined other witnesses during this period. As was the custom in all Inquisition trials, Maria Luisa had an initial opportunity to give her side of the story. In her first interrogation she was asked if she knew, or could guess, why she had been arraigned before the tribunal.[16]

Once again, Maria Luisa said she suspected that Agnese Eletta and Katharina von Hohenzollern might have slandered her. She also said the Jesuit padres Leziroli, Benedetti, and Paolo Mignardi[17] could have played some role in having charges brought against her. "Padre Leziroli because, in his naivety, he may have gotten mixed up about the extraordinary things; Padre Benedetti, because he claimed that the late sister Maria Agostina had an extraordinary soul and was a saint; Padre Mignardi, because he said that there was a nun who ruled over Sant'Ambrogio." Here, Maria Luisa was alluding to herself as Sant'Ambrogio's Reverend Mother. "I also suspect that Sister Maria Giuseppa . . . might have spoken about me disrespectfully." When she was probed on this point, Maria Luisa declared these women to be her "enemies," who wished her nothing but ill. Finally, she named the convent's estate manager, Pietro Bartolini, and her confessor, Padre Peters, as possible adversaries—the last of these on the grounds that he hadn't wanted her to devote her energies to the convent as she did.

The following day, Maria Luisa volunteered information on the main charges she suspected had been raised against her.[18] She started with her lesbian relationships, which, in contrast to the statement she had made in March, she now addressed openly. However, she placed the blame on Agnese Eletta, saying that when she had been a girl of twelve or thirteen, Agnese Eletta forced her to perform acts she found deeply repellent. As soon as Maria Luisa arrived in Sant'Ambrogio, she said, the older nun had come to her and examined her private parts. Eletta claimed her aunt, the mother founder, had given her "the privilege" of "imparting chastity by this means." This had led to "immodest acts."

Maria Luisa then told an entirely new story about the origin of her visions, saying she had been trying to protect herself from Agnese Eletta's sexual predilections. "I began to conceive of some dreams in which the late abbess told me what was necessary to prevent such wrongdoing." Maria Luisa told Padre Leziroli about these "dreams" in confession, and he "believed in them, treating them as if they were visions and revelations." The abbess at the time, Agnese Celeste della Croce, was likewise convinced that they were genuine. Still, at least this meant Maria Luisa was able to keep Agnese Eletta at a distance for a little while. As she was undertaking the spiritual exercises in preparation for professing her vows, she told Padre Leziroli during confession that all the visions were her "inventions," "and not true things." But the confessor dismissed this as an expression of her "scruples and modesty," and cleaved to the authenticity of the visions against her wishes. Maria Luisa also told the extraordinary confessor, Padre Peters, that she had only been pretending. He praised her "spirited manner" and forgave the offense. But he said that she must use "such stratagems only in extreme cases."

Maria Luisa distanced herself from the false cult of the founder, Maria Agnese Firrao. She tried to convince the court that she had only invented her visions in order to help her combat the false cult of Firrao: an attempt to present herself as the Inquisition's enthusiastic ally. It had been her aim, she said, to get Sant'Ambrogio to recognize the 1816 verdict. Everything she did was done to achieve this end— even taking over the role of novice mistress. That way, at least she could try to immunize the convent's younger generation against the dangerous Firrao virus.

Maria Luisa claimed that at Christmas 1854, when a "secret procession" was due to take place in honor of Maria Agnese, she had invented "one of the usual dreams." Her goal was to prevent this procession, and influence the elections for abbess, vicaress, and the other offices as she wished. With the help of another vision, foretelling that Cardinal Protector Patrizi would be poisoned if he didn't come to the convent for the election, Leziroli finally managed to draw the cardinal to Sant'Ambrogio. "The cardinal came, and everything was done according to my dream."

In her interrogation on June 13, 1860, the defendant steered the subject back to the case of the late Maria Agostina and her supposed visions. Maria Luisa said she had fought against these from the start, believing them to be deceptions.[19] "The abbess, the nuns and Padre Benedetti believed in them. They annoyed me tremendously. I was the only one who did not believe in the visions." On several occasions, Benedetti used his sermons to criticize an "arrogant soul" in the convent, who harped on about her own holiness, but refused to acknowledge that of another. "I was well aware that Padre Benedetti was aiming this speech at me." With the help of more visions, she managed to get the Jesuit general to remove Benedetti from his position as confessor. After this, she could do as she pleased with Maria Agostina. When the latter carried on talking about the mother founder, and the founder's ring that had healed her, "I decided not to invent any more dreams, because they weighed on my conscience. Instead, I would wear a ring, to expose her illusions and make her confess." She got the first heavenly ring from the statue of the Madonna in the choir: "I took the ring she wore on her finger, which looked like a little rose with a small red gemstone in the middle."

In fact, the ring brought her immense power in the convent.[20] "Bigot young women" who thought they were something special were refused entry to the novitiate, supposedly on the mother founder's orders. Those who had already been taken in were now removed. But the ring also helped her discipline more seasoned nuns. "Using the ring, I made all kinds of revelations, in order to keep them in check."

Maria Luisa also continued to portray Katharina von Hohenzollern as deranged—a strategy she had begun to adopt in March. On June 14, she flatly denied ever having given the princess an obscene letter in German—the Americano's obscene letter. This had all been a figment of Katharina's imagination. When Katharina continued to talk nonsense, Maria Luisa even sent for the princess's spiritual guide, Cardinal Reisach, and begged him to exert his influence on her. The cardinal had managed to calm the princess temporarily. Reisach told her Katharina was to be pitied: her nerves were in a terrible state. Her life's many sufferings had filled her head with fanciful ideas.

It would have been quite surprising for a high-ranking cardinal of the Curia to hurry to the convent at the request of a mere vicaress, and to discuss his charge's mental state with her in rather disrespectful terms. This would mean that there must have been a very close bond of trust between Maria Luisa and the cardinal. How could this have come about? Perhaps Maria Luisa was talking up her acquaintance with Reisach to give the Inquisition the impression that she was already on a firm footing with one of the cardinal inquisitors, Sallua's superior. Her subtext here was: watch out! The cardinal is keeping an eye on you. The reference may have been a tactical maneuver—but perhaps there was more to it than this.

Cardinal Reisach had a pronounced weakness for women with mystical gifts, and frequently took their visions and auditions to be the real thing. Even while he was still the archbishop of Munich and Freising, he had been an eager follower of the stigmatized seer Louise Beck[21] in Altötting. She passed on messages from the Virgin and the "poor souls" to the people of the world. These "poor souls" were people who had died and remained in purgatory, awaiting final redemption. In the nineteenth century, a lot of Catholics believed they would be able to send messages to the living once they had passed on, either telling them to pray for their salvation from the purifying flames, or warning them of sinful behavior. The spirit of Juliane Bruchmann, the late wife of the Redemptorists' provincial, acted as mediator between the Virgin Mary and Louise Beck.[22] Her spirit, or soul, was known as the "mother," while Louise Beck was the "child." Beck's followers, who had to subordinate themselves entirely to this "higher guidance," were known as "children of the mother." Many of the Redemptorists, and believers outside the order, followed the cult. Reisach, too, became a child of the mother in 1848. Following a lifetime confession, he had fallen under Louise Beck's religious spell. Is it not plausible, then, that after Reisach had moved to Rome in 1855, Maria Luisa had taken the place of Louise Beck, and he had found a new saint to follow?

After mentioning Reisach, Maria Luisa brought the subject back to the princess's sudden illness, starting with the scene in the choir on December 8, which she claimed was still incomprehensible to her. Maria Luisa gave the following version of events:

Katharina: "Take pity on your soul; say yes to what I am saying."
I replied: "Are you not well? Stay calm."
And she: "No! You must answer yes, for the love of Jesus Christ and the Madonna. I have prayed so hard for you—convert! I won't say anything; I am fond of you," and countless other things of this sort.
I told her she should not upset herself, and asked what I should

As a cardinal member of the Inquisition and a confidant of the pope, Cardinal Reisach was able to intervene in the trial at any point.

do. In the middle of this conversation I was called away, and the scene was ended.

The "violence of this act" caused Katharina to suffer a stroke two or three days later. The whole poisoning business had been nothing more than the imaginings of a sick mind—and perhaps also a result of the stroke, which had caused severe damage to the princess's brain. Maria Luisa also claimed that Katharina's exit from Sant'Ambrogio had gone without a hitch. Nobody put any kind of obstacle in the princess's way. When he came to collect Katharina, her cousin Hohenlohe told Maria Luisa the princess was so upset at the death of her young relative (the queen of Portugal) that he now had to take her to his country villa in Tivoli. However, both she and the abbess feared that when she left, the confused princess might try to pin something on them in connection with the cult of the mother founder.

In an attempt to ward off this accusation, Maria Luisa consistently tried to shift the blame for this cult, which she called "fanciful," onto Padre Leziroli.[23] She said that he alone had been responsible for the veneration of the mother founder's relics: her hair, a tooth, numerous items of clothing, scourges, writings, and letters had been treated as relics in Sant'Ambrogio. Leziroli had also written a saint's life of Firrao. He had sermonized about her constantly, and included her as a saint in the liturgy. He had believed her writings to be the product of divine inspiration, and the nuns always called him "the Mother's vicar." Maria Luisa's own attempts to put a stop to this false cult had, alas, been in vain.

In her interrogations throughout the first half of June, Maria Luisa also distanced herself from any responsibility for the policy of secrecy that the visitators and inquisitors had encountered at every turn in Sant'Ambrogio. She claimed that the confessors and the abbess were solely to blame for the nuns having hidden (and in some cases destroyed) the mother founder's writings, Leziroli's saint's life, and texts by the Jesuit Giuseppe Pignatelli. The abbess also told her she had no need to fear the Visitation: "We will have to bear the burden, if they keep coming back. We will do as they ask; I will say yes and no, as they wish, and this virtue will see us victorious."

Maria Luisa repeatedly told the court she was ready to beg for forgiveness, while at the same time making it very clear she had done all this because she believed "neither in the mother founder nor in her cult." She was just doing everything she could to stop the nuns venerating a false saint. As she couldn't display her opposition to this openly in Sant'Ambrogio, she had proceeded with extreme caution, "but not in order to claim holiness or anything else for herself." It had simply been necessary to act as she had done, "to provide a remedy for this sickness."

Just as in March 1860, the Dominican Sallua remained unconvinced by Maria Luisa's account of events in Sant'Ambrogio: "She began to speak about the main charges *ex se*; she reported every incident and conversation in a way that was favorable to her, and did not correspond to the truth of the witness hearings," he told the cardinals in his *Ristretto*.[24]

EVIDENCE AND FIRST CONFESSIONS

During her first interrogations, Maria Luisa denied all guilt. Now Sallua began to confront her with the evidence and the witness statements; now the investigating court started calling the shots. Its task was to prove the charges that had been formulated during the informative process, point by point. Ideally, this would be topped off with a confession from the defendant.

Over the course of several days, the investigating court gave Maria Luisa a series of "harsh warnings" as it confronted her with witness statements that corroborated each other in detail. Only then, during the month of June, did she gradually begin to confess her responsibility for the offenses with which she had been charged.[25] Still, her confessions remained incomplete, and her statements often contradicted each other.

Her first admission concerned her participation in the cult of Firrao. In her interrogation on June 24, 1860, she said:[26] "I freely confess that I supported and spread the veneration and the cult of the mother founder in various ways, and through various pretenses." But, at least to begin with, she had only been doing what was required of the nuns, as they had been instructed by the confessors—in particular, Padre Leziroli. Everyone in Sant'Ambrogio had joined in the "adoration" and "glorification" of Maria Agnese Firrao. She herself had only gone along with all these "deceptions" because she didn't know any better: ever since she was young, since she entered the convent, this was all she had learned from the example of the older nuns and superiors, and the readings from the founder's texts.

Maria Luisa was also finally prepared to confess to her own pretense of holiness. "Not just with my tongue, but with my heart I confess that I feigned all these things." She said she had been motivated by "pride." She wanted to appear "favored by the Lord" in order to gain power, so that she, too, would be venerated within Sant'Ambrogio.

The inquisitors were particularly interested in the practice of confession in Sant'Ambrogio. When questioned, Maria Luisa admitted forcing the novices to make a detailed confession of all their sins before they entered the convent, especially their "dishonesties"—by which she especially meant their sexual transgressions. She also made the novices confess to her before their weekly confession, and then told them what they could and couldn't say to the father confessor. And she had dispensed absolution. For this, the novices had to fall to their knees as she "gave them the blessing, assigned a penance and let them take Communion." She used the "information" gleaned from these confessions to steer individual nuns in whatever direction she thought best. "It is true that the father confessors Peters and Leziroli imparted to me what they had heard from the novices and some of the nuns in confession."[27] This proved to the investigating court that the seal of the confessional had been continually broken, via "intimate communication" between Maria Luisa and the confessors.

Maria Luisa then confessed to the financial misdemenors of which she had been accused. She had embezzled the "money from heaven" from the nuns' dowries. She had also failed to observe fast days and other Church commandments, such as the obligatory Liturgy of the Hours. She admitted to having a relationship with the Americano, though without making it clear exactly how far this relationship had gone. Kreuzburg, she said, came to the parlatory every day, and wrote her a letter after each meeting. These letters were very muddled. He was unable to believe that "one day, once he had been released from the devil, he could become a Jesuit." He kept giving in to the "vice of dishonesty." "He went to the Pincio, where he met women and sinned with them." In several of his letters, he wrote "that we nuns tended toward this same vice; that even we harbored unclean desires. Once he even made one of these claims about me personally."

MARIA LUISA AND HER NOVICES

On June 21, 1860, Maria Luisa was questioned about the lesbian practices and initiation rites in Sant'Ambrogio.[28] Before giving her testimony, she wept bitter tears, and knelt in humility to beg for forgiveness for what she now had to describe. "As I said yesterday evening towards the end of the hearing, I want to confess all the wicked deeds I committed. When Agnese Eletta was still in Sant'Ambrogio, after her so-called conversion, I began to allow myself deceitful intimacies with her, in that I studied her private parts very closely with my eyes, and also touched them with my hands."

Then she explained how she had happened upon the idea of "these villainies":

When we were taken to Santi Quattro Coronati, at the time of the Republic, the nuns' most important task was to rescue and take with them the writings of the mother founder, and her father confessors and spiritual guides. I was given three large bundles; I read some of them, and found the following instructions from the mother founder to Sister Maria Maddalena: she said she entrusted her daughters to her. Maddalena must consider how much her daughters had cost her; Maria Agnese had paid for them with her spirit and her body, since she had nourished them with her milk. Maddalena should always keep in mind that nuns who entered the convent at an advanced age and knew something of the world should be examined and purified.

But what sort of purification was this?

I asked the late Sister Maria Crocifissa, who was then vicaress. By and by, under the seal of secrecy, she told me how these things were done. She said that Sister Maria Maddalena entered the convent because the mother founder had called her in an extraordinary way. As she was of an advanced age, and had knowledge of worldly matters, the founder examined and purified her through touching various parts of her body with her own.

So that I might better understand how this worked, Maria Crocifissa gave me the example of Elijah,[29] saying, "Just as Elijah laid himself over the child, causing warmth to enter his body and bring him back to life, so God gave the mother founder the gift of being able to impart her virtue, her spirit, her purity, by laying herself over a nun. She would examine the nun and made the sign of the cross in her private parts, to purify her. And as she did this she filled her with a special liquor."

I recall reading in the letters from the mother founder that she also recommended Maria Maddalena should carry out this purification. With regard to the late Maria Giuseppa, who entered the convent at an advanced age, she told Maddalena to treat her at least once a week in this way. So I imagine that those of the older nuns who are still living also know of this—at least Sister Maria Caterina and Sister Maria Gertrude. They have told me many times of the slander against the late Sister Maria Maddalena during the Holy Office's trial, where she was accused of dishonest and terrible things. After the trial, some people painted satirical verses under the window of the convent. She suffered very much from the slander. . . .

I confess that, being steeped in these precepts, I committed the acts I have described with Agnese Eletta.

I also committed the same deceitful acts with Sister Maria Giacinta as I had with Agnese Eletta, and although these did not go as
far as with Agnese Eletta, they were more frequent and lasted longer. But with this nun there were no visions or strange occurrences.

I have spoken of these disgraces, and let me say that in
Sant'Ambrogio, where things have always been this way, it will
be impossible to stamp out these precepts and practices, because
they are rooted in the holiness of the mother founder. As long as
there is the vaguest memory of her, this depravity will remain in
Sant'Ambrogio.

According to Maria Luisa's testimony there was a tradition going back
to Agnese Firrao, of Sant'Ambrogio's abbess performing lesbian initiation rites with each new entrant to the convent—particularly if they
were already sexually experienced. Sallua must have been delighted
with this testimony, particularly as it supported his historical reconstruction of the original case against Firrao. Sexual intercourse had
taken place, under the pretext of purifying the novices' sexual organs,
during which vaginal fluid—the "liquor"—was exchanged. The requirements for the offense of female sodomy were thus fulfilled. As the
vicaress and novice mistress, Maria Luisa was a senior nun, and she
therefore engaged in this element of Firrao's "reform program" as a
matter of course. She believed that sexual purification was one of the
essential features of the Regulated Third Order of Holy Saint Francis
at Sant'Ambrogio, independently of the specific people involved.

This argumentation, however, didn't completely convince the tribunal. The mention of Maria Maddalena's sexual practices, which
were so widely known in the city that ordinary people had written
rude verses about them on the convent wall, set the inquisitors thinking. After all, Maria Luisa had entered the convent under the aegis of
this abbess. Was her induction to these practices really just theoretical?

SEXUAL ABUSE

On July 20, 1860, Maria Luisa was finally ready to tell the whole
truth.[30]

When I was in the convent of Santi Quattro Coronati, I received the writings of the mother founder and her spiritual guides to keep safe. When I read these, I came across descriptions that she had given to her father confessor. She said the Lord had appeared to her and entrusted the institute to her, with the solemn injunction to oversee the keeping of the vows, and chastity most of all. For this purpose the Lord had filled her with a liquor. He had poured this over her person and left it with her, so that she could use it to purify her daughters and make them holy, particularly those who had entered the convent as adults or had already sinned in their worldly lives.

I read about this matter in various letters; in two of these the mother founder said she had twice seen this liquor flowing from the mouth and from the ribs of the Lord, and had used it to purify Mother Maddalena. Thus the Lord had chosen Mother Maddalena to replace the founder in the institute. I also read letters from the founder to Maria Maddalena, where she urged her to oversee and carry out this command from the Lord. Elijah was mentioned in these letters, as I said before.

In another letter, the mother founder told her father confessor that she lacked feeling, and said that the Lord no longer appeared to her. She also said she had to take in a particular lady from Venice, who was given the name Sister Maria Giuseppa. She must be purified. The Virgin Mary appeared to her five times, and five times she allowed the founder to suck at her breast, to draw out the liquor which the founder must then use to purify Maria Giuseppa. She spoke of five times, because the name Maria has five letters.

I confess that with Maria Giacinta, I performed the same acts the mother founder said she had performed with the Madonna.

Now the purification of the sexual organs of newly veiled nuns had acquired a Mariological dimension. The nuns linked the act of suckling at the breast to *Maria Lactans*, a widespread image from the mysticism and piety of the Middle Ages, showing the Mother of God feeding the faithful with milk from her breasts.[31]

Maria Luisa was keen to bring the matter to a close with this statement, but the inquisitors now pressed her to testify in full. Only after being severely reprimanded was she finally prepared to do this.

I entered the convent of Sant'Ambrogio at the age of 13 or 14. The abbess at the time was Maria Maddalena; she lived from that April until Christmas, when she died. During those months I was the only postulant in the convent (apart from one who only stayed a very short time), so I had the attention and the affection of the old lady all to myself. The mother abbess gave me special affection and attention; she wanted to have me in the cell next to hers, and kept me in her company almost the whole day. She was constantly instructing me on the virtues and the philosophy of the institute, and speaking of the persecution and the holiness of the mother founder. She called me "her little lamb," "her treasure"; she kissed and embraced me. She was very strict, when she taught me humility and decorum, saying that one day I should be like her. Her attention and the affection she showed me were so great that some of the nuns grew jealous and told me how lucky I was, for they were hardly permitted to exchange even a few words with the abbess.

A few months later ... I was called by the late vicaress, Sister Maria Crocifissa ... after lunch. She told me that the mother abbess wanted to give me a gift. She sent me into the abbess's bedroom; she was lying on the bed in a swoon.

Maria Crocifissa said to me: "See how the mother abbess hides her virtue and her holiness? She lets the nuns believe that she wants to rest, but really she is sunk in prayer. Now she is illuminated by the Lord, who allows her to comprehend all manner of things, and see into people's hearts; this is why she can speak so well of virtue. Do you see? The way her face is so enflamed is a sign of God's love."

She made me go nearer to the bed and kiss her hand. Then she began to undress the abbess completely and to touch her in her private parts with her hands. She showed me a white liquid that appeared as she did so, saying: "This is a heavenly liquor, imparted to her by the Lord."

She also told me that if I loved the abbess and was her little lamb, I must take heed to steal this liquor from her, so I could become like her. She made me bend my head down to the abbess's private parts. I was gripped by fear and showed my disgust, saying: "and what if she then throws me out?"

Maria Crocifissa replied: "On the contrary, afterwards you can be sure she will not expel you, because this is a precious gift for you, which the Lord has commanded her to bestow."

She then bade me lick this liquid with my tongue. She took my hand and made me dip my fingers in this liquid, with which I had to make three signs of the cross on my forehead and lips with my own hand. Then she signed herself in the way I have described, and laid her head on Maria Maddalena's private parts. Then she covered her up and we walked away slowly, but the abbess, Maria Maddalena, called to me, and I went back to her bed. Maria Crocifissa went away and left me alone with her.

The abbess started saying, very lovingly: "Little thief of my heart, come here, what have you stolen from me? I know everything."

I trembled, expecting a terrible scolding, but she got up and sat on the bed. She embraced me and said that I should have no fear, because what I had done was the will of God, and the Lord had given me a great gift. But this was only the beginning, and she had received the command to give this gift fully. She held me in her arms and spoke at length to me, with tender words; then she got out of bed and, invoking the obedience due to her, demanded that I lie down. In the meantime, she made signs with her hands and eyes towards heaven, as one might in prayer. Finally she got into bed too, undressed me and laid herself on me, and touched me in a shameful way with her hands. Through vigorous movements of her body on mine, the liquid from her private parts flowed into mine, which afterwards felt quite moist.

She said to me several times: "My daughter, receive . . . this heavenly liquor."

After some time she got up. She had performed this act several times and rested a little in between. She asked what I was thinking, and said that I should have no fear: this was not a sin, but a holy thing and a gift from God. She also said that to the world these were wicked acts, but they had been commanded by the Lord as a gift for me.

After the last of these acts she remained in bed; I knelt beside her, and she laid her hands on my head; with the tone of a mother superior she said to me: "Daughter, you have received a great gift; in the name of God I command you to safeguard and to propagate it. Every evening you must put a finger into your private parts and then make the sign of the cross with your damp finger on your forehead and lips. In this way many gifts of God will be imparted to you."

Then she blew three times into my mouth. Finally, as she continued her affectionate expressions and embraces, she asked me to take her breast in my mouth and suckle on it, which I did. The last thing she did was to lay a veil of secrecy over everything: under no circumstances was I to speak about this to anyone.

Later, she asked me about my prayers, and also whether I was practicing every evening the things she had taught me. She said I should be sure not to speak to the father confessor, Padre Leziroli, about it: one had only to confess sins, and not gifts. These were special gifts that the Lord had bestowed upon me through her, which would benefit the institute, as I would see later.

Sister Maria Crocifissa was the one who had introduced me to these acts with the abbess, and so when I read the letters from the mother founder and her spiritual guides, which I was to keep safe in the convent of Santi Quattro Coronati, it was to her that I turned for explanation, as stated elsewhere.

The above-named abbess wanted to hear about the whole of my previous life and the things that had happened to me. Then she advised me what I should say to the father confessor. When I had been to confession, she demanded an account of what I had said to the father confessor. This is the system that was used in Sant'Ambrogio, and I myself practiced it with the novices.

I do not know whether the abbess did what I have reported above with other nuns; it might have happened with the late Sister Maria Metilde, because I could see that they were very close.

As soon as the abbess died, I made use of what she had taught me and, although I was still a novice, I tried to behave like a mother superior. I invented revelations and commands from the abbess. I made Sister Anna submit to me, and forced her to give me an account of her conscience every evening—then I blessed her with my scapular. Now I remember that, after doing the things I have spoken of, Abbess Maria Maddalena kept me with her on my own and, as well as the usual instructions, took my hand and put it into her private parts seven or eight times. Afterwards she told me to make the sign of the cross, so that I might receive gifts.

Maria Luisa now retracted her earlier accusations against Agnese Eletta. It hadn't been Agnese Eletta wanting her to touch her private parts—it was she, Maria Luisa, who had forced Eletta to perform the sexual acts she had described. She confirmed "under sacred oath" that everything she had said about her introduction to the practice of sexual purification at the hands of Mother Maria Maddalena was true. The young novice mistress was therefore clearly to blame for the "moral deviance" and "acts of sodomy" that had taken place later, as the investigating judges recorded in the *Ristretto*.

A young girl was required to perform sexual acts by her superior, the abbess. Later, the former victim, Maria Luisa, became a perpetrator herself. By engaging in the homosexual acts she used to bless, purify, and heal her partners, she was following a "sacred" tradition that had begun with Agnese Firrao, and had been upheld by the subsequent leaders of Sant'Ambrogio's community, ending with Maria Luisa. This tradition spanned more than six decades and, according to the mother founder's instructions, must not be interrupted.

In the nineteenth century, sexual relationships among monks and nuns, and between confessors and penitents, were a commonplace in anticlerical literature, which drew a connection between celibate lifestyle, religious mania, and sexual deviance.[32] The difficulty of the source material makes it impossible to clarify the extent to which these clichés may have had a basis in reality. But in today's terminology, what went on in Sant'Ambrogio constituted sexual abuse. The preconditions for this, generally speaking, are an imbalance of power.[33] Perpetrators usually use sexual abuse to satisfy both their own sexual needs and their need for power and recognition. In this sense, Maria Luisa seems to have achieved a great deal, playing on her winning personality and her sexual attractiveness. Abuse is often preceded by a special devotion to the abuser.[34] But this doesn't mean her victims consented to sexual acts with "knowledge, willingness and competence."[35] The novices were duty bound to obey the novice mistress and vicaress. For many of them, the madre vicaria was an ersatz mother, and Maria Luisa systematically exploited their emotional dependency. She also used secrets from the confessional to manipulate her opponents, and render her victims submissive. Maria Luisa further increased her power by bringing the confessors under her control: the nuns had to view their instructions as absolutely binding. She also swore those who participated in these acts to absolute secrecy: nobody on the outside must ever learn of them, not even the confessor—particularly not him!—or the heavenly blessing would lose its unique, holy quality. This way, she succeeded in committing the nuns to keep absolute silence. Swearing victims to secrecy and threatening dire consequences if they tell is another typical marker of sexual abuse.[36]

The crucial factor, however, was the religious authority that Maria Luisa assumed. She gave her behavior a religious elevation by claiming it was the will of God. Speaking out against Maria Luisa's revelations wouldn't just have been a rebellion against the commandment of obedience, but against the heavenly powers, and ultimately against the will of God. The nuns and the confessors would have been risking their immortal souls, the salvation of which was the true goal of their earthly existence. To the people who received letters from the Virgin Mary, the threats these letters contained were real and existential. This fear allowed Maria Luisa to disguise her crimes and moral misdemeanors as spiritual and medical treatment or, just as easily, as the work of the devil. The nuns' faith in the sacred led them to allow Maria Luisa to abuse them.

On the one hand, the nuns of Sant'Ambrogio weren't really able to speak about sexuality, as it could play no part in a life dedicated to God—but on the other, they honored numerous saints whose mystical experiences were described using metaphors of love and eroticism. In this milieu, it may not have seemed at all strange to interpret what they felt during an exchange of intimacies as a sanctifying spiritual experience, rather than forbidden lust. During their hearings, many of the nuns brought up the fact that they felt ashamed and guilty about undressing for the doctor. This speaks for the likelihood of a cloistered upbringing leading to an immature form of sexuality. In the insular environment of Sant'Ambrogio (which was what sociologists would call a "total institution")[37] there was nothing to correct the worldview its nuns all shared. The confessors and Patrizi had completely failed in their duties as supervisory authorities, not least because their own piety followed the same popular trends as that of Sant'Ambrogio's nuns.

Maria Luisa also admitted to the other endearments and "improper intimacies and practices" mentioned by numerous witnesses. She admitted all the "obscene acts" that had taken place during her tenure as novice mistress, which the court put to her *per singolo* (case by case) from the transcripts of the novices' hearings. She did, however, attempt to give at least some excuse for her behavior, by claiming that many of the novices had "shown her an exaggerated love." They had fussed around her constantly, repeatedly embracing her, "one kissing her shoulder, another her breast, a third her arm." At first, she had only reacted to these professions of love, but this had only caused them to escalate.

Maria Luisa also admitted to a custom she had introduced as novice mistress, whereby the night before they professed their vows, novices would sleep with her in her cell. On those nights, "two beds were made into one." After the novices lay down, she pretended to have spiritual conversations—sometimes with God, sometimes with the Virgin—in which these heavenly figures gave her various commands. At this, the novices would begin kissing and caressing her. Abbess Maria Veronica had been well aware of this. She had even told her to "let them do it." Once, she allegedly helped to push the beds together in Maria Luisa's cell.

The investigating judges found the descriptions of sexual practices and Maria Luisa's abuse so shocking that they omitted their own summary and a full commentary on this statement from the *Ristretto*. They twice referred the cardinals to the "shameless and obscene deeds," "excesses and disgusting offences," and "perverse precepts"—as they termed the homosexual acts—described in the transcripts of the hearings, which were attached to their report. The "Most Reverend Judges" were simply advised to read these statements for themselves.

JESUIT CONFESSORS AND THEIR VERY SPECIAL BLESSING

Now the court turned its attention to Maria Luisa's father confessor. However, before she addressed her special relationship with Padre Peters, the former madre vicaria wanted to put it into context. In order to understand what had happened between Maria Luisa and Padre Peters, the inquisitors first had to hear about another of Sant'Ambrogio's secrets: the Jesuit blessing. She revealed this to the Inquisition on June 26, 1860.[38]

In the old writings of the mother founder and her first companions . . . I read the following: so that the convent would not fall into the hands of the Holy Office again, as had happened to the mother founder, and to preserve the spirit of the institute that she had founded with advice and guidance from Padre Pignatelli, it turned out to be necessary always to have a Jesuit father confessor. (The mother founder had always had Jesuits as spiritual guides, and wanted to retain their spirit.) He must instill the Jesuit spirit into the nuns of our institute, and could thereby awaken extraordinary things. . . .

Agnese Firrao had sworn her community into a very special practice, saying: "My daughters, if you do this, you will preserve the institute. You know how much it costs—if you do not do it, you will be ruined."

As proof of this, I can tell you what the late sisters Maria Crocifissa and Maria Francesca confided to me. They said Padres Marconi, Doz[39] and Santinelli[40] had instilled the spirit of the Mother, and God's spirit, in Mother Maria Maddalena by a unique method. This spirit was then also instilled in Teresa Maddalena.

The spirit is instilled in the following way: the father confessor kisses the penitent on the forehead, the face and the lips; then he makes the sign of the cross on her throat with his tongue. Sometimes he puts his tongue into the penitent's mouth and kisses her on the heart, on the side where we usually have the crucifix. Before these acts are begun, the penitent nun falls on her knees before the father confessor, who remains standing. He gives her the blessing, using the words that I have written down. Sometimes during the aforementioned blessing, the nun falls into ecstasies. Then the father confessor falls upon his knees and, supporting her with his right arm, he performs the acts I have just described.

I did not only find these acts and the words of the blessing in the Mother's writings; the late nuns also explained them to me, just as I have described them now. They also performed these acts . . . I think that these things were done with great secrecy, since I did not notice the other nuns doing anything of this sort.

As with the sexual blessings, Maria Luisa didn't hang back. She was keen to follow in the mother founder's footsteps with this special

Jesuit blessing as well, and she enlisted Padre Peters to carry it out. Maria Luisa said that for around three years she had been fabricating heavenly letters. These encouraged the confessor to give her the extraordinary blessing, just as his Jesuit predecessors had given it to the previous heads of Sant'Ambrogio. She put these letters into the little casket, to which Peters believed he had the only key. Of course, Maria Luisa had a second key, as she admitted to the court.

> In these letters I called on him to instill in me the spirit of the mother founder and the spirit of God, in the way I described above. And indeed I fell on my knees before Padre Peters and he dispensed the blessing. However, I did not go into ecstasies, but remained clearly composed. After the blessing, he would also kneel down; sometimes he carried out one of the above actions, sometimes another. Then he had to go, as the letters decreed. How many times this happened I cannot say, because it happened whenever the opportunity arose. As far as I remember, he only put his tongue in my mouth twice. This did not trouble my conscience, and I also never confessed it.

In Sant'Ambrogio, as the court learned, these "sensual and intimate acts" were known by the term *benedizione straordinaria*—an extraordinary blessing.[41] Maria Luisa ascribed a fourfold effect to the blessing:[42] "1. Insight; 2. Spiritual meditation; 3. Transformation; 4. Substantial communication." She went on to say that this "substantial communication must take place seven times a year between the father confessor and the nun, and the other actions together with the blessing a total of 33 times within a year."

But what was this special communication? Maria Luisa had also gleaned this information from the mother founder's documents. There she read "that the *comunicazione sostanziale* takes place when the father confessor puts his tongue in the mouth of the penitent nun; this was like the laying on of hands that the apostles practiced with the disciples to instill in them the Holy Spirit. . . . Regarding the other actions, it was written that as the Lord gave potency to the water of Holy Baptism, and the oil of Confirmation, so He had embued all the above-named actions with the power to instill in the penitent nun the energies and the gifts described above."

In these old writings from just after the convent was founded, Maria Luisa discovered the names of five Jesuits who had dispensed this extraordinary blessing, which was reserved for the abbesses of Sant'Ambrogio. Giuseppe Marconi, José Doz, Agustín Monzon,[43] Brunelli,[44] and Nicola Benedetti had upheld this special tradition by giving the blessing during confession. Maria Luisa's list didn't specifically include the Jesuit Padre Pignatelli, who was later canonized by Pius XII. But she made it clear that the spirit of the institute, which was passed on through the "substantial communication" of French kissing, originated with none other than Pignatelli—whatever this statement might mean. And although Maria Luisa was a mere vicaress, rather than the abbess, she was keen to perpetuate the tradition and add another Jesuit to the list: Padre Peters.

It wasn't just the form but the supposed pretense of the *benedizione straordinaria* that went far beyond that of a blessing a priest might say during Mass, or following the absolution of sins in the confessional. Heavenly gifts of grace were conveyed in Sant'Ambrogio. This gift of divine mercy was even connected with the idea of "transformation." This suggests that the being and substance of the nuns receiving this blessing were transfigured, just as a priest is at his ordination. The office of priest and bishop has been handed down through the Catholic Church since the time of the apostles, in an unbroken line of benedictions that preserves the Faith's tradition. In Sant'Ambrogio's extraordinary blessing, the hand of benediction was replaced with a French kiss. To the nuns of Sant'Ambrogio, the Jesuit blessing seemed more important than the consecration of an abbess, the ceremony through which the Church installs a mother superior. And this special blessing, received in an encounter with a man, then allowed the abbess to conduct the homosexual "purification" and "care" of the sisters in her charge. Here, of course, it was bodily fluids as well as the convent's spirit that passed from one nun to another. The goal was an unbroken line of tradition from one abbess to the next. In a sense, the mother founder had devised an alternative, exclusively feminine model of succession.

But the women of Sant'Ambrogio couldn't do without men entirely. Each new abbess required a new act of Jesuit inspiration: the spirit still had to be breathed into her through a French kiss with a padre from the Society of Jesus. This may have originated in an attempt by individual Jesuits to protect the spirit of their own order (which was suppressed in 1773, and only permitted to resume in 1814), by preserving it in a community of Franciscan women. Firrao's reform came during the Society of Jesus's suppression. This would have made the Regulated Third Order Franciscan nuns *female Jesuits* in disguise— something that has never existed in the Church, and certainly couldn't exist at this time. So the special protection the community of Sant'Ambrogio received from Jesuits and Jesuit pupils after 1814 comes as no surprise. Leo XII was as much a friend to the Jesuits as Pius IX, Patrizi, and Cardinal Reisach.

THE CONFESSOR'S AFFAIR WITH ALESSANDRA N.

The heavenly letters and the Jesuit blessing's intense physical contact, with all its erotic implications, gave Maria Luisa an unusual power over her confessor. Padre Peters was putty in her hands. The Madonna's letters enabled her to guide him in whatever direction she pleased. She spoke about this to the Inquisition on June 26, 1860.[45]

> As Padre Peters had realized my resistance to the extraordinary, he told me that a respected, leading Jesuit padre had been deceived by a penitent, which had left him badly humiliated. I was gripped by curiosity. Through one of the usual letters, I informed him that if that padre were to perform an act of humility, by telling me everything, he would have the comfort of being able to convert that soul. For a while he held back, but I pressed him, saying that this act of grace was dependent upon him telling his story. Finally he gave in. I found a letter in the above-mentioned casket; the letter explained all that had happened between the padre and his penitent. But I was not satisfied with this, and requested another letter from him, in which he told me the whole story from beginning to end.
>
> He said he had been deceived as to the holiness of his penitent, Alessandra N., who lived in Rome in 1848 and 1849, and had been taken in by her stories of miracles. This made him bend to commit obscene acts with her, such as kissing, improper touching and embracing. She once fell on her knees and took his manhood in her

mouth, and finally they did shameful things together. And then he also explained how these last actions were carried out.

The name Alessandra N. must have caught the inquisitor's attention: in the course of the informative process, he had stumbled upon the rumor that Peters had conducted a sexual relationship with a woman named Alessandra. The nuns had obviously been whispering about this affair behind their hands. Now he was hearing the juicy details from Maria Luisa; she had clearly paid close attention to everything Peters said in his letters to the Madonna.

> In this letter he said that Alessandra N. had deceived many father confessors, and with her artfulness had stopped any of them being able to speak about it to the others. This Alessandra was still living in Rome some years ago, and came to the convent to visit one of my novices. I saw her, and she asked me if I gave confession to Padre Peters, but I marched her out. This Alessandra had a reputation as a pious woman, and used to dress all in black. But the curate of Sant'Adriano warned the people about her, so they might protect themselves from her.
>
> The same letter also said that from this union of the flesh a natural effect had come to pass, but that this mark had disappeared again, in a manner unknown and undiscovered by them (namely Padre Peters and the penitent Alessandra).

Neither Maria Luisa's testimony nor the letter clarified what exactly Padre Peters meant by a "natural effect" of intercourse. This could have been a pregnancy, which disappeared in an inexplicable fashion, or, if Alessandra had been a virgin at the time she slept with the Jesuit padre, a bloodstain on the sheets from where her hymen was broken. Maria Luisa went on:

> At Padre Peters' wish I returned the letter to him, but sealed, and with the word *Gratia* written on it. Knowing about all this made me worry that, when Padre Peters instilled the spirit of the mother founder into me in the aforementioned way, he might take it further. So the few times it happened—twice to be exact—after I had read the aforementioned letter, I was cautious and fearful. After

that, I wrote a letter (I can't remember whether in the name of the guardian angel or the Blessed Virgin) saying that God's mercy had been granted to him through my prayers, and that because of his resistance to extraordinary things, he could cease to dispense his blessing.

For the investigating judge, this was evidence that Padre Peters had committed another offense. In the context of his work as confessor, he had previously conducted a sexual relationship with a woman called Alessandra. In order to construct a specific charge against the Jesuit, Sallua and his colleagues now required further information.

But it was July 28, just over a month later, before Maria Luisa managed to summon up the necessary "composure" to continue testifying on this subject.[46] To this end, she submitted handwritten statements detailing her memory of the correspondence between the Jesuit and the Virgin Mary.[47] As the defendant explained, Alessandra had used "many extraordinary things" to "deceive" Peters, who had believed in her.

> Alessandra had made him great and extraordinary promises, which moved him to overcome his misgivings and not feel ashamed of being seen with her and going about with her, because she had persuaded him to be with her. At this time, great and surprising things occurred, as he said himself. "The acts consisted of long and ardent embraces, kisses, mutual caressing and touching of her clitoris[48] with my hand and fingers." (These are the padre's words.)
>
> Suddenly she embraced him and fell in a swoon between his naked thighs. Then she took his naked member and put it in her mouth. The "divine marriage" was carried out as follows: "Alessandra lay down on the bed and I" (Padre Peters) "stretched myself out on her, putting my member into the sex[49] of the unfortunate Alessandra. During this vehement operation that I had to carry out, she pretended to be in God. But from the expression and pallor of her face, from the odious way she writhed constantly during the act, I could well see that it was a deception and not anything divine. But I cannot explain how a bloodstain could vanish before my eyes, without anybody touching it. It must surely have been the work of the devil, because it cannot have been any natural process."

Once, the good old woman came into the room and surprised him *in flagrante* during one of these odious acts, causing a great scandal. He held it to be a great miracle that he was able to escape the scandal as he did. From the letter I gathered that this old lady rented a room to him, in which the two of them lived. The old lady must have seen something, because she tried to chase them out of the house—this was written in the letter, though I cannot remember the exact words. The letter explained that Alessandra always returned his kisses and embraces. I don't remember whether it said the terrible acts with the mouth and the others of the matrimonial bed happened just once, or several times. Nor can I remember whether the letter said the union began with this action, or was completed by it. But I am sure the mutual touching and embracing that was described in such detail happened many times.

Maria Luisa's testimony suggested that Peters hadn't just broken his vow of celibacy; he was also guilty of *Sollicitatio*. Interestingly, this affair had taken place in 1848–1849. In the wake of the Roman Revolution, the Jesuits had been driven out of the city once more. Peters probably used his superiors' absence to disappear amid the bustle of the city, take a room with his lover, and remain undisturbed with her in their love nest. The affair probably only came to an end when the revolution was quelled, restoring order in the Church, and allowing the pope to return to Rome. Now that Peters's superiors were back on the scene, he had to go back to his order's house and the oversight of his abbot.

MARIA LUISA AND PADRE PETERS: BLESSING OR BEDDING?

Instead of addressing her relationship with Padre Peters head-on, Maria Luisa had told the Inquisition two very interesting stories: the secret of the special Jesuit blessing, and Peters's affair with Alessandra. Now the judges pressed her to make a specific statement about her relationship with the Jesuit padre. In her interrogation on July 24, 1860, she finally gave them the information they wanted.[50]

She had, she claimed, faked her "extraordinary malady" on a regular basis. She would then call on her confessor for support day and night.

Whenever he came into my cell, I would pretend to be out of my senses; he would fall on his knees, take my hand, press and kiss it. It is understandable why we were alone together. As he did this, I sometimes acted as if I was coming to myself again—or sometimes I did not. And if I did not, he would repeat these acts until I was recovered. Then he would sit on the bed while I told him of some vision or prophecy or about my terrible headaches—he had to use the blessing to release me from these. Or else we spoke of some gift or mercy that the Lord would bestow upon him.

Sometimes I let him find letters about the above-mentioned blessing or other things under my pillow, or in my drawer, or my writing box. Sometimes I had the abbess give him letters before he entered the convent. Our conversations about visions and prophecies went on for hours, and were repeated according to what I had prophesied. During these conversations, he would give me the extraordinary blessing that I spoke of above, and which I had set out for him in the letters from the Madonna.

He dispensed the blessing in the following way: he began by laying his hands on my head, and then he blessed me in the name of the Holy Trinity, the Madonna, and in his own name as my father confessor and protector. Then he fell on his knees and gave me an ardent kiss. Then he stretched out his right hand and at the same time laid his face upon my breast, on the side where the heart is. Then he kissed me on the mouth and on the face, and laid his head on my throat, under my chin. He remained there as our faces touched and he supported my face with his hands.

This all happened every time Padre Peters came in, sometimes several times a day—except for the sign of the cross he made on my throat, as I will now describe. He only did this twice. As the letters instructed, he lifted my *guimpe* [the part of the habit that covers the neck and chest] and made the sign of the cross on my skin with his tongue, from the lowest part of my throat to my chin. Sometimes, acting on the instructions in my letters, he also kissed my feet. On many occasions the letters said he should kiss my heart, and this he also did.

Sometimes, as I was pretending to be overcome by visions and divine conversations, I lifted myself up a little and moved on the bed. He held me in a vehement embrace, and I remained lying on his breast for a while; sometimes he kissed me. For my part, I was quite wary and pretended not to be conscious of these acts, so that he would not doubt my affected purity and holiness.

Sometimes Padre Peters stayed longer, and sometimes not so long. It might be a few hours, half a day or a whole day. Sometimes he also stayed for part of the night and, once, a whole night. Padre Peters came to my cell to care for me . . . four or five times a month, and this went on for several years. It started shortly after he had begun to stand in as my confessor, and carried on once he became confessor to the convent.

Maria Luisa later corrected her statement about the frequency of the visits:

It is sadly true that I allowed Padre Peters to enter the enclosure. We would withdraw somewhere from lunchtime until the hour of Ave Maria, and sometimes later. There was rarely a day when this did not happen. . . . Two or three times, when the acts I have described between myself and Padre Peters took place in my cell, as I lay in bed, Padre Peters pulled down the covers and kissed the upper part of my habit, to kiss my heart. He kissed me there over and over, and held his face against my heart for a long time. The whole time we were together was thus a continuous series of kisses and embraces and other acts, as I said above, so I cannot say how long it lasted each time. I can only say that I lay on the bed on my side, opposite him. As the bed was very low, he could repeat the above-mentioned acts in comfort and keep his face against mine.

During these acts he repeated the following phrases: "My daughter, my beloved daughter, firstborn, favored, my delight, my bliss, my treasure."

When he kissed my heart, he said: "Pure heart, sacred heart, immaculate heart, my treasure," and similar.

This always happened in the context of pastoral care and in confession. Maria Luisa's testimony suggested that Padre Peters was guilty

of the serious offense of *Sollicitatio* with her, too. Sallua made a detailed
note of the confessor's misconduct "concerning those acts which, as
the expression goes, took place behind closed doors, between confessor and penitent."[51]

Maria Luisa, on the other hand, was more concerned with her
reception of the extraordinary blessing.

> Once, during these intimacies, I made myself seem very inflamed
> by the love of God. Padre Peters held me in his embrace; I was
> lying with my head on his breast. Suddenly he put his hand under
> my scapular and then into the slit in my habit. He pushed my cru-
> cifix aside and rubbed my breast, particularly on the side of the
> heart for a very long time. Meanwhile, he redoubled his kisses, his
> caresses, his exclamations. Many other times during these inti-
> macies, he drew the crucifix aside and touched my heart with his
> hand. Once, he put his tongue into my mouth and I made an effort
> to trap it with my own. I almost always kept my head on the Jesuit
> padre's breast, though almost always while pretending to faint or to
> speak with the Lord or the Madonna.

Padre Peters kissed and embraced her with tremendous "ardor." He
put his tongue in her mouth "with great vehemence." "Afterwards he
was eager to tell me all about it, and said that during that night he had
seen a great beauty in me, like that of the Madonna."

The terms "ardor" and "vehemence," which Maria Luisa used several times, were intended to emphasize that—unlike her—the Jesuit
padre had been very sexually excited. She tried to convey to him
that this extraordinary blessing he was permitted to give her, as the
Blessed Virgin's favorite daughter, was something entirely different
from his relationship with Alessandra. There, was filth; here, purity.
There, was lust; here, a blessing. There, desire; here, faith.

> I never believed these deeds were sinful: I say this with complete
> certainty. When I invited Padre Peters to carry out those acts, via
> the letters from the Madonna, I was trying to do him a kindness—
> and, at the same time, make him consider the evil he had commit-
> ted with Alessandra. The letters said he was doing these things
> on God's orders and as His minister. He was therefore commit-

ting no such sin as he had with Alessandra. Or rather: by behaving so differently, I was able to assure him of the goodness of these acts. Through them, as I said to him many times, he could make amends for many things. He would receive mercy, merits of the highest order, and glory by communication—principally on those occasions when he put his tongue in my mouth. I repeated all these things very often in the letters to Padre Peters from the Madonna, the Lord and the guardian angel. I wanted to convince him of my holiness by this means. I continued to use this system to the very end, and it never troubled my conscience.

The investigating judges didn't accept Maria Luisa's distinction between blessing and bedding, and kept coming back to this issue in the hearings. But Maria Luisa stuck to her story: the padre had wanted more, it was true, but she had (among other things) sewn up her scapular so he could no longer touch her chest with his hands. However, he "parted it, so it seemed to me, using his teeth, and put his hand to my breast and touched me there for some time."[52] On July 28, 1860, she begged that Sallua had to believe her when she said that she and the Jesuit had done nothing that resembled what had passed between Peters and Alessandra.[53] When his hands wandered "further down" from her chest, she had given up her ecstasies and come to immediately. She repeated this on August 14, 1860, this time in writing.[54] The Jesuit had not touched her on the bosom "with his hand or in any other way"; nor had he touched any other "shameful part" of her body. There had been no "act more shameful" than those she had already described.

On September 18, 1860, Maria Luisa finally admitted that she had conducted a passionate relationship with Padre Peters.[55] She had *wanted* the Jesuit to commit all these acts with her. She was simply in love with him.

"MY ONLY DEFENSE IS JESUS CHRIST"

Katharina's poisoning was another subject on which Maria Luisa only made a full confession after the interrogating judge had questioned her for almost a month, and had confronted her with evidence and incriminating witness statements.[56] On July 3, 1860, Maria Luisa related her version of the poisoning attempts to the court.

"In order to give a proper answer to this difficult question, there are a few things I must say first. The late Sister Maria Saveria boasted of many visions and revelations of the mother founder . . . and claimed that the princess was ill disposed towards me and Padre Peters. . . . She . . . ordered me . . . to do away with . . . the princess." Maria Saveria told her to mix "12 grains of opium with a medicine such as cassia or tamarind." On several occasions after this, Saveria apparently gave her "some little packets of very finely ground glass," saying she should "put it into the princess's soup, to make her ill." Maria Luisa confessed to having kept a few of these little packets. She had "put this glass powder into the princess's soup two to three times a week." But she threw away a "packet of white powder" that she had been told to administer to the princess.

By claiming that the initiative had come from the late Maria Saveria, Maria Luisa was trying to shift a portion of the blame away from herself. Sallua could, after all, neither interrogate nor punish a dead woman. But something in this testimony caught his attention: For the first time, Maria Luisa had provided a concrete motive for the murder, even if she had placed it in the mouth of a deceased nun. The princess had wanted to harm Maria Luisa and Padre Peters, and ultimately bring ruin on the whole convent. This was probably a reference to the vicaress's clandestine relationship with Peters, which would have caused a scandal if it had become known outside the walls of Sant'Ambrogio.

But, as Maria Luisa stressed many times over, it wasn't for her own sake that she had tried to poison the princess. She was only doing it to protect her confessor. "I decided to release Padre Peters from his fears, because he told me that if the princess left the convent, she would ruin him, me, and the whole community. I thought it was now necessary to put Sister Maria Saveria's plan into action. I went to the convent dispensary and inquired about some medicaments."

But in spite of the poisons she had been fed, Katharina didn't die. It was looking increasingly unlikely that the prophecy Maria Luisa had spread throughout the convent—that the princess would be dead by Christmas—would be fulfilled. Maria Luisa was now forced to claim that Katharina's survival was the result of her intercession with God. Once more, she stressed that Padre Peters would have been the only one to benefit from the princess's demise.

The investigating judges remained skeptical about the truth of this statement. Maria Luisa had lied to the court too often already, or told them only half-truths. And her claim that the Jesuit confessor was the sole instigator, and would have been the one to profit most from Katharina's death, was a very serious allegation. When they interrogated Padre Peters about this, the tribunal wanted to be as certain of the facts as possible. But as they started to press Maria Luisa on this point, she stood her ground, saying: "I confirm everything that I said in the previous hearing."

On July 6, the defendant finally cracked and gave a full confession. For the inquisitors, this was definitive proof that she had made several attempts to murder Princess Katharina von Hohenzollern, using various poisons: tartar emetic; ground glass, with and without spongia; alum; opium; quicklime; and oil varnish. She had also obtained turpentine and belladonna (deadly nightshade), but had not used them. The only reason she stopped giving the princess the brown opium powder was because the doctors stopped prescribing cassia, into which the drug could easily be mixed. And when she came under suspicion as a murderess, Maria Luisa shifted the blame onto the devil, who she said had assumed her form.

She also described how her accomplice Maria Ignazia had gradually distanced herself from her. "Maria Ignazia was distraught by the whole affair, and told me I should be careful, as I was in danger of ending up before the Holy Office. Anyone who killed other people would be punished by death." Finally, this was the proof Sallua needed that Maria Luisa had forced one of her charges into becoming her accomplice by invoking the religious duty of obedience.

Maria Luisa also confessed to the renewed attempts on Katharina's life in the summer of 1859. She had "administered further poisons to the princess during her final days in the convent, putting them in her chocolate and other things. However, this was not done with the intention of killing her. The aim was to make her so ill that she was forced to remain in her cell, and was thus unable to leave the convent." Maria Luisa had been terribly afraid of Katharina going. Padre Peters had said to her several times: "If she leaves, and talks about our affairs—the extraordinary blessing, the mother founder, and so on—it will spell the end for us both, and for the whole community."

She then returned a third time to her confessor's involvement in the poisoning attempts. "I alone am guilty of carrying out the poisoning—but the reason for it and the decision to do it came from the great fears that Padre Peters expressed to me. As a result of what I said to him in general, and what he learned from other nuns, a few facts about the poisoning of the princess were certainly known to him." This statement seriously incriminated Padre Peters. He had the most to fear if Katharina should leave Sant'Ambrogio and talk. He had been the real *spiritus rector* of the whole poisoning campaign.

Maria Luisa finally reinforced her point a fourth time:

> What you have read out about Padre Peters is also true. Since I have sworn to tell the truth, you should know that in his replies to my letters, he said I must pray to the Lord and ask Him to do away with the princess at once (he really wrote this), to save us all from the ruin that was to come.
>
> As I wept to see the princess dying, he saw me and said: "You are mad! There have been so many prayers for her to die; it is a mercy."
>
> It is the truth and nothing but the truth that, having uttered these words, he expressed his regret that she was not yet dead.
>
> After the princess had left, he said he always trod warily when he entered the convent. If the princess had gone straight to Austria, we would have had nothing to fear, but the fact that she had gone to Tivoli and then to Rome made him suspicious that something might happen to the convent.

It was only at the very end of her interrogation that Maria Luisa was finally prepared to admit what the real catalyst of the whole affair had been.

> It is true that I received the letter in German from the above-named Pietro Americano. I took it to the princess, so she could read it to me. The princess was troubled by the letter and told me that bad things were written in it and I should throw it away. I took the letter and sealed it and gave it to the padre, so he would not suspect I had shown it to the princess. When the princess told

Padre Peters about it, I claimed it had been the devil in my form. Padre Peters had sworn me to the strictest silence on the subject of this Pietro. I invented this story about the devil so that nobody would find out I had spoken to the princess about it—which I had in fact done.

In conclusion, Maria Luisa asked the court to inform Katharina von Hohenzollern and her cousin, Archbishop Hohenlohe, of her confession and her regret. "I would like to beg both of them for forgiveness." Here the notary added, by way of commentary: *"She wept as she said this."* She also begged forgiveness for making the novice Maria Ignazia into her accomplice. The notary commented: *"Here, she wept and sobbed even harder."*

At the end of this interrogation, the defendant was subjected to intense questioning about the attempts on other nuns' lives. "I am guilty of many murders, I committed such crimes many times." She admitted she had been afraid Maria Giacinta might tell the princess about the poisons she had given her, and the shameful acts she had committed with Giacinta. She had therefore tried to induce her death, using a drastically increased dose of a strong medicine. Maria Luisa also confessed that she had prevented anyone calling a doctor for the sick Maria Costanza in time to save her. And she admitted to murdering Sister Maria Agostina, because she was envious of her visions and ecstasies. Having heard everything the judges had read out to her from the files, she confirmed that she had developed an intense dislike of Maria Agostina. She had systematically humiliated and bullied the young nun, eventually destroying her both psychologically and physically.

In Maria Agostina's case, the poison had been the "Elixier Le Roi." Exactly what this was is no longer clear. Suggestions range from a highly alcoholic monastic liqueur, made in Chartreuse and called "Elixier," to a secret potion made from all kinds of unknown ingredients. The sick woman had told Maria Luisa it was "like a bolt of lightning that set her on fire from head to toe." This reaction could well have been the effect of high-percentage alcohol, and the essential oils contained in the Elixier Le Roi, on a person who was already in a weakened state.

The Inquisition had now obtained a confession from Maria Luisa on all the charges. She didn't demand to have the witnesses reexamined in her presence—which meant that she also didn't make use of the grace period to which she was legally entitled, to prepare a written counterstatement. She turned down the offer of a defense counsel, despite the prospect of draconian punishments. Her defense was handed over to the court-appointed lawyer for those who had been accused by the Holy Office, Giuseppe Cipriani.[57] He reviewed the *Ristretto* and signed it off.

Maria Luisa's concluding statement read: "Filled with disgust at my offences, I acknowledge that I deserve all punishments that will be visited upon me by the popes. I therefore request that they may be exercised without delay, for I seek only forgiveness and salvation. . . . My only defense is Jesus Christ."

CHAPTER SEVEN

"That Good Padre Has Spoiled the Work of God"

The Interrogations of the Father Confessor and the Abbess

GIUSEPPE LEZIROLI: A CONFESSOR BEFORE THE COURT

According to canon law, there were two people responsible for everything that had happened in Sant'Ambrogio: the abbess, and the convent's spiritual director. The nuns were duty-bound to obey them in all things, and had to follow their instructions as if they came from Jesus Christ Himself. This was particularly the case for the spiritual director, who, as an ordained priest, acted *in persona Christi*. While the mother superior was responsible for maintaining discipline and ensuring strict adherence to the Rule, the confessor's area of responsibility was faith and pastoral care. There had to be a clear division between these two spheres. In particular, the nuns had to be sure that what they said in confession would be kept secret, and not passed on to the abbess or her vicaress. There had already been a serious violation of this basic Church norm. And in the course of the informative process, further serious allegations had been made—both against Abbess Maria Veronica, and the principal confessor and spiritual director, Giuseppe Leziroli. Therefore, the Inquisition brought charges against them both on February 27, 1861.[1]

Leziroli had been born on March 19, 1795, in Rimini. He entered the novitiate of the Society of Jesus in Reggio Emilia in 1817.[2] Having been ordained as priest in February 1822, he spent two years working in Terni, three in Fano, and a further year in Tivoli. In 1831, his superiors sent him to Rome. He was first employed as a spiritual director in the Collegio Romano, and its seminary. In 1839, he was installed in Sant'Ambrogio as the principal confessor and spiritual director. He was always assisted in this task by a second Jesuit padre. From 1856 to November 1859, this was Padre Giuseppe Peters.

Leziroli's interrogations extended over roughly four months, from March 16 to July 19, 1861.[3] Like all defendants who appeared before the Holy Tribunal, he was first given the opportunity to speak spontaneously. His defense strategy was very simple: "What I can say about myself is that I started well, but was deceived in the end." This deceit was connected with a nun to whom he had been a "spiritual companion," and who, he soon saw, "possessed gifts and was capable of extraordinary things." He promptly informed Cardinal Patrizi of this, and Patrizi advised him to be cautious. But the cardinal vicar apparently left it at that. At least, Leziroli didn't mention any other interventions by Patrizi.

As Sallua noted in his report, Leziroli claimed to have instructed this nun that, were she to be visited by an apparition, she should defend herself by speaking the following words: *"Our Father, may the sign of the cross release us from our enemies."* Five months later, Saint Stanislaus appeared to this sister.[4] He led her to the place where the late abbess, Maria Maddalena, subsequently started appearing to her on a regular basis. "When she came to this place with Saint Stanislaus, Maria Maddalena appeared to her with a cross in her hand, and commanded her to venerate it with the words *Adoramus te Christi*." As they venerated the cross together, she spoke the words Leziroli had given her. This convinced him that "it could not be the work of the devil, but must be the work of God." He therefore "always believed what she told him" about all her subsequent visions, and "never doubted her honesty."

This nun was none other than Maria Luisa. Leziroli had heard from two or three other sisters that they had seen Maria Luisa "with a sullen face" in a particular place, although she was actually elsewhere and "in a good mood." This led him to believe that the devil had assumed her form. "The sum of all these facts meant that I allowed myself to be deceived. Nothing more."

This made the father confessor look very gullible, for an educated

Jesuit—his attitude was almost naive. When he was questioned further about when and how he realized he had been deceived, the padre stated that it had only happened two or three weeks after he had been released from his duties in Sant'Ambrogio, in December 1860. This was when his fellow Jesuit, Peters, told him that Maria Luisa had commissioned "certain rings" through the lawyer Franceschetti, "which she caused to appear on her finger as if they were gifts received in heaven." The rings from the heavenly marriage were thus revealed as being of earthly manufacture. "From this I concluded that everything else must have been a deception, too." He immediately burned all the papers to do with Maria Luisa's holiness. He did, however, keep his manuscript on the life of the mother founder, as he remained absolutely convinced of her holiness.

THE APOSTLE OF SAINT AGNESE FIRRAO

Now the interrogation turned to the most important charge against Leziroli: the promotion of the cult of Agnese Firrao, who had been convicted of feigned holiness.[5] The judges were particularly keen to know about Leziroli's work, *Sulle memorie della vita di Suor Maria Agnese di Gesù*, which he had composed over the course of many years. This manuscript, the draft for a saint's life of Firrao, had been handed over to the Inquisition by the Jesuit general, Petrus Beckx, along with the letter he had received from the Virgin Mary.[6]

To prepare for Leziroli's interrogation, the judges tasked the Carmelite monk Girolamo Priori with an evaluation of this manuscript, on April 24, 1861.[7] Priori had worked as a consultor for the Holy Office since 1852, and he had also been prior general of his order in Rome since 1856.[8] Priori's judgment was damning: he said this "mendacious biography" of the false saint Maria Agnese Firrao should by all means be burned. In addition to numerous "mercies, privileges and ecstasies," the Jesuit had presented Firrao's heroic virtue in a manner that was normally reserved for a *propositio* by the Sacred Congregation of Rites. Either Leziroli was angling for a papal beatification of Maria Agnese (whom he already venerated as blessed), or he was hoping to get her beatified through his *Memorie* alone, without the Church's blessing, which was a staggering presumption.

In his false saint's life, Leziroli gave a very detailed description of Agnese Firrao's mystical wedding to Christ in heaven. This was an attempt to legitimate a new nineteenth-century mystic using a strategy that had worked for the great mystics of the Middle Ages. A mystical union with Christ was supposed to serve as unequivocal proof of sainthood, although this had been hotly debated within the Church even in relation to the "classical" female mystics. The Carmelite's evaluation of Leziroli's text pointed out that it "compromised" Giuseppe Pignatelli, Agnese Firrao's sometime confessor, "many times over." Leziroli depicted Pignatelli as a committed believer in the true holiness of Agnese Firrao. Priori saw the serious threat that this presented to the process for Pignatelli's own beatification, which had just been opened in Rome. If the Jesuit Pignatelli had really supported a false saint, then he himself could not be a saint. (In fact, Pignatelli was eventually beatified in 1933, and canonized in 1954.) In Priori's view, Leziroli's terrible manuscript had to be taken out of circulation immediately. Of course—as was customary for a Holy Office evaluator—he left the decision on the final *Damnatio* up to the congregation of cardinals.

With this unequivocal votum up his sleeve, Sallua asked Leziroli exactly what his purpose had been in writing his life of Firrao. The padre answered that the mother founder had been a "nun filled with virtue," possessed of "extraordinary gifts," and people must not be allowed to forget this. But in the first instance, he said, his work had only been meant for use within the convent. He had wanted to present Maria Agnese to the nuns of Sant'Ambrogio as a shining example. Of course, he and the nuns all knew that Pius VII had condemned her as a false saint—but they thought he had only arrived at this verdict because Firrao's enemies had slandered her reform of the Third Order of Holy Saint Francis. Even the pope himself, as Sister Maria Caterina had explained to him, had believed the slander. Leziroli also claimed that, as he was basing his text on Firrao's memoirs and the stories told by her first companions, he was only setting down in writing things that were already familiar to the nuns from oral sources.

Then there was the matter of the mother founder's continued contact with her daughters in Rome, from exile in Gubbio. The Jesuit justified this by claiming it had been permitted by Leo XII—something that Cardinal Giuseppe Pecci,[9] the bishop of Gubbio from 1841 to 1855, had certainly known. Leziroli was probably drawing on the papal brief of 1829, in which the pope released the nuns of Sant'Ambrogio from all censures and canonical judgments. Even if the brief contained no specific mention of the mother founder, this was obviously how the nuns had interpreted Pope Leo XII's words. But for contact to have been permitted, Agnese Firrao's exile would have to have been revoked—which clearly wasn't the case.

Leziroli was honoring Sant'Ambrogio's long tradition of defying the 1816 Inquisition decree, without fundamentally questioning its validity. The *cantus firmus* of his testimony was that Agnese Firrao was a true saint. The investigating judges also recorded that Leziroli claimed he himself had been miraculously healed. Maria Luisa had written to tell him that this healing was the result of Saint Maria Agnese's intercession.

Leziroli stubbornly defended his "saint's life" before the tribunal. Its real purpose, he said, had been to preserve the most important information on Maria Agnese's life and work for posterity, "in case the Lord should decide her innocence must be revealed." He still had faith in all the old sources: Firrao's personal testimonial, and the statements from her companions. However, he did admit "that everything pertaining to visitations and mercies after her death must be removed from the life of Sister Maria Agnese di Gesù, for this is an illusion." "All of this" came from what Maria Luisa, the false saint, had told him while he was in his "blinded" state.

In fact, these pages were already missing from the *Memorie* the court showed him, and which he identified as his work. Leziroli said that Padre Peters had cut out the incriminating pages after they learned of Maria Luisa's deception.

Sallua then turned his attention to the practical ways in which Firrao was venerated in Sant'Ambrogio. The confessor conceded the nuns had called her *Beata, Santa Madre* (Blessed, Holy Mother), especially after her death. He himself had only referred to her as *Beata* in private. In public, and particularly in the liturgy, he merely called her "most pious, virtuous and favored mother," taking care never to say "blessed, holy or venerable." But in subsequent interrogations, Leziroli was forced to admit that, after her death, he also called the mother founder *Beata* in public. He explained to the court that when he said this, he meant that Maria Agnese had already achieved heavenly glory. During the benediction for the sick, he therefore incorporated the phrase "at the intercession of Your servant Agnes" into the liturgical wording for the intercession of the saints. He also advised the nuns: "Trust in your holy mother!"

Leziroli also had to admit to "reworking" the prayers to Saint Joseph, the Virgin Mary, and other saints, at the nuns' request, to include a prayer for the return of the mother founder from exile. After her death, he inserted the name Maria Agnese into the Litany of the Saints, as "blessed by heaven," as if she had already achieved divine glory. From the Inquisition's point of view, this meant he had arrogated responsibilities to himself that belonged solely to the pope and the Roman congregations in charge: the changing of liturgical texts, and raising the dead to the altars.

Leziroli was firmly convinced that Agnese Firrao's visions had been genuine. She once wrote to him from Gubbio to say she had seen the late abbess, Maria Maddalena, "going up to heaven." He spoke to Cardinal Pecci about her vision, and Pecci replied: *"She does seem to be an exalted spirit, but only God knows this for certain."* The Jesuit was sure "that the Lord, who keeps His promises, would one day glorify His servant." Agnese Firrao was still a saint in Leziroli's eyes, Inquisition judgment or no. And so he allowed the mother founder's contact relics to be venerated in Sant'Ambrogio, and petitioned for the return of her body from Gubbio. Firrao's confessor there wrote and told him her body had shown no signs of decay a full ten days after her death. Leziroli's aim was to create a saint's grave as a place of veneration inside the walls of Sant'Ambrogio.[10]

Sallua wrote: "The defendant was shown many unanimous witness statements, saying he had promoted the veneration and the cult of the mother founder in various ways, acting on his conviction that she was a saint." Leziroli was unable to refute the overwhelming evidence, and had to confess. "Very well, everything you have read to me is correct."

He argued that his behavior was purely the result of Maria Luisa's deception. The tribunal saw this the other way around: when Maria Luisa told the Jesuit about her visions and the other supernatural phenomena connected to the mother founder, she had been preaching to the choir. Everything she said fit with the image he had already formed of the "saint" Maria Agnese. He was only too willing to let Maria Luisa help him set more jewels into the crown of Maria Agnese's sainthood. Leziroli didn't feel he had been deceived by Agnese Firrao, whose spiritual guide he had been for a decade and a half, but only by Maria Luisa. She had a duty of obedience to him, but she had manipulated him using her supposedly divine powers. Leziroli gave a telling picture of the beautiful young vicaress's strategy of communication and control. Looking back, he expressed his horror and disappointment at having been taken in by this deception. But he may not have been aware, as he did this, that Maria Luisa was consciously serving the expectations or projections he and many other nineteenth-century men of the cloth had of gifted women.[11]

THE CONFESSOR AND "SAINT" MARIA LUISA

The next charge concerned Maria Luisa's pretense of holiness.[12] The investigating judges asked Leziroli how Maria Luisa had managed to assume such a position in the convent. The defendant said that in 1849, the mother founder had written to tell him she "disapproved" the "extraordinary things" Maria Luisa was claiming. This corroborated the statements the older nuns had given during the informative process. There may have been a kind of competitive envy at work here: skepticism from Sant'Ambrogio's old saint about the new one, who was threatening to outstrip her.

Leziroli, as he told the tribunal, emphatically rebuffed the mother founder's criticism. He had put Maria Luisa to the test a number of times, and had seen clear signs that his faith in the authenticity of her supernatural experiences was justified. He viewed her as "a unique treasure" and saw to it that this "privileged soul" was given the appropriate offices in the convent.

Leziroli then took Cardinal Vicar Patrizi into his trust, having informed him of Maria Luisa's special gifts. Patrizi instructed him to forbid Maria Luisa "all these things," which, Leziroli claimed, he promptly did. But the investigating judges took a rather different view on the matter, and accused him of not having followed Patrizi's orders. There was an obvious reason for the court to take this attitude to Leziroli's statement about Patrizi: the judges had to get the head of the Roman Inquisition, their most senior overseer, out of the firing line.

But if Patrizi had been so critical of Maria Luisa, why was he present when she was elected as vicaress? Had he really believed that if he didn't go, the devil would possess his servant and poison him with chocolate, as Maria Luisa had prophesied? Patrizi's visit had perpetuated the "system of visions," Leziroli explained, because it was taken as recognition of Maria Luisa's holiness.

Leziroli subsequently admitted that in many cases he had acted on the visions of the supposed saint. He had casually handed out dispensations from fasting and attending Divine Office, and supported Maria Luisa's recruitment of young nuns. He put pressure on Maria Giuseppa during confession, because she refused to believe in Maria Luisa's holiness. In general, he had been imprudent with the seal of the confessional, and had actually broken it several times. He had been unstinting in his claims that the heavenly letters were genuine. Last but not least, he had staged the scene in which the nuns venerated the madre vicaria as she lay, seemingly unconscious, on her bed, wearing valuable rings and giving off a lovely fragrance.

The court was particularly interested in what Leziroli knew about the relationship between Padre Peters and Maria Luisa. On June 13, 1861, Leziroli told how Peters's unusually intensive "pastoral" support had come about.[13]

While she was still a novice, Maria Luisa showed a note which, she said, she had been commanded to write by the late abbess, Maria Maddalena. It instructed the novice mistress at the time to let Maria Luisa lie in bed for three days, as she was going to suffer from a very severe headache, a sunstroke ... and in fact, this did then happen. She continued to suffer from this illness, which in recent years was declared extraordinary and supernatural. She therefore had need of a confessor and his blessing, rather than a doctor. I was called upon once to care for her during an attack of this illness, and recited litanies and blessed her, to give her comfort, which she said she felt.

A few days later, she told me the mother founder had appeared to her and said: "That good padre has spoiled the work of God. The suffering was supposed to last a day longer, in order to receive the reward of two more jewels for the ring." The mother founder also said she should now suffer for one more day, which indeed she did.

I also heard tell that during her suffering she fell into a swoon, and spoke with divine beings. But at this time she gave confession to Padre Peters; it was he who was present on these occasions, and not myself.

I would also like to mention that Padre Peters once told me an angel with a sword in his hand had appeared to Maria Luisa. She had taken the sword from the angel's hand and wounded her breast, to share in the suffering of the Madonna.

This was probably a reference to an image that was widespread in nineteenth-century Catholicism of the "seven sorrows of Mary." On devotional cards, these sorrows were symbolized by seven swords in Mary's breast.[14] Maria Luisa's vision was her attempt to position herself as close as possible to the Virgin Mary by reenacting her suffering. The scene in which Mary stands under her son's cross with his favorite disciple, and the *Pietà*, where she holds the body of Jesus in her arms, play a central role in the history of piety. The *Mater Dolorosa* became a model for the experience of suffering, particularly the suffering of women.[15] Perhaps Maria Luisa was searching for a substitute for the wounds of Christ, the stigmata that she lacked. There were numerous reports that the mother founder had received the stigmata.

On Holy Saturday 1857, Maria Luisa and Peters sent for the abbess and Leziroli, to demonstrate to them the authenticity of her ecstasies, and the purity of Padre Peters's care. This certainly worked in Leziroli's case. He recounted his experience of the vision to the Inquisition.

After Maria Luisa had been called, Padre Peters kissed her ring, which at that time was set with a simple cross. At this, she fainted, and the mother abbess supported her and laid her on a chair. In this state, without saying anything, she made movements of her body, and her head most of all, which suggested honor, affection and veneration. She lowered her head, as if some being, invisible to us, was giving her a kiss. Padre Peters gave an explanation of these acts, saying that at that moment, she was transported to God, and was perhaps being embraced. She remained in this condition for around three quarters of an hour, before coming to and telling us she had seen the choir of angels, the apostles, and the risen

Christ.... During the ecstasy, as I recall, Padre Peters told me to go into the adjoining room, because—as he claimed—he had to receive some manner of secret communication from Maria Luisa. I withdrew for a few minutes.

Leziroli could say nothing, however, about Peters's continual breaking of the *clausura,* the exact quality of the extraordinary blessing, and the possible sexual dimension of Peters's relationship with Maria Luisa.

In Agnese Eletta's case, this was rather different. The Jesuit had to confess that she had slept in Maria Luisa's cell for a year or more with his knowledge and permission—naturally, following a divine instruction.

I ordered the abbess to let the two of them sleep in the same room, because it was a command from God. I also revealed this command to the novice Maria Giacinta, who had to sleep in the mistress's cell as well, to serve as secretary. She actually slept there for a few months.

With regard to the novices, I only heard that the evening before they received their habits and professed their vows, they spent a few hours in spiritual conversation with the mistress in her room, and then went to bed. I heard nothing else about the intimacies that occurred between the nuns.

This account downplayed his own role in the affair, and didn't convince the investigating judge. Sallua presented Leziroli with testimonies from several nuns who said they had made more than one complaint about "immoral" and "improper" acts and intimacies between Maria Luisa and the novices. Leziroli replied: "As I believed Maria Luisa to be an innocent soul, who could not commit such acts, I attributed these things to the devil. It is true that I was shocked to be told that Maria Luisa treated a nun *on the sexual organs.* But because I was led to believe that this instantly healed the nun, I was reassured."

Leziroli stubbornly insisted that he had acted "in good faith throughout this business." The court, however, rejected this claim, and gave the Jesuit a caution. Even in his concluding statement, he refused to make any confession of guilt. He could only bring himself to state: *"Alas, God gave me this blindness as punishment for my sins."*

LEZIROLI AND THE POISONINGS

The third and final charge concerned the poisoning attempts. The court put it to Leziroli that he hadn't taken Katharina von Hohenzollern seriously, on the several occasions she had expressed serious doubts about Maria Luisa's virtue and holiness, and about the devil having assumed her form. He had also dismissed the princess's "complaints" as ridiculous—particularly those concerning the Americano's obscene letter. If Leziroli had only believed Katharina, the poisoning attempts would never have occurred. In the court's view, a substantial portion of the blame for the criminal acts that had been committed in Sant'Ambrogio fell to the convent's spiritual formation director, and his negligence. In his interrogation on June 14 and 15, 1861, Leziroli answered this charge at some length.[16]

> The story of the letter you are asking about . . . is true. The princess did not believe it was the devil in the shape of the mistress who had given her the letter, so she came to me on December 3 to speak to me about it. She said she refused to believe it was an illusion created by the devil. But at the time I was convinced of Maria Luisa's innocence, and did everything I could to convince the princess it was the devil, and not Maria Luisa, who had given her that letter. . . .
>
> Later, Maria Luisa told me that on the morning of the Immaculate Conception, the princess had thrown herself at her feet after Communion, and begged her to tell the truth. Maria Luisa felt very offended by this, and gave her a curt answer, saying: "You don't know who I am."
>
> Maria Luisa then told me the Lord had revealed to her that he would send a terrible illness and death to the princess, as punishment for her pride and her stubbornness, because she opposed Maria Luisa. I was to pray to God that Cardinal Reisach would not visit the princess before the start of her illness. At that time, we were expecting a visit from the cardinal to the princess.
>
> In fact, the princess suffered a stroke a day or two after the Immaculate Conception . . . and just two or three days later she was on her deathbed. Padre Peters told me there was a suspicion that one of the nuns in the convent had given her something poisonous. The sick woman had handed him a little glass of liquid, which had

been fed to her, and she told him she believed it contained something harmful. The above-named padre had it analyzed, and alum was found in it. Maria Luisa told Padre Peters, and later myself, that the cook had accidentally put alum in the broth instead of salt.

Padre Peters asked me if he should undertake a more thorough investigation, to establish whether the princess really had been poisoned. But I said no, because I was firmly convinced of Maria Luisa's holiness and innocence.

Leziroli made several attempts to exonerate his fellow Jesuit: "But I must also confess that Padre Peters relied on my authority, so I am guiltier than he."

The judges refused to accept that Leziroli hadn't been aware of the details of the poisoning. They confronted him with numerous witness statements that contradicted what he had said. Finally he had to admit that, shortly after the prophecy of Katharina's death, he learned that the novice mistress had not only asked Agnese Celeste about the effects of various poisons, but had also ordered a series of poisonous substances from various apothecaries in Rome. But once again, he saw the devil at work in Maria Luisa's shape.

Even the poisoning of Sister Maria Agostina didn't cause him to doubt the madre vicaria's integrity during his time in Sant'Ambrogio.[17] It was only after the Apostolic Visitation, when he was dismissed from his post as the convent's confessor, that he began to suspect that both Katharina von Hohenzollern and the late Sister Maria Agostina had been given "something harmful" to cause their illnesses, and Agostina's death. He didn't believe it was a case of poisoning. He only started to have his doubts when, following the Visitation, Padre Peters told him Maria Luisa had prevented him from seeing the sick woman, when Maria Agostina had expressly asked Leziroli for him.

Eventually, the regular confessor and spiritual director of Sant'Ambrogio made a detailed admission of guilt.[18]

First, he confessed that he had endorsed the holiness, the visions, stigmata, and many other supernatural gifts of the condemned Sister Maria Agnese Firrao, both in writing and verbally. He had promoted her cult in various ways, and had invoked her as a saint. "I admit that I did wrong, and ask for forgiveness."

Second, he confessed to promoting the feigned holiness of Sister Maria Luisa in various ways, through writing, verbal statements, and

reprehensible actions. He had believed the supposedly divine correspondence to be real, even though the subject matter of these divine
missives was sometimes unworthy of God and the saints. He had
come to the defense of this "saint," with her visions and her heavenly
marriage and divine rings, against the nuns' doubts and fears, which
later proved to be justified. And he had made himself an accomplice to
Maria Luisa's crimes, immoral acts, and other misdemeanors, which
he now recognized as such. "I do not know how I can explain my great
confusion and blindness at that time. I remain confused, and admit
that, unfortunately, I have erred."

Third, he confessed that he was guilty of knowing about, endorsing, and assisting in the expulsion of Sister Agnese Eletta from the
convent. "For this, too, I beg forgiveness."

Finally, he confessed to promoting precepts and practices that were
out of line with healthy theology and morality. Some had been wrong
and dangerous, and their use in Sant'Ambrogio had had serious consequences, such as blasphemy and perjury. "For this I also ask God
and the Holy Office for forgiveness."

The tribunal stated that he was guilty on several charges, and in
conclusion the Jesuit replied that although he had erred, he had not
done so consciously. Leziroli recognized that the Inquisition's judicial proceedings had been perfectly correct, and the transcript was
an accurate record of his interrogation. Like Maria Luisa, he declined
a defensive process with a reexamination of the witnesses, as well as
any further defense. The answers he had given had been his defense.
He was happy just to allow the assigned counsel, Giuseppe Cipriani,
to review the files. On September 13 and 17 respectively, the fiscal,
Antonio Bambozzi, and then Cipriani, checked the draft *Ristretto* for
Leziroli's interrogation, countersigned it, and released it for printing.
In October 1861, copies were made on the Inquisition's secret internal press, and distributed to its deciding authority: the consultors, the
cardinals, and the pope.

MARIA VERONICA MILZA: AN ABBESS BEFORE THE COURT

Sallua began his witness examination of Abbess Maria Veronica in
mid-January 1860 as part of the informative process. She pulled the

wool over his eyes several times. It was only when Sallua confronted her with witness statements from her fellow nuns that she admitted to "intentional omissions, lies, and several counts of perjury." The Dominican therefore called her a "model of wickedness."[19] On March 16, following the preferral of charges, the cardinal vicar had her secretly moved to the conservatory of Santa Maria del Rifugio, near Santa Maria in Trastevere. The pope stipulated that neither she nor the other nuns from Sant'Ambrogio were permitted to wear the habit of the Regulated Third Order. Instead, she was given a simple black tunic.

The abbess's interrogation as a defendant lasted from March 22 until July 31, 1861.[20] Adelaide Milza (her secular name) told the court that she came from Sonnino in the province of Latina.[21] She had been born in 1806, and was the daughter of Giuseppe Milza, since deceased. She came to Rome at the age of nineteen, and spent a year in the convent of Santa Pudenziana.[22] She wasn't able to profess her vows there, as she wished, and so in October 1827 she went to the reformed Sisters of the Third Order of Holy Saint Francis in Borgo Sant'Agata. She was clothed in February 1828, and in October of the same year the entire community moved to the convent of Sant'Ambrogio, where she professed her vows. Over the years, she was entrusted with many offices and duties there. She was under-mistress, nurse, novice mistress, and was twice elected vicaress, before taking over the office of abbess at New Year 1854–1855.[23]

Just after the start of the Apostolic Visitation to Sant'Ambrogio in the fall of 1859, the vicegerent had instructed the convent's superiors to hand over all documents and objects from the mother founder, Agnese Firrao. The abbess was noticeably reticent, even at this stage. When she was interrogated as a defendant, she was forced to admit she hadn't obeyed this instruction. In fact, she had ordered her nuns to hide or burn Firrao's writings to prevent them from falling into the Holy Office's hands, for fear that this "could be the ruin of herself and the institute." She had asked Maria Colomba to throw the incriminating files on the fire immediately; Colomba replied, "Stay calm, I will take care of it." One of Maria Agnese's letters from 1838 contained an extremely disparaging remark about the family of a servant of the bishop of Gubbio. She said he was neglecting her in such a way "that she will be found dead one of these days." She called the confessor a false "flunky." These phrases, in the abbess's opinion, were unworthy of a saint, and must not be seen by the Holy Tribunal.

Maria Veronica also said that the nuns of Sant'Ambrogio had systematically bribed the mother founder's father confessors in Gubbio. They used little favors and larger "gifts" to gain the confessors' support for their forbidden correspondence with Maria Agnese in exile. The inquisitor emphatically rejected the abbess's claim that this contact had been allowed, in spite of the 1816 judgment.

The court listed a whole series of documents from the Roman Inquisition's archive to prove the prohibition had remained in place. More important, these documents were supposed to prove that the nuns of Sant'Ambrogio had always been aware of this fact. And the files all said the same thing: the convent's superiors repeatedly sought to have the 1816 ban on communication officially lifted, even after 1829. In December 1831, for example, they appealed to Cardinal Giacomo Giustiniani.[24] He had been a cardinal member of the Roman Inquisition since February of that year, and was promoted to become prefect of the Congregation of the Index in 1834. They asked whether Firrao might not be permitted "to communicate with the nuns of the convent she founded, by direct or indirect means." This plea was rejected by the Holy Office, as were others from September 17, 1834, and August 12, 1846.[25]

With the juridical illegitimacy of the correspondence thus clarified, the abbess was called upon to explain what constituted Sant'Ambrogio's "famed spirit of perfection," and what relation this bore to the mother founder's supernatural gifts. Maria Veronica replied that it was only because Firrao had been a soul chosen by God that she was able to found an institute of such great holiness. She cited the wound in the founder's side as conclusive proof of her holiness, and the spirit of Sant'Ambrogio that stemmed from it.

The investigating judge was particularly struck by the abbess's "dishonesty" when it came to the biography of Firrao written by Abbot Marconi. In her first hearings, Maria Veronica had denied the existence of this work many times over. Sallua now produced several witness statements that revealed just how familiar she was with the biography. Her reply is typical of her behavior before the Holy Office's tribunal: "What I said only appears to be a contradiction: by a life of Maria Agnese, I meant a printed book. When I said there was none, I thought you were asking me about a published work. Now I understand that this also included manuscripts, and in truth I must say that these did indeed exist, although I do not believe they were the work of Abbot Marconi."

Nor did the court believe her when she said she had always acted in "good faith and conscience." Her excuse was far more reticent than Padre Leziroli's: she claimed she had simply been following the convent's tradition, and the example of others. The abbess thus denied any personal responsibility for perpetuating the cult of Firrao, blaming everything on the structures and system of Sant'Ambrogio.

When she was questioned about Maria Luisa's feigned holiness, Maria Veronica praised this sister's "innocence, virtue and simplicity," and "celebrated her holiness and her supposedly supernatural gifts."[26] Her unequivocal belief in "saint" Maria Luisa's authenticity was based on the heavenly letters and, not least, on the authority of the confessor. She quoted Padre Leziroli as saying that "even if an angel were to come down from heaven and tell him the opposite, he would not believe it." And the learned theologian Padre Peters, "a man in whom even cardinals confide, and rightly so," had spent days at a time with Maria Luisa during her ecstasies. He had sacrificed many hours from his theological studies to attend to her—which confirmed to the abbess that Maria Luisa was something "out of the ordinary."

There had been a clear reversal of roles in Sant'Ambrogio. The Rule said that the vicaress should be nothing more than a dependent helpmeet to the abbess, but Maria Veronica had been elected abbess by the grace of Maria Luisa. And it wasn't just that she had been chosen on the strength of Maria Luisa's vision; in the course of her time in office, she proved to be a puppet in Maria Luisa's hands. One symptom of this role reversal was the way in which blessings were dispensed. Normally, an abbess would bless her nuns. In Sant'Ambrogio, however, the vicaress blessed the abbess on a daily basis. "Every evening I received the blessing from Maria Luisa, in the following way: I knelt down, kissed the ring on her hand, and she made the sign of the cross three times on my forehead and heart, pressing her hand to my breast. Maria Luisa told the father confessors of this practice, and because of the comfort it brought me, they said I might continue with it."

With the support of a few of the older sisters, the abbess made at least one attempt to revolt against Maria Luisa's regime. Significantly, this was when Agnese Eletta was expelled from Sant'Ambrogio. The abbess and Maria Costanza appealed against this decision to Cardinal Vicar Patrizi—but he just informed the spiritual director, Leziroli, of what they had told him. Leziroli gave the abbess and the older nuns a telling off, and threatened certain punishment from God if these accusations against Maria Luisa went any further. After this they gave in, and bowed to the Sant'Ambrogio system.

Maria Veronica also knew about Maria Luisa's highly problematic recruitment of young nuns, as she admitted to the court. She gave the example of Angelica Volpiani from Ferrara, who was taken into the convent following pressure from the novice mistress and Leziroli, even though the girl's mother was against it. She was hurriedly clothed and given the name Maria Agostina. The abbess had relented and given her assent to the acceptance of this attractive and powerful young woman, although from the outset Angelica Volpiani had made an unfavorable impression on her. In the abbess's view, this young woman had no vocation. The order's rules stated that as the mother superior, Maria Veronica should have rejected her on these grounds. And Maria Agostina's tragic fate showed just how disastrous it had been to ignore the rules: in the truest sense of the words, Maria Luisa drove her to her death.

Even before the convent had won Katharina von Hohenzollern as a novice, Maria Luisa told the abbess of "various revelations, particularly coming from the Madonna." The Virgin was adamant they should take Katharina, writing in one letter: *"The princess must be mine, whether sick or well."* Unfortunately, the abbess could say nothing of the exact circumstances in which the princess had been recruited—the role of Cardinal Reisach, for example.

The letter from the Virgin was part of Maria Luisa's plan to found an offshoot of Sant'Ambrogio, where she could become an abbess herself. Agnese Eletta, the vicaress's former bedfellow, told the prioress of San Pasquale that in 1857, Maria Luisa had foretold that she would "go to France with a Signora for a new founding."[27] When Katharina von Hohenzollern came to Rome in the summer of that year, Maria Luisa must have heard about her search for a suitable convent, her poor state of health, and, most important, the substantial convent fund Katharina had established after the death of her second husband. But there was only one person in Rome who could have given her this information: Katharina's spiritual guide and confessor, Cardinal Reisach. And after the princess entered Sant'Ambrogio, Reisach seems to have convinced her to add a clause to her will stipulating that "a convent of the same institute is to be founded, the first founder of which must be the madre vicaria, Maria Luisa." Hohenlohe provided this information during his hearing on April 19, 1860, adding that the sealed testament was in Reisach's hands.[28]

"The princess must be mine, whether sick or well," wrote the Virgin. In reality, this was a monstrous demand: it wasn't Mary in heaven but Maria Luisa in Sant'Ambrogio who wanted to possess Katharina. And the princess did seem like a gift from heaven, to help her fulfill her lust for power.

CONFESSIONS

The abbess was not to be swayed from her firm belief in Maria Luisa's holiness and the authenticity of the supernatural phenomena that surrounded her, despite the judge pointing out the "disconnections and contradictions" in her statements. It was only after he had given her a "severe and at the same time paternal warning" that she confessed to having acted unjustly, and begged the court for forgiveness. "I realize that I have done wrong. I was truly blind in allowing Maria Luisa to err in so many ways. I realize that I am guilty of knowing about her errors and illusions. I therefore beg forgiveness.... I ask God, the Holy Tribunal, and in particular His Eminence the cardinal vicar for forgiveness: I deceived him for a long time, by keeping all these things from him. I now thank the Lord for opening my eyes and showing me the abyss in which I and the entire community found ourselves. He removed the blindfold from my eyes, and I feel like a completely new person."

She now answered the charges in detail, saying she had not only been informed of the intimate acts between Maria Luisa and Padre Peters; she had actively encouraged these.[29] From the outset, she had noted the "delight" with which Padre Peters had looked upon the beautiful vicaress. Once, the cardinal vicar came to the convent unannounced while Peters was in Maria Luisa's cell. She herself had quickly hidden him, so that Patrizi wouldn't suspect any wrongdoing. And she was the one who had allowed the padre to enter the enclosure.

Then the abbess came to the poisoning of Katharina von Hohenzollern.[30] At first, the novice mistress had been able to "quell the princess's mistrust with her flattery and sweet words." But at that moment when the princess "told the father confessor about the Americano's letter, which contained vile words," Maria Luisa's hatred for her had grown immeasurably. "She was further enraged by the princess's act of humility, when she came to her on the morning of the feast of the Immaculate Conception and begged her to tell the truth." The abbess admitted she had acted wrongly, increasing her own guilt in the whole affair by believing Maria Luisa's version of events instead of Katharina's. She had been blinded by the vicaress's apparent holiness.

Maria Ignazia's statements on the poisoning were read out to the abbess, and she corroborated them before the court. "They are indeed correct ... and represent the precise facts," she said—though admittedly with the caveat that she could only judge this so far as she herself had been informed about the affair. "A few facts concerning how the poisons were administered were unknown to me, or I could not believe them when other people told me."[31] Maria Ignazia had in fact exonerated the abbess on some fundamental points, saying that she had no active involvement in the attacks, and knew nothing about various important details of the poisonings. The tribunal accepted this. There were some facts that couldn't be denied, because the body of evidence was so overwhelming—but Maria Veronica claimed she had followed the confessors' instructions, and had simply written these off as "illusions created by the devil."

In spite of this partial exoneration, the abbess accepted ultimate responsibility for the attempts on Katharina von Hohenzollern's life. As the mother superior of Sant'Ambrogio, she was to blame for everything that happened there. She saw Maria Luisa's feigned holiness as the key to all her crimes and immoral acts. If she had spoken out against the false cult of Maria Luisa in time, none of these other terrible things would have happened. However, there is no way of knowing whether the abbess came to this conclusion on her own, or if she was just agreeing with Sallua and the Inquisition, who believed that false faith almost automatically led to false actions.

In any case, the abbess placed a great deal of blame on Padre Peters.[32] In her eyes, he was the principal promoter of Maria Luisa's holiness. He was also the person most deeply involved in everything that had gone wrong, through the heavenly letters and his "improper" intimacies with the madre vicaria. And he had the most to lose if the case became public knowledge. Maria Veronica said he had been deeply perturbed, and had told her anxiously: "The cardinal vicar knows something." In an attempt to stop anything coming to light, Padre Peters had sworn the nuns, including herself, to secrecy. She and the nuns had obediently lied or refused to speak to the visitators, and had even kept their promise when they were first called to appear before the Inquisition. Peters had officially informed her in writing that she must tell all; face-to-face, however, he had told her she should reveal nothing.

At the end of the abbess's interrogation, Sallua summarized her confession into five points. One: she had admitted to actively encouraging the cult of Firrao. Two: she had also lent her enthusiastic support to Maria Luisa's feigned holiness. Three: she had abused her office with regards to the enclosure. Four: she had blindly and falsely believed in the supposed apparitions of the devil. This "deception" had been repeatedly used to commit numerous offenses and slander innocent parties. Five: she was to blame for various false precepts and scandalous practices in Sant'Ambrogio. This covered a whole gamut of deviant religious and social behavior, from lesbian initiation rites to amorous relationships with men, and the continual breaking of the rules on fasting, confession, and Divine Office.

Maria Veronica gave a "sincere" confession (as the court noted with satisfaction), acknowledging her guilt on all points. "I confess that I have done wrong, although I must say, there were some things I would not have done had I known that they were evil. I beg forgiveness, and to be assigned a punishment, so that I might atone for my mistakes." She raised no objection to the possible punishments the judge mentioned to her, "because I wish to make reparations to God and the Holy Tribunal."

The abbess declared the trial against her to be legitimate, and declined a reexamination of the witnesses and a defensive process, as well as a period in which to retract her confession. Nor did she take advantage of the right to instruct her own defense counsel. The

Holy Office called in its lawyer once again, just as it had done for Maria Luisa and Padre Leziroli. Giuseppe Cipriani read over the files and signed them off on September 16, 1861. The fiscal, Antonio Bambozzi, had already done this on September 12. The *Ristretto* for the abbess's interrogation could now be printed for the cardinals and consultors. They were given their copies in October 1861, and used them to reach their verdict on Maria Veronica Milza.

"During These Acts
I Never Ceased My Inner Prayer"

The Interrogation of Giuseppe Peters

PADRE PETERS'S TRUE IDENTITY

Padre Giuseppe Peters had been Sant'Ambrogio's second confessor since 1856. The decree of February 27, 1861, which marked the official start of the offensive process, brought charges against him and Padre Leziroli. Both Jesuits were forbidden from making contact with each other, and from taking confession from men or women. The interrogation of Padre Peters began on March 11, and lasted until August 2, 1861.[1]

When he first appeared before the Holy Office, Peters accepted the decisions it had made in his case up to that point "with reverence"— the phrase all defendants were expected to use.[2] But there was a surprise to come, when the court began proceedings by taking down, as customary, his personal details. The name Giuseppe Peters, by which the Jesuit was known in Sant'Ambrogio and many other places besides, was just a pseudonym. He had adopted this alias on the advice of superiors of the Society of Jesus, when he started his novitiate in Switzerland. They had suggested he change his name to help him avoid police investigation by the Protestant government of Prussia. He continued to use the name Peters, which was easy for Italians to pronounce, in his day-to-day activities—particularly pastoral care. But when it came to "matters of importance"—books and votums for the pope, or for one of the Roman congregations—he always used his real name: Joseph Kleutgen.

In the convent, acting as confessor and spiritual advisor, he was simply the pious Jesuit Giuseppe Peters. But when he was writing books, debating issues central to the Catholic Church, providing inspiration to cardinals like Reisach, or advising the pope, he was the great theologian and philosopher Joseph Kleutgen—an illustrious master of the arts of scholastic argument and distinction. This posed a special challenge to the Roman Inquisition's investigating court. They weren't dealing with some naive little Jesuit padre; this defendant was a skilled rhetorician, and a member of a far-reaching social, political, and theological network.[3]

Joseph Wilhelm Carl Kleutgen[4] came into the world on April 9, 1811, in Dortmund, Germany. He was the second of five children born to Wilhelm and Anna Catharina (née Mergendahl) Kleutgen. His formative years coincided with one of the greatest periods of upheaval in modern Church history.

The French Revolution of 1789, and the secularization of Germany in 1803, shattered the thousand-year-old structure of the German Catholic *Reichskirche* and swept away the spiritual basis of classical Catholicism as well.[5] When Germany's prince-bishoprics were dissolved, most of the country's Catholics came under Protestant rule. Kleutgen's hometown of Dortmund, which was part of the archbishopric of Paderborn, became Prussian. There was no more religious unity within the various German states. The 1648 Peace of Westphalia meant each state had been governed according to the motto *cuius regio, eius religio*, but now the Christian denominations were competing with each other within states, each attempting to mark out its own territory. Ecumenical approaches to the problem were the exception rather than the rule. In Germany, the nineteenth century is often called the second age of confessionalization. While Protestants and Catholics were equal in number and—on paper—had equal rights, Catholics were de facto denied entry to higher offices. The result was Catholic inferiority, as authoritarian Protestants marginalized Catholicism's influence in government and society. The Catholic population became increasingly ghettoized.

It was the early 1830s before the bishoprics were reestablished in Germany, allowing at least partial restoration of the Church's outward structure. Internally, the Catholic Church of the early nineteenth century was characterized by spiritual turmoil and theological uncertainty. Wildly different models of Catholic faith vied with each other for supremacy. There were enlightened and liberal Catholics, adherents of a state church, and Romantics. German Catholics also became more strongly oriented toward Rome, a movement that eventually crystalized into Ultramontanism.

Following the July Revolution of 1830, there was an increasing polarization within Catholicism. On the one side stood the liberals, who sought to reconcile the Church and the world, faith and knowledge; on the other, the intransigents, for whom all new ideas were polluted by the malignant spirit of the revolution. They held the modern world and the old Church to be fundamentally irreconcilable. These Church-political parties and groups followed different theological or philosophical models. For the intransigents, who were strongly canonical theologians, Romantics, and new scholastics, Saint Thomas Aquinas held the answers to all questions. They therefore rejected modern philosophy and its representatives—like Immanuel Kant and his school—as dangerous heretics. The modernizers, on the other hand, believed that new questions called for new answers, which could only be found by engaging with modern philosophy, from Descartes to Kant. This was the position held by theologians like Johann Sebastian Drey[6] in Tübingen, Johann Baptist Hirscher in Freiburg, Georg Hermes[7] in Bonn, and Anton Günther in Vienna.

Joseph Kleutgen, along with a whole generation of young Catholics, found himself in the middle of this great quest to reform Catholicism. At first, he seems to have had relatively liberal leanings. After finishing school in 1830, he went to Munich University to study philosophy and classical philology. There he joined the student fraternity "Germania," which was influenced by the emotionalism around contemporary notions of liberty. Through Germania, he became involved in student unrest, which led to the temporary closure of Munich University and the expulsion of students from outside the city. Kleutgen was judged to be a subversive, and forced to leave the city on the Isar River. He had fallen victim to the spirit of Carlsbad, which saw dangerous revolutionary ideas behind every national movement for liberty. Led by the Austrian chancellor, Prince Clemens Wenzel von Metternich, the most important states of the German confederation had met in the Bohemian spa town in 1819. There they had formulated the "Carlsbad Decrees," which included extreme restrictions on freedom of speech, and a strict oversight of the universities. But Kleutgen did not stay "liberal" for long.

Following the premature deaths of two of his contemporaries, he underwent a radical change of religious direction. Now he regarded only the strictest ecclesiasticism as truly Catholic. All experiments with freedom were passé; Kleutgen allied himself wholeheartedly to what he saw as Catholicism's eternal values: the pope in Rome, and the *Theologie der Vorzeid*. This was to become the title of his major work, the four volumes of which appeared between 1853 and 1870. In 1832, he began to study theology in Münster. Within the faculty, he immediately sided with the reactionary opponents of the Hermesians. Following their teacher, Georg Hermes, the Hermesians had a sort of bourgeois Catholicism, which sought to reconcile faith and reason, attachment to the Church and modern philosophy. Hermes had worked as a professor of theology in both Münster and Bonn. In 1834, three years after his death, he was denounced by Metternich and other right-wing Catholics, and Pope Gregory XVI added him as "revolutionary" to the *Index of Forbidden Books*. In condemning Hermes, the chancellor and the pope also met the religious sensibilities of the young Kleutgen.

Kleutgen made his basic standpoint clear in one of his very first theological text, his *Memorandum* of 1833.[8] His thought was born of an anxious search for security in an age of upheaval and uncertainty. It was, after all, only just over three years since the July Revolution. Kleutgen didn't want to keep searching for new answers to new questions. He was weary of the Enlightenment's "independent thought" and was looking for eternal truths. "People left the old literature to molder in libraries, and the pope on the other side of the mountains. They ignored all the achievements of the past, believing the only way to attain salvation is to lay an entirely new foundation," he complained. He saw this "double dispensation," from being "led by the supreme head of the Church" and from "looking at the Church's past," as the fundamental problem in the Catholicism of his time. He placed the blame for this on the widespread "mania for liberty," which he attributed to modern philosophy in general, and in particular the thought of the French Revolution, which perforce ended in chaos and the guillotine.

For Kleutgen, true freedom "blossomed" "precisely from obedience."[9] The *Theology of Times Past* provided eternally valid answers to contemporary questions. For him, the only true philosophy was that which took "its form from Greece's most acute thinker [Aristotle], its ideas from the leading light of Christianity [Augustine], and its instruction from Thomas Aquinas." This theology ranged from Anselm of Canterbury in the eleventh century to writing produced in the mid-eighteenth century.[10]

Combating Catholic authors whom he believed had been infected by the spirit of the Enlightenment, and defending the *Theology of Times Past* against all modern concepts, became Kleutgen's life's work. His goal was nothing less than the comprehensive restoration of scholastic thought; new scholasticism would become the official Catholic philosophy.[11] Kleutgen rose to become the leading proponent of new scholasticism. At the same time, he began to view the pope as the eternal rock of Peter, to which he could cling through all the storms of the modern world. The dogmatization of papal infallibility and the primacy of jurisdiction, at the First Vatican Council of 1870, was very much in line with the program he had sketched out in 1833 as a young man of twenty-two.

From April 1833 Kleutgen, a member of the Paderborn Diocese, continued his studies at the seminary there, and in February 1834 he was ordained as a subdeacon. In April of the same year, however, he entered the Jesuit novitiate of the order's German province. At the time, the Society of Jesus was banned in Germany, so the novitiate was located in Brig, in Valais, Switzerland. Dortmund, Kleutgen's hometown, was part of Prussia, and the Prussian ambassador to Bern demanded that Kleutgen go immediately to Berlin to answer for his involvement in the events connected with the "Germania" fraternity. Kleutgen didn't give himself up to the Prussian authorities—who, among other things, expected him to do military service. Instead, he heeded the advice of his order's superior and took Swiss citizenship under the pseudonym Joseph Peters.[12]

From 1836 to 1840, Kleutgen studied philosophy and theology at the Jesuit University in Fribourg. He was ordained as a priest in 1837. From 1841 to 1843, he worked as a teacher at the Jesuit school in Brig, the Spiritus Sanctus College. When the school was nationalized in 1843, there came a crucial turning point in Kleutgen's biography: he was called to Rome to work in the administration of the Jesuit order. He began work there as an employee of the order's secretary, and confessor at the Collegium Germanicum. From 1847, he also taught rhetoric at the Germanicum. The 1848 Revolution forced him and the rest of the Jesuits underground. But in 1850, when the pope returned from Gaeta, Kleutgen was made a consultor to the Congregation of the Index, where he had a substantial influence on the condemnation of high-profile modern theologians.[13] From 1858 to 1862, he was secretary of the order—an influential position, involving a close working relationship with the Jesuit general, Petrus Beckx. This gave him a nuanced insight into the Society's politics. At the same time, he used his position to build up a network of important contacts both inside and outside the Roman Curia.

In 1847, Kleutgen started using his given name again on official documents, although the pseudonym Peters remained in brackets in the order's internal list of members.[14] As he ascended through the Jesuit hierarchy, and achieved his greatest successes in Church politics and theology under the name Kleutgen, he was also working as the second confessor in Sant'Ambrogio.

Kleutgen's biography was shaped by sickness and failure, conflicts and persecution. A serious illness stopped him attending school for two years, and meant he had to put off taking his final exams. After his father's death in 1825, his mother embarked on a new marriage, and bore five more children, meaning Kleutgen had a total of nine siblings. Two of them caused trouble for him within the Church. A half-brother who also wanted to become a Jesuit was dismissed from the Society for morally reprehensible conduct in Fribourg. Another, a priest in the Diocese of Paderborn, converted to Protestantism. He married and started working as a Lutheran pastor in Kleutgen's hometown of Dortmund. Having a "heretic" for a brother—a man who had converted and betrayed the "true" Catholic Church—must have been a bitter pill for the Catholic hard-liner to swallow. In addition to these personal catastrophes, Kleutgen was a member of the Society of Jesus, which meant he spent his whole life being subjected to persecution and oppression from "anti-clerical and anti-Jesuit propaganda."[15]

The experience of persecution, coupled with a fragile mental state, may well have forced him into a kind of habitual defensive position. This made it almost impossible for him to compromise and develop a flexible attitude to the challenges of his age and to look for compromises. He wrote to a friend: "It seems to me that for some time now, divine providence has created circumstances in which everyone is forced into a decision. 'Whoever is not for me is against me.' Half measures will not work any longer. Anyone who is reluctant to declare himself a Roman Catholic with all his heart soon finds himself on the opposing side. Our times demand this division."[16]

In the past, Kleutgen has been characterized as a "depressive" with an "underdeveloped sense of self-worth" who required "strict order and clear authority" to stabilize his personality. He found this in the Jesuits, the Ultramontanist papal Church, and, not least, the *Theology of Times Past.*[17]

How did all this fit with his role as Padre Peters in Sant'Ambrogio, the man who believed in miracles? Had he managed to reconcile the different norms and expectations of his two lives? If he had, then Peters's behavior in Sant'Ambrogio—his belief in holy women, letters from the Virgin, and heavenly rings—would be simply the practical application of Kleutgen's theological and philosophical concepts. Or, in reverse, Kleutgen's theology would be a justification of Peters's behavior. Miracles and apparitions of the Virgin Mary, and the tangible materialization of the supernatural in the natural world, were concomitant with the new scholastics' approach and their understanding of the natural and the supernatural.[18] In this respect, Peters's piety and religious practice followed what made perfect theological sense to Kleutgen.

But there is one crucial dimension of the Sant'Ambrogio affair that cannot simply be integrated into this theory: Peters's moral, sexual, and criminal misdeeds, in particular his lax attitude to the seal of the confessional, and the offense of *Sollicitatio.* These clearly weren't covered by the rigid moral theology of new scholasticism that he stood for. They were much more than "venial sins," or mere human weakness—failings that didn't compromise a theological principle, and could therefore be charitably overlooked.

So there was a degree of conflict between the roles of Peters and Kleutgen. Did he perhaps have two separate identities? Was Peters-

Kleutgen a dissociative personality who, as Padre Peters, could allow himself to do all the "bad" things the prominent theologian Kleutgen could not—things Kleutgen would have condemned? This scenario has shades of Jekyll and Hyde about it. But Peters gives us no reliable symptoms for this kind of retrospective psychiatric diagnosis, which medical historians could reach in cases of "possession" like the Americano, for example.[19] Kleutgen knew exactly what Peters was doing, and vice versa. Admittedly—at least, according to the anti-Jesuit polemic of the time—the Society of Jesus's military structure, and the rigorous ethic of achievement within the pope's mobile response troop, sometimes led to a kind of double morality. The Jesuits were often accused of using extreme sophistry to justify completely contradictory actions, or pervert a norm into its exact opposite.[20] Did this flexible morality also sanction the adoption of two completely different roles by a member of the Society of Jesus?

THE DEFENDANT'S SPONTANEOUS ADMISSIONS

Like other defendants in inquisition trials, when Kleutgen was first brought before the Inquisition, he was given the opportunity to make a spontaneous statement before being confronted with the specific charges against him. The investigating judge asked the standard question: "Do you have anything to say for yourself?" The Jesuit replied that he thought it probably had something to do with his work as a confessor in Sant'Ambrogio.[21] But he didn't follow this up with any off-the-cuff admissions, as the tribunal had hoped. Instead, he gave them an elaborate prepared statement. It was no surprise that as a successful theological author he had approached this task with a pen in his hand. He presented the court with a lengthy memorandum, which he read out in the sessions on March 18 and 26, and signed to approve its inclusion in the files. His dossier outlined seven instances in which he acknowledged that he had displayed "a lack of caution and tact."[22]

The first point concerned Maria Luisa's visions, and his belief in their authenticity. He said the young nun told him that the three late abbesses—Maria Agnese, Maria Maddalena, and Maria Agnese Celeste della Croce—had appeared to her. They wanted to provide her, "or rather, the whole community, with support in respect of spiritual and worldly needs." These visions had occurred very frequently up to the year 1857, when Maria Luisa told him that God had agreed they should cease. However, she later spoke of many other apparitions: sometimes of the Lord, sometimes of the Virgin Mary, or other saints, who always told her of the present glory of Maria Agnese Firrao in heaven, and her future glorification on earth. "I remember two points very well: 1. That Maria Agnese was esteemed particularly highly in heaven because of the greater than average suffering she had endured on earth; 2. that, displaying her stigmata, she said that these stigmata would one day speak." The Inquisition's decree of 1816 had played no role in this context. Later, however, he heard it said in Sant'Ambrogio that false witnesses had been called in the mother founder's trial, and those who had persecuted and accused Maria Agnese, God had immediately punished with death. "But I know that no word of disrespect for the authority was spoken in my presence."

He had viewed the veneration of Maria Agnese as "private invocation," which was "normally permitted" for "deceased persons who died with a good reputation." He took Maria Luisa's "apparitions or revelations" to be supernatural, and, because there must be no contradiction between theory and moral conduct, he decided to give his "tacit consent" to the cult.

I do not say this in order to justify myself entirely, but to show that it was rather a lack of rational consideration than insubordination that led me to err. Let it be known: when I said I acted in good faith, I did not mean the good faith that excuses all guilt. How could I then confess that I have earned punishment? I only meant that I do not hold myself to be guilty of that malice that some things possess by their very nature. I have, however, lacked discretion, in speaking of extraordinary things (however infrequently) with some of the nuns, and with Senor Franceschetti. I am to blame for the lack of caution that led me to uphold the strict secrecy that Maria Luisa had imposed upon me. I should instead have demanded the freedom to speak with educated and experienced men. Not to have done this was the cause of all my errors, and I acknowledge I am guilty of this.

Kleutgen's dossier skillfully shifted the blame onto Maria Luisa and her divinely ordered secrecy. He believed her visions were real. However—and this was the voice of the academically trained theologian—he should have spoken to experts on mysticism, who could have provided him with the criteria for distinguishing between true and false mystics. But he failed to address the central question of why he, an ordained cleric, allowed himself to be sworn to secrecy by a woman. This turned the hierarchical system of the Catholic Church on its head. There was supposed to be a clear distinction between shepherds and sheep, clerics and laity, the Church that taught and the Church that listened. Only priests could impose silence as a penance—and, according to Paul, women had had to stay quiet in church in any case.

In the second paragraph of his summary, Kleutgen turned to the splendid reputation that Maria Luisa enjoyed throughout the convent. It was only when a few sisters who had "noticed something extraordinary" came to him with their observations, "that I must have shown I believed in it." Of course, two "events that were held to be very extraordinary" had become general knowledge. First, Maria Luisa owned rings that she claimed were gifts from heaven, and second, her body started to give off a heavenly fragrance. Kleutgen denied actively encouraging the nuns to venerate the divine ring. But he couldn't explain how, in that case, all the nuns ended up kissing the ring. "If I remember rightly, I said nothing about the ring, though I knew she was wearing it on this day. I thus tolerated this extraordinary fact, at least implicitly, through my conduct. I did not want to humiliate Maria Luisa, and did not give sufficient consideration to the rest."

The third point of Kleutgen's written statement related to the heavenly letters. In the last months of 1856, when he had only just begun serving as second confessor, Maria Luisa started to bring him pieces of writing, "which had been dictated to her, as she claimed, during visitations." To begin with, these were just a few lines long, and gave answers to some of the questions that he had asked beforehand. But gradually they became "proper letters," several pages in length. Maria Luisa told him that during the inspired writing of these letters, she had understood nothing of their content. At first, Maria Luisa wrote these letters during her visions: she was the inspired scribe, a mere tool with no will of her own, whose pen was guided by a divine being. Later, the divine beings supposedly began to write their own letters, giving them to Maria Luisa when she was transported to heaven. She brought the letters, "which were no longer in her handwriting, but in another, very beautiful hand," back to earth with her, to the convent of Sant'Ambrogio.

The Jesuit's belief in the authenticity and heavenly origin of the letters had been unshakable. As he wrote in his dossier: "I blame myself for my recklessness in taking these letters to be the writings of heavenly persons, and, in my replies, accepting what they demanded of me."

So Kleutgen's belief in the letters was not just theoretical. He put the Virgin Mary's instructions into practice—even when she made unreasonable demands on him. His obedience to these supernatural instructions even made him reveal one of his life's greatest secrets: the affair with Alessandra N. This was an open acknowledgment that he had broken his vow of celibacy, making him a fallen priest, and therefore extremely vulnerable. But he thought his secret was safe in heaven, with the Mother of God.

Kleutgen believed Maria Luisa to be a pure soul, fundamentally incapable of lies and deceit. Of course, he said, he had been mistrustful at the start, but his doubts had evaporated in light of "certain things that happened in regard to the heavenly letters." He had always sealed his replies in such a way "that I thought it impossible they could be opened without damaging the paper and the seal. But they were returned to me intact, just as I had left them." As the letters gave precise answers to questions he had asked in his sealed replies, somebody must have assimilated the contents without opening them. This could only have happened by supernatural means. There had thus been no doubt in his mind that the letters genuinely came from heaven.

Kleutgen had experienced a second phenomenon for which he could find no natural explanation. Once, he received a heavenly letter in which some of the text was struck through, which upset his aesthetic sensibilities a great deal. The beautiful letter had been defaced. He carried this letter around with him all day, and so had no idea how, when he looked at it again that evening, the line through the text could have disappeared. There was no correction of any kind to be seen. He had spoken to Maria Luisa about the ugly line, and she had simply advised him to take another look that evening. He could only comprehend the improvement as a supernatural phenomenon. He had also believed the "beautiful handwriting, which was new to me" to be divine. Naturally, he had inquired whether any of the nuns in Sant'Ambrogio was capable of creating an artwork of such heavenly beauty, and had been told that the novice Maria Francesca was a gifted calligrapher. Twice he had asked her whether she had anything to do with the letters, "but she denied everything. I thought her a good and simple soul, so I did not suspect she could be deceiving me." For Kleutgen, this proved the heavenly origins of the letters. Once again, the supernatural was manifesting itself in the natural world.

The Jesuit gave a detailed statement on the content of the letters. Many were religious texts and meditations on Church feasts, with texts for blessings and prayers to be used, or commands from above regarding the regulation of the convent's business and financial affairs. Other heavenly letters provided responses to his "doubts in respect of the sister's spirit," and "gradually explained the mercies that had been bestowed upon her in the course of her life." But far more important for Kleutgen was the fact that the letters reflected his hope of a radical turning point in the course of history, which he saw as having been on a trajectory of decline since the start of the nineteenth century. His longings and the will of God were seemingly of one accord.

> Due to the evil of our century and the regrettable state of all peoples of the world, ever since I was a young man I had cherished the thought and the hope that the Lord would renew the earth through a great reversal. One day I spoke with the sister about the lamentable state of the world, thinking she would understand, and this might motivate her to prayer. She took the opportunity to simulate a revelation, which, so to speak, gradually grew within her. In short, she said the Lord wanted to change the state of the world, by letting His kingdom blossom once more on the earth, and he therefore wanted to destroy and rebuild the earth with His mighty hands.

Kleutgen said he had burned the majority of the heavenly missives as soon as he had read them; the remainder he had kept in a little chest in the convent, to which he had the only key. Following the Apostolic Visitation, when the novice mistress's "deceptions" became clear to him, he entreated Franceschetti to bring him this casket, and then destroyed all the letters. He had obviously never considered there might be another key.

Kleutgen's fourth point was a detailed response to the accusation that he had been inside Sant'Ambrogio's enclosure too often, and had spent time there alone with Maria Luisa. A man's unauthorized entry into the enclosure of a women's convent was a serious offense, and tended to arouse suspicions of sexual misconduct. Kleutgen therefore made attempt after attempt to explain that he had always had a good reason for entering the enclosure of Sant'Ambrogio. "I never went into the convent unless asked by the mother abbess, or at least by somebody acting on her behalf. I believe I never took it upon myself to ask if I might enter, but always waited to be sent for." Whenever he had stayed overnight, or spent several hours there during the day, it had always been for the pastoral care of nuns who were mortally ill or dying.

In the three years from November 1856 to October 1859, seven of Sant'Ambrogio's nuns had been seriously ill. Five of them had come close to death. Two who survived had been described as "dying" rather than sick by the doctors. "So it can come as no surprise that during this whole period I spent ten or 12 nights in the convent. Particularly as I encouraged the sisters to call upon me rather than Padre Leziroli at these times, out of consideration for his age and his frail state of health. I would like to point out that several times, the doctor told me I should stay, but I declined."

Then Kleutgen came to the point that lay at the heart of his frequent visits to the enclosed part of the convent: his relationship with Maria Luisa. He had never sought the company of this young nun of his own accord, he said; the requests for special pastoral assistance had always come from the convent and those in charge. He had only helped Maria Luisa through her supernatural travails because the abbess had asked him to. And in fact, he had often succeeded in healing her with his blessings. He saw this as conclusive proof of the "reality of the sickness." Several times, Maria Luisa had had no pulse. She had been unconscious, and it seemed to him that she was being visited by heavenly beings. "There were a few occasions during these episodes when I remained in the convent not just overnight, but also the following morning; in 1859 I stayed for several days at a time. This was not only to keep watch over her, but also because the nuns had begged me to, saying that the sister was only able to rise from her bed again thanks to my blessings. Even so, after the malady had vanished, it would sometimes return."

Still, it was possible—the Jesuit slyly conceded—that he had given in to Maria Luisa and the abbess on too many occasions, when they requested his pastoral care and extraordinary blessing. Perhaps he had entered the enclosure too often for that reason. He should have found out more about what "the experts" had written on this topic: another of the learned theologian's typical arguments. He claimed that in all the time he was there providing pastoral support, he had never knowingly violated the convent's enclosure—though because "extraordinary things" were happening there, he should have been more careful.

Then the Jesuit turned to his relationship with Maria Luisa:

I come now to the main point of my confession, a testimony I cannot give without great embarrassment and bitter pain. I admit, to my shame, that in summer 1857 I kissed Sister Maria Luisa's hands, her feet, face, mouth and heart—from the outside, through her habit—thinking that she was out of her senses. And while she was in that state, which to me seemed ecstatic, I also embraced her. In saying this, I am repeating the confession of guilt I have already made at the feet of the Savior. Before Him, I confess: 1. that I did not do these things with the intent to commit further acts obscene in nature; 2. that it was not impure passion which induced me to do this; 3. that I felt no immoral love and no affection for this person that would tend to be any kind of greatr confidentiality; 4. that these things I performed were acts of veneration, always done on my knees and with great reluctance; 5. that I honestly and firmly believed the sister was out of her senses, and that she was aware of nothing; 6. as a result, I never spoke about this with her; 7. finally, during the year in which these events took place, and in the two years following, my behavior when in the presence of, or speaking to, this or any other sister was never too free or overly familiar. I always conducted myself with due religious dignity and modesty.

As Kleutgen mentioned in the fifth point of his dossier, he performed these actions several times in Maria Luisa's cell, as she was lying in bed, seemingly oblivious to them. But she had certainly not been naked: not only was she "modestly dressed," she was also covered. The letters from the Virgin gave a "very clear" description of the exact form of "pastoral" assistance Maria Luisa required, and of the special "blessings." Kleutgen believed he was simply fulfilling the will of heaven. It had of course been clear to him that the actions prescribed by the heavenly letters should "not usually be carried out because of the great danger" attached to them. "God would never normally have willed these things; but this was not only a special case, it was a unique case. The matter could be concluded within a short space of time, when the sister would enter a state of deep peace. And when this happened, these things did in fact cease."

According to Kleutgen, this was the whole of the "sad story." What he'd done might look erotic and sexual, but it was actually a special, unique form of pastoral care expressly willed by God. He had never experienced any sort of desire or lust: what he felt was more like "reluctance." And now, as he added by way of conclusion, it was no longer for him to judge whether his had been an excusable error.

In the sixth point of his declaration, Kleutgen touched on Peter Kreuzburg.[23] He admitted they had known each other for around twenty years. Kreuzburg had come to Rome in 1857 against Kleutgen's will, even though he had written to the Americano saying he wasn't able to care for him there. Before Kreuzburg even arrived on the Tiber, Kleutgen had asked Sister Maria Luisa to pray for him. And later, the Americano took it upon himself to go to Sant'Ambrogio and meet Maria Luisa there—which seemed to have a very good effect on his spiritual well-being.

Then the Jesuit brought up the letter that Kreuzburg had written in German, and which Katharina had translated for Maria Luisa. Kleutgen claimed he first learned of this letter's existence from Cardinal Reisach in the fall of 1858. He denied that Katharina had informed him of its "indecent expressions, rudeness and deceit." Maria Luisa had given him the letter, which he glanced over before burning it. This was Kleutgen's attempt to stop the Inquisition accusing him of breaking the seal of the confessional. He was also denying the chronological—and therefore potentially causal—connection

between the obscene letter, Katharina's outrage, and the start of
Maria Luisa's attempts to poison her.

Kleutgen concluded with the seventh point in his dossier, which
concerned the character of the plaintiff. He said Reisach had
informed him of Katharina von Hohenzollern-Sigmaringen's plans
for a cloistered life shortly after her arrival in Rome. She was adamant
that she wanted to enter a Roman convent but, in view of her poor
health, Kleutgen had been extremely skeptical from the beginning.
Reluctantly, however, he had eventually suggested various convents
in Rome: Torre di Specchio,[24] the Salesian Sisters of the Ordo Visitationis, the Teresians,[25] and Sant'Ambrogio. Kleutgen painted himself
as the voice of reason, having always had his doubts about Katharina's vocation and her determination to enter a convent. He had been
against the princess's acceptance into Sant'Ambrogio to the very last,
but she enjoyed the highest level of protection in Rome, and he had
finally had to accept the wisdom of his superiors' decision.

> The princess complained because I alone spoke out against it,
> while Their Eminences Patrizi and Reisach, and even her friends
> and relatives supported her, against expectations. I was reluctant
> to agree, for I could imagine the difficulties a person of her stand-
> ing, her age and *nation* might encounter in that convent. I was
> also mindful of what some people had told me, and what I had
> observed myself: namely that, perhaps not by nature, but because
> of the many illnesses she had suffered, she had a vivid imagina-
> tion and was highly sensitive. She was also not given to persever-
> ance. Although Sister Maria Luisa claimed the princess had a true
> and firm vocation, I was worried for the princess because of Maria
> Luisa. I had no specific reason for this, but I knew that for such
> a lady as the princess, extraordinary occurrences—no matter how
> she interpreted them—could easily be problematic.

Kleutgen's words exposed his defense strategy: he was suggesting that
the princess's testimonies and complaints were not to be taken seriously. Katharina was sick and hysterical; her mind was playing tricks
on her. The next stage of his argumentation followed on from this:
the poisoning attempts, too, were nothing but a figment of the ailing
princess's imagination. The Jesuit rejected any connection between

the administration of poisoned medicine and the start of Katharina's serious illness on December 9, 1858. "Although the princess fell ill and suffered a congestion of the heart after she had taken some medicine, her illness should in no way be attributed to this medicine." Her family had a history of weak hearts: the princess's father had died of one, and many symptoms of the same illness had been diagnosed in her.

In his dossier, Kleutgen also named Maria Giuseppa, Giuseppa Maria, Maria Giacinta, and Maria Ignazia as witnesses who had raised accusations of poisoning.

> And so, if everything seems to point to the fact that no poison was administered, there are also grounds for believing that the nuns I have mentioned were mistaken about this. The princess had expressed her suspicions *before* her illness, and those sisters knew it. In addition, these nuns have made various other claims which have proved to be untrue.... If I had not found that everything had been resolved two or three days later, I too would have been unsettled. But it seemed as though a storm had taken place, after which the community had returned to its usual state of perfect calm.

Eventually, he said, Katharina herself had also calmed down. However, the skirmishes taking place in Italy in the spring and summer of 1859 had sent her over the edge again. When she finally expressed her wish to leave the convent, nobody stood in her way. And as for the discussions in the convent about whether the devil had had a hand in the whole affair: well, Kleutgen had never taken an active part in them.

Kleutgen's spontaneous statement addressed seven of the charges brought against him at the end of the informative process, down to the last detail. Only two charges remained: breaking the seal of the confessional, and *Sollicitatio*. There is no way the Jesuit could have composed his text without precise knowledge of what had taken place in the trial up to that point, including the testimonies of individual witnesses, and the charges being brought against him.

Of course, there was the theoretical possibility that, as the former confessor of Sant'Ambrogio, Kleutgen could have spoken to the witnesses during the informative process, which had lasted for more than a year. There was evidence that he had done this in the case of the lawyer Franceschetti. It was, however, out of the question that he could have been in contact with any of the nuns. Since he had been stripped of his role as confessor, he was forbidden from ever entering Sant'Ambrogio again. But the fact that the Jesuit seems to have been familiar with every detail of the witness statements, and the charges the investigating tribunal were planning to bring against him, suggests he had read Sallua's *Relazione informativa* of January 1861. This document contained a summary of the investigation's findings—but it was top secret, meant only for the eyes of the Inquisition's cardinals and consultors, and the pope. How had Kleutgen come by his information? Who had broken the *secretum sancti Officii*?

A CARDINAL BREAKS THE SECRET OF THE HOLY OFFICE

Theoretically, this could have been any one of around four dozen people: Pope Pius IX, the twelve cardinal members of the Inquisition, the thirty consultors and qualifiers, the commissary, his two deputies, the assessor, the fiscal, and the notary. They were the only people who had received a copy of the secretly printed *Relazione*. But as breaking the secret of the Holy Office would incur severe sanctions from the Church, up to and including excommunication, the document must have been leaked by somebody who was particularly indebted to Kleutgen.

The first people to spring to mind are the members of the Society of Jesus, who were known for their strong sense of solidarity during this period. And in fact there were two Jesuits in the 1860–1861 cohort of consultors: Cornelis van Everbroeck[26] and Camillo Tarquini.[27] Van Everbroeck had been a professor at the Collegio Romano since 1825, and a consultor of the Holy Office since 1836; Tarquini had also gained a professorship at the Collegio Romano in 1852, and had been a consultor since 1856. Both knew Kleutgen through his work in the Jesuits' generalate.

Among the highest tribunal's twelve cardinals, one is particularly suspicious: August, Count Reisach, whom Pius IX had made a cardinal member of the Inquisition specifically for this trial. It was Reisach who had enlisted Kleutgen, under the name of Peters, as a confessor for Katharina von Hohenzollern, and had seen to it that the princess was placed in Sant'Ambrogio. It was Reisach whom Kleutgen had informed about the soup poisoned with alum. It was Reisach who, for this very reason, must have had an interest in his associate Kleutgen mounting the best possible defense, so that Reisach wouldn't find himself in the firing line as well. Everything points to the German cardinal being Kleutgen's informant, and possibly even letting him see a copy of the secret *Relazione.*

Sant'Ambrogio and Katharina von Hohenzollern weren't Kleutgen's only connections with Reisach. The Jesuit padre was, in fact, the German cardinal's closest theological advisor. Reisach's behavior as archbishop of Munich and Freising in Bavaria had made his position untenable, and in 1855, at the request of the Bavarian king, Pius IX promoted him away from Germany, making him a cardinal of the Curia. Reisach's inflexible attitude to a pragmatic solution for the relationship between Church and state had brought him into conflict with the Bavarian government. He had also personally annoyed King Ludwig I[28] with his anti-ecumenical attitude to the funeral ceremonies for the protestant Queen Karoline,[29] Ludwig's father's second wife. On top of this, he was at odds with many of his fellow bishops. Reisach, who had been educated by the Jesuits in Rome, rejected the formation of a German conference of bishops in 1848, calling it an antipapal association. He saw this as a renewal of the German bishops' self-confidence, and a move toward a new German national church.[30] His fondness for mystical phenomena, in particular his dependence on the stigmatized seer Louise Beck, also met with opposition from the German episcopate.

But Reisach placed a large part of the blame for his deportation to Rome on the Munich church historian Ignaz von Döllinger and his theological friends. Döllinger was a former Ultramontanist who had become a liberal. Once in Rome, Reisach tried to exact revenge on them, doing his best to expose and silence their whole movement through indexing and other papal censures.

In order to see this agenda through, he needed an alliance of comrades who would provide him with theological arguments. His most important ally, a man who shared all his views and gave him theological advice, was Joseph Kleutgen. They had been close friends since

1856. The Curia cardinal had the necessary contacts and the requisite influence on Church politics—he even had the ear of Pope Pius IX. The Jesuit, meanwhile, contributed the philosophical know-how for the votums, papers, and summaries they had to produce. Reisach wanted a strictly papal Church; Kleutgen provided the spiritual framework for this with his *Theology of Times Past*. It was no coincidence that the cardinal, who was described as a "warm advocate" of the Jesuit, financed the Italian edition of his major work.[31]

The obvious conclusion is that, when Reisach's most important intellectual authority found himself in a tight spot, the cardinal wouldn't leave him there, particularly as the political background of the Sant'Ambrogio case couldn't have escaped him. The constellation of people involved made this an even more likely scenario: the liberal, pro-Italian Archbishop Hohenlohe and the theologically progressive Benedictine Maurus Wolter on the one side; the papalists Reisach, Cardinal Patrizi, and the Jesuit Kleutgen on the other. The whole thing also had the air of a classic conflict between religious orders. The Benedictines of Saint Paul Outside the Walls were striving for a reconciliation between the Church and the modern world, while the Jesuits, under the influence of new scholasticism, came down ever more firmly on the side of separation. If Reisach viewed Kleutgen not simply as a confessor accused of moral failings—if he saw this as the theological and Church political movement for which they both stood being arraigned before the highest tribunal—then it would be no surprise if he, as a member of the court, was keeping the Jesuit defendant up to date on the internal results of the investigation. Loyalties within his own coterie were more important than the interests of the Church as a whole, the confidence of his own clientele more valuable than the confidentiality of the court files. He must have been well aware that breaking the *secretum Sancti Officii* carried the automatic punishment of excommunication. Reisach apparently accepted this risk in order to give his man the best chance of defending himself.

Even if Kleutgen never told the Inquisition directly about the special quality of his relationship with Reisach, he did make an indirect admission that the cardinal had kept him up to speed on the trial. He explained that he "had heard, from stories told by His Eminence Cardinal Reisach, that the princess had exaggerated somewhat in her statements. Some of her written submissions about the convent had contained a series of inaccuracies."[32] Kleutgen was letting the court know that he was in the picture on Katharina von Hohenzollern's denunciation, at least—and that his information came from a cardinal member of the Inquisition, who was also a close friend of his. In his interrogation on March 28, 1861, the Jesuit claimed that Katharina herself had provided him with the text of her denunciation.[33] But what could possibly have moved the princess, for all her credulity, to take this step? In any case, Kleutgen was also in possession of information that went far beyond the contents of Katharina's *Denunzia,* as his dossier demonstrated. Kleutgen knew how the informative process had concluded—and this couldn't have come from Katharina. Only the members of the Inquisition had access to this information.

It could be that Kleutgen let the reference to Reisach slip in an unguarded moment, in his eagerness to defend himself. But a more likely scenario is that the Jesuit revealed this information strategically, in order to send a clear message to the Dominican Sallua and the other investigating judges: watch out, I know exactly what you've been doing, and my friend the cardinal will be keeping a close eye on you as well.

Kleutgen stuck to his exceedingly confident standpoint throughout his interrogations. He wanted to be treated as a witness and not a defendant in this trial. But, in spite of his constant repetition of this, and all the protection he received from behind the scenes, he didn't get his way. The cardinals and the pope had decided he was one of the main suspects—and that was an end to it.

AND AFTER ALL, THE CULT OF FIRRAO WAS PERMITTED

Once Kleutgen had made his submissions, the first part of the offensive process was over. The ball was now in the Inquisition's court. Would the judges manage to undermine the Jesuit's position? Would they persuade him to respond to the charges and make a genuine confession, as they had ultimately done with each of the other three defendants?

The judges faced a more difficult task with Kleutgen than they had with the other defendants. For one thing, they were dealing with an experienced theologian, an absolute master of the art of rhetoric and scholastic distinction. And for another, he also had insider information on the course of the trial. He was able to construct a targeted defense, and adapt it to changing circumstances. This possibility, which is a given in modern legal proceedings, was unusual for the Inquisition—a fact that led people in Rome to accuse it of handing down arbitrary judgments. Third, Kleutgen's work as an evaluator for the Congregation of the Index meant that he was familiar with the practices and processes of Catholic Congregations, and was acquainted with numerous members of the Congregation of the Index and the Roman Inquisition.

The Jesuit's interrogations dragged on, and the main line of questioning branched off into numerous individual issues. Kleutgen repeatedly submitted written statements, containing corrections, clarifications, or partial retractions of his verbal evidence from the previous day. Like the other defendants, he was accused of having venerated Maria Agnese Firrao as a saint, and of promoting her cult within the convent of Sant'Ambrogio. At the start of April 1861, he made quite a tortuous verbal argument against this, and in his interrogation on April 16 he produced an elaborate written statement.[34] This text made it clear that there was no way the Jesuit would be forced to go on the defensive. Instead, he was attempting to turn the interrogation into a scholastic debate.

The *Quaestio* was: is the cult of Firrao permitted, or not? The court proposed a thesis, called the *Propositio*: the cult of Firrao is forbidden. Kleutgen took up the role of the opponent, whose job it was to refute this theory. As is usual in scholastic publications, he took on all the conceivable arguments in favor of the court's thesis and sought to refute them with his *Contradictiones*. He then arrived at a *Solutio*, the answer to the question.[35]

Kleutgen presented a lengthy disquisition on why he had believed that it was "no longer forbidden" to venerate Maria Agnese Firrao as a saint. Up to this point, he said, he had avoided a detailed discussion of this before the Holy Tribunal, fearing that "to speak about this at length might have seemed disrespectful to the authority. But now, when I am not only permitted, but commanded to provide such an explanation, I can speak freely."

Kleutgen's statement rubbed salt into the Inquisition's wound, which had been festering ever since its 1816 judgment against the mother founder had been disregarded. In Sant'Ambrogio, people had behaved as if the *Damnatio* had never existed. And where would the Church be if every nonentity nun and little confessor could simply ignore the judgments of the highest Catholic religious authority, and go unpunished? The second Sant'Ambrogio trial would set this ignominy right, once and for all.

In the first stage of his argument, Kleutgen gave four reasons that, from his point of view, justified the veneration of Maria Agnese as a saint: "1. The Rule of the reformed sisters was reinstated by Leo XII, after the mother founder was convicted. 2. The constitutions were also reinstated by His Eminence the cardinal vicar after the conviction. 3. The Church authority gave its express permission for the nuns to read two volumes written by Maria Agnese, primarily containing instructions for convent life. 4. I believed the correspondence with the founder had been permitted for a long time by a papal act."

Kleutgen's second step was to preempt a possible objection from his opponents that the church authority had merely declared Firrao's texts to be exemplary, while continuing to regard the author herself as a false saint. The Jesuit's *Contradictio* was:

> Although her life and her teachings did not always agree, so that one might condemn the life and devalue the teaching, it would be very unlikely that an evil and duplicitous woman could write volumes on the spiritual life without the poison that filled her somehow revealing itself in these books. And if this is difficult, then it also appears unlikely that a false and villainous woman . . . could write regulations, constitutions and tracts on piety, teaching how and in what spiritual disposition all private and communal parts of convent life are to be approached, without these prescriptions contradicting healthy religious teachings in the slightest. But if this should prove possible after all, then the Church authorities (I, at least, believed this) would never approve such writings.

There was no doubt that the Church had approved three texts: the Rule, the constitution, and two volumes of spiritual exhortations.

Kleutgen then imagined the objection his opponents might raise to the connection he drew in his *Contradictio* between teaching and life, author and text. This, too, he refuted, by demonstrating that the Church authority would have given the nuns of Sant'Ambrogio a "double obligation" that they could never fulfill. But, he argued, the prudence of this same Church authority made it impossible for it to impose commandments that couldn't be fulfilled.

> If the superiors continued to demand that the judgment be followed, what expectation would this place on the nuns? Almost every day they had to hear Maria Agnese's words in the choir, in the chapter house, in the refectory. These words were in their heads day and night; they had to love and honor them as the true expression of God's will. But at the same time they had to take care not to express any good opinion of the person who spoke to their hearts through these writings, and who inculcated these same things in them through her very frequent letters. They had to convince themselves they could become holy, and give thanks to God, so long as they were permeated by the spirit of the Rule, and the constitution, and Maria Agnese's other writings. But at the same time, they must not doubt that these instructions for a spiritual life came from a heart that was filled not with God's grace, but with wickedness and bitter gall.

Such a "double obligation" would have torn these pious women apart. Ergo, the Church could not have demanded it.

It was only then that Kleutgen presented, with great relish, his most important argument for the veneration of Agnese Firrao having been permitted. "Leo XII accepted the Rule again, and encouraged the reform to flourish once more. This pope permitted the relationship between the nuns and their mother founder." Leo XII had also given the nuns back their constitution and Maria Agnese's other writings through the power of *Sanatio*, the retrospective redress of a failure of justice. The Jesuit was unashamedly criticizing the Inquisition's decision of 1816: "I thought that the superiors, not wishing to see any contradiction in these files, had discerned that in the trial against Maria Agnese, something had happened that can sometimes happen." In plain terms, this meant that the Holy Office had made an error, and the pope had repaired this failure of justice in 1829. Kleutgen went on: "I did not doubt the Holy Office's competence in reviewing legal matters." He was aware that Maria Agnese had repented, from a letter she had sent to the Holy Office. "But I never heard that this document was formally delivered to the convent by the Church authority." If this had happened, the nuns wouldn't have indeed been able to say that they knew nothing.

This was strong stuff. Kleutgen was accusing the Holy Office of dilettantism and incompetence in seeing through the decisions it had reached. He refused to accept the judges' counterargument, that there had never been any doubt within the convent about the uninterrupted validity of the 1816 decree (even if there was a possibility the official letter wasn't delivered).

> I cannot believe that such simple and virtuous women consciously set themselves against the authority. When I came to the convent . . . I discovered that Maria Agnese was, in fact, still being venerated as a saint. . . . Finally, to be brief, I and many others who knew Maria Agnese found her order's veneration of her to be completely normal; other padres before me had tolerated it. In the first few months, I noticed that Cardinal della Genga, Inquisitor General and Prefect of the Congregation of Bishops and Regulars (who also exercised his authority over the convent, though on what mandate I do not know) knew about this veneration and did not put an end to it. On closer consideration, it seemed to me that the main cause of this veneration lay in the attitude of the responsible authority.

So the highest office of the Catholic hierarchy had approved, or at least tolerated, the cult of Firrao. The obedient nuns had just been implementing these guidelines from above.

Sallua tried to argue against this, saying that the "highest authority"—by which the Holy Office meant itself—had never uttered a single word that could be interpreted as leniency toward Firrao, or any kind of pardon.[36] But Kleutgen steamrollered over his objection. When he talked about the "highest authority," he didn't mean the Holy Office: the highest Catholic authority was obviously the pope. And that had been Leo XII, who had delegated responsibility for the convent to the cardinal vicar. According to canon law, he was responsible for Sant'Ambrogio, as its protector. Other high-ranking members of the Curia were also involved here, particularly Cardinal Gabriele della Genga, the pope's nephew, and Cardinal Nicola Clarelli Paracciani, another of the convent's enthusiastic visitors and supporters.

The investigating judge had to grit his teeth and admit that Leo XII had confirmed the convent's Rule, but he also stressed that this didn't mean the pope had rehabilitated Firrao as an author. The judgment upon her remained valid until her death. "And so the Church authority, in accepting or permitting the use of this Rule and the constitution never—*even indirectly*—thought that the author had written these through divine inspiration, or in fact that they had even sprung from her own mind." Most of her texts had been copied from elsewhere.

The scholarly debate continued. However they might try and reinterpret it, the judges were unable to deny the existence of Leo XII's brief. Kleutgen tried to argue that it represented indirect permission to venerate Maria Agnese as a saint—which was hardly something the brief suggested. The Jesuit admitted to having glorified Agnese Firrao himself, and argued that he was justified in this, for the reasons he had set out. The judges accused him of "ecclesiastical arrogance."

Kleutgen refused to climb down on this matter—and, ultimately, Sallua was unable to refute him. On a factual level, all anybody had were claims, interpretations, and readings: it was Kleutgen's word against Sallua's, and so the matter remained undecided. At the end of this disputation, the Jesuit was prepared to make only the most minimal of confessions. He said that the judges shouldn't take his text, which argued that the veneration of Maria Agnese was permitted, to imply that there was no cause to criticize his behavior. He had merely wanted to give the court some arguments for his "good faith" in the legitimacy of the cult. He stuck to his guns on the issue of Leo XII's confirmation of the Rule and the constitutions as well as on the rehabilitation of Firrao he had derived from it, maintaining that text and author could not be separated. An orthodox Rule could not be written by a heretic. And vice versa: a false saint could not write a sacred constitution. The Catholic Church's teaching authority couldn't contradict itself by approving a text and, at the same time, condemning its author.

On the central question of whether the cult of Firrao was allowed, Kleutgen had cheerfully passed the buck to the Church authority—or rather, to various Church authorities, and ultimately the pope. But if the Church had sanctioned the cult of Saint Maria Agnese, even indirectly, by confirming the Rule and lifting all its previous censures and prohibitions against Sant'Ambrogio (in the words of Leo XII's brief), then perpetuating the cult could no longer be a charge in an Inquisition trial.

The other defendants and witnesses who admitted to following the cult of Firrao also accepted the Inquisition's premise that this was a punishable offense. Kleutgen, on the other hand, called this supposition into question. The practiced theologian Joseph Kleutgen used theological argumentation to justify the spiritual practice of the confessor Giuseppe Peters. There was no conflict between these two rules. Peters and Kleutgen were perfectly in tune.

THEOLOGY AND FRENCH KISSING

Was Maria Luisa a genuine saint? The inquisitors devoted a particularly long time to this question.[37] From the day of his first interrogation, March 11, through to July, they questioned Kleutgen continually on this issue. He gave them a lengthy back-and-forth, constantly quibbling and splitting hairs. Confronted with incriminating witness statements, he would answer evasively. The following day, he would submit a well-structured text, admitting only to what the evidence had already shown. Everything else, he denied. Then the game would begin all over again.

In his second interrogation on March 12, 1861, Kleutgen submitted a handwritten text, in which he put this uneducated nun's excellent theological knowledge down to her holiness, and the authenticity of her supernatural experiences.[38] "In order to speak of the experiences that I took to be superhuman, I made Sister Maria Luisa talk about the most sublime mysteries of our religion: not just the Holy Trinity in general, but the intra-Trinity procession of divine beings,[39] and the qualities of God and their relation to each other.[40] She spoke about creation,[41] salvation[42] and, above all, the working of God in the soul."[43]

Only people with a robust philosophical and theological education would be able to discuss these demanding subjects. The *processiones ad intra*—the ontological origins of the Trinity—are still one of the most difficult issues in the dogma on God and the Trinity. Any knowledge Maria Luisa was able to demonstrate here certainly wasn't the result of years of study. Kleutgen argued that she could only have acquired it through her translation into heaven, and an immediate encounter with God.

"I must say that I never noticed her make an error, and that the sister spoke about all these mysteries with admirable clarity. She answered my objections with precision and a quick wit, always using the correct expressions—often those that only learned men know. I could not think but that this insight had been instilled in her directly; I knew for a fact that before she joined the convent, she had only a pauper's schooling, and I could not discover where she could have got such an education inside the convent." For him, this had been compelling evidence both for Maria Luisa's holiness, and the authenticity of the heavenly letters.

Here, the Jesuit voluntarily moved on to an issue in which Sallua had a burning interest. The sum total of the Inquisition's *corpus delicti* on the letters was the heavenly epistle to Beckx, intended to bring down the theologians Passaglia and Schrader. Sallua wanted to know how the Virgin, or rather Maria Luisa, had come up with the idea for this letter, seeing that it required a detailed knowledge of the relationships within the Gregorian University and the Jesuit order.

The Dominican was, of course, able to make a few deductions himself. The Jesuits were fundamentally divided on the theological direction their order should take. While Passaglia advocated a pluralistic model, Kleutgen favored a monopoly for new scholasticism. The blow to Passaglia must have come at a very opportune moment for Kleutgen.

As usual, the Jesuit's answer was long-winded and full of qualifying clauses. Yes, he had once spoken about Passaglia's theology to Maria Luisa, though without mentioning him by name. Then how had Maria Luisa come by the name of this Jesuit theologian? It was quite simple: Maria Luisa knew all about the theological dispute within the Society of Jesus from her visits to heaven. But Kleutgen then admitted he had spoken to Maria Luisa directly about Schrader and Passaglia, their relationship with each other, and their theological positions. Of course, he added, by this time the whole affair had become public knowledge anyway, and Maria Luisa could have heard the relevant information from "other persons." To the question of exactly how the supernatural letter about Passaglia had come about, Kleutgen gave the cryptic reply: "I believe it happened as you say, although I have no clear memory of these details."

The judges weren't satisfied with this, and demanded more precise answers. And so the Jesuit said that the madre vicaria had claimed the Virgin Mary wrote the Passaglia letter in heaven, in her presence. Kleutgen stressed that in the conflict with Passaglia, the Jesuit general had to support "the teaching of Saint Thomas." This gave Sallua Kleutgen's motive for inspiring the letter. Maria Luisa knew of his heart's desire the resurrection of scholasticism—and tried to serve him in this aim by writing a letter from the Virgin. Significantly, Kleutgen didn't reveal whether he had reacted in any way to learning that the heavenly letters, and therefore also the letter to Beckx, were earthly forgeries.

Sallua also put several questions to Kleutgen about the special Jesuit blessing, which had caught the tribunal's attention in Maria Luisa's testimony. Having given evasive answers during several interrogations, Kleutgen once again submitted a written document on April 22, 1861.[44] In this, he admitted to dispensing the extraordinary Jesuit blessing, which involved embraces and kisses. He called it a "ministry": an "extraordinary" and "superhuman" pastoral service. He had always carried out these acts in good faith, and in obedience to the Virgin Mary. God had chosen Sister Maria Luisa, through the Blessed Virgin, to vanquish the wickedness of the world and rebuild God's kingdom. "And God determined that I should assist her in a particular way, protecting and safeguarding her." The actions involved in the blessing had admittedly "confused" him at first, but the heavenly letters had always reassured him. They told him that God demanded these actions only at this particular stage; it was part of a process that would lead to the "perfect connection" of Maria Luisa's soul to God. The letters also spoke of a "union" between himself and Maria Luisa, but this was of a purely spiritual nature. There had been no suggestion of any other kind of "love," or of a physical union.

The reference to other sorts of love gave the Inquisition the perfect opportunity to inquire about the exact circumstances of the affair between Kleutgen, at that time in his mid-thirties, and a certain Alessandra N. Kleutgen now had to reveal his lover's full name: Alessandra Carli.

Alessandra and her twin brother, Domenico, had been born to Isabella Fellitti and Carlo Buonafede Carli in 1814 in Comacchio, which now belongs to the province of Ferrara. In 1835, her father was appointed vice consul for the United States in Rome. Alessandra came from a prosperous family, and may well have come to the Eternal City with her parents.[45]

Kleutgen answered in writing, as he did on all delicate topics—and this time not in Italian, but in Latin.[46] He was unable to deny the sexual details that Maria Luisa had already given the judges. Now everything came down to how these facts were interpreted. After the Jesuits had been driven out of Rome in 1848, Kleutgen said, he temporarily became a secular priest, and spent two months living with Alessandra Carli as man and wife, in her apartment in Rome. He presented himself as the victim of a seductress. He, the poor innocent priest, had fallen for Alessandra's feminine wiles. At the time, he had so little experience of acting as confessor to female penitents. Up until that point, he had always lived in protected monastic houses, hardly ever coming into contact with "worldly people," let alone young women. Using "false revelations and promises," Alessandra had persuaded him to commit "shameless and improper acts" with her. But during sexual intercourse, he had never had "any debauched or bad intentions," and "during these acts never ceased my inner prayer." He had "not wanted to offend God."

Kleutgen's interpretation was designed to convince the court that the whole affair had been purely mechanical, with no eroticism, excitement, or the involvement of libido. From a moral-theological point of view, it was an attempt to mitigate the fact that he had broken his vow of celibacy and chastity.[47] Up until the mid-nineteenth century, any sexual misconduct on the part of a priest would be made public, and punished by the Church authorities, as a matter of course. Enlightenment thought influenced the perception of priests, who were seen as educators of the people and moral examples. But the rise of Ultramontanism brought with it a renewed, cultish overelevation of priests, who were now more strongly associated with sexual purity. While sexual impurity and defilement through intercourse with a woman didn't make priests unworthy of their cult status according to canon law, they did in the eyes of conservative churchgoing citizens. This meant their sins couldn't be allowed to become public. When a vow of chastity was broken by an ordained man, or in a consecrated place, the moral theology of the time termed it a "*sacrilegium.*"[48] Kleutgen must have done everything in his power to keep his misstep a secret.

For the tribunal, of course, the crucial task here was to clarify whether Kleutgen's sexual relationship with Alessandra Carli was in any way connected to his function as her father confessor. This would have made it the serious offense of *Sollicitatio.* But the Jesuit continued to skirt around this central point. Yes, he had met Alessandra when she came to him for confession. No, nothing had ever happened in the confessional itself. Yes, they had slept together in Alessandra's apartment. In short: he, the inexperienced Jesuit, had been the victim of an experienced woman. He had been attacked by the devilish serpent, working its evil through Eve. Yes, he had "sometimes spoken with Alessandra about such delusions." But later he, too, had become "deluded."

These excuses got him nowhere: the court then made him confess that, having described this whole affair by order of heavenly letters, he had received replies from the Virgin Mary. They told him his relationship with Alessandra had involved a dirty, lustful sexual union. By contrast, with Maria Luisa he would be permitted to experience a pure, divine, lustless relationship with a woman. And Kleutgen had never denied this juxtaposition.

So what sort of divine experiences had he had with Maria Luisa? Were they really so different—simply divine—from the sexual dalliance with Alessandra that he'd described with such sadness? The Jesuit attempted to whitewash the facts the court presented to him using theological distinctions. He did his best to come up with "just" causes for his actions. Once again, he denied having felt any sensual, bodily lust, or *delectatio carnalis.*[49] The embraces, caresses, and kisses he had dispensed had left him quite cold; he had merely been fulfilling his pastoral duty.

The new scholastic had read his Thomas Aquinas thoroughly, and Aquinas had provided him with eternally valid answers to all questions of dogma and moral theology. Aquinas's *Summa Theologiae* declared that an unchaste glance, touch, embrace, or kiss "in and of itself" was not a mortal sin. It only became so when "lust" entered the equation.[50]

In light of the unanimous witness statements, Kleutgen eventually had to concede that he had conducted an erotic relationship with Maria Luisa. He confessed that, unfortunately, it was true that "during the night, in the room he had been assigned, he embraced, kissed and held Maria Luisa, and also put his tongue into her mouth." The Jesuit gave a noncommittal answer to why he hadn't just kissed Maria Luisa on the mouth—why he had left his tongue in her mouth for a long time. In his defense, he said he had only "seldom put his tongue in Maria Luisa's mouth." Still, this meant it had been more than just one kiss. He also confessed to "using the following expressions during the kisses: 'Thou my daughter, my love, first-born, beloved daughter, my delight, my bliss, my treasure.' And as he kissed her heart: 'Thou pure heart, sacred heart, immaculate heart, my treasure.'"[51]

"My treasure"—phrases like this strongly suggest an erotic fascination. At the same time, some of Kleutgen's exclamations had religious connotations, like the "immaculate heart of Mary."[52] This combination of sex and religion arose again and again in Sant'Ambrogio. The dividing lines between sexual acts and the religious interpretation of these acts had been equally fluid for Maria Luisa and the women with whom she shared her bed. Sexual and religious experiences both involve transcendence and the dissolution of boundaries, meaning that there is a structural relationship between the two. In both religious and sexual experiences, there is a sensual, physical precondition for any transcendental experience. But Catholic moral theology has always disputed this connection: real ecstasies can only occur "when they are related to Christ." Only then are religious transcendental experiences considered good, while erotic ecstasies are fundamentally sinful.[53]

Kleutgen wanted his exclamations to be interpreted exclusively as religious rapture, with no sexual content, as we can see from his testimony on May 28:

This did take place. But by way of explanation, I would like to add the following:[54] I ... never had an impure or tender affection for this nun. And because I had to force myself to commit the acts to which I have admitted, I almost always spoke such words with a cold heart, even feeling troubled or bored. I was trying to convince myself that I must show homage and also fatherly love to this soul that I believed holy. I felt this reverent affection only seldom, and weakly—and it was not an outburst of lust, but absolutely ruled by my will.

In his interrogation on June 1, he added that none of the other acts he had committed with Maria Luisa should be interpreted as signs of his lust. True, Maria Luisa had put the finger that wore the heavenly ring into his mouth, for the purposes of veneration, but he had never "sucked" it.[55] For him, a reverent kiss was a religious act, while sucking was something erotic and lustful.

However, Kleutgen couldn't convince the Inquisition that his encounters with Maria Luisa had been exclusively religious and lust-free. Everything they had done together had clear sexual connotations in the judges' eyes. This was a case of "fornication"—as could be seen from the repeated, lingering French kisses.

In the moral theology of the nineteenth century, kissing with tongues was a mortal sin "in intent and in the deed itself."[56] Even partners who were joined in holy matrimony weren't allowed to kiss this way. It was interpreted (with good reason) as an anticipation of sex; this also made it a mortal sin even when it didn't result in ejaculation, or "pollution." More recent publications in cultural studies make this point of view seem not unreasonable: here, French kissing is viewed as an analogy of sexual congress, due to the direct contact of inner organs it involves.[57]

All his powers of scholastic distinction were no help to the learned Jesuit in light of this fact. He couldn't reinterpret the French kiss as a cold act of will, performed in the course of carrying out a divine command. According to his own new scholastic moral theology, it was an expression of pure lust. And if this was a mortal sin for married couples, then how much worse was it for a monk who had taken a vow of chastity, and was sharing this kiss with a virgin dedicated to God?

The crucial issue of seduction in the confessional was, of course, something that also had to be addressed in the case of Kleutgen's relationship with Maria Luisa. Several interrogation transcripts from the end of May and beginning of June 1861 start with remarkably similar questions: Did he know any other confessor who had dispensed a special blessing with similar sexual connotations? Did he know any other confessor who had spent nights alone in a cell with a young nun? Did he know any other confessor who had torn apart his penitent's scapular in order to kiss her naked breast? Did he know even a single confessor who had put his tongue in a nun's mouth for minutes at a time? And so on.[58]

The Jesuit's justifications were of no use here, either. He denied any chronological or other connection between the sacrament of penance that he dispensed to Maria Luisa, and the embraces, kisses, and other touches. He claimed that Maria Luisa had never let him "enter the *clausura*" after confession, which always took place through the grille between the convent's inner and outer parlatory. It was only much later, when he had visited the sick and given them the sacraments, that he visited Maria Luisa in the convent to give her pastoral support. When the court challenged this, he put forward a particularly weak argument, saying he hadn't "paid very much attention to the exact circumstances of confession." Nor had he ever been conscious of "acting wrongly, or abusing the sacraments."[59]

Kleutgen may have forced the inquisitors onto the back foot over the veneration of Agnese Firrao, but he couldn't pull off the same thing when it came to Maria Luisa's false holiness. This wasn't a general cult; it was a case of him personally venerating the beautiful young nun as a saint and an attractive woman. It was an attack on his own moral and pastoral integrity. He couldn't play off Church authorities like Popes Leo XII and Pius VII against each other to undermine the authority of the Inquisition. Kleutgen was a master of disputation in matters of objective fact, but he was unconvincing when it came to subjective misconduct and moral failings. All his attempts at reassurance and scholarly distinction came to nothing. He was even forced to admit that the heavenly letters had told him about Maria Luisa's lesbian relationship with Maria Giacinta—though he had naturally ascribed these "bad deeds" to the devil in Maria Luisa's form. Moreover, in the discussion about French kissing, the court had turned his own scholastic theology against him.

Once again, the question arises of how far the figures of Peters and Kleutgen were united, and how much his testimony was worth. A naive father confessor might have believed in the authenticity of the heavenly letters. But it was surprising that a highly educated Jesuit theologian, as Kleutgen most certainly was, had been taken in by letters that demanded immoral acts of him.

On the other hand, this belief was in line with the well-regarded brochure of 1846, *Über den Glauben an das Wunderbare* (On the Belief in Miracles). The author of this text, who used the pseudonym J. W. Karl, was none other than the young Kleutgen: Joseph Wilhelm Carl were his three forenames. Even at that time, he had mounted an enthusiastic defense of miraculous apparitions, stigmata, and women with mystical gifts. He pointed out that "the gift of miracles is one of the favors bestowed upon the Church by its divine benefactor."[60] It shouldn't be considered improbable "that the saints, and the queen of saints herself, might come down from heaven."[61] But the unusual apparitions that were part of a mystic's life should be approached with extreme caution. It was better to ask three times than to believe too easily. The crucial criterion for judging these divine works was their "wholesome purpose."[62] "Gullibility and precipitate eagerness in these cases" were a great "evil." "We call those people gullible who believe in miraculous apparitions without further ado, before they have been properly investigated."[63] Kleutgen, alias Karl, emphasized the important role played by these female mystics' "spiritual guides."[64] They had to examine all supernatural phenomena with the utmost care. For if "even men whose role is to lead and teach the people" allowed themselves to be gullible and impulsive, "then how much greater and more dangerous will be the outrage of the pious, and the scorn of the unbelievers, if a deception or sham should be discovered!"[65]

This confirms that Kleutgen sincerely believed in the reality of supernatural phenomena, and that this belief had a theological foundation. Visions, apparitions, and letters from the Virgin were quite self-evidently real to him. But then why didn't Peters, working in Sant'Ambrogio in 1857, stick to the criteria that Kleutgen had set down in 1846? Why didn't he ask "three times"? Why was he, a priest and a spiritual guide, "gullible" and more than "impulsive"? The answer may well have been: because he was blinded by his love for Maria Luisa.

NEW SCHOLASTIC CONVOLUTIONS

As it had been for the other three main defendants, the third point to be covered in Kleutgen's hearings was the poisoning of Katharina von

Hohenzollern, and the Jesuit's possible entanglement in the murder plot. Kleutgen also applied his tried and tested strategy to this charge: first, denial, then admitting as little as possible, and finally trying to cast anything he had been forced to admit in a different light in an attempt to mitigate what he had done. After a long back-and-forth, involving extensive discussions and written explanations, the court recorded the following facts pertaining to this charge.[66]

From the outset, Kleutgen had been well informed about the contents of the letter from the Virgin that Maria Luisa made Maria Francesca write for her on December 8, 1858. He also knew about other such prophecies. Since he believed in the authenticity of these letters, he had to assume that the princess's death had been ordained by heaven, and that furthermore she was threatened with eternal damnation. As a good pastor, he should have acted immediately to try and save Katharina's soul, even if he didn't believe he could save her earthly life.

As her father confessor, Kleutgen had also always known that the princess was afraid she was being poisoned in Sant'Ambrogio. However, he didn't take her concerns seriously. He told the Inquisition several times that he believed they were the product of an overwrought noblewoman's imagination. The Jesuit also regarded the Americano's ominous letter as the catalyst for the whole affair. But as Maria Luisa consistently denied having shown Katharina the letter, and because the heavenly letters said it was a satanic trick, Kleutgen chose to believe their version of events.

The Jesuit also knew that some of the nuns suspected Katharina was being murdered with a cocktail of various poisons. Although there were a great many rumors about the poisoning, he had remained convinced that the princess was not being given "any genuine poison." But he then had to admit he had been concerned for his own future, should Katharina decide to talk about the secrets of Sant'Ambrogio outside the convent. Once he had even broached the subject directly with Maria Luisa, and had also communicated his fears to her in writing.

Then the court confronted Kleutgen with Maria Luisa's testimony, which claimed that his fears were the real catalyst for the poisoning attempts. She had set the whole thing in motion as a favor to him, to release him from his concerns. Kleutgen's answer, as was only to be expected, was extremely evasive. "I repeat that I expressed my fears about the princess in the manner I have stated." But what exactly did that mean? Was he afraid *for* the princess, which should have been his duty as a confessor? Or was he afraid *of* what she might say about him and Maria Luisa if she made it out of the convent alive?

There had, Kleutgen continued, been a "huge misunderstanding" regarding the words he had used about the princess's impending death. "I said we should pray for God to show us the truth, because I believed in Maria Luisa's innocence. And as the princess had fallen seriously ill, I may possibly have expressed the opinion that her death might be God's way of putting an end to things that had disturbed both the princess and the community." In plain terms, this meant that Kleutgen had not acted to bring about Katharina's demise; he merely hoped that God would see to this Himself. Then it wouldn't be his fault, but that of a higher power.

The court was, of course, very interested in the exact nature of the "fears and distress" that Kleutgen felt at the prospect of any revelations Katharina von Hohenzollern might make. The Jesuit admitted that he had told Maria Luisa, and probably also the abbess, about these fears. But he had never used the "wicked words" that the witness statements accused him of uttering. And then he passed the buck on to the novice mistress, testifying that his concerns stemmed exclusively from "Maria Luisa's revelations."

He also firmly denied ever having told the nuns to pray for the princess's death. When he had said that the princess was in danger of dying on that particular night, he was "merely repeating Doctor Marchi's words." The court accused him of declaring that the sick woman had to die "as a punishment from God." The Jesuit replied: "This much is true. When I denied that the time of the princess's death was prophesied, I was referring to the prophetic letter. I do not remember Maria Luisa telling me in person that the princess would fall ill that very day. But from what I now recollect, I must conclude that she at least revealed the day the princess was likely to die."

So Kleutgen knew about Katharina's impending death. Her demise would certainly have been advantageous to him: she was party to his secrets, and this would have silenced her once and for all. But the investigating court couldn't prove that he was directly involved in the poisoning attempts.

However, using his authority as father confessor, Kleutgen had sworn the nuns and the abbess to secrecy, and this (among other things) suggested to the court that he was the real initiator of the whole poisoning affair.[67] He instructed them not to tell in the context of the Apostolic Visitation or the Holy Office's tribunal anything about the "extraordinary" things that happened to Maria Luisa, or about his relationship with her. And in fact, many of the sisters kept quiet about everything for a long time. By following their confessor's instruction, some even committed perjury.

This was a monstrous affront to the authority of the highest tribunal. Before the Inquisition, defendants and witnesses were supposed to behave as though they were standing before Christ Himself, the judge of mankind. The investigating judges felt they had come under attack from Kleutgen, and they asked a number of particularly probing questions on this point. At first the Jesuit flatly denied having sworn the nuns to secrecy on the subject of Maria Luisa's holiness, and all that was bound up with it. But, after being presented with countless witness statements, he eventually had to admit that it was true.

Now Kleutgen started splitting hairs once again, frantically trying to find some theological justification for remaining silent before the court. He finally resorted to a piece of moral-theological pedantry around the principle that a witness only had to answer the specific questions he was explicitly asked. He didn't have to volunteer information that would incriminate somebody else. Kleutgen claimed this was what he'd meant when he swore Maria Giuseppa to secrecy: he told her she shouldn't voice her suspicion that Maria Luisa had given Katharina poison *unless she was asked*. Nor did the abbess have any need to speak about those "facts" that Maria Luisa "had revealed to her out of a sense of duty."

Kleutgen claimed he knew "with pure certainty" that he "never *recommended* to the sisters, as a group or individually, that they remain silent on this or that." "And still less did I instruct them to conceal the events that had taken place."[68] It was obvious that his statements contradicted each other, and Sallua immediately pointed this out. The Jesuit backtracked and admitted that he was now "getting a little unsure." "Perhaps" he had told a nun, when she asked, "that she could choose to remain silent on these matters before the authority." "But

I am sure I did not do this because I believed that the extraordinary will of God provided us with a dispensation in this matter. I may just have applied a principle badly." In the following interrogation session, he then contradicted this statement, saying that, at the time, it looked "as if God wanted the matter to remain secret for the time being." "Although this does not release us from our duty to the authority, it could be that God permitted the sisters error."

Even the inquisitors, who were schooled in theology, did not and would not follow the logic of this tortuous argument. Sallua made no bones about what he thought of Kleutgen's flimsy excuses, and worked out exactly what his real motives were—with evident enjoyment, as the files show. This had nothing to do with subtle theological principles and possible issues with the pastoral application of ethical ground rules. The Jesuit was simply afraid that if the nuns gave open and honest testimonies, "a trial would be brought about the poison." Then his own involvement in the whole affair, and in particular his amorous relationship with Maria Luisa, would become public knowledge. It would spell the end of his career in the Catholic Church. This, and nothing else, was what he was desperate to avoid.

In spite of this, Kleutgen carried on making evasive statements. His strategy rested on admitting errors of understanding, but denying errors of will. He was unable to refute the facts that the court presented to him: they were corroborated by numerous witness statements. But he denied having committed these crimes willingly, and with intent. And intent was ultimately impossible to prove in judicial proceedings of this kind. In the end, it was too much for the Inquisition, and they simply recorded that the facts of this case were clear. But Kleutgen refused even to acknowledge this. His characteristic conclusion was: *"I have spoken of my actions, and leave the Holy Tribunal to pass judgment upon them."*[69]

THE COURT'S FINAL PROPOSITION

In the case against Joseph Kleutgen, the court considered the following charges had been proven—through partial confessions, witness statements, and circumstantial evidence:[70]

1. Kleutgen had not only permitted, but also encouraged, the false holiness and the cult of Agnese Firrao, who was convicted in 1816.

2. He had "used numerous unauthorized means to proclaim and support . . . the feigned holiness of the convicted Sister Maria Luisa Ridolfi."

3. He had also "permitted a long-running heavenly correspondence to take place. . . . After you were removed from the convent, you attempted to come into possession of all these letters so that you could burn them, which you subsequently did."

4. The next charge related to Kleutgen's pretension that God had chosen him as an "extraordinary minister," "to protect Maria Luisa as if she were a saint, destined for great things, for the destruction of evil and creation of good. You . . . gave Maria Luisa eager assistance during her extraordinary malady and her many ecstasies, which lasted for hours."

5. "You entered the *clausura* in order to perform the extraordinary ministry mentioned above. When she went into a feigned ecstasy, you supported and embraced her many times, kissing her face and sometimes her throat; sometimes you put your tongue into her mouth. At other times you touched her on the chest, on the side of her heart, and performed acts of veneration."

6. As Kleutgen had also practiced these and other intimacies with his penitent Maria Luisa in the context of dispensing the sacrament of penance, he had become guilty of "*sollecitazione con falso dogma*"—seduction in the confessional, using false dogma.

7. When Maria Luisa claimed to have received money from heaven, Kleutgen regarded this as a miracle and evidence of her holiness.

8. "You arranged for an American, an acquaintance of yours whom you had declared to be possessed, to have contact with Maria Luisa, and allowed him to conduct fanciful, immoral conversations with her, and to write her letters, although these were then ascribed to the devil for their wicked contents."

9. The court believed there was sufficient evidence to prove that Kleutgen had sworn the nuns to secrecy. He had also imposed this duty on the abbess after he was dismissed as father confessor, telling her to remain silent on anything that he believed could cause harm to a third party.

10. "You practiced intimate acts with Maria Luisa and another penitent known to you." The court had not been convinced by Kleutgen's claim that he had always performed these actions "without passion or debauched urges, without affection, not even with slightly impure affection, but using willpower alone."

11. Furthermore, the Jesuit was found guilty of regarding Maria Luisa's revelations as genuine, and acting accordingly.

12. "You accepted the truth of prophecies made by Maria Luisa, both verbally and in writing, regarding the illness and death of a novice, and her eternal damnation." He had also ignored all kinds of justified indications that she was being poisoned, portraying the whole thing as an illusion, and as the machinations of the devil. Interestingly, the court didn't name the victim here. Nor did it state whether Kleutgen was involved in the attempts on her life.

13. "Finally, you were requested to answer some questions and propositions regarding moral theology and the doctrine of the Church. You gave appropriate answers, but not on all points." Therefore the Inquisition's congregation of cardinals had judged his "doctrine and morality in relation to the facts and misdemeanors of the case at hand to be neither honest nor healthy."

In conclusion, Sallua recorded that Kleutgen had undergone a "properly-conducted interrogation." He had "essentially" confessed to the misdemeanors with which he had been charged. For the other defendants, this passage stated that they had given complete and detailed confessions. But at least, at the end of his hearings, the Jesuit seems to have indicated that he would submit to whatever judgment the Inquisition passed on him. He was evidently hoping this would result in a degree of leniency.

The main goal of the Inquisition trial—a comprehensive confession of guilt from the defendant on all charges—was not achieved in Kleutgen's case, as we may guess from Sallua's words:

> In addition to your answers, you submitted many handwritten pages during these 14 separate hearings, and explained the sequence of facts that relate to you in this case. In a few of these texts, and particularly in the first, you gave a partial spontaneous explanation of the facts of which you were accused, and with which you have been charged. Although your answers sometimes denied these or were incomplete, when you then heard the facts of the case read out, you declared that you did remember them, and confessed to them. Your objections were then confined to a few exaggerations with regard to the nature and the number of these deeds, as you yourself stated.

The sheer number of charges the Inquisition had proved suggested Kleutgen would receive a severe punishment. But would it really hand this man, whose friends included senior members of the Curia, a lengthy prison sentence?

A PROXY WAR?

This was the end of the offensive process for the defendant Joseph Kleutgen. Sallua had now completed his task. The consultors and the congregation of cardinals were asked to judge the Jesuit's guilt and fix a sentence, based on the *Ristretto* of October 1861.[71]

But in Kleutgen's case, this was no simple matter. Just as the father confessor Giuseppe Peters had been revealed as the eminent theologian Joseph Kleutgen, there was another dimension waiting to be discovered behind the Sant'Ambrogio trial, too. There was a much larger issue at stake here: namely, the fundamental orientation of the Catholic Church in the nineteenth century. The key to this secret level is provided by Katharina von Hohenzollern's new confessor, the Benedictine Maurus Wolter. He had already tipped Sallua off about the ominous Americano's connection with a certain Kleutgen, during the extrajudicial investigation.

Following her rescue from Sant'Ambrogio, Katharina was just glad to have escaped her convent hell. But, under the sacrament of confession, her new confessor had enjoined her to make a denunciation to the Inquisition. Her *Denunzia* was an act of penance, and a moral obligation, as she emphasized several times. This meant it fulfilled the conditions for the Holy Office to take the case further. Taking revenge on enemies, destroying an opponent's good reputation, and any similarly base motives had to be ruled out from the start. But what motive could Wolter have had for assigning Katharina this penance? Why did the Benedictine insist she make a denunciation to the highest religious tribunal? Was it really just a matter of obtaining justice for Katharina, and exposing the "Sant'Ambrogio system," which had already had deadly consequences?

The hint that Wolter provided about Kleutgen's relationship with the Americano helps to answer these questions. And the fact that a high-ranking cardinal of the Curia like Reisach stepped in to help Kleutgen with his defense suggests that there was much more at stake in this trial than the sexual transgressions of Sant'Ambrogio's second confessor. It was no coincidence that Reisach went to Tivoli immediately after Katharina had been released from Sant'Ambrogio. He was afraid that something dangerous was brewing there, and he was keen to sound out the situation and rescue what he could from it.[72]

An entire Church-political and theological faction was on trial in the Sant'Ambrogio case. The members of this faction belonged to a Jesuit network, and their goal was the strict centralization and uniformity of the Catholic Church. Their theological superstructure was provided by new scholasticism. They envisaged an absolute papal monarchy, together with the eradication of all collegial, episcopal, and centrifugal movements within Catholicism. Their piety, set against the background of the new Marian dogma of 1854, was influenced by sentiment, extraordinary religious phenomena, and apparitions—as opposed to the "cold" rationalism of enlightened religious practice.

The first person who should be named as a member of this network is Cardinal Reisach himself. He had placed Katharina in Sant'Ambrogio, and had direct contact with Maria Luisa via Kleutgen. He knew about Sant'Ambrogio's "secret," and the plans to use Katharina's generous dowry to help found an offshoot of the Regulated Third Order of Holy Saint Francis under Firrao's reform, with

Maria Luisa as abbess. Cardinal Patrizi, whose brother was a Jesuit, was another member. As the convent's long-serving cardinal protector, he was kept informed of the two saints and their cult, thanks to Leziroli. The fact that he failed to intervene and call a halt to all this meant he at least tolerated it. Kleutgen was also part of the network, as a confessor working "on the ground," and as the group's chief theologian. And, last but not least, the pope himself might be added to this list. He had attempted to avoid an Inquisition trial for as long as possible in order to protect his Jesuit friends. When a trial before the Holy Office became unavoidable, Pope Pius IX appointed Patrizi as its head, and made Reisach a cardinal member. This gave them the final say over Kleutgen's fate. It was a clear signal from the pope of exactly where his personal and political sympathies lay.

Katharina also found herself allied to a political and theological network—though she was probably never aware that this level of the trial even existed. She was rightly convinced of the integrity of her actions. The terrible things that had happened to her in Sant'Ambrogio, the cult of the mother founder and Maria Luisa, with all its excesses, and the fact that more murders could well be committed in the convent, were quite enough to justify her complaint to the Inquisition.

But it was no coincidence that, when she reached Tivoli, her cousin Hohenlohe sought out the Benedictine Maurus Wolter to be her new confessor. Wolter was an outspoken opponent of the Jesuits. Hohenlohe had a long-standing connection with the Benedictines of Saint Paul Outside the Walls, and had been good friends with its abbot, Pappalettere, since at least 1853. He was also "firmly opposed" to the adversaries of Anton Günther.[73] When Johann Baptist Baltzer,[74] who was Günther's student and a professor of dogmatic theology in Breslau, made a trip to Rome in 1853, he wrote to his ally Franz Peter Knoodt[75] that Hohenlohe was entirely on the Güntherians' side, if only "out of opposition to the Jesuits."[76]

Anton Günther was born in northern Bohemia in 1783. He broke off his novitiate with the Jesuits and became a secular priest in 1821. A fundamental estrangement ensued between the Society of Jesus and its onetime protégé. Günther rejected various offers of professorships, and moved to Vienna in 1824, where he became an independent scholar.[77] Starting from Descartes' maxim "I think, therefore I am," Günther arrived at a "revised theory of spiritual self-awareness," rejecting the scholastic principle that faith came before thought.[78] For him, faith came both "before and after thought."[79] In modern parlance, Günther propagated something like an anthropological turn in theology.[80] His thought had huge appeal for educated Catholics, who wanted to link modern philosophy and Catholic belief, and proceed from self-awareness to religious awareness.

Günther's main opponents were the new scholastics, whom he attacked ferociously, accusing them of flagrant pantheism. Aristotelianism and Christianity were, he said, as irreconcilable as inimical brothers in Rebecca's womb.[81] Philosophy was reduced to the status of a "stable girl": this was "thin science" versus "fat faith."[82] In Günther's view, the world was created as a complete counterimage of God. He worked from the principle that God was different from, but not superior to, the world. "But scholasticism insists on the superiority of God, and thus accepts *mysteries* as truths that are above reason, and the concept of the *supernatural* as a reality that is above nature, and the concept of the *miracle* as an event that breaks through the laws of nature."[83] Günther argued against the central categories of new scholastic philosophy, which his pupil Knoodt described as "reheated sauerkraut with no new sausage."[84] Günther saw mysticism as the logical consequence of these new scholastic errors. They led to a deification of humans. But mysticism, the "wayward daughter of scholasticism," was far worse than its mother, festooning itself all the more "with the heathen jewels of nature" and ending "in madness."[85]

From a political perspective, Günther had some quite liberal leanings. In 1848, for example, he declared himself in favor of a constitutional monarchy for Austria—though admittedly without actually calling for a revolution. This gave Kleutgen and his movement several reasons to act against him: Günther despised new scholasticism, mysticism, and the Jesuits, but he also espoused ideas of liberty, which made him an enemy of the pope.

Cardinal Johannes von Geissel from Cologne[86] denounced Günther to the Roman authorities, supported by Cardinal Othmar von Rauscher from Vienna,[87] much to the delight of Rome's hard-liners. The Congregation of the Index then tasked Joseph Kleutgen, of all people, with working up the case.[88] The Jesuit had been a consultor for the Index since July 1850.[89] On April 26, 1853, he provided them with a 130-page extract from Günther's works, printed in secret by the congregation, on the basis of which he made an unequivocal plea for the Viennese philosopher to be condemned.[90]

The networks of those defending and accusing Anton Günther then began to take shape, both in Germany and in the Curia. The Viennese philosopher was backed by Cardinal Friedrich, prince of Schwarzenburg,[91] who had been prince-archbishop of Prague since 1850, and Cardinal Melchior von Diepenbrock, prince-bishop of Breslau since 1845, who both came to Rome to speak in Günther's favor. They received a great deal of support from Gustav zu Hohenlohe-Schillingsfürst, who, as papal chamberlain, had a hotline to Pius IX. The Benedictine monks of Saint Paul Outside the Walls—among them a whole series of Günther's pupils—also supported their teacher.

Alongside Geissel and Rauscher, Günther's opponents included the archbishop of Munich: August, Count Reisach. He was particularly keen for Günther to be indexed. Not content with a simple ban on his books, Günther's adversaries pushed for an official condemnation of his erroneous teachings in the form of a papal brief. The prefect of the Congregation of the Index, Cardinal Giacomo Luigi Brignole,[92] and the cardinal secretary of state, Luigi Lambruschini,[93] were also members of this anti-Güntherian, Jesuit-inspired network, for which Kleutgen supplied the theology.

In the face of this fearsome opposition, Günther's Roman supporters, Hohenlohe and Pappalettere, told the Viennese theologian that the only way for him to escape being indexed was to come to Rome at once, and clear things up with the pope in person. They thought Pius IX might be won over face-to-face, on account of his "emotional, sanguine" personality. But under no circumstances should Günther hope for a positive outcome to the Index trial. It was impossible to avoid a ban via this official route, following a "maneuver by the Jesuit faction."[94] He therefore had to bypass the usual trial process, and resolve things as people had done in early modern times. He must seek an audience with the ruler—in this case, the pope—and prostrate himself at his feet.

Günther didn't follow the advice of his Roman advocates. He was in poor health, and didn't feel able to make the trip to Rome. He left the decision to the Congregation of the Index, which had chosen a new, surprisingly liberal prefect, Cardinal Girolamo D'Andrea,[95] on

July 4, 1853. D'Andrea would save numerous modern thinkers and writers from the Index.[96] And at first, Günther wasn't indexed; the matter seemed to have been shelved. Pius IX had clearly been receptive to the arguments of the Viennese philosopher's Roman friends.

But then the mood in Rome became increasingly unfavorable toward the liberals. In an address on December 9, 1854, Pius IX outlined his intentions for the dogma of the Immaculate Conception, which he had announced the previous day: "The Blessed Virgin, who overcame and destroyed all heresies, grant that this pernicious error of rationalism, which so troubles and plagues not only civil society, but also the Church in these sad times, may be torn out by the root and disappear." Unfortunately there were "certain men pre-eminent in learning, who . . . hold human reason at so high a value, exalt it so much, that they very foolishly think it is to be held equal to religion itself. Hence, according to the rash opinion of these men, theological studies should be treated in the same manner as philosophical studies."[97] This was a reference to Anton Günther and others like him. The pope also promoted two of Günther's principal accusers, Rauscher and Reisach, to the rank of cardinal on December 17, 1855. And just three days later, Pius IX made Reisach a member of the Congregation of the Index. The Viennese theologian's most forceful opponent had now become one of his judges.

This unleashed a spate of votums within the Congregation of the Index. Following on from his excerpts from Günther's works, Kleutgen authored many more detailed votums of the Viennese philosopher and his pupils. On April 23, 1854, there was a censor's report on the first five volumes of *Lydia*, the yearbook of the Vienna School of philosophy. Four more detailed votums, totaling over three hundred printed pages, were produced for the conclusive meeting on January 8, 1857.[98] In the Congregation of the Index, the hard-liners around Kleutgen and Cardinal Reisach called for a papal brief formally condemning Günther. Abbot Pappalettere, who had been a consultor of the Congregation of the Index since August 1856, and the Tyrolean Alois Flir,[99] who had also been a consultor since February 1856, sided with the Index prefect, Cardinal D'Andrea, in calling for an acquittal.

In the end, the two sides reached a typical Roman compromise. There was no ceremonial condemnation via a papal brief—but nor was there an acquittal. Nine of Günther's works were banned in a simple Index decree on January 8, 1857.[100] But the decree was only publicized on February 17, once Günther had submitted to it. Cardinal D'Andrea may have lost the battle, having failed to prevent the indexing, but he published the judgment with an "addendum unique in the 400-year history of the Index." This said that on February 10, Günther had "submitted uprightly, piously and laudably."[101] The usual wording was simply "He submitted laudably."[102]

Kleutgen immediately informed like-minded comrades in Germany of the judgment. He was deeply dissatisfied with the lenient Index decree, and wanted to see a condemnation of Günther himself, rather than just his works. The things Günther had written, he said, were "injurious to the dogma."[103] With the help of Cardinal Geissel, who visited Rome in the spring of 1857, Reisach and Kleutgen managed to bypass the Congregation of the Index and its head, D'Andrea, and persuade the pope to produce a formal condemnation of Günther, ignoring the judgment that had already been enacted in the case. Hohenlohe could do nothing to stop Geissel from convincing Pius IX in an audience to publish the brief *Eximiam Tuam*. This appeared on June 15, 1857, and solemnly condemned Anton Günther's teachings.[104] It was also a personal attack on the Viennese philosopher, and called his Catholicism into question.

Kleutgen and Reisach had scored a total victory. Having failed to get their way through a proper court procedure, they persuaded Pius IX to revise his own judgment. This shows just how tractable this pope was, and how erratic in his decisions, which depended in each case on who had the pontiff's ear. Since 1854, the liberals in Rome had hardly any access to Pius IX. He now trusted only the hard-liners and those with a Jesuit education.

Günther's pupils in Germany and Rome knew who was to blame for their defeat: the new scholastics, and Kleutgen in particular. Günther spoke of the Jesuits as "rotten Aristotelians, who deserve to be slaughtered." Sadly, they were still blithely going about their business in Rome, without having "scraped the old muck from their shoes."[105]

There was now very little Günther's pupils and friends could achieve for their mentor through Pope Pius IX. A resumption of the censorship trial with the aim of a revision was impossible: the Congregation of the Index couldn't call a papal brief into question. But the defeated Güntherians in Rome wanted some kind of revenge.

They even considered denouncing their adversaries, in particular the Jesuits' chief thinkers, Kleutgen and Perrone, and getting them added to the *Index of Forbidden Books* as well. But this was a hopeless undertaking from the start: the new scholastics had a majority within the Congregation, and enjoyed the highest protection from the pope.

But with Kleutgen's involvement in the Sant'Ambrogio case, the Güntherians had a unique opportunity to teach the movement's chief ideologue a lesson, after all. This was much better than getting his books banned by the minor Congregation of the Index. It was a chance to get Kleutgen himself condemned by the Inquisition, and make it impossible for him to exert his influence again in Rome, or anywhere else. Once he had been convicted of heresy, complicity in an attempted murder, and seduction in the confessional—and with his notorious disregard for the verdicts of the highest Catholic authority exposed—he would be silenced once and for all. Or so Hohenlohe, Wolter, and Pappalettere hoped. At the very least, his days of damaging the liberal cause in the Catholic Church would be over: after this, he could no longer be a censor for the Congregation of the Index and the Inquisition, or provide advice and inspiration to the pope.

CHAPTER NINE

"Sorrowful and Contrite"

The Verdict and Its Consequences

CONSULTORS, CARDINALS, POPE: THE VERDICT

Once the investigating court had concluded the offensive process, it turned to the deciding level of the Holy Tribunal once more. The judges had summarized the interrogations of Maria Luisa, the abbess, Leziroli, and Kleutgen into four written *Ristretti*, listing the misdemeanors for which they had obtained confessions or conclusive proof. Based on these, the consultors of the congregation had to formulate a suggested decision. Then the cardinals would arrive at a verdict, which the Holy Office's assessor would present to the pope for a final pronouncement.

The consultors always met on a Monday, and on January 27, 1862, they discussed the case of Sant'Ambrogio at length.[1] There were sixteen members present.[2]

First, they addressed the consistent disregard that the nuns and confessors of Sant'Ambrogio, and their supporters in the Curia, had shown for the verdict passed on Agnese Firrao in 1816. The Holy Roman and Universal Inquisition saw this as an assault on its authority, and the wound had to be treated. The consultors were united on the first point of their *votum*: under threat of the harshest punishment, the nuns and confessors—in particular the special devotee of Firrao,

Padre Leziroli—should be made to acknowledge once and for all that the decree against Firrao of February 8, 1816, had "never been lifted." From that moment on, nobody would ever be allowed to say it had. There was to be no more veneration of Agnese Firrao, "whether verbal or written, private or public, direct or indirect, through word or deed."

In the second point of their *votum*, the consultors declared themselves unanimously in favor of dissolving Sant'Ambrogio. The pope had already been considering this, in any case. Furthermore, the nuns and confessors should be given an ultimatum: they must hand over every copy of the order's Rule and constitutions, and all Firrao's other writings to the Holy Office at once, on pain of excommunication.

Turning their attention to the principal defendant, the former novice mistress and vicaress Maria Luisa Ridolfi, all the consultors present agreed that the charge of pretense of holiness had been clearly proven. The heresy of Molinosism was at work here once again, and was named as the root cause of all the other crimes. Maria Luisa should therefore make a formal abjuration of her faults before the Inquisition, and should be sentenced to monastic imprisonment in absolute isolation. She should not be allowed to communicate with anyone outside the convent walls. She must also stay away from the convent gate and the outer walls; this was a total ban on contact with the outside world. For three years, she should take only bread and water on Fridays, and for the rest of her life she must pray the Rosary every Saturday and beg forgiveness for her sins. She should also be assigned an "educated, clever" confessor, who would lead this lost soul back onto the right path.

The consultors couldn't agree on how long Maria Luisa should remain in prison. Four voted for a sentence of ten years, with strict fasting and other ascetic exercises. She should also be made to wear a cilice. In view of the severity of her crimes—in particular the poisoning attempts, and the "sin of sodomy"—one member was in favor of lifelong imprisonment, and denying her the sacraments. In his opinion, she should only be allowed to receive Holy Communion on the feasts of Easter, Pentecost, and Christmas.

Abbess Maria Veronica Milza should also renounce her errors and misdemeanors in a ceremony before the Inquisition. After this, she should remain in monastic imprisonment and no longer be permitted to wear the black veil of a choir nun. She should be barred forever from making any contact with the former nuns and confessors of Sant'Ambrogio, or any other persons who had been connected to the convent. The length of the abbess's sentence was the only thing the consultors couldn't agree on. While ten of them advocated a term of three years, another four wanted to leave the decision entirely up to the cardinals. After serving her sentence, Maria Veronica should be accommodated in a suitable house of pious women, and live there as a simple nun.

The consultors had a lengthy discussion on the fate of Giuseppe Leziroli, the first father confessor and spiritual director of Sant'Ambrogio. All were naturally agreed that he should perform a vigorous ceremonial abjuration, the *abjuratio de vehementi*.[3] But they couldn't agree on whether he should be banned from acting as a confessor for a limited period only. Two of the consultors wanted to ban him from taking confession from women. Five thought he should still be allowed to take confession from monks. But in all eventualities, he should be prohibited from contacting the nuns, and anyone else connected with Sant'Ambrogio, for the rest of his life.

When it came to sentencing Leziroli, six consultors voted for a term of five years' imprisonment. Four voted for one year, and one even argued for a single month. One consultor—probably a Jesuit—even tried to exonerate Leziroli entirely, and argued for a lenient punishment on these grounds. Another raised serious accusations against him, and advocated a drastic escalation of his punishment. He saw the Jesuit as the principal perpetrator in this case, since he was the driving force behind the propagation of Agnese Firrao's false holiness. And this was "a false doctrine, wayward, erroneous and unjust to the Holy See, as well as a suspected heresy." This consultor suggested ten years' imprisonment in a house belonging to the Jesuit order, with ten years of silence and ten days of spiritual exercises every year as penance. One consultor abstained from this controversial discussion altogether. As the consultors were divided on Leziroli's case, the cardinals were asked for their thoughts.

Eleven of the consultors voted that Joseph Kleutgen should perform the *abjuration de formali*, the most rigorous renunciation the Inquisition could demand—though one argued for the *abjuratio de vehementi*. This should be followed by ten days of spiritual exercises in a house belonging to the Society of Jesus, to be chosen by the order's general. He was also to serve his sentence there, rather than in the Inquisition's cells.[4]

The length of Kleutgen's sentence was the subject of some debate. Four consultors wanted to leave the decision up to the cardinals; three argued for five years; two for three years, and another two for ten years. Four consultors viewed his "sexual intercourse with virgins"—which he claimed to have performed with noble, spiritual intentions—as a heresy against the Decalogue's commandment: "Thou shalt not commit fornication."[5] These four viewed his sexual acts with Maria Luisa, including the French kisses and the special erotic blessing in the context of confession, as the effects of the same "Molinosistic heresy" already condemned elsewhere. They thought that, as a convicted heretic, Kleutgen should serve out his sentence in a correctional facility, the Pia Casa di Penitenza at Corneto,[6] rather than in a Jesuit house. Two of these four consultors were in favor of five years in Corneto, one suggested ten years, and the last just a single year.

One consultor (probably one of the two Jesuits) argued that Kleutgen had been deceived, and had corrected himself as soon as he had realized his error. Numerous bishops and cardinals had repeatedly praised Sant'Ambrogio as an exemplary convent. Kleutgen, the consultor said, had merely started following a tradition that had been sanctioned by the Church authorities, without asking too many questions. This consultor also tried to shield Kleutgen from the charge of heresy: "As far as I am aware, no religious verdict has been passed in this case, only a criminal verdict." This would have made Kleutgen a morally unreliable priest—possibly even one who was involved in criminal actions—but not a heretic. However, the consultor was unable to get this suggestion past his colleagues.

The consultors may not have been able to agree on the length of Kleutgen's sentence, but they were all certain that he should be banned from taking confession from men or women. He should also be forbidden from contacting any of the nuns from Sant'Ambrogio. Petrus Beckx, the Jesuit general, should appoint a suitable spiritual guide for Kleutgen, who, acting under the secret of the Holy Office, would inform him of the heretical principles that he had been accused of following. He should then renounce them all.

The Inquisition might have been expected to pass a long sentence for the offense of *Sollicitatio*—particularly as contemporary Catholic writing presented seduction in the confessional as a disgusting crime. An 1853 Catholic encyclopedia stated that monastic priests convicted of this should be punished with "exile, the galleys, life imprisonment, degradation and being delivered up to the secular judges."[7] But in reality the Roman Inquisition treated these priests with extreme leniency: they were usually just assigned a penance, and had to spend a few days saying psalms. Members of their order who also happened to be consultors or cardinals of the Holy Office often made sure that the defendants could lie low in another monastery for a while.[8]

The cardinals of the Holy Office considered the case of Sant'Ambrogio on February 5, 1862, on the basis of the votum from the consultors' meeting.[9] They passed their advisors' suggested decision on the first point (inculcating the validity of Firrao's 1816 conviction) without further discussion. And the cardinals even went one step further than the consultors, who had suggested that all memory of the former convent of Sant'Ambrogio, and its mother founder, Agnese Firrao, should be destroyed. They ruled that her corpse should be exhumed from its grave in San Marziale in Gubbio, and placed in an anonymous, unidentifiable grave in a public graveyard.

The judgment that the sixteen consultors had suggested on Maria Luisa Ridolfi was passed with no alterations, and the sentence was set at twenty years. The cardinals also agreed with the consultors' proposal for Abbess Maria Veronica Milza. Her sentence was to be one year; after this, she should be allowed to move to another suitable convent, with the permission of the cardinal vicar. Giuseppe Leziroli also received a year's sentence, and a lifetime ban on taking confession. Joseph Kleutgen was to be given three years. He would also receive a special caution regarding the moral principles against which he had offended. The judgments against the abbess and the novice mistress were to be communicated privately to the nuns and confessors of the former convent.

On the evening of February 5, the Holy Office's assessor, Raffaele Monaco La Valletta, read out the cardinals' verdicts in the case of Sant'Ambrogio in a private audience with Pius IX.[10] The pope approved the decisions, with a few small changes. He requested that the exhumation and reburial of Firrao's body be conducted under the supervision of the bishop of Gubbio, and with the greatest secrecy, to avoid any public furor. The pope reduced Maria Luisa's sentence to eighteen years—a comparatively mild punishment, considering she had confessed to the murder of several nuns. At the time, this would have incurred the death penalty in many countries. Pius IX reduced Kleutgen's sentence to two years.

Was two years really an appropriate punishment for the serious offenses Kleutgen had committed? It's clear where the pope's sympathies lay in this trial. Kleutgen was an important theological advisor who, with Reisach acting as mediator, wrote texts and votums that allowed Pius IX to implement his policies and support his claim to universal power in the Church and the Papal States. The padre was part of his Jesuit network. Kleutgen and the Jesuits shored up the pope's sovereignty—this called for care and leniency.

On February 12, another assembly of the cardinals made an addendum to the judgment.[11] Sallua was unclear on whether the "formal and definite abjuration" in Kleutgen's and Leziroli's cases also meant they should be suspended from their priestly duties. This wasn't stipulated in the text of the judgment, so the judges had to fall back on customary law. The Holy Office consistently forbade priests who had to abjure from celebrating Mass for a certain period. In the normal course of things, they were expected to lead Mass on a daily basis. The cardinals erred on the side of caution here and left the decision up to the pope, who banned both Jesuits from celebrating Mass for twenty days. The cardinals also noted that the previous week, they had discussed the destruction of Firrao's grave in Gubbio, but not the final resting places of the two other abbesses, Maria Maddalena and Agnese Celeste della Croce. These women had also been venerated as living saints in Sant'Ambrogio. Their bodies would now also be exhumed and reburied in an anonymous place, without a headstone or any other marker.

These measures amounted to nothing less than a complete *damnatio memoriae*: everything that held the slightest memory of Sant'Ambrogio was to be wiped from history. This time, the Holy Office's tribunal wanted to leave the field of battle as the ultimate victor. All graves that might be regarded as memorials had to be removed. All written records of the convent and, most importantly, its two false saints, had to disappear off the face of the earth—or rather, into the most secret of all church archives, where the public wouldn't be able to read them.

The ceremonial abjuration was the high point of an Inquisition trial. The Spanish Inquisition's public *auto-da-fés,* as captured in many famous paintings, shape our idea of these events to this day.[12] Galileo Galilei was forced to abjure on June 22, 1633, when the Inquisition made him renounce views based on his scientific observations. The event was made famous by, among other works, Bertolt Brecht's play *Life of Galileo*: "I, Galileo Galilei, teacher of mathematics and physics at The University of Florence, renounce what I have taught, that the sun is the centre of the universe and motionless in its place, and that the Earth is not the centre and not motionless."[13] However, there was no such public *abjuratio* in the case of Sant'Ambrogio. The ceremony was conducted in secret, and the public was not admitted. The convent's secret was to be kept even (and especially) after the judgment.

Sallua was charged with arranging this. He immediately had to summon the four guilty parties before the Holy Office and announce to them the cardinals' decision, which had been ratified by the pope. He informed them of their sentences, received their abjurations, heard them renounce the crimes of which they had been convicted, and released them from the punishment of excommunication. He then had to inform the rest of the nuns of the verdict. Each of the individual points to be renounced corresponded to one of the main charges listed in the closing summation of each *Ristretto*. The *abjuratio de formali* was an established ritual, and always followed the same pattern.

Joseph Kleutgen's abjuration took place on February 18, 1862, in the Palace of the Holy Office.[14] Present were the two investigating judges, Vincenzo Leone Sallua and Enrico Ferrari, the Holy Office's scribe, Pacifico Gasparri,[15] and Giacomo Vagaggini, acting as notary.[16]

Kleutgen, whom the court continued to address as Peters, knelt down. A copy of the Gospels lay in front of him. Sallua read out the verdict in a loud, clear voice:

We have resolved to pronounce upon you the final verdict stated below. For this our final verdict we have called upon the holy names of our Lord Jesus Christ and his glorious mother, the Virgin Mary; we who sit in judgment will pronounce from these files of the case and the other cases before us between Monsignore Antonio Bambozzi, as the appointed Fiscal of this Holy Office on the one side, and you, Padre Giuseppe Peters, on the other.

We affirm, render, decide and declare that we condemn you, Padre Giuseppe Peters, for what you have confessed. You have been found guilty by the Holy Office of claiming the false holiness of the late condemned Sister Maria Agnese Firrao in each and every way. You supported and claimed the false holiness of the condemned Sister Maria Luisa Ridolfi in various unlawful and criminal ways, with words, writings and deeds. You are guilty of seduction, through committing acts with her while you were her confessor. You broke the *clausura* in order to care for her. You claimed, wrote and revealed views and principles that were unhealthy and do not correspond to healthy theology. You believed in a supposedly heavenly correspondence and encouraged it, to further the above-mentioned aims. Finally, you are guilty of further offences that fall within the traditional jurisdiction of this highest religious tribunal, and of offences that have been assigned to our jurisdiction. You have therefore brought upon yourself all the censures and punishments that are imposed and decreed for such offences by the Sacred Canons and other special or universal decrees.

But as you have admitted the above-mentioned errors of your own volition, and have asked for forgiveness, we are pleased to release you from excommunication, to which you are subject for these offences, provided that you first abjure, detest and condemn the above-mentioned errors and heresies, and that you abjure any further errors, heresies and sects opposed to the Holy Catholic and Apostolic Roman Church, with sincere heart and unfeigned faith, as we command in this our final verdict, and as you must perform in the manner that we will convey to you.

And so that these offences do not go unpunished—so that you will be more cautious in future and serve as an example to others, following your formal abjuration, we sentence you to: eternal dis-

qualification from hearing Holy Confession, and eternal disquali-
fication from any kind of spiritual guidance; a 20-day suspension
from reading Holy Mass; ten days of spiritual exercises. We sentence you to remain two years in a house of your order, to be determined by your order's General. You are prohibited from entering
into any form of communication with the nuns or any persons who
visited the former convent of Sant'Ambrogio. The General will
provide you with a suitable pastoral guide, to set you right on the
honest principles of morality. We also assign the salutary penance
that, during the two years of your imprisonment, you will say a
Requiescat three times a month, and the Rosary of the Blessed Virgin Mary once a week.

We affirm, render, decide, declare and punish in this way, and in
every other better way that the law allows and compels.

The transcriber noted that Padre Kleutgen heard and understood the
verdict, and spoke no word against it. Kleutgen, still kneeling, then
laid his hand on the Gospels and spoke the usual words of abjuration:

"I know that nobody who is not of this Faith will be saved, which
the Holy Catholic and Apostolic Church observes, believes, preaches,
confesses and teaches. I recognize that I have committed grave errors
against the Church. I greatly regret this."

Next, the Jesuit had to renounce individually all the offences the
investigating court had listed in its closing statement. He had to state
that he detested them, and acknowledge that they were condemned
by the Holy Roman Catholic Church. Still kneeling, he then read out
the abjuration proper:[17]

Now that, sorrowful and contrite, I am certain of the falsity of the
above-mentioned errors and heresies, and of the truth of the Holy
Catholic Faith, I abjure them with sincere heart and unfeigned
faith. I detest and condemn the above-mentioned errors and heresies and in general all further errors, all further heresies and sects
opposed to the Holy Catholic and Apostolic Roman Church. I
accept and promise to serve all punishments that have been or will
be imposed upon me by the Holy Office. If I should break any of
my promises or oaths (God forbid!), I will submit to all punishments imposed and enacted upon me by the Sacred Canons and
other universal and specific constitutions against such offences.

May God and His Holy Gospels, upon which I lay my hand, help me. I, Padre Giuseppe Peters, have abjured, sworn, promised and pledged as above. I have signed with my own hand the record of the abjuration, which I have spoken word for word, here in the knowledge of the truth and with a clear conscience, in Rome, on this day, February 18, 1862. Padre Giuseppe Peters.

Giuseppe Leziroli had made his "sorrowful and contrite" abjuration the previous day, February 17, 1862. He, too, had come to the tribunal's palace, knelt, and placed his hand on the Gospels as instructed.[18] Maria Luisa and the abbess abjured on February 14—the latter in the "House of Women," Santa Maria del Rifugio, and the former in the Buon Pastore jail.[19]

After just over two and a half years, the Inquisition trial in the case of Sant'Ambrogio was formally at an end. The tribunal could assume that the defendants had realized their crimes, abjured the errors of faith and morality associated with them, and accepted their just punishments. But there was an exceptional feature to this trial that went beyond the Inquisitors' everyday experience. In the Sant'Ambrogio case, the pope had made the religious authority of the Holy Office into a criminal court for capital crimes, although they didn't fall within its jurisdiction. The indissoluble connection between the heresy and the murder charges had made this seem imperative. But, unlike heretical views, crimes could not be corrected through abjuration. This balancing act was palpable, at least indirectly, throughout the whole trial. Following its tradition as a religious tribunal, the court intended to guide the perpetrators both to a verbal renunciation and a practical acceptance of the judgment. This would reconcile them with themselves and, more importantly, with the Church.

Anyone searching the Sant'Ambrogio case files for the Holy Tribunal's public announcement of the judgment will be disappointed. When Agnese Firrao was condemned as a false saint in 1816, the judgment was published on a *bando*. But there is no known *bando* for the judgment in the second Sant'Ambrogio trial in 1862. It was a relatively common practice for the Inquisition to avoid any kind of public notification, particularly for cases in which members of the Church hierarchy were involved. The motive for this is not far to seek.

One of the reasons for publishing the 1816 judgment against Firrao was that the case had already attracted international attention, with a flurry of articles appearing north of the Alps as well. In this case, it was necessary for the highest religious authority to take a visible stand against the offense of feigned holiness. After the chaos of the Napoleonic period, it was also a sign that the Catholic judicial apparatus was functioning again, having been almost entirely broken down over the previous twenty years. The present case was quite different: only a small number of people in Rome knew anything about it. Publishing the judgment on a *bando* would have made the case public for the first time, and that was something the Holy Office was obviously keen to avoid. This was part of the same strategy that had seen them destroy the graves of Firrao and the women who had succeeded her as abbess.

But perhaps the *type* of offenses that had come to light in the Sant'Ambrogio case also made publication seem inopportune. The pope and the Holy Office could easily have made a public condemnation of Maria Luisa's pretense of holiness. There was a long tradition of this. But the public should hear as little as possible of the sexual scandal, which ranged from sodomy to *Sollicitatio*. This was a matter of maintaining respect for the Church as an honest institution, and for the sacrament of penance.

In the end, the judges' decisions were only announced internally, thus protecting the defendants from the sensation-hungry press.[20] This applied above all to the perpetrators who were in the public eye, which meant Kleutgen in particular. He held important offices in the hierarchy of the Society of Jesus, and was also a theologian, an author, and a censor for the Index. Of the four defendants, he had the most to gain from the judgment being kept secret. This meant his sexual transgressions, in particular the seduction in the confessional, would never reach the public's ears. The mere fact that he had made an internal abjuration could mean anything at all. This was a huge gray area that allowed for all kinds of interpretations—something that would be demonstrated a decade and a half after the judgment.

Keeping the case out of the public eye also allowed the Holy Office to draw a veil over the fact that some of the Curia's most senior members had been caught up in it. An internal resolution of this embarrassing episode avoided the possibility of public gossip about friends of the pope—namely Cardinals Patrizi and Reisach. This was a plausible enough reason for the pope and the Inquisition not to publish the judgment.

Ultimately, the Holy Office only achieved its noble aim with two

of the four defendants. Padre Leziroli spent his year of imprisonment in the retreat house of Saint Eusebius.[21] In November 1863, he
returned to Sant'Andrea al Quirinale in Rome,[22] where the Jesuits
had a novitiate. There he was employed in various functions within
his order, although the prohibition on preaching and taking confession remained in place for the rest of his life.

The superiors of Leziroli's order made many failed attempts to persuade Pius IX to lift this ban. The pope didn't believe Leziroli could
be rehabilitated. He is supposed to have said: "He is a holy man, so he
may pray for us, but he is much too simple to rule over the conscience
of the faithful."[23] After the disaster of Sant'Ambrogio, Pius IX simply couldn't let Leziroli loose on believers again. But the padre could
continue to contribute to the good of the Church with his prayers and
silent Masses, without the participation of the community. The padre
seems to have resigned himself to his fate with humility, as one would
expect of a pious monk. He died, seemingly at peace with himself and
the Church, on April 27, 1878, in Castel Gandolfo in the Albanian
mountains, where the pope's summer residence was located.[24]

Maria Veronica Milza, the former abbess of Sant'Ambrogio, completed her year of monastic imprisonment. The Holy Office then
ordered her to be transferred to the convent of the Mantellates on
the Via della Lungara in Rome, on January 28, 1863. The nuns there
were sisters of the Third Order of the Servites, also known as the
Servants of Mary.[25] Two years later, Maria Veronica put in a request
to the highest religious tribunal to be admitted to this convent as a
simple nun. The cardinals granted her request in their meeting on
July 14, 1865. They tasked the prior general of the Servites, Girolamo
Priori, with arranging for Maria Veronica's acceptance and profession
of vows, following a month of spiritual exercises.[26] The former abbess
had found her place as a simple nun in a new order, and seems finally
to have accepted the judgment against Sant'Ambrogio.

A FOUNDER INSTEAD OF A NUN

But what of the plaintiff? The things Katharina experienced in 1858
and 1859 engraved themselves on her memory, as the detailed report
she dictated to Christiane Gmeiner in 1870 shows. After more than a

decade, everything she had gone through was still as real to her as if it had happened yesterday. The awful fear of death she had experienced speaks from every line. Still, she never said anything in public about her time in Sant'Ambrogio.

Even within her family, where of course everyone knew about the affair, Katharina played it down. "This convent episode in my aunt's life," her niece Marie von Thurn und Taxis-Hohenlohe remembered, "awakened my great curiosity, but nobody at home liked to talk about it."[27] It was only much later, after her aunt's death, that she finally learned more about the story. By this point, as oral histories are wont to do, it had changed a great deal—but the beautiful madre vicaria, her holiness and her sham miracles, still lay at its core. The princess, however, now bore the religious name Sister Ludovica, rather than Sister Luisa Maria. And the seducer was no longer an American, but (as in a classic murder mystery) the gardener, whom Katharina had caught in flagrante. Then, of course, there was the poisoning. A "small young nun" managed to get a message to the Vatican. And Hohenlohe rescued his cousin without further ado, storming into the convent that same night armed with a papal brief, hurling "anathemas" at the recalcitrant nuns. The princess wasn't taken to Tivoli, but straight to Pope Pius IX in the Vatican.[28] These embellishments suggest that Katharina did little to correct the development of the legend within her family. She clearly wanted nothing more to do with this aspect of her biography, nor did she want to be reminded of it.

The more time elapsed following these terrible events, the more the princess tried to find excuses for Kleutgen's behavior. She must have remained oblivious to the fact that her denunciation had been the stick that stirred the theological wasp's nest of Güntherians and new scholastics, enabling Wolter to take his revenge on Kleutgen. Most importantly, she never learned of Maria Luisa's testimony, which painted Kleutgen as the real initiator of the poisoning attempts. If she had, she could hardly have judged her former confessor so charitably.

In her *Erlebnisse* (Experiences) dictated in 1870, Katharina was troubled by the question of how a "sensible man, an experienced priest, a great scholar" like Kleutgen could have fallen for a hoax perpetrated by "an uneducated nun" like Maria Luisa. "The certainty with which Kleutgen believed in her holiness is astonishing, as it can have been manifested to him through nothing more than what she told him of it. But he would rather believe the most audacious claims than cast doubt upon her virtue." The princess was sure that anyone would think "such a deception impossible"—and yet the Jesuit had been "completely deceived."

She saw two main reasons for this. Women, she said, were naturally possessed of a fine, unerring sense for the detection of superficiality and dishonesty in members of their own sex, and could see through the "cunning and subtlety" with which they "sought to hide their failings." But this quality was often absent in "knowledgeable, worthy men." While they cast a "serious and critical" eye on all other facts and relationships, these men were blind when it came to women. "There may be a feature of the female character, which a man lacks completely, and which is therefore almost unfathomable to him": namely, the ability "to present themselves differently, to take on an appearance that in no way corresponds to the reality." Katharina's second reason was that Kleutgen was totally inexperienced in pastoral care. "He had not lived much in the world. His main work was scholarly research. From the books by which he was almost always surrounded, he could have gained no knowledge of the world or of people."[29]

A decade later, in 1879, the Sant'Ambrogio affair appeared in the German press for the first time, following a statement by the Church historian Johann Friedrich, who had become an Old Catholic (a movement that had come into existence in the wake of the First Vatican Council as a protest against the new infallibility dogma). But even then, Katharina refrained from speaking of it in public. This was the era of the *Kulturkampf*, an attempt by the Prussian government to undermine the Catholic Church's influence over its state. Against this backdrop, Friedrich claimed that the Inquisition had sentenced Kleutgen to six years in jail as a result of his involvement in the poisoning of "a princess von Hohenzollern."[30] The princess wrote Kleutgen a sympathetic letter on March 23, 1879, in which she reminded him of "many a proof of priestly diligence and sympathetic concern" that he had shown her twenty years earlier. She said she had gathered from the press with "active regret" "that you have become the focus of lies and persecutions." Katharina assured the Jesuit of her sympathy, and added that she would "remember [him] with respect." She seemed to have forgotten the disappointment she had expressed over her former confessor in her denunciation of 1859. Instead, she reiterated the conclusion she had reached in her *Erlebnisse*: the Jesuit hadn't been a perpetrator, but a victim of Maria Luisa, like herself. In her letter, she remembered sadly "that we both experienced a very painful deception. We have both had to gaze into an abyss of errors committed by an unhappy soul, estranged from God."[31]

How did Pius IX behave toward Katharina? From the outset, the pope played a double game. For as long as he could, he internally conveyed the impression that the denunciation was not to be taken seriously. But in his personal dealings with the princess, Pius IX was affection personified. Once Katharina had spent some time with her cousin in Tivoli, and was on the road to recovery, the pope even allotted her an apartment in the papal palace. He jokingly called her the "Prioress of the Quirinal"[32] and, when she expressed a desire to make a pilgrimage to the Holy Land, he lent her his wholehearted support. This was actually quite convenient for him: it meant the plaintiff in the Sant'Ambrogio case would be absent from Rome from February 12, 1860, until well into the summer, and could take no further part in the trial. Three German Benedictines from Saint Paul Outside the Walls accompanied her on her journey to Palestine: her confessor, Maurus Wolter, his brother Placidus, and Anselm Nickes[33]—all of them pupils of Günther.[34] On September 29, 1860, the pope bade Katharina and the Wolter brothers farewell in a private audience.[35] Katharina's influence on the trial was eliminated long before it entered its most crucial phase. And from then on, she devoted her energy to another religious project: with Pius IX's support, the Wolter brothers and Katharina wanted to found a Benedictine monastery. They first considered Altenburg, in the district of Mülheim am Rhein, then the village of Materborn in Kleve, and finally Beuron on the upper Danube.[36]

After many trials and tribulations, two marriages, and two attempts at convent life, the princess had finally found her true calling. God had put her to the test many times, but now He had given her her life's work. In retrospect, she began to interpret her awful experiences in Sant'Ambrogio as a benevolent act of divine providence. Without the poisoning attempts, she would never have fled from the convent; without her escape, she would never have met Wolter Brothers; without them, she would never have come to know Benedictine spirituality or become the founder of a Benedictine monastery.

Princess Katharina during the last years of her life. She entered the history
books as the founder of the Benedictine abbey of Beuron.

At least, the princess described her experiences to her family on
several occasions as providential, as her niece Maria von Thurn
und Taxis-Hohenlohe mentions in the memoir of her youth. After
leaving Sant'Ambrogio, Katharina had been "a poor stray creature,"
"without husband or child, without a goal, wandering through life
looking for a path to follow, a work to which she could commit herself." Then she encountered the Wolter brothers, "two enthusiasts
in whom the fire of the first confessors burned." Their aim was to
renew the order of Saint Benedict. "And there it was: her path, the
work that was worthy of her, and of her illustrious name and her
burning heart! With unprecedented passion, she threw herself into
this task. All her worldly wealth was poured into the service of the
order. Her rare spirituality, her iron will, the influence that her rank
and family gave her—all this now belonged to the two padres and
their great plans."[37]

The princess was to have her convent after all. The usual roles were
reversed here: as a rule, powerful men founded convents for pious

women, but here, a powerful woman was founding a monastery for pious men. The founding of Catholic monasteries was prohibited in the Kingdom of Württemberg and the Grand Duchy of Baden—a ban that lasted from German secularization in the early nineteenth century to the end of the German empire in 1918. However, Katharina was still able to do this within the Hohenzollern Duchies. The former Augustine abbey of Beuron on the Danube had been secularized in 1802, and now belonged to Katharina's stepson, Karl Anton von Hohenzollern-Sigmaringen. The princess bought it from him for the order of Saint Benedict in 1863.[38] By 1868, the priory of Beuron had been made an independent Benedictine abbey, and Maurus Wolter was elected as its first abbot. During the *Kulturkampf*, from 1875 to 1887, the monastery was suppressed and the monks had to flee abroad. While they were away, the princess—as a good founder should—took care of the maintenance and administration of the buildings and lands. Once the conflict between state and Church was over, the monks were able to return to Beuron without any problems, and the Benedictine tradition continued almost uninterrupted.

For twelve years, Katharina had been "the protector of the abandoned monastery." But when the Benedictines returned, she made the surprising decision to leave Beuron forever, and move to Freiburg. Her official line was that her baby had grown up, and she could now leave it to take care of itself. She longed for "complete freedom of my heart in silence and seclusion." The climate was milder in Freiburg, she said, and she could obtain treatment from doctors in the university town whenever she needed it.[39] But were these her real motives? There were rumors within her family about an increasing estrangement between the princess and Abbot Wolter. They wondered "what was going on between Saint Francis and Saint Clara?" On leaving the upper Danube valley, Katharina was said to have cried: "No, you will never have me here again, living or dead!"[40] The day the princess left Beuron, July 7, 1890, marked the end of the abbey's founding phase. And it was to be a double farewell: the following day, July 8, Maurus Wolter died suddenly.[41] His brother Placidus, whom Katharina had also met in Rome, was elected as the new abbot.

"What she was to Beuron is engraved for all time in the history of this blossoming archabbey." This is how the princess's biographer, Karl Theodor Zingeler, described her life's crowning achievement.[42]

Katharina went down in history as the founder of the Benedictine Abbey of Beuron, which became the center of the important Beuronese Benedictine Congregation, and the famous Beuron Art School. The latter had a historical impact far beyond the confines of the Church.[43]

Princess Katharina Wilhelmine Maria Josepha von Hohenzollern-Sigmaringen, née Hohenlohe-Waldenburg-Schillingsfürst, died in Freiburg on February 15, 1893, at the age of seventy-six. She was interred in the royal tomb in Sigmaringen.[44] Her final resting place in the family vault befitted her status—though as the founder of a monastery, she could have been laid to rest in a founder's grave beneath the high altar of the abbey church. She had already selected the place there for her sarcophagus.[45] In spite of the apparent bad blood between abbot and founder in their final years, the princess's name remains associated with a monastic success story unparalleled to this day. By contrast, her failure as a Catholic nun, and the convent scandal bound up with this, have been largely forgotten. Katharina—and of this she was firmly convinced—had found the place designated for her by God. Once again, He had worked in mysterious ways, and turned a curse into a blessing.[46]

A CARDINAL'S POISON PARANOIA

Hohenlohe, Katharina's rescuer, made use of the unique chance that Kleutgen's involvement in the Sant'Ambrogio affair gave him to take his revenge for the condemnation of Anton Günther. The Jesuit may have been formally convicted, but the titular bishop of Edessa ultimately failed in his aim. And Kleutgen's friends and supporters—the cardinals Patrizi and Reisach and their Jesuit network, including the pope himself—knew exactly who had placed their comrade in this hot water. They may well have believed that Hohenlohe initiated the Sant'Ambrogio trial as a strategic move against new scholasticism and its chief thinkers. Whatever his motive, Hohenlohe had now taken up a clear position within the complex factions of the Roman Curia.

The case of Sant'Ambrogio acted as a catalyst for political and theological polarization within the Roman milieu. When Hohenlohe had arrived in Rome in 1846, his thought had still been informed by the "religious romanticism of a seminarian" and an "enthusiasm for the Jesuit mastery of spiritual exercises." The members of the Society of Jesus did everything they could to win over the German nobleman for their Counter-Reformation order. But, disillusioned by the flunkyism of the papal Curia, Gustav Adolf's initial "desire to enter the Jesuit order, and fascination with the closed nature of Thomist philosophy," soon grew into a preference for a more open, liberal Church.[47] Hohenlohe's charm allowed him to establish a good connection with Pius IX, even though the two men were starting to diverge politically and theologically. When the pope made his escape from the Revolution of 1848, Hohenlohe accompanied him into Neapolitan exile. Pius IX didn't forget this, and, after his return to Rome, Hohenlohe was admitted to his innermost circle.

But, following the judgment of 1862, there was a growing distance between Hohenlohe and the pope, who turned increasingly toward the Curia's Jesuit-dominated faction—in matters that went far beyond Church politics. His personal relationship with Hohenlohe also deteriorated. The German came from a noble family, and following an intervention from King Wilhelm I of Prussia he was made a cardinal in 1866, but he no longer had any influence in the Vatican. Hohenlohe had firmly positioned himself as a liberal, an opponent of new scholasticism, and a bitter enemy of the Jesuits. Now the empire struck back. Hohenlohe was sidelined. Nobody dragged one of I Nostri—"one of our own," as the members of the Jesuit network described themselves—before the Holy Roman Inquisition and went unpunished. Each of Hohenlohe's candidacies for a bishop's see in Germany was shot down by the Jesuit faction. From 1868 to 1881, he made every effort to become bishop of Freiburg, and when this finally came to nothing, he was convinced it wasn't the cathedral chapter there but his enemies in the Curia who were to blame. "The Jesuits have the pope so wrapped around their little finger that there is nothing to be done for me."[48]

This lasting snub made Hohenlohe increasingly anti-Jesuit. He was the strongest opponent of papal infallibility within the Roman Curia, seeing it as a typical move by the Jesuit faction. "It is a bad time now, especially here," he wrote to his brother Chlodwig, during the First Vatican Council. This meeting defined the infallibility and universal jurisdiction of the pope as dogma. "Stupidity and fanaticism join hands and dance the Tarantella, making such a caterwaul that one cannot bear to look or listen."[49] Despite being a cardinal of the Curia, he felt he had been sidelined, shut out of the preparations, advice, and discussions. The supporters of the infallibility dogma, led by the Jesuits, had arranged things so that "the cardinals who do not belong to their faction are given as little as possible to do."[50]

Hohenlohe didn't take part in the final vote on the new dogma. He found its definition of papal infallibility "inopportune." In his view, the council wasn't free, and therefore the dogma was invalid. The day Pius IX "imposed" his agenda upon the council spelled the end of "the conciliar existence of this sad gathering." As far as Hohenlohe was concerned, the First Vaticanum was no longer an ecumenical council. Up to this point, his argument had been no different from those of other opposing bishops and cardinals; around four fifths of the German episcopate had declined the infallibility dogma, and had left Rome before the final vote. But then Hohenlohe began an anti-Jesuit tirade, speaking with heavy sarcasm of the council's progress without the now absent dissenting foreign bishops: "One can only imagine all the decisions being made in these meetings. Perhaps they are declaring the infallibility of the Jesuits and all their schemes."[51]

Hohenlohe felt more and more isolated in Rome, and increasingly withdrew from public life. He spent most of his time at the Villa D'Este in Tivoli, which became his Tusculum. Here, he soon made a name for himself as a patron of the arts. The composer Franz Liszt spent a long time in Hohenlohe's idyllic country manor, which the liberals celebrated as the "last echo of a life that was once so potent, like that of the Farnese and other Renaissance cardinals."[52] For Hohenlohe, it was an escape from Vatican intrigues and political machinations. The Curia cardinal was on the losing side, and his notion of a Church that was open to the world had no place in Pius IX's Curia. Hohenlohe saw Rome as dominated by a pathological idea of the Church, of which Sant'Ambrogio was an extreme manifestation.

Once Rome had been occupied by Italian troops, Hohenlohe called for an agreement between the Italian king and the pope, and the Curia therefore began to view him as a traitor. In 1872, as a cardinal of the Curia, he even got Prince Otto von Bismarck to propose him as the German ambassador to the Holy See. This made things impossible for him with both the Church and the state. For six years, from 1870 to 1876, he remained exclusively in Germany. He became an "aristocratic vagabond," "haunting" the various residences of his many relatives and their extended family, like the Hohenzollerns in Berlin, and making marriage plans for all his single nieces.

Katharina von Hohenzollern and her onetime savior became increasingly estranged during these years. She couldn't understand Hohenlohe's opposition to the dogma of infallibility, or to Pius IX, with whom she remained in regular correspondence. She still had the greatest reverence for the pope, and spoke to him of her cousin's "blindness." "The poor man," she said, was "not really aware of the great inconsistencies in his life, or he would not tarry so far from his post."[53]

Since 1862, Hohenlohe had lost his head for politics completely. He gradually fell victim to a persecution complex, imagining a murderous Jesuit hiding behind every tree. The poison that had been administered to Katharina in Sant'Ambrogio had made the cardinal extremely paranoid about being poisoned himself. Hohenlohe was convinced that Kleutgen had been the real initiator of the attacks on his cousin, and placed him at the end of a long line of famous Jesuit poisoners. The idea that Jesuits not only prayed their adversaries into the grave, but also did away with them using poison, had been part of the standard repertoire of anti-Jesuit polemic for centuries.[54] Unlike his great adversary Cardinal Reisach, Hohenlohe was unable to get a glimpse into the court files. He therefore didn't know the exact outcome of the Inquisition's investigation, which exonerated Kleutgen to some degree on this charge.

In 1878, the Old Catholic Johann Friedrich claimed that the Jesuit had been convicted by the Inquisition for his involvement in the poisoning of a Princess von Hohenzollern in the convent of Sant'Ambrogio. This information may have originated with Hohenlohe: Friedrich had been the cardinal's council theologian during the First Vatican Council of 1870.[55] Frustrated that Kleutgen and his movement were now steering the Church despite the Sant'Ambrogio affair, and that a convicted heretic was helping draft papal dogma, Hohenlohe had told the German theologian the whole story of the poisoning.[56] And Friedrich then discredited the triumphant new scholastic Kleutgen in the press, calling him a poisoner and a murderer—which was, in all likelihood, exactly what Hohenlohe had intended.

But in the cardinal's eyes, the Jesuits had more than just the near-death of his cousin Katharina on their conscience. He was convinced they were trying to poison him as well. This meant he stopped eating and drinking anything at receptions and dinners outside his own household. Even when staying with his relatives, he no longer trusted the servants, imagining that they had all been bribed by the Jesuits. Marie von Thurn und Taxis-Hohenlohe reported that, when he came to visit, her uncle had not accepted anything at all to eat or drink, "not even a glass of water, as he always imagined the Jesuits were trying to poison him. He could not bear them, and thought they were trying to pay him back for this."[57]

It was only when his secretary and servant, Gustavo Nobile, whom he trusted absolutely and made his sole heir, had tasted food in his presence that Hohenlohe would eat it. His fear of poisoning was so great that every time he celebrated Holy Mass, Nobile had to try the Host and the Communion wine at the start of the service. Only if the taster still felt quite well at the start of the offertory did Hohenlohe allow them to be carried to the altar.[58]

Still, by the time of the conclave that followed Pius IX's death in 1878, the cardinal seemed to have regained some political influence. His first aim was to get the liberal cardinal Alessandro Franchi elected as pope.[59] When this proved impossible, he steered the Franchi group toward Gioacchino Pecci, who was then elected and became Pope Leo XIII. In return, Leo XIII made Franchi his cardinal secretary of state. Hohenlohe believed he could once again wield great political influence in the Vatican, through this member of the anti-Jesuit faction. However, Franchi died unexpectedly after only five months in office. Rumors immediately began circulating through the Curia that the Jesuits had had a hand in this. Hohenlohe was firmly convinced that Franchi had been poisoned by a member of the Society of Jesus.[60]

Three and a half decades after the poisonings in Sant'Ambrogio, Hohenlohe's life was still shaped by his poisoning paranoia and his terror of the Jesuits. He even spoke of a "war of annihilation" being waged against him in the Vatican, and of "scoundrels" in the Curia.[61] He tried to harm the Jesuits to the same degree he felt he was being persecuted by them. In March 1896, six months before his death, he heard that Cardinal Georg Kopp[62] had finally persuaded Hohenlohe's brother, Reich Chancellor Chlodwig zu Hohenlohe-Schillingsfürst, to readmit the Jesuits to the German Empire. They had been banned there since 1872. Hohenlohe was outraged: "If this happens, I will excommunicate both of them"—the cardinal and the reich chancellor.[63]

Hohenlohe died of a heart attack on October 30, 1896, and was buried in the German graveyard, the Campo Santo Teutonico, in the shadow of Saint Peter's.[64] With him died a model of Catholicism that favored reconciliation with Protestants and the modern nation-states, the pragmatic solution of the Roman Question, and, above all, a simple, late-Enlightenment faith, suspicious of any tendency toward exaggerated mysticism, pseudo-Catholic irrationalism, and exalted forms of piety. The judgment in the Sant'Ambrogio affair had also been a judgment against a pathological form of Catholic mysticism, and at that time the skeptical Hohenlohe had had the authority of the Holy Office behind him. But Hohenlohe himself was now defamed as being un-Catholic. There was no longer a place for someone like him in a Church where—as he remarked—"infallibility . . . has become an epidemic."[65]

FRIENDS IN HIGH PLACES

Hohenlohe's political and theological opponents in the College of Cardinals, Reisach and Patrizi, fared rather differently. Their careers were not affected in the slightest by the Sant'Ambrogio affair. On the contrary, they continued to rise unhindered through Pius IX's Curia. And no wonder: after all, neither of them had been in the dock, where they really belonged. Instead, the pope had installed them as judges of the highest religious tribunal specifically for this trial, even though both cardinals actually bore the ultimate responsibility for the catastrophe.

Reisach had introduced Katharina von Hohenzollern to the sisters of the Regulated Third Order of Holy Saint Francis. And he must have known what was going on there, since the convent's second confessor was none other than his close friend Kleutgen. Reisach apparently also had direct contact with Maria Luisa. The Virgin Mary had written a letter foretelling the founding of an offshoot of Sant'Ambrogio, with help from the "dowry of a foreign princess" who would enter the convent. This fact suggests the cardinal had informed the madre vicaria of the existence of Katharina's convent fund—something only he knew about.

Reisach's sympathies for the mysticism in Sant'Ambrogio in general, and for Maria Luisa in particular, were of a piece with his dependence on the stigmatized medium Louise Beck in Altötting. Even though the affair of "higher guidance" had overshadowed his personal life and made it impossible for him to continue as archbishop of Munich and Freising, or in Germany more generally, he didn't learn from his mistakes. He allowed himself to be hoodwinked by Maria Luisa, just as he had by Louise Beck before her. And Reisach must have known that the goings-on in the convent wouldn't remain hidden from Katharina for long: she was an educated lady, who came from an enlightened, aristocratic, interdenominational milieu. But his veneration of living female saints and mystical mediums blinded him to the approaching catastrophe.

In spite of this, he was still on the winning side in his struggle against modern theology and for new scholasticism. He was also very successful in his advocation of Ultramontanism, and a strict centralization of the Catholic Church. His problematic piety and a penchant for false mysticism didn't hamper his rise through Pius IX's Curia. In fact, he and the pope were united by their belief in the working of the supernatural in the natural world, and their weakness for the supernatural in general. Pius IX also gave Reisach a substantial role in the preparations for the First Vatican Council, making him the head of the influential Commission for the Secular Policy of the Church. In return, the cardinal made sure that only new scholastics were called as consultors, deliberately excluding renowned liberal German academic theologians.[66] Reisach had been promoted to cardinal bishop of Sabina in 1868, and Pius IX gave him the honor of being named first president of the Council on November 27, 1869. But Reisach wasn't able to take up this politically important office. Nor was he granted the opportunity to experience the greatest triumph of his lifelong labors: the dogmatization of papal infallibility. He fell ill in the fall of 1869, and retired to the Redemptorist monastery of Contamine-sur-Arve in Savoy, where he died on December 16, 1869. His final resting place was a tomb in his titular church, Sant'Anastasia in Rome.[67] When Pius IX announced the new dogma in the Vatican amid thunder and lightning on July 18, 1870, one of the most important advocates of papal infallibility had been dead for more than six months.

As cardinal protector of Sant'Ambrogio, Patrizi was also party to the convent's secret. His mother had been an enthusiastic devotee of Agnese Firrao, so the young Costantino may even have known about the mother founder a great deal earlier. Leziroli and the abbess started sending him written updates on the continuing veneration of Firrao, and Maria Luisa's visitations, after the Revolution of 1848. The cardinal was also the recipient of at least one letter from the Virgin. Patrizi was part of the network that kept a protective hand over the convent (which at this point had officially been suppressed), and tacitly tolerated its inhabitants' consistent disregard for the Inquisition's decree of 1816. In spite of this, no allegations were made against the cardinal secretary of the Inquisition during the trial. Even a highly motivated Dominican inquisitor like Sallua couldn't investigate the head of his own authority. The members of the tribunal enjoyed self-evident immunity; any inquiry into their affairs was taboo.

Costantino Patrizi was able to continue establishing his position as "the most influential Roman cardinal of the Pian era." His bigotry was notorious. When Pius IX returned, exhausted, from his exile in Gaeta, and requested a cup of meat broth to fortify him, Patrizi was deeply dismayed. The pope was trying to break the fast: his return fell on a Friday, a fast day. Visions were as much a part of his piety as they were Pius IX's.[68]

While people admired Patrizi for his piety and his strictness, they also maligned his modest intellectual abilities and lack of political skill. Patrizi was the "epitome of the donkey's ignorance combined with the stubbornness of a mule, the whole united with a strong dose of piety, which towers above his bigotry, and borders on fetishism."[69] Despite this, Patrizi's heritage, his excellent connections, the Jesuits' support, and the numerous offices he held made him the most influential cardinal in the city of Rome. While remaining cardinal vicar, he also became prefect of the Congregation of Rites, and secretary of the Holy Office. In 1860 he was made a cardinal bishop, and was given the suburbicarian episcopal sees of Porto and Santa Ruffina. In 1870, when he was cardinal bishop of Ostia and Velletri, he even became deacon of the College of Cardinals. He died on December 17, 1876. An insider in Rome is said to have remarked after his death: "With him, the College of Cardinals and Church have lost no leading light, but they have lost a model of piety and priestly virtue."[70]

Patrizi's wealth of offices makes the fact that he probably never understood the real background and implications of what happened in Sant'Ambrogio all the more tragic.[71] Patrizi wasn't honored with all these titles because of his abilities or services, but because of his noble pedigree and his spiritual kinship with Pius IX. If competence and professionalism, rather than patronage and clientelism, had determined how leading roles in the Curia were assigned, and if the cardinal protector of Sant'Ambrogio had really understood his duty, Maria Luisa probably wouldn't have been allowed to perpetuate her false cult and gain such a hold over the convent. This was a personal failure by Patrizi, but it was also the failure of a system that didn't perceive his incompetence, and even rewarded it by continuing to promote him through the clerical hierarchy of the Curia.

A SAINT IN THE MADHOUSE

Maria Luisa Ridolfi must have been an extremely self-confident and attractive young woman. Many people spoke of her extraordinary beauty and her winning charm. She was well aware of the effect she had on both men and women, and made deliberate use of her attractiveness. She wound the Americano around her little finger. She spent the night in bed with the learned theologian Joseph Kleutgen, who put her beauty and grace on a par with the Virgin Mary's. But her physical allure wasn't her only weapon: Maria Luisa also had an irresistible charisma. Even the Princess von Hohenzollern, who was not easily moved, had been wholly enthusiastic about her to begin with.

Maria Luisa came from a humble background, which she had tried to escape through her entry into a convent.[72] As a young girl, she was sexually abused by the then abbess of Sant'Ambrogio, and immediately afterward started to have visions and ecstasies, which gradually escalated over the years. It is impossible to say for sure whether these supernatural activities were an awful reaction to the things she had experienced. But the possibility is suggested by the fact that in the nineteenth century, Marian visions were frequently associated with a "collection of symptoms: poverty, dependency, sickness, the role of a social outsider, or a crucial experience of physical and emotional vulnerability."[73] The stigmatized seer Maria von Mörl's mystical experiences started after she was abused by her father.[74] Maria Luisa's suffering—in her case, severe headaches—was something else she had in common with other ecstatic women, like the "bride of suffering" Anna Katharina Emmerick. However, Maria Luisa took things even further. She used the "language of the ecstatic body" not just as a "feminine crisis-management strategy" and a "way of expressing suffering," but in a conscious and targeted way to manipulate those around her.[75]

Maria Luisa never wanted to find herself standing in the shade again. She wasn't going to carry on being one of life's losers. It was only natural that she should follow the example of female mystics from history, and portray herself as a nun with a direct line to God. And she had the perfect environment for this: supernatural phenomena weren't exactly rare in Sant'Ambrogio, as things stood. Backed by a divine authority, Maria Luisa was gradually able to accumulate power, first within the convent, and then in parts of the Curia. Her direct connection to heavenly powers made her closer to God than any priest or bishop, and even the pope himself. She could always answer objections from ordained men by saying: and did the Mother of God tell you that herself? And—as crazy as it sounds—Maria Luisa and her feminine, mystical strategy made some headway in the masculine, clerical hierarchy of the Catholic Church.[76]

The fact that theologians and cardinals genuinely believed in Maria Luisa is only understandable against the backdrop of the miracle addiction of Rome's religious milieu in the second half of the nineteenth century. In the apocalyptic mood stirred up by the gradual shrinking of the Papal States, and the prospect of Rome's occupation by Italian nationalist troops, people expected heavenly powers to intervene at any moment, to protect the pope and the Curia. And naturally, the pope himself performed miracles on an almost daily basis, as more than a few of his contemporaries believed.[77]

But Maria Luisa wanted more. She wasn't content with controlling the simple, pious women in Sant'Ambrogio, and manipulating men of the cloth. She wanted to create a legacy that would forever be associated with her name. And so she began to formulate a plan that would make her the next Agnese Firrao: she would found a new convent, an offshoot of Sant'Ambrogio, with herself as abbess. But she needed money for this—a lot of money, and the protection of influential churchmen.

Part of the tragedy of this beautiful young nun's story is that it was the preparations for this masterstroke that led to catastrophe. Cardinal Reisach had finally put the money to finance the new institution within her reach. Katharina von Hohenzollern was very wealthy, and had put her widow's inheritance into a convent fund. The Virgin Mary soon laid claim to her: "She must be mine, the princess." But nobody had reckoned with the German noblewoman's mentality, which was radically different from that of her Italian sisters. The princess saw through Maria Luisa, and the story ended with poisoning attempts and a trial before the Holy Office.

The churchmen who had previously hung on Maria Luisa's lips and breasts, and venerated her as a living saint, now dropped her like a hot potato. The Holy Office's all-male tribunal believed them when they said they'd been deceived. Their claims chimed with contemporary clichés about women: what else could one expect from the weaker sex, the daughters of Eve, who were so easily seduced by evil and then seduced men in turn? The powerful men, the cardinal protectors, members of the Curia, and father confessors, should have realized what was going on from the start. They should have provided pastoral support to Maria Luisa when she was abused as a child and young woman, supporting her on a personal and a spiritual level. Now she alone would be punished for all the things that the churchmen's false faith had allowed to happen, while the eminent gentlemen themselves got off scot-free.

Of course, we must not forget that Maria Luisa had confessed to several murders, and a secular court might well have sentenced her to death.[78] In accordance with the regular criminal law of the Papal States in the nineteenth century, "every planned and premeditated killing" carried the death penalty as well. A poisoner couldn't expect the authorities to be any more lenient—in fact, while executions were usually carried out by beheading, the law stipulated an even worse fate for those who had poisoned their victims. They were executed by being shot in the back.[79]

But the blood of priests and members of religious orders was seldom shed. In the Papal States, they held the so-called *privilegium fori*, according to which they couldn't be tried before a secular court for civil or criminal offenses.[80] It was very rare for them to be handed over to the jurisdiction of secular courts and executed. This only really happened to those who stubbornly refused to abjure in cases of heresy, or had committed a capital offense and were dismissed from the priesthood. And the Inquisition tribunal wasn't looking for capital crimes: its sole focus was heresy, next to which murder and attempted murder were almost classed as secondary offenses, the results of false belief.

Maria Luisa was never allowed to speak publicly about the involvement of clerics in the whole affair. The young nun remained alone, imprisoned in cloistered isolation and cut off from the world.[81] During the trial, from December 1859 until May 1860, Maria Luisa was held in the convent of Purificazione, where her "strange behavior" was noted. The abbess then requested that she be transferred elsewhere. The first five years of her monastic imprisonment in Buon Pastore, from 1862 to 1867, seem to have passed without incident. However, she then became "restless," and started behaving oddly. She roamed the convent day and night, upsetting the nuns with her crazy talk. She started to become violent, and finally could no longer be controlled. She even endangered a nun's life by trying to "compress her throat."

In light of this, on July 29, 1868, the Holy Office decided to place Maria Luisa in the Casa della Penitenza alle Terme prison.[82] People there soon began to have serious doubts about her mental health. "Here she has been living in quite an animal fashion, and showing clear signs of mental confusion," as a report to the cardinals of the Inquisition stated.[83] The prison physician, Doctor Caetani, described Maria Luisa as "a woman as excited as a wild animal, who suffers excessive outbreaks of the nervous system. However, I do not believe I have been able to discern a true madness."[84] Expert knowledge was necessary to reach a conclusive diagnosis here.

The tribunal followed the doctor's suggestion on January 20, 1869, and had Maria Luisa committed to the Ospizio dei Dementi,[85]

Rome's lunatic asylum. The doctors there diagnosed a mental "disharmony," in addition to physical weakness. Maria Luisa's mind had been thrown completely off balance, and she displayed strong kleptomaniac tendencies. She stole everything she could find, and stubbornly denied having done so. She had developed a kind of mantra, denying over and over again that she had ever had a religious vocation. She claimed to have lived an orderly, secular life. She had evidently repressed her convent past, and all the experiences bound up with it. The doctors told her several times that she had entered a convent at the age of thirteen. "But she understood nothing"—or she refused to understand.

Maria Luisa didn't seem to be responding to any kind of therapy, so the doctors suggested she be allowed to live with her family under house arrest. Pius IX approved this decision on June 30, 1869, with the proviso that her father must guarantee to keep watch over her and prevent her from causing any more damage. She should continue to live as a nun at home. It was impressed upon her that she should give no cause for future complaints.

After little more than a year, in mid-1870, Domenico Ridolfi appealed to the Holy Office, telling them he couldn't keep his daughter with him any longer. She had plunged his entire household into chaos, and was "unruly." "She just roamed around all day when she was at home, crashing about and screaming, she treated her sisters like whores, laying hands on them. . . . She denied God and hell," he complained. Following a ruling on July 1, 1870, Maria Luisa was taken back to Buon Pastore.

Just a few weeks later, in October 1870, Italian troops occupied Rome and released her. She claimed to have been imprisoned on purely religious grounds. She explained to the Italian authorities that her trial before the Holy Office eight years previously had merely been a "question of religious conflict between Franciscans and Dominicans," into which she had been drawn quite innocently. The picture she painted of herself as the victim of an arbitrary, inhuman religious court, made use of existing prejudices against the Inquisition. As far as Rome's new lay administration was concerned, she was preaching to the choir.

Finally, on October 23, 1871, Maria Luisa's case was brought to trial before the civil court of Rome. Maria Luisa, represented by her

lawyer, Orlando Fiocchi, was pitted against the Holy Office, represented by the lawyer Severino Tirelli.[86] The former novice mistress
requested the return of her dowry, to the sum of 1,300 scudi, plus an
adequate pension and the restitution of her honor, which had been
damaged by her wrongful conviction. In a modern state like Italy,
a person couldn't be punished for divergent religious beliefs that
opposed the papal system. Maria Luisa and her lawyer made good use
of this principle.

Severino Tirelli, the Holy Office's lawyer, made it clear that the
judgment of 1862 had covered not only religious but capital offenses.
However, he didn't go into detail. The Church was desperate to
avoid any further aggravation of the already tense situation between
state and Church that had developed since 1870. Revelations about
Sant'Ambrogio would have been just what the new Italian bureau-
cracy was waiting for. Tirelli was thus quick to offer a settlement
on behalf of the Inquisition—though not without mentioning the
immense costs that Maria Luisa had racked up for the Holy See since
1859, and referring pointedly to the asylum doctors' evaluation of her
mental state. Her accommodation in various jails and institutions had
cost a total of 4,473.76 scudi. Nevertheless, the Church was prepared
to return the dowry of 500 scudi that Maria Luisa had paid on her
entry to Sant'Ambrogio. Maria Luisa didn't accept this offer, insist-
ing she wanted the 1,300 scudi she originally requested. However,
on May 2, 1872, the tribunal ruled that she should receive 500 scudi,
which corresponded to 2,687 Italian lire.

The money doesn't seem to have lasted long. Maria Luisa had not
only parted ways with the Church; she had fallen out with her family as well. And once she had been "freed," she couldn't return to the
asylum or a convent jail. She was mentally and physically broken.
The judgment of Sant'Ambrogio, and the distance she had fallen as a
result, had caused her—if we believe her father—to lose all faith. The
woman who had once been the Virgin Mary's favorite daughter could
find no place for herself in this world. The former saint landed first in
the madhouse, and then in the gutter.

If we believe Marie von Thurn und Taxis-Hohenlohe, then before
Maria Luisa vanished from history, there was one final encounter
between the former novice mistress and her former novice Luisa
Maria, Katharina von Hohenzollern. It must have been during the

princess's visit to Rome in the spring of 1872 that a "poor woman" visited her apartment.[87] "She invited her in—and there stood the madre vicaria. Her heart stood still. But the unhappy, broken, and aged woman, who had retained none of her former beauty, threw herself at her feet and beseeched her for forgiveness. She had recently left prison and was in the depths of misery, literally on the point of starvation." Katharina, who had inwardly "already forgiven her," did not refuse her pleas for help, and saved the unhappy woman from "complete despair."[88]

From this description, it would seem that forgiveness had at least brought an end to the conflict that had been the catalyst for the Sant'Ambrogio trial. There was no more enmity between the two women: the "saint" Maria Luisa and the "unbeliever" Katharina, the poisoner and her victim. And neither of the two former nuns would have to face the Final Judgment unreconciled. But this may have just been wishful thinking. Marie von Thurn und Taxis-Hohenlohe's story of reconciliation cannot be corroborated by other sources. Even if it were true, it would probably have made little difference to the fact that the Sant'Ambrogio affair left Maria Luisa a broken woman. The story of the former madre vicaria and novice mistress faded away into the darkness of history. In her case, the Inquisition ultimately achieved its aim of *Damnatio memoriae*.

A HERETIC WRITES DOGMA

Unlike Maria Luisa, Kleutgen got away incredibly lightly, despite the serious nature of the charges against him. He himself said later that the Holy Office had sentenced him to "five years of imprisonment in the Inquisition's cells" for *formalem haeresim* (formal heresy). But the cardinals and the pope had rendered the judgment increasingly lenient, and in the end it was reduced to just two years of incarceration in a Jesuit house outside Rome.[89] Kleutgen served his sentence in a sanitorium and house of retreat in Galloro, a picturesque location near the Castle of Ariccia on Lake Nemi, in the Alban Hills southeast of Rome. At the time, this house was frequently used for rest and recuperation by the editors of the *Civiltà Cattolica*, the Jesuit journal.[90]

Kleutgen had close connections with this group, and in Galloro he also had the requisite leisure time to press ahead with his *Theology of Times Past*. In short, his stay there didn't bear the slightest resemblance to incarceration "in the Inquisition's cells." Unlike Maria Luisa, who fell into a void, Kleutgen was caught by his order's community, which had plenty of influence within the Curia of Pope Pius IX.

After just a year and a half, in October 1863, Kleutgen returned to Rome. There he resumed his work as a teacher of rhetoric at the Collegium Germanicum.[91] Outwardly, the affair seemed to have caused him only minimal damage. He may no longer have been assigned a place in the order's leadership, but he was allowed to return to his beloved Germanicum, and had enough time to complete his major work on new scholasticism. His influence on Church policy, in particular the development of the Catholic magisterial authority, was undiminished. Even Kleutgen himself marveled at this in retrospect: "Remarkably, those very cardinals who had not long since convicted me *ob formalem haeresim*, afterwards treated me just as if nothing had happened."

Cardinal Reisach in particular proved very well disposed to Kleutgen, visiting him in Galloro in 1862–1863. When the pope asked Reisach to "procure a theological evaluation on a very important matter," Reisach asked Kleutgen, who took on the job at once. Reisach handed the text to the pope and another senior member of the Curia, and both were "astonished" at the quality of the votum. In response to their inquiries, Reisach revealed the secret of the censor's identity. In light of the "aptitude" displayed in this *votum*, Pius IX allowed Kleutgen to return from exile to Rome straightaway. Not long before, the Jesuit general Petrus Beckx had also gone to the pope to beg for mercy on Kleutgen's behalf.[92] Even as a condemned man and a heretic, Kleutgen had proved faithful to the cause, and the pope was merciful.

But what was this extremely important theological matter that led to the Jesuit's immediate reprieve? Reisach had a hand in two pieces of Church policy during 1862–1863 to which Kleutgen may have contributed a votum. One was the brief *Gravissimas inter*, of December 11, 1862, and the other was the brief *Tuas libenter*, of December 21, 1863. Both papal documents rested on a concept that Kleutgen had developed as a censor of the Congregation of the Index during the 1850s.

Pius IX proclaimed the dogma of the Immaculate Conception, and had
himself and his successors declared infallible by the First Vatican Council.
He was beatified in the year 2000 by Pope John Paul II.

His idea made it easier to defame modern, non-new-scholastic theologians as unorthodox, and place them on the *Index of Forbidden Books*.

Very soon after Kleutgen had been convicted of heresy, Pius IX
enshrined this model, which had initially been used only within
the Congregation of the Index, as official Church doctrine. It was
the concept of the "ordinary magisterium," which is still of central
importance today.[93] Of course, at the same time Joseph Kleutgen
was "inventing" this concept, Giuseppe Peters was acting on religious
convictions that the Inquisition would later class as heretical.

The ordinary magisterium makes its first doctrinal appearance in
1863, in *Tuas libenter*. This brief was principally directed against the
Munich Church historian Ignaz von Döllinger, and his speech at
the academic conference he had organized in Munich.[94] The conference had been intended to bridge the divide within German theology between Roman and German theologians, new scholastics and
modern thinkers—though after Döllinger's caustic opening address,
this was clearly doomed to failure. Döllinger called Italian theology

"gloomy and church-yardish." The "old tenement knocked together by the scholastics" had fallen into disrepair. A new structure could only be built using both "eyes of theology": history and philosophy.[95]

Prior to *Tuas libenter*, the concept of an ordinary magisterium had been unknown. There was only the sacred magisterium of the councils and the pope. On the rare occasions when there was no other option, and it was the only way to secure a religious truth, this teaching authority would turn a tenet into a formal dogma. Among other things, this led to the articles of the creed being set down in writing by the Church's early councils. But theologians were free to discuss all questions of faith that hadn't been defined by the sacred magisterium. The essential task of this sacred magisterium was to act as a shepherd, observing and protecting tradition, rather than adding to the *Depositum fidei*.[96] "The Deposit of Faith was not something presented by the magisterium; rather, the bishops were able to testify to it because it was believed."[97]

Going against this tradition, Kleutgen defined the relationship between the papal magisterium and the teaching authority of the theologians in a completely new way. In addition to the sacred magisterium, he proposed an ordinary magisterium for the pope and Curia that would be exercised daily, and would be equally binding. Döllinger's address, which had made a plea for theology's freedom from Roman paternalism, was the catalyst that set this in motion. The Munich historian believed that in future only dogmatic errors, offenses "against the clear universal teaching of the Church," should be denounced and investigated in Rome. Theologians should be given complete freedom in all other fields, which made up the majority of their work—including the freedom to make mistakes. The theological weapons of reason and argument were the only things that should be used against errors that had not been defined solemnly by the Church's magisterial decision.[98]

The new scholastic and Ultramontanist camp saw this as an attack on them. They wrote an opposing statement, and denounced Döllinger's speech and the entire conference to Rome. And Rome, unfortunately for Döllinger, was home to his old archenemy, who had spent years waiting for a chance to have his revenge: Cardinal Reisach. Reisach believed that in 1855 the Munich theologian had used his influence on the Bavarian government to get Reisach "promoted" away from Munich. The denunciation of Döllinger offered Reisach the opportunity to take revenge on an academic he believed was blinded by his pride in his own intellect. He now had the pope on his side. And, once again, he enlisted Kleutgen in his mission—hence Reisach's visit to Galloro.

The real incendiary power of Kleutgen's idea was revealed in the *Tuas libenter* brief, which said that in Germany there was a widespread "false opinion against the old school." It also referred to the "false" philosophy practiced in connection with this.[99] The term "old school" was at least an indirect allusion to the first volume of Kleutgen's *Theologie der Vorzeid*, which had been published in Münster in 1853. But the reference to "false" philosophy may have been directed at Jakob Frohschammer,[100] who was teaching in Munich at that time, and had been placed on the *Index* for philosophical errors a few years previously, at Kleutgen's urging. He was one of new scholasticism's most steadfast opponents in Germany, and was also an enemy of the Jesuits. It was no coincidence that *Tuas libenter* was addressed to the archbishop of Munich, Gregor von Scherr.[101] He was not only responsible for the area in which the Munich conference had taken place, but also for Frohschammer, who taught there. Kleutgen at least inspired this brief, if he didn't write it. In any case, the newly accessible sources in the Archive of the Congregation for the Doctrine of the Faith allow us to identify him as the real "inventor" of the ordinary magisterium of the pope and Curia.

Jakob Frohschammer's work *Ueber den Ursprung der menschlichen Seelen* (On the Origin of Human Souls) was denounced to the Congregation of the Index in 1855.[102] Thomas Aquinas famously taught that the human embryo was progressively imbued with a soul: it gained first a plant and then an animal soul, and a human soul developed after this. The question discussed among theologians was whether this progression should be thought of in creationist or generationist terms—whether God had to perform an act of creation for each of the three successive souls, or whether the succession proceeded automatically as the fetus developed, from the initial spark it received from its parents in the act of conception. Frohschammer argued in favor of the generationist position.

The secretary of the Congregation of the Index looked over the matter, and initiated a trial. The votum was entrusted to none other than Joseph Kleutgen. He clearly thought the Munich philosopher's work on generationism was an open-and-shut case, as his report showed: it was barely eight pages long. But the question of generationism versus creationism was far from the focus of Kleutgen's interest. For him, this was more about the fundamental question of what counted as binding doctrine, and what didn't. Creationism had never been defined by the Church as an article of faith, which was why Frohschammer assumed that he was permitted to argue for an alternative model. Kleutgen opposed this view, saying that since the seventh century at the latest, it had been the unanimous doctrine of the pope, bishops, and good theologians that generationism was "close to heresy." At the very least, it had been viewed "as erroneous and highly audacious." It was this seemingly uninterrupted consensus within the Church that meant Frohschammer's work had to be judged heretical.[103]

But Kleutgen's argumentation convinced neither the consultors nor the cardinals.[104] There was therefore a second trial, for which two more censors were engaged: the Franciscan Friar Minor Conventual Angelo Trullet,[105] and the Benedictine Bernard Smith.[106] Kleutgen was forced to position himself. He now returned to the idea of a double magisterium, which he had developed in his *Theologie der Vorzeid*. It was something he had first considered in a dispute with the moral and pastoral theologian Johann Baptist Hirscher.[107] Kleutgen's second votem on Frohschammer essentially just explained the argument he had already advanced in his book.

It would be a misunderstanding and an extraordinary presumption, Kleutgen said, to claim that the Church only considered something binding when it acted as the highest judge in a religious dispute, exercising its power as sacred teaching authority. Rather, the Church believed that everything it presented in its role as ordinary teaching authority was binding. It thus had a "double magisterium." Unlike Thomas Aquinas, however, Kleutgen wasn't referring to one magisterium of shepherds, and one of the theologians. For him, both teaching authorities, sacred and ordinary, belonged exclusively to the shepherds, and ultimately to the pope. "The ... ordinary and perpetual ... consists of that very enduring Apostolate of the Church. The other is extraordinary, and exercised only at particular times, for example when false teachers cause unrest within the Church. It is at once a teaching authority and a judging authority."[108]

For Kleutgen, this also settled the question of whether somebody true to the Catholic faith was allowed to form his own views in areas "where one cannot prove through the agreement of theologians, or in any other way," that something "belongs to the doctrine of the Catholic Church in the strictest sense." According to Kleutgen, the Church certainly didn't recognize "the freedom exercised by certain people, to teach anything that is not technically classed as heretical." In his *Theology of Times Past*, Kleutgen had proposed to Hirscher that freedom of thought and teaching wasn't just limited by the dogma, but by the ordinary magisterium. He now repeated this in his votum on Frohschammer. There could be no "intemperance of opinion and teaching in the Church" regarding tenets that hadn't been explicitly defined as dogma by the sacred magisterium. Creationism might not have been formally defined, but it had been consistently espoused by the ordinary and enduring magisterium. According to Kleutgen, this authority belonged first to the pope, in everything he said, and then to the bishops, who were scattered across the globe and taught with one accord. It also belonged to the Roman Congregations, and, finally, "respected" theologians.

Interestingly, the second evaluator, Angelo Trullet, accused Kleutgen of introducing entirely new criteria and benchmarks for evaluating theology and censoring books. This was an attempt to pass a law criminalizing something that previously hadn't been a crime at all.[109] Trullet refused to recognize an ordinary magisterium. In his eyes, therefore, this couldn't be a reason to condemn Frohschammer. Trullet said that creationism hadn't been formally defined, so of course theologians were permitted to argue for generationism.

But the Congregation of the Index didn't accept this. The third censor, Bernard Smith, came down on Kleutgen's side and agreed with the idea of the ordinary magisterium. Frohschammer's generationist text was placed on the *Index of Forbidden Books* in March 1857 for contradicting the ordinary magisterium Kleutgen had developed, which, before that point, nobody had heard of.

Having been indexed and humiliated in other ways by the Church authorities, Frohschammer wrote two programmatic texts that completely rethought the relationship between reason and faith, science and Church authority. They were also heavily critical of the Congregation of the Index.[110] These books were duly denounced in Rome and investigated by the Congregation of the Index. But once again, Frohschammer hadn't denied any officially defined doctrine. The consultor Piotr Semenenko's[111] votum therefore concluded that Frohschammer's theology might be unusual, but it was completely orthodox.[112] When the Congregation of the Index definitively refused to ban these works, too, Kleutgen resorted to a process already tested in the Günther trial. Via Reisach, he managed to bypass the Congregation of the Index, and got the pope himself to condemn Frohschammer's teachings in the brief *Gravissimas inter* (December 11, 1862). Kleutgen may have written an early draft of this brief in Galloro.[113]

Kleutgen's conviction in the Sant'Ambrogio trial didn't impact his influence on Church politics, or the implementation of his theology. Even while he was serving his sentence in Galloro, his concept of the ordinary magisterium found its way into Pius IX's doctrinal documents. But how was Kleutgen affected on a personal level? Did being convicted of heresy really leave him cold?

Kleutgen was discomfited by the fact that the highest religious tribunal had condemned him as a heretic. He was, after all, an obsessively correct theologian who thought of himself as hyper-orthodox. His entire life had been dedicated to obeying the pope in all things. As an influential consultor for the Congregation of the Index, he was usually the one classing other people as heretics, bringing theological and personal destruction down upon them. The judgment was a brutal blow, to which he was unable to reconcile himself. He was in danger of falling from the rock to which he had clung in fear through the storms of the nineteenth century, and being plunged back into the roaring waves. The Holy Father, whom he feared and idolized at the same time, and whom he had only ever tried to please, had chastised him and branded him a disobedient son. Ultimately, Kleutgen had "not been able to bear this reprimand." From then on, he was a "broken man."[114]

The Jesuit must have found it difficult to accept that he had failed to live up to his own moral and theological standards.[115] He wanted to be an exemplary and strictly moral priest, but he had succumbed to the temptations of a woman several times over. He knew the criteria for judging the authenticity of revelations, but had still taken the "divine" letters at face value in spite of their absurd contents. He knew French kissing was immoral, but had still put his tongue into the mouth of a young nun for minutes at a time. He was at home in

the exalted heights of theological speculation, following in the footsteps of Saint Thomas Aquinas—but he wasn't equal to the human,
all-too-human lowlands of pastoral care in a convent.

And the site of this disaster had not been somewhere in the prov-
inces, but the center of Christianity, the pope's own city. The longer
Kleutgen stayed in Rome, the more he associated it with his unhappiness and "nameless suffering."[116] More than once, he complained
"about the hated city of Rome, the site of my great fall." By the summer of 1869, he was convinced he had to turn his back on the Eternal City once and for all. He believed he could no longer be of "any
particular use" there. "It seems better for me and the community," he
wrote, "if I live out my days in greater seclusion, in some house of my
order."[117]

With permission from the general of his order, he retired to
Viterbo—but he soon returned to Rome to play a decisive role in
the First Vatican Council. As a simple priest, he couldn't become a
Council Father or a member of any of the conciliary commissions.
Only cardinals, bishops, and the heads of monastic communities
could perform these roles. Kleutgen served as council theologian to
one of his fellow Jesuits, the apostolic vicar of Calcutta, Archbishop
Walter Steins.[118] Steins was a member of the dogmatic commission,
which considered potential constitutions and definitions to be issued
by the Council. In this role, Kleutgen helped to shape the Council's
two dogmatic constitutions on the Catholic Faith and the Church of
Christ, and the dogma of papal infallibility. Without the First Vatican Council, his concept of the ordinary magisterium could never
have gained so much weight, nor had such an effect on history.

The pope intended this Council as an opportunity for the Church
to position itself against the hostile modern world and its rationalism. Its most important task was to clarify the relationship between
faith and reason, and to rebuff what Catholics in Rome viewed as the
erroneous ideas of many German- and French-speaking theologians.
These fundamental theological problems were discussed extensively
in the draft *De doctrina catholica*. However, this draft was far too ver-
bose for most of the Council Fathers, and they rejected it. On the
wishes of Pius IX, Joseph Kleutgen was tasked with revising it, as part
of the constitution on the Faith. He was then largely responsible for
the wording of the final text.[119]

It was only to be expected that Kleutgen's concept of the double magisterium would surface again, in the revelatory constitution *Dei filius*, which was adopted on April 24, 1870. "Further, by divine and Catholic faith, all those things must be believed which are contained in the written word of God and in tradition, and those which are proposed by the Church, either in a solemn pronouncement or in her ordinary and universal teaching power, to be believed as divinely revealed."[120]

Kleutgen also had a crucial influence on the constitution *Pastor aeternus* of July 18, 1870, in which the dogma of papal infallibility and papal primacy were defined. He drafted the wording for the definition of infallibility, which met with "the highest acclaim from the fathers." The man who later became prefect of the Congregation of the Index, Cardinal Andreas Steinhuber,[121] was also convinced that the final text of the dogma was shaped by Kleutgen: "A goodly number of the principles defined were formulated by him."[122]

The wording Kleutgen suggested was: "Therefore all that is taken or taught to be beyond doubt in matters of faith and virtue everywhere in the world, under the leadership of the bishops bound to the Apostolic Throne, and what the bishops define should be believed and taught by all, with the agreement of the pope or by the pope himself, when he speaks *ex cathedra*, must be taken as infallible."[123] It is debatable whether Kleutgen, as some people have claimed, really bore "the main responsibility for the detailed preparation of the constitution *Pastor aeternus*."[124] This would mean that the final wording of the new dogma was directly attributable to him. But what we do know is that Kleutgen was a man who had been convicted of formal heresy, and was now exerting an active influence on the conception of the infallibility dogma.

Kleutgen wasn't able to remain in Rome for long: Italian troops occupied the pope's city in the summer of 1870, bringing the First Vatican Council to an abrupt end. The Council was postponed indefinitely, and Kleutgen was forced to flee to Viterbo. Still, he claimed: "Despite the suspension of the Council, I shall work on the *Schema de Ecclesia*, though this is to be kept secret."[125] Kleutgen set off on an odyssey through northern Italy and South Tyrol. He was in poor health, feeling physically and spiritually exhausted. He went first to Brixen, though the climate there was "too extreme for me, as I am in

any case much weakened and extremely susceptible."[126] He felt root-
less, in need of a sanctuary. He longed for the Germanicum in Rome,
and at the same time hated the city because it reminded him of the
disaster of Sant'Ambrogio. Kleutgen kept moving, staying in Görz,
Bad Innichen, Lengmoos near Bozen, Trento. . . . [127] He had become
a drifter, unable to find peace anywhere. When one day he arrived
at the pastor's house in Lengmoos he looked like a homeless person,
"all ragged from head to foot, from hat to shoes," even though he was
really "an orderly man" as the pastor there remembered.[128]

After eight long years, the summer of 1878 brought a turning point:
Kleutgen was finally allowed to return to his beloved Germanicum.
His delight in being made prefect of studies, and reinstated as a consultor to the Congregation of the Index, was ultimately greater than
his fear of Rome.[129] Time seems to have healed the rift of 1862, at least
to some degree. Leo XIII, the new pope, also issued the encyclical
Aeterni Patris on August 4, 1879.[130] This document declared the philosophy of Thomas Aquinas, and with it the new scholasticism that
Kleutgen had always advocated, to be the only legitimate philosophy
of the Catholic Church. Whether Kleutgen was directly involved in
composing the encyclical or not, this was official approbation of his
life's work from the Church's teaching authority.[131] Theologically, he
had achieved his aim.

It had been a long road to the recognition of new scholasticism as
the only legitimate Catholic theology. Kleutgen had faced heavy opposition, even from within the Jesuit order—in particular from Carlo
Passaglia. Kleutgen had not shrunk from inspiring Maria Luisa to produce the letter from the Virgin Mary denouncing Passaglia, his main
theological opponent in the Society, as a homosexual, and thereby
silencing him. First, new scholasticism became the Jesuit theology, and
then Leo XIII finally made it the theology of the Catholic world.

But Kleutgen's happiness in Rome did not last. The city that had
seen his greatest personal humiliation was also witness to his ultimate
doom. While giving a lecture in March 1879, he suffered a stroke
that left him paralyzed down one side. Having been "*defeated*"—as
he wrote—"I will sadly have nothing more to do with the Gregorian
University."[132] On the other hand, he claimed he was quite glad to be
leaving Rome—that "den of robbers."[133] He began another odyssey:
Castel Gandolfo; Terlago near Trento; Mantua; Venice; Chieri; and

finally, in July 1881, Saint Anton near Kaltern, in South Tyrol. Kleutgen felt obsessively compelled to continue writing theological works in spite of his disability, but the paralysis made it very difficult. After the summer of 1881, he was "almost completely unable to write."[134] His hands refused to obey him. Over New Year 1882–1883, he suffered another stroke, which robbed him of his speech.

Joseph Wilhelm Carl Kleutgen died on the evening of January 13, 1883, and was buried on January 15 in the graveyard in Kaltern.[135] His gravestone proclaimed he was a "man of outstanding gifts, respected scholarship, distinguished by moral integrity and famed in the academy for his many published works."[136]

It is questionable whether a priest convicted by the Inquisition of seduction in the confessional can really be lauded for his moral integrity. And a respected scholar perhaps shouldn't have believed in letters from the Virgin Mary announcing the murder of a nun. But Kleutgen was without doubt a gifted theologian and a prolific author—here the inscription is correct. Leo XIII is said to have dubbed him the "prince of scholasticism," because his works contributed to making the *Theology of Times Past* the only model recognized by the Church.[137] Kleutgen's gravestone obviously overlooks the really salient aspect of his biography: his life's great scandal. Just a short time after being convicted of formal heresy by the highest religious authority, this man was helping to formulate Church doctrine—including the new dogma of papal infallibility that remains binding for Catholics to this day.

> When the Roman pontiff speaks *ex cathedra*, that is, when, in the exercise of his office as shepherd and teacher of all Christians, in virtue of his supreme apostolic authority, he defines a doctrine concerning faith or morals to be held by the whole church, he possesses, by the divine assistance promised to him in blessed Peter, that infallibility which the divine Redeemer willed his church to enjoy in defining doctrine concerning faith or morals. Therefore, such definitions of the Roman pontiff are of themselves, and not by the consent of the church, irreformable.

And the final sentence of the dogma of 1870 reads: "So then, should anyone, which God forbid, have the temerity to reject this definition of ours: let him be anathema."[138]

Epilogue

The Secret of Sant'Ambrogio as Judged by History

Pius IX and the Inquisition avoided publishing the judgment in the Sant'Ambrogio case, keeping the convent's secret hidden behind the walls of the Palazzo del Sant'Ufficio.

However, they failed to keep the case out of the public eye altogether: despite the order of secrecy, the liberal Italian press still got wind of it. In 1861, when the dissolution of Sant'Ambrogio was made public, the newspapers published articles that indulged in all kinds of speculation about the affair. They took great delight in using Sant'Ambrogio to criticize the backwardness of the Curia's legal practices, and to call into question the legitimacy of a religious court. But these newspapers had been told that the dissolution of the convent was simply due to the continued veneration of Firrao. The names of the principal defendants, and the other offenses, don't seem to have been made public. Sant'Ambrogio provided the liberal press with the perfect opportunity to attack the Catholic Church, and the pope's secular rule over the Papal States. What remained of his territory was still standing in the way of Italian unification, even if the Marches and Umbria had already joned the *Risorgimento*.

The *Civiltà Cattolica* reprinted a *Giornale di Roma* report from May 13, 1861, criticizing coverage of the case by "bad" newspapers. It referred to the editors as "people raking through the muck." By contrast, the Catholic *Civiltà* portrayed the dissolution of the convent as an appropriate reaction to the pretense of holiness and continued veneration of Agnese Firrao.[1] The international press paid little attention to the case. All that remained of the Sant'Ambrogio scandal was a memory of the cult of Agnese Firrao, as websites about Rome's tourist attractions confirm.[2]

But the fact that the case received very little publicity was also due to the front pages being taken over by other Church-political events. There was the papal condemnation of the Munich conference in 1863,[3] and the *Syllabus errorum* in 1864, in which Pius IX took a sweeping blow at modern thinkers and their values—like the freedom of religion and conscience.[4] Finally, preparations for the First Vatican Council absorbed the public's interest. When Kleutgen was drafted in to work on preparing the two constitutions, Ignaz von Döllinger's 1870 *Römische Briefe vom Concil* suggested that the Jesuits must be very short-staffed if they had to resort to using a man who had been "convicted some time ago by the Holy Office for an indecent affair in a convent."[5] Interestingly, Döllinger's hint was picked up by the German newspaper *Der Spiegel* in 1962, in a lead article on the opening of the Second Vatican Council. At this point, there was talk of Kleutgen having been imprisoned for six years.[6]

The Sant'Ambrogio affair only reappeared in the press in the spring of 1879.[7] The Munich-based Church historian Johann Friedrich had been a high-profile opponent of the infallibility dogma, and had therefore been excommunicated in 1871. He subsequently allied himself to the Old Catholic Church. Writing in the *Deutscher Merkur*, he now raised serious allegations against Kleutgen. At the time, controversies were raging between the Old Catholics,[8] and what they called the "New Catholics," who defended papal infallibility as it was defined in 1870. Friedrich was aiming for a public vilification of the Jesuit, whom he saw as one of the driving forces behind the dogma. He claimed that the Inquisition had sentenced Kleutgen to six years in jail for his part in the poisoning attacks on a Princess von Hohenzollern, but had later been reprieved by the pope.[9]

The orthodox *Neue Zeitung* issued a sharp rebuttal to Friedrich, accusing him of the most shameless lies. The Old Catholic retaliated by starting a libel suit against the paper. In the trial that followed, the *Neue Zeitung*'s editors landed a surprising coup. They submitted as evidence a text dated March 7, 1879, from the Holy Office's chancellery.

It was written by Giovenale Pelami,[10] the Holy Office's notary, and it confirmed that Kleutgen had "never been charged with poisoning or involvement in an attempted murder by poison, and was certainly never interrogated or convicted for this."[11] It was certainly true that he hadn't been convicted of poisoning Katharina von Hohenzollern. But the Holy Office's statement that he hadn't been interrogated on this matter was manifestly untrue. And the notary was careful not to mention any other charges, or the sentence that Kleutgen had actually been given by the Inquisition. In its March 15 edition, the *Neue Zeitung* argued that there could be no truth in Friedrich's accusations, because the pope had entrusted Kleutgen with important work for the Council. "It would be entirely unthinkable for the pope to confer this honor on somebody who had been convicted of mixing poisons."[12] But Pius IX evidently had no problem drawing on the services of a convicted heretic to formulate dogma. Leo XIII had sworn the Jesuit to silence on the matter, so Kleutgen himself stayed out of the argument.[13] If he had taken up the gauntlet, things might have been rather different.

The Curia's strategy in the Sant'Ambrogio case was clear, at least during the lifetimes of its protagonists: the whole awkward affair was swept under the carpet for as long as possible. The Church authorities suppressed every memory of the convent and what had happened there as permanently as they could. When there was no other option, they did everything in their power to play the case down. If necessary, the formal truth could be told, but the really interesting facts were deliberately omitted.

There is a similar tendency in the historiographical treatment of the case. Strictly orthodox, Ultramontanist works of history—in particular, those with Jesuit leanings—have consistently attempted to defuse or ignore the incendiary nature of the Sant'Ambrogio affair. They have painted it as just one case of feigned holiness among many. Where there was any doubt, the blame has fallen on the women who pretended to be saints, while the Jesuit confessors have been painted as the victims of slander. This has sometimes even been interpreted as one of those divine tests of faith to which men of religious orders are often subjected.

A classic example of this is the biography of Kleutgen written by Johann Hertkens[14] and the Jesuit Ludwig Lercher[15] in 1911, to celebrate the hundredth anniversary of his birth. Their book claimed that as extraordinary confessor, the Jesuit had been to Sant'Ambrogio only three or four times a year. Apart from these confessional days, he hadn't given much thought to the sisters there. The biography's message was that Kleutgen had nothing to do with the whole affair. It was therefore "easy to understand how he could know and say little of the whole nebulous business." Kleutgen had let himself be deceived by the nuns over the mother founder's feigned holiness and the practices associated with this, it was true—but this had only been in the course of the trial, and "not while he was hearing confession." This phrase is telling; it brings with it the unspoken suggestion of *Sollicitatio*. The biographers state that Kleutgen vigorously defended himself against all charges before the Inquisition, but then, as befitted a man of the cloth, humbly submitted to the judgment of the *Suprema*. There are no further details of the charges and the verdict. A brief summary tells us: "The outcome of the trial otherwise caused only minor damage, if any, to Padre Kleutgen's reputation and people's respect for him." He "remained a man trusted by higher and lower prelates, able to advise them on the thorniest of issues."[16] Kleutgen's fellow Jesuits even saw "a marvelous quality of divine providence" in the trial. Providence "tests those it favors, and turns and guides every suffering in a glorious chain of events to the advantage of those it has tested—and, at the same time, to the advantage of many others, and the Church as a whole." It was only the fact that he was convicted, and the time he had spent away from Rome as a result, that had given the Jesuit sufficient leisure to finally complete his monumental *Theologie der Vorzeid*.[17]

In his semi-official account of the First Vatican Council, the Jesuit Theodor Granderath[18] only mentioned Sant'Ambrogio in a footnote. It was an explanation of why Kleutgen, "although known as a first-rate theologian, [was] not called in for the preparatory work." As an extraordinary confessor to the "Benedictine nuns" of the "convent of Saint Ambrose" in Rome, he had been "severely punished" by the Holy Office. The nuns had venerated as a saint "a sister who had died at the start of the century, to whom people had attributed extraordinary, supernatural gifts even during her lifetime," and the confessors had "missed this . . . due to the cleverness of the nuns' superiors."[19] This was, at least, a reference to Firrao's feigned holiness and her continued veneration, though the Franciscan nuns had become Benedictine, and everything else remained unclear. The reader is not told why Kleutgen had to be punished "severely."

The study by the Jesuit Franz Lakner, published in 1933, also follows this tradition.[20] He kept all details of the case from his readers—even the fact that Kleutgen was in any way involved in the Sant'Ambrogio affair. In an attempt to make the whole matter seem banal, he merely noted that the Holy Office had passed a "remarkable judgment" on Kleutgen, which had forced him to leave Rome for a time in 1862. However, this transpired to be an act of divine "providence," which provided him with "sufficient peace and leisure" to write his major theological work.

In a biographical entry on Kleutgen for the *Jesuiten-Lexikon* published in 1934, the German Jesuit Ludwig Koch demonstrated a complete lack of knowledge about the case.[21] He stated nebulously that Kleutgen had been extraordinary confessor to the Benedictines of Saint Ambrose. "Shortly before 1870" he had been caught up in a "denunciation for abusive devotions, and suspended." Readers could interpret "abusive devotions" in whatever way they wanted. The real core of the Sant'Ambrogio affair had thus vanished completely. In the obituaries published in 1883[22] and 1911,[23] in the *Civiltà Cattolica* (a paper belonging to Kleutgen's Jesuit network), the case wasn't even mentioned.

It's easy to understand why Jesuit historians played down or even omitted the affair from their works. It was partly done to protect their own order, and the theology for which Kleutgen stood. This damaging picture—the father of new scholasticism as a criminal and seducer, and the Jesuits and their friends in the Curia as a society of gullible bigots—should on no account be allowed to enter the public imagination. This kind of history writing wasn't about hard facts, or the ideal of "objective" truth. It was almost entirely apologist, like many other "historical" works.

But historical texts about Katharina von Hohenzollern also displayed a tendency to gloss over the attempts on the princess's life, and the Inquisition trial that followed. Even the work by her official biographer, Karl Theodor Zingeler, follows this pattern.[24] On her time in Sant'Ambrogio, he says succinctly: "In December the princess became very ill. She was given the last rites, and—because it was thought her time had come—they also conducted the ceremony for the profession of vows." Against expectations, Zingeler goes on, Katharina recovered and remained in the convent until July 26. Then she left Sant'Ambrogio with the support of her cousin, Archbishop Hohenlohe.[25] At his country seat in Tivoli, she met the German Benedictine priest Maurus Wolter, who was also recuperating there, and who immediately became her new confessor. Zingeler styles this meeting as the turning point in her life: after many trials and tribulations, the princess found her true calling through Wolter's Benedictine spirituality, and became the founder of Beuron.[26] There is no word about the poisoning, or her dramatic cry of "Save, save me!" There is no mention of the denunciation she made to the Inquisition on the express instruction of her confessor, Father Wolter—even though Zingeler must have known about this: in the foreword to his book he thanks "Fräulein Christiana Gmeiner, who was the princess's confidante for so many years," and who wrote a detailed report in 1870 of the princess's experiences in Sant'Ambrogio.[27]

In 1912, when Zingeler's biography was published, it was obviously hard for the Catholic milieu and the royal house of Sigmaringen to bear the involvement of a Catholic noblewoman in this sort of affair. With the fierce disputes that the crisis of modernism had brought with it still raging,[28] it was easiest to remain silent about the whole thing. In any case, the image of Katharina as a poisoning victim and plaintiff in an Inquisition trial didn't fit with the idea of her as the immaculate founder of a monastery. She was a heroine, whose efforts had given life to the first Benedictine monastery in the southwest of Germany since secularization.

After the Old Catholics had made their attack on Kleutgen and the Jesuits, nobody wrote openly about the Sant'Ambrogio affair until the Second Vatican Council, when Benedictine historians referred to it in connection with the opening of the Catholic Church. Prior to this, even they had glossed over it. Anselm Schott made no mention at all of the Sant'Ambrogio case in his biography of Maurus Wolter.[29] He claimed it was the pope himself, not Hohenlohe, who made the Benedictine Katharina's confessor, and opened up "the new and higher path" that he then followed toward the founding of Beuron. It was only Virgil Fiala, in a 1963 book marking the hundredth anniversary of Beuron Abbey, who addressed Katharina's experiences in Sant'Ambrogio directly. He wrote that the princess had suffered a life-threatening illness in December 1858—and he named its cause. She had discovered "serious errors made by the young and beautiful madre vicaria," who had then made an unsuccessful attempt to win Katharina over with her "flatteries." After that, "every attempt to report this to the outside world was prevented. Indeed, there was even an attempt to 'help along' her poor health"—that is, to poison her.

In his contribution, Fiala also quoted a letter from the princess to Abbot Maurus Wolter, written on December 11, 1878. He had discovered this in the Beuron archive.[30] Here, Katharina addressed the poisoning attacks directly: "It is now the anniversary—20 years! of when I drank the lethal draught in Sant'Ambrogio." Having been rescued, she had met Maurus Wolter, who had blessed the princess with holy fragments from the True Cross, "after which I was returned almost immediately, miraculously, to health." The path to the founding of Beuron began with a miracle from God. In the Beuron jubilee publication, Katharina's traumatic experiences in the Regulated Third Order of Holy Saint Francis, with its exalted, sick forms of piety, was painted as the negative foil to the healthy spirituality of the Benedictines. And the miraculous healing performed by Padre Maurus wasn't an unusual mystic practice in the Sant'Ambrogio mold, but a Church-approved, long-established blessing. Splinters from the cross of Jesus contained in a small monstrance (so-called Fragments of the True Cross) were frequently used for blessings: for example, the blessing of the fields on the Feast of the Ascension.[31] God had turned the evil intentions of Sant'Ambrogio's superiors to good, through Katharina's meeting with Maurus Wolter. Without the poisonings, there would have been no cry for help; without the cry for help, no salvation; without salvation, no chance to meet Wolter; without this meeting, no founding of Beuron. One hundred years after the Inquisition trial, the Benedictine Virgil Fiala was making the same argument that Katharina had once put forward. And this meant he had to tell the story of the poisoning.

But this was the exception. The tendency to keep the affair from the public gaze ultimately won out, as the three editions of the German Catholic lexicon, *Lexikon für Theologie und Kirche,* from the 1930s, 1960s, and 1990s show. There is no mention of Sant'Ambrogio in the articles on Joseph Kleutgen[32] or Katharina von Hohenzollern.[33] According to these, Katharina's stay in Rome was simply the occasion of her meeting with Maurus Wolter, and Kleutgen was an important new scholastic theologian. This is the picture German Catholics wished to present in the three editions of their most important reference work. The darker aspects of both lives were retouched or painted out. Sant'Ambrogio simply didn't fit into the picture.[34]

Still, the secret that surrounded the whole affair was revealed, at least in part, in a theological dissertation in 1976. Konrad Deufel was the first writer to have reliable sources on the case at his disposal, having discovered Christiane Gmeiner's report from 1870 in the Hohenzollern royal house and seigniory archive in Sigmaringen.[35] Here were seventy-eight pages written by somebody immediately connected with the affair—even if the report had been composed long after the events it described, and may be of limited value as a source. Over just three pages, Deufel gave a short summary of Katharina's *Erlebnisse* disclosing key facts about the denunciation and the Inquisition trial. Deufel was also able to access letters written by Kleutgen and Andreas Steinhuber (who later became a Jesuit cardinal), in the archive of the Low German Jesuit province. These revealed that Kleutgen had told his order he had been convicted *ob formalem haeresim*. But the Jesuit deliberately left his brothers in the dark about exactly what his misdemeanors had been. Steinhuber therefore speculated that Kleutgen had "uttered some sentence during the interrogation that the judges took to be heretical."[36]

Deufel's study has received some harsh criticism for its technical deficiencies.[37] In his review of the book, Herman H. Schwedt calls the Inquisition trial, as sketched by Deufel, a "modern-day witch trial" in which witnesses (meaning Kleutgen) were "convicted alongside the defendants."[38] He also unjustly condemns Deufel for regarding "the much-discussed attempt by the novice mistress to poison Katharina von Hohenzollern as a fact," although there was no public announcement of a conviction for attempted murder, and such cases lay entirely outside the Holy Office's jurisdiction.[39] Still, Deufel's initial, brief reconstruction of the Sant'Ambrogio affair, supported by a certain amount of source material, did achieve some recognition, and has been cited in many subsequent books. Giacomo Martina draws on Deufel in his lengthy monograph on Pius IX,[40] as does Elke Pahud de Mortanges in her study on Jakob Frohschammer,[41] and Aidan Nichols in his *Conversation of Faith and Reason*, which mentions "The Kleutgen Fiasco."[42]

Deufel claimed that the mystery surrounding the case up to that point, and in particular the reason for Kleutgen's fall from grace, had been "largely illuminated" by the report from the Sigmaringen state archive. Information from Rome, he said, could "only provide something new in the formal sense."[43] This has proved inaccurate. The opening of the Congregation for the Doctrine of the Faith's archives by John Paul II in 1998 made the Holy Roman Inquisition's files accessible to researchers for the first time. The files from the Sant'Ambrogio trial, which had been hidden for a century and a half in the most secret of all Church archives, finally saw the light of day. At last, the secret could be revealed—and what had sounded like an outrageous fantasy turned out to be a true story of a convent in scandal.

Acknowledgments

The Nuns of Sant'Ambrogio would not have been written without the support I received from many sides. Thanks are therefore due to:

The Historisches Kolleg in Munich: this unique establishment for historians afforded me working conditions that made a year's residency go by in a flash. I would like to thank the board of trustees for the faith they placed in me; the Fritz Thyssen Foundation for financing my year at the college; the managing director, Dr. Karl-Ulrich Gelberg, for the smooth organization of everything; Dr. Elisabeth Müller-Luckner for all the stimulating conversations; Gabriele Roser and Elvira Jakovina for making life in the college so pleasant; and my two student assistants, Edith Ploethner and Franz Quirin Meyer, for a great many books, photocopies, and intelligent questions. I would also like to thank my fellow stipend recipients for the interesting insights into their subjects and research aims. Dr. Elisabeth Hüls made the workshop "Wahre und falsche Heiligkeit" (True and False Holiness) in January 2012 into a wonderful forum. It is also thanks to her that the conference volume, *"Wahre" und "falsche" Heiligkeit. Mystik, Macht und Geschlechterrollen im Katholizismus des 19. Jahrhunderts* was published so quickly, appearing as volume 90 in the series *Schriften des Historischen Kollegs, Kolloquien* in spring 2013. Many things that *The Nuns of Sant'Ambrogio* touches upon are given in-depth consideration there, from a variety of perspectives. I would like to thank all the conference participants and moderators for contributing their ideas to the workshop and reworking their chapters for the conference volume.

The foundations: I discovered the files on the Sant'Ambrogio case in the Archive of the Congregation for the Doctrine of the Faith (ACDF) in 1999. At that time, researchers were seldom permitted to make copies, so it was necessary first to gain a proper understanding of the files, and then to write parts of them out. The Gerda Henkel Foundation kindly financed this effort. And without years of support from the German Research Foundation (DFG) for my studies in this archive, I would never have been able to bring this case to light, let alone work on it.

The archives: even after twenty years as a professor of Church history, my fascination for archive work remains undiminished. This is partly thanks to the archivists. I would like to thank Monsignore Dr. Alejandro Cifres, the director of the ACDF, and his colleagues Daniel Ponziani, Fabrizio De Sibi, and Fabrizio Faccenda for making the central collections available and providing helpful answers to all my questions. Dr. Johan Ickx, who spent many years at the ACDF and is now the head of the Secretariat of State's historical archive, was always an important contact, particularly as his wife, Elizabeth Ickx-Lemens, took on the task of copying out parts of the collections relevant to Sant'Ambrogio. This book also makes use of material from a number of other archives. Along with many other people, I would like to thank Dr. Clemens Brodkorb from the Archiv der Deutschen Provinz der Jesuiten in Munich, and Birgit Meyenberg from the Sigmaringen state archive, for making files available and responding conscientiously to all inquiries. Prof. Dr. Peter Walter used his profound knowledge of the theological history of the nineteenth century to help me date the Passaglia affair, among other things. I spent a fascinating afternoon with Prof. Dr. Christa Habrich, who gave me an exemplary introduction to the world of poisons. If I should ever find myself needing to commit the perfect murder, I will certainly consult her again. I thank her, and with her everyone who, whether as archivist, librarian, colleague, or private individual, has provided me with pieces of the great puzzle of Sant'Ambrogio.

The Seminar for Middle and Modern Church History: my year in Munich would not have been possible without my team in Münster. Everyone there, but particularly my managing director, PD Dr. Thomas Bauer, and my substitute for the year, Prof. Dr. Klaus Unterburger, kept me free of any obligations. In working on the manuscript, I was able to rely on translations provided by Alex Piccin und Elisabeth-Marie Richter, among others. During the editing process and while conducting difficult research, I was as always grateful to have recourse to the expertise and vast experience of my collaborators in scientific communication. The conversations I had with them were hugely beneficial—and not just to the manuscript. I would therefore like to thank Dr. Holger Arning, Sarah Brands, and Katharina Hörsting. I am also grateful to Dr. Judith Schepers und Birgit Reiß from my seminar, and to Sabine Höllmann, for their thorough proofreading. And these thanks would not be complete without mentioning two collaborators in particular: Dr. Maria Pia Lorenz-Filograno, my "Signora di Sant'Ambrogio," for her translations, research, checks, and motivation, and Dr. Barbara Schüler, for her criticism, copyediting, polishing, and general organization of everything.

The first readers: curious to know how the "true story" would come across, and how different people would react to it, we gave the manuscript to people with an interest in history but who were not experts in the field. I would like to thank Michael Pfister, Christiane Richter, Christa Schütte, und Heribert Woestmann, among others, for their nuanced opinions and suggestions.

C. H. Beck: as an author, I feel I am in the best of hands with my long-standing editor, Dr. Ulrich Nolte. I am greatly honored that my book has been published by C. H. Beck in its 250th anniversary year.

Munich, September 2012
Hubert Wolf

Notes

The material from the Roman archives is largely written in Italian and Latin. Translations into German have been commissioned by the author, placing an emphasis on faithfulness and readability. The English translations of all quotes have been made from the German. In the notes, the Italian titles of these sources have been retained (where these exist), as they appear in the archives. It has not always been possible to provide page numbers. All emphases within the quotations are taken from the originals and set in italics, whether they were originally underlined or picked out in some other way. All names mentioned in the text, with the exception of the popes and famous figures from world history, are given a biographical note; if no details for a person could be found, no special mention is made. The full versions of all abbreviated archive collections and book titles used in the notes can be found in the "Sources and Literature" section.

PROLOGUE *"Save, Save Me!"*

1. Fogli manoscritti consegnati in atti dalla Principessa Caterina de Hohenzollern il 15. Settembre 1859. Sommario della Relazione informativa no. XXII; ACDF SO St. St. B 7 c.
2. Christiane Gmeiner started work as a governess for Princess Rosa zu Hohenlohe-Bartenstein, born Countess von Sternberg, in March 1870. She accompanied her to Prague. Katharina had obviously recommended her confidante for this task. HZA Archiv Bartenstein, box 130, addendum 56.
3. Erlebnisse von S. Ambrogio, von Fräulein Ch. Gmeiner notiert im Jahr 1870; StA *Sigmaringen*, Dep 39 HS I Rubr 53 no. 14 UF 9m, p. 76.

CHAPTER ONE *"Such Turpitudes"*

1. Cf. Stefanie Kraemer and Peter Gendolla (eds.), *Italien. Eine Bibliographie zu Italienreisen in der deutschen Literatur. Unter Mitarbeit von Nadine Buderath* (Frankfurt am

Main, 2003). There is also an extensive bibliography online: www.lektueren
.de/Lehrveranstaltungen/Bibliographie%20Italienreisen.pdf (5/18/2012).

2. On the following, cf. Weitlauff (ed.), *Kirche*; Wolf, *Kirchengeschichte*, pp. 114–21;
Zovatto (ed.), *Storia*, pp. 508–15. The relevant sections of the *Handbuch der Kirchengeschichte*, vol. 6/1 are still also worth reading, as is Schmidlin, *Papstgeschichte*, vol. I. On the suppression of the Jesuits, see Hartmann, *Jesuiten*, pp. 84–90; Martina, *Storia*. The concepts used in the following section for theological and ecclesiastico-political directions, such as "enlightened," "intransigent," "liberal," "modern," "establishmentarian," and "Ultramontanist" are not entirely unproblematic, as they were the object of serious controversy themselves at the time. They also have a different meaning outside their religious context, and imply different values according to one's standpoint.

3. Ercole Consalvi was born in 1757. He was the cardinal secretary of state from 1800 to 1806, and again from 1814 to 1823. He died in 1824. For more on him, see Wolf (ed.), *Prosopographie*, pp. 340–46.

4. Cf. Giacomo Martina, "Gregorio XVI," in *DBI* 59 (2003), online: www.treccani .it/enciclopedia/papa-gregorio-xvi_(Dizionario-Biografico) (5/22/2012); Reinermann, *Metternich*, pp. 524–48; Georg Schwaiger, "Gregor XVI." in *LThK*, 3rd ed., vol. 4 (1995), pp. 1023–24; Wolf, *Index*, pp. 105–16.

5. Mauro Capellari, Il trionfo della Santa Sede e della Chiesa contro gli assalti dei Novatori (Venice, 1799).

6. Cf. Hasler, *Pius IX*. Ickx, *Santa Sede*, pp. 293–568; Lill, *Ultramontanismus*, pp. 76–91; Martina, *Pio IX*, 3 vols; Weber, *Kardinäle*, 2 vols; Wenzel, *Freundeskreis*, pp. 190–355; Wolf, *Index*; Wolf, *Kirchengeschichte*, pp. 137–52.

7. Cf. Seibt, *Rom*, pp. 111–89.

8. Cf. Franz Hülskamp and Wilhelm Molitor, *Piusbuch. Papst Pius IX. in seinem Leben und Wirken* (Münster, 3rd ed., 1877), p. 7.

9. Diary entry from November 10, 1852; Gregorovius, *Roman Journals*, p. 3.

10. Cf. *Descrizione topografica*, pp. 201–8; Hergenröther, *Kirchenstaat*; Kruft/Völkee, Einführung, in Gegorovius, *Tajebücher*, pp. 21–30; Sombart, *Campagna*; Stefani, *Dizionario corografico*; Weber, *Kardinäle* vol. 1, pp. 1–183. On the development of Rome from 1870 to the present, see Seronde-Babonauz, *Rome*.

11. This biography of Katharina von Hohenzollern is principally based on the (admittedly rather hagiographic) description of her life by Zingeler, *Katharina*; also Deufel, *Kirche*, pp. 56–67; Fiala, *Jahrhundert*, pp. 47-52; Gustav Hebeisen, "Hohenzollern, Katharina," in *LThK*, 1st ed., vol. 5 (1933), p. 106 (for the date of her trip to Rome and meeting with Reisach); Wenzel, *Freundeskreis*, pp. 359–81.

12. On the House of Hohenlohe and its various lines, cf. *Adelslexikon*, vol. 5, pp. 302–7; Taddey, *Unterwerfung*, pp. 883–92; Zingeler, *Katharina*, p. 3.

13. Fiala, *Jahrhundert*, p. 48; Zingeler, *Katharina*, p. 4.

14. See Garhammer, *Regierung*, pp. 75–81; Garhammer, *Seminaridee*, pp. 11–74; Anton Zels, "Reisach," in Gatz (ed.), *Bischöfe*, pp. 603–6.

15. Hofbauer, who was born in 1751, was the first German Redemptorist. He died in 1820. See Werner Welzig, "Hofbauer," in *NDB* 9 (1972), pp. 376–77.

16. Adam Müller was born in 1779. He studied in Göttingen and Berlin, where he

came into contact with the literary Romantics. In 1815, he entered the Austrian civil service, and was knighted in 1826, becoming Ritter von Nitterdorf. He died in 1829. See Silvia Dethlefs, "Müller Ritter von Nitterdorf" in *NDB* 18 (1997), pp. 338–41.

17. The Collegio Romano was founded in Rome in 1551 by Ignatius of Loyola, as the Jesuits' central training institute. In 1773, following the suppression of the Society of Jesus, it passed into the hands of the secular priests. In 1824 it was returned to the Jesuits by Leo XII. In the mid-nineteenth century, the Jesuits' school lay on the Piazza del Collegio Romano, off the main street, the Via del Corso. Since 1873, the former Collegio Romano has been known as the Gregorian Pontifical University. This was also when it moved to Via del Seminario, between the Piazza Veneziana and the Trevi Fountain. Cf. Ricardo García-Villoslada, *Storia del Collegio Romano* (Rome, 1954); Benedetto Vetere and Alessandro Ippoliti (eds.), *Il Collegio Romano. Storia di una costruzione* (Rome, 2001). On the history of the Gregorian University, cf. Robert Leiber and Ricardo García-Villoslada, "Gregoriana," in *LThK*, 2nd ed., vol 4 (1960), pp. 1195–96; Steinhuber, *Geschichte*, 2 vols. The Collegium Germanicum is a seminary led by Jesuits, which was founded in 1552 by Pope Julius III. In 1580, the Collegium Germanicum was merged with the Collegium Hungaricum, and since then it has carried the official name Pontificum Collegium Germanicum et Hungaricum de Urbe. The seminary lies on the Via Leonida Bissolati in Rione Sant'Eustachio. Cf. Schmidt, *Collegium*.

18. Garhammer, *Regierung*, p. 79. The Collegio Urbano de Propaganda Fide lies in the Rione Borgo, on the Via Urbano VIII, near Lungotevere Vaticano, and is now called the Pontificio Collegio Urbano. On the Congregation for the Propagation of Faith, cf. Nikolaus Kowalsky, "Propaganda-Kongregation," in *LThK*, 2nd ed., vol. 8 (1963), pp. 793–94.

19. Cf. Wenzel, *Freundeskreis*, p. 360.

20. Marie zu Hohenlohe-Waldenburg-Schillingsfürst was born in 1855 in Venice, and married Prince Alexander von Thurn und Taxis (1851–1939) in 1875. She spent a large part of her youth in Italy, and died at Schloss Lautschein in 1934. See Hans Friedrich von Ehrenkrook (ed.), *Genealogisches Handbuch der Fürstlichen Häuser*, vol. 1 (Glücksberg, 1951), p. 432.

21. Thurn und Taxis-Hohenlohe, *Jugenderinnerungen*, p. 76.

22. Franz Erwin von Ingelheim, born in 1812, was the fourth son of the Imperial Austrian and Royal Bavarian privy councilor Friedrich Karl Joseph von Ingelheim. He died in 1845. See Harald Kohtz, "Von Ingelheim. Ritter—Freiherren—Grafen," in François Lachenal/Harald T. Weise (ed.), *Ingelheim am Rhein 774–1974. Geschichte und Gegenwart* (Ingelheim am Rhein 1974) pp. 299–312 (family tree p. 308); Josef Meyer (ed.), *Das große Conversations-Lexikon für die gebildeten Stände* 15 (1850), p. 1019.

23. On the House of Hohenzollern-Sigmaringen and Prince Karl, cf. Platte, Hohenlohe-Sigmaringen, pp. 10 and 17 (family tree); Gustav Schilling, *Geschichte des Hauses Hohenzollern in genealogisch fortlaufenden Biographien aller seiner Regenten von den ältesten bis auf die neuesten Zeiten, nach Urkunden und andern authentischen Quellen* (Leipzig, 1843), pp. 300–306.

24. Contract between Katharina von Hohenzollern and Prince Karl Anton von Hohenzollern-Sigmaringen, February 5, 1854; HZA Archiv Waldenburg Wa 270, smaller estates 206.

25. Cf. Alfred Hillengass, *Die Gesellschaft vom heiligen Herzen Jesu* (Société du Sacré Cœur de Jésus). Eine kirchenrechtliche Untersuchung (Kirchenrechtliche Abhandlungen 89) (Stuttgart, 1917); Provinzial-Correspondenz 22 (1873), online: www.zefys.*staatsbibliothek*-berlin.de/amtspresse/ansicht/issue/9838247/1856/4/ (6/27/2012)

26. Quoted in Zingeler, *Katharina*, p. 68.

27. Ibid., p. 70.

28. Ibid., p. 69. On Reisach's elevation to cardinal, cf. Garhammer, *Erhebung*, pp. 80–101.

29. Katharina's stay in the pope's city even made it into the *Augsburger Allgemeine Zeitung*. The paper reported her presence in Rome, saying she was "received by His Holiness in the Vatican with great honor." Cf. *Augsburger Allgemeine Zeitung*, no. 197, October 24, 1857, p. 4743. The writer was the philologist Albert Dressel in Rome, according to the editors' copy in the DLA. The "Palazzo alle Quattro Fontane" probably refers to the Palazzo Albani del Drago, which stands at the crossroads of the Via delle Quattro Fontane and the Via XX Settembre.

30. Cf. Schlemmer, *Gustav*, pp. 373–415; Weber, *Kardinäle*, vol. I, pp. 306–28 and elsewhere; Wolf, *Eminenzen*, pp. 110–36; Wolf, *Gustav*, pp. 350–75. Katharina's father was Karl Albrecht, the third Prince zu Hohenlohe-Waldenburg-Schillingsfürst (1776–1843). Gustav Adolf's father was Franz Joseph zu Hohenlohe-Schillingsfürst (1787–1841). Franz Joseph and Karl Albrecht were cousins, and their fathers were brothers, making Gustav Adolf and Katharina second cousins. Cf. *Genealogisch-historisch-statistischer Almanach* 17 (1840), pp. 432–40.

31. Chlodwig zu Hohenlohe-Schillingsfürst was born in 1819, and was made minister of Bavaria in 1866. He was the president of the Bavarian Council of Ministers until 1870. In 1871 he became a member of the Reichstag, and served as the German ambassador in Paris from 1874 to 1885. From 1894 to 1900, he was the German imperial chancellor. He died in 1901. Cf. Stalmann, *Fürst Chlodwig*.

32. Diepenbrock was born in 1798, and was ordained a priest in 1823. He became prince-bishop of Breslau in 1845, was made a cardinal in 1850, and died in 1853. Cf. Erwin Gatz, "Diepenbrock," in Gatz (ed.), *Bischöfe*, pp. 686–92.

33. Döllinger was born in 1799. After his ordination in 1822, he became a professor of canon law and church history, first in Aschaffenburg, and then in Munich. He was excommunicated in 1871, after speaking out against the infallibility of the pope to the priesthood. He died in 1890. Cf. Bischof, *Theologie*.

34. Schulte, *Lebenserinnerungen*, vol. I, p. 49.

35. Zingeler, *Katharina*, p. 70.

36. Thurn und Taxis-Hohenlohe, *Jugenderinnerungen*, pp. 75–76.

37. Cf. Zingeler, *Katharina*, p. 73. This was a community of Salesian Sisters of the Order of the Visitation, the Ordo Visitationis Beatae Mariae Virginis. This Latin name gave rise to the popular term "Visitationists" for these sisters. Cf.

Angelomichele De Spirito and Gaincarlo Rocca, "Visitandine (Ordine della Visitazione)," in *DIP* 10 (2003), p. 160. The Visitationists in Rome initially lived in the convent dell'Umilità, next to the Quirinal Palace, before purchasing the Villa Palatina on the hill of the same name in 1857. Cf. "Visitazione della Madonna o Salesiane," in Moroni, *Dizionario* 101 (1851), pp. 145—60, here p. 158; Antonio Nibby, *Itinerario di Roma de delle sue vicinanze* (Rome, 7th ed., 1861), p. 136.

38. Busch, *Frömmigkeit*, p. 307. Cf. also Menozzi, *Sacro Cuore*, pp. 7—106.

39. Lempl, *Herz Jesu*, p. 1.

40. Thurn und Taxis-Hohenlohe, *Jugenderinnerungen*, p. 77.

41. The postulate (postulatio), in the canon law of religious institutes, is a trial period of convent life before the novitiate. Cf. Albert Gauthier, "Postulatio," in *DIP* 7 (1983), pp. 138—41; Dominikus Meier, "Postulat II," in *LThK*, 3rd ed., vol. 8 (1999), p. 458.

42. *Erlebnisse von S. Ambrogio*; StA Sigmaringen, Dep 39 HS 1 Rubr 53 no. 14 UF 9m, pp. 1—4.

43. Ibid., p. 4. The enclosure was particularly strict for nuns. They were allowed to leave it only in an emergency, and only with the written permission of the bishop—otherwise they were excommunicated. The same punishment befell anyone entering the enclosure without the bishop's permission, with the exception of the bishop himself, the prelates of the order for the purposes of visitation, the father confessor, the doctor, and craftsmen carrying out repairs. Cf. Raymond Hostie, "Clausura," in *DIP* 2 (1975), pp. 1166—83; Sägmüller, *Kirchenrecht*, pp. 742—43.

44. *Erlebnisse von S. Ambrogio*; StA Sigmaringen, Dep 39 HS 1 Rubr 53 no. 14 UF 9m, p. 6.

45. On the forms of devotion in nineteenth-century Italy, see Zovatto (ed.), *Storia*, pp. 478—532.

46. The toothbrush came into use at the end of the seventeenth century, and became particularly popular among the upper classes. It was only at the start of the eighteenth century that dentists recognized its worth, though it still wasn't widely used. Cf. Rudolf Hintze, *Beiträge zur Geschichte der Zahnbürste und anderer Mittel zur Mund- und Zahnpflege* (Berlin, 1930), pp. 32—53.

47. At the start of the modern era, Germany led the way in the processing of cotton. During the Industrial Revolution, England took over the lead in cotton processing within Europe. The fact that in the mid-nineteenth-century Roman nuns had no idea where cotton came from was probably a result of less and less cotton being grown in Italy over the course of the eighteenth century. By the end of the American Civil War, it had almost completely disappeared from Italy. Cf. Alwin Oppel, *Die Baumwolle. Nach Geschichte, Anbau, Verarbeitung und Handel, sowie nach ihrer Stellung im Volksleben und in der Staatswirtschaft* (Leipzig, 1902).

48. *Erlebnisse von S. Ambrogio*; StA Sigmaringen, Dep 39 HS 1 Rubr 53 no. 14 UF 9m, p. 7, with note I.

49. Ibid., p. 1.

50. Ibid., p. 17. "Clothing" refers to the ceremony when a postulant takes the habit of the order, usually at the start of her novitiate. Cf. Matías Augé Benet et al.,

"Vestizione," in *DIP* 9 (1997), pp. 1951–59; Evelyne Menges, "Einkleidung," in *LThK*, 3rd ed., vol. 3 (1993), p. 553.

51. *Augsburger Allgemeine Zeitung*, no. 282, October 9, 1958, p. 4560. The author was once again the philologist Albert Dressel in Rome, as the editorial copy in the DLA reveals.

52. The period in which a person practices the ways of convent life, prior to professing their vows, is known as the novitiate. Even before they have taken their vows, novices are bound by the rules. Cf. Raymond Hostie, "Noviziato," in *DIP* 6 (1980), pp. 442–63.

53. Cf. the overviews in ACDF SO St. St. B 6 n and B 7 c, and the collection ACS, Collegio di Sant'Ambrogio.

54. *Erlebnisse von S. Ambrogio*; StA Sigmaringen, Dep 39 HS 1 Rubr 53 no. 14 UF 9m, p. 76.

55. Ibid., p. 75.

56. Ibid., p. 76.

57. Cf. Sägmüller, *Kirchenrecht*, p. 743. A Cologne newspaper gave a particularly interesting report of Katharina's withdrawal from Sant'Ambrogio and the pope's reaction. The paper emphasizes "how little the Holy Father was saddened by the princess's decision." *Kölnische Zeitung*, no. 323, November 21, 1859.

58. *Erlebnisse von S. Ambrogio*; StA Sigmaringen, Dep 39 HS 1 Rubr 53 no. 14 UF 9m, p. 76.

59. Cf. Hohenlohe to Pappalettere, August 1, 1859, quoted in Wenzel, *Freundeskreis*, pp. 361–62.

60. See Norbert M. Borengässer, "Wolter," in *BBKL* 14 (1998), pp. 55–62; Hermann Arthur Lier, "Wolter," in *ADB* 44 (1898), pp. 170–72; Suso Mayer, "Zur Einführung. Der Verfasser und sein Werk," in Maurus Wolter OSB, *Elementa. Die Grundlagen des Benediktinischen Mönchtums* (Beuron, 1955), pp. 5–33; Petzolt, *Wolter*, pp. 335–43. On Maurus Wolter's work in 1858–1859, up to his stay in Tivoli, see Lapponi, *Diario*, pp. 152–79.

61. Ernst Wolter was born in 1828 and was ordained in 1851. In 1856, he became a conventual monk in the abbey of Saint Paul Outside the Walls, taking the name Placidus. As the cofounder of Beuron, he became its second archabbot in 1890. He died in 1908. Cf. Virgil Fiala, "Wolter, Placidus," in *DIP* 10 (2003), p. 619.

62. Pappalettere was born in 1815, took his vows in 1836, and became a lecturer in philosophy and abbot of Subiaco. In 1853 he became the custodian of the abbey of Saint Paul Outside the Walls, and in 1855 a consultor of the Congregation of the Index. From 1858 until 1863 he was the abbot of Montecassino, though his sympathy for the nation of Italy led Pius IX to remove him from office. In 1875 he became the prior of the Basilica di San Nicola in Bari, and died there in 1883. Cf. Wolf (ed.), *Prosopographie*, pp. 1122–24.

63. Cf. Wenzel, *Freundeskreis*, pp. 125–357. The abbey of Saint Paul lies on the Via Ostiense, around two kilometers from the Aurelian city walls. The basilica of Saint Paul Outside the Walls is right next to the monastery. This is one of four Papal Basilicas in Rome, supposedly erected over the grave of the apostle Paul. Today, it is one of the seven pilgrim churches in Rome.

64. Thurn und Taxis-Hohenlohe, *Jugenderinnerungen*, p. 82.
65. Letter from Katharina von Hohenzollern-Sigmaringen to Angelo Pescetelli, August 14, 1859, quoted in Wenzel, *Freundeskreis*, p. 362.
66. Letter from Katharina von Hohenzollern-Sigmaringen to the German fathers of Saint Paul, September 14, 1859; quoted in Wenzel, *Freundeskreis*, pp. 362–64, here p. 362.
67. *Erlebnisse von S. Ambrogio*; StA Sigmaringen, Dep 39 HS 1 Rubr 53 no. 14 UF 9m, p. 78.
68. Denunzia della Principessa Hohenzollern, August 23, 1859; ACDF SO St. St. B 6 a, fol. 2r–51r. Subsequent information also taken from this text. Katharina von Hohenzollern didn't just provide a verbal denunciation. She prepared a set of written allegations, and required several days to compose them, which is why the individual parts have different dates. The section on the secrets of Sant'Ambrogio is dated August 7; the section on the Americano, August 12; Maria Luisa's false holiness, August 14; and finally the poisoning, September 1, 1859.
69. In the classic language of the Inquisition, the value-neutral term "denunziante" is used for the plaintiff. See for example the "Relazione informative con Sommario." At the start of the "Elenco delle persone e testimoni esaminati in questa causa," Katharina is referred to as "denunziante"; ACDF SO St. St. B 7 c.
70. Diderot's novel, initially unpublished, was written in 1760 and only appeared after his death, under the title *La religieuse* (Paris, 1796). See Denis Diderot, *The Nun* (London, 1797). Manzoni's "La Monaca di Mona" was written in 1823, as part of *Fermo e Lucia*, and was published posthumously in 1954. Cf. Alessandro Manzoni, *The betrothed* (London, 1997). Recommended further reading: Enrichetta Caracciolo, *I misteri del chiostro napoletano. Memorie* (Florence, 1864); Maria Monk, *Awful disclosures of Maria Monk or The hidden secrets of a nun's life in a convent* (Paisley, 1836). This strongly anti-Catholic book is about the sexual abuse of nuns by priests, and it was later revealed that its story was invented. Another story appears in Vincenzo Petra, "Le lusinghe monacali," in *Novelle* (Naples, 1862), S. 9–21. There was another manuscript about coercion in religious orders published in 1990, though the text was written in the seventeenth century: Arcangela Tarabotti and Francesca Medioli (eds.), *L'Inferno monacale* (Turin, 1990).
71. *Erlebnisse von S. Ambrogio*; StA Sigmaringen, Dep 39 HS 1 Rubr 53 no. 14 UF 9m, p. 12.
72. Katharina von Hohenzollern, Relazione riguardante Sr. M. Agnese fondatrice del monastero di S. Ambrogio, August 7, 1859; ACDF SO St. St. B 6 a, fol. 4r–6v. Subsequent quotations also taken from this text, unless otherwise stated.
73. *Erlebnisse von S. Ambrogio*; StA Sigmaringen, Dep 39 HS 1 Rubr 53 no. 14 UF 9m, p. 7.
74. Cf. Weiß, *Redemptoristen*; Weiß, *Weisungen*, pp. 161–62 and elsewhere.
75. *Erlebnisse von S. Ambrogio*; StA Sigmaringen, Dep 39 HS 1 Rubr 53 no. 14 UF 9m, p. 10.
76. Ibid., p. 12.

384 · Notes to pages 27–43

77. Katharina von Hohenzollern, Relazione sopra l'Indemoniato, August 12, 1859; ACDF SO St. St. B 6 a, fol. 7r–10r. Subsequent quotations also taken from this text.

78. Katharina von Hohenzollern, Relazione sopra Sr. M[ari]a Luisa di S. Francesco Saverio Madre vicaria in S. Ambrogio, August 14, 1859; ACDF SO St. St. B 6 a, fol. 11r–19v (handwritten original). A printed transcript can be found in Sommario del Ristretto Informativo no. IV, January 1861; ibid., B 7 c. Subsequent quotations also taken from this text.

79. Walkowitz, *Formen*, p. 443.

80. The *rota* was a rotating hatch in the wall next to the convent's gate, through which objects could be passed in and out of the enclosure. Cf. *Pierer's Universal-Lexikon*, vol. 14 (Altenburg, 1862), p. 385.

81. Katharina von Hohenzollern, Tutto il seguente sono notizie che precedono la malattia, September 1, 1859; ACDF SO St. St. B 6 a, fol. 36r–39r.

82. Katharina von Hohenzollern, Esposizione di alcuni fatti della mia vita, August 23, 1859; ACDF SO St. St. B 6 a, fol. 20r–31r. Subsequent quotations also taken from this text.

83. Cf. Roger Aubert, "Die Römische Frage," in *Handbuch der Kirchengeschichte*, vol. 6/1, pp. 696–705; Gall, *Europa*, pp. 46–56, here pp. 46–48.

84. Fogli manoscritti consegnati in atti dalla Principessa Caterina di Hohenzollern il 15. Settembre 1859. Sommario della Relazione informativa no. XXII; ACDF SO St. St. B 7 c. Subsequent quotations also taken from this text.

85. Stephanie von Hohenzollern-Sigmaringen was born in 1837, and was the eldest daughter of Prince Karl Anton von Hohenzollern-Sigmaringen. In 1858 she married King Pedro V of Portugal, though she died in 1859 without having provided him with an heir. See the *Deutsche Staats-Wörterbuch*, ed. Johann Caspar Bluntschli and Karl Ludwig Brater, vol. 8 (Stuttgart/Leipzig, 1864), p. 168 (Portugal entry); Platte, *Hohenzollern-Sigmaringen*, p. 23 (picture of Stephanie).

86. Denunzia della Principessa Hohenzollern, Domande e risposte; ACDF SO St. St. B 6 a, fol. 40r–43v.

87. Esame di Msgr. Hohenlohe, April 18 and 19, 1860; ACDF SO St. St. B 6 m, fol. 1–10. Subsequent quotations also taken from this text unless otherwise stated.

88. Costituto di Katharina von Hohenzollern, August 21, 1859; ACDF SO St. St. B 6 a, fol. 76.

89. Il Gesù is the Jesuit order's mother church, situated on what is today the Corso Vittorio Emanuele II. The monastery or rather the Jesuits' professed house is directly connected to it. This was also the seat of the Jesuit general. Today it is known as the Collegio internazionale del Gesù. Cf. Ernst Platner/Carl Ludwig von Ulrichs, *Beschreibung Roms. Ein Auszug aus der Beschreibung der Stadt Rom* (Stuttgart/Tübingen, 1845), pp. 557–58.

90. The original here has the Latin expression "in visceribus Christi." Praying "in visceribus Christi" means beseeching Christ to the bottom of His heart. Possibly also an allusion to the liturgical song "per viscera misericordiae Dei nostri." Cf. "in visceribus," in *Dizionario etimologico*, online: www.etimo.it (5/16/2012). For a detailed explanation of the word "viscera," which originally meant intes-

tines, but is often used in the sense of the innermost part of a man, standing metaphorically for the heart and for love, cf. Bardo Weiß, *Die deutschen Mystikerinnen und ihr Gottesbild. Das Gottesbild der deutschen Mystikerinnen auf dem Hintergrund der Mönchstheologie,* vol. 3 (Paderborn, 2004), p. 2039.

91. Cf. the list of furniture and cult objects of the dissolved convent of Sant'Ambrogio, of which thirty-two pieces were marked as "from the dowry of Princess Hohenzollern." ASV, Archivo Partiolare di Pio IX, Oggetti vari 1733 (S. Ambrogio Monastero Inventario).

CHAPTER TWO *"The 'Delicatezza' of the Matter as Such"*

1. Sallua was named titular bishop of Chalzedon in 1877, and died in Rome in 1896. Cf. Wolf (ed.), *Prosopographie,* pp. 1299–1303. Santa Sabina is an early Christian Basilica in Rione Ripa, on the square of the same name, near the Lungotevere Aventino.

2. Enrico Ferrari entered the Dominican order in Faenza in 1830. After gaining his doctorate in theology in Bologna, he first became a lecturer, then in 1851 the second *socius* of the Holy Office. In 1870 he became first *socius,* and in 1877 a consultor of the Congregation for Bishops and Religious Orders. Ferrari died in 1886 in Rome. Cf. Wolf (ed.), *Prosopographie,* pp. 570–72.

3. De Ferrari died in Rome in 1874. Cf. ibid., pp. 396–415.

4. Cf. ibid., pp. 1606–8 (lists of offices).

5. Monaco La Valletta became a consultor of the dogma commission in preparation for the First Vatican Council in 1866. He was made a cardinal in 1868 and died in 1896. Ibid., pp. 1016–19.

6. Esame della Principessa Hohenzollern, Septermber 15, 1859, Sallua's Nota Bene; ACDF SO St. St. B 6 a, fol. 48v.

7. Sallua's *Relazione* for the *Congregazione Segreta* on November 16, 1859; ACDF SO St. St. B 6 b, fol. 1r–9r. Subsequent quotations also taken from this text.

8. Cf. "Congregazioni Cardinalizie attuali," in Moroni, *Dizionario* 14 (1842), pp. 151–299, here p. 235. See also Pianciani, *Rome,* vol. 2, p. 38.

9. Relazione sommaria degli atti principali nella causa contro le Monache Riformate in S. Ambrogio, no. I: Denunzia della Principessa Hohenzollern. Saggie providenze ordinate da Sua Santità; ACDF SO St. St. B 6 e 1.

10. Cf. Wilhelm Koch/Josef Krieg, "Häresie," in *LThK,* 1st ed., vol. 4 (1932), pp. 823–25.

11. Ristretto informativo con Sommario. Il Santo Padre prende cognizione della denunzia e manifesta il Suo oracolo; ACDF SO St. St. B 7 c.

12. On the Vicariate of Rome, the cardinal vicar, the vicegerent, and the Tribunal of the Vicariate, cf. Boutry, *Souverain,* pp. 210–13 (with extensive bibliography).

13. See Wolf (ed.), *Prosopographie,* pp. 1134–37.

14. Cf. Weber, *Kardinäle,* vol. 1, pp. 299–303 and vol. 2, p. 716.

15. *Erlebnisse von Sant'Ambrogio,* StA Sigmaringen, Dep 39 HS 1 Rubr 53 no.14 UF 9m, p. 1. The relevant regulations for the election to convent offices can be found in the *Regola della Riforma delle Monache del Terz'Ordine di S. Francesco,* January 24, 1806, Cap. XII: "Del Protettore"; ACDF SO St. St. B 6 r1.

16. Relazione informativa con Sommario, Il Card. Vicario ordina alcuni esami; ACDF SO St. St. B 7 c. Subsequent quotations also taken from this text.

17. On San Pasquale on the Via Anicia, see "Conservatorii di Roma," in Moroni, *Dizionario* 17 (1842), pp. 9–42, here pp. 23–25; Luigi Grifi, *Breve Ragguaglio delle Opere Pie di Carità e Beneficenza ospizi e luoghi d'istruzione della città di Roma* (Rome, 1862), p. 21. There was also a conservatory housed here, which served as a retreat for women.

18. On the Gubbio Inquisition, see Menichetti, *Storia,* vol. 2, pp. 70–72; Adriano Prosperi, "Gubbio," in *DSI* 2 (2011), p. 741.

19. On the convent of San Marziale in Gubbio, and the Church of Saint Andreas, see Menichetti, *Storia,* vol. 2, p. 49.

20. Lettere e scritti del P. Leziroli Gesuita Consegnati dall'Em[inentissim]o Cardinal Vicario, here a letter from abbess M. Metilde to Patrizi, undated [1854], in which she complains of Agnese Eletta's lack of respect toward Leziroli; ACDF SO St. St. B 6 a, fol. 4r–92r, here fol. 90rv.

21. Esame della Priora di San Pasquale, October 17, 1859; ACDF SO St. St. B 6 a, fol. 52r–55r.

22. Esame di Sr. Agnese Eletta, October 18, 1859; ACDF SO St. St. B 6 a, fol. 55r–59r.

23. Letter from the prioress of San Pasquale, Maria Luisa di Gesù, to Sallua, October 19, 1859; ACDF SO St. St. B 6 a, fol. 58r.

24. Esame di Sr. Agnese Eletta, October 21, 1859; ACDF SO St. St. B 6 a, fol. 59r–62v. Subsequent quotations also taken from this text.

25. Friendships between nuns were prohibited as part of maintaining their vow of chastity. Nuns had to remain at a physical and emotional distance from each other. This rule was couched in terms of the exclusive dedication of nuns to their bridegroom, Christ. Cf. Brown, *Immodest Acts,* p. 8; Hüwelmeier, *Närrinnen,* pp. 18–196 (on the taboo of "particular friendships"); Schneider, *Zelle,* pp. 140–53.

26. Card from the Mother Superior of San Pasquale, Maria Luisa di Gesù, to Sallua, October 30, 1859; ACDF SO St. St. B 6 a, fol. 64r.

27. Esame di Sr. Agnese Eletta, November 3, 1859; ACDF SO St. St. B 6 a, fol. 63r.

28. Foglio manoscritto consegnato dalla Sr. Agnese Eletta, undated [before November 3, 1859]; ACDF SO St. St. B 6 a, fol. 65r, 67v, 86rv. Subsequent quotations also taken from this text. Cf. also the printed summary in "Sommario del ristretto informativo," no. XII, which underlines the significance of this document, at least in Sallua's eyes. Ibid., B 7 c.

29. Cf. Gousset, *Moraltheologie,* vol. 1, pp. 120–24 and pp. 278–96.

30. Ibid., p. 280.

31. Cf. Riegler, *Moral,* pp. 531–34.

32. Cf. Reinhard, *Lebensformen,* pp. 61–67.

33. Cf. Gousset, *Moraltheologie,* vol. 1, pp. 288–89. Tellingly, the term "il pessimo" arises in the case of Sant'Ambrogio for female same-sex acts: Relazione sommaria degli atti principali assunti nella causa contro le monache riformate in S. Ambrogio, Titolo VI: Complicità, massime e insinuazioni erronee dei PP.

Confessori Leziroli e Peters; ACDF SO St. St. B 6 e 1: "N. B. L'Inquisita nei suoi costituti grava specialmente la madre Maria Maddalena di enormi turpezze commesse con essa lei nell'età di 15 anni, e Maria Crocifissa come sua istitutrice in *rebus pessimis* facendo l'una e l'altra derivare cotali azioni e massime quali doni ed insegnamenti della beata Fondatrice."

34. Walkowitz, *Formen*, p. 444.

35. The term "lesbian" is used here, although this is an identity that only came into being at the end of the nineteenth century. Cf. Judith M. Bennet, "'Lesbian-Like' and the Social History of Lesbianisms," in *Journal of the History of Sexuality* 9 (2000), pp. 1–24, in particular pp. 10–17; Gertrud Lehnert, "Lesbianismus/Lesbischer Feminismus/Lesbian Studies," in Kroll (ed.), *Gender Studies*, pp. 230–32; Rich, *Heterosexuality*, pp. 139–68; Christine Steiniger, "Lesbische Liebe," in Lissner et al. (eds.), *Frauenlexikon*, pp. 632–38.

36. The Christian sexual morality of the nineteenth century prohibited any unusual satisfaction of sexual urges "absolutely and under threat of eternal damnation, with no advice for those who are not abstinent, other than to marry." Cf. Stapf, *Moral*, p. 421. This is based on 1 Corinthians 6:9, according to which whores, idol worshippers, adulterers, effeminate men, and molesters of boys will not enter the kingdom of heaven. Any kind of fornication outside marriage was a "great sin against the Father," which was why the Church and its lawmakers had always maintained an absolute prohibition of sexual satisfaction outside marriage. 1 Corinthians 7:9 says that those who cannot remain abstinent should marry. Cf. ibid., p. 422; Riegler, *Moral*, pp. 528–31. For a view of the Catholic position in a greater historical context, cf. Reinhard, *Lebensformen*, pp. 67–86.

37. Cf. Cattaneo, "Vitio," pp. 55–77; Pierroberto Scaramella, "Sodomia," in *DSI* 3 (2010), pp. 1445–50.

38. Cf. Louis Crompton, "The Myth of Lesbian Impunity. Capital Laws from 1270 to 1791," in *Journal of Homosexuality* 6 (1980/81), pp. 11–25.

39. Reinhard, *Lebensformen*, p. 87. Cf. also Brooten, *Love*; Rich, *Heterosexuality*, pp. 1445–50.

40. Thomas Aquinas, *Summa theologiae* II-II, Quaestio 154, article 11.

41. According to the Italian jurist Prospero Farinacci (1554–1618); quoted in Brown, *Immodest Acts*, p. 14.

42. Cf. Gousset, *Moraltheologie*, vol. 1, p. 292.

43. According to the Italian priest Ludovico Maria Sinistrari, toward the end of the seventeenth century; quoted in Brown, *Immodest Acts*, p. 18.

44. Esame di Sr. Agnese Eletta, November 3, 1859; ACDF SO St. St. B 6 b, fol. 63r, 65r, 67v, 68rv (original files). Subsequent quotations also taken from this document. A printed version of the interrogation can be found in "Sommario del ristretto informative," no. XII; ibid., B 7 c.

45. Nicola Benedetti was born in 1807 and entered the Society of Jesus in 1826. In 1843 he took up the office of spiritual. He died in 1866. Cf. Mendizábal, *Catalogus*, p. 62.

46. Memorie di tutte le cose più rimarchevoli occorse in questo nostro S. Istituto

nelle diverse epoche incominciando dal principio della fondazione; ACDF SO St. St. B 6 s I, fol. 576.

47. Annuario Pontificio 1860, p. 32.
48. Relazione sommaria degli atti principali, Titolo VI: Complicità dei PP. Confessori; ACDF SO St. St. B 6 e I.
49. Maurus Wolter to Sallua, September 17, 1859; ACDF SO St. St. B 6 a, no folio [after fol. 47v].
50. This was Theodor Caspar Heinrich Wegener from Coesfeld. He was born in 1831 and ordained as priest in 1855. He went to Rome to study in 1859. Cf. *Schematismus der Diözese Münster 1860* (January) (Münster, 1860), p. 131. There he "probably entered the circle of those devotees of Emmerick, who paid for her headstone in the Dülmen cemetery." Cf. Franz Flaskamp, "Theodor Wegener," in *Heimatblätter der Glocke,* no.135, May 16, 1963, Supplement, p. 537. Wegener may have returned to his home city of Münster in 1861: on June 19, 1861, he was admitted to the Congregation of the Virgin Mary, Consoler of the Afflicted of Kevelaer. Cf. *Schematismus der Diözese Münster* 1864 (August) (Münster, 1864), pp. 10 and 96. In March 1866, he was finally transferred to Haltern. Cf. *Schematismus der Diözese Münster* 1872 (January) (Münster, 1872), pp. 38 and 139. In Haltern he funded the creation of a Via Crucis on the Annaberg, and wrote the prayerbook *Annabüchlein oder Andacht zur heiligen Anna* (two editions, 1884 and 1890). In 1885 he entered the Augustinian order as Padre Thomas Villanova, and from then on devoted himself to research for the beatification process of Anna Katharina Emmerick. Cf. *Chronik Annaberg,* online: http://eservice2 .gkd-re.de/bsointer160/DokumentServlet?dokumentenname=160l3776.pdf (7/13/2012). Wegener died in 1917.
51. On the Campo Santo in the nineteenth century, cf. Erwin Gatz, *Anton de Waal und der Campo Santo Teutonico* (Römische Quartalschrift Supplementheft 38) (Rome, 1980), pp. 8–35.
52. The Church of San Nicola in Carcere lies on the Via del Teatro di Marcello, on a spot where a jail was situated in the Middle Ages. Cf. Armellini, *Chiese*, pp. 475–82.
53. Letter from the priest of San Nicola in Carcere to Sallua, October 11, 1859; ACDF SO St. St. B 6 a, fol. 50rv.
54. The art historian Ludwig Pollak recalled that most residents of the Via di Monte Tarpeo rented rooms. "In the winter of 1893–1894, I lived in the tallest house on this narrow street, number 61 (?), on the top floor, and for what was admittedly a very sparsely furnished room that was impossible to heat, I paid 30 Lire a month." Ludwig Pollak, *Römische Memoiren: Künstler, Kunstliebhaber und Gelehrte 1893–1943,* ed. Margarete Merkel Guldan (Rome, 1994), pp. 93–94. "The Via di Monte Tarpeo rose along the front of the Church of the Consolazion, with a flight of steps. It then bent to the right, and descended again at the south-west point of the Tabularium. This street, descending to the Campo Vaccino, was opened under Gregory XIII, as the inscription on the slope shows, where the famous verses of the Aeneid describing what were then the new buildings of the capital are also written." Cf. Ernst Platner, *Beschreibung der*

Stadt Rom. Vol. 3: *Die sieben Hügel, der Pincio, das Marsfeld und Trastevere* (Stuttgart/ Tübingen, 1837), p. 26.

55. Sallua's note, November 5, 1859; ACDF SO St. St. B 6 a, fol. 69rv.

56. Sallua speaks of "una denunzia assai grave e corredata di molti argomenti di verità." Ristretto informativo con Sommario; ACDF SO St. St. B 7 c. He also speaks of a "denunzia assai gravante e circostanziata." Notes for the congregation of cardinals, November 16, 1859; ibid., B 6 b.

57. It is difficult to say whether Sallua was using "more solito" as a specifically legal term, or just a turn of phrase. On the legal term, see Gerhard Dilcher, "Das mittelalterliche Stadtrecht also Forschungsproblem," in Jörg Wolff (ed.), *Kultur- und rechtshistorische Wurzeln Europas* (Mönchengladbach, 2006), pp. 227–42, here p. 237, where customary law is described as "more solito, more maiorum, secundum antiquam consuetudinem." Cf. also Simon Teuscher, *Erzähltes Recht: lokale Herrschaft, Verschriftlichung und Traditionsbildung im Spätmittelalter* (Historische Studien 44) (Frankfurt am Main, 2007), p. 178, which explains "more solito" and also "more consueto" as a legal mode established through custom. As a turn of phrase, it means "as usual": "more solito 'secondo il solito costume,' in base alla solita consuetudine, come di consueto," Paride Bertozzi, *Dizionario dei brocardi e dei latinismi giuridici* (Assago, 6th ed., 2009), p. 123.

58. Cf. Friedrich Münter, *Gemischte Beyträge zur Kirchengeschichte* (Copenhagen, 1798), p. 155: "Everyone who enters the Congregation, whether as a cardinal or a consultor, must take an oath of secrecy, from which they only have dispensation when they learn of matters that would damage and spoil the Inquisition itself or could hinder the course of proceedings. Breaking this silence carries a sentence of *Excommunicatio latae sententiae*, which the pope alone can revoke. Otherwise, this transgression is viewed and punished as a personal offense against the pope." Cf. also Maria Pia Fantini, "Segreto," in *DSI* 3 (2011), pp. 1490–91. The phrasing of the oath can be found in ACDF SO St. St Q 2 c, fol. 15r–16r: "Ego N de N &c. constitutus coram vobis Rev.mo P. Sac. Theologiae Mag.o F. N de N Inquisitore N tactis per me Sacrosanctis Dei Evangeliis coram me propositis, iuro ac promitto fideliter exercere munus, & officium Vicarii, vel, Consultori— Sanctae Inquisitionis huius civitatis N., & non revelare, nec loqui, aut tractare— verbo, vel scriptis, aut alias quovis modo de iis, quae concernent causas Sancti Officii, nisi cum dominis Consultatoribus aliisque Officialibus dicti S. Officii, sub poena periurii, & excommunicationis latae sententiae, a qua non nisi ab Eminentissimis, & Reverendissimis Dominus Cardinalibus Inquisitoribus generalibus absolvi possim. Sic me Deus adiuvet, & haec sancta illius Evangelia, quae propriis manibus tango."

59. Fogli consegnati dal Sig. Cardinale Vicario Patrizi al P. Sallua, November 5, 1859; ACDF SO St. St. B 6 a, fol. 73r–92r. Individually: fol. 74r–75v, no. 1, letter from Abbess Maria Agnese Celeste della Croce to Cardinal Vicar Patrizi, October 6, 1848; fol. 76r–77v, no. 2, letter from Abbess Maria Agnese Celeste della Croce to Cardinal Vicar Patrizi, December 30, 1848; fol. 78r–79r, no. 3, letter from Abbess Maria Agnese Celeste della Croce to Cardinal Vicar Patrizi, March 30, 1849; fol. 80r–81v, no. 4, note from Padre Leziroli to Cardinal Vicar

Patrizi, undated; fol. 82r–83r, no. 5, letter from Leziroli to Cardinal Vicar Patrizi, July 9, 1849; fol. 83v, Leziroli's reply to Cardinal Vicar Patrizi, relating to text no. 4, July 9, 1849; fol. 84rv, no. 6, letter from Sister Maria Metilde de' dolori di Maria SS.a to Cardinal Vicar Patrizi, undated; fol. 85r–87v, no number, probably from Leziroli to Cardinal Vicar Patrizi, unsigned; fol. 88r, no number, letter from Leziroli to Cardinal Vicar Patrizi, July 29, 1849; fol. 90rv, no number, letter from Sister Maria Metilde de' dolori di Maria SS.a to Cardinal Vicar Patrizi, [no month] 11, 1854; fol. 91rv, no number, letter from Agnese Eletta of the Holy Family to Cardinal Vicar Patrizi, undated; fol. 92r, no number, letter from Sister Maria Metilde de' dolori di Maria SS.a to Cardinal Vicar Patrizi, [no month] 21, 1854.

60. Vita della Serva di Dio. La M. Maria Agnese di Gesù. Fondatrice delle Monache Riformate del Terz'Ordine del Padre San Francesco; ACDF SO St. St. B 6 q 1. Kunigunde Anna Helena Maria Josepha, Countess of Lausitz, Princess of Saxony, was born in 1774, and married Giovanni Patrizi-Naro Marchese Montoro. She died in 1828. Cf. *Diario di Roma,* no. 85, 1828.

61. Sallua's communication to the cardinal vicar, undated; ACDF SO St. St. B 6 a, fol. 105r–106r.

62. Sallua's note, November 5, 1859; ACDF SO St. St. B 6 a, fol. 69r. On the *Congregazione Segreta,* cf. Prattica del S. Tribunale del S. Offizio nel formare i Processi diversa da quella di tutti gli altri Tribunali Ecclesiastici e Secolari; ibid., Q 2 m, fasc. 3a, no folio.

63. Sallua's *relazione informativa* for the *Congregazione Segreta,* November 16, 1859; ACDF SO St. St. B 6 b, fol. 1r–9r.

64. Fascicolo dei Decreti, Decretum Feria IV, November 16, 1859; ACDF SO St. St. B 6 w f. In this fascicle, which is part of the court files from the Sant'Ambrogio case, there is a copy of all relevant decisions and suggested decisions by the consultors, cardinals, and the pope. The originals are held in the series ACDF SO Decreta 1859–1862.

65. See "Congregazioni Cardinalizie attuali," in Moroni, *Dizionario* 14 (1842), p. 234.

66. "According to the intention or opinion." This Latin expression is used in the documents of the Roman Curia to clarify, limit, or change a decision by referring to the original intent of that decision. Cf. http://www.treccani.it/vocabolario/ad-mentem (5/17/2012).

67. Antonio Ligi-Bussi was born in 1799 and became a Franciscan Minorite. In 1851 he was made titular archbishop of Konya and vicegerent. Cf. *Notizie per'anno 1857,* p. 217.

68. Fascicolo dei Decreti, Decretum Feria IV, November 16, 1859; ACDF SO St. St. B 6 w f.

69. Fascicolo dei Decreti, Decretum Feria III. loco IV, December 6, 1859; ACDF SO St. St. B 6 w f.

70. Brevissimi cenni delli atti nella causa di S. Ambrogio, undated [probably December 8, 1859]; ACDF SO St. St. B 6 n 1, no folio.

71. Sallua's audience with the pope on December 8, 1859, and the pope's decision on December 11, 1859; ACDF SO St. St. B 6 w f.

72. Relazione informativa, Elenco delle persone e testimoni esaminati in questa causa, January 1861; ACDF SO St. St. B 7 c.
73. Vita della serva di Dio. La Maria Agnese Firrao di Gesù; ACDF SO St. St. B6 q 1.
74. Cf. Wolf, *Inquisition*, pp. 547–60.
75. Cf. Schwerhoff, *Inquisition*.
76. Cf. Claus Arnold, *Die Römische Zensur der Werke Cajetans und Contarinis (1558–1601). Grenzen der theologischen Konfessionalisierung* (Römische Inquisition und Indexkongregation 10) (Paderborn, 2008), pp. 171–332; Klaus Ganzer, "Aspekte der katholischen Reformbewegungen im 16. Jahrhundert," in Ganzer, *Kirche auf dem Weg durch die Zeit. Institutionelles Werden und theologisches Ringen. Ausgewählte Aufsätze und Vorträge,* ed. Heribert Smolinsky und Johannes Meier (Reformationsgeschichtliche Studien und Texte. Supplemental vol. 4) (Münster, 1997), pp. 181–211, here pp. 187–91.
77. Cf. Del Col, *Inquisizione*, pp. 509–698; Tedeschi, *Prosecution*.
78. Cf. Angenendt, *Toleranz*, p. 263; Trusen, *Inquisitionsprozeß,* pp. 168–230, here p. 168.
79. Over the four centuries from 1542 to 1966, in which the Roman Inquisition was the highest tribunal of the Catholic Church, individual elements of its procedure were altered. Relatively little is known about the Inquisitorial trial, its possible varieties and historical developments, because the archive of the Roman Inquisition has only been accessible to researchers since 1998. Cf. the relevant entries in the collections *L'Apertura, L'Inquisizione, L'Inquisizione e gli storici*, and *A dieci anni.* There has been an official guide to the procedure behind book censorship and the Inquisition's involvement in creating the *Index of Forbidden Books* since 1752, the *Sollicita ac Provida* brought in by the pope. Cf. Wolf, *Index*, pp. 46–58; Edition and introduction in Wolf/Schmidt (ed.), *Benedikt XIV.* There are no normative guidelines available for a trial by the Holy Office. This means researchers have to take the more painstaking path of analyzing historical sources, and attempting to distill the basic structures of these tribunals from individual trials before the Suprema over the course of the centuries. To date, hardly any work has been done on the Inquisition trials of the nineteenth century, and thus on the immediate context of the Sant'Ambrogio case. There is the added problem that the jurisdictions of the numerous courts and tribunals in the Church and the Papal States were never precisely distinguished from each other, and an official Curia court law was never decreed. Cf. Agostino Borromeo, "Congregazione del Sant'Uffizio," in *DSI* 1 (2011), pp. 389–91, here p. 390: "Conosciamo poco e male l'azione svolta dalla Congregazione nel XIX e nel XX secolo." See also Adriano Prosperi, "Inquisizione romana," in *DSI* 2 (2011), p. 826: "La storia della Congregazione è storia della sua composizione, dei suoi poteri e delle sue funzioni nel loro modifi carsi attraverso i tempi e i luoghi, ma è anche, naturalmente, storia di come e dove e a carico di chi quei poteri e quelle funzioni sono stati esercitati. Se si tiene conto di questi aspetti . . . appare tanto più singolare la mancanza di ricerche storiche adeguate fino a tempi recenti."
80. Norme per procedere nelle cause del S. Officio (inizio XIX secolo); ACDF SO St. St. D 2 i, no folio [following fol. 105v]. This lists the offenses that fall under

the Inquisition tribunal's jurisdiction, according to the inquisitors themselves. They include heresy, seduction in the confessional box, polygamy, and the issue of Jews in general.

81. One consequence of this was that handbooks were written by skilled and experienced inquisitors. Cf. Andrea Errera, "Manuali per inquisitori," in *DSI* 2 (2011), p. 821; Angelo Turchini, "Il modello ideale dell'inquisitore. La *Pratica* del cardinale Desiderio Scaglia," in Del Col and Paolin (eds.), *Inquisizione*, pp. 187–98.

82. The cardinal secretary was the formal leader of the proceedings. Cf. Hinschius, *Kirchenrecht*, vol. I, p. 451. More extensive information in Schwedt, *Kongregationen*, pp. 49–61, here p. 54: "Among the cardinals, the highest-ranking, managing cardinal has held the title of 'secretary' of the Congregation during the last 200 years. In the 16th century, the highest-ranking cardinal of the *S. Officium* signed letters and so on as *unus ex Inquisitionibus Generalibus*. It appears that this title was only made official in the first decades of the 17th century, meaning it was no longer dependent on changes of rank within the college of cardinals (for example, through the promotion of a titular church to a cardinalate). So we can speak of the fixed Curia office (independent of changes in rank) of secretary *S. Oficii* during this time. However, it took until the 18th century for this term to be officially entered into the Roman Lists."

83. On the Congregation of Cardinals, cf. "Congregazioni Cardinalizie attuali," in Moroni, *Dizionario* 14 (1842), pp. 233–34; Agostino Borromeo, "Congregazione del Sant'Uffizio," in *DSI* I (2011), S. 389–91; *Pratica della Curia Romana, che comprende la giurisdizione dei tribunali di Roma*, vol. 2 (Rome, 1815), p. 94; Wolf, *Einleitung*, pp. 36–37. On its members, see *Annuario Pontificio 1860*, pp. 267–69 and *Notizie per l'anno 1861*, pp. 279–81.

84. Cf. Blouin, *Archives*, p. 7; Wolf, *Einleitung*, p. 41.

85. Cf. Wolf, *Einleitung*, p. 36. On the conference of consultors and how it operated, see Luigi De Sanctis, *Roma Papale* (Florence, 1865), p. 274: "Ecco come si tengono le congregazioni del S. Uffizio. Ogni lunedì mattina alle 8 le carrozze papali, chiamate volgarmente frulloni, vanno a prendere i consultori, e li conducono al palazzo dell'Inquisizione. Là presieduti dal P. Commissario, e seduti intorno alla tavola ellittica, discutono sulle cause, e dànno i loro voti. Il voto de' consultori è soltanto consultivo." Cf also "Congregazioni Cardinalizie attuali," in Moroni, *Dizionario* 14 (1842), p. 233: "La prima [Congregazione] tiene nel lunedì mattina nel palazzo del tribunale, coll'intervento de' consultori, di monsignor assessore, del p. commissario, del primo compagno di questo, del fiscale ecc., all'effetto di leggere i processi, e le lettere degl'inquisitori *de partibus*; prendonsi le opportune provvidenze, e si preparano le materie per la congregazione de' Cardinali." On the consultors in the years 1860–1861, see *Annuario Pontificio 1860*, pp. 267–69, and *Notizie per l'anno 1861*, pp. 279–81.

86. The office of assessor came into being in 1553, and was dependent on that of the commissary. Only later did it gain specific functions, primarily providing a link between the congregation of cardinals and the investigating court. The assessor presented the *Causae* to be decided to the cardinals, noted the decisions from

the first part of the meetings—in which the notary did not take part—and then relayed them to the notary for recording. He gave a talk in the plenary meetings, and prepared a summary for the cardinals and the pope, to enable them to make a decision. Cf. "Congregazioni Cardinalizie attuali," in Moroni, *Dizionario* 14 (1842), p. 233; Agostino Borromeo, "Congregazione del Sant'Uffizio," in *DSI* 1 (2011), pp. 398–91; Andrea Del Col, "Assessore," in *DSI* 1 (2011), p. 107; Hinschius, *Kirchenrecht*, vol. 1, p. 451.

87. The assessor's audience with the pope replaced the Thursday meeting known as *Coram Sanctissimo, Feria quinta.* "Congregazioni Cardinalizie attuali," in Moroni, *Dizionario* 14 (1842), p. 233. Cf. also Bangen, *Curie*, p. 122: "Of the specific cases, only the most important belonged here [the *Coram Sanctissimo*]; the rest the assessor presented to the pope for approval after the cardinals' meeting." See also Hinschius, *Kirchenrecht*, vol. 1, p. 448, note 5: For "the decisions made during the meetings *in plano* (in the pope's absence), his approval was gained afterwards, except in the few important cases, which the congregation alone was given to decide, or the matters that were to be dealt with *de stilo* (according to a fixed and constant praxis)."

88. Cf. Carl Joseph Anton Mittermaier, *Das deutsche Strafverfahren in der Fortbildung durch Gerichts-Gebrauch und Partikular-Gesetzbücher* (Heidelberg, 1827), p. 322.

89. "Die heutige römische Curie. Ihre Behörden und ihr Geschäftsgang," in *Zeitschrift für das Recht und die Politik der Kirche*, vol. 2 (Tauchnitz, 1847), pp. 195–250, here p. 216.

90. Hinschius, *Kirchenrecht*, vol. 1, p. 451.

91. The commissary was always a Dominican and acted as an ordinary judge, heading the investigating court and leading the trials. He brought the case to trial, divided the work between the consultors, and chaired their meetings. Cf. "Congregazioni Cardinalizie attuali," in Moroni, *Dizionario* 14 (1842), p. 233; Luigi De Sanctis, *Roma papale* (Florence, 1865); Andrea Del Col, "Commissario," in *DSI* 1 (2011), p. 351; Hinschius, *Kirchenrecht*, vol. 1, p. 451; Pianciani, *Rome*, vol. 2, p. 38. See also "P. Commissario e impiegati del S.O."; ACDF SO St. St. Q 2 d (1), no. 4, no folio.

92. Also called *Primo* and *Secondo Compagno.* According to Hinschius, *Kirchenrecht*, vol. 1, p. 451, note 1, two committee members, also Dominicans, formed the investigating court alongside the *Commissarius Sancti Officii.* There is a rough list of the specific duties of these officials in a note "P. Commissario e impiegati del S.O."; ACDF SO St. St. Q 2 d (1), no. 4, no folio: "Fare Processi, ricevere denunzie, e fare esami, ed i Ristretti di Roma, overo quando gli atti siano denunzie, siano esami superiori al numero di tre. Materie da disbrigarsi da tutti i sostituti in generale, ed in particolare dipendentemente dal Cappo Notaro. In generale. Ricevere tutti gli atti che occorrono; fare ristretti delle denunzie, stendere i Ristretti facendo le incombenze prescrittesi, fare i Biglietti per le distribuzioni, e pieghi, e riassumere se vi siano altri privilegii contro le Persone di cui devono fare il Ristretto; e quello che riceve le denunzie deve farne anche il Ristretto." Cf. also "Congregazioni Cardinalizie attuali," in Moroni, *Dizionario* 14 (1842), p. 225.

93. Cf. Andrea Del Col, "Notaio," in *DSI* 2 (2011), p. 118.
94. Research on the role of the fiscal, also called *Advocatus* or *Procurator fiscalis*, and corresponding to the modern-day state prosecutor, is still in its early days. Cf. Beretta, *Galilée*, p. 56; Lucia Piccinno, "Fiscale," in *DSI* 2 (2011), p. 607.
95. Cf. Vincenzo Lavenia, "Processo," in *DSI* 3 (2011), pp. 1257–63, here p. 1262.
96. Wolf (ed.), *Prosopographie*, p. 1247.
97. Ibid., p. 1136.
98. Riflessione e chiarimenti sull'elezione del Card[inal]e Segretario del S. Offizio; ACDF SO St. St. Q 2 d (1).
99. Cf. Blouin, *Archives*, pp. 3–11; *L'Apertura* (various relevant entries); Schwedt, *Archiv*, pp. 267–80. Rules of use: *Congregazione per la Dottrina della Fede, Archivio. Regolamento per gli Studiosi* (Vatican City, 2003).
100. Cf. Malena, *Inquisizione*, pp. 289–306, here p. 291, with notes 8–17; Ponziani, *Fonti*, pp. 59–66; Ponziani, *Misticismo*, pp. 323–49.
101. On the *Stanza Storica* see Blouin, *Archives*, p. 10; recently a database with an inventory has been made available in the ACDF.
102. As a way of publishing the verdict, the *bandi* gradually faded into the background, when the Editio Stereotypa in Rome started publishing the *Acta Sanctae Sedis* in 1865. From January 1, 1909, the Typis Poliglottis Vaticanis publishing house started producing the *Acta Apostolicae Sedis*. The AAS is still the official legal gazette of the Holy See, in which important decisions of the Holy Office are also published.
103. On the conditions a *Denunzia* had to fulfill, see ACDF SO St. St. Q 2 m (trasferito a Q d c) 3a, no folio; Battistella, *S. Officio*, p. 57; Elena Brambilla, "Denunzia," in *DSI* 1 (2011), pp. 467–69; Masini, *Arsenale*, p. 12.
104. See ACDF SO St. St. Q 2 m; Masini, *Arsenale*, p. 25.
105. Denunzia della Principessa Hohenzollern, August 23, 1859; ACDF SO St. St. B 6 a, fol. 2rv: "Sponte personaliter comparuit coram Rmo P. M.o Vincentio Leone Sallua Ord. Praed: Socio Rmi P. Commi. S. Off: sistente in Domo Illmi a Rmi DD. Archichiespicopi Edesseni, sdenusina in Ssmi D.i Nostri Pii Pape IX. In neique Illma Princeps Femina Catharina Filia quindam Principis Cordi Alberti Hohenlohe Vilua Principis Hohenzollern, nunc Soror Aloysia Maria a S. Joseph dopos Roma, aetatis suae annorum 42, qui potiit audiai, eique data facultate, et jurata de veritate dicenda tactis SS. Dei Evangeliis exposuit ut infra. Per obbligo di coscienza impostomi dall'attuale mio Confessore mi presento a questo S. Tribunale per deporre quanto appresso. Previa la facoltà del Sommo Pontefi ce sono uscita per motivo di salute del monastero di S. Ambrogio di Roma dove avervi vestito l'Abito delle Riformate del Terzo Ordine del P. S. Francesco il giorno 29 Settembre 1858. Dopo uscita dal suddetto Monastero mi sono portata in Tivoli per respirare aria migliore prendendo stanza presso le Sorelle della Carità. Quivi ho preso a mio Padre Spirituale, e Confessore il Monaco Cassinese D. Mauro Wolter per essere più intesa facilmente nella mia lingua naturale tedesca."
106. "Suor Luisa Maria di S. Giuseppe (Catharina Principessa de Hohenzollern)"; ibid.

107. See for example Esame di Msgr. Hohenlohe, April 18, 1860; ACDF SO St. St. B 6 m, fol. 1.

108. Esame di Sr. Agnese Eletta, October 18, 1859; ACDF SO St. St. B 6 a, fol. 55.

109. Esame di Msgr. Hohenlohe, April 18, 1860; ACDF SO St. St. B 6 m, fol. 1.

110. There is no real agreement among researchers on the distinction between the informative and offensive processes. Some differentiate between two phases of the trial: the informative on the one hand, and the offensive and defensive on the other. Cf. Battistella, *S. Officio*, p. 57. Other academics, e.g., Vincenzo Lavenia, "Processo," in *DSI* 3 (2011), pp. 1257–63, here p. 1262, consider the first phase as characterized by two elements, an informative and an offensive process. The *repetitio testium* (reexamination of witnesses) belongs to the second phase, which can therefore be considered as the defensive trial. The members of the Holy Office clearly spoke of a *processo informativo* and a *processo costitutivo*, when differentiating between informative and offensive processes (*costitutivo* because this phase consists of *costituti*, hearings). This can be seen in ACDF SO St. St. Q 2 d, no. 10, quoted in Garuti, *Inquisizione*, pp. 381–417, here p. 403, note 112.

111. The scribe was called a *Sommista*. His function and duties are not entirely clear. There is an explanation in Charles-Louis Richard and Jean Joseph Giraud, *Biblioteca sacra ovvero Dizionario universale delle scienze ecclesiastiche . . . per la prima volta . . . tradotta ed ampliata da una società di ecclesiastici*, 29 vols., here vol. 18 (Milan, 1837), p. 170: "Sommista, così chiamasi nella cancelleria romana l'ufficiale il quale ha l'incarico di fare le minute, e di far apporre ad esse il suggello. Il sommista ammette nelle bolle delle clausole che non è permesso agli abbreviatori di ricevere, giusta le regole della cancelleria." See also Andrea Del Col, "Assessore," in *DSI* 1 (2011), p. 107, who explains how the assessor of 1621 was required "a procurarsi un uomo fidato che potesse preparare i sommari (sommista), in modo da concludere le cause più celermente."

112. Cf. Carmignani, *Elementi*, p. 239: "Nel processo inquisitorio, siccome il giudice esamina i testimonj insciente il reo . . . e siccome la publicazione degli atti si fa per via della loro comunicazione ai difensori del reo . . . ; la difesa nel *fatto* si pratica per via del *processo difensivo*, e la difesa nel *diritto* per via di allegazioni scritte. Il processo difensivo o sottomette ad *articoli interrogatorj* i testimonj già prodotti dal querelante, il che si denomina *processo rispettivo*; o produce nuovi estimonj per via di *capitoli*, detti perciò *a repulsa*." Cf. also Giuseppe Giuliani, *Istituzioni di diritto criminale*, vol. 1 (Macerata, 3rd ed., 1856), p. 635: "Il complesso degli esami fatti ai testimonj fiscali sugli articoli proposti dal reo chiamavasi processo *ripetitivo*: il complesso poi dei nuovi atti a difesa appellavasi processo *difensivo*."

CHAPTER THREE *"I Am the Little Lion of My Reformed Sisters"*

1. Inventario del Monastero di S. Ambrogio della Massima 1710; ASV, Visita Apostolica 97, no. 21, Chapter 9. The Sacra Congregazione della Visita Apostolica, founded in 1592, had to make regular checks on the spiritual and material condition of Catholic convents and monasteries, and report back to the pope. On the working methods of the Congregation and its inventories, cf. Pagano,

Visite, pp. 317–464. The "Pescheria" referred to here is either the church of Sant'Angelo della Pescheria, or the street of the same name, Via di Sant'Angelo della Pescheria. This street, named for the fish market that was once sited there, led east to the convent of Sant'Ambrogio.

2. Cf. ACS, Collegio di Sant'Ambrogio. A few cloistered Catholic communities have the office of a general procurator, who functions as the order's plenipotentiary representative to the Holy See, and is housed in the General Curia of that order. The Cassinense Congregation of the Original Observance, also called the Congregation of Subiaco, was founded by Pietro Casaretto (1810–1878) in the first half of the nineteenth century. Important marks of Casaretto's reform included the *vita communis*, strict asceticism, and missionary work. In 1856 Casaretto asked the pope if he could set up his own college in Rome. After a long search for an appropriate building, in 1861 he learned that the Franciscan convent of Sant'Ambrogio was to be dissolved. On May 14, 1861, the pope gave the convent over to him. Cf. "Casaretto," in *Biographia Benedictina*, online: http://www.benediktinerlexikon.de/wiki/Casaretto,_Pietro (10/11/2011); G. Paolo Carosi, "Subiaco," in *DIP* 9 (1997), pp. 538–41; "Pietro Casaretto e gli inizi della Congregazione Sublacense (1810–1880). Saggio storico nel I Centenario della Congregazione (1871–1972)," in *Studia monastica* 14 (1972), pp. 349–525. On the monasteries of the Congregation Subacio, cf. the statistics in *DIP* 1 (1974), p. 1331.

3. Cf. Bianchi, *Notizie*; Cutrì, *Scuola*; Gurisatti and Picchi, *S. Ambrogio*, pp. 49–60; Lombardi, *Roma*, pp. 235–40; Pietrangeli, *Rione XI*, pp. 56 and 90.

4. Cf. Dreuille, *S. Ambrogio*, p. 21.

5. The semiofficial history of the popes contains an entry for the year 803 that mentions a "monasterio sanctae Mariae quae appellatur Ambrosii"—a convent of the Virgin Mary which was renamed "Ambrosius." Louis Duchesne, *Le Liber Pontificalis. Texte, Introduction et commentaire*, vol. 2 (Paris, 1892), p. 23. Various sources from the early Middle Ages mention another, smaller church next to the Church of the Virgin Mary, Santo Stefano, the existence of which has also been proved by archaeologists.

6. Dreuille, *S. Ambrogio*, p. 29.

7. Ibid., p. 32.

8. The Visitation of 1710 advised the building of the novitiate wing, which was completed over the years that followed. "Inventario del Monastero di S. Ambrogio della Massima 1710"; ASV, Visita Apostolica 97, no. 21. From this point on, Sant'Ambrogio fulfilled all the structural requirements for a strictly enclosed convent. For a detailed account, see Dreuille, *S. Ambrogio*, pp. 49–74. Also Armellini, *Chiese*, pp. 110–11; Lombardi, *Roma*, p. 240.

9. Cf. Dreuille, *S. Ambrogio*, p. 77.

10. The "Conservatorio di Sant'Eufemia" was inhabited by *Zitelle* (maidens) and was destroyed by French troops in 1812. In 1814, Pius VII had the *Zitelle* of Sant'Eufemia accommodated in Sant'Ambrogio della Massima, and in 1828 Leo XII had them moved so that the Reformed Franciscans could settle there. Cf. Dreuille, *S. Ambrogio*, from pp. 77–78; "Francescano, Ordine religioso,"

in Moroni, *Dizionario* 26 (1844), pp. 48–199, here p. 195; Giancarlo Rocca, "Zitelle," in *DIP* 10 (2003), p. 682.

11. See the corresponding articles in *DIP* 4 (1977), pp. 446–511 and 823–911; Gieben (ed.), *Francesco*; Heimbucher, *Orden*, vol. 2, pp. 9–53; Edith Pásztor, "Franziskaner," in *LexMA* 4 (1999), pp. 800–7.

12. On the variants of the Third Order, cf. Degler-Spengler, *Terziarinnen*, pp. 609–62, with extensive bibliography; Giovanni Parisi and Rafaele Pazzelli, "Terz'ordine regolare di San Francesco," in *DIP* 9 (1997), p. 1077; Pazzelli, *San Francesco*; Pazzelli, *Terz'Ordine*. On the basis of the Rule, cf. the *Regola del Terz'Ordine claustrale di san Francesco d'Assisi* (Rome, 1898).

13. The research on these Regulated Third Order nuns is extremely modest, which may be not least because of the "all too various forms of existence" that individual Tertiary convents created for themselves "from the beginning." "Each house observes its own statutes or constitutions in addition to the Third Order Rule, laid down by its founder or spiritual leaders." Degler-Spengler, *Terziarinnen*, p. 610. On the order's habit, see Sales Doyé, *Trachten*, particularly the tables on pp. 133–35 and 137.

14. The nuns of Sant'Ambrogio are sometimes wrongly referred to as "Poor Clares" in the literature. Cf. for example Pietrangeli, *Rione XI*, p. 56.

15. Cf. the requirements of the Rule from 1806: Regola della Riforma delle Monache del Terz'Ordine di S. Francesco; ACDF SO St. St. B 6 r1. On the daily routine, the Divine Office, the convent offices, and the stages of postulant, novice, and professed nun, cf. the relevant articles in *DIP*.

16. Costituto Sr. Maria Luisa, June 11, 1860; ACDF SO St. St. B 6 n, fol. 1–4.

17. Agnese Firrao's biography is based on the collections "Copia dell'antico piccolo ristretto per il P. Priori" and "Vita della Serva di Dio. La M. Maria Agnese di Gesù" among other sources; ACDF SO St. St. B 6 e1 and B 6 q1.

18. Carlo Odescalchi was born in 1785, into the famous northern Italian royal dynasty. He was ordained as priest in 1808 and wanted to enter the Jesuit order in 1814, though his family prevented this. In 1838 he gave up all his Curia offices and his cardinalship to become a Jesuit in Verona. After a short time as a chaplain and missionary in northern Italy, he died in 1841. See Wolf (ed.), *Prosopographie*, pp. 1064–66.

19. Appendice al Ristretto informative; ACDF SO St. St. B7 f. The church and the convent of Santa Apollonia were founded in 1582 on the estate of the Roman noblewoman Paluzza Pierleoni, and consecrated in 1585. Cf. *Roma antica*, vol. 1, p. 181.

20. *Notizie per l'anno 1789*, p. 25. On Santa Chiara on the piazza of the same name in Rione della Pigna, see Armellini, *Chiese*, p. 187.

21. See *Diario ordinario di Roma*, no. 2200, January 30, 1796, p. 12.

22. Ibid., no. 2226, from April 30, 1796, pp. 16–19.

23. A reading of the few surviving "Atti della Segreteria del tribunal del Vicariato" in the ASVR did not turn up any reference to this investigation.

24. *Diario ordinario di Roma*, no. 2270, from October 1, 1796, p. 23.

25. There is no detailed biographical information on Salvadori/Salvatori. Giuseppe

Loreto Marconi claimed to have spoken about the miracles with "Signor Don Domenico Salvatori," father confessor at the Seminario Romano, during the beatification process of Benedict Labre. Cf. *Beatificationis et canonizationis V.S.D. Benedicti Josephi Labre: summarium super dubio . . . de virtutibus theologalibus . . . positio super virtutibus . . .* (Rome, 1828), p. 785.

26. Copia dell'antico ristretto per il Rmo P. Priori; ACDF SO St. St. B 6 e 1.

27. Albani was born in 1750, became a cardinal in 1801, and was cardinal secretary of state from 1829 to 1831. He died in 1834. See *DBI* 1 (1960), online: http://www.treccani.it/enciclopedia/giuseppe-andrea-albani_(Dizionario_Biografico) (5/22/2012).

28. In the *Notizie per l'anno* from 1786, p. 35, to 1788, p. 35, Marconi appears as a lecturer in "*Teologia morale*" at the Collegio Romano. In the later *Notizie per l'anno* from 1789, p. 35, to 1808, p. 109, Abbot Marconi appears as a lecturer in "*Sagra Scrittura*." He also features in connection with the founding of the Conservatorio Borromeo. Cf. "Conservatori di Roma," in Moroni, *Dizionario* 17 (1842), pp. 9–42, here p. 33. Surprisingly, there are barely any references to Marconi's life and work in the secondary literature, and no biography of him, although he wrote numerous books that were read abroad as well as in Italy, including the *Vita* of Benedict Joseph Labre (*Ragguaglio della vita del servo di Dio Benedetto Giuseppe Labre* [Rome, 1783]), which was translated into German, English (*Account of the Life of the Servant of God, Benedict Joseph Labre, Frenchman* [London, 1785]), French, Dutch, Polish, and Spanish. Marconi was confessor to Labre, and to Karl Emmanuel, king of Sardinia, and spiritual guide to the king's wife, Marie Clotilde, who was declared an Honorable Servant of God on April 10, 1808. Cf. "Maria Clotilde di Francia," in Moroni, *Dizionario* 42 (1847), pp. 316–18; Luigi Bottiglia, *Erbauliche Lebensgeschichte der Dienerin Gottes Marie Clotilde von Frankreich, Königin von Sardinien.* Translated from the French, 3 vols. (Augsburg, 1819). As well as Firrao's life story, Marconi was said to have written the biography of Margherita Muzi, "vergine di specciata virtù." Cf. Qualifica del volume manoscritto sulle memorie della vita di Suor Maria Agnese di Gesù del Rmo P. Maestro Girolamo Priori Priore Generale de' Carmelitani Calzati Consultore del S. Offizio; ACDF SO St. St. B7 f.

29. Pignatelli was born in 1737 and entered the Society of Jesus in 1753. After his novitiate in Tarragona, he studied philosophy and theology and was ordained in 1762. In 1803 the Russian superior (the Jesuits had not been suppressed in Russia) made him provincial of Italy. When Napoleon's troops took Parma in 1804, the Jesuits had to leave town and move to Naples. Pius VII had granted special permission for the Society of Jesus to exist within the Kingdom of the Two Sicilies. Over the following two years, many Jesuits who had become secular priests in 1773 returned to the order. They founded a community in Saint Pantaleon near Rome, and soon there were other settlements in Tivoli and a novitiate in Orvieto. During his final two years, Pignatelli suffered from gastric bleeding. He died in 1811, was beatified in 1933 by Pope Pius XI, and finally canonized by Pius XII in 1954. See Giuseppe Boreo, *Istoria della vita del Ven. Padre Giuseppe M. Pignatelli della Compagnia di Gesù* (Rome, 1856, and Monza, 1859); José

Antonio Ferrer Benimeli, *José Pignatelli S.J. 1737–1811. La cara humana de un santo* (Bilbao, 2011); Johannes Hellings, *De heilige schakel: de zelige Joseph Pignatelli S. J.* ('s-Hertogenbosch, 1935); Konstantin Kempf, *Joseph Pignatelli. Der neue Selige der Gesellschaft Jesu* (Einsiedeln, 1933); José M. March, *El restaurador de la Compañía de Jesús Beato José Pignatelli y su tiempo*, 5 vols. (Barcelona, 1935); Agostino Monçon, *Vita del servo di Dio P. Giuseppe M. Pignatelli della Compagnia di Gesù* (Rome, 1833); Robert Nash, *Saint of the Displaced. St. Joseph Pignatelli* (Dublin, 1955); Sommervogel, *Bibliothèque*, vol. 9, p. 770. See also Qualifica del volume manoscritto sulle memorie della vita di Suor Maria Agnese di Gesù del Rmo P. Maestro Girolamo Priori Priore Generale de' Carmelitani Calzati, Consultore del S. Offizio; ACDF SO St. St. B 7 f. Following the Firrao case, the Inquisition researched Pignatelli and went over his canonization process with a fine-tooth comb. The files are under S. Cong. ne de'Riti per la causa del Pignatelli P. Giuseppe della Comp. di Gesù 1845–1846; ACDF SO St. St. B 6 u 1.

30. This was probably the Conservatorio Borromeo, which Marconi founded and led with the support of Cardinal Vitaliano Borromeo. Cf. "Conservatorii di Roma," in Moroni, *Dizionario* 27 (1848), pp. 9–42, here p. 33: "Il sacerdote d. Giuseppe Marconi ... vedendo alcune fanciulle di tenera età oppresse dalla miseria e dall'infermità ... caritatevolmente le riunì in un locale terreno sul colle Esquilino presso via Graziosa ... e fu detta *la casa delle povere fi gliuole della scuola della divina carità*." Cardinal Borromeo "acquistò le case contigue al suddetto luogo, che ridusse in forma di conservatorio, gli assegnò rendite, e lo dichiarò erede dei suoi beni liberi, meno alcuni legati. Per questo motivo il conservatorio prese il nome di *Borromeo*, e le alunne furono chiamate *Borromee*. . . . Il medesimo ne affi dò la cura allo stesso Giuseppe Marconi." The Via Graziosa lies on the hill from Esquilin down into Rione Monte. It stretches from the Piazza della Suburra (on the corner between Via Urbana and Via Leonina) to Via Panisperna. Today it is part of the Via Cavour.

31. Approbation of the Rule and the ceremonial in Pius VII's papal brief: "Nuper dilectae in Christo Filiae" of January 26, 1806; ACDF SO St. St. B 6 r 1, no folio. Cf. also Erasmo Pistolesi, *Vita del sommo pontifice Pio VII*, vol. 2 (Rome, 1824), p. 24.

32. See Mark 6: 35–44; Mark 8: 1–10.

33. Angela Merici was born between 1470 and 1475, became the founder and author of the Rule of the community of Saint Ursula in 1535–1536, and died in 1540. See Karl Suso Frank, "Merici, Angela," in *LThK*, 3rd ed., vol. 1 (1993), p. 647. Cf. also Käthe Siebel-Royer, *Die heilige Angela Merici. Gründerin des ersten weiblichen Säkularinstitutes* (Graz, 1966).

34. Mary Ward was born in 1585, and founded the "Congregatio Jesu," a women's order for the education of girls with a Jesuit Rule, in 1609. She died in 1645. See Imolata Wetter, "Ward, Mary," in *DIP* 10 (2003), pp. 583–86; on the intervention of the Inquisition, see also p. 584; Wetter, *Ward*; Gabriela Zarri, "Ward, Mary," in *DSI* 3 (2011), p. 1707.

35. Merenda was born in 1752. A Dominican, he had been commissary of the *Sanctum Officium* since 1801, but was unable to perform this office between July 1814 and August 1815. He died in 1820. See Wolf (ed.), *Prosopographie*, pp. 991–93.

36. Vita della Serva di Dio. La M. Maria Agnese di Gesù; ACDF SO St. St. B 6 q 1.

37. Napoleon also had the entire archive of the Inquisition transported to Paris. It only returned to Rome—relatively incomplete—after 1815. Cf. Andrea Del Col, "Archivi e serie documentarie: Vaticano," in *DSI* 1 (2011), pp. 89–91, here p. 90; Wolf, *Einleitung*, p. 38. The corresponding series in the Vatican's secret archive are entitled "Epoca Napoleonica." Cf. Karl August Fink, *Das Vatikanische Archiv. Einführung in die Bestände und ihre Erforschung unter besonderer Berücksichtigung der deutschen Geschichte* (Bibliothek des Deutschen Historischen Instituts in Rom 20) (Rome, 2nd ed., 1951), pp. 87–88.

38. Relazione informativa con Sommario, Cenni storici sull'antica causa, e relative condanna della Fondatrice Sr. Maria Agnese Firrao, e di altre religiose; ACDF SO St. St. B 7 c. Subsequent quotations also taken from this text.

39. A search of the ACDF, in particular the "SO Decreta" collection, yielded no results.

40. Little is known about Pietro Marchetti. The "Appendice al Ristretto informativo, Sommario no. II" speaks of the verdict the cardinals gave on him on May 15, 1816: "Insuper addiderunt, quod scribatur Episcopo Tudertino, ut sub alio praetextu removeat in sua Dioecesi sacerdotem Petrum Marchetti ab audiendis confessionibus sacramentalibus, et a quacumque directione animarum"; ACDF SO St. St. B 7 f. According to this text, he belonged to the diocese of Todi in Umbria. The "Relazione sommaria degli atti principali assunti nella causa contro le monache riformate in S. Ambrogio" refers to him as "Pietro Marchetti di Rieti Cameriere Dogmatico di Nostro Signore," and in another place "D. Pietro Marchetti di Rieti Cameriere Segreto di Nostro Signore"; ibid., B 6 e 1. From the *Notizie per l'anno,* 1819, p. 141, 1820, p. 132, and 1821, p. 146, it emerges that he was one of the pope's Camerieri Segreti Soprannumerari, which is surprising given that this was only three years after he was condemned by the Holy Office.

41. Relazione informativa con Sommario, Cenni storici sull'antica causa; ACDF SO St. St. B 7 c. Marconi's Saint's Life is essentially a "Proposition," which the Congregation for Canonization put together, often over decades and usually long after the death of a "servant of God," to justify the proposed saint's *fama sanctitatis* with evidence of their virtues and miracles, documenting these in as much detail as possible. Cf. Gotor, *Chiesa*; Samerski, *Himmel*, pp. 81–83.

42. Cf. Adelisa Malena, "Quietismo," in *DSI* 3 (2011), pp. 1288–94; Anthony Meredith, "Quietismus," in *TRE* 28 (1997), pp. 41–45; Modica, *Dottrina*; Petrocchi, *Quietismo*; Schwedt, *Quietisten*, pp. 579–605. On the combination of Quietism and Satanism, cf. Orlandi, *Fede*.

43. Louis Cognet, "Quietismus," in *LThK*, 2nd ed., vol. 8 (1963), pp. 939–41, here p. 939.

44. Cf. "Conservatorii di Roma," in Moroni, *Dizionario* 17 (1842), pp. 9–42, here p. 40.

45. The Venerabile Arcispedale di Santo Spirito in Sassia was the largest hospital in Rome, with 645 beds and around thirty medical staff. The hospital for internal medicine was situated under the Bridge of Angels on the Vatican side, and was housed in several large buildings. Cf. L. Tutschek, "Aerztliche Mittheilungen aus Rom," in *Aerztliches Intelligenz-Blatt,* no. 12, March 19, 1865, p. 163.

46. Cf. Wolf, *Einleitung*, pp. 21 and 46–64.

47. Notificazione di affetata santità, February 14, 1816; ACDF SO St. St. B7 a (printed copy). There is a copy of the *bando* in the Biblioteca Casanatense, Per. Est. 18/115, no. 82. Subsequent quotations also taken from this text.

48. Santa Maria del Rifugio, called Sant'Onofrio, is in Trastevere, on the street of the same name, Salita di S. Onofrio. Cf. Armellini, *Chiese*, p. 493. The institution "goes back to 1703, and owes its origins to the devout priest Alexander Bussi.... Set up on broader foundations than other refuges, the conservatorium took in girls of 13–20, if they were orphans with no other means of support. The general custom of taking girls at a younger age is of course very praiseworthy; it is also very helpful that there is a place such as that we are presently visiting, to keep the older members out of danger. They number about 50, and are raised to be pious, hard-working and accustomed to the work done here. They buy their uniforms themselves from the wages they receive for their labor, which consists of making household linen, embroidery and ornaments for priests." Cf. Jean Joseph Gaume, *Rom in seinen drei Gestalten, order das alte, das neue und das unterirdische Rom*, vol. 2 (Regensburg, 1848), pp. 284–85.

49. Cf. Andreas Heinz, "Der Rosenkranz. Das immerwährende Jesus-Gebet des Westens," in *Liturgisches Jahrbuch* 55 (2005), 4, pp. 235–47.

50. Assembly of the consultors of the Holy Office, January 22, 1816; ACDF SO St. St. B 7 a.

51. On Molinos and Molinosism, see Gotor, *Chiesa*, pp. 115–20; Heppe, *Geschichte*, pp. 110–35 and 272–82; Adelisa Malena, "Molinos, Miguel de," in *DSI* 2 (2011), p. 1059; Modica, *Dottrina*, pp. 17–42 and 117–36 ("Santità finta e atti sessuali illeciti"); Romeo, *Inquisizione*, pp. 87–94 (also on the role of confessors in cases of female false saints); Schwedt, *Quietisten*, pp. 579–605.

52. Cf. Jacobson Schutte, *Saints*, pp. 201–21.

53. Cf. Hans-Wolf Jäger, "Mönchskritik und Klostersatire in der deutschen Spätaufklärung," in Harm Klueting et al. (eds.), *Katholische Aufklärung— Aufklärung im katholischen Deutschland* (*Studien zum achtzehnten Jahrhundert* 15) (Hamburg, 1993), pp. 192–207; Franz Quarthal, "Aufklärung und Säkularisation," in Nicole Priesching and Wolfgang Zimmermann (eds.), *Württembergisches Klosterbuch. Klöster, Stifte und Ordensgemeinschaften von den Anfängen bis in die Gegenwart* (Ostfildern, 2003), pp. 125–38.

54. Sommario del Ristretto contro il P. Leziroli, no. I: Cenni storici delle vicende di Sr. Maria Agnese Firrao, e del Monastero di S. Ambrogio estratti dagli Annali manoscritti, che comprendono la Storia dell'Istituto dall'anno 1804 fino a tutto il 1857 divisi in 26 fascicoli e pagine 628 in foglio; ACDF SO St. St. B 7 e. The women named as Firrao's accomplices, Sisters Maria Maddalena Ragazzoni, Teresa Maddalena della Vergine del Dolori, Maria Crocifissa Pantanelli, and Agnese Celeste Rabuer, were sent to various other convents. See Copia dell'antico piccolo ristretto per il Rmo P. Priori; ebd., B 6 e I; Vita della Serva di Dio. La M. Maria Agnese di Gesù; ibid., B 6 q I.

55. The convent in Rione Castro Pretorio, built in the seventeenth century, and the church of Santa Maria della Concezione ai Monti next to it, no longer exist. They were pulled down in order to lengthen the Via Cavour. See Armellini, *Chiese*, p. 404; Ottorino Montenovesi, "Il monastero della Concezione ai

Monti," in *Archivi d'Italia e rassegna internazionale degli archivi: periodico della Bibliothèque des annales institutorum* 26 (1959), pp. 313–41.

56. Relazione informativa con Sommario, Cenni storici sull'antica causa; ACDF SO St. St. B 7 c. Interestingly, Agnese Firrao seems to have defended herself vehemently against the charge of Molinosism. Cf. Copia dell'antico piccolo ristretto per il P. Priori; ibid., B 6 e 1.

57. Sommario del Ristretto contro il P. Leziroli, no. 1: Cenni storici; ACDF SO St. St. B7 e. Agnese Firrao had a strong following in England. The Franciscan Peter Bernadine Collingridge conducted a lively correspondence with her, and visited her in Rome several times, together with Bishop John Milner. A copy of Marconi's saint's life even found its way into the Clifton diocesan archive. The only surviving portrait of Firrao may also have been commissioned by one of her English devotees. Collingridge reports a man called Charles Butler entreating him to get a "miniature of Sister Agnes." Cf. John Berchmans Dockery, *Collingridge. A Franciscan Contribution to Catholic Emancipation* (Newport, 1954), pp. 285–87; Bernard Ward, *The Eve of Catholic Emancipation. Being the History of the English Catholics During the First Thirty Years of the Nineteenth Century,* vol. 2: 1812–1820 (London, 1911), pp. 113–16.

58. For example, *The Orthodox Journal and Catholic Monthly Intelligencer,* no. 40, September 1816, p. 370; *Gazzetta di Milano,* no. 56, February 25, 1816, p. 216; *Österreichischer Beobachter,* no. 62, March 2, 1816, p. 339; *Baireuther Zeitung,* no. 58, March 7, 1816, p. 214; *Lemberger Zeitung,* no. 31, March 11, 1816, p. 141; *Real-Zeitung,* no. 21, March 12, 1816, p. 88; *Journal de la Province de Limbourg,* no. 75, March 28, 1816, p. 1.

59. She died in 1824. See Clemens Emling and Anna Katharina Emmerick, *Mystikerin der Nächstenliebe* (Kevelaer, 2011); Anna von Krane, *Anna Katharina Emmerick. Leben und Wirken der Seherin von Dülmen* (Leipzig, 2008); Weiß, *Seherinnen,* pp. 48–56.

60. Cf. Winfried Hümpfner (ed.), *Tagebuch des Dr. med. Franz Wilhelm Wesener über die Augustinerin Anna Katharina Emmerick unter Beifügung anderer auf sie bezüglicher Briefe und Akten* (Würzburg, 1926), p. 198.

61. Cf. Peter Groth, "Die stigmatisierte Nonne Anna Katharina Emmerick—Eine Krankengeschichte im Zeitalter der Romantik—zwischen preußischer Staatsraison und 'katholischer Erneuerung,'" p. 110, online: http://www.in-output.de/AKE/akekrank2.html (5/17/2012).

62. *Journal de la Province de Limbourg,* no. 75, March 28, 1816, p. 1.

63. This was probably the wife of the Marchese Luigi Costaguti, who was a member of the pope's noble guard. Cf. *Notizie per l'anno* 1828, p. 216; "Vessillifero di Santa Romana Chiesa," in Moroni, *Dizionario* 94 (1859), pp. 98–130, here p. 109.

64. This was probably Baroness Piccolomini's first lady-in-waiting. Cf. *Diario di Roma,* no. 71, 1828, p. 4. A Faustina Ricci appears among Rome's "Signore della carità" (ladies of charity), responsible for the fourth prefecture of Santa Maria in Trastevere. Cf. *Piano dell'istituto generale della carità e sua appendice* (Rome, 1816), p. 48. For a Faustina Paracciani from Montepulciano, who married a Ricci and went to Rome, see Archivio di Stato di Firenze, Fondo Raccolta Ceramelli Papiani, Fasz. 6748 (Famiglia Ricci), online: http://www.archiviodistato.firenze.it/ceramellipapiani2/index.php?page=Famiglia&id=6339 (7/10/2012).

65. Mattei was born in 1744. He became archbishop of Ferrara in 1777, and cardinal *in petto* in 1779 (an appointment made public in 1782). He became prefect of the Congregation of Ceremonies in 1815, prefect of the Congregation for the Fabric of Saint Peter, and died in 1820. See Wolf (ed.), *Prosopographie*, pp. 963–67.

66. Vita della Serva di Dio. La M. Maria Agnese di Gesù; ACDF SO St. St. B 6 q 1.

67. Charles Emanuel was born in 1751 and married Marie Clotilde of France in 1775. He became king of Sardinia and duke of Savoy in 1796, before abdicating in 1802. He left the throne of Sardinia to his brother Victor Emanuel I, but kept the Duchy of Savoy. He entered the Society of Jesus in 1815 and died in 1819. See Giuseppe Locorotondo, "Carlo Emanuele IV di Savoia, re di Sardegna," in *DBI* 20 (1977), online: http://www.treccani.it/enciclopedia/carloemanuele-iv -di-savoia-re-di-sardegna .%28Dizionario-Biografico%29/ (7/5/2012).

68. Marie Clotilde of France was born in 1759 and died in 1802. See Luigi Bottiglia, *Erbauliche Lebensgeschichte der Dienerin Gottes Marie Clotilde von Frankreich, Königin von Sardinien*. Translated from the French, 3 vols. (Augsburg, 1819); Pietro Cavedoni, "Biografia della Venerabile Maria Clotilde di Borbone, Regina di Sardegna," in *Continuazione delle Memorie di religione, di morale e di letteratura*, vol. 2 (Modena, 1833), pp. 93–159; "Maria Clotilde di Francia," in Moroni, *Dizionario* 42 (1847), pp. 316–18.

69. Sommario del Ristretto contro il P. Leziroli, no. I: Cenni storici; ACDF SO St. St. B 7 e.

70. Almost all the Jesuits who had been connected with Firrao were dead by 1816. Francesco Antonio Spaziani, the ceremonial master *supra numerum* of the papal chapel (*Notizie per l'anno* 1784, p. 34, to 1792, p. 162) and lecturer in moral theology in the Propaganda Fide College (ibid., 1786, p. 37, to 1801, p. 146), died in 1810. Marconi and Pignatelli died in 1811, and José Doz in 1813. When Pignatelli saw his end was near, he passed the role of Firrao's spiritual guide onto the Jesuit father Agustín Monzon. Cf. Sommario del Ristretto contro il P. Leziroli, no. I: Cenni storici; ACDF SO St. St. B 7 e.

71. Lorenzo Litta was born in 1756 and became titular bishop of Thebes in 1793. The same year, he also became nuncio to Poland, and in 1797 apostolic delegate and ambassador to Saint Petersburg. He was made a cardinal in 1801, and was prefect of the Congregation of the Index from 1803 to 1816. He was cardinal vicar in Rome from 1818 until his death in 1820. See Wolf (ed.), *Prosopographie*, pp. 873–77.

72. Vita della Serva di Dio. La M. Maria Agnese di Gesù; ACDF SO St. St. B 6 q 1.

73. Sommario del Ristretto contro il P. Leziroli, no. I: Cenni storici; ACDF SO St. St. B 7 e.

74. Della Genga became titular Bishop of Tyrus in 1794, and nuncio to Cologne the same year. In 1814 he became extraordinary nuncio in Paris. He was made a cardinal in 1816, and became cardinal vicar in Rome in 1820. He was elected pope in 1823, and died in 1829. See *Notizie per l'anno* 1820, p. 25; Wolf (ed.), *Prosopographie*, pp. 464–66.

75. Della Genga was Protector of the Collegio Umbro-Fuccioli in 1822. The convent of Regulated Third Order nuns under Firrao's reform had been housed in the Collegio Fuccioli in Borgo Sant'Agata before Firrao was convicted in 1816.

Cf. *Notizie per l'anno* 1822, p. 27. Pius VII's brief of January 24, 1806, set out his responsibilites; Regola della Riforma delle Monache del Terz'Ordine di S. Francesco, Cap.XII. Del Protettore e Visitatore; ACDF SO St. St. B 6 r 1.

76. Ristretto con Sommario dei Costituti sostenuti dall'inquisita Abbadessa Sr. Maria Veronica Milza; ACDF SO St. St. B 7 d.

77. Appendice al Ristretto informativo: Sr. Maria Luisa riferisce della Relazione e premura, che aveva Leone XII per il monastero di S. Ambrogio; ACDF SO St. St. B 7 f.

78. There seem to have been several miraculous images in Sant'Ambrogio. Another picture of the Virgin was venerated there in the eighteenth century. Cf. ACDF SO St. St. B 6 s; Bianchi, *Notizie*; Dreuille, *S. Ambrogio*, pp. 30 and 78; "Ragguaglio storico intorno alla sacra Immagine della SS. Vergine Consolatrice venerate nella chiesa di Sant'Ambrogio delle Monache riformate del terz'Ordine di S. Francesco." The picture named here came from the estate of Cardinal Francesco Saverio de Zelada, who died in 1801. See Wolf (ed.), *Prosopographie* (1701–1813), p. 1324. It was purchased by the Abbess Maria Maddalena's father, Alessandro Ragazzoni. She evidently brought the picture with her to the convent.

79. Ragguaglio storico; ACDF SO St. St. B 6 s. Other senior religious and secular dignitaries, like the archbishop of Naples, Luigi Cardinal Ruffo-Scilla, or King Charles Emanuel IV of Sardinia, paid homage to the picture on several occasions. On Ruffo-Scilla, see Ekkart Sauser, "Ruffo-Scilla," in *BBKL* 17 (2000), p. 1172.

80. Clarelli Paracciani was born in 1799 and became a consultor of the Congregation of Cardinals in 1821. He was made a cardinal in 1844, prefect of the Congregation for Bishops and Religious Orders in 1860, and prefect of the Congregation for the Fabric of Saint Peter's in 1870. He died in 1872. See Wolf (ed.), *Prosopographie*, p. 337.

81. Sommario del Ristretto contro il P. Leziroli, no. I: Cenni storici; ACDF SO St. St. B 7 e.

82. Appendice al Ristretto informativo: Sr. Maria Luisa riferisce della Relazione e premura, che aveva Leone XII per il monastero di S. Ambrogio; ACDF SO St. St. B 7 f.

83. Wiseman, *Recollections*, pp. 261–63, here p. 262.

84. See H. W. van Os, "Krönung Mariens," in *LCI* 2 (1970), pp. 671–76; Heinrich Schauerte and Torsten Gebhard, "Corona," in *Marienlexikon* 2 (1989), pp. 96–97. For the coronation inscription engraved on the miraculous image, see Dreuille, *S. Ambrogio*, illustration 40.

85. "But the pope became a special custodian and helper to the Society of Jesus, which had been reinstated by his predecessor." Schmidlin, *Papstgeschichte*, vol. 1, p. 460. See also Martina, *Pio IX*, vol. 1, p. 243.

86. ASV, Monasteri femminili soppressi, S. Ambrogio Busta 1, vol. 3, Visitatio Apostolica 1824.

87. Ristretto con Sommario dei Costituti del P. Leziroli, In nota, October 1861; ACDF SO St. St. B 7 e.

88. "Leone Papa XII. per la futura memoria del fatto." Leo XII's brief, January 30, 1829; ACDF SO St. St. B 6 r 1.

89. As a monsignore, Cinotti belonged to the Camerieri Segreti Soprannumerari, and was the author of several important works. See *Notizie per l'anno* 1861, p. 377.

90. Perrone was born in 1794 and entered the Society of Jesus in 1815. In 1823 he became a professor at the Collegio Romano, and in 1830 professor at the Jesuit college in Ferrara. He was made rector of the college in 1850, and died in 1876. See Erich Naab, "Perrone," in *BBKL* 7 (1994), pp. 227–29.

91. Sommario del Ristretto contro il P. Leziroli, no. I: Cenni storici; ACDF SO St. St. B 7 e.

92. "Dopo aver narrato molte altre di queste particolarità dice, che anche il Card. della Genga stando in Roma andava spesso a visitare e conferire coll'Abbadessa Maria Maddalena. Più dice di aver letto molte lettere, che il Cardinale le scriveva da Ferrara dove era Vescovo, e che essa lo dirigesse, come era pur noto alle vecchie etc." Appendice al Ristretto informativo: Sr. Maria Luisa riferisce della Relazione e premura, che aveva Leone XII per il monastero di S. Ambrogio; ACDF SO St. St. B 7 f. Gabriele della Genga, born in 1801, became prefect of the Congregation for Bishops and Religious Orders and a member of the Holy Office in 1852. He became prefect of the Congregation for Consultations of Regulars in 1856, and died in 1861. Cf. Weber, *Kardinäle*, vol. I, p. 456; Wolf (ed.), *Prosopographie*, pp. 467–68.

93. Ristretto con Sommario dei Costituti sostenuti dall'inquisita Abbadessa Sr. Maria Veronica Milza; ACDF SO St. St. B 7 d.

94. "Stato Pontificio. Roma 21 settembre. Domenica 15 del corrente, giorno sacro al glorioso nome della Vergine SS.ma, l'Em. Cardinal Pacca, vescovo ostiense e decano del S. Collegio, si portò con treno nella chiesa di Sant'Ambrogio, detta volgarmente *alla Massima*, ove consecrò il nuovo arcivescovo di Berito monsignor Gabriele della Genga Sermattei canonico della basilica patriarcale Lateranense. L'Em. S. fu assistita nell'augusta ceremonia dai monsignori Genovesi, arcivescovo di Mitilene, e Mazenod, vescovo d'Iconia. Il sacro rito fu amministrato con dignità e decoro." *Gazzetta Privilegiata di Milano*, no. 272, September 21, 1833, p. 1193.

95. Cf. Schmidt, *Konfessionalisierung*, pp. 131–51.

96. Cf. Wolf, *Ketzer*, pp. 141–90 and pp. 379–82.

97. The account of pretense of holiness that follows is based primarily on Bottoni, *Scritture*; Del Col, *Inquisizione*, pp. 659–80; Gotor, *Chiesa*, pp. 139–41 (with extensive bibliography); Anne Jacobson Schutte, "Finzione di santità," in *DSI* 2 (2011), pp. 601–5; Schutte, *Saints*; Modica, *Dottrina*; Prosperi, *Tribunali*, pp. 430–64; in particular Zarri (ed.)'s excellent anthology, *Finzione*.

98. Zarri, *Santità*, p. 14.

99. Gotor, *Chiesa* is essential reading here; also Samerski, *Himmel*, pp. 61–92.

100. See Miguel Gotor, "Canonizzazione dei santi," in *DSI* 1 (2011), pp. 257–60.

101. Zarri, *Santità*, p. 15.

102. See Samerski, *Himmel*, pp. 492–99.

103. See Del Col, *Inquisizione*, p. 660.

104. Miguel Gotor, "Canonizzazione dei santi," in *DSI* 1 (2011), p. 258; Gotor, *Chiesa*, pp. 110–20.

105. Cf. Overbeck and Niemann, *Stigmata*. Therese Neumann, who was born in

1898, lived in the Bavarian village of Konnersreuth. In an attempt to put out a fire on a neighboring farm, she injured her spine and was confined to bed. She suffered visual disturbances, epileptic fits, indications of paralysis, and deafness. On the day Saint Thérèse of Lisieux was beatified, in April 1923, she was suddenly able to see again, and when Saint Thérèse was canonized in 1925, her paralysis disappeared. In 1926 Thérèse Neumann, who was already venerated as a saint by the people, began to display stigmata. She died in 1962. See Armin Strohmeyr, *Glaubenszeugen der Moderne. Die Heiligen und Seligen des 20. und 21. Jahrhunderts* (Düsseldorf, 2010), pp. 135–38. Cf. Paola Giovetti, *Teresa Neumann di Konnersreuth. Biografia di una grande mistica del nostro tempo* (Milan, 3rd ed., 1990). Padre Pio was born in 1887 and received the stigmata in 1918. A great wave of veneration followed. He died in 1968 and was canonized in 2002. See Del Col, *Inquisizione*, p. 815; Turi, *Stigmate*, p. 84. A very critical view of Padre Pio's stigmata can be found in Luzzatto, *Padre Pio*, pp. 54–96.

106. Zarri, *Santità*, p. 15.

107. The concept of confessionalization goes back to Heinz Schilling and Wolfgang Reinhard, who added the concept of "social disciplining" to Ernst Walther Zeeden's theories of "Konfessionsbildung" (the formation of denominations) in the late 1970s and early 1980s. This turned the process of forming denominations "from a phenomenon of church history to a fundamental socio-historical process of early modernity." Cf. Reinhard, *Konfessionalisierung*, pp. 419–52, here p. 420; also Reinhard, *Konfession,* pp. 107–24.

108. Cf. Reinhard, *Konfessionalisierung,* p. 427.

109. Zarri, *Santità*, p. 20.

110. Del Col, *Inquisizione*, p. 661. Cf. also Gennari, *Misticismo*.

111. Figures given in Weiß, *Seherinnen*, p. 44, note 6.

112. Cf. David Blackbourn, *Marpingen*, pp. 50–56.

113. The Archive of the Roman Inquisition, which functioned as the city Inquisition for Rome and as the central head office of the numerous local Inquisitions, particularly in Italy, was not accessible to researchers until 1998. Academic investigation of the phenomenon of pretense of holiness therefore initially concentrated on the cases that had been dealt with by the local Inquisitions. A list of cases and further reading can be found in Malena, *Inquisizione*, p. 289, note 3. There was a clear emphasis here on the seventeenth century and the first half of the eighteenth century, as the concept of "affettata, falsa, finta, pretesa, simulata santità" was closely connected to the period of confessionalization. Jacobson Schutte, *Saints*, p. xii. Cf. also Malena, *Inquisizione*, pp. 289–306. The nineteenth century, the second age of confessionalization, was surprisingly overlooked for a long time. Cf. Blaschke, *19. Jahrhundert*, pp. 38–75. In the Archive of the Congregation for the Doctrine of the Faith, the highest concentration of cases of pretense of holiness clearly falls in the early modern period. Processi del Santo Officio per affettata santità (1617–1771); ACDF SO St. St. B 4 p. Venerazione di persone non canonizzate o beatificate (1615–1783); ibid., B 4 b 1. Cf. also Del Col, *Inquisizione*, pp. 814–16.

114. Wietse de Boer, "Sollecitazione in confessionale," in *DSI* 3 (2011), pp. 1451–55;

Georg Holzherr, "Sollizitation," in *LThK*, 2nd ed., vol. 9 (1964), p. 868; Julius Krieg, "Sollicitatio ad turpia," in *LThK*, 1st ed., vol. 9 (1937), pp. 656–57; Adriano Prosperi, "Sessualità," in *DSI* 3 (2011), pp. 1417–20.

115. Congregazione per la Dottrina della Fede, Archivio. Regolamento per gli Studiosi (Vatican City), 2003, p. 3 (no. 12); Schwedt, *Archiv*, pp. 267–80.

116. Esami di Franceschetti, December 22, 1859, and January 7, 1860; ACDF SO St. St. B 6 b, fol. 18r–28r.

117. The quotation from Paul comes from 1 Corinthians 15:42, and the Psalms quotation from Psalm 16:10. Cf. Angenendt, *Corpus incorruptum*, pp. 320–48; Angenendt, *Heilige*, pp. 149–52 and elsewhere.

118. Relazione informativa, January 1861, Titolo I, Sallua's summary; ACDF SO St. St. B 7 c.

119. Esami di Maria Veronica, January 13 and 16, 1860; ACDF SO St. St. B 6 c. Subsequent quotations also taken from this text.

120. The veneration of Firrao in Sant'Ambrogio was typical for a saint whose relics weren't available: the image of a saint often came to stand for their "presence." Over the course of church history, people—in particular mystics—frequently reported having visions in front of these pictures. "It was not only that saints most often manifested themselves in the same attitude and with the same appearance as their images; they also identified themselves with these images and animated them." Angenendt, *Heilige*, p. 188. Cf. also Anton Legner, "Vom Glanz und von der Präsenz des Heiltums—Bilder und Texte," in Anton Legner and Louis-Ferdinand Peters, *Reliquien. Verehrung und Verklärung. Skizzen und Noten zur Thematik und Katalog zur Ausstellung der Kölner Sammlung Louis Peters im Schnütgen-Museum* (Cologne, 1989), pp. 33–147.

121. The term "litany" denotes a particular form of prayer; after every invocation of a saint there follows an unchanging response from the people. Cf. Balthasar Fischer, "Litanei," in *LThK*, 3rd ed. vol. 3 (1997), p. 954. In the Litany of the Saints, following the usual introduction of the *Kyrie eleison*, all the different classes of saints are entreated to intercede—some being invoked by name, and the rest addressed in general. A strict order of rank is adhered to: "First the most blessed Virgin Mary is called upon, then follows a series of holy angels, the patriarchs and prophets, the holy apostles and evangelists, the holy martyrs, the holy bishops, confessors and doctors of the church, the holy priests and levites, the holy monks and hermits, and finally the holy virgins and widows. Then follows the naming of evils that are particularly important to avoid, then the naming of the reasons for which we hope to be heard." Carl Kammer, *Die Litanei von allen Heiligen* (Innsbruck, 1962), p. 7.

122. Relazione informativa con Sommario, Titolo I: Sallua quotes from the interrogation of the abbess on January 13, 1860; ACDF SO St. St. B 7 c.

123. Esami di Maria Caterina, Maria Gertrude, and Maria Colomba, late January–early February 1860; ACDF SO St. St. B 6 c.

124. Relazione informativa con Sommario, Titolo I: La condannata Sr. Agnese Firrao è sempre stata in venerazione di Santa in vita e dopo morte presso le monache di S. Ambrogio; ACDF SO St. St. B 7 c.

125. On the process and history of canonization, see Angenendt, *Heilige*, pp. 74–80 and passim; Sieger, *Heiligsprechung.*

126. Relazione informativa con Sommario, Sommario no. II: Esame di Suor Maria Caterina di S. Agnese, January 31, 1860; ACDF SO St. St. B 7 c.

127. In the Italian sources, his name is often incorrectly spelled "Mosferzon." Paul MacPherson was born in 1756, ordained as priest in 1779, and worked in various parishes before becoming the procurator in Edinburgh in 1792. The following year he became an agent in Rome, before being ordered to leave by the French in 1798. He returned to Edinburgh, but was back in Rome by 1800. He was rector of the Scottish College there from 1818 to 1826, and 1834 until his death in 1846. See *Edinburgh Review*, no. 119, January–April, New York, 1864, p. 98; *Journal and Appendix to Scotichronicon and Monasticon* (Glasgow, 1869), p. 595; David McRoberts, *Abbé Paul MacPherson, 1756–1846* (Glasgow, 1946).

128. Placido Zuria was born in 1769. He entered a Camaldolese order, becoming a lecturer in theology at San Michele in 1795, and in 1817 professor of moral theology at the Patriarchal Seminary in Venice. In 1822 he was made a consultor of the Congregation for the Index, in 1823 a cardinal, and in 1824 cardinal vicar of the diocese of Rome and prefect of the Congregation for the Residential Obligation of Bishops. He died in 1834. See Wolf (ed.), *Prosopographie*, pp. 1596–1600. Giacomo Filipo Fransoni was born in 1775, became nuncio to Portugal in 1822, and titular bishop of Nazianz in the same year. He was made a cardinal in 1826, became prefect of the Congregation for Church Immunity in 1830, and prefect of the Congregation for the Propagation of the Faith in 1834. In 1851 he became a member of the preparatory commission for the dogma of the *Immaculata*. He died in 1856. See ibid., pp. 614–16.

129. Quoted by Sallua in his summary: Relazione informativa con Sommario, Titolo I; ACDF SO St. St. B 7 c.

130. Relazione informativa con Sommario, Titolo II: Relazione continuata per oltre 40 anni, e direzione temporale e spirituale della Firrao verso le Monache di S. Ambrogio, e la totale dipendenza di queste da quella fino alla sua morte; ACDF SO St. St. B 7 c. Subsequent quotations also taken from this text.

131. Sallua's handwritten note to the inquisitor of Gubbio, November 29, 1859; ACDF SO St. St. B 6 a, fol. 49r.

132. Bruno Brunelli must have been born between 1805 and 1810, as he entered the subdeaconate of the diocese of Gubbio in 1830, and was ordained in 1832. He died in 1878. With thanks to the Gubbio diocesan archive for their information.

133. The fascicle contains the interrogations carried out by the local inquisitor in Gubbio, from folio 37; ACDF SO St. St. B 6 b.

134. See Nikolaus Gihr, *Die heiligen Sacramente der katholischen Kirche.* Vol. 2: *Die Buße, die letzte Ölung, das Weihesacrament und das Ehesacrament* (Freiburg i. Br., 2nd ed., 1903).

135. Jeffrey Burton Russell, *Prince of Darkness: Radical Evil and the Power of Good in History* (New York, 1988), p. 114.

136. This would have been the "translation of relics." Cf. Hans-Jakob Achermann, "Translationen heiliger Leiber als barockes Phänomen," in *Jahrbuch für Volkskunde* 4 (1981), pp. 101–11; Martin Heinzelmann, "Translation (von Reliquien)," in

LexMA 8 (1999), pp. 947–49. On saints' graves, cf. Angenendt, *Heilige*, p. 460 (index).

137. See Angenendt, *Heilige*, pp. 149–89.

138. Contact relics are "secondary relics." These are objects or pieces of clothing with which the saint has come into contact during his/her lifetime. Cf. Arnold Angenendt, "Reliquien/Reliquienverehrung II: Im Christentum," in *TRE* 29 (1998), pp. 69–74.

139. On hagiographies as accounts of the lives of saints, and the academic research conducted on these, see René Algrain, *L'hagiographie. Ses sources, ses méthodes, son histoire* (Paris, 1953). A particular category of a saint's life is termed a "Vita." A Vita is written by an author who knew the saint personally, or wrote about their life with the help of information from eyewitnesses. This should be differentiated from a "legend," a saint's biography written by authors distant in time, showing little or no historicity. Cf. Peter Dinzelbacher, "Der Kampf der Heiligen mit den Dämonen," in *Santi e demoni nell'alto medioevo occidentale (secoli V–XI)* (*Settimane di studio del centro italiano di studi sull'alto medioevo 36*), vol. 2 (Spoleto, 1989), pp. 647–95, here p. 653.

140. Relazione informativa con Sommario, Titolo III: Scritti ed altri oggetti conservati nel monastero di S. Ambrogio nonostante la proibizione. Perquisizione dei medesimi; ACDF SO St. St. B 7 c. Subsequent quotations also taken from this text unless otherwise stated.

141. Esame di Sr. Maria Veronica, January 13, 1860; ACDF SO St. St. B 6 c.

142. Some of these documents can be found in ACDF SO St. St. B 6 w a to B 6 w e.

143. Relazione informativa con Sommario, Titolo IV: Brevi riflessi sù di alcuni scritti interessanti al merito della causa; ACDF SO St. St. B 7 c. Subsequent quotations also taken from this text.

144. Cf .the testimonies of various nuns. Maria Nazarena stated: "The mother founder wrote to us that the Lord had revealed His will to her, and we were travelling the path of perfection in our institute. Her message was read aloud to us, as instructed. I have no doubt that she was inspired by the Lord when she wrote these texts." Esame di Sr. Maria Nazarena, February 9, 1860; ACDF SO St. St. B 6 d. Sister Maria Gertrude, a longtime companion of the founder, told of her many miracles and extraordinary gifts, and said: "We all had a high opinion of the founder's holiness; although she herself read no books, she received everything that she wrote through inspiration from God." Esame di Sr. Maria Gertrude, April 12, 1860; ACDF SO St. St. B 6 g.

145. Cf. Helmut Gabel, "Inspiration III," in *LThK*, 3rd ed., vol. 5 (1996), pp. 535–38.

146. Ceremonials of Sant'Ambrogio; ACDF SO St. St. B 6 h I, fol.9.

147. Gabriel Ghislain, "Capitolo delle Colpe, in *DIP* 2 (1975), pp. 176–79; Hans-Jürgen Becker, "Schuldkapitel," in *LexMA* 7 (1999), pp. 1581–82.

148. Ristretto informativo con Sommario, Titolo IV; ACDF SO St. St. B 7 c.

149. Cf. Bernard-D. Marliangeas, *Clés pour une théologie du ministère. In persona Christi, in persona Ecclesiae* (Théologie Historique 51) (Paris, 1978); Egidio Miragoli (ed.), *Il sacramento della penitenza. Il ministero del confessore: indicazioni canoniche e pastorali* (Milan, 1999), pp. 25–40.

150. Engelbert Krebs, "Laienbeichte," in *LThK*, 1st ed., vol. 6 (1934), pp. 340–41, here p. 341.

151. Relazione informativa con Sommario, Titolo V: Quale parte e responsabilità risulti a carico dei PP. Confessori Leziroli e Peters circa i titoli suddetti; ACDF SO St. St. B 7 c. Subsequent quotations also taken from this text unless otherwise stated.

152. Relazione informativa con Sommario, Sallua's summary of Titolo V; ACDF SO St. St. B 7 c. Leziroli's work "Sulle memorie della vita di Suor Maria Agnese di Gesù" is also held in the archive, at B 7 f.

CHAPTER FOUR *"Wash Me Well, for the Padre Is Coming"*

1. Relazione informativa con Sommario, Titolo VI: Affettata Santità della M. Vicaria Sr. Maria Luisa di S. Francesco Saverio Maestra delle Novizie; ACDF SO St. St. B 7 c. Subsequent quotations, including those from individual interrogations, also taken from this text.

2. On visions and supernatural apparitions, cf. Dinzelbacher, *Vorbedingungen*, pp. 57–86; Zahn, *Einführung*, pp. 462–575.

3. Cf. Busch, *Frömmigkeit*, pp. 132–42.

4. Regola della Riforma delle Monache del Terz'Ordine di S. Francesco, Cap. IX: Degli Uffizi; ACDF SO St. St. B 6 r 1.

5. Leziroli to Patrizi, undated; ACDF SO St. St. B 6 a, fol. 102rv. Memorie di tutte le cose più rimarchevoli occorse in questo nostro S. Istituto nelle diverse epoche incominciando dal principio della fondazione; ibid., B 6 s 1, fol. 621.

6. Sommario della Relazione informativa, no. V: Esame di Sr. Maria Crocifissa, April 25, 1860; ACDF SO St. St. B 7 c.

7. John 20:22.

8. See Luke 22:14–20 and 1 Corinthians 11:23–25.

9. This feast was observed on August 15, according to the liturgical calendar. Cf. Adolf Adam, "Das Hochfest 'Aufnahme Marias in den Himmel,'" in *Klerusblatt* 64 (1984), 8, pp. 201–4.

10. See the second verse of the hymn to the Virgin, "Die schönste von allen"; Gotteslob. Edition for the diocese Rottenburg (Ostfildern), 1975, no. 895.

11. A scapular is part of a nun's habit, resembling an apron worn over the tunic. Cf. Giancarlo Rocca, "Scapolare," in *DIP* 8 (1988), pp. 1015–18.

12. On these eschatological places, see Auffahrt, *Himmel*, pp. 515–23; Lang, *Himmel*, pp. 524–33. On the period of purification, the particular judgment and the *interzessio* (the saint's intercession with God on behalf of the deceased), cf. Angenendt, *Heilige*, pp. 106–8.

13. Cf. Speyer, *Verehrung*, p. 50.

14. It is frequently conjectured that mystics make regular use of intoxicants to achieve their ecstatic state. Cf. Peter Gerlitz, "Mystik I," in *TRE* 23 (1994), pp. 533–47, here pp. 543–44.

15. Cf. Wolfgang Beinert et al. (eds.), *Das kirchliche Amt in apostolischer Nachfolge. Grundlagen und Grundfragen*, 3 vols. (Freiburg i. Br., 2004–2008); Max Seckler, "Der Begriff der Offenbarung," in *Handbuch der Fundamentaltheologie*, ed. Walter Kern,

Hermann Josef Pottmeyer and Max Seckler, Vol. 2: Traktat Offenbarung (Freiburg i. Br., 1985), pp. 60–83.

16. On mysticism in general, cf. Bürke, *Mythos*; Leppin, *Mystik*; McGinn, *Writings*; Wehr, *Mystik*; Zahn, *Einführung*. On mysticism in the Franciscan orders, cf. Freyer, *Mystik*.

17. Helga Unger, "Mystik," in Lissner et al. (eds.), *Frauenlexikon*, pp. 795–805, here p. 795.

18. Christoph Weber describes visions and ecstasies as the means to an "obscure feminine recapture of words and power in the Catholic Church." Weber, *Ultramontanismus*, p. 31.

19. Dinzelbacher, *Frauenmystik*, pp. 251–84; Alois Stöger, "Erscheinungen," in *Marienlexikon* 2 (1989), pp. 395–98, here p. 398; Helga Unger, "Mystik," in Lissner et al. (eds.), *Frauenlexikon*, p. 804. On the problematization of "true" and "false" mysticism, cf. Lhermitte, *Mystiker*. On the difference between *Revelatio privata* and *Revelatio publica*, cf. Georg Essen, "Privatoffenbarung," in *LThK*, 3rd ed., vol. 8 (1999), pp. 603–4.

20. Cf. Dinzelbacher, *Frauenmystik*; Schmökel, *Hochzeit*; Weiß, *Ekstase*.

21. The martyr Agnes of Rome was wearing a heavenly ring to symbolize her marriage to Christ as early as the second century AD. Cf. Marianne Heimbach-Steins, "Brautsymbolik II: Brautmystik," in *LThK*, 3rd ed., vol. 2 (1994), p. 665. The sensual and erotic dimension of this tradition, in which a female mystic wed her divine bridegroom, reached its high point in the Middle Ages with Mechthild of Magdeburg. Cf. Gisela Vollmann-Profe, "Mystische Hohelied-Erfahrungen. Zur Brautmystik Mechthilds von Magdeburg," in *Das Hohelied. Liebeslyrik als Kultur(en) erschließendes Medium?* (Bern, 2007), pp. 57–68; Weiß, *Ekstase*, pp. 462–68. On the cultural-historical and liturgical significance of the ring in general, see Rupert Berger and Michael Schmauder, "Ring," in *LThK*, 3rd ed., vol. 8 (1999), pp. 1192–94.

22. Craveri, *Sante*, pp. 65–85; Dinzelbacher, *Mystik*, pp. 356–64; Doornik, *Katharina*, pp. 37–46; Poppenburg, *Leben*.

23. Raymond of Capua was born in 1330. He was a Dominican, who became Catherine of Siena's confessor since 1347, and was made provincial of Lombardy in 1379. From 1380 to 1399 he was Master General of the part of the Dominican order that had remained faithful to Rome. He died in 1399 and was beatified in 1899. See Walter Senner, "Capua," in *BBKL* 7 (1994), pp. 1279–81.

24. Raymond of Capua, *Life*, pp. 75–76.

25. The "Legenda minor" also emphasized this: "After this clear vision, Catherine constantly saw the ring on her finger, although it remained invisible to us." Caffarini, *Caterina*, p. 90. The invisible ring was to help Catherine fulfill her difficult duties in the world, in spite of all hostility and persecution. It thus became a sign of legitimation for her ecclesiastico-political mission, which was not without its dangers. See also Malan, *Geschichte*, pp. 232–33.

26. Wilhelm Horkel, *Spiritismus. Geheimnisse des Jenseits* (Stuttgart, 1987); Felizitas Küble, "Voodoo, Spiritismus, magische Kulte. Ritual aus der Finsternis," in *Theologisches* 42 (2012), 1/2, pp. 27–44; Sawicki, *Leben*.

27. Cf. Nils Freytag and Diethard Sawicki, "Verzauberte Moderne. Kulturge-

schichtliche Perspektiven auf das 19. und 20. Jahrhundert," in Nils Freytag and Diethard Sawicki, *Wunderwelten. Religiöse Ekstase und Magie in der Moderne* (Munich, 2006), pp. 7–24; Weiß, *Redemptoristen*, pp. 31–38.

28. On Brentano's enthusiasm for mystical phenomena, and in particular for Anna Katharina Emmerick, cf. Wolfgang Frühwald, *Das Spätwerk Clemens Brentanos (1815–1842). Romantik im Zeitalter der Metternich'schen Restauration* (Tübingen, 1977); Gerd-Klaus Kaltenbrunner, *Die Seherin von Dülmen und ihr Dichter-Chronist. Clemens Brentano, Anna Katharina Emmerich und die Folgen einer seltsamen Seelen-Symbiose* (Gersau, 1992); Thomas a Villanova Wegener, "Anna Katharina Emmerich und Clemens Brentano. Zur Orientierung einer viel besprochenen Frage," Dülmen 1900, online: http://sammlungen.ulb.unimuenster.de/hd/content/pageview/827203 (6/26/2012)—there is also a section here on Clemens Brentano's biography.

29. See Dussler, *Feneberg.*

30. 2 vols., Stuttgart 1829. Friederike Hauffe was born in 1801 and died in 1829, in Löwenstein. Her "gifts," strongly reminiscent of mystical phenomena, were in her case treated as symptoms of somnambulism, and even connected with occultism.

31. Cf. Görres, *Mystik.* Cf. also Naab, *Auflösung,* pp. 53–74; Weiß, *Ort,* pp. 79–130.

32. Weiß, *Ort,* p. 94.

33. Ibid., p. 95. The miraculous fragrance was one of the classic attributes of true sainthood in the Church tradition. Cf. Angenendt, *Heilige,* p. 10, 119–22, and passim.

34. Weiß, *Ort,* p. 119.

35. Cf. Thurston, *Phenomena,* Weiß, *Seherinnen,* pp. 43–48.

36. Weiß, *Ort,* p. 120.

37. Karl, *Glauben,* p. 7.

38. Ibid., p. 6.

39. Ibid., p. 9.

40. Ibid., p. 24.

41. Relazione informativa con Sommario, Titolo VI: Affettata Santità della M. Vicaria Sr. Maria Luisa; ACDF SO St. St. B 7 c. Subsequent quotations also taken from this text unless otherwise stated.

42. Letter from Leziroli to Patrizi, undated; ACDF SO St. St. B 6 a, fol. 101rv.

43. The annals have the title: Memorie di tutte le cose più rimarchevoli occorse in questo nostro S. Istituto nelle diverse epoche incominciando dal principio della fondazione (January 3, 1857), 628 pp.; ACDF SO St. St. B 6 s 1.

44. On the rose as the flower of the Virgin, and rose perfume, see Angenendt, *Heilige,* pp. 119–22; "Rose," in Forstner and Becker (eds.), *Lexikon,* pp. 280–82. On the lily, see Margarete Pfister-Burkhalter, "Lilien," in *LCI* 3 (1971), pp. 101–3.

45. Franceschetti gave the Holy Tribunal some very important information in his hearings on December 7 and 22, 1859, and on January 7, May 9, and June 19, 1860. Sommario della Relazione informativa, no. VII: Esami di Franceschetti; ACDF SO St. St. B 7 c.

46. The Paolo was a Roman silver coin weighing four grams. It was introduced by

Paul III to replace the Giulio. On the value of the coin in Rome, see Johann Jacob Volkmann, *Historisch-kritische Nachrichten von Italien: welche eine genaue Beschreibung dieses Landes, der Sitten und Gebräuche, der Regierungsform, Handlung, Oekonomie, des Zustandes der Wissenschaften, und insonderheit der Werke der Kunst . . . enthalten,* vol. 2 (Leipzig, 1771), p. 764: "The money in Rome is very easy to work out, as it uses the decimal system, and as a consequence there are very few fractions. All bills are worked out in Scudi and Baiocchi. A Scudo is worth ten Paoli, and a Paolo ten Baiocchi. A Baiocco is five Quattrini, a copper coin only used by poor people. The decimal numbers are uncommonly good for calculations." See also the detailed article "Monete pontificie," in Moroni, *Dizionario* 46 (1847), pp. 104–25.

47. The Baiocco was a coin in the Papal States, weight 12 grams. It was worth $\frac{1}{100}$ of a scudo and $\frac{1}{10}$ of a paolo. See *Meyers Großes Konversations-Lexikon* 2 (1905), p. 284.

48. Relazione informativa con Sommario, Titolo VI: Affettata Santità della M. Vicaria Sr. Maria Luisa: Perquisizione delli anelli nei luoghi comodi del Noviziato; ACDF SO St. St. B 7 c.

49. Relazione informativa con Sommario, Titolo VI: Affettata Santità della M. Vicaria Sr. Maria Luisa; ACDF SO St. St. B 7 c. Subsequent quotations also taken from this text unless otherwise stated.

50. The general "is chosen by the General Assembly, which has to meet after the death of a general, and, once elected, he holds the position for life. The general is . . . of course bound by the order's constitution and canon law, in particular obedience to the Pope, and can only exercise his power within the bounds of the constitutions. But in individual cases, and in certain circumstances, he can also dispense with these, and the decisions of general congregations, and in accordance with the constitution possesses . . . the entire and immediate plenipotentiary power of the government. In this respect, the highest executive of the Society of Jesus can be called monarchical. However, his power is not absolute, but constitutional." "General (Praepositus generalis)," in Koch, *Jesuiten-Lexikon,* vol. 1, pp. 656–59, here p. 656. On the organization of the Society of Jesus, see Hartmann, *Jesuiten,* pp. 19–29; Martina, *Storia;* Sommavilla, *Compagnia.*

51. Beckx died in 1887. See "A.R.P. Petrus Beckx †," in *Stimmen aus Maria Laach* 32 (1887), p. 265; Koch, *Jesuiten-Lexikon,* vol. 1, pp. 170–72; Schoeters, *Beckx;* Sommervogel, *Bibliothèque,* vol. 1, pp. 1118–25.

52. Appendice al Ristretto infomativo, Esame di Beckx, March 1860; ACDF SO St. St. B 7 f.

53. Esame di Sr. Maria Veronica, February 15, 1860; ACDF SO St. St. B 6 d, fol. 48 f.

54. Appendice al Ristretto informativo, Esame di Beckx, March 1860; ACDF SO St. St. B 7 f.

55. Lettera della Vergine Maria al Preposito Generale della Compagnia di Gesù; ACDF SO St. St. B 6 z, fol. 4rv (original letter); Appendice al Ristretto informativo, Sommario no. I; ACDF SO St. St. B 7 f (printed version).

56. For example, Prince Kraft zu Hohenlohe-Ingelfingen said that Pius spoke

French during audiences as a matter of course; *Aus meinem Leben*. Vol. 2: *1856–1863* (Berlin, 1905), p. 160.

57. See Carlin, *Ecclesiologia*, pp. 29–34, here p. 30.

58. Passaglia died in 1887. See ibid., pp. 11–52; Martina, *Storia*, pp. 145–64; Peter Walter, "Passaglia," in *LThK*, 3rd ed., vol. 7 (1998), p. 1414; Walter, *Passaglia*, pp. 165–82, here pp. 165–71.

59. Schrader died in 1875. See Schauf, *Schrader*, pp. 368–85; Peter Walter, "Schrader," in *LThK*, 3rd ed., vol. 9 (2000), p. 248.

60. See Wolf (ed.), *Repertorium Indexkongregation*, p. 406.

61. See Giovagnoli, *Teologia*, pp. 107–9.

62. Appendice al Ristretto informativo, Sommario no. II: Lettera consegnata dal P. Leziroli, August 5, 1857; ACDF SO St. St. B 7 f.

63. Cf. Schneider, *Feminisierung*, pp. 123–47. Cf. also Duby, *Modell*, pp. 187–220.

64. Borutta, *Antikatholizismus*, pp. 218 and 366–89.

65. Cf. Horst, *Dogma*, pp. 95–114.

66. Apostolic Constitution from Pius IX, "Ineffabilis Deus," issued on December 8, 1854; full English text online: http://www.papalencyclicals.net/Pius09/p9ineff.htm (08/29/2013). On the position of the Roman school on the new dogma of the Virgin, see Schumacher, *Konzept*, pp. 207–26.

67. "Das Dogma und die Civilisation," in *Augsburger Postzeitung*, no. 210, August 2, 1855, p. 694, and no. 211, August 3, 1855, p. 698. The article originally appeared in the German edition of the *Civiltà Cattolica*, 1855, pp. 204–29. Interestingly, the *Augsburger Postzeitung* names the author as Giuseppe Calvetti, a friend of Joseph Kleutgen, who died in 1855 at the age of just thirty-eight. Cf. Schäfer, *Kontroverse*, p. 66.

68. Schwedt, *Döllinger*, p. 133.

69. Alois Stöger, "Erscheinungen," in *Marienlexikon* 2 (1989), pp. 395–98. Cf. also Bernhard Schneider, "Ein deutsches Lourdes? Der 'Fall' Marpingen (1876 und 1999) und die Elemente eines kirchlichen Prüfungsverfahrens," in Schneider (ed.), *Maria und Lourdes. Wunder und Marienerscheinungen in theologischer und kulturwissenschaftlicher Perspektive* (Münster, 2008), pp. 178–97.

70. Blackbourn, *Marpingen*, p. 54.

71. Cf. Cavarzere, "Suppliche," pp. 145–68, here p. 160; Schreiner, "Maria als Symbolgestalt," p. 122; Schreiner, *Maria. Jungfrau*, p. 132. Text of the letter: Epistolae B. Virginis Mariae ad Messanenses veritas vindicate ac plurimis gravissimorum scriptorium testimoniis et rationibus erudite illustrate (Viterbo, 2nd ed., 1632). A letter composed in Latin to the city of Florence, and a letter from Mary to Ignatius of Antioch also belong to this genre.

72. Cf. Blackbourn, *Marpingen*, pp. 17–113; Ludwig Boer, "Briefe," in *Marienlexikon* 1 (1988), pp. 584–89; Stübe, *Himmelsbrief*. On the connection between mystical experiences and heavenly letters, see Spamer, *Himmelsbriefe*, pp. 184–92.

73. Text of the letter: Camille Fraysse, "Les Lettres d'origine céleste aux pays de Baugé," in *Revue de Folklore Français* 5 (1933/34), pp. 119–22, here p. 120. Ludwig Boer claims that Pierre Bizet's work *Lettre de la S. Vierge trouvée dans la Chapelle provisoire de Notre-Dame d'Afrique* (Algiers, 2nd ed., 1860) (defending the authen-

ticity of a letter apparently from the Virgin in heaven, preserved in Algiers) was placed on the *Index of Forbidden Books* in 1862. Cf. Ludwig Boer, "Briefe," in *Marienlexikon* 1 (1988), p. 588. However, this could not be substantiated by the Münster research on book censorship.

74. Relazione informativa con Sommario, Titolo VII: Sr. M. Luisa per più anni sostiene la vantata sua Santità presso il suo confessore P. Giuseppe Peters col mezzo di scritti, e lettere pretese sopranaturali; ACDF SO St. St. B 7 c.

75. Esame di Sr. Maria Francesca, February 18, 1860; ACDF SO St. St. B 6 d, fol. 25r—29r. Subsequent quotations are taken from this text.

76. Bittner, *Himmel*; Graf, *Himmel*, pp. 10—23; Riedel, *Kirchenrechtsquellen*, pp. 166—75. On the apocryphal letters from Christ, cf. Johann Michl's overview, "Briefe, apokryphe," in *LThK*, 2nd ed., vol. 2 (1958), pp. 688—93, here p. 688.

77. The title "rosa mystica" is a cipher for the Mother of God. This is how Mary is referred to in the Laurentian litany, and elsewhere. See Walter Dürig, *Die Lauretanische Litanei. Entstehung, Verfasser, Aufbau und mariologischer Inhalt* (St. Ottilien, 1990).

78. In the Christological hymn of the apostle Paul's Epistle to the Colossians (Colossians 1:15—20), Christ is called the "firstborn of every creature." The various creeds of the first four centuries speak of "one Lord Jesus Christ, the only son of God, eternally begotten of the Father."

79. Esame di Sr. Maria Francesca, February 20, 1860; ACDF SO St. St. B 6 d, fol. 30v—34r.

80. Since 1856, the situation in the Papal States had escalated. Piedmont's involvement in the Crimean War, fighting alongside the French, gave the nascent Italian national state the opportunity to take more of a stand against papal rule. At the start of June 1859, there was an uprising in Bologna, which rapidly spread to many other cities in the Papal States. Cf. Schmidlin, *Papstgeschichte*, vol. 2, pp. 66—80.

81. Meaning Saint Agatha of Catania, who was martyred during the persecution of the Christians by Emperor Decius. She refused to enter into marriage with the city prefect, Quintianus, and renounce the Christian faith, and her breasts were cut off as punishment. Cg. Maria-Barbara von Stritzky, "Agathe von Catania," in Steimer (ed.), *Lexikon*, pp. 24—25.

82. From the context, it is unclear whether this refers to Gertude of Nivelles or Gertrude of Helfta, also called Gertrude the Great. Cf. Matthias Werner, "Gertrud von Nivelles," in Steimer (ed.), *Lexikon*, p. 109; Margot Schmidt, "Gertrud von Helfta," in ibid., p. 108.

83. Esame di Sr. Maria Francesca, February 21, 1860; ACDF SO St. St. B 6 d, fol. 34r—40r.

84. Esame di Sr. Maria Francesca, February 22, 1860; ACDF SO St. St. B 6 d, fol. 40r—45r.

85. Sommario della Relazione informativa, no. VII: Esami di Franceschetti, December 22, 1859, January 7 and May 9, 1860; ACDF SO St. St. B 7 c.

86. A summary also appears in Relazione informativa con Sommario, Titolo VII: Sr. M. Luisa per più anni sostiene la vantata sua Santità presso il suo confessore

P. Giuseppe Peters col mezzo di scritti, e lettere pretese sopranaturali; ACDF SO St. St. B 7 c. Subsequent quotations also taken from this text, with additional material from individual interrogation transcripts.

87. Sommario della Relazione informativa, no. X: Esame di Sr. Agnese Celeste, March 29, 1860; ACDF SO St. St. B 7 c.

88. Sommario della Relazione informativa, no. X: Esame di Sr. Giuseppa Maria, March 31, 1860; ACDF SO St. St. B 7 c. Subsequent quotations also taken from this text.

89. Sommario della Relazione informativa, no. X: Esame di Sr. Maria Fortunata, May 7, 1860; ACDF SO St. St. B 7 c.

90. Sommario della Relazione informativa, no. X: Esame di Sr. Maria Fortunata, May 14, 1860; ACDF SO St. St. B 7 c.

91. Sommario della Relazione informativa, no. X: Esame di Sr. Maria Veronica, May 23, 1860; ACDF SO St. St. B 7 c.

92. Relazione informativa con Sommario, Titolo IX: Disonestà con false massime praticate da Sr. M. Luisa con alcune religiose; ACDF SO St. St. B 7 c. Subsequent quotations also taken from this text.

93. Text by Maria Giacinta, added to the files at her hearing on March 24, 1860; ACDF SO St. St. B 6 e, fol.77r–79v.

94. Cf Scala, *Exorzismus*, pp. 357–86.

95. Sommario della Relazione informativa, no. XIV: Esame di Sr. Giuseppa Maria, April 2, 1860; ACDF SO St. St. B 7 c.

96. Sommario della Relazione informativa, no. XIV: Esame di Sr. Maria Francesca, February 22, 1860; ACDF SO St. St. B 7 c.

97. Sommario della Relazione informativa, no. XIV: Esame di Sr. Agnese Celeste, March 27, 1860; ACDF SO St. St. B 7 c.

98. Sommario della Relazione informativa, no. XIV: Esame di Sr. Maria Fortunata, May 7, 1860; ACDF SO St. St. B 7 c.

99. Relazione informativa con Sommario, Titolo IX: Disonestà con false massime praticate da Sr. M. Luisa con alcune religiose; ACDF SO St. St. B 7 c.

100. Esame di Franceschetti, September 12, 1860; ACDF SO St. St. B 6 m.

101. Relazione informativa con Sommario, Titolo X: Massime erronee e pratiche perniciose; ACDF SO St. St. B 7 c. Subsequent quotations also taken from this text.

102. Regola della Riforma delle Monache del Terz'Ordine di S. Francesco, Cap. V: Del Confessore, e dei Sagramenti della Confessione, e Comunione; ACDF SO St. St. B6 r 1. See also Cornelius M. Rechenauer, *Seelenleitung, Beichte und Kommunionempfang in Frauenklöstern und den übrigen religiösen Genossenschaften mit Laienoberen* (Regensburg, 1909), pp. 9–18.

103. Regola della Riforma delle Monache del Terz'Ordine di S. Francesco, Cap. VI: Del cibo, e dell'astinenza; ACDF SO St. St. B 6 r 1.

104. Relazione informativa con Sommario, Titolo VIII: Perquisizione degli oggetti; ACDF SO St. St. B 7 c.

105. Relazione informativa con Sommario, Titolo X: Massime erronee e pratiche perniciose, Sallua's closing votum; ACDF SO St. St. B 7 c.

106. Esame di Sr. Giuseppa Maria, February 18, 1860; ACDF SO St. St. B6 h, fol. 104–5. Giuseppa Maria stressed that she was repeating Maria Luisa's address word for word.
107. Sommario della Relazione informativa, no. XV: Esame di Sr. Maria Veronica, May 19, 1860; ACDF SO St. St. B 7 c.
108. Relazione informativa con Sommario, Titolo X: Massime erronee e pratiche perniciose; ACDF SO St. St. B 7 c.
109. Relazione informativa con Sommario, Titolo VI: Affettata Santità della M. Vicaria Sr. Maria Luisa, Sallua's introduction; ACDF SO St. St. B 7 c.

CHAPTER FIVE *"An Act of Divine Splendor"*

1. Ristretto con Sommario dei Costituti Sr. Maria Veronica Milza, Sommario VI: Estratto dagli Esami di Sr. Maria Ignazia; ACDF SO St. St. B 7 d.
2. Relazione informativa con Sommario, Titolo XI: Avvelenamento, Sallua's introduction; ACDF SO St. St. B 7 c.
3. Sallua accorded this matter its own, short charge: "Relazione sospetta di Sr. M. Luisa con un tal Dottore di medicina Mario Kreisburg," within the larger context of Titolo XI. Relazione informativa con Sommario, Titolo XII; ADCF SO St. St. B 7 c. Subsequent quotations also taken from this text unless otherwise stated.
4. Cf. "Teufel," in Gerlach, *Lexikon,* pp. 200–3; Dinzelbacher, *Realität,* pp. 151–75; Schwerhoff, *Hexerei,* pp. 325–53, and the relevant articles in *LThK,* 2nd ed., vol. 10 (1965), pp. 1–5.
5. Marshman, *Exorcism,* pp. 265–81; William Nagel, "Exorzismus III," in *TRE* 10 (1982), pp. 751–56; *Rituale Romanum Pauli V Pontificis Maximi iussu editum* (Rome 1614–15), Tit. VIII; Adolf Rodewyk, "Exorzismus", in *LThK,* 2nd ed., vol. 3 (1959), pp. 1314; Scala, *Exorzismus,* pp. 350–436.
6. This refers to the Spiritus Sanctus College in Brig, founded by the Jesuits in 1662. In 1773 it was dissolved following the prohibition of the Jesuit order. After the ban was lifted, many well-known personalities studied at the Jesuit boarding school, until it was finally nationalized in 1834. Cf. *300 Jahre Kollegium Brig. 1662/63–1962/63. Festschrift zur Jubiläumsfeier der kantonalen Mittelschule des Ober-wallis* (Brig, 1963); Strobel (ed.), *Regularklerus,* pp. 384–407. The lists of pupils still available contain only the names of students who received a prize for their final exams. The archive material therefore doesn't prove whether Kreuzburg attended the college.
7. Cf. Michael Rosenberger, "Levitation," in *LThK,* 3rd ed., vol. 6 (1997), p. 864.
8. Cf. Relazione di Luigi Franceschetti al Santo Uffizio intorno a cose intese ovedute di una persona creduta indemoniata, June 19, 1860; ACDF SO St. St. B 6 m, fol. 52r–65v.
9. The biography of Kreuzburg that follows is based on various sources: Census 1850 and Census 1860; NARA Washington. Passport applications for Peter Kreuzburg and his children; ibid, Death Register of Pau for the year 1889; Archives de la Communauté d'agglomération Pau-Pyrénées, online: http://archives.agglo-pau.fr/ (5/2/2012).

10. Relazione informativa con Sommario, Titolo XI: Avvelenamento; ACDF SO St. St. B 7 c.

11. The feast of the Immaculate Conception (*Immaculata Conceptio*) is celebrated on December 8. Cf. Theodor Maas-Ewerd, "Marienfeste," in *LThK*, 3rd ed., vol. 6 (1997), pp. 1370–74, here p. 1371; Franz Courth, "Unbefleckte Empfängnis Marias," in *LThK*, 3rd ed., vol. 10 (2001), pp. 376–79.

12. Sommario della Relazione informativa, no. XXIII: Esame di Sr. Giuseppa Maria, April 2, 1860; ACDF SO St. St. B 7 c.

13. Sommario della Relazione informativa, no. XXVI: Esame di Sr. Maria Giacinta, March 17, 1860; ACDF SO St. St. B 7 c.

14. There are many references in the literature to this ritual as a sign of penitence, for example in the Barnabite orders. Cf. Wilhelm David Fuhrmann, *Handwörterbuch der christlichen Religions- und Kirchengeschichte*, vol. 1 (Halle, 1826), p. 208; Pierre Hélyot, *P. Hippolyt Hélyots ausführliche Geschichte aller geistlichen und weltlichen Kloster- und Ritterorden führ beyderley Geschlecht*, vol. 4 (Leipzig, 1754), p. 129. The ritual was also used by the Benedictine nuns of the Perpetual Adoration. Cf. Joseph Huguet, *Die Andacht zum allerheiligsten Herzen Jesu in Beispielen. Oder die Vortrefflichkeit der Gebete und Andachtsübungen zu Ehren des allerheiligsten Herzens Jesu, nachgewiesen durch viele Beispiele und Wunder aus dem Leben der Heiligen unserer Zeit* (Regensburg, 1863), pp. 164–66.

15. Cf. Paolo Regio, *La miracolosa vita di S. Francesco di Paola* (Naples, 1581), p. 91; Giuseppe Maria Perrimezzi, *La Vita di San Francesco di Paola, fondatore dell'ordine de' Minimi* (Venice/Milan, 1764), p. 279.

16. Sommario della Relazione informativa, no. XXV: Esame di Sr. Maria Francesca, February 21, 1860; ACDF SO St. St. B 7 c (printed version); ibid., B 6 d, fol. 34r–40r (original).

17. Sommario della Relazione informativa, no. XXV: Esame di Sr. Maria Francesca, February 22, 1860; ACDF SO St. St. B 7 c; ibid., B 6 d, fol. 40r–45r (original).

18. Relazione informativa con Sommario, Titolo XI: Avvelenamento; ACDF SO St. St. B 7 c.

19. Esame di Sr. Agnese Celeste, March 27, 1860; ACDF SO St. St. B 6 e, fol. 52–54. Cf. also Sommario della Relazione informativa, no. XXVII; ibid., B 7 c.

20. On the individual poisons used, see the relevant entries in the various volumes of *Hagers Handbuch*; on the use of quicksilver and atropine, see Eikermann, *Frauen*, here also especially the general remarks on murder by poisoning.

21. The statements from the nuns were very reliable, and corroborated each other in detail, in terms of the poisons used, their preparation, the places where the poisons were mixed, and where the ingredients came from. But regarding the dates of the individual acts of the tragedy, and therefore the chronology of the whole affair, the statements differed quite fundamentally. They mixed up days of the week, confused the sequence of events, and made a jumble of the dates. But this was by no means intentional; it is quite typical of witness statements during police investigations or before a court. Recent neurological research suggests that this is simply an effect of the way human memory works. Places and things are frequently remembered exactly, while dates are easily confused. In recent

historical research, this means that the chronological value of sources reliant on memory, like autobiographical texts and witness statements, is regarded with a certain degree of skepticism. Cf. Fried, *Schleier*, pp. 49—56 and passim.

22. Sommario della Relazione informativa, no. XVI: Esame di Sr. Maria Giuseppa, April 2, 1860; ACDF SO St. St. B 7 c.

23. Sommario della Relazione informativa, no. XXVI: Esame di Sr. Maria Giacinta, March 21, 1861; ACDF SO St. St. B 7 c.

24. Sommario del Ristretto dei Costituti Sr. Maria Veronica Milza, no. VI: Estratto dagli esami di Sr. Maria Ignazia; ACDF SO St. St. B 7 d.

25. Sommario della Relazione informativa, no. XXVII: Esame di Sr. Agnese Celeste, March 27, 1860; ACDF SO St. St. B 7 c.

26. Sommario della Relazione informativa, no. XXVII: Esame di Sr. Maria Giuseppa, March 9, 1860; ACDF SO St. St. B 7 c.

27. Sommario della Relazione informativa, no. XXVI: Esame di Sr. Maria Giacinta, March 21, 1861; ACDF SO St. St. B 7 c.

28. Faiola and the surrounding mountains were notorious in Italy as the home of bands of robbers. See Hermann Reuchlin, "Das italienische Brigantentum," in *Unsere Zeit. Deutsche Revue der Gegenwart. Monatsschrift zum Conversationslexikon* New Series 6 (1870), pp. 145—66; Heinrich Wilhelm Thiersch, *Friedrich Thiersch's Leben.* Vol. 1: 1784—1830 (Leipzig, 1866), p. 247.

29. Sommario della Relazione informativa, no. XXVII: Esame di Sr. Agnese Celeste, March 28, 1860; ACDF SO St. St. B 7 c.

30. Sommario della Relazione informativa, no. XXVII: Esame di Sr. Maria Giuseppa, March 9, 1860; ACDF SO St. St. B 7 c.

31. Sommario del Ristretto dei Costituti relativi a Sr. Maria Veronica Milza, no. VI: Estratto dagli esami di Sr. Maria Ignazia; ACDF SO St. St. B 7 d.

32. Relazione informativa con Sommario, Titolo XI: Avvelenamento; ACDF SO St. St. B 7 c. Subsequent quotations also taken from this text.

33. Sommario del Ristretto dei Costituti relativi a Sr. Maria Veronica Milza, no. VI: Estratto dagli esami di Sr. Maria Ignazia; ACDF SO St. St. B 7 d.

34. Relazione informativa con Sommario, Titolo XI: Avvelenamento; ACDF SO St. St. B 7 c.

35. Sommario della Relazione informativa, no. XVII: Esame di Sr. Agnese Celeste, March 28, 1860; ACDF SO St. St. B 7 c.

36. See Judith 13:8. Judith decapitated the warlord Holofernes to save the besieged people of Israel.

37. Opium was administered to Katharina in two different forms. First she was given opium tincture, then raw opium, shaped into balls—called opium pills in the source material. In both these forms, opium tastes bitter enough to be disgusting. The two ounces of raw opium that Franceschetti was told to procure is a huge amount, given the fact that the daily dosage should be a maximum of 500 milligrams, any higher dose being lethal. Mixing the opium with cassia was a promising strategy, because the pureed flesh of the *cassia fistula* pods was both very pleasant-tasting and the same color as raw opium. Katharina had been given cassia several times as a laxative for her digestive problems, and the cassia made an excellent base for the opium because it was impossible to taste the

drug in this mixture—particularly when it also had tamarind mixed with it. The "sour date" was taken for a "lovely sister" to the cassia, and also had a laxative effect.

38. Sommario del Ristretto dei Costituti relativi a Sr. Maria Veronica Milza, no. VI: Estratto dagli esami di Sr. Maria Ignazia; ACDF SO St. St. B7 d. Subsequent quotations also taken from this text unless otherwise stated.

39. Relazione informativa con Sommario, Titolo XI: Avvelenamento; ACDF SO St. St. B 7 c.

40. Esami del Dr. Marchi, December 3 and 5, 1860; ACDF SO St. St. B 6 m, fol. 81–87.

41. Esame del Dr. Riccardi, December 5, 1860; ACDF SO St. St. B 6 m, fol. 85.

42. In the nineteenth century, illnesses like neuralgia and "weak nerves," which could lead to mental and physical breakdown, were increasingly treated with strong stimulants or sedatives. Chloroform, which was used as a narcotic for the first time in 1847, was used both for these cases and in women's medicine, where it was frequently used to treat menstrual cramps. In many cases, medicinal use turned into addiction, as for Georg Trakl, who turned to chloroform in periods of nervous tension. Cf. Mike Jay, *High Society: Mind-Altering Drugs in History and Culture* (London, 2010); "Report of the Committee on Chloroform," *The Lancet*, July 1864, pp. 49–50.

43. Relazione informativa con Sommario, Titolo XI: Avvelenamento; ACDF SO St. St. B 7 c. Subsequent quotations also taken from this text.

44. Cf. John 13:1–17; Thomas Schäfer, "Fußwaschung," in *LThK*, 2nd ed., vol. 4 (1960), pp. 476–78.

45. Relazione informativa con Sommario, Titolo XI, Sallua's introduction to this charge; ACDF SO St. St. B 7 c.

46. Sommario della Relazione informativa, no. XXVIII: Esame di Sr. Maria Ignazia, March 2, 1860; ACDF SO St. St. B 7 c. Subsequent quotations also taken from this text.

47. Veronica Giuliani lived from 1660 until 1727, and received the stigmata in 1696. It was only after a long struggle, against opponents including the Roman Inquisition, that the Capuchin nun was beatified in 1804, and canonized in 1839. Maria Luisa was drawing a parallel with a female mystic whose recognition from the Church had been the result of a long fight. On Veronica Giuliani, see Ekkart Sauser, "Giuliani," in *BBKL* 12 (1997), p. 1277.

48. *The Lives of S. Veronica Giuliani, Capuchin Nun: And of the Blessed Battista Varani, of the Order of S. Clare, the Saints and Servants of God, Second Series* (London, 1874), pp. 126–27. (Text taken from the original Italian by the Abate Filippo Maria Salvatori, Rome, 1839.)

49. Relazione informativa con Sommario, Titolo XI: Avvelenamento; ACDF SO St. St. B 7 c.

50. Sommario della Relazione informativa, no. XXIX: Esame di Sr. Maria Ignazia, March 7, 1860; ACDF SO St. St. B 7 c.

51. Relazione informativa con Sommario, Titolo XI, from the subtitle: Sr. M. Luisa tenta con veleni ed in altre maniere procura ed influisce nella infermità e morte

di altre religiose; ACDF SO St. St. B 7 c. Subsequent quotations also taken from this text.

52. This was probably Vincenzo Stocchi, who was born in Sinalunga in 1820, entered the Jesuit novitiate, and was ordained as priest in 1851. Stocchi spent three years teaching rhetoric in Senigallia, was later employed in practical pastoral care, and died in 1881. Cf. Sommervogel, *Bibliothèque,* vol. 7, pp. 1582–83.

53. Sommario della Relazione informativa, no. XXVII: Esame di Sr. Maria Giuseppa, March 10, 1860; ACDF SO St. St. B 7 c.

54. Sommario della Relazione informativa, no. XXIX: Esame di Sr. Maria Ignazia, March 5, 1860; ACDF SO St. St. B 7 c.

55. Relazione informativa con Sommario, Titolo XI: Avvelenamento; ACDF SO St. St. B 7 c.

56. Sommario della Relazione informativa, no. XXX: Esame di Sr. Giuseppa Maria, April 3, 1860; ACDF SO St. St. B 7 c.

57. Relazione informativa con Sommario, Titolo XI: Avvelenamento; ACDF SO St. St. B 7 c. Subsequent quotations also taken from this text.

58. Relazione informativa con Sommario, Titolo XIII: Sr. Maria Luisa più volte ha fatto comparire somme di denaro ricevute miracolosamente dal Cielo; ACDF SO St. St. B 7 c. Subsequent quotations also taken from this text.

59. A Scudino is a gold coin from the Duchy of Modena, worth two thirds of a Roman scudo. Cf. Oskar Ludwig Bernhard Wolff, *Neues elegantestes Conversations-Lexikon für Gebildete aus allen Ständen,* vol. 5 (Leipzig, 1842), p. 369.

60. Sommario della Relazione informativa, no. XXXI: Esame di Franceschetti, September 12, 1860; ACDF SO St. St. B 7 c.

61. Relazione informativa con Sommario, Titolo XIV: I Padri Confessori Leziroli e risultano fautori, complici e conniventi; ACDF SO St. St. B 7 c. Subsequent quotations also taken from this text. On the role of the Jesuits as confessors for nuns, see Moos, *Disziplinierung,* pp. 82–86.

62. Relazione informativa con Sommario, Titolo XI: Avvelenamento; ACDF SO St. St. B 7 c.

63. Relazione informativa con Sommario; ACDF SO St. St. B 7 c. Subsequent quotations also taken from this text.

64. Decision by the Assembly of the Cardinals, Feria IV, February 27, 1861; ACDF SO St. St. B 6 w f.

65. Cf. ACDF SO St. St. B 6 z, fol. 1. Bambozzi, who was born around 1795, was director general of all prisons in Rome from 1856. He died in 1863. See Wolf (ed.), *Prosopographie,* pp. 103 and 1609.

66. The assessor's private audience with the pope, and the latter's decision, Feria IV, Febraury 27, 1861; ACDF SO St. St. B 6 w f.

67. Decision by the cardinals, Feria IV, March 6, 1861; ACDF SO St. St. B 6 w f.

CHAPTER SIX *"It Is a Heavenly Liquor"*

1. Decision by the pope, December 6, 1859; ACDF SO St. St. B 6 wf. Fascicolo dei Decreti, Decretum Feria III. Loco IV, December 6, 1859; ibid., B6 wf.

422 · Notes to pages 210—215

Relazione sommaria degli atti principali, Sua Santità ordina che Sr. M. Luisa sia traslocata in altro monastero; ibid., B 6 eı. The convent of Purificazione was a former nunnery with a church attached. The Roman nobleman Mario Ferro Orsini bought the land from the Carthusian monks of Santa Maria degli Angeli alle Terme, and had the church and convent built. The sisters of Saint Clara of Assisi moved in in 1600. Cf. "Purificazione della B. V. Maria. Congregazione di monache," in Moroni, *Dizionario* 56 (1852), p. 99.

2. Ristretto dei Costituti di Sr. Maria Luisa con Sommario, Parte I: Atti spontanei emessi da Sr. M. Luisa durante la sua dimora nell monastero della Purificazione; ACDF SO St. St. B 6 u. Cf. also Esami di Sr. Maria Luisa, March 20 and 26, 1860; ibid., B 6 f. Subsequent quotations also taken from this text unless otherwise stated.

3. Costituto di Sr. Maria Luisa, June 11, 1860; ACDF SO St. St. B 6 n, fol. 1—4.

4. Cf. ACDF SO St. St. B 6 w l.

5. The source material doesn't specify which feast of the Madonna this was. The following feasts are likely candidates: Solemnity of Mary, Mother of God (January 1); the Feast of the Annunciation (March 25); the Feast of the Assumption (August 15); the Holy Name of the Blessed Virgin Mary (today on September 12; then on September 8); the Immaculate Conception (December 8). The first of the churches mentioned, San Silvestro, is on the Quirinal Hill and was most recently renewed under Pope Gregory XIII. San Quirico is at 31, Via di Tor de' Conti, and is dedicated to the three-year-old Quiricus and his mother, Julitta, who suffered martyrs' deaths under Emperor Diocletian. Cf. Alfred von Reumont, *Römische Briefe von einem Florentiner. vol. 3: Neue Römische Briefe 1837—1838, Erster Teil* (Leipzig, 1844), pp. 386—87.

6. Cf. Morichini, *Istituti,* vol. 2, pp. 88—89; http://pallottinespirit.org/charism/congregational-history/ (5/2/2012).

7. "Si dotano 3 zitelle povere ogni anno, una dalla collegiata, l'altra dalla confraternita del ss. Rosario, la 3a dalla confraternita della SS. Annunziata e del Carmine." "Viterbo," in Moroni, *Dizionario* 102 (1861), pp. 3—421, here p. 65.

8. Archpriest Pastacaldi was secretary to Cardinal Vincenzo Macchi. Cf. *Giornale arcadico di scienze, lettere ed arti,* vol. 68 (Rome 1836), p. 366.

9. The Basilica lies on the street of the same name in Rione Celio, halfway between the Colosseum and the Piazza San Giovanni in Laterano. The buildings also include a convent, occupied by Augustine canonesses since 1560. The church and convent are known for the impressive frescoes depicting the legend of Saint Sylvester. See Maria Giulia Barberini, *I Santi Quattro Coronati a Roma* (Rome, 1989).

10. Ristretto dei Costituti di Sr. Maria Luisa, Part I, summary of Maria Luisa's own handwritten report; ACDF SO St. St. B 6 u. Subsequent quotations also taken from this text.

11. Cf. Feldbauer, *Geschichte*, pp. 30—36; Traniello and Sofri, *Weg.*

12. Cf. Behringer, *Hexen*; Schwaiger (ed.), *Teufelsglaube.*

13. On impurity through menstruation, see Angenendt, *Pollutio*, pp. 52—93.

14. Cf. Müller, *Dogmatik*, pp. 680—713.

15. Fascicolo dei Decreti, Decretum Feria IV, May 2, 1860; ACDF SO St. St. B 6 w f. Buon Pastore lay on the Lungara, and was founded by a Barefoot Carmelite in the first half of the seventeenth century. It was known as La Scalette. In 1838, this correctional institution for women was handed over to the Sisters of the Good Shepherd (Religieuses de la Congrégation de Notre-Dame-de-Charité du Bon Pasteur d'Angers). They took in those who entered freely and showed the will to reform. Women whose husbands wanted them locked away, to which the cardinal vicar had to give his assent, also found themselves in La Scalette. However, the institute also served as a prison for women under investigation. "A stay in this house is supposed to work wonders, and the Good Shepherd sets many lost sheep back on the right track. In Rome, many touching stories are told about it. Apart from those women who are sent there, they also take in those who go of their own accord and wish to live apart from society. Both are released when, as a result of their good conduct, it appears suitable. The way of life there is semi-nunlike: retreats; prayer and song; work, the profit from which the women keep; readings during the midday and evening meals. Talking is only permitted during leisure hours. Only visits from fathers, mothers, guardians or husbands are received. Most pay an annuity, which varies according to their circumstances. The nuns are all French; Italians would scarcely do so well. The number of these is twelve; the penitents number up to 70. It is said that the nuns of Notre Dame de Charité will be charged with the rest of the penitentiaries and correctional facilities for women; judging by the successes in this limited area to date, such a measure can only be for the best." Alfred von Reumont, *Römische Briefe von einem Florentiner.* Vol. 3: *Neue Römische Briefe 1837–1838, Erster Teil* (Leipzig, 1844), pp. 188–89. See also "Conservatorio di S. Croce della Penitenza alla Longara detto del Buon Pastore," in Moroni, *Dizionario* 17 (1842), pp. 20–21.
16. Costituto di Sr. Maria Luisa, June 11, 1860; ACDF SO St. St. B 6 n.
17. Paolo Mignardi was born in 1790 in Macerata, and professed his vows in 1842 after entering the Jesuit order. He died in 1860. See Mendizábal, *Catalogus,* p.46.
18. Costituto di Sr. Maria Luisa, June 12, 1860; ACDF SO St. St. B 6 n.
19. Costituto di Sr. Maria Luisa, June 13, 1860; ACDF SO St. St. B 6 n.
20. Costituto di Sr. Maria Luisa, June 14, 1860; ACDF SO St. St. B 6 n. Subsequent quotations also taken from this text.
21. Louise Beck was born in 1822, and according to her own account had visions of saints, "poor souls," and her guardian angel even as a child. Her stigmata appeared in Easter week 1846, and she then sought help from the Redemptorist provincial, Franz von Bruchmann, who became her spiritual guide. She died in 1879. See Weiß, *Redemptoristen,* pp. 522–77, 649–52, and 668–71.
22. Franz Ritter von Bruchmann was born in 1798. He entered the Redemptorists in 1831, after his wife, Juliane, died in October 1830. They had not been married long. Bruchmann was provincial of the Bavarian Redemptorists from 1814 to 1865, and died in 1867. See Weiß, *Redemptoristen,* pp. 573–75.
23. Ristretto dei Costituti di Sr. Maria Luisa, Parte II: Si riportano i detti e i fatti deposti ex se dall'Inquisita durante i costituti; ACDF SO St. St. B 6 u.

24. Ristretto dei Costituti di Sr. Maria Luisa, Parte II, closing summary; ACDF SO St. St. B 6 u.

25. Ristretto dei Costituti di Sr. Maria Luisa, Parte IV: Risposte; ACDF SO St. St. B 6 u. Subsequent quotations also taken from this text unless otherwise stated.

26. Ristretto con Sommario, Sommario dei Costituti di Sr. Maria Luisa, no. III: Costituto di Sr. Maria Luisa, June 24, 1860; ACDF SO St. St. B 6 u.

27. Ristretto con Sommario, Sommario dei Costituti di Sr. Maria Luisa, no. X: Costituto di Sr. Maria Luisa, August 22, 1860; ACDF SO St. St. B 6 u.

28. Ristretto con Sommario, Sommario dei Costituti di Sr. Maria Luisa, no. II: Costituto di Sr. Maria Luisa, June 21, 1860; ACDF SO St. St. B 6 u.

29. 2 Kings 4:32–37.

30. Ristretto con Sommario, Sommario dei Costituti di Sr. Maria Luisa, no. VI: Costituto di Sr. Maria Luisa, July 20, 1860; ACDF SO St. St. B 6 u.

31. Peter Morsbach, "Lactatio," in *Marienlexikon* 3 (1991), p. 702; Schreiner, *Maria. Jungfrau,* pp. 78–213.

32. See for example Otto von Corvin, *Der Pfaffenspiegel. Historische Denkmale des Fanatismus in der römisch-katholischen Kirche* (Leipzig, 1845); Manuel Borutta, *Antikatholizismus. Deutschland und Italien im Zeitalter der europäischen Kulturkämpfe* (Göttingen, 2nd ed., 2011), pp. 155–218.

33. Cf. Wipplinger and Amann, *Missbrauch,* p. 29. It has been impossible to prove statistically whether sexual abuse was more common in institutions governed by the Catholic Church than in society in general. Cf. Christian Pfeiffer, "Drei Promille aller Täter. Eine Außenansicht," in *Süddeutsche Zeitung,* March 15, 2010.

34. Klemm, *Mißbrauch,* pp. 12–23, here p. 18.

35. Criteria according to Wipplinger and Amann, *Missbrauch,* p. 32.

36. Cf. Klemm, *Mißbrauch,* p. 30; Richter-Appelt, *Folgen,* p. 230.

37. Cf. Richard Utz, "'Total Institutions,' 'Greedy Institutions.' Verhaltensstruktur und Situation des sexuellen Missbrauchs," in Marion Baldus and Richard Utz (eds.), *Sexueller Missbrauch in pädagogischen Kontexten. Faktoren. Interventionen. Perspektiven* (Wiesbaden, 2011), pp. 51–76. See also the entries in Ammicht Quinn et al. (eds.), *Verrat.*

38. Ristretto con Sommario, Sommario dei Costituti di Sr. Maria Luisa, no. I: Costituto di Sr. Maria Luisa, June 26, 1860, und Ristretto dei Costituti di Sr. Maria Luisa, Parte II; ACDF SO St. St. B 6 u.

39. José Doz was born in 1738 in Tarazona, Spain, and entered the Society of Jesus in 1752. When the Jesuits were expelled from Spain, Doz was deported to Italy, where he died in 1813. See Sommervogel, *Bibliothèque,* vol. 9, p. 242.

40. Luigi Santinelli was born in 1760 in Sant'Angelo in Vado (Pesaro). He entered the Society of Jesus and professed his vows in 1824, and died in Rome in 1842. See Mendizábal, *Catalogus,* p. 22.

41. Ristretto dei Costituti di Sr. Maria Luisa, Parte IV; ACDF SO St. St. B 6 u.

42. Ristretto con Sommario, Sommario dei Costituti di Sr. Maria Luisa, no. I: Costituto di Sr. Maria Luisa, June 26, 1860; ACDF SO St. St. B 6 u.

43. Agustín Monzon (sometimes written Monzón, Monton, or Monçon) was born

in 1750, and began his novitiate with the Jesuits in 1765 in Spain. After the order was prohibited there, he was sent to Italy. He professed his vows there in 1814. He wrote the "Vita del servo Dio P. Giuseppe M. Pignatelli," though this was only published posthumously in Rome, in 1833. Monzon died in 1824. See Sommervogel, *Bibliothèque,* vol. 5, pp. 1203–4.

44. Brunelli may have been an ex-Jesuit who became a secular priest after the Society of Jesus was banned. It is unlikely that this was the canon Giovanni Brunelli, who worked as the archivist in the Ospedale di Santo Spirito from 1755 to 1786. Cf. Giuseppe Flajani, *Methodo di medicare alcune malattie* (Rome, 1786), p. 31. Francesco Brunelli, who took up office as the Father of Santa Maria del Carmine and San Giuseppe in 1822, is also a very unlikely possibility, as he probably rejoined his order when the ban was revoked in 1814. Cf. *Notizie per l'anno* 1822, p. 195.

45. Ristretto con Sommario, Sommario dei Costituti di Sr. Maria Luisa, no. I: Costituto di Sr. Maria Luisa, June 26, 1860, ACDF SO St. St. B 6 u.

46. Ristretto con Sommario, Sommario dei Costituti di Sr. Maria Luisa, no. VIII: Costituto di Sr. Maria Luisa, June 28, 1860; ACDF SO St. St. B 6 u.

47. Ristretto con Sommario, Sommario dei Costituti di Sr. Maria Luisa, no. VIII: Costituto di Sr. Maria Luisa, July 28, 1860, Fogli manoscritti consegnati in sudetto costituto; ACDF SO St. St. B 6 u.

48. In the Italian original, the clitoris here is referred to as "membro" (member).

49. In the Italian original, "vagina" is also referred to as "membro."

50. Ristretto con Sommario, Sommario dei Costituti di Sr. Maria Luisa, no. VIII: Costituto di Sr. Maria Luisa, July 24, 1860; ACDF SO St. St. B 6 u.

51. Ristretto dei Costituti di Sr. Maria Luisa, Parte IV; ACDF SO St. St. B 6 u.

52. Ristretto con Sommario, Sommario dei Costituti di Sr. Maria Luisa, no. VII: Costituto di Sr. Maria Luisa, July 24, 1860; ACDF SO St. St. B 6 u.

53. Ristretto con Sommario, Sommario dei Costituti di Sr. Maria Luisa, no. VIII: Costituto di Sr. Maria Luisa, July 28, 1860, Fogli manoscritti consegnati in sudetto costituto; ACDF SO St. St. B 6 u.

54. Ristretto con Sommario, Sommario dei Costituti di Sr. Maria Luisa, no. IX: Costituto di Sr. Maria Luisa, August 14, 1860, Fogli manoscritti consegnati in sudetto costituto; ACDF SO St. St. B 6 u.

55. Costituti di Sr. Maria Luisa, September 18, 1860; ACDF SO St. St. B 6 o, fol. 116.

56. Ristretto dei Costituti di Sr. Maria Luisa, Parte IV; ACDF SO St. St. B 6 u. Ristretto con Sommario, Sommario dei Costituti di Sr. Maria Luisa, no. IV: Costituto di Sr. Maria Luisa, July 3, 1860, and no. V: Costituto di Sr. Maria Luisa, July 6, 1860; ibid., B 6 u. Subsequent quotations also taken from this text.

57. Cipriani was born in 1812 and ordained in 1838. He became an *advocatus reorum* in 1843. See Boutry, Souverain, p. 680; Wolf (ed.), *Prosopographie,* pp. 330–31.

CHAPTER SEVEN *"That Good Padre Has Spoiled the Work of God"*

1. Cardinals' decision, Feria IV, February 27, 1861; ACDF SO St. St. B 6 wf.

2. See the Ristretto dei Costituti del P. Giuseppe Leziroli, Parte I: Sulla venera-

tion e culto della fondatrice Sr. Maria Agnese Firrao; ACDF SO St. St. B 7 e. Prov. Rom. Summ. Vitae 1846–1889, p. 559; ARSI. See also *Catalogus Provinciae Romanae Societatis Iesu* . . . (Rome, 1844–1875); Mendizábal, *Catalogus,* p. 88; Sommervogel, *Bibliothèque,* vol. 4, p. 1771.

3. Ristretto con Sommario dei Costituti del P. Giuseppe Leziroli, October 1861; ACDF SO St. St. B 7 e. Subsequent quotations also taken from this text.

4. Saint Stanislaus Kostka was born in 1550. At the age of fifteen, he ran away from home to Vienna, to join the Jesuit order. In the novitiate he distinguished himself by being joyful, pious, and striving for perfection. He died in 1568, probably from the exertions of his escape. He was beatified in 1670 and canonized in 1726. Leziroli probably praised this Jesuit saint particularly highly to the nuns. See Bernhard Stasiewski, "Stanislaus Kostka," in *LThK,* 2nd ed., vol. 9 (1964), pp. 1017–18.

5. Ristretto dei Costituti del P. Giuseppe Leziroli, Parte I: Sulla veneratione e culto della fondatrice Sr. Maria Agnese Firrao; ACDF SO St. St. B 7 e. Subsequent quotations also taken from this text.

6. Appendice al Ristretto informativo, Esami di Beckx, carried out by Monaco La Valletta, March 1, 5, 8, and 14, 1861; ACDF SO St. St. B 7 f and Costituti Peters, ibid., B 6 z, fol. 2r–9v.

7. Appendice al Ristretto informativo, Qualifica del Volume manoscritto "Sulle memorie della Vita di Sr. Maria Agnese di Gesù" del Rmo Maestro Girolamo Priori, October 20, 1861; ACDF SO St. St. B 7 f.

8. Girolamo Priori lived from 1810 to 1883. See Boutry, *Souverain,* pp. 737–38; Wolf (ed.), *Prosopographie,* pp. 1220–22.

9. Cardinal Giuseppe Pecci was born in 1776. He came from Gubbio, where he was made a canon in 1800, a vicar general in 1821, and the administrator of the bishopric in 1839. Pecci (no relation to Cardinal Gioacchino Pecci, later Pope Leo XIII) was in Gubbio throughout Firrao's exile, working in important canonical offices. He died in 1855. See Weber, *Kardinäle,* vol. 2, p. 503 and elsewhere.

10. Interventions by Cardinal Giuseppe Pecci, the bishop of Gubbio, Cardinal Gabriele della Genga, the nephew of Pope Leo XII, and Cardinal Vicar Patrizi were all unsuccessful.

11. Cf. Anderson, *Piety,* p. 702.

12. Ristretto dei Costituti del P. Giuseppe Leziroli, Parte II: Circa l'affettata santità di Sr. M. Luisa, massime erronee ed altri addebiti; ACDF SO St. St. B 7 e. Subsequent quotations also taken from this text.

13. Sommario del Ristretto di P. Leziroli, no. IV: Costituto di P. Leziroli, June 13, 1861; ACDF SO St. St. B 7 e.

14. Cf. Elke Bayer, "Sieben Schmerzen Mariens," in *Marienlexikon* 6 (1994), pp. 157–58.

15. Cf. Schreiner, *Maria. Jungfrau,* pp. 95–100; Karl Woschitz, "Schmerzensmutter," in *Marienlexikon* 6 (1994), pp. 28–29.

16. Sommario del Ristretto di P. Leziroli, no. V: Costituto di P. Leziroli, June 14 and 15, 1861; ACDF SO St. St. B 7 e.

17. Ristretto dei Costituti del P. Leziroli, Parte III: Attentato avvelenamento; ACDF SO St. St. B 7 e.

18. Ristretto dei Costituti del P. Leziroli, conclusion: Il P. Leziroli si rende a pieno confesso su tutti i punti delle conclusioni fi scali e domanda perdono; ACDF SO St. St. B7 e. Subsequent quotations also taken from this text.

19. "Un mostro d'iniquità." Relazione informativa con Sommario, Titolo VI: Affettata santità, Sallua's introduction; ACDF SO St. St. B 7 c.

20. Ristretto con Sommario dei Costituti sostenuti dall'Inquisita Abbadessa Sr. Maria Veronica Milza, September 1861; ACDF SO St. St. B7 d.

21. Sonnino is a town in the Latina province in Latium. Robbers plied their trade in the surrounding area. Among them was the famous Gasparone of Sonnino, who was an uncle of the secretary of state to Pope Pius IX, Cardinal Giacomo Antonelli. Cf. Aurelio Bianchi-Giovini, *Il Diario di Burcardo. Quadro dei costume della Corte di Roma. Aggiuntavi la Storia del Legno della Croce. Una biografi a del cardinale Antonelli ed altri documenti analoghi* (Florence, 1861), p. 76; Hermann Reuchlin, "Das italienische Brigantentum," in *Unsere Zeit. Deutsche Revue der Gegenwart. Monatsschrift zum Conversationslexikon,* New Series 6 (1870), pp. 145–66.

22. The church of Santa Pudenziana lies near Santa Maria Maggiore, in what was then the Via di S. Pudenziana and is now the Via Urbana. The convent next to it belonged to the Cistertians and later the Augustine nuns B.M.V. (*Canonichesse regolari di S. Agostino*). It was the site of the house of S. Pudente, a Roman senator who, legend has it, was converted by Saint Peter. In AD 164, the house was converted by Pope Pius I, first into an oratory and then into a church. It did not attain its present appearance until 1598. Cf. Anon, *Corografia di Roma, ovvero descrizione: e cenni istorici de suoi monumenti colla guida ai medesimi mercé di linee stradali, corredata di elenchi* (Rome, 1846), p. 28; Armellini, *Chiese,* pp. 565–69.

23. Ristretto dei Costituti di Sr. Maria Veronica, Parte I: Sulla veneratione e culto della fondatrice Sr. Maria Agnese Firrao; ACDF SO St. St. B 7 d. Subsequent quotations also taken from this text.

24. Giustiniani was born in 1769 and became the titular bishop of Tyrus in 1817. He became bishop of Imola in 1826, and a cardinal in the same year. He died in 1843. See Boutry, *Souverain,* pp. 393–95; Wolf (ed.), *Prosopographie,* pp. 701–5.

25. Sommario del Ristretto della Abbadessa, no. I: Documenti sull'espressa proibizione fatta alla Firrao di mai più avere comunicazione colle pretese sue fi glie. Documenti che mostrano non essere mai stata né revocata questa proibizione, né tollerata alcuna corrispondenza; ACDF SO St. St. B 7 d.

26. Ristretto dei Costituti di Sr. Maria Veronica, Parte II: Sull'affettata santità e doni straordinari di Sr. Maria Luisa Ridolfi ; ACDF SO St. St. B 7 d. Subsequent quotations also taken from this text.

27. Esame della Priora di San Pasquale, October 17, 1859; ACDF SO St. St. B 6 a, fol. 52r.

28. Esame di Msgr. Hohenlohe, April 19, 1860; ACDF SO St. St. B 6 m, fol. 7f.

29. Sommario del Ristretto della Abbadessa, no. IV: Risposte sull'ingresso del P. Peters in clausura, undated; ACDF SO St. St. B 7 d. Subsequent quotations also taken from this text.

30. Sommario del Ristretto della Abbadessa, no. V: Risposta sulla storia dei pretesi veleni attribuiti ad illusioni diaboliche, undated; ACDF SO St. St. B 7 d. Subsequent quotations also taken from this text.

31. Ristretto dei Costituti relativi a Sr. Maria Veronica, Parte II, conclusion; ACDF SO St. St. B 7 d. Subsequent quotations also taken from this text unless otherwise stated.

32. Sommario del Ristretto della Abbadessa, no. VII: Risposta ad una contestazione fiscale sul segreto imposto dai PP. Confessori; ACDF SO St. St. B 7 d.

CHAPTER EIGHT *"During These Acts I Never Ceased My Inner Prayer"*

1. Costituti del P. Peters; ACDF SO St. St. B 6 y and B 6 z.

2. Ristretto con Sommario relativo ai Costituti del P. Giuseppe Peters, Parte I: Sulla veneratione e culto della fondatrice Sr. Maria Agnese Firrao; ACDF SO St. St. B 6 i.

3. On the networks around the Curia, see Wolfgang Reinhard, *Freunde und Kreaturen. Verflechtung als Konzept zur Erforschung historischer Führungsgruppen. Römische Oligarchie um 1600* (Munich, 1979).

4. There is no modern biography of Kleutgen with sufficient historical as well as theological aspirations. Deufel's 1976 study, *Kirche,* provides much important information, but has also been heavily criticized for its errors. Cf. Walter, "Zu einem neuen Buch," pp.318–56, and Schwedt, "Rez. Zu Deufel," pp. 264–69. But read alongside the corrections made by Peter Walter in particular, the book can certainly be useful. See also Belz, *Michelis,* pp. 46–53; Finkenzeller, *Kleutgen,* pp. 318–44; Lakner, *Kleutgen,* pp. 183–202 (still worth reading); Langhorst, *Jugendleben* (on Kleutgen's youth); Schäfer, *Kontroverse,* pp. 37–53; Walter, *Philosophie,* pp. 145–75 (essential); Wolf (ed.), *Prosopographie,* pp. 806–17. There are several different dates given for Kleutgen's birth, probably because his gravestone has it as September 11, 1811. According to the church books of the former Dominican monastery in Dortmund, Joseph Wilhelm was born on April 9, 1811, the son of the merchant Wilhelm Kleutgen. The name "Carl" was added subsequently. Erzbistumsarchiv Paderborn Matrikelbestand der Dortmunder Propsteipfarrei St. Johannes Baptist I/5. In spite of intensive research, no picture of Kleutgen has yet come to light.

5. Blaschke, *19. Jahrhundert,* pp. 38–75; Lill, *Ultramontanismus,* pp. 76–94; Wolf, *Kirchengeschichte,* pp. 92–121. Subsequent information also taken from this last text.

6. Johann Sebastian Drey was born in 1777. He was professor of apologetics, dogmatic theology, and the history of dogma at the Katholische Landes-Universitat of Ellwangen, which existed for only a few years before being integrated into the University of Tübingen. In 1819, Drey cofounded the journal *Tübinger Theologische Quartalschrift.* He died in 1853. See Abraham P. Kustermann, "Drey," in *LThK,* 3rd ed., vol. 3 (1995), p. 373.

7. Hermes was born in 1775 and became professor of dogmatic theology in Münster in 1807. He moved to Bonn in 1820, and died in 1831. See Hubert Wolf,

"Hermes, Georg," in *RGG*, 4th ed., vol. 3 (2000), p. 1664. On Hermesianism, see Nichols, *Conversation*, pp. 23–41 (a chapter significantly entitled "A Kantian Beginning: Georg Hermes"); Hubert Wolf, "Hermesianismus," in *RGG*, 4th ed., vol. 3 (2000), pp. 1667–68. On Hermes's indexing, see Schwedt, *Urteil.*

8. On the dating of this, see Walter, *Philosophie*, pp. 146–47.
9. Kleutgen, *Memorandum*, pp. 5–11, here pp. 7–8.
10. Kleutgen, *Schulen*, p. 193; Kleutgen, *Theologie*, vol. I, pp. 18–19. On Kleutgen's role in the rise of new scholasticism, see Marschler, *Scheeben*, pp. 459–84; Steck, *Kleutgen*, pp. 288–305; Walter, *Philosophie*; Weiß, *Moral.*
11. Cf. Lakner, *Kleutgen*, p. 200.
12. Cf. Finkenzeller, *Kleutgen*, p. 322.
13. Cf. Wolf (ed.), *Prosopographie*, pp. 806–17 (list of votums).
14. Cf. Lakner, *Kleutgen*, p. 192.
15. Walter, "Zu einem neuen Buch," p. 320.
16. Kleutgen to Franz Hülskamp, May 16, 1868; quoted in Deufel, *Kirche*, pp. 92–93.
17. Cf. Deufel, *Kirche*, p. 182, note 22, and pp. 91–93. This "psychologizing" view drew the criticism of Walters at the time, who wanted to see more consideration of the historical context in which Kleutgen was operating. Cf. Walter, "Zu einem neuen Buch," pp. 319–20.
18. On the new scholastic understanding of miracles, cf. Albert Lang, *Fundamentaltheologie*, 2 vols. (Munich, 1962), here vol. 1: *Die Sendung Christi, II. Hauptstück: Das Problem der übernatürlichen Offenbarung*, Chapter 3: "Das Wunder als das entscheidende Offenbarungskriterium," pp. 111–31. On the significance of Mariology in Kleutgen's theology, see Haacke, *Maria*, pp. 97–110.
19. Cf. Burkhard Peter, "On the History of Dissociative Identity Disorders in Germany: The Doctor Justinus Kerner and the Girl from Orlach, or Possession as an 'Exchange of the Self,'" in *Journal of Clinical and Experimental Hypnosis* 59 (2011), pp. 82–102.
20. Cf. for example Blaise Pascal's caustic criticism of the probabilism and laxism of Jesuit morality in his "Lettres provinciales" of 1656.
21. Costituto di P. Kleutgen, March 11, 1861; ACDF SO St. St. B 6 z.
22. Sommario del Ristretto di P. Peters, no. II: Fogli originali consegnati nel Costituto, March 18, 1861; ACDF SO St. St. B 6 gı. The printed version: ibid., B 6 i. Subsequent quotations also taken from this text.
23. Sommario del Ristretto di P. Peters, no. III: Fogli originali consegnati nel Costituto, March 26, 1861; ACDF SO St. St. B 6 i. Subsequent quotations also taken from this text.
24. The "Honorable House of gate de' Specchi" is the home of the congregation of lay brothers founded by Francesca Romana. Cf. Oblate di S. Francesca Romana dette di Tor de' Specchi, in Moroni, *Dizionario* 30 (1845), pp. 196–203; Friedrich Wilhelm Bautz, "Franziska von Rom," in *BBKL* 2 (1990), pp. 113–14; http://www.tordespecchi.it (10/8/2013).
25. The Teresians, also called Barefoot Nuns, were a Carmelite order founded by Teresa of Avila in Spain, in 1562. Cf. *Pierer's Universal-Lexikon*, vol. 17 (Altenburg, 1863), p. 494.

26. Van Everbroeck was born in 1784, and became professor of canon law, liturgy, and Chaldean, and later church history, at the Collegio Romano in 1825. In 1856 he was made a theologian of the Apostolic Penitentiary, and he died in 1863. See Wolf (ed.), *Prosopographie*, pp. 534–36.

27. Camillo Tarquini was born in 1810, and was professor of church law at the Collegio Romano from 1852 to 1869, and again from 1871 to 1873. He was made a cardinal in 1873, and died in 1874. See ibid., pp. 534–36.

28. Ludwig I, the son of Maximilian I Joseph and Princess Auguste Wilhelmine Maria von Hessen-Darmstadt, was born in 1786 and crowned king of Bavaria in 1825. He died in 1868. See Andreas Kraus, "Ludwig I." in *NDB* 15 (1987), pp. 367–74.

29. Princess Karoline Friederike Wilhelmine was Maximilian I Joseph's second wife, and became the first queen of Bavaria in 1806, after Bavaria had been declared a kingdom. The marriage produced eight children. The marriage contract stipulated that Karoline did not have to give up her protestant faith, and would receive her own protestant preacher. She died in 1841 and was interred beside her husband in Munich's Theatinerkirche. The protests against the unworthiness of her burial—the entire Catholic clergy appeared in secular clothes—finally led her stepson Ludwig I to soften his attitude toward the protestant church in Bavaria. See Manfred Berger, "Karoline Friederike Wilhelmine von Baden," in *BBKL* 23 (2004), pp. 199–207.

30. Cf. Garhammer, *Regierung*, pp. 84–90.

31. Cf. Deufel, *Kirche*, pp. 259–60.

32. Ristretto con Sommario relativo ai Costituti del P. Giuseppe Peters, Parte I: Sulla veneratione e culto della fondatrice Sr. Maria Agnese Firrao; ACDF SO St. St. B 6 i.

33. Costituto di P. Peters, March 28, 1861; ACDF SO St. St. B 6 z.

34. Sommario del Ristretto di P. Peters, no. V: Fogli consegnati nel Costituto, April 16, 1861; ACDF SO St. St. B 6 i. Subsequent quotations also taken from this text.

35. On scholastic disputation, see Uwe Gerber, "Disputatio," in *TRE* 9 (1982), pp. 13–15; Hanspeter Marti, "Disputatio," in Gert Ueding (ed.), *Historisches Wörterbuch der Rhetorik*, vol. 2 (Tübingen, 1994), pp. 866–80.

36. Ristretto con Sommario relativo ai Costituti del P. Giuseppe Peters, Parte I: Sulla veneratione e culto della fondatrice Sr. Maria Agnese Firrao; ACDF SO St. St. B 6 i. Subsequent quotations also taken from this text.

37. Ristretto con Sommario relativo ai Costituti del P. Giuseppe Peters, Parte II: Risposte sulla santità affettata di M. Luisa e sugli altri addebiti relativi; ACDF SO St. St. B 6 i. Subsequent quotations also taken from this text.

38. Sommario del Ristretto di P. Peters, no. I: Fogli consegnati dall'Inquisito P. Peters nel Costituto, March 12, 1861; ACDF SO St. St. B 6 i.

39. On the so-called "processiones ad intra" cf. the tract on the Trinity in Perrone, *Praelectiones Theologicae*. Vol. 4: *De Deo uno et trino*, pp. 209–360.

40. On the qualities of God, His unity, His knowledge, and will, as well as His love and His aim and the connection between these qualities, see the "Tractatus de

deo eiusque attributis," in Perrone, *Praelectiones Theologicae*. Vol. 4: *De Deo uno et trino*, pp. 5–208.

41. The theology of creation reflects how we can understand the creed of God as "creator of heaven and earth," as the Niceno-Constantinopolitan Creed acknowledges Him to be. Cf. Perrone, *Praelectiones Theologicae*. Vol. 5: *De Deo creatore*.

42. Soteriology is the theory of the salvation of mankind through Jesus Christ. The theory originally made a unity from Christ the man and his deeds, in a biblical and patristic sense. In late scholasticism, the creation of the dogma of Christology, the theory of Jesus as a man, caused a separation between Christology and Soteriology. Cf. Müller, *Dogmatik*, p. 372. Giovanni Perrone did not give Soteriology its own tract, merely touching upon the question in his Christology tract "de incarnatione," where he presents Jesus Christ as the true Messiah in an apologetic debate "adversus hebraeos." Cf. Perrone, *Praelectiones Theologicae*. Vol. 6: *De incarnatione et cultu sanctorum*, pp. 5–104.

43. The working of God in the soul is addressed in new scholastic dogma as part of the theory of grace, and the question of how God's grace works in man. Cf. Perrone, *Praelectiones Theologicae*. Vol. 7: *De gratia christi*.

44. Sommario del Ristretto di P. Peters, no. VI: Fogli consegnati nel Costituto, April 22, 1861; ACDF SO St. St. B 6 i.

45. Nothing further is known about Alessandra Carli; Archivio della Cattedrale di Comacchio, Stato d'anime della città di Comacchio del 1826–27, fol. 41. On her father's business, see *Notizie per l'anno 1835*, p. 263; *Notizie per l'anno 1845*, p. 355.

46. Costituti di P. Peters, no. N: Fogli consegnati nel Costituto, April 23, 1861; ACDF SO St. St. B 6 z.

47. Cf. Denzler, *Lust*.

48. See Götz von Olenhusen, *Klerus*, pp. 236–37 and elsewhere; Klee, *Grundriß*, pp. 90–94, here p. 92.

49. See the relevant explanations in the "Tractatus IX: De sexto praecepto Decalogi" by Alphons of Liguori, *Homo Apostolicus instructus in sua vocatione ad audiendas confessiones sive praxis et instructio confessariorum* (Turin, 1870), p. 178. On Alphons of Liguori and his reception, see Weiß, *Moral*.

50. Thomas Aquinas, *Summa Theologiae* IIa–IIae, Quaestio 154, article 4.

51. Ristretto con Sommario relativo ai Costituti del P. Giuseppe Peters, Parte II; ACDF SO St. St. B 6 i.

52. The veneration of the heart of the Virgin Mary is closely connected to the Sacred Heart of Jesus. The Oratorian Johannes Eudes began celebrating a feast of the Heart of Mary in addition to the Heart of Jesus feast in his order in 1646. Pius VII gave it his official approbation at the start of the nineteenth century, and set the date for it as August 22, the octave day of the Assumption. Cf. Karl-Heinrich Bieritz, *Das Kirchenjahr. Feste, Gedenk- und Feiertage in Geschichte und Gegenwart* (Munich, 1991), p. 150. In the Sant'Ambrogio period, Rome officially recognized a liturgical veneration of the Heart of Mary in 1805. This was then instated in all the institutions that requested it. See Theodor Maas-Ewerd, "Herz Mariä. I. Verehrung," in *LThK*, 3rd ed., vol. 5 (1996), pp. 60–61, here

p. 60. On the dedication to the immaculate heart of Mary, see also Franz Courth, "Marianische Gebetsformen." Die Herz-Mariä-Weihe," in Wolfgang Beinert and Heinrich Petri (ed.), *Handbuch der Marienkunde*, vol. 1 (Regensburg, 2nd ed., 1997), pp. 550–52.

53. The theory of the connection between religion and sexuality is put forward by the psychologist and protestant theologian Christina Bachmann, among others. Cf. Christina Bachmann, *Religion und Sexualität. Die Sehnsucht nach Transzendenz* (Stuttgart, 1994), here pp. 118 and 226. On the relationship between religion, sexuality, and ecstasy, cf. Klaus Peter Köpping, "Ekstase," in Christoph Wulf (ed.), *Vom Menschen. Handbuch Historischer Anthropologie* (Weinheim and Basel, 1997), pp. 548–68; Wunibald Müller, *Ekstase. Sexualität und Spiritualität* (Mainz, 1992).

54. Costituto di P. Peters, May 28, 1861; ACDF SO St. St. B 6 z.

55. Costituto di P. Peters, June 1, 1861; ACDF SO St. St. B 6 z.

56. Pierre Dens, *Theologia moralis et dogmatica*, vol. 4 (Dublin, 1832), no. 297 I. See also "Baiser," in Abbé Migne, *Encyclopédie Théologique*, vol. 31 (Paris, 1849), p. 293: "Kisses . . . on unusual parts of the body, for example on the chest, the bosom, or *more columbarum* [in the manner of doves], in which one puts the tongue into the mouth, are to be censured. They are viewed as an expression of lustful intentions, or at least as leading to a serious danger of lust, meaning one cannot save oneself from the mortal sin."

57. Otto Best, "Zungenkuss," in Best, *Lexikon*, p. 254; Elberfeld, *Geschichte*.

58. Costituti di P. Peters, May 28 and June 4, 1861; ACDF SO St. St. B 6 z.

59. Ristretto con Sommario relativo ai Costituti del P. Giuseppe Peters, Parte II: Risposte sulla santità affettata di M. Luisa e sugli altri addebiti relativi; ACDF SO St. St. B 6 i.

60. Karl, *Glauben*, p. 9.

61. Ibid., p. 14.

62. Ibid., p. 28.

63. Ibid., p. 30.

64. Ibid., p. 37.

65. Ibid., p. 31.

66. Ristretto con Sommario relativo ai Costituti del P. Giuseppe Peters, Parte IV: Sulle asserite predizioni, rivelazioni ed operazioni del Demonio relative alla malattia ed avvelenamento della novizia Principessa; ACDF SO St. St. B 6 i. Subsequent quotations also taken from this text.

67. Ristretto con Sommario relativo ai Costituti del P. Giuseppe Peters, Parte III: Sul segreto imposto alle monache circa le cose straordinarie e sù di altri addebiti; ACDF SO St. St. B 6 i. Subsequent quotations also taken from this text unless otherwise stated.

68. Sommario del Ristretto di P. Peters, no. X: Fogli consegnati nel Costituto, July 1, 1861; ACDF SO St. St. B 6 i.

69. Ristretto con Sommario relativo ai Costituti del P. Giuseppe Peters, Parte V: Istanze e contestazioni Fiscali; ACDF SO St. St. B 6 i.

70. Costituti di P. Kleutgen; ACDF SO St. St. B 6 y, fol. 189–195. Subsequent quotations also taken from this text.

71. Ristretto con Sommario relativo ai Costituti del P. Giuseppe Peters già confessore delle Monache Riformate in Sant'Ambrogio, October 1861; ACDF SO St. St. B 6 g (handwritten version) and ibid., B 6 i (printed copy).

72. Letter from Hohenlohe to Pappalettere, August 1, 1859, quoted in Wenzel, *Freundeskreis*, pp. 361–62.

73. Letter from Gangauf to Postelmayr, November 25, 1853, quoted in ibid., p. 161.

74. Baltzer was born in 1803, and became a priest and lecturer at the Catholic Theological Seminary in Bonn in 1829. He went to Breslau as an extraordinary professor of dogmatic theology, and gained tenure there in 1831. He became a canon in Breslau in 1846, and from 1860 was persecuted by the prince-bishop of Breslau, Heinrich Foerster. He was relieved of his office and barred from drawing a salary. In 1870 he joined the Old Catholic movement, though he died a year later. See Friedrich Wilhelm Bautz, "Baltzer," in *BBKL* 1 (1975), p. 361; Ernst Melzer, "Baltzer," in *ADB* 2 (1875), p. 33

75. Knoodt was born in 1811 and became an extraordinary professor in Bonn in 1845, achieving tenure two years later. In 1878 he became the vicar general of the Old Catholics' Diocese, and he died in 1889. See Herman H. Schwedt, "Knoodt," in *BBKL* 4 (1992), pp. 163–65; Paul Wenzel, "Knoodt," in *NDB* 12 (1979), p. 211.

76. Baltzer to Knoodt, November 21, 1853, quoted in Wenzel, *Freundeskreis*, p. 161.

77. Cf. Wolf, *Ketzer*, pp. 52–58.

78. Reikerstorfer, *Günther*, p. 266.

79. As Pritz puts it. *Glauben*, p. 266.

80. See ibid., pp. 348–75; Schäfer, *Kontroverse*, pp. 28–36.

81. Philosophisches Jahrbuch von Dr. A. Günther und Dr. J. E. Veith, *Lydia* 4 (1854), p. 603.

82. Wenzel, *Anliegen*, p. 204.

83. Ibid., p 206.

84. Quoted in ibid., p. 211, note 445.

85. Quoted in ibid., pp. 213 and 216.

86. Geissel was born in 1796. He became bishop of Speyer in 1837, bishop coadjutor in 1841, archbishop of Cologne in 1845, and cardinal in 1850. He died in 1864. See Eduard Hegel's article on him in Gatz (ed.), *Bischöfe*, pp. 239–44.

87. Rauscher, who was born in 1797, became archbishop of Seckau in 1849 and prince-archbishop of Vienna in 1853. He was made a cardinal in 1855, and died in 1875. See Erwin Gatz's article on him in ibid., pp. 596–601.

88. The account of the trial against Günther in Rome is based on the excellent study by Herman H. Schwedt, with additional material from sources released by the Vatican ACDF archive in 1998. Schwedt, *Verurteilung*, pp. 301–43. See also Schoeters, *Beckx*, pp. 146–51. On the theological disagreement between Kleutgen and Günther, see Schäfer, *Kontroverse*.

89. See Wolf (ed.), *Prosopographie*, pp. 806–17, here p. 807.

90. See ACDF Index Causes célèbres 4, Günther.

91. Schwarzenberg was born in 1809. He became prince-bishop of Salzburg in 1836, cardinal in 1842, and prince-bishop of Prague in 1850. He died in 1885. See Erwin Gatz, in Gatz (ed.), *Bischöfe*, pp. 686–92.

92. Brignole was born in 1797 and made a cardinal in 1834. He was the prefect of the Congregation of the Index from 1851 to 1853, and died in 1853. See Weber, *Kardinäle*, vol. 2, pp. 443–44 and elsewhere.

93. Lambruschini was born in 1776, became a cardinal in 1831, and was cardinal secretary of state from 1836 to 1846. He died in 1854. See ibid., pp. 475–76 and elsewhere.

94. Schwedt, *Verurteilung*, p. 309.

95. D'Andrea was born in 1812. He became titular bishop of Mèlitene and nuncio to Switzerland in 1841. He was made a cardinal in 1852, and served as prefect of the Congregation of the Index from 1853 to 1861. In 1866 he was suspended from the office of bishop, and from his cardinalate in 1867, with the loss of all his earnings. His rehabilitation and his death both came in 1868. See Wolf (ed.), *Prosopographie*, pp. 379–83.

96. Cf. Ickx, *Santa Sede*, pp. 593–94 (index); Wolf, *Index*, pp. 173–74.

97. Pius IX's Encyclical of December 8, 1864, full English text: http://www .papalencyclicals.net/Pius09/p9quanta.htm and his Syllabus of Errors (the collection of the eighty most important errors of our time): http://www .papalencyclicals.net/Pius09/p9syll.htm.

98. ACDF Index Prot. 121, nos. 18 and 19 (*Lydia*); ibid., Causes célèbres 4.

99. Flir was born in 1805. He became a professor of philology and aesthetics in Innsbruck in 1835, and in 1856 he was made a consultor of the Congegation of the Index. He was named auditor of the Roman Rota in 1858, though he died in 1859 before taking up office. See Wolf (ed.), *Prosopographie*, pp. 591–93. On the relationship between Hohenlohe, Flir, and Günther, see Rapp (ed.), *Briefe*, p. 28.

100. Wolf (ed.), *Bücherverbote*, pp. 248–50; Wolf (ed.), *Repertorium Indexkongregation*, pp. 361–64.

101. "Ingenue, religiose, ac laudabiliter se subjecit"; bando, January 8, 1857; Wolf (ed.), *Bücherverbote*, p. 249.

102. Cf. for example the bando of June 12, 1856; ibid., pp. 245–46. This was the judgment on Louis-Hilaire Caron. The decree contained the statement: "Auctor laudabiliter se subjecit et opus reprobavit."

103. Letter from Kleutgen to Schlüter, January 10, 1857; quoted in Deufel, *Kirche*, p. 245.

104. ASS 8 (1847), pp. 445–48.

105. Wenzel, *Anliegen*, p. 211, note 445.

CHAPTER NINE *"Sorrowful and Contrite"*

1. Fascicolo dei Decreti, Feria II., January 27, 1862, Votum DD. Consultorum; ACDF SO St. St. B 6 w f. Subsequent quotations also taken from this text. An inventory of the objects and description of the rooms was produced after Sant'Ambrogio was dissolved. Inventario degli oggetti sacri e mobiliari rimasti nel soppresso monastero delle Riformate in S. Ambrogio con succinta descrizione dei locali che lo compongono; ibid., B 6 i 1.

2. Cf. *Annuario Pontificio* 1862, pp. 261–63. The consultors of the Holy Office were:

Ignazio Alberghini, Giuseppe Primavera (Fiscal), Gaetano Bedini, Giuseppe Berardi, Andrea Bizzarri, Annibale Capalti, Luigi-Maria Cardelli, Giuseppe Cipriani (Advocatus Reorum), Luigi Ferrari, Giacinto De Ferrari (Commissary), Girolamo Gigli, Pietro Silvestro Glauda, Camillo Guardi, Vincenzo Jandel, Luigi Jannoni, Antonio Ligi-Bussi, Paolo Micallef, Raffaele Monaco La Valletta (Assessor), Bonfiglio Mura, Salvatore de Ozieri, Giuseppe Papardo del Parco, Girolamo Priori, Antonio Maria da Rignano, Giovanni Battista Rosani, Vincenzo Leone Sallua (first *socius*), Camillo Tarquini, Augustin Theiner, Luigi Tomassetti, and Cornelis van Everbroeck. The members of the congregation on January 27, in addition to the assessor and the commissar, the fiscal Antonio Bambozzi (in place of Primavera) and the advocatus reorum, were the consultants Cardelli, Glauda, Guardi, Jandel, Jannoni, Micallef, de Ozieri, Papardo, Priori, da Pignano, Tarquini, Van Everbroeck; ACDF SO Acta Congregationis 1861—1862, Consulta habita Feria II. January 27 1862.

3. Theologians and canon lawyers differentiated between four types of abjuration. The *de formali* was called for if the defendant's heresy could be established with certainty; *de vehementi* was used for Catholics "strongly" suspected of heresy; *de levi* was for Catholics who were "slightly" suspected of heresy; finally, the abjuration *violenta suspicione haeresis* was for those who had come under suspicion of heresy through saying or doing something that could give the judge reason to think they were a heretic. Cf. "Abiura," in Moroni, *Dizionario* 1 (1840), pp. 32—33; Elena Brambilla, "Abiura," in *DSI* 1 (2011), pp. 5—6.

4. Cf. Maria Messana, "Carcere," in *DSI* 1 (2011), pp. 269—71.

5. The Decalogue merely reads: "Thou shalt not commit adultery" (Exodus 20:14). In Catholic moral theology this commandment has been gradually extended to include an entire catalogue of sexual misdemeanors, including prostitution. This sin comprises all "animal lust," called forth through "mingling of the sexes outside marriage." Prostitution is condemned in Christianity on the basis of 1 Corinthians 6:9 and Ephesians 5:5. Cf. Stapf, *Moral*, p. 445.

6. The Pia Casa di Penitenza in Corneto was a correctional facility for convicted priests, around forty miles from Rome. The house was set up by Pope Urban VIII, and later extended by Pius VI. Up to thirty-eight prisoners could be accommodated here. The house was a safe, clean, and orderly jail. See "Carceri ecclesiastiche," in Moroni, *Dizionario* 9 (1841), pp. 261—63, here p. 262; Carlo Luigi Morichini, *Degli istituti di carità per la sussistenza e l'educazione dei poveri e dei prigionieri in Roma. Libri tre. Edizione novissima* (Rome, 1870), p. 738, note 1; Jean Joseph François Poujoulat, *Toscana e Roma. Lettere,* 2 vols. (Milan, 1840), here vol. 2, pp. 161—62.

7. It continues: "The guilty priest shall be punished for this crime without regard to his standing, office, special privileges or exemptions, according to the magnitude of the sin and the aggravating circumstances, with suspension, loss of active and passive eligibility election rights, privation or dismissal. But whosoever falsely denounces a priest for such a crime, be he priest or laity, cannot be absolved by priests or bishops (except *in articulo mortis*), but only by the Apostolic See." Three constitutions are mentioned as legal sources: *Universi Dominici* by

Gregory XV (August 30, 1622), *Sacramentum poenitentiae* by Benedict XIV (June 1, 1741), and *Apostolici muneris*, also by Benedict XIV (February 8, 1745). Cf. "Sollicitatio ad turpia," in Heinrich Josef Wetzer and Benedikt Welte (eds.), *Kirchen-Lexikon oder Encyklopädie der katholischen Theologie und ihrer Hilfswissenschaften*, vol. 10 (Freiburg i. Br., 1853), p. 241.

8. See Luigi De Sanctis, *Roma papale. Descritta in una serie di lettere con note* (Florence, 1865), p. 373. De Sanctis further describes the practice of the tribunal: after acceptance of the denunciation, the tribunal investigates the reputation of the woman; if she does not enjoy a good reputation, the denunciation is taken to be slanderous. Only following three denunciations by honorable women is the case discussed before the Congregation. If the man denounced is a respectable person, he is secretly requested to appear before the Inquisition and make a spontaneous confession of his sin. The Holy Office then accepts his confession and—De Sanctis remarks critically—"tutto è finito," everything is all right again. There are numerous denunciations for *Sollicitatio* in the ACDF, but very few judgments against confessors.

9. Fascicolo dei Decreti, Assembly of the Cardinals Feria IV, February 5, 1862; ACDF SO St. St. B 6 w f. Seven cardinals took part in the meeting: Fabio Maria Asquini, Alessandro Barnabò, Anton Maria Cagiano, Prospero Caterini, Anton Maria Panebianco, Patrizi, and Reisach; ACDF SO Decreta 1862, Feria IV, February 5, 1862. According to the *Annuario Pontificio* 1862, p. 261, members of the congregation were: Filippo de Angelis, Giacomo Antonelli, Fabio Maria Asquini, Alessandro Barnabò, Anton Maria Cagiano, Prospero Caterini, Clarelli Paracciani, Domenico Lucciardi, Anton Maria Panebianco, Patrizi (secretary), Rauscher, and Reisach.

10. Fascicolo dei Decreti, assessor's audience with Pius IX, February 5, 1862; ACDF SO St. St. B 6 w f.

11. Fascicolo dei Decreti, Assembly of the Cardinals Feria IV, February 12, 1862, and the assessor's private audience with Pius IX on the same day; ACDF SO St. St. B 6 w f.

12. Maria Sofia Messana, "Autodafé, Spagna," in *DSI* 1 (2011), pp. 124–26.

13. Bertolt Brecht, *A Life of Galileo* (trans. Deborah Gearing and Mark Ravenhill) (London, 2013). On the Galileo trial, see Beretta, *Galilée*; Beretta (ed.), *Galilée en procès*; Wolf, *Kontrolle*, pp. 1017–19 and 1024–27.

14. Costituti di P. Peters; ACDF SO St. St. B 6 y, fol. 195–203.

15. Pacifico Gasparri was a scribe for the Holy Office from January 1851. See Wolf (ed.), *Prosopographie*, p. 650.

16. Giacomo Vagaggini, who came from Toscana, became secretary to the Holy Office's assessor in 1848. In 1851 he became a substitute for the Holy Office's notary, and he died in 1885. See Wolf (ed.), *Prosopographie*, p. 1517.

17. Costituti di P. Peters, Abjuratio, February 18, 1862; ACDF SO St. St. B 6 y, fol. 197.

18. Costituti di P. Leziroli, Abjuratio, February 17, 1862; ACDF SO St. St. B 6 s, fol. 98–105.

19. Costituti di Sr. Maria Luisa, Abjuratio, February 14, 1862; ACDF SO St. St. B 6 o, fol. 76–78; the abbess's *Abjuratio*, February 14, 1862; ibid., B 6 r, fol. 77–81.

20. Cf. Norbert Lüdecke, "Kidnapping aus Heilssorge? Der lange Schatten des Edgardo Mortara," in Reinhold Boschki and Albert Gerhards (eds.), *Erinnerungskultur in der pluralen Gesellschaft. Neue Perspektiven für den jüdisch-christlichen Dialog (Studien zum Judentum und Christentum)* (Paderborn, 2010), pp. 303–20.

21. The church and the house of retreat attached to it are located on the Esquiline Hill, on the Via Napoleone III, where it crosses the Piazza Vittorio Emanuele II. It was in the hands of the Jesuits until 1870. See Anon., *Le case di esercizi spirituali stabilite a norma di ciò che prescrive s. Ignazio di Lojola e si pratica nella Casa di S. Eusebio in Roma* (Rome, 1855); Augustin Theiner, *Geschichte der geistlichen Bildungsanstalten. Mit einem Vorworte, enthaltend Acht Tage im Seminar zu St. Euseb in Rom* (Mainz/Vienna, 1835).

22. The round church and the Jesuit novitiate building connected to it were commissioned by Camillo Panfili, a nephew of Pope Innocent X, in 1678, from plans drawn up by Bernini. See Armellini, *Chiese*, p. 185.

23. Quoted from Galletti, *Memorie*, vol. 2, p. 455.

24. Sommervogel, *Bibliothèque*, vol. 4, p. 1771.

25. The convent and its church of Santa Maria della Visitazione and San Francesco di Sales are in Trastavere, on the Via della Lungara. They were built for the nuns of the order of the Visitation of Mary in 1669, at the request of Clement IX. The order remained there from 1673 until 1793. After the nuns moved to the convent of Santa Maria dell'Umiltà next to the Quirinale, the complex was bought by a silk merchant from Sorrento, Vincenzo Masturzi, in 1794. He gave it to a community of pious women led by his daughter. Seven years later, the community was permitted to found a new convent of the Servants of Mary. In 1873, the convent was expropriated by the Italian government, and later converted into a women's prison. See Armellini, *Chiese*, p. 655; "Serve di Maria SS. Addolorata o Servite," in Moroni, *Dizionario* 64 (1853), pp. 191–99.

26. Fascicolo dei Decreti, Assembly of the Cardinals Feria IV, June 14, 1865, ACDF SO St. St. B 6 w f.

27. Thurn und Taxis-Hohenlohe, *Jugenderinnerungen*, p. 77.

28. Ibid., pp. 77–79.

29. *Erlebnisse von S. Ambrogio*; StA Sigmaringen, Dep 39 HS 1 Rubr 53 no. 14 UF 9m, pp. 49–50.

30. *Deutscher Merkur. Organ für katholische Reformbewegung*, no. 12, March 22, 1879, p. 95. Cf. also Deufel, *Kirche*, p. 62.

31. Copy of a letter from Princess Katharina von Hohenzollern to Padre Kleutgen, March 23, 1879; ADPSJ Abt. 47, no. 541.

32. Thurn und Taxis-Hohenlohe, *Jugenderinnerungen*, p. 80; Zingeler, *Katharina*, p. 83.

33. Johann Peter Anselm Nickes was born in 1825 and studied in Bonn. Having gained his doctorate in theology and philosophy, he entered the Benedictine monastery of Saint Paul in Rome, where he taught morality and Greek. He died in 1866. See Kosch, *Deutschland*, vol. 2, p. 3247.

34. Zingeler, *Katharina*, pp. 79 and 82.

35. Virgil Fiala, "Wolter, Maurus," in *DIP* 10 (2003), pp. 617–19. See also *Kölnische Zeitung*, no. 297, October 25, 1860: "The widowed Princess Katharina von Hohenzollern-Sigmaringen, for whose use the Holy Father has set aside an

apartment in the Quirinal Palace since her return from Naples, has left Italy for Germany. She is followed by Monsignor Hohenlohe, Privy Counsellor to His Holiness."

36. Zingeler, *Katharina,* pp. 82–93.

37. Thurn und Taxis-Hohenlohe, *Jugenderinnerungen,* pp. 81–82.

38. See Virgil Fiala, "Beuron," in *DIP* I (1974), pp. 1427–30; Fiala, *Bemühungen,* pp. 718–33; Fiala, *Beuron,* pp. 135–44; Fiala, *Jahrhundert;* Kopf, *Klösterliches Leben,* p. 28; Petzolt, *Gründungs- und Entwicklungsgeschichte;* Reinhardt, *Bemühungen,* pp. 734–44. Karl-Anton von Hohenzollern-Sigmaringen was born in 1811 and was the Minister-president of the kingdom of Prussia from 1858 to 1862. He died in 1885.

39. Letter from Katharina von Hohenzollern to Prince Leopold, February 14, 1890, quoted in Zingeler, *Katharina,* pp. 199–201.

40. Thurn und Taxis-Hohenlohe, *Jugenderinnerungen,* pp. 83–84.

41. Cf. Zingeler, *Katharina,* pp. 201–4.

42. Ibid., p. 210.

43. Cf. Fiala, *Jahrhundert;* Wenzel, *Freundeskreis;* Zingeler, *Katharina.* Zingeler's biography has the telling subtitle: "The Benefactor of Beuron." On the Benedictine congregation of Beuron, see *Beuron 1863–1963;* Petzolt, *Gründungs- und Entwicklungsgeschichte;* Schöntag (ed.), *250 Jahre.* On the Beuron School of Art, see Siebenmorgen, *Anfänge.*

44. See Zingeler, *Katharina,* pp. 207–8.

45. See Thurn und Taxis-Hohenlohe, *Jugenderinnerungen,* p. 84.

46. "But it has been the miraculous guidance of divine providence itself that brought her to the same, and through a special act of providence manifestly laid out the innermost experiences and suffering of her recent past to Your paternal gaze." Katharina von Hohenzollern-Sigmaringen to the German Fathers of Saint Paul, September 14, 1859; quoted in Wenzel, *Freundeskreis,* pp. 362–64, here p. 362.

47. Fink, *Tagebücher,* p. 474. With regard to the following, see also Fink, *Kardinal,* pp. 164–72; Kraus, *Hohenlohe,* pp. 165–75; Schlemmer, *Gustav,* pp. 373–415; Wolf, *Gustav,* pp. 350–75.

48. Quoted in Wolf, *Gustav,* p. 359. On the allocation of the Freiburg archbishop's seat, see Josef Becker, "Zum Ringen um die Nachfolge Erzbischofs Hermann von Vicaris 1868. Die Voten der Domkapitulare Orbin, Schmidt, Haitz und Kössing," in *Freiburger Diözesanarchiv* 88 (1968), pp. 380–427.

49. Letter from Gustav to Chlodwig zu Hohenlohe-Schillingsfürst, November 26, 1869; quoted in Curtius (ed.), *Denkwürdigkeiten,* vol. 2, pp. 1–2.

50. Letter from Gustav to Chlodwig zu Hohenlohe-Schillingsfürst, November 26, 1869; quoted in ibid., vol. 1, p. 404.

51. Letter from Gustav zu Hohenlohe-Schillingsfürst to Cardinal Schwarzenberg, July 18, 1870, quoted in ibid., p. 365.

52. Kraus, *Hohenlohe,* p. 175.

53. Katharina von Hohenzollern to Pius IX, undated (April 1873), quoted in Zingeler, *Katharina,* p. 169, note 1.

54. See Duhr, *Jesuiten-Fabeln*, pp. 425–53, the case of Kleutgen, pp. 451–53. Gustav zu Hohenlohe-Schillingsfürst shared his anti-Jesuit stance with his brother Chlodwig. See Pfülf, *Hohenlohe*, pp. 1–22.
55. Friedrich was born in 1836, and was excommunicated in 1871 for his refusal to recognize the infallibility dogma. He played a substantial role in establishing the Old Catholic faculty in Bern in 1874. He returned to Munich in 1875, and died in 1917. See Kessler, *Friedrich*.
56. Letter from Steinhuber to Langenhorst, May 1883; ADPSJ section 47, no. 541.
57. Thurn und Taxis-Hohenlohe, *Jugenderinnerungen*, p. 91. See also p. 79: he was a man "who smelled poison everywhere." On Hohenlohe's poison paranoia, see Schlemmer, *Gustav*, pp. 388–90; Weber, *Quellen*, pp. 140–41.
58. Cf. Bülow, *Denkwürdigkeiten*, vol. 1, p. 11; Weber, *Quellen*, p. 141, note 203. There is no further information on Gustavo Nobile.
59. On the 1878 conclave, see Schmidlin, *Papstgeschichte*, vol. 2, pp. 338–46. Franchi was born in 1819 and was made a consultor of the Council's ecclesiastico-political preparatory commission in 1867. In 1868 he became a papal nuncio in Spain, and in 1874 prefect of the Congregation for the Propagation of the Faith. He became cardinal secretary of state in March 1878, and died later that year. See Weber, *Kardinäle*, vol. 2, p. 466; Weber, *Quellen*, pp. 137–42; Wolf (ed.), *Prosopographie*, pp. 609–11.
60. Cf. Lill, *Akten*, p. 95, note 2; Wolf, *Gustav*, p. 368.
61. Letter from Gustav zu Hohenlohe-Schillingsfürst to Hermann zu Hohenlohe-Langenberg, May 13, 1895; quoted in Schlemmer, *Gustav*, p. 383.
62. Georg Kopp was born in 1837 and was vicar general in Hildesheim from 1872 to 1881. From 1881 to 1887 he was bishop of Fulda, and in 1887 he was made prince-bishop of Breslau. He became a cardinal in 1893, and died in 1914. See Gatz (ed.), *Bischöfe*, pp. 400–4.
63. Quoted in Kraus, *Tagebücher*, p. 657.
64. The gravestone is a relief tablet with an inscription, portrait, and coat of arms. Cf. Albrecht Weiland, *Der Campo Santo Teutonico in Rom und seine Grabdenkmäler* (Römische Quartalschrift Supplementheft 43) (Rome, 2nd ed., 1988), pp. 555–57 and illustration 85.
65. Quoted in Kraus, *Tagebücher*, p. 575.
66. Cf. Weber, *Quellen*, pp. 19–21.
67. Cf. Anton Zeis, in Gatz (ed.), *Bischöfe*, pp. 603–6, here p. 606. The church is in the Rione Campitelli on the square of the same name, not far from the Bocca della Verità.
68. Cf. Weber, *Kardinäle*, vol. 1, pp. 299 and 500.
69. Cf. Aubert, *Pontificat*, p. 285. The quotation comes from Diomede Pantaleoni (1810–1885), who was counted as a liberal during the pontificate of Pius IX.
70. Louis Teste, *Préface au Conclave* (Paris, 1877), p. 80; quoted in Aubert, *Pontificat*, p. 285.
71. Cf. Weber, *Quellen*, p. 265, note 137.
72. Tribunale civile e correzionale di Roma, copy of a file on a legal dispute between the Holy Office and Maria Ridolfi before the Tribunale civile e correzionale di

Roma on October 23, 1871. Here, the lawyer Severino Tirelli, representing the Holy Office, looks back over Maria Luisa's fate. ACDF SO St. St. B 6 w l.

73. Gißibl, *Zeichen*, p. 109.

74. Maria von Mörl, who was born in 1812, was a sickly child. Her ecstasies began in 1832. At the age of twenty-four she received the wounds on her hands and feet, attracting many visitors, pilgrims, and curious onlookers. She died in 1868, in a Third Order convent in Kaltern, where she had lived since her father's death in 1840. Cf. Priesching, *Mörl*, p. 16.

75. Gißibl, *Zeichen*, p. 110. See also Priesching, *Mörl*, pp. 105–7.

76. Gender studies research is especially helpful in explaining these phenomena. Cf. Braun and Stephan (eds.), *Gender-Studien*; Opitz, *Um-Ordnungen*; Weiß, *Weisungen*, pp. 243–46.

77. Cf. for example Huguet, *Geist*, pp. 385–422, here the chapter "Übernatürliche Begebenheiten im Leben Pius IX." On the veneration of the pope and the miracles his contemporaries ascribed to him, cf. Zinnhobler, *Pius IX*, pp. 386–432.

78. The basis for criminal law in central Europe until well into the nineteenth century was the *Constitutio Criminalis Carolina*, the procedure for the judgment of capital crimes issued by Charles V and the Holy Roman Empire. There were different methods of execution for different crimes: arsonists, enchanters, witches, sodomites, and those who stole from churches were burned; traitors were quartered; murderers were beheaded or broken on the wheel. Until the end of the eighteenth century the death penalty was applied to a wide range of offenses. The first outspoken opponent of the death penalty was the Italian jurist Cesare Beccaria, whose work *Dei delitti e delle Pene* was published in Naples in 1764. Over the course of the nineteenth century, the death penalty was scrapped in many countries, and replaced by life imprisonment. However, it was still enforced during the wars that established the nation-states of Europe to secure power interests. Cf. Karl Hilgenreiner, "Todesstrafe," in *LThK*, 1st ed., vol. 10 (1938), pp. 194–95; Oliver Michael Timothy O'Donovan, "Todesstrafe," in *TRE* 33 (2002), pp. 639–46. The punishments generally meted out to priests can be found in Hinschius, *System*.

79. See Gregory XVI, "Regolamento sui delitti e sulle pene," September 20, 1832, in Sergio Vinciguerra (ed.), *I regolamenti penali di Papa Gregorio XVI per lo Stato Pontificio (1832)* (Padua, 2000), pp. 83–121, here pp. 88 and 111.

80. The *Privilegium fori* was gained through the profession of vows. Cf. Sägmüller, *Kirchenrecht*, p. 740 and generally pp. 188–90. See also Richard Puza, "Privilegium fori," in *LexMA* 7 (1999), pp. 228–29. On the legal situation in the Papal States, see Raffaele Ala, *Il foro criminale*, vol. 8 (Rome, 1826), pp. 131–34.

81. Tribunale civile e correzionale di Roma, Comparsa conclusionale (concluding statement) by Severino Tirelli, October 23, 1871; ACDF SO St. St. B 6 w l. Subsequent quotations also taken from this text.

82. The jail was housed in a building near the Baths of Diocletian. It had originally been built by Pope Clement XI in 1705 for the department of nutrition. The "Casa di detenzione alle Terme" diocleziane was opened in 1834 and housed men as well as women who had been sentenced to between one and three years'

imprisonment. From 1854, the women's section was overseen by the Sisters of Divine Providence and the Immaculate Conception. Cf. Monica Calzolari, "La Casa di detenzione alle Terme diocleziane di Roma (1831–1891)," in Livio Antonielli (ed.), *Carceri, carcerieri, carcerati. Dall'antico regime all'Ottocento* (Soveria Mannelli, 2006), pp. 49–78; Carlo Luigi Morichini, *Degli istituti di carità per la sussistenza e l'educazione dei poveri e dei prigionieri in Roma*, vol. 3 (Rome, 1870), pp. 702–10.

83. Tribunale civile e correzionale di Roma, Comparsa conclusionale by Severino Tirelli, Pro secreta Em.orum, undated [probably July 25, 1868]; ACDF SO St. St. B 6 w l.

84. Tribunale civile e correzionale di Roma, Comparsa conclusionale by Severino Tirelli, Attestazione del Dr. Caetani, January 14, 1869; ACDF SO St. St. B 6 wl. "Dr. Caetani" was probably Placido Gaetani, who came from Alatri and worked as a doctor in the hospital of San Gallicano. Cf. Annibale Taddei, *Manuale di notizie risguardanti le scienze, arti, e mestieri della città di Roma per l'anno 1839* (Rome, 1838), p. 62.

85. According to a report by the German doctor Karl Finkelnburg at about the year 1866, the asylum, which was officially named "Manicomio Santa Maria della Pietà," had stood on the right bank of the Tiber since 1728, and was significantly expanded under Pius IX to encompass the area around Giancolo, including the Villa Barberini. "The old main building, the entrance and front of which on the Via San Michele was gloomy and blackened with age, presenting a very unfriendly first impression to visitors, has also been expanded and completely renovated inside. Both of the strictly separated sections for men and women are now divided into four quarters corresponding to the character of their inhabitants: *Tranquilli, Suicidi* (unclean people), *Agitati* and *Furiosi*.... Dr. Viale, the pope's personal physician, has been the medical head of the institution since 1860.... A prelate is naturally charged with the overall administration, and a small number of monks and nuns serve the house, and keep watch over the patients.... Viale conducts the medical treatment of the mentally disturbed entirely according to the principles of the French school—but his *Traitement moral* is characterized by great mildness, the rejection of any physical force, and ingenious attempts to bring out the patient's moral sense of self." *Allgemeine Zeitschrift für Psychiatrie und psychisch-gerichtliche Medicin, herausgegeben von Deutschlands Irrenärzten* 23 (1866), pp. 398–401.

86. Tirelli came from Cerreto Guidi (Tuscany) and, having completed his baccalaureate in 1835, his diploma in *Facultatis Juris Utriusque* in 1838, and his law degree, he became a lawyer in the Papal States in 1850. See *Annuario Ecclesiastico* (Rome, 1898), p. 101; *Annuaire pontifical catholique* (Paris, 1899), pp. 376 and 458; *La gerarchia cattolica la cappella e la famiglia pontificie per l'anno 1888 con appendice di altre notizie riguardanti la Santa Sede* (Rome, 1888), p. 636; http://www.prometheos.net /immagini/cataloghi/ ... /udite.pdf (8/1/2012).

87. See Zingeler, *Katharina*, pp. 167–168.

88. Thurn und Taxis-Hohenlohe, *Jugenderinnerungen*, p. 83.

89. At least, this is how Kleutgen painted it in retrospect. Letter from Kleutgen to

Steinhuber, who was then rector of the Collegium Germanicum, May, 1883; ADPSJ section 47, no. 541, fol. 8.

90. The sanctuary church of Santa Maria di Galloro was built between 1624 and 1633, with the convent connected to it being added between 1632 and 1634. Until 1798 it was occupied by the Vallombrosians. They returned in 1801 after the era of the Roman Republic, and remained until 1809. In 1816 the convent was given over to the Jesuits. Following a temporary return by the Vallombrosians, it was handed back to the Jesuits in 1824. They still occupy the building today, using it as a house of retreat. Cf. Giuseppe Boero, *Istoria del santuario della beatissima Vergine di Galloro* (Rome, 1842; 2nd ed., 1852; 3rd ed., 1863); Girolamo Pecchiai, *Il santuario di Galloro e la miracolosa immagine di Maria Santissima che in esso si venera. Cenni storico-descrittivi* (Rome, 1910); Francesco Petrucci, "Il Cavalier Gianlorenzo Bernini e il santuario di Galloro," in *Documenta Albana* (Series II) 10 (1988), pp. 59–73; Schäfer, *Kontroverse*, p .66, note 53.

91. Letter from Patrizi to Pius IX, undated, which refers to a plea from Beckx of October 16, 1863; ACDF SO St. St. B7 a, fascicle on Kleutgen. Peter Walter also found evidence that Kleutgen returned to Rome in 1863; Walter, "Zu einem neuen Buch," p. 323. Deufel, *Kirche*, p. 63, assumes that Kleutgen remained in Galloro for two years. Kleutgen is known to have sent letters from Galloro between September 4, 1862, and May 8, 1863. Cf. Schäfer, *Kontroverse*. See also Imkamp, *Studienjahre*, p. 178, note 28; Lakner, *Kleutgen*, p. 196, note 59; Walter, *Kleutgen*, p. 146.

92. Letter from Steinhuber to Langenhorst, May 1883; ADPSJ section 47, no. 541. Steinhuber quotes here from Kleutgen's communication with him. The biography of Kleutgen that Langenhorst wanted to write, for which Steinhuber provided this information, was never published.

93. See Wolf, *Erfindung*, pp. 236–59.

94. According to Bischof, *Theologie*, pp. 95–105.

95. Döllinger, *Rede*, pp. 25–59, here pp. 42 and 47–48.

96. See Congar, *Bref historique*, p. 108; Congar, *Tradition*, pp. 218–19.

97. Unterburger, *Lehramt*, p. 136.

98. Döllinger, *Rede*, p. 58.

99. Pius IX's brief *Tuas libenter*, of December 21, 1863; complete Latin text in ASS 8 (1874), pp. 436–42; English translation of exerpts from *Tuas libenter* available in The Daughters of Saint Paul, *Papal Teachings: The Church, Selected and Arranged by the Benedictine Monks of Solesmes* (Boston, 1962).

100. Jakob Frohschammer was born in 1821 and ordained in 1847. He became professor for philosophy in Munich in 1855, was suspended in 1863, and died in 1893. See Pahud de Mortanges, *Philosophie*.

101. Gregor von Scherr was born in 1804 and ordained in 1829. He professed his vows in the Benedictine monastery of Metten in 1833, and in 1838 he was made prior. He became the abbott there in 1840. From 1856 until his death in 1877 he was archbishop of Munich and Freising. See Anton Zeis, in Gatz (ed.), *Bischöfe*, pp. 654–56.

102. Jakob Frohschammer, *Ueber den Ursprung der menschlichen Seelen. Rechtfertigung des Generatianismus* (Munich, 1854).

103. Kleutgen, votum on Frohschammer, *Ueber den Ursprung* . . . , November 19, 1855; ACDF Index Prot. 119 (1854–1857), fol. 443r–446v.

104. On the whole trial, see Pahud de Mortanges, *Philosophie*, pp. 33–69. Subsequent information also taken from this text.

105. Angelo Trullet was born in 1813. He was a Franciscan, and became a consultor of the Congregation of the Index in 1854. He died in 1879. See Wolf (ed.), *Prosopographie*, pp. 1505–8.

106. Bernard Smith was born in 1812. He was a Benedictine, and became a consultor of the Congregation of the Index in 1852. He died in 1892. See ibid., pp. 1390–98.

107. Johann Baptist Hirscher was born in 1788. He became a priest of the diocese of Rottenburg in 1810, and a professor of moral theology in Tübingen in 1817. He moved to Freiburg in 1839, when he also became a capitular. Hirscher was caught up in a number of indexing trials and was persecuted by the new scholastics for his liberal, Enlightenment thinking. He died in 1865. See Köster, *Hirscher*.

108. Kleutgen, second votum on Frohschammer, *Ueber den Ursprung* . . . , February 7, 1856; ACDF Index Prot. 119 (1854–1857), fol. 758r–794v. Subsequent information also taken from this text.

109. Trullet, votum on Frohschammer, *Ueber den Ursprung* . . . , August 26, 1856; ACDF Index Prot. 119 (1854–1857), bound after fol. 799r, unpaginated, 222 pp. in a secret printing.

110. Froschammer's piece "Einleitung in die Philosophie und Grundriss der Metaphysik. Zur Reform der Philosophie" (Introduction to the Philosophy and Outline of Metaphysics: On Reforming Philosophy) was published in 1858, and his "Ueber die Freiheit der Wissenschaft" (On the Freedom of Science) in 1861. On both texts, see Pahud de Mortanges, *Philosophie*, pp. 72–140. See also Frohschammer's "Autobiographie," in Adolf Hinrichsen (ed.), *Deutsche Denker und ihre Geistesschöpfungen* (Berlin, no date [1888]), pp. 35–45.

111. Piotr Adolf Konstanty Semenenko was born in 1814, and was a member of the Congregation of the Resurrection. He became a consultor of the Congregation of the Index in 1857, and a consultor for the Holy Office in 1873. He died in 1886. See Wolf (ed.), *Prosopographie*, pp. 1361–65.

112. Semenenko, votum on Frohschammer, *Ueber die Freiheit* . . . , November 29, 1861; ACDF Index Prot. 122 (1862–1864), no number, 36 pp., printed document, esp. fol. 3. Cf. Pahud de Mortanges, *Philosophie*, pp. 206–19.

113. Ibid., pp. 263–91. Pius IX's brief *Gravissimas Inter* of December 11, 1862; complete Latin text in ASS 8 (1874), pp. 429–35.

114. Walter, *Kleutgen*, p. 146.

115. See Deufel, *Kirche*, p. 63, note 246. Cf. Kleutgen's letters from Rome, in which he began to distance himself from the city to a certain extent from the 1860s onward. Kleutgen, *Briefe*.

116. Letter from Kleutgen to Steinhuber, August 29, 1869, quoted in Deufel, *Kirche*, pp. 286–88, here p. 286.

117. Ibid., p. 63, note 246.

118. Walter Steins was born in 1810. He entered the Jesuit novitiate in Nijvel in 1832, and was ordained in 1842. In 1852 he went to India as a missionary, where he was made bishop of Calcutta. Steins died in 1881. See the Biografisch Archiv van de Benelux, Steene-Stekke, Fiche 646, pp. 444–46.

119. Cf. Mai, *Bischof,* p. 126; *Mansi* 53, pp. 286–331; Schatz, *Vaticanum I,* vol. 2, pp. 313–55; Walter, "Zu einem neuen Buch," p. 325.

120. Vaticanum I, dogmatic constitution *Dei filius* on the Catholic faith, April 24, 1870. English translation online: http://www.inters.org/Vatican-Council-I-Dei-Filius (11/17/2013).

121. Andreas Steinhuber was born in 1825. He was ordained in 1851 and entered the Society of Jesus in 1857. After spending some time as a professor of dogmatics in Innsbruck, and rector of the Collegium Germanicum, he embarked on a classic Curia career before dying in 1907. See Wolf (ed.), *Prosopographie,* pp. 1415–18.

122. Letter from Steinhuber to Langenhorst, April 1883; ADPSJ section 47, no. 541, fol. 10f.

123. *Mansi* 53, p. 313 A.

124. Beumer, *Konstitution,* p. 354, note 60. See also [Kleutgen], *Lehrgewalt.*

125. Letter from Kleutgen to Steinhuber, January 7, 1871, quoted in Deufel, *Kirche,* p. 69.

126. Letter from Kleutgen to Steinhuber, February 24, 1872, quoted in ibid., p. 71.

127. Kleutgen's itinerary: ibid., pp. 78–79.

128. Letter from Pastor Glatz to Father Felchlin, March 6, 1883, quoted in ibid., p. 72.

129. Cf. Deufel, *Kirche,* p. 74.

130. Leo XII's encyclical *Aeterni Patris* of August 4, 1879; Latin text in ASS 12 (1879/80), pp. 436–42. English translation online: http://www.papalencyclicals.net/Leo13/l13cph.htm (11/17/2013).

131. Steinhuber even claimed Kleutgen had written a "draft" of this. Letter from Steinhuber to Langenhorst, April 1883; ADPSJ section 47, no. 541. Winter states that "the 1st draft probably" came from Kleutgen: Eduard Winter, "Kleutgen," in *LThK,* 1st ed., vol. 6 (1934), p. 46. Walter, on the other hand, says it is "uncertain" whether he was involved in the preparations: Peter Walter, "Kleutgen," in *LThK,* 3rd ed., vol. 6 (1997), p. 135.

132. Letter from Kleutgen to Steinhuber, September 12, 1879, quoted in Deufel, *Kirche,* p. 75.

133. Pastor Glatz from Lengmoos remembers this expression of Kleutgen's in the retrospective written in 1883; ibid., p. 76.

134. Letter from Kleutgen to Schneemann, July 16, 1881, quoted in ibid., p. 77.

135. Cf. Finkenzeller, *Kleutgen,* p. 324.

136. The text of the Latin inscription can be found in Hertkens, *Kleutgen,* p. 90; Lakner, *Kleutgen,* p. 200.

137. Lakner, *Kleutgen,* p. 200.

138. The first dogmatic constitution on the Church of Christ Pastor aeternus of July 18, 1870; English translation online: http://www.papalencyclicals.net/Councils/ecum20.htm#Chapter 4. On the infallible teaching authority of the Roman pontiff.

EPILOGUE *The Secret of Sant'Ambrogio as Judged by History*

1. Cf. *Civiltà Cattolica*, May 25, 1861, pp. 621–23.
2. See http://www.romafelix.com/sambrmass.htm (11/24/2013).
3. Cf. Bischof, *Theologie*, pp. 62–105.
4. Cf. Wolf, *Syllabus*, pp. 115–39.
5. See Quirinus [Ignaz von Döllinger], *Römische Briefe vom Concil* (Munich, 1870), p. 286. These letters were first published as articles in the *Augsburger Allgemeine Zeitung*, and were later published by Döllinger in book form.
6. See the article "Gottes eigenes Konzil. Zweitausend Jahre Apostel, Päpste und Politik im Namen Christi" in *Der Spiegel*, no. 43, October 24, 1962.
7. There is a collection of articles from this period in ADPSJ section 47, no. 541.
8. On Old Catholicism, see Conzemius, *Katholizismus*; Schulte, *Altkatholizismus*.
9. *Deutscher Merkur. Organ für katholische Reformbewegung*, no. 12, March 22, 1879, pp. 95–96. See also Hertkens, *Kleutgen*, p. 81–82. In his history of the First Vaticanuum Friedrich therefore also mentioned the "infamous Jesuit Kleutgen"; cf. Friedrich, *Geschichte*, vol. 3/2, p. 757.
10. Giovenale Pelami was born in 1819, and became the Holy Office's substitute notary in 1844. He was its chief notary from 1870 to 1886, and died in 1888. See Wolf (ed.), *Prosopographie*, p. 1151.
11. *Neue Zeitung für das katholische Deutschland*, no. 63, March 14, 1879. Cf. also Deufel, *Kirche*, p. 62. Latin text in [Dr.] Liesen, "P. Joseph Kleutgen," in *Der Katholik* 63 (1883), first half, pp. 523–43, here p. 529; also Hertkens, *Kleutgen*, p. 82.
12. *Neue Zeitung für das katholische Deutschland*, no. 64, March 15, 1879.
13. Cf. Deufel, *Kirche*, p. 62.
14. Johann Hertkens was born in 1843. He was a chief pastor, biographer, and teacher of homiletics. He died in 1909. See Herrmann A. L. Degener (ed.), *Wer ist's? Zeitgenossenlexikon enthaltend Biographien nebst Bibliographien* (Leipzig, 4th ed., 1909), p. 573; *Biographisches Jahrbuch und deutscher Nekrolog*, vol. 14 (Berlin, 1909), p. 36*.
15. Ludwig Lercher was born in 1864, entered the Society of Jesus in 1891, and was a professor of dogmatics at the University of Innsbruck. He died in 1937. See Franz Daxecker, "Lercher," in *BBKL* (online); Koch, *Jesuiten-Lexikon*, vol. 2, p. 1098.
16. See Hertkens, *Kleutgen*, pp. 77–80.
17. Ibid., p. 81.
18. Theodor Granderath was born in 1839, entered the Society of Jesus in 1860, and was professor of dogmatic theology at the Gregorian University and the Saint Ignatius College in Valkenburg. He died in 1902. See Koch, *Jesuiten-Lexikon*, vol. 1, p. 723.
19. Granderath, *Geschichte*, vol. 2, pp. 363–64, note 6. Schäfer still took up Granderath's position in 1961 (*Kontroverse*, p. 47, note 90).
20. Lakner, *Kleutgen*, p. 195–96. Franz Lakner was born in 1900, and entered the Society of Jesus in 1922. He was ordained in 1929. He later became professor of dogmatic theology in Innsbruck, and died in 1974. See Klaus Schatz, "Lakner," in *NDB* 13 (1982), p. 424.

21. Koch, *Jesuiten-Lexikon*, p. 998. Ludwig Koch was born in 1878 and entered the Society of Jesus in 1897. He was a writer and editor, editing the Sunday newspapers *Leo* and *Sonntagsstimmen*. He also worked for the *Stimmen der Zeit*. He died in 1936. See Paul Duclos, "Koch," in *BBKL* 4 (1992), pp. 220–21.

22. "Cronaca Contemporanea," in *Civiltà Cattolica*, Series XII 1 (1883), pp. 633–36.

23. "Un Ristoratore della Filosofi a scolastica. Giuseppe Kleutgen S. J. (9 aprile 1811–13 gennaio 1883)," in *Civiltà Cattolica* 62 (1911), pp. 34–45.

24. Zingeler was born in 1845, took his final exams as an external candidate in Bonn, and went on to study philosophy. The hereditary prince Leopold von Hohenzollern employed him in 1871 as tutor to his two eldest sons, and brought him to Sigmaringen. Later, he became head of the royal archive there. In this role, he produced several works about the house of Hohenzollern. He died in 1923. See Chr. Zingeler, "Karl Theodor Zingeler, 1845–1923," in *Zollerheimat* 2 (1933), pp. 40–42.

25. Zingeler, *Katharina*, p. 75.

26. Ibid., p. 77; similarly Zingeler, *Karl Anton*, pp. 159–60. The curator of the Rottenburg Diocesan Museum, Anton Pfeffer (1879–1961) also follows Zingeler's portrayal. Cf. Pfeffer, *Gründerin*, pp. 9–14.

27. Zingeler, *Katharina*, p. v (preface).

28. Cf. Arnold, *Geschichte*; Loome, *Catholicism*; Wolf and Schepers (eds.), *Jagd*.

29. Schott, *Leben*, pp. 17–18. Anselm Schott was born in 1843, ordained in 1867, and entered the Benedictine abbey of Beuron in 1868, where he professed his vows in 1870. He made his name as the editor of the widely used missal *Messbuch für Laien*, which was popularly known as "Schott." He died in 1896. See Angelus Häussling, "Schott," in *LThK*, 3rd ed., vol. 9 (2000), p. 242.

30. Fiala, *Jahrhundert*, pp. 51–52. Fiala was born in 1911. He gained his doctorate in Vienna in 1937, and took temporary vows in 1938, followed by a full profession of vows in 1949. He was ordained the same year. He worked as a lecturer in theology in Beuron, and from 1960 in the State Library of Württemberg, the state library in Stuttgart. He died in 1978. See Aegidius Kolb (ed.), *Bibliographie der deutschsprachigen Benediktiner 1880–1980*, vol. 2 (Sankt Ottilien, 1987), pp. 575–76. Wilhelm Freiherr Koenig von und zu Warthausen's article "Die Errettung einer 'Lebend Begrabenen'" in the *Schwäbische Zeitung*, no. 162, July 17, 1965, was based on Fiala's piece in Beuron's centenary publication.

31. Cf. Damianus Schaefers, "Kreuz IX: Geschichte der Kreuzreliquien," in *LThK*, 2nd ed., vol. 6 (1961), pp. 614–15.

32. Eduard Winter, "Kleutgen," in *LThK*, 1st ed., vol. 6 (1934), p. 45. Winter, a professor at the University of Prague, summarizes that Kleutgen is "of outstanding merit for the reanimation of scholastic theology and philosophy in Germany, through clear and sober argumentation on the basis of tradition." Leonard Gilen, "Kleutgen", in *LThK*, 2nd ed., vol. 6 (1961), p. 340. The Jesuit Gilen credits Kleutgen with the "scientific overcoming of Hermesianism," though Kleutgen's real objectives were "to construct a positive philosophy with its source in the thought of scholasticism and patristics." Peter Walter, "Kleutgen," in *LThK*, 3rd ed., vol. 6 (1997), p. 135.

33. Gustav Hebeisen, "Hohenzollern, Katharina," in *LThK*, 1st ed., vol. 5 (1933), p. 106. Hebeisen, who was the director of the Sigmaringen Archive at the time, characterizes her as a "princess inclined to idiosyncrasy and struck by blows of fate," who was not always easily understood. He also writes that although Katharina planned on three occasions to enter a religious order, none of these plans came to fruition, due to ill health and Reisach advising against it. Eberhard Gönner, "Hohenzollern, Katharina," in *LThK*, 2nd ed., vol. 5 (1960), p. 435. Peter Thaddäus Lang, "Hohenzollern, Katharina," in *LThK*, 3rd ed., vol. 5 (1996), p. 217. Lang puts Katharina's failure to lead a cloistered life down to her "bad constitution."

34. The insight yielded by modern research on encyclopedias, that lexicons have never been neutral collections of information, but have always also been the "locus of what a society held to be worthy of knowing," also proves correct here. Cf. Ines Prodöhl, *Die Politik des Wissens. Allgemeine deutsche Enzyklopädien zwischen 1928 und 1956* (Berlin, 2011), p. 1.

35. Cf. Deufel, *Kirche*, pp. 56–63.

36. Cf. Fried, *Schleier*, pp. 13–46.

37. Cf. Walter, "Zu einem neuen Buch," pp. 318–56.

38. Cf. Schwedt, "Rez. zu Deufel," pp. 264–69, here pp. 267–68.

39. Neither of these objections is valid. First, there are many known cases handled by the Roman Inquisition and the Congregation of the Index in which a judgment was made, but not publicized for some reason. For example, John Zahm's work *Evolution and Dogma* was banned in 1898, but this ban wasn't published. Cf. Mariano Artigas et al., *Negotiating Darwin The Vatican Confronts Evolution, 1877–1902* (Baltimore, 2006), pp. 124–202. Second, it is a mistake to speak of objective limits to the jurisdiction of an early-modern court, which the Roman Curia still was, even in the nineteenth century. The absolute ruler, in this case the pope, could declare an authority or an office responsible for whatever he liked, which in this case Pius IX certainly did.

40. Martina, *Pío IX*, vol. 2, p. 243.

41. Pahud de Mortanges, *Philosophie*, p. 254.

42. Nichols, *Conversation*, pp. 117–19.

43. Deufel, *Kirche*, pp. 17–18.

Sources and Literature

Sources

Munich, Archiv der Deutschen Provinz der Jesuiten (ADPSJ)
Abt. 47 no. 541

Neuenstein, Hohenlohe-Zentralarchiv (HZA)
Archiv Bartenstein Bü 130, Nachträge 56
Archiv Waldenburg Wa 270, kleinere Nachlässe 206

Sigmaringen, Staatsarchiv (StA)
Dep 39 HS 1 Rubr 53 no. 14 U F 9m Erlebnisse von S. Ambrogio, von Fräulein
   Ch. Gmeiner notiert im Jahr 1870, Darstellung des in S. Ambrogio Erlebten
   von März 1858 bis 26. Juli 1859
FAS HS 1–80 T 13 no. 70 Tod der Fürstin Katharina von Hohenzollern
Sa T 2 Fo 167 Katharina von Hohenzollern

Rome, Archivum Congregationis Sublacensis (ACS)
Collegio di Sant'Ambrogio
Scatola Piante

Rome, Jesuit Archive (ARSI)
Catalogus Provinciae Austriae Societatis Iesu ineunte anno . . . , Rome
   1844–1878
Catalogus Provinciae Romanae Societatis Iesu ineunte anno . . . , Rome
   1844–1878
Glossario gesuitico. Guida all'intelligenza dei documenti, Rome 1992
Provinciae Romanae Summ. Vitae 1846–1889
Schedario unificato. Schede della Antica e Nuova Compagnia

Sanctum Officium (SO)
Acta Congregationis 1861–1862
Decreta 1859–1862
Stanza Storica (St. St.)
   B 4 b 1 Venerazione di persone non canonizzate obeatificate
      (1615–1783)
   B 4 p Processi del S. Offizio per affettata santità (1617–1771)

B 6 a to B 6 z
B 6 a 1 to B 6 z 1
B 6 w a to B 6 w n ⎬ Causa contra le Monache e Direttori del Monastero
B 6 w 1 di S. Ambrogio in Roma
B 7 a to B 7 f

D 2 i Norme per procedere nelle cause del S. Offizio (inizio XIX secolo)
Q 2 c and Q 2 m Prattica del Sagro Tribunale del S. Offizio nel formare i Processi diversa da quella di tutti gli altri Tribunali Ecclesiastici e Secolari
Q 2 d Istruzione per Monsignore Assessore del S. Offizio

Vatican City, Archive of the Congregation for the Doctrine of the Faith (ACDF)
Congregation of the Index (Index)
Causes célèbres 4, Günther
Protocolli (Prot.)
119 (1854–1857); 121 no. 18 and no. 19; 122 (1862–1864)

Vatican City, Vatican Secret Archive (ASV)
Archivio Particolare di Pio IX
Oggetti vari 1733: S. Ambrogio Monastero Inventario
Monasteri femminili romani soppressi
S. Ambrogio Busta 1–6
Visita Apostolica
97 no. 21 Inventario del Monastero di Sant'Ambrogio della Massima 1710

Consultation from Archives, Libraries, and Private Persons
Archives de l'État de Fribourg / Staatsarchiv Freiburg, Switzerland
Archivio della Cattedrale di Comacchio
Archivio della Curia Vescovile di Gubbio
Archivio Storico del Vicariato di Roma (ASVR)
Biblioteca Casanatense Rome
Deutsches Historisches Institut Rome, Library, Dr. Thomas Hofmann
Deutsches Literaturarchiv Marbach (DLA)
Erzbischöfliches Archiv Munich
Erzbistumsarchiv Paderborn
Herb Depke, Cary, North Carolina
Kollegium Spiritus Sanctus, Brig
Mediathek Wallis, Sitten
Medizinhistorisches Museum, Ingolstadt, Prof. Dr. Christa Habrich
National Archives and Records Administration (NARA), Washington, D.C.
Staatsarchiv Wallis
Stadtarchiv Dortmund
Università La Sapienza Rome, Osservatorio sul moderno, Prof. Dr. Gaia Remiddi und Maria Teresa Cutrì

Literature

Acta Sanctae Sedis [*ASS*]. Rome, 1865–1908.

A dieci anni dall'apertura dell'Archivio della Congregazione per la Dottrina della Fede: Storia e Archivi dell'Inquisizione (Roma, 21–23 febbraio 2008) (Atti dei Convegni Lincei 260). Rome, 2011.

Adelslexikon, ed. Deutsches Adelsarchiv. vol. 5: Has-I, compiled by Walter von Hueck. Limburg, 1847.

Allgemeine Deutsche Biographie [*ADB*], edited by Historische Commission beider Königlichen Akademie der Wissenschaften, vols. 1–56. Leipzig, 1875–1910. Online: http://www.deutsche-biographie.de/index.html.

Ammicht Quinn, Regina, Hille Haker, and Maureen Junker-Kenny (eds.). *Struktureller Verrat. Sexueller Missbrauch in der Kirche* (Concilium. Internationale Zeitschrift für Theologie 40, 3). Mainz, 2004.

Anderson, Margaret L. "Piety and Politics. Recent Work on German Catholicism." *The Journal of Modern History* 63 (1991), pp. 681–716.

Angenendt, Arnold. "Corpus incorruptum. Eine Leitidee der mittelalterlichen Reliquienverehrung." *Saeculum* 42 (1991), pp. 320–48.

——. *Heilige und Reliquien. Die Geschichte ihres Kultes vom frühen Christentum bis zur Gegenwart*. Munich, 1994; 2nd ed., 1997.

——. "Pollutio. Die 'kultische Reinheit' in Religion und Liturgie." *Archiv für Liturgiewissenschaft* 52 (2010) vol. 1/2, pp. 52–93.

——. *Toleranz und Gewalt. Das Christentum zwischen Bibel und Schwert*. Münster, 2006.

Annuario Pontificio. Rome, 1860–.

Armellini, Mariano. *Le Chiese di Roma. Dalle loro origini sino al secolo XVI*. Rome, 1887.

Arnold, Claus. *Kleine Geschichte des Modernismus*. Freiburg i. Br., 2007.

Aubert, Roger. *Le Pontificat de Pie IX (1846–1878)* (Histoire de L'Église 21). Paris, 1952.

Auffahrt, Christoph. "Himmel—Hölle—Fegefeuer I." In: Markschies and Wolf (eds.), *Erinnerungsorte*, pp. 515–23.

Bangen, Johann Heinrich. *Die römische Curie, ihre gegenwärtige Zusammensetzung und ihr Geschäftsgang. Mit einer Sammlung von Belegstücken und Formularen*. Münster, 1854.

Battistella, Antonio. *Il S. Officio e la riforma religiosa in Bologna*. Bologna, 1905.

Behringer, Wolfgang. *Hexen. Glaube, Verfolgung, Vermarktung*. Munich, 4th ed., 2005.

Belz, Willi. *Friedrich Michelis und seine Bestreitung der Neuscholastik in der Polemik gegen Joseph Kleutgen* (Studien zur Problemgeschichte der antiken und mittelalterlichen Philosophie 9). Leiden, 1978.

Beretta, Francesco. *Galilée devant le Tribunal de l'Inquisition. Une relecture des sources*. Fribourg, Switzerland, 1998.

Beretta, Francesco (ed.). *Galilée en procès, Galilée réhabilité*. Saint-Maurice, 2005.

Best, Otto F. *Vom Küssen. Ein sinnliches Lexikon* (Reclam Bibliothek 20056). Leipzig, 2003.

Beumer, Johannes. "Die dogmatische Konstitution 'Pastor aeternus' und ihr Rückgriff auf die Theologie der Vorzeit." *Estudios Eclesiásticos* 45 (1970), pp. 339–58.

Beuron 1863–1963. Festschrift zum hundertjährigen Bestehen der Erzabtei St. Martin. Beuron, 1963.

Bianchi, Giovanni A. *Notizie dell'origine, e dell'antichità del ven. monastero di S. Ambrogio detto della Massima e della sagra immagine di Maria Vergine chenella chiesa dello stesso monastero conservasi.* Rome, 1755.

Biographisch-Bibliographisches Kirchenlexikon [BBKL], founded and ed. Friedrich Wilhelm Bautz. Continued by Traugott Bautz. Herzberg, 1990. Online: http://www.bautz.de/bbkl.

Bischof, Franz Xaver. *Theologie und Geschichte. Ignaz von Döllinger (1799–1890) in der zweiten Hälfte seines Lebens* (Münchener Kirchenhistorische Studien 9). Stuttgart, etc., 1997.

Bittner, Maximilian. *Der vom Himmel gefallene Brief Christi in seinen morgenländischen Versionen und Rezensionen.* Vienna, 1905.

Blackbourn, David. *The Marpingen Visions: Rationalism, Religion and the Rise of Modern Germany.* London, 1995.

Blaschke, Olaf. "Das 19. Jahrhundert: Ein Zweites Konfessionelles Zeitalter?" *Geschichte und Gesellschaft* 26 (2000), pp. 38–75.

Blouin, Francis X. *Vatican Archives. An Inventory and Guide to Historical Documents of the Holy See.* Supplement 1: *The Archives of the Congregation for the Doctrine of the Faith, Including the Archives of the Former Congregation of the Holy Office and the Archives of the Former Congregation for Forbidden Books.* Ann Arbor, 2003.

Borutta, Manuel. *Antikatholizismus. Deutschland und Italien im Zeitalter der europäischen Kulturkämpfe.* Göttingen, 2nd ed., 2011.

Bottoni, Elena. *Scritture dell'anime. Esperienze religiose femminili nella Toscana del Settecento* (Temi e Testi 76). Rome, 2009.

Boutry, Philippe. *Souverain et pontife. Recherches prosopographiques sur la Curie romaine à l'âge de la restauration (1814–1846)* (Collection de l'École française de Rome 300). Rome, 2002.

Braun, Christina von, and Inge Stephan (eds.). *Gender-Studien. Eine Einführung.* Stuttgart/Weimar, 2nd ed., 2006.

Brooten, Bernadette J. *Love Between Women. Early Christian Responses to Female Homoeroticism.* Chicago, 1996.

Brown, Judith C. *Immodest Acts: The Life of a Lesbian Nun in Renaissance Italy.* New York and Oxford, 1986.

Buhlmann, Nicolaus U., and Peter Styra (eds.). *Signum in Bonum. Festschrift für Wilhelm Imkamp zum 60. Geburtstag* (Thurn und Taxis Studien—Neue Folge). Regensburg, 2011.

Bülow, Bernhard Fürst von. *Denkwürdigkeiten,* 4 vols., ed. Franz von Stockhammern. Berlin, 1930–1931.

Bürke, Georg. *Vom Mythos zur Mystik. Joseph Görres' mystische Lehre und die romantische Naturphilosophie.* Einsiedeln, 1958.

Busch, Norbert. *Katholische Frömmigkeit und Moderne. Die Sozial- und Mentalitätsgeschichte des Herz-Jesu-Kultes in Deutschland zwischen Kulturkampf und Erstem Weltkrieg* (Religiöse Kulturen der Moderne 6). Gütersloh, 1997.

Caffarini, Tommaso. *Caterina von Siena. Erinnerungen eines Zeitzeugen. Die Legenda Minor,* ed. Werner Schmid. Passau, 2001.

Carlin, Gianluca. *L'ecclesiologia di Carlo Passaglia (1812–1887). Mit einer deutschen Zusammenfassung* (Dogma und Geschichte 2). Münster, 2000.

Carmignani, Giovanni. *Elementi di diritto criminale*. Milan, 1863.

Cattaneo, Massimo. "'Vitio nefando' e Inquisizione romana." In: Marina Formica and Alberto Postigliola (eds.), *Diversità e minoranze nel Settecento. Atti del Seminario di Santa Margherita Ligure 2–4 giugno 2003* (Biblioteca del XVIII secolo 4). Rome, 2006, pp. 55–77.

Cavarzere, Marco. "Suppliche di denuncia e censura ecclesiastica alla metà del Seicento (1620–1650)." *Archivio italiano per la storia della pietà* 20 (2007), pp. 145–68.

Conciliorum Oecumenicorum Decreta [COD]/Dekrete der Ökumenischen Konzilien, ed. Giuseppe Alberigo et al., vol. 3. Paderborn, 3rd ed., 1973.

Congar, Yves. "Bref historique des formes des 'magistère' et de ses relations avec les docteurs." *Revue des sciences philosophiques et théologiques* 60 (1976), pp. 99–112.

———. *Die Tradition und die Traditionen*. Mainz, 1965.

Conzemius, Victor. *Katholizismus ohne Rom*. Zurich, 1969.

Coreth, Emerich, Walter M. Neidel, and Georg Pfligersdorffer. *Christliche Philosophie im katholischen Denken des 19. und 20. Jahrhunderts*, 3 vols. Graz, 1987–1990.

Craveri, Marcello. *Sante e streghe. Biografie e documenti dal XIV al XVII secolo*. Milan, 1980.

Curtius, Friedrich (ed.). *Denkwürdigkeiten des Fürsten Chlodwig zu Hohenlohe-Schillingsfürst*. 2 vols. Stuttgart/Leipzig, 1907.

Cutrì, Maria Teresa. Ex scuola in via Sant'Ambrogio 4. Online: http://w3.uniroma1
.it/archiscuole/SCUOLE%20WEB/SCUOLE%20PDF/SCUOLE%20I%20
PDF/27%20-%20ex%20scuola%20in%20via%20Sant%20Ambrogio%204%20%20
%28MTC%29.pdf.

De Giorgio, Michela. "Das katholische Modell." in: Duby and Perrot (eds.), *Geschichte*, vol. 4, pp. 187–220.

Degler-Spengler, Brigitte. "Die Regulierten Terziarinnen in der Schweiz." In: *Helvetia Sacra Abteilung V: Der Franziskusorden*. vol. 1: *Die Franziskaner, die Klarissen und die regulierten Franziskanerterziarinnen in der Schweiz. Die Minimen in der Schweiz*. Bern, 1978, pp. 609–62.

Del Col, Andrea. *L'Inquisizione in Friuli. Mostra storica* (Inquisizione e società. Strumenti 1). Trieste, 2000.

———. *L'Inquisizione in Italia. Dal XII al XXI secolo*. Milan, 2006.

Del Col, Andrea, and Giovanna Paolin (eds.). *L'Inquisizione romana. Metodologia delle fonti e storia istituzionale. Atti del seminario internazionale, Montereale Valcellina, 23 e 24 settembre 1999*. Trieste, 2000.

Denzinger, Heinrich, and Peter Hünermann. *Enchiridion Symbolorum Definitionum et Declarationum de rebus fidei et morum*. Freiburg i. Br., 43 ed., 2010.

Denzler, Georg. *Die verbotene Lust. 2000 Jahre christliche Sexualmoral*. Munich, 3rd ed., 1991.

Descrizione topografica di Roma e Comarca. Loro monumenti commercio industria, agricoltura, istituti di pubblica beneficenza, santuarii acque potabili e minerali, popolazione uomini illustri nelle scienze lettere ed arti. Rome, 1864.

Deufel, Konrad. *Kirche und Tradition. Ein Beitrag zur Geschichte der theologischen Wende im 19. Jahrhundert am Beispiel des kirchlich-theologischen Kampfprogramms P. Joseph Kleutgens S. J. Darstellung und neue Quellen* (Beiträge zur Katholizismusforschung. B: Abhandlungen). Munich, 1976.

Dinzelbacher, Peter. *Christliche Mystik im Abendland. Ihre Geschichte von den Anfängen bis zum Ende des Mittelalters*. Paderborn, 1994.

——. "Die Realität des Teufels im Mittelalter." In: Peter Segl (ed.), *Der Hexenhammer. Entstehung und Umfeld des Malleus maleficarum von 1847*. Cologne/Vienna, 1988, pp. 151–75.

——. "Körperliche und seelische Vorbedingungen religiöser Träume und Visionen." In: Tullio Gregory (ed.), *I sogni nel medioevo. Seminario internazionale Roma 2–4 ottobre 1983* (Lessico Intellettuale Europeo 35). Rome, 1985, pp. 57–86.

——. *Mittelalterliche Frauenmystik*. Paderborn, 1993.

Dizionario biografico degli Italiani [DBI], ed. Istituto della Enciclopedia Italiana. Rome, 1960–. Online: http://www.treccani.it/biografie.

Dizionario degli Istituti di Perfezione [DIP], ed. Guerrino Pelliccia and Giancarlo Rocca, 10 vols. Rome, 1974–2003.

Dizionario Storico dell'Inquisizione [DSI]. ed. Adriano Prosperi, aided by Vincenzo Lavenia and John Tedeschi, 3 vols. and 1 vol. Apparati. Pisa, 2010.

Döllinger, Ignaz von. "Rede über Vergangenheit und Gegenwart der katholischen Theologie." In: *Verhandlungen der Versammlung katholischer Gelehrter in München vom 28. September bis 1. Oktober 1863*, ed. Pius Gams. Regensburg, 1863, pp. 25–59.

Doornik, Nicolaas G. M. van. *Katharina von Siena. Eine Frau, die in der Kirche nicht schwieg*. Freiburg i. Br., 1980.

Dreuille, Mayeul de. *S. Ambrogio della Massima. Maison Padrenelle de St. Ambroise. XXII siècles d'histoire. La plus ancienne maison religieuse de Rome*. Parma, 1996.

Duby, Georges, and Michelle Perrot (eds.). *Geschichte der Frauen. vol. 4: 19. Jahrhundert*, ed. Geneviève Fraisse and Michelle Perrot. Frankfurt am Main, 1997; reprint, Berlin, 2012.

Duhr, Bernhard. *Jesuiten-Fabeln. Ein Beitrag zur Kulturgeschichte*. Freiburg i. Br., 2nd ed., 1891.

Dussler, Hildebrand. *Johann Michael Feneberg und die Allgäuer Erweckungsbewegung. Ein kirchengeschichtlicher Beitrag aus den Quellen zur Heimatkunde des Allgäus*. Nürnberg/Kempten, 1959.

Eikermann, Erika. "Heilkundige Frauen und Giftmischerinnen—eine pharmaziehistorische Studie aus forensisch-toxikologischer Sicht. Darlegung einzelner Giftmordfälle aus dem 19. und 20. Jahrhundert, Beschreibung der verwendeten Gifte und ihrer Geschichte." Dissertation, University of Bonn, 2004.

Elberfeld, Ingelore. *Küss mich—eine unterhaltsame Geschichte der wollüstigen Küsse*. Königstein im Taunus, 2001.

Feldbauer, Gerhard. *Geschichte Italiens. Vom Risorgimento bis heute*. Cologne, 2008.

Fiala, Virgil. "Beuron." In: Quarthal et al. (compilers), *Benediktinerklöster*, pp. 135–44.

——. "Die Bemühungen um Wiederzulassung der Benediktiner in Baden und Hohenzollern während des 19. Jahrhunderts." In: Quarthal et al. (compilers), *Benediktinerklöster*, pp. 718–33.

——. "Ein Jahrhundert Beuroner Geschichte." In: *Beuron 1863–1963*, pp. 39–230.

Fink, Karl August. "Kardinal Hohenlohe und das römische Milieu in der zweiten Hälfte des 19. Jahrhunderts." In: Martin Schmidt and Georg Schwaiger (eds.), *Kirchen und Liberalismus im 19. Jahrhundert* (Studien zur Theologie und Geistesgeschichte des neunzehnten Jahrhunderts 19). Göttingen, 1976, pp. 164–72.

——. "Zu den Tagebüchern von Franz Xaver Kraus," *Theologische Quartalschrift* 138 (1958), pp. 471–80.

Finkenzeller, Josef. "Joseph Kleutgen (1811–1883)." In: Fries/Schwaiger (ed.), *Theologen*, vol. 2, pp. 318–44.

Forstner, Dorothea, and Renate Becker (eds.). *Neues Lexikon christlicher Symbole*. Innsbruck, 1991.

Freyer, Johannes-B. (ed.). *Mystik in den franziskanischen Orden* (Veröffentlichungen der Johannes-Duns-Skotus-Akademie für franziskanische Geistesgeschichte und Spiritualität 3). Kevelaer, 1993.

Fried, Johannes. *Der Schleier der Erinnerung. Grundzüge einer historischen Memorik*. Munich, 2004.

Fries, Heinrich, and Georg Schwaiger (eds.), *Katholische Theologen Deutschlands im 19. Jahrhundert*, 3 vols. Munich, 1975.

Gall, Lothar. *Europa auf dem Weg in die Moderne 1850–1890* (Oldenbourg Grundriss der Geschichte 14). Munich, 3rd ed., 1997.

Galletti, Pietro. *Memorie stoṛiche intorno alla Provincia romana della Compagnia di Gesù dall'anno 1814 all'anno 1870*. Vol. 2: *1849–1870*. Rome, 1939.

Garhammer, Erich. "Die Erhebung von Erzbischof Reisach zum Kardinal. Gründe, Hintergründe, Konsequenzen." *Römische Quartalschrift* 81 (1986), pp. 80–101.

———. "Die Regierung des Erzbischofs Karl August Grafen von Reisach (1846–1856)." In: Georg Schwaiger (ed.), *Das Erzbistum München und Freising im 19. und 20. Jahrhundert*. Munich, 1989, pp. 75–124.

———. *Seminaridee und Klerusbildung bei Karl August Graf von Reisach. Eine pastoralgeschichtliche Studie zum Ultramontanismus des 19. Jahrhunderts* (Münchener kirchenhistorische Studien 5). Stuttgart, 1990.

Garuti, Adriano. "La Santa Romana e Universale Inquisizione: strutture e procedure." In: *L'Inquisizione. Atti del Simposio internazionale*, pp. 381–417.

Gatz, Erwin (ed.). *Die Bischöfe der deutschsprachigen Länder 1785/1803 bis 1945. Ein biographisches Lexikon*. Berlin, 1983.

Gennari, Casimiro. *Del falso misticismo*. Rome, 1907.

Gerlach, Walter. *Das neue Lexikon des Aberglaubens*. Frankfurt am Main, 1998.

Gieben, Servus (ed.). *Francesco d'Assisi nella storia. Secoli XVI–XIX*. Rome, 1983.

Giovagnoli, Agostino. *Dalla teologia alla politica. L'itinerario di Carlo Passaglia negli anni di Pio IX e Cavour* (Biblioteca di storia contemporanea). Brescia, 1984.

Gißibl, Bernhard. "Zeichen der Zeit? Wunderheilungen, Visionen und ekstatische Frömmigkeit im bayerischen Vormärz." In: Nils Freytag and Diethard Sawicki (eds.), *Wunderwelten. Religiöse Ekstase und Magie in der Moderne*. Munich, 2006, pp. 83–114.

Görres, Joseph von. *Mystik, Magie und Dämonie*. In: Joseph Bernhart (ed.), *Die Christliche Mystik in Auswahl*. Munich/Berlin, 1927.

Gotor, Miguel. *Chiesa e santità nell'Italia moderna* (Storia moderna). Rome/Bari, 2004.

Götz von Olenhusen, Irmtraud. *Klerus und abweichendes Verhalten. Zur Sozialgeschichte katholischer Priester im 19. Jahrhundert: Die Erzdiözese Freiburg* (Kritische Studien zur Geschichtswissenschaft 106). Göttingen, 1994.

Gousset, Thomas M. J. *Moraltheologie zum Gebrauche der Pfarrer und Beichtväter*. Vol. 1: *Enthaltend die Abhandlungen über die menschlichen Handlungen, über das Gewissen, über die Gesetze, über die Sünden, über die Tugenden und über die zehn Gebote Gottes*. Aachen, 1851.

Graf, Georg. "Der vom Himmel gefallene Brief Christi." *Zeitschrift für Semitistik und verwandte Gebiete* 6 (1928), pp. 10–23.

Granderath, Theodor. *Geschichte des Vatikanischen Konzils. Von seiner ersten Ankündigung bis zu seiner Vertagung.* Vol. 2: *Von der Eröffnung des Konzils bis zum Schlusse der dritten öffentlichen Sitzung.* Freiburg i. Br., 1903.

Gregorovius, Ferdinand. *The Roman Journals of Ferdinand Gregorovius, 1852–1874,* edited by Friedrich Althaus and translated from the second German edition by Mrs. Gustavus W. Hamilton. London, 1907.

Greschat, Martin (ed.). *Gestalten der Kirchengeschichte,* 14 vols. Stuttgart, 1993.

Gurisatti, Giulia, and Domenico Picchi. "S. Ambrogio della Massima." *Quaderni dell'Istituto di storia dell'architettura* 27 (1982), pp. 49–60.

Haacke, Rhabanus. "Maria in der neuscholastischen Theologie am Beispiel Joseph Kleutgens." In: Rhabanus, *Beiträge zur Marienkunde* (Siegburger Studien 21), Siegburg, 1988, pp. 97–110.

Hagers Handbuch der pharmazeutischen Praxis für Apotheker, Arzneimittelhersteller, Drogisten, Ärzte und Medizinalbeamte, 2 vols. Berlin, 2nd ed., 1938; 1 supplementary vol., Berlin, 1949; 2 supplementary vols., Berlin, 1958.

Handbuch der Kirchengeschichte, ed. Hubert Jedin. vol. 6, no. 1: *Die Kirche zwischen Revolution und Restauration,* ed. Roger Aubert et al. Freiburg, 1971.

Hartmann, Peter C. *Die Jesuiten.* Munich, 2001.

Hasler, August Bernhard. *Pius IX. (1846–1878). päpstliche Unfehlbarkeit und 1. Vatikanisches Konzil. Dogmatisierung und Durchsetzung einer Ideologie* (Päpste und Papsttum 12), 2 vols. Stuttgart, 1977.

Heimbucher, Max. *Die Orden und Kongregationen der katholischen Kirche,* 2 vols. Munich, 3rd ed., 1965.

Heppe, Heinrich. *Geschichte der quietistischen Mystik in der katholischen Kirche.* Berlin, 1875.

Hergenröther, Joseph. *Der Kirchenstaat seit der Französischen Revolution. Historisch-statistische Studien und Skizzen.* Freiburg i. Br., 1860.

Hertkens, Johann. *P. Joseph Kleutgen S. J. Sein Leben und seine literarische Wirksamkeit. Zum Säkulargedächtnis seiner Geburt (1811–1911),* compiled and edited by P. Ludwig Lercher. Regensburg, 1910.

Hinschius, Paul. *Das Kirchenrecht der Katholiken und Protestanten in Deutschland,* 5 vols. and 1 half-vol. Berlin, 1869–1897.

———. *System des katholischen Kirchenrechts mit besonderer Rücksicht auf Deutschland. vol. 5, Erste Abteilung* (Das Kirchenrecht der Katholiken und Protestanten in Deutschland). Berlin, 1893.

Horst, Ulrich. "Das Dogma von der Unbefleckten Empfängnis Marias (1854). Vorgeschichte und Folgen." In: Weitlauff (ed.), *Kirche,* pp. 95–114.

Huguet, Paul, and Franz Thalhaus. *Der Geist Pius IX. oder die schönsten Züge aus dem Leben dieses großen Papstes. Deutsch bearbeitet, mit Anmerkungen und Zusätzen und mit einer historisch-politischen Skizze: der Papst-König.* Vienna, 1866.

Hüwelmeier, Gertrud. *Närrinnen Gottes. Lebenswelten von Ordensfrauen.* Münster, 2004.

Ickx, Johan. *La Santa Sede tra Lamennais e San Tommaso d'Aquino. La condanna di Gerard Casimir Ubaghs e della dottrina dell'Università Cattolica di Lovanio (1834–1870)* (Collectanea Archivi Vaticani 56). Vatican City, 2005.

Imkamp, Wilhelm. "'Fervens ad laborandum … !' Die römischen Studienjahre des Dr. Carl Sonnenschein." *Römische Quartalschrift* 71 (1976), pp. 175–98.

Jacobson Schutte, Anne. *Aspiring Saints: Pretense of Holiness, Inquisition and Gender in the Republic of Venice, 1618–1750.* Baltimore/London, 2001.

Kessler, Ewald. *Johann Friedrich (1836–1917). Ein Beitrag zur Geschichte des Altkatholizismus* (Miscellanea Bavarica Monacensia 55). Munich, 1975.

Klee, Heinrich. *Grundriß der katholischen Moral,* ed. Heinrich Himioben. Mainz, 1843.

Klemm, Hans-Jürgen. "Was ist sexueller Mißbrauch? Aktuelle Diskussion und Definitionsfragen." In: Klemm/Heidrun Gaßmann (ed.), *Sexueller Mißbrauch bei Menschen in Abhängigkeitsverhältnissen. Tabu und Wirklichkeit.* Bielefeld, 1996, pp. 12–23.

[Kleutgen, Joseph, using the pseudonym] J. W. Karl, *Ueber den Glauben an das Wunderbare.* Münster, 1846.

[Kleutgen, Joseph], *Die oberste Lehrgewalt des Römischen Bischofs. Von einem römischen Theologen.* Trier, 1870.

Kleutgen, Joseph. *Die Philosophie der Vorzeit,* 2 vols. Münster, 1860–1863, 2nd ed., 1878.

——. *Die Theologie der Vorzeit.* Münster, 1853–1870, 2nd ed., 1867–1874.

——. *Kleinere Werke.* Vol. 2: *Briefe aus Rom.* Münster, 1869.

——. "Memorandum." In: Kleutgen, *Zu meiner Rechtfertigung.* Münster, 1868, pp. 5–11.

——. *Ueber die alten und die neuen Schulen.* Mainz, 1846.

Koch, Ludwig. *Jesuiten-Lexikon. Die Gesellschaft Jesu einst und jetzt,* 2 vols. Löwen-Heverlee, 1962.

Kopf, Paul. "Klösterliches Leben in Baden-Württemberg von 1803–2003 und dessen Positionierung in die Zukunft." *Freiburger Diözesanarchiv* 123 (2003), pp. 25–45.

Kosch, Wilhelm. *Das Katholische Deutschland. Biographisch-Bibliographisches Lexikon,* 2 vols. Augsburg, 1937.

Köster, Norbert. *Der Fall Hirscher. Ein "Spätaufklärer" im Konflikt mit Rom?* (Römische Inquisition und Indexkongregation 8). Paderborn, 2007.

Kraus, Franz Xaver. "Hohenlohe (1897)." In: Kraus, *Essays,* vol. 2, Berlin, 1901, pp. 165–75.

——. *Tagebücher,* ed. Hubert Schiel. Cologne, 1957.

Kroll, Renate (ed.) *Metzler Lexikon Gender Studies—Geschlechterforschung: Ansätze, Personen, Grundbegriffe.* Stuttgart, 2002.

L'Apertura degli Archivi del Sant'Uffizio Romano (Roma, 22 gennaio 1998) (Atti dei Convegni Lincei 142). Rome, 1998.

L'Inquisizione. Atti del Simposio internazionale (Città del Vaticano, 29–31 ottobre 1998), ed. Comitato del Grande Giubileo dell'Anno 2000. Vatican City, 2003.

L'Inquisizione e gli storici: un cantiere aperto. Tavola rotonda nell'ambito della conferenza annuale della ricerca (Roma, 24–25 giugno 1999) (Atti dei Convegni Lincei 162). Rome, 2000.

Lakner, Franz. "Kleutgen und die kirchliche Wissenschaft Deutschlands im 19. Jahrhundert." *Zeitschrift für katholische Theologie* 57 (1933), pp. 161–214.

Lang, Bernhard. "Himmel—Hölle—Fegefeuer II." In: Markschies and Wolf (eds.), *Erinnerungsorte,* pp. 524–33.

Langhorst, August. "Aus dem Jugendleben des P. Joseph Kleutgen." *Stimmen aus Maria Laach* 25 (1883), pp. 105–24, 393–403, and 489–510.

Lapponi, Massimo. "Il diario di D. Mauro Wolter monaco di S. Paolo." *Benedictina* 47 (2000), pp. 151–79.

Lempl, Thomas. *Das Herz Jesu. Eine Studie über die verschiedenen Bedeutungen des Wortes "Herz" und über den Gegenstand der kirchlichen Herz-Jesu-Andacht.* Brixen (Bressanone), 1909.

Leppin, Volker. *Die christliche Mystik.* Munich, 2007.

Lexikon der Christlichen Ikonographie [LCI], founded by Engelbert Kirschbaum and edited by Wolfgang Braunfels, 8 vols. Freiburg i. Br. 1968–1976; Special edition, Freiburg i. Br., 1990

Lexikon des Mittelalters [LexMA], 9 vols., Stuttgart/Weimar, 1999.

Lexikon für Theologie und Kirche [LThK]. 1st edition, ed. Michael Buchberger, 10 vols., Freiburg i. Br., 1930–1938. 2nd edition, ed. Josef Höfer and Karl Rahner, 10 vols. and an index vol., Freiburg i. Br., 1957–1967. 3rd edition, ed. Walter Kasper et al., 10 vols., Freiburg i. Br., 1993–2001.

Lhermitte, Jean. *Echte und falsche Mystiker.* Lucerne, 1953.

Lill, Rudolf. "Der Ultramontanismus. Die Ausrichtung der gesamten Kirchen auf den Papst." In: Weitlauff (ed.), *Kirche,* pp. 76–94.

Lill, Rudolf (compiler). *Vatikanische Akten zur Geschichte des deutschen Kulturkampfes. Leo XIII. 1. Teil: 1878–1880.* Tübingen, 1970.

Lissner, Anneliese, Rita Süssmuth, and Karin Walter (eds.). *Frauenlexikon. Tradition, Fakten, Perspektiven.* Freiburg i. Br., 1988.

Lombardi, Ferruccio. *Roma. Chiese, Conventi, Chiostri. Progetto per un inventario 312–1925.* Rome, 1993.

Loome, Thomas Michael. *Liberal Catholicism. Reform Catholicism. Modernism: A Contribution to a New Orientation in Modernist Research.* Mainz, 1979.

Luzzatto, Sergio. *Padre Pio. Miracoli e politica nell'Italia del Novecento.* Turin, 2007.

Mai, Paul. "Bischof Ignatius von Senestréy als Mitglied der Deputation für Glaubensfragen auf dem I. Vatikanum." *Verhandlungen des Historischen Vereins für Oberpfalz und Regensburg* 109 (1969), pp. 115–43.

Malan, Emil Chavin von. *Geschichte der heiligen Katharina von Siena (1347–1380).* Regensburg, 2nd ed., 1874.

Malena, Adelisa. "Inquisizione, 'Finte Sante,' 'Nuovi Mistici.' Ricerche sul Seicento." In: *L'Inquisizione e gli storici,* pp. 289–328.

Mansi, Joannes. *Dominicus, Sacrorum Conciliorum Nova et Amplissima Collectio,* vol. 53. Graz, 1961.

Marienlexikon, commissioned by the Institutum Marianum Regensburg e. V., edited by Remigius Bäumer und Leo Scheffczyk, 6 vols. St. Ottilien, 1988–1994.

Markschies, Christoph, and Hubert Wolf (eds.). *Erinnerungsorte des Christentums.* Munich, 2010.

Marschler, Thomas. "Scheeben und Kleutgen—ihr Verhältnis im Spiegel zweier unveröffentlichter Briefdokumente." In: Buhlmann/Styra (ed.), *Signum,* pp. 459–84.

Marshman, Michelle. "Exorcism as Empowerment: A New Idiom." *The Journal of Religious History* 23 (1999), issue 3, pp. 265–81.

Martina, Giacomo. *Pio IX (1846–1878),* 3 vols. Rome, 1986–1990.

——. *Storia della Compagnia di Gesù in Italia (1814–1983).* Brescia, 2003.

Masini, Eliseo. *Sacro Arsenale ovvero pratica dell'uffizio della Santa Inquisizione; coll'inserzione di alcune regole fatte dal P. Inquisitore Tommaso Menghini Domenicano, e di diverse annotazioni del dottore Gio. Pasqualone . . . in questa quarta impressione aggiuntavi la settima denunzia fatta dal suddetto padre perli sponte Comparenti, impressa in Ferrara 1687 . . .* Rome, 1730.

McGinn, Bernard. *The Essential Writings of Christian Mysticism.* New York, 2006.

Mendizábal, Rufo. *Catalogus Defunctorum in renata Societate Iesu ab a. 1814 ad a.1970.* Rome, 1972.

Menichetti, Piero Luigi. *Storia di Gubbio. Dalle origini all'Unità d'Italia.* Città di Castello, 1987.

Menozzi, Daniele. *Sacro Cuore. Un culto tra devozione interiore e restaurazione cristiana della società* (Sacro sancto. Nuova serie 5). Rome, 2001.

Modica, Marilena. *Infetta dottrina. Inquisizione e quietismo nel Seicento* (Sacrosancto. Nuova serie 13). Rome, 2009.

Moos, Peter von. "Kirchliche Disziplinierung zwischen Mittelalter und Moderne. Adriano Prosperis 'Tribunali della coscienza' aus mediävistischer Sicht." *Zeitschrift für Historische Forschung* 27 (2000), pp 75–90.

Morichini, Carlo Luigi. *Degl'istituti di pubblica carità ed istruzione primaria e delle prigioni in Roma,* vol. 2. Rome, 1842.

Moroni, Gaetano. *Dizionario di erudizione storico-ecclesiastica da S. Pietro sino ai nostri giorni,* 103 vols. Venice, 1840–1861. Online: http://www.cortedeirossi.it/libro/biblio/moroni.htm.

Müller, Gerhard Ludwig. *Katholische Dogmatik. Für Studium und Praxis der Theologie.* Freiburg i. Br., 2nd ed., 1994.

Naab, Erich. "Die Auflösung der 'mystischen Theologie' und 'Die christliche Mystik' von Görres" *Revista Española de Teología* 65 (2005), pp. 53–74.

Neue Deutsche Biographie [NDB], edited by Historische Kommission bei der Bayerischen Akademie der Wissenschaften, 24 vols. to date. Berlin 1953–. Online: http://www.deutsche-biographie.de/index.html.

Nichols, Aidan. *Conversation of Faith and Reason. Modern Catholic Thought from Hermes to Benedict XVI.* Chicago, 2011.

Notizie per l'anno 1716–1859. Rome, 1716–1859.

Opitz, Claudia. *Um-Ordnungen der Geschlechter. Einführung in die Geschlechtergeschichte* (Historische Einführungen 10). Tübingen, 2005.

Orlandi, Giuseppe. *La fede al vaglio. Quietismo, satanismo e massoneria nel Ducato di Modena tra Sette e Ottocento* (Deputazione di storia patria per la antiche province modenesi 101). Modena, 1988.

Overbeck, Gerd, and Ulrich Niemann. *Stigmata. Geschichte und Psychosomatik eines religiösen Phänomens.* Darmstadt, 2012.

Pagano, Sergio. "Le visite apostoliche a Roma nei secoli XVI–XIX. Repertorio delle fonti." *Ricerche per la storia religiosa di Roma* 4 (1980), pp. 317–464.

Pahud de Mortanges, Elke. *Philosophie und kirchliche Autorität. Der Fall Jakob Frohschammer vor der römischen Indexkongregation (1855–1864)* (Römische Inquisition und Indexkongregation 4). Paderborn, 2005.

Pazzelli, Raffaele. *Il Terz'Ordine Regolare di S. Francesco attraverso i secoli. Rielaborazione critica e sviluppo dell'opera storica di Raniero Luconi.* Rome, 1958.

———. *San Francesco e il Terz'Ordine. Il movimento penitenziale prefrancescano e francescano.* Padua, 1982.

460 · Sources and Literature

Perrone, Giovanni. *Praelectiones Theologicae*. 9 vols., Regensburg, 1854.

Petrocchi, Massimo. *Il quietismo italiano del Seicento*. Rome, 1948.

Petzolt, Stephan. *Die Gründungs- und Entwicklungsgeschichte der Abtei Beuron im Spiegel ihrer Liturgie (1863–1908)*. Würzburg, 1990.

———. "Maurus Wolter—ein Leben im Geist der Liturgie." *Erbe und Auftrag* 66 (1990), pp. 335–43.

Pfeffer, Anton. *Die Gründerin der Erzabtei Beuron. Fügung und Führung in einem Frauenleben* (Aus Schwabens Vergangenheit 2). Stuttgart, 1932.

Pfülf, Otto. "Hohenlohe als Ankläger des Jesuitenordens." *Stimmen aus Maria Laach* 72 (1907), pp. 1–22.

Pianciani, Luigi. *La Rome des papes. Son origine, ses phases successives, ses moeurs intimes*, 3 vols. London, 1859.

Pietrangeli, Carlo. *Rione XI—S. Angelo, Guide Rionali di Roma*. Palombi, 1984.

Platte, Helmut. *Das fürstliche Haus Hohenzollern-Sigmaringen* (Deutsche Fürstentümer 9). Werl, 2003.

Ponziani, Daniel. "Fonti per una storia dei misticismi nel XX secolo. La serie 'Devotiones variae' dell'Archivio del Sant'Ufficio (1912–1938)." *Ricerche di storia sociale e religiosa*, Nuova Serie 79 (2011), pp. 59–66.

———. "Misticismo, santità e devozione nel 'secolo dei lumi.' Percorsi di ricerca nell'Archivio della Congregazione per la Dottrina della Fede." In: Hubert Wolf (ed.), *Inquisition und Buchzensur im Zeitalter der Aufklärung* (Römische Inquisition und Indexkongregation 16). Paderborn, 2011, pp. 323–49.

Poppenburg, Annette. *Das Leben der heiligen Katharina von Siena. Untersuchung und Edition der mittelniederdeutschen Legendenhandschrift* (Westfälische Beiträge zur niederdeutschen Philologie 9). Bielefeld, 1999.

Pottmeyer, Hermann J. *Der Glaube vor dem Anspruch der Wissenschaft. Die Konstitution über den katholischen Glauben "Dei Filius" des 1. Vatikanischen Konzils und die unveröffentlichten theologischen Voten der vorbereitenden Kommission* (Freiburger theologische Studien 87). Freiburg i. Br., 1968.

Priesching, Nicole. *Maria von Mörl (1812–1868). Leben und Bedeutung einer "stigmatisierten Jungfrau" aus Tirol im Kontext ultramontaner Frömmigkeit*. Brixen (Bressanone). 2004.

Pritz, Joseph. *Glauben und Wissen bei Anton Günther. Eine Einführung in sein Leben und Werk mit einer Auswahl aus seinen Schriften*. Vienna, 1963.

Prosperi, Adriano. *Tribunali della coscienza. Inquisitori, confessori, missionari* (Biblioteca di cultura storica 214). Turin, 1996.

Quarthal, Franz, et al. (compilers) *Die Benediktinerklöster in Baden-Württemberg* (Germania Benedictina V). Augsburg, 1975.

Rapp, Ludwig (ed.). *Briefe aus Rom von Dr. Alois Flir*. Innsbruck, 1864.

Raymond of Capua. *Life of Saint Catherine of Siena by the Blessed Raymond of Capua Her Confessor*. New York, no date.

Reikerstorfer, Johann. "Anton Günther (1783–1863) und seine Schule." In: Coreth et al (ed.), *Philosophie*, vol. 1, pp. 266–84.

Reinermann, Alan J. "Metternich and Reform: The Case of the Papal State, 1814–1848." *The Journal of Modern History* 43 (1979), pp. 524–48.

Reinhard, Wolfgang. "Konfession und Konfessionalisierung. 'Die Zeit der Konfessionen" (1530–1620/30) in einer neuen Gesamtdarstellung." *Historisches Jahrbuch* 114 (1994), vol. 1, pp. 107–24.

——. *Lebensformen Europas. Eine historische Kulturanthropologie.* Munich, 2nd ed., 2006.

——. "Was ist katholische Konfessionalisierung?" In: Wolfgang Reinhard and Heinz Schilling (eds.), *Die katholische Konfessionalisierung* (Schriften des Vereins für Reformationsgeschichte 198). Gütersloh, 1995, pp. 419–52.

Reinhardt, Rudolf. "Die Bemühungen um Wiederzulassung der Benediktiner in Württemberg während des 19. Jahrhunderts." In: Quarthal et al. (compilers), *Benediktinerklöster*, pp. 734–44.

Religion in Geschichte und Gegenwart [RGG]. *Handwörterbuch für Theologie und Religionswissenschaft*, 4th edition, ed. Hans Dieter Betz et al., 8 vols. and an index vol. Tübingen, 1998–2007.

Rich, Adrienne. "Compulsory Heterosexuality and Lesbian Existence." In: *Blood, Bread, and Poetry: Selected Prose, 1979–1985*, New York, 1986.

Richter-Appelt, Hertha. "Differentielle Folgen von sexuellem Missbrauch und körperlicher Misshandlung und die Bedeutung von Replikationsstudien." In: Wipplinger and Amann (eds.), *Missbrauch*, pp. 229–49.

Riedel, Wilhelm. *Die Kirchenrechtsquellen des Patriarchats von Alexandrien.* Leipzig, 1900.

Riegler, Georg. *Christliche Moral. Nach der Grundlage der Ethik des Maurus von Schenkl*, 2 parts in 3 vols, Augsburg, 1825–1826. Part 2, vol. 1: *Allgemeine Pflichtenlehre.* Augsburg, 1826.

Roma antica, e moderna o sia Nuova descrizione di tutti gl'edificj antichi, e moderni, tanto sagri, quanto profani della città di Roma formata con l'autorità del cardinal Baronio, . . . Abbellita con duecento, e più figure di rame, e con curiosenotizie istoriche . . . Distinta in 14. rioni . . . Divisa in tre tomi . . . Tomo primo[-terzo]. Rome, 1750.

Romeo, Giovanni. *L'Inquisizione nell'Italia moderna* (Storia moderna). Rome/Bari, 2002.

Sägmüller, Johann Baptist. *Lehrbuch des katholischen Kirchenrechts.* Freiburg i. Br., 1930.

Sales Doyé, Franz von. *Die alten Trachten der männlichen und weiblichen Orden sowie der geistlichen Mitglieder der ritterlichen Orden.* Leipzig, 1930; reprint, Darmstadt, 2012.

Samerski, Stefan. "Wie im Himmel so auf Erden"? *Selig- und Heiligsprechung in der Katholischen Kirche 1740 bis 1870* (Münchener Kirchenhistorische Studien 10). Stuttgart, 2002.

Sawicki, Diethard. *Leben mit den Toten. Geisterglauben und die Entstehung des Spiritismus in Deutschland 1770–1900.* Paderborn, 2002.

Scala, Monika. *Der Exorzismus in der Katholischen Kirche. Ein liturgisches Ritual zwischen Film, Mythos und Realität.* Regensburg, 2012.

Schäfer, Theo. *Die erkenntnistheoretische Kontroverse Kleutgen-Günther. Ein Beitrag zur Entstehungsgeschichte der Neuscholastik.* Paderborn, 1961.

Schatz, Klaus. *Vaticanum I*, 3 vols., Paderborn, 1992–1994.

Schauf, Heribert. "Clemens Schrader (1820–1875)." In: Fries and Schwaiger (eds.), *Theologen*, vol. 2, pp. 368–85.

Schlemmer, Martin. "Gustav Adolf zu Hohenlohe-Schillingsfürst. Schlaglichter aus dem Hohenlohe-Zentralarchiv Neuenstein." In: *Kirche und Gesellschaft im Wandel der Zeiten. Festschrift für Gabriel Adriányi zum 75. Geburtstag*, ed. Hermann-Josef Scheidgen, Sabine Prorok, and Helmut Rönz. Nordhausen, 2012, pp. 373–415.

Schmidlin, Joseph. *Papstgeschichte der neuesten Zeit.* Vol. 1: *Papsttum und Päpste im Zeitalter der*

Restauration (1800–1846). Munich, 3rd ed., 1933. Vol. 2: *Papsttum und Päpste gegenüber den modernen Strömungen. Pius IX. und Leo XIII. (1846–1903).* Munich, 1934.

Schmidt, Peter. *Das Collegium Germanicum in Rom und die Germaniker. Zur Funktion eines römischen Ausländerseminars (1552–1914).* Tübingen, 1984.

———. "Et si conservi sana . . . —Konfessionalisierung und Sprache in den Briefen der römischen Inquisition." In: *Historische Anstöße. Festschrift für Wolfgang Reinhard zum 65. Geburtstag,* ed. Peter Burschel et al. Berlin, 2002, pp. 131–51.

Schmökel, Hartmut. *Heilige Hochzeit und Hoheslied.* Wiesbaden, 1956.

Schneider, Bernhard. "Feminisierung der Religion im 19. Jahrhundert. Perspektiven einer These im Kontext des deutschen Katholizismus." *Trierer Theologische Zeitschrift* 111 (2002), pp. 123–47.

Schneider, Michael. "Die Zelle im monastischen Leben." *Erbe und Auftrag* 86 (2010), pp. 140–53.

Schoeters, Carolus. *P.-J. Beckx S. J. (1795–1887) en de "Jezuieten-Politick" van zijn Tijd.* Antwerp, 1965.

Schöntag, Wilfried (ed.). *250 Jahre Abteikirche Beuron. Geschichte, geistliches Leben, Kunst.* Beuron, 1988.

Schott, Anselm. *Leben und Wirken des hochwürdigsten Herrn Dr. Maurus Wolter, Erzabtes von Beuron.* Stuttgart, 1891.

Schreiner, Klaus. "Die lesende und schreibende Maria als Symbolgestalt religiöser Frauenbildung." In: Gabriela Signori (ed.), *Die lesende Frau* (Wolfenbütteler Forschungen 121). Wolfenbüttel, 2009, pp. 113–54.

———. *Maria. Jungfrau, Mutter, Herrscherin.* Vienna, 1994.

Schulte, Johann Friedrich von. *Der Altkatholizismus.* Gießen, 1887; reprint, Aalen, 1965.

———. *Lebenserinnerungen,* 3 vols. Gießen, 1908–1909.

Schumacher, Joseph. "Das mariologische Konzept in der Theologie der Römischen Schule", in: *Trierer Theologische Zeitschrift* 98 (1989), vol. 3, pp. 207–26.

Schwaiger, Georg (ed.). *Teufelsglaube und Hexenprozesse.* München, 1987.

Schwedt, Herman H. "Das Archiv der römischen Inquisition und des Index." *Römische Quartalschrift* 93 (1998), pp. 267–80.

———. *Das römische Urteil über Georg Hermes (1775–1831). Ein Beitrag zur Geschichte der Inquisition im 19. Jahrhundert* (Römische Quartalschrift 37, Supplement). Rome, 1980.

———. "Die römischen Kongregationen der Inquisition und des Index: die Personen (16.–20. Jahrhundert)." In: Tobias Lagatz/Sabine Schratz (ed.), *Censor Censorum. Gesammelte Aufsätze von Herman H. Schwedt* (Römische Inquisition und Indexkongregation 7). Paderborn, 2006, pp. 49–61.

———. "Die Verurteilung der Werke Anton Günthers (1857) und seiner Schüler." *Zeitschrift für Kirchengeschichte* 101 (1990), vols. 2–3, pp. 301–3.

———. "Quietisten und ein verbotenes Buch des Inquisitors R. Grillenzoni (1688)." In: Buhlmann/Styra (ed.), *Signum,* pp. 579–605.

———. "Rezension zu Konrad Deufel: Kirche und Tradition." *Römische Quartalschrift* 72 (1977), pp. 264–69.

———. "Vom ultramontanen zum liberalen Döllinger." In: Georg Denzler/Ernst Ludwig Grasmück (ed.), *Geschichtlichkeit und Glaube. Gedenkschrift zum 100. Todestag Ignaz von Döllingers.* Munich, 1990, pp. 107–97.

Schwerhoff, Gerd. *Die Inquisition. Ketzerverfolgung in Mittelalter und Neuzeit.* Munich, 3rd ed., 2009.

———. "Hexerei, Geschlecht und Regionalgeschichte." Überlegungen zur Erklärung des scheinbar Selbstverständlichen." In: Gisela Wilbertz, Gerd Schwerhoff, and Jürgen Scheffler (eds.), *Hexenverfolgung und Regionalgeschichte. Die Grafschaft Lippe im Vergleich* (Studien zur Regionalgeschichte 4/Beiträge zur Geschichte der Stadt Lemgo 4). Bielefeld, 1994, pp. 325–53.

Seibt, Gustav. *Rom oder Tod. Der Kampf um die italienische Hauptstadt.* Berlin, 2001.

Seronde-Babonaux, Anne-Marie. *Rome, croissance d'une capitale: de l'urbs à la ville.* Aix-en-Provence/Paris, 1980.

Siebenmorgen, Harald. *Die Anfänge der Beuroner Kunstschule.* Sigmaringen, 1983.

Sieger, Marcus. *Die Heiligsprechung. Geschichte und heutige Rechtslage* (Forschungen zur Kirchenrechtswissenschaft 23). Würzburg, 1995.

Sombart, Werner. *Die römische Campagna, Eine sozial-ökonomische Studie.* Leipzig, 1888.

Sommavilla, Guido. *La Compagnia di Gesù.* Milan, 1985.

Sommervogel, Carlos. *Bibliothèque de la Compagnie de Jésus. Première Partie: Bibliographie,* 9 vols.; *Seconde Partie: Histoire,* 3 vols. Brussels/Paris, 1890–1900.

Spamer, Adolf. "Himmelsbriefe der deutschen Mystik." In: *Volkskundliche Ernte. Hugo Hepding dargebracht am 7. September 1938 von seinen Freunden* (Gießener Beiträge zur deutschen Philologie 60). Gießen, 1938, pp. 184–92.

Speyer, Wolfgang. "Die Verehrung der Heroen, des göttlichen Menschen und des christlichen Heiligen. Analogien und Kontinuitäten." In: Peter Dinzelbacher and Dieter R. Bauer (eds.), *Heiligenverehrung in Geschichte und Gegenwart.* Ostfildern, 1990, pp. 48–66.

Stalmann, Volker. *Fürst Chlodwig zu Hohenlohe-Schillingsfürst 1819–1901. Ein deutscher Reichskanzler.* Paderborn, 2009.

Stapf, Joseph Ambrosius. *Die christliche Moral als Antwort auf die Frage: Was wir thun müssen, um in das Reich Gottes einzugehen,* vol. 2. Innsbruck, 1841.

Steck, Karl Gerhard. "Joseph Kleutgen und die Neuscholastik." In: Erich Fries (ed.), *Festschrift für Joseph Klein zum 70. Geburtstag.* Göttingen, 1967, pp. 288–305.

Stefani, Guglielmo. *Dizionario corografico dello Stato Pontificio.* Rome, 1856.

Steimer, Bruno (ed.). *Herders Lexikon der Heiligen.* Freiburg i. Br., 2003.

Steinhuber, Andreas. *Geschichte des Collegium Germanicum Hungaricum in Rom,* 2 vols. Freiburg i. Br., 1895.

Strobel, Ferdinand (ed.). *Der Regularklerus. Die Gesellschaft Jesu in der Schweiz* (Helvetia Sacra 7). Bern, 1976.

Stübe, Rudolf. *Der Himmelsbrief. Ein Beitrag zur allgemeinen Religionsgeschichte.* Tübingen, 1918.

Taddey, Gerhard. "Unsere unglückliche Unterwerfung unter die württembergische Despotie betreffend. Die Mediatisierung der hohenlohischen Fürstentümer." In: *Alte Klöster—Neue Herren. Die Säkularisation im deutschen Südwesten 1803.* Vol. 2: *Aufsätze Teil 1: Vorgeschichte und Verlauf der Säkularisation,* ed. Hans Ulrich Rudolf. Ostfildern, 2003, pp. 883–92.

Tedeschi, John. *The Prosecution of Heresy. Collected Studies on the Inquisition in Early Modern Italy* (Medieval & Renaissance Texts & Studies 78). Binghamton, 1991.

Theologische Realenzyklopädie [TRE], 36 vols. Berlin/New York, 1977–2004.

Thurn und Taxis-Hohenlohe, Marie von. Jugenderinnerungen (1855–1875). Vienna, 1936.

Thurston, Herbert. The Physical Phenomena of Mysticism. London, 1952.

Traniello, Francesco, and Gianni Sofri. Der lange Weg zur Nation. Das italienische Risorgimento. Stuttgart, 2012.

Trusen, Winfried. "Der Inquisitionsprozeß. Seine historischen Grundlagen und frühen Formen." In: Zeitschrift der Savigny-Stiftung für Rechtsgeschichte. Kanonistische Abteilung 74 (1988), pp. 168–230.

Turi, Anna Maria. Stigmate e stigmatizzati. Rome, 1990.

Unterburger, Klaus. Vom Lehramt der Theologen zum Lehramt der Päpste? Pius XI., die Apostolische Konstitution "Deus scientiarum Dominus" und die Reform der Universitätstheologie. Freiburg i. Br., 2010.

Walkowitz, Judith R. "Gefährliche Formen der Sexualität." In: Duby and Perrot (eds.), Geschichte, vol. 4, pp. 417–49.

Walter, Peter. "Carlo Passaglia. Auf dem Weg zur Communio-Ekklesiologie." In: Peter Neuner and Gunther Wenz (eds.), Theologen des 19. Jahrhunderts. Eine Einführung, Darmstadt, 2002, pp. 165–82.

———. "Die neuscholastische Philosophie im deutschsprachigen Raum." In: Coreth et al (eds.), Philosophie, vol. 2, pp. 131–94.

———. "Zu einem neuen Buch über Joseph Kleutgen SJ. Fragen, Berichtigungen, Ergänzungen." Zeitschrift für katholische Theologie 100 (1978), pp. 318–56.

Weber, Christoph. Kardinäle und Prälaten in den letzten Jahrzehnten des Kirchenstaates. Elite-Rekrutierung, Karriere-Muster und soziale Zusammensetzung der kurialen Führungsschicht zur Zeit Pius' IX. (1846–1878), 2 vols. (Päpste und Papsttum 13, I and II). Stuttgart, 1978.

———. Quellen und Studien zur Kurie und zur vatikanischen Politik unter Leo XIII. Mit Berücksichtigung der Beziehungen des Hl. Stuhles zu den Dreibundmächten. Tübingen, 1973.

———. "Ultramontanismus als katholischer Fundamentalismus," in: Wilfried Loth (ed.), Deutscher Katholizismus im Umbruch zur Moderne (Konfession und Gesellschaft 3), Stuttgart, 1991, pp. 30–45.

Wehr, Gerhard. Die deutsche Mystik. Leben und Inspiration gottentflammter Menschen in Mittelalter und Neuzeit. Cologne, 2011.

Weiß, Bardo. Ekstase und Liebe. Die Unio mystica bei den deutschen Mystikerinnen des 12. und 13. Jahrhunderts. Paderborn, 2006.

Weiß, Otto. "Der Ort der 'christlichen Mystik' im Gesamtwerk von Görres und im Denken seiner Zeit." In: Weiß, Kulturen, Mentalitäten, Mythen. Zur Theologie und Kulturgeschichte des 19. und 20. Jahrhunderts, Manfred Weitlauff, Hubert Wolf, and Claus Arnold, Paderborn (eds.). 2004, pp. 79–130.

———. Deutsche oder römische Moral? Oder: Der Streit um Alfons von Liguori. Ein Beitrag zur Auseinandersetzung zwischen Romanismus und Germanismus im 19. Jahrhundert. Regensburg, 2001.

———. Die Redemptoristen in Bayern (1790–1909). Ein Beitrag zur Geschichte des Ultramontanismus (Münchener theologische Studien. I. Historische Abteilung 22). St. Ottilien, 1983.

———. "Seherinnen und Stigmatisierte." In: Weiß, Kulturen, pp. 43–77.

————. *Weisungen aus dem Jenseits? Der Einfluss mystizistischer Phänomene auf Ordens- und Kirchenleitungen im 19. Jahrhundert.* Regensburg, 2011.

Weitlauff, Manfred (ed.). *Kirche im 19. Jahrhundert.* Regensburg, 1998.

Wenzel, Paul. *Das wissenschaftliche Anliegen des Güntherianismus. Ein Beitrag zur Theologiegeschichte des 19. Jahrhunderts.* Essen, 1961.

————. *Der Freundeskreis um Anton Günther und die Gründung Beurons. Ein Beitrag zur Geschichte des deutschen Katholizismus im 19. Jahrhundert.* Essen, 1965.

Wetter, Immolata. *Maria Ward unter dem Schatten der Inquisition.* Munich, 2003.

Wipplinger, Rudolf, and Gabriele Amann. "Sexueller Missbrauch: Begriffe und Definitionen." In: Wipplinger and Amann (eds.), *Missbrauch,* pp. 17–44.

Wipplinger, Rudolf, and Gabriele Amann (eds.). *Sexueller Missbrauch. Überblick zu Forschung, Beratung und Therapie. Ein Handbuch.* Tübingen, 2005.

Wiseman, Nicholas Patrick. *Recollections of the Last Four Popes and of Rome in Their Times.* London, 1858.

Wolf, Hubert. "Der 'Syllabus errorum' (1864). Oder: Sind katholische Kirche und Moderne unvereinbar?" In: Weitlauff (ed.), *Kirche,* pp. 115–39.

————. "'Die liebenswürdigste aller Eminenzen.' Kardinal Gustav Adolf von Hohenlohe-Schillingsfürst." *Römische Quartalschrift* 90 (1995), pp. 110–36.

————. *Einleitung 1814–1917. In vier Sprachen (Deutsch, Italienisch, Englisch, Spanisch)* (Römische Inquisition und Indexkongregation. Grundlagenforschung: 1814–1917). Paderborn, 2005.

————. "Gustav Adolf zu Hohenlohe-Schillingsfürst. Kurienkardinal, Freiburger Erzbischofskandidat und Mäzen 1823–1896." *Lebensbilder aus Baden-Württemberg,* vol. 18, Stuttgart, 1994, pp. 350–75.

————. *Index. Der Vatikan und die verbotenen Bücher.* Munich, 2006, 2007.

————. "Inquisition." In: Markschies/Wolf (ed.), *Erinnerungsorte,* pp. 547–60.

————. "Katholische Kirchengeschichte im 'langen' 19. Jahrhundert von 1789 bis 1918." In: *Ökumenische Kirchengeschichte.* Vol. 3: *Von der Französischen Revolution bis 1989,* Thomas Kaufmann et al. (eds.). Darmstadt, 2007, pp. 91–177.

————. *Ketzer oder Kirchenlehrer? Der Tübinger Theologe Johannes Evangelist Kuhn (1806–1887) in den kirchenpolitischen Auseinandersetzungen seiner Zeit* (Veröffentlichungen der Kommission für Zeitgeschichte B 58). Mainz, 1992.

————. "Kontrolle des Wissens? Kirche im Spannungsfeld zwischen Forschung und Zensur." In: Heinz Finger, Reimund Haas, and Hermann-Josef Scheidgen (eds.), *Ortskirche und Weltkirche in der Geschichte. Kölnische Kirchengeschichte zwischen Mittelalter und Zweitem Vatikanum. Festgabe für Norbert Trippen zum 75. Geburtstag* (Bonner Beiträge zur Kirchengeschichte 28), Cologne/Weimar/Vienna 2011, pp. 1017–37.

————. "'Wahr ist, was gelehrt wird' statt 'Gelehrt wird, was wahr ist'? Zur Erfindung des 'ordentlichen' Lehramts." In: Thomas Schmeller, Martin Ebner, and Rudolf Hoppe (eds.), *Neutestamentliche Ämtermodelle im Kontext* (Quaestionesdisputatae 239), Freiburg i. Br., 2010, pp. 236–59.

Wolf, Hubert (ed.). *Prosopographie von Römischer Inquisition und Indexkongregation 1701–1813;* vol. 1: *A-K;* vol. 2: *L-Z.* By Herman H. Schwedt, with Jyri Hasecker, Dominik Höink and Judith Schepers (Römische Inquisition und Indexkongregation. Grundlagenforschung III: 1701–1813). Paderborn, 2010.

466 · Sources and Literature

———. *Prosopographie von Römischer Inquisition und Indexkongregation 1814–1917*; vol. 1: A–K; vol. 2: L–Z. By Herman H. Schwedt, with Tobias Lagatz (Römische Inquisition und Indexkongregation. Grundlagenforschung III: 1814–1917). Paderborn, 2005.

———. *Römische Bücherverbote. Edition der Bandi von Inquisition und Indexkongregation 1814–1917.* Herman H. Schwedt, edited by Judith Schepers and Dominik Burkard (Römische Inquisition und Indexkongregation. Grundlagenforschung I: 1814–1917). Paderborn, 2005.

———. *Systematisches Repertorium zur Buchzensur 1814–1917.* vol. 1: *Indexkongregation*; vol. 2: *Inquisition.* With Sabine Schratz, Jan Dirk Busemann, and Andreas Pietsch (Römische Inquisition und Indexkongregation. Grundlagenforschung II: 1814–1917). Paderborn, 2005.

Wolf, Hubert, and Bernward Schmidt (eds.). *Benedikt XIV. und die Reform des Buchzensurverfahrens. Zur Geschichte und Rezeption von "Sollicita ac provida"* (Römische Inquisition und Indexkongregation 13). Paderborn, 2010.

Wolf, Hubert, and Judith Schepers (eds.). *"In wilder zügelloser Jagd nach Neuem". 100 Jahre Modernismus und Antimodernismus in der katholischen Kirche* (Römische Inquisition und Indexkongregation 12). Paderborn, 2009.

Zahn, Josef. *Einführung in die christliche Mystik* (Wissenschaftliche Handbibliothek. Erste Reihe: Theologische Lehrbücher 28). Paderborn, 1908.

Zarri, Gabriella. "'Vera' santità, 'simulata' santità: ipotesi e riscontri." In: Zarri (ed.), *Finzione*, pp. 9–36.

Zarri, Gabriella (ed.). *Finzione e santità tra medioevo ed età moderna.* Turin, 1991.

Zingeler, Karl Theodor. "Karl Anton von Hohenzollern und Fürstin Katharina von Hohenzollern (Prinzessin von Hohenlohe). Die Erzabtei Beuron." *Deutsche Revue. Eine Monatsschrift* 36 (1911), issue 1, pp. 156–68.

———. *Katharina von Hohenzollern, geb. Prinzessin Hohenlohe. Die Stifterin von Beuron.* Kempten/Munich, 1912.

Zinnhobler, Rudolf. "Pius IX. in der katholischen Literatur seiner Zeit. Ein Baustein zur Geschichte des Triumphalismus." In: Georg Schwaiger (ed.), *Konzil und Papst. Historische Beiträge zur Frage der höchsten Gewalt in der Kirche. Festgabe für Hermann Tüchle.* Paderborn, 1975, pp. 387–432.

Zovatto, Pietro (ed.). *Storia della spiritualità italiana.* Rome, 2002.

Illustration Credits

Endpaper: Giovanni Battista Falda, *Nuova pianta e alzata della città di Roma,* 1676 [Reprinted in 12 sheets: Rome: Danesi, 1931]. Scaled-down reproduction of sheet 9 of the reprint, from the copy held in the German Historical Institute in Rome / Historische Bibliothek, shelfmark: Lb 937 (5, 2–2°), photography by Claudio Cassaro.

221 Photograph of Cardinal Reisach. Marie von Thurn und Taxis-Hohenlohe, *Jugenderinnerungen (1855–1875)*, Vienna, 1936, plate X.

335 Photograph of Princess Katharina von Hohenzollern-Sigmaringen. © Raccolte Museali Fratelli Alinari (RMFA)—collezione Palazzoli, Florence.

353 Photograph of Pope Pius IX.

Index

Printed in the United States
by Baker & Taylor Publisher Services